George H. Whitney

Bible Geography

George H. Whitney

Bible Geography

ISBN/EAN: 9783337828509

Printed in Europe, USA, Canada, Australia, Japan

Cover: Foto ©Lupo / pixelio.de

More available books at **www.hansebooks.com**

OF

BIBLE GEOGRAPHY.

BY

Rev GEORGE H. WHITNEY, D.D.

TWELFTH THOUSAND.

REVISED EDITION.

Illustrated by nearly One Hundred Engravings, and Forty Maps and Plans.

NEW YORK: EATON & MAINS.
CINCINNATI: CURTS & JENNINGS.

PREFACE.

SACRED Geography and Sacred History are inseparably connected. Geographical allusions abound in every part of the Holy Scriptures. The "Lands of the Bible" are the living monuments of the Divine authenticity of the Book which speaks of their mountains and plains, of their rivers and pools, their cities, their peoples, and their tombs. Within the past few years Christian scholars of various lands have given a new impulse to the exploration of sacred localities, and thus has been illustrated more forcibly than ever before the connection between the two great branches of Bible study above indicated.

The places mentioned in Scripture were once by many considered as beyond the sphere of the merely scientific explorer. Their soil must be pressed by the feet only of priest-ruled devotees, and their holy relics touched only by believers who accept every thing and question nothing. Thus "sacred places" multiplied, and sites both true and false became mingled in indistinguishable confusion. The same theory had already obtained in reference to the books of the Bible. Concerning the books, however, it was long ago determined that the records of those who claimed to write as they were inspired by the Holy Ghost might be and should be judged, as were the works of all other authors, by every method known to criticism. Thus far the books have stood the test, and now it is still further desired by the enlightened believer in the Bible that the sacred volume shall continue to be tested by modern exploration and discovery amid the sites of Scripture lands.

Profane history speaks to us to-day with an emphasis made doubly strong by the unearthing of some of the identical sites concerning which its records were made. Nearly two thousand years ago the volcano of Italy buried several splendid cities beneath its rain of death. History made the record, and for centuries their site was lost. Yesterday strong arms went out with spade and pick; to-day the streets of Pompeii, its forum, suburbs, baths, dwellings, and theaters, its people and their customs, are all before our gaze. Classic art, long buried, is lifted out of her ashy grave, and steps forth from her winding-sheet of fire. So, too, the forum of ancient Rome, the palace of the Cæsars, the Mausoleum of Halicarnassus, the Punic and other edifices of Africa, are dug up, and compelled to speak out in attestation of the veracity of those who penned their annals.

Sacred localities must be treated thus. Many of them have already been thus explored. All Palestine is a land of ruins; it is pre-eminently the Memorial Land. Its hill-tops, covered with heaps of stone, are so many Mizpehs that "witness" the partings of pious chieftains and the assemblies of the people of God. Its plains, claimed as once "folds for flocks" and as

PREFACE.

gardens for "roses"—long ago blasted by the presence of the oppressor—to-day teach with equal force the accuracy of the historian and the inspiration of the prophet. The dwelling-places of the tribes, the cities set upon a hill, the hamlets that nestled among the fastnesses of the rocks; the "water-courses," now choked with the rubbish of centuries, have all left their traces of the heaven-chosen people that built them. More impressive than all is the geography of the Holy City itself, as it is delineated by Psalmists, Prophets, Apostles, and by our blessed Lord, in their prayers and hymns, in their warnings and their wanderings. But there are other sites and other peoples besides those of Palestine of which we take cognizance. The seats of primeval life—the "garden" where first God's voice was heard on earth; the "plain" chosen by sinful man whereon to build the monument of his fall; the palaces and temples dedicated to false gods; the exceeding great cities of earliest civilization, Babylon, Nineveh, Susa, Zoan, Memphis, Tyre, and Zidon, and many scores of other cities, together with the customs of their people, the wells they digged, the walls they reared, and the tombs their heroes filled—all these share our consideration.

While it is certainly cause of gratulation to American students of the Bible that the pioneer in modern researches in the Holy Land was our own learned and lamented Dr. Robinson, yet it is with the sincerest gratitude that we here make mention of the London Society, known as the "Palestine Exploration Fund," whose efforts have accomplished so much in Jerusalem. and which give promise of results equally important throughout Western Palestine. Since the first edition of this Hand-book was published, explorations and discoveries of great importance have also been made in the Sinaitic peninsula by Professor E. H. Palmer, and in Moab by Tristram; while the thorough survey of Eastern Palestine has been begun by the American Palestine Exploration Society. The results reached by these various researches are noted in this edition.

The present volume proposes to bring the geography of the sacred record within reach of the great mass of Bible readers and students to whom the larger and more costly Biblical *Dictionaries* and *Cyclopædias* are inaccessible. It contains the name, pronunciation, and meaning (as far as ascertainable) of every place, nation, and tribe mentioned in both the canonical and apocryphal Scriptures, with historical and descriptive notes.

Very many sites in Bible Lands have been clearly identified, others are yet wholly unknown, and concerning a few others contradictory theories exist among the best geographers. These different theories are, in a number of instances, presented side by side in these pages. It has been the author's aim not to establish particular theories, but to arrive at the truth.

So far as practicable each article is based on the following analysis: 1. Name. 2. Number of map where found. 3. Meaning. 4. Situation. 5. Bible allusions. 6. Bible events. 7. Modern name, condition, etc. The best authorities have been consulted, and the latest information concerning the various localities, is here recorded. This information has been obtained not only from published statements, but also in many cases from the lips of travelers fresh from the sites herein described.

The numerous attractive maps, which have been lithographed expressly for this volume, together with the many engravings, will be found invaluable aids to the student. No other book, it is believed, contains within the same space so much information, with illustrations so complete concerning

PREFACE. 7

the important subject of which it treats. As a special instance showing the connection between History and Geography, the reader is referred to the article on JERUSALEM, which contains an account of the recent excavations made in the Holy City.

A list of the principal works consulted in the preparation of this Handbook, and for the use of which the writer now makes his earnest acknowledgment, is here appended:

Ayre's "Treasury of Bible Knowledge;" Dr. Burt's "The Land and its Story;" Dr. Butler's "St. Paul in Rome;" Dr. Barclay's "City of the Great King;" "Baker's Ismailia;" "Bibliotheca Sacra;" Conybeare and Howson's "Life of St. Paul;" Clark's "Bible Atlas," with Grove's "Index;" Dr. Durbin's "Observations in the East;" De Lanoye's "Rameses the Great;" "Early Travels in Palestine;" Farrar's "Life of Christ;" Gibbon's "Decline and Fall of the Roman Empire;" Gesenius's "Hebrew Lexicon;" Dr. Hanna's "Life of our Lord;" Herzog's "Encyclopædia;" Inglis's "Bible Text Cyclopædia;" Josephus's "Works;" Kitto's "Biblical Cyclopædia," "Scripture Lands," and "History of the Bible;" Keil's "Commentary;" Kiepert's "Map of Palestine;" Layard's "Nineveh;" Lewin's "Life and Epistles of St. Paul;" M'Clintock and Strong's "Cyclopædia;" Macgregor's "Rob Roy on the Jordan;" Newman's "Thrones and Palaces of Babylon and Nineveh;" "Ordnance Survey of Jerusalem;" Dr. Olin's "Travels;" Paine's "Tabernacle and the Temple;" Dr. Porter's "Hand-book for Syria and Palestine" and "Giant Cities of Bashan;" Ritter's "Geography of Palestine," (Gage's translation;) Dr. Robinson's "Biblical Researches" and "Greek Lexicon of the New Testament;" Rawson's "Bible Hand-book;" Dr. Smith's "Dictionary of the Bible" and "Classical Dictionary;" Dr. Strong's "Harmony of the Gospels;" Smith's (S.) "Temple and the Sepulcher;" Dr. Stanley's "Sinai and Palestine" and "History of the Jewish Church;" "Statements of the Palestine Exploration Fund;" "Statements of the American Palestine Exploration Society;" Tristram's "Land of Israel," and "The Land of Moab;" Thomson's "The Land and the Book;" Tischendorf's "Septuagint;" "The Desert of the Exodus;" Van de Velde's "Map of Palestine;" Wheeler's "Geography of Herodotus."

The Author here takes occasion to express his warmest thanks for the many valuable suggestions received, during the several years' labor bestowed upon this volume, from the Rev. J. H. Vincent, D.D., at whose solicitation the work was undertaken.

To Pastors, as a convenient book of reference for the study-table; to Superintendents, Teachers, and Sunday-school scholars, as also to the general reader, this Hand-book of Bible Geography is offered with a sincere desire and the humble hope that it may in some measure assist in the better understanding of that Sacred Volume whose truths it aims to illustrate.

G. H. W.

HACKETTSTOWN, N. J., *November*, 1881.

LIST OF FULL PAGE ENGRAVINGS.

	PAGE
PLAN OF JERUSALEM IN THE TIME OF SOLOMON	2
ANTAKIA (ANTIOCH IN SYRIA)	24
THE AREOPAGUS (OR MAR'S HILL) AND ACROPOLIS	30
ATHENS RESTORED, AS SEEN FROM THE PNYX	32
BABYLON (restored)	43
BIRS-NIMRUD	47
BETHLEHEM	64
MOUNT CARMEL	82
CORINTH RESTORED, AS VIEWED FROM THE ACROCORINTHUS	92
DAMASCUS	97
THE PYRAMIDS	112
PYLONS AND PORTICO OF A GREAT TEMPLE (restored according to the Egyptian Commission)	116
TEMPLE OF DIANA (restored)	124
THEATER AT EPHESUS	127
THE SEA OF GALILEE	140
MOSQUE AT HEBRON (MACHPELAH) AND PART OF THE TOWN	173
PLAN OF ANCIENT JERUSALEM	194
SOLOMON'S TEMPLE (according to Rev. T. O. Paine)	To face 197
HEROD'S TEMPLE (according to Rev. T. O. Paine)	204
MOSQUES IN THE HARAM INCLOSURE AT JERUSALEM	226
PLANS ILLUSTRATING EXCAVATIONS AT JERUSALEM	235
JAFFA [ANCIENT JAPHO OR JOPPA)	248
BATHING PLACES OF PILGRIMS ON THE JORDAN	254
WILDERNESS OF KADESH	261
THE MONASTERY OF MAR SABA—GORGE OF THE KIDRON	272
THE GRAND RANGE OF LEBANON	280
LUDD, (ANCIENT LYDDA)—RUINS OF THE CHURCH OF ST. GEORGE	288
NAZARETH	325
NEBY YUNUS, KOYUNJIK, AND RUINS OPPOSITE MOSUL	334
VIEW OF THEBES (restored) DURING THE INUNDATION	340
PALESTINE FROM THE MEDITERRANEAN	350
PROFILE SECTIONS OF PALESTINE	354
ISLE OF PATMOS, WITH THE HARBOR OF LA SCALA AND THE TOWN OF PATINO	367
PERSEPOLIS	372
VIEW FROM JEBEL TAHUNEH	395
THE COLOSSUS AT RHODES	399
THE DEAD SEA—VIEW FROM 'AIN JIDY (EN-GEDI) LOOKING SOUTH	421
LONGITUDINAL SECTION OF THE DEAD SEA FROM NORTH TO SOUTH	425
NABLOUS (ANCIENT SHECHEM)	436
THE NILE—THE SPEOS OF IBSAMBOUL	444
THE RAS SUFSAFEH FROM THE PLAIN OF ER RAHAH	448
SECTIONS OF JEBEL MUSA AND JEBEL SERBAL	452
MOUNT TABOR	461
TARSUS	466
RUINS OF TYRE	480

LIST OF FULL PAGE MAPS.

	PAGES
No. 1. SCRIPTURE WORLD	16, 17
No. 2. EGYPT AND THE WILDERNESS	50, 51
No. 3. CANAAN IN PATRIARCHAL AGES	76
No. 4. DOMINIONS OF DAVID AND SOLOMON	105
No. 5. THE HOLY LAND	156, 157
No. 6. ENVIRONS OF JERUSALEM	210
No. 7. MODERN JERUSALEM	216
No. 8. TRAVELS OF ST. PAUL	264, 265
Nos. 9-11. JERUSALEM AT THREE EPOCHS	222, 223
No. 12. GENTILE NATIONS	302, 303
No. 13. THE DOMINIONS OF SOLOMON	358
No. 14. KINGDOMS OF JUDAH AND ISRAEL	359
No. 15. TERRITORY OF ASMONEAN KINGS	359
Nos. 16-19. THE FOUR EMPIRES	410, 411
No. 20. THE GOSPEL HISTORY	470
No. 21. THE SEA OF GALILEE	471
Nos. 22-32. THE TABERNACLE AND THE TEMPLE	240, 241

ARABIC GLOSSARY.

The following Arabic words occur in various parts of this volume.

Abu, father.
'Ain, pl. *'Ayûn*, fountain.
Ard, plain.
Báb, door; gate.
Bahr, sea.
Balad, village.
Bakshish, present.
Beit, pl. *Buyût*, house.
Belád, district.
Bír, well.
Birkeh, pl. *Burák*, pool.
Deir, convent.
Emír, pl. *Umarâ*, prince.
El-Ghor, valley—the name applied to the northern part of the Jordan Valley. The southern continuation of the same valley is called *El-Arabah*.
Ibn, pl. *Beni*, son.
Jámi'a, mosque.
Jebel, pl. *Jibál*, mountain.
Jisr, bridge.
Ká'a, plain.
Kabr, pl. *Kubûr*, sepulcher.
Kády, judge.

Kefr, village.
Khán, caravansary.
Khurbeh, a ruin.
Kubbeh, dome.
Kurn, pl. *Kurûn*, a horn.
Kul'ah, castle.
Kusr, castle.
Már, saint.
Merj, pl. *Murûj*, meadow.
Mihráb, prayer-niche.
Moslem, Mohammedan.
Nahr, pl. *Anhur*, river.
Nakhleh, pl. *Nukhl*, palm-tree.
Neby, prophet.
Neb'a, fountain.
Nukb, pass.
Rás, head, cape.
Selám, peace.
Sheikh, *Shuyúkh*, chief, elder.
Tell, pl. *Tulúl*, dim. *Tuleil*, hill.
Tín, fig.
Turfa, tamarisk.
Um, mother.
Wády, valley, water-course.
Wely, saint's tomb.

A CONCISE CHRONOLOGICAL TABLE.

A. M.		B. C.
	The creation of the world	4004
056	Birth of Noah	2948
1656	The deluge	2348
2008	Birth of Abraham	1996
2083	Call of Abraham	1921
2107	Cities of the Plain destroyed	1897
2108	Birth of Isaac	1896
2168	Birth of Jacob	1836
2298	Jacob and his family go into Egypt	1706
2433	Birth of Moses	1571
2513	The Exodus	1491
2514	The giving of the law	1490
2553	Entrance of Israel into Canaan	1451
2561	Death of Joshua	1443
2909	Appointment of Saul as king	1095
2949	Accession of David as king of Judah	1055
2956	David king over all Israel	1048
2959	David captures Jerusalem	1045
2990	Accession of Solomon	1015
3001	Dedication of the temple	1004

The dates above given are according to Archbishop Usher; the following are according to Winer.

		B. C.
Accession of Rehoboam, Jeroboam I., Abijam		975
Abijam		957
Asa		955
Nadab		954
Baasha		953
Elah		930
Zimri, Omri, Tibni, Ahab		928
Ahab		918
Jehoshaphat		914
Ahaziah of Israel		897
Joram of Israel		896
Joram of Judah		889
Ahaziah of Judah		885
Jehu, Athaliah,		884
Joash of Judah		878
Jehoahaz of Israel		856
Joash of Israel		840
Amaziah		838
Jeroboam II		825
Uzziah		809
Zachariah		772
Shallum, Menahem,		771
Pekahiah		760
Pekah, Jotham,		758
Ahaz		741
Hoshea		729
Hezekiah		725
Samaria taken, and the kingdom of Israel ended		721
Accession of Manasseh		696
Amon		641
Josiah		639
Jehoahaz of Judah, Jehoiakim,		609
Jehoiachin, Zedekiah,		598

	B. C.
Jerusalem taken, and Judah carried captive to Babylon	588
Return of the Jews under Zerubbabel, according to the decree of Cyrus	536
The second temple begun	534
Death of Cyrus	529
Accession of Darius Hystaspis to the throne of Persia	521
The temple finished and dedicated	516
Accession of Xerxes	485
Artaxerxes Longimanus	465
Ezra proceeds to Jerusalem	459
Nehemiah appointed governor	445
Death of Darius Codomannus, the last king of Persia, and end of the Persian monarchy	330
Death of Alexander the Great	323
Antiochus Epiphanes obtains the crown of Syria	175
The statue of Jupiter Olympus set up in the temple at Jerusalem	167
The temple cleansed by Judas Maccabeus	164
Jonathan succeeds his brother Judas Maccabeus	161
Simon succeeds Jonathan	143
and establishes Jewish freedom	142
John Hyrcanus succeeds	135
Aristobulus I., first of the Asmonean family who had the title of king	107
Alexander Jannæus	105
Alexandra	79
Hyrcanus II	70
Aristobulus II	69
Hyrcanus restored	63
Antigonus	
Herod, called the Great, declared king of Judea by the Roman Senate	40
Herod begins to rebuild the temple at Jerusalem	21
Birth of Jesus CHRIST	6(?)
Death of Herod	4

	A. D.
Archelaus dethroned, Insurrection of Judas of Galilee,	6
Death of Augustus Cæsar	14
Pontius Pilate procurator of Judea	25
The Crucifixion	31(?)

The dates of the birth and death of our Lord are variously given by different chronologers.

Pontius Pilate deprived of his government	36
Death of Tiberius: Caligula becomes Emperor	37
Conversion of St. Paul	38
Herod Antipas banished to Gaul	39
Claudius Emperor	41
Death of Herod Agrippa I	44
Council of apostles and elders in Jerusalem	51
Felix procurator of Judea	52
Death of Claudius: Nero Emperor	54
Felix removed; Festus procurator	60/61
Vespasian Emperor	69
Jerusalem taken by Titus	70

BIBLE GEOGRAPHY.

Ab'ana, (Map 5,) *stony,* (marg. AM'ANA,) a river of Damascus. "Top of Amana," Sol. Song iv, 8. It was called by the Greeks *Chrysorrhoas,* "golden stream." Rising in the Anti-Libanus, near *Zcbdány,* and passing by the site of ancient Abila, it flows through the city of Damascus. From the main stream, which runs through the city, no less than seven large canals are taken at different elevations, to irrigate the surrounding orchards and gardens. Leaving the noted Assyrian ruin *Tell es-Salahiyeh* on its left bank, after a course of fifty miles it loses itself in the lake or marsh *Bahret el-Kibliyeh.* It is one of the rivers which the proud Naaman preferred to the waters of Israel, 2 Kings v, 12. It is identified as the modern *Barada.* Mr. Porter calculates that not less than fourteen villages and 150,000 souls are dependent on this important river. A thrilling and deeply interesting account of Abana has recently been given by J. Macgregor, M.A., who in his well-known craft, the "Rob Roy," explored the river from the mountains of Lebanon to Lake Ateibeh.

Ab'arim, (Map 5,) (regions) *beyond.* In Jer. xxii, 20, the name signifies the "*passages*" A chain of mountains east of Jordan. Peor, Nebo, and Pisgah belong to it. Pisgah is a ridge, Nebo a peak. Moses died there, Deut. xxxiv, 1, 5. It affords a splendid prospect, xxxiv, 1, 3. Other allusions, Num. xxi, 20; xxvii, 12; xxxiii, 47, 48; Deut. xxxii, 49. "Field of Zophim on top of Pisgah," where Balaam prophesied, Num. xxiii, 14.

Ab'don, *servile,* a Levitical city of Asher, Josh. xxi, 30; 1 Chron. vi, 74. It is probably identical with the ruined site *Abdeh,* eight or nine miles northeast of Accho.

A'bel. In 1 Sam. vi, 18, "the great stone of Abel, whereon they set down the ark of the Lord." It was near Beth-Shemesh. The word thus translated "the great Abel" signifies *meadow,* or *mourning.* The alteration of a letter would make it "the great stone;" and this is in accordance with the context, (14, 15.) The term is used almost exclusively with some adjunct, to be supplied if not expressed, as in 2 Sam. xx, 14, 18.

A'bel, and **A'bel-Beth-Ma'achah,** (Map 5,) *meadow of the house of Maachah,* a town in the north of Palestine, near Dan. It is called ABEL-MAIM (*meadow of water*) in 2 Chron. xvi, 4. Sheba fled to it and was slain, 2 Sam. xx, 14–18. It was spoiled by Ben-Hadad, 1 Kings xv, 20; 2 Chron. xvi, 4. It was taken by Tiglath, 2 Kings xv, 29. Probably it is identical with the modern *Abil-el-Karub,* in the region of the upper Jordan, near Dan.

A'bel-Kera'mim, *meadow of vineyards,* a place east of the Jordan, whither the victorious Jephthah pursued the invading Ammonites with great slaughter, Judg. xi, 33. Probably the place of the present ruins of *Merj Ekkeh.* (See M'Clintock and Strong's *Cyclopedia.*)

A'bel-Maim. See A'BEL.

A'bel-Meho'lah, (Map 13,) *meadow of dancing,* a place in or near the valley of the Jordan northward, Judg. vii, 22; 1 Kings iv, 12. The original residence of Elisha, 1 Kings xix, 16-19. Perhaps the spot now occupied by the ruins of *Khurbet esh-Shuk.*

A'bel-Miz'raim, *meadow,* or, probably, *mourning of the Egyptians,* a place generally considered to be east of the Jordan, where Joseph mourned for his father, Gen. l, 11. Jerome identifies the place with *Beth Hoglah,* on the west bank of the river: it is more likely to have been south of Hebron, but its site is unknown. See ATAD.

A'bel-Shit'tim, (Map 2,) *Acacia meadow,* the last station of the Israelites before entering Canaan, Num. xxxii, 49; in the low level of Moab by the Jordan. Generally called Shittim, Num. xxv, 1; Josh. ii, 1. Acacia groves still remain in the vicinity, but there is no town.

A'bez, *whiteness, luster,* or *tin,* a town of Issachar, near the border, Josh. xix, 20. Probably it is *Kunebiz,* called also *Karm en-Abiz,* which lies three English miles south-west of *Iksal.* Possibly, however, it may be a corruption of Thebez, now *Tûbás,* not far from Engannim and Shunem.

Ab'ila, (probably the same as Abel,) *a grassy place.* A city called Abila of Lysanias, to distinguish it from other Syrian cities of the same name. It is in the center of the Anti-Libanus, eighteen Roman miles from Damascus, on the road to Heliopolis or Baalbec, and was the capital of Abilene. Its site has been identified with *Sûk-Wady-Barada,* a small village on the right bank of the river Barada, the ancient *Abana,* which breaks just by through a picturesque mountain gorge. Inscriptions have been found here; and there are the remains of a tomb called *Kabr Habil,* " the tomb of Abil." Abila was in Christian times a bishop's see, and was sacked by the Moslems 634 A.D.

Abile'ne, (Map 20,) *father of the apartment,* or *of mourning,* a small district of Palestine, among the eastern declivities of Anti-Libanus, described Luke iii, 1, as under the government of Lysanias when John the Baptist commenced his ministry. It is hardly possible to determine its exact limits. Abila was its capital. See ABILA.

Ab'salom's Pillar, (Map 7,) *the father of peace,* a monument in memory of Absalom in the valley of Kidron or the King's Dale, 2 Sam. xviii, 18. It is twenty-four feet square at the base, and forty feet high. It is ornamented on each side with two columns and two half-columns of the Ionic order, with pilasters at the corners. To the top of the architrave, eighteen feet, it is cut from the rock; above this, mason work of large stones rises about twenty feet, making a total elevation of about forty feet. Its present Mohammedan name is *Tantur Faraon.*

Ac'cad, *fortress,* (some say a *bond,*) one of the four cities said to be the beginning of Nimrod's kingdom, Gen. x, 10. Its location cannot be identified accurately. Perhaps *Nisibin,* the ancient Nisibis, on the *Khabour* river, marks the site. But Rawlinson considers Akkad the name of the primitive Hamite race, whose original seat was Babylonia, and from whose language was derived the trunk Shemitic stream of tongues; and locates this city at about seven miles west by north of Bagdad, where there is now a vast pile of ruins with the name of *Aker Kûff.*

Ac'caron, 1 Macc. x, 89. The Greek form of Ekron.

Ac'cho, (Map 5,) *heated sand;* or Ptolemais, now *St. Jean d'Acre,* a town of Phenicia given to Asher. The Canaanites remained in it, Judg. i, 31.

BIBLE GEOGRAPHY. 13

The Church at Accho was visited by Paul, Acts xxi, 7. It is now a place of some importance. See PTOLEMAIS.

Acel'dama, (Map 7,) *field of the blood*, a piece of land originally called "The Potters' Field," which was purchased with the money given to Judas for betraying Christ, Matt. xxvii, 8; Acts i, 18, 19. Various spots have been supposed to be this field. That now bearing the name is on the southern face of the valley of the son of Hinnom, at the eastern end; a ruined edifice stands on it.

Achai'a, (Map 8,) *grief, trouble, noise*, (derivation uncertain,) a region of Greece. The Churches in Achaia visited by Paul, Acts xvii; xix, 21; Rom. xvi, 5; 1 Cor. xvi, 15. They contributed to the saints at Jerusalem, Rom. xv, 26. For towns of, see CENCHREA, CORINTH.

Ach'metha, (Map 1,) *a city*, or *station*, or *fortress*, (derivation uncertain,) a city of Persia. Cyrus's decree for rebuilding the temple at Jerusalem was found here, Ezra vi, 2. See ECBATANA.

A'chor, (Map 5,) *trouble*, a valley near Jericho, where Achan was stoned; and from the trouble brought by Achan upon Israel it had its name, Josh. vii, 24, 26. Yet from that trouble, sanctified, a new career of victory began, Hosea ii, 15. See also Josh. xv, 7; Isa. lv, 10. It is now called *Wady-el-Kelt*. Perhaps the same as Cherith, 1 Kings xvii, 3-7.

Ach'shaph, *fascination*, a city of Canaan, (Josh. xi, 1; xii, 20,) in the division of the land allotted to Asher, Josh. xix, 25. Perhaps it is the modern *Kesâf*, on the northeast edge of the *Hûleh*, or it may be the same with the modern *Chaifa*.

Ach'zib, (Map 5,) *deceit, falsehood*, a town of Asher, Josh. xix, 29. Now *Es-Zib*. Another Achzib was in Judah, Josh. xv, 44; Micah i, 14. This probably is identical with Chezib, Gen. xxxviii, 5.

Ac'ra, (Map 7,) *a summit* or *citadel*. An eminence north of the temple at Jerusalem. The *Acropolis* of Jerusalem. There is much controversy as to its precise location; but the middle of the Mohammedan quarter seems the most probable site.

Acrab'bim. See MAALEH–ACRABBIM.

Ad'adah, *festival*, according to some, *boundary*, a town in the extreme south of the portion of Judah, Josh. xv, 22. Probably identical with '*Ad-'adah*, a ruin near *Tuweirah el Foka*, south-west of the Dead Sea.

Ad'am, *red, red earth*, a city near the Jordan, by which the waters were cut off when Israel passed over—*beside* Zaretan, Josh. iii, 16; 1 Kings vii, 46.

Ad'amah, *earth*, (so called from its *reddish* color,) a fenced city of Naphtali, Josh. xix, 36. Probably the same as that called Adami, (xix, 33,) a city near the border of Naphtali, between Zaanaim and Nekeb.

Ad'ami, *human*, a place on the border of Naphtali, Josh. xix, 33. Unknown. See NEKEB.

A'dar, *greatness, splendor*, a border town of Judah, Josh. xv, 3. It would seem to be the same with Hazar-Addar, Num. xxxiv, 4; possibly '*Ain el-Kudeirât*.

Ad'asa, 1 Macc. vii, 40, 45; Josh. xv, 37, (called by Josephus *Adazer, Adaco, Acoduco*,) a town in the tribe of Judah, near which Judas Maccabeus vanquished and slew the Syrian general Nicanor. It was near Beth-horon, according to Josephus; and according to Jerome, near Gophna. Some good authorities think it possibly identical with Hadashah, which see.

Ad'dan, *humble*, or, perhaps, *lord*, a place from which some who could not show their genealogy returned with Zerubbabel, Ezra ii, 59. In Neh vii, 61 it is called Addon.

Ad'ida, 1 Macc. xii, 38; xiii, 13; Ezra ii, 33; a fortified town built upon an eminence in the Sephela, not far from the Mediterranean, west of Beth-horon, and north-west of Jerusalem. Simon Maccabeus encamped near it during his war with Tryphon. It is possibly identical with Hadid and Adithaim.

Aditha'im, *double prey,* or *double ornament,* a city in the plain country of Judah, Josh. xv, 36; mentioned between Sharaim and Gederah. Possibly identical with Adida and Hadid.

Ad'mah, *earth, red earth,* a city in the vale of Siddim, Gen. x, 19. Invaded by Chedorlaomer, Gen. xiv, 2. Destroyed with Sodom, Deut. xxix, 23; Hosea xi, 8. It is conjectured to have been somewhere near the middle of the southern end of the Dead Sea.

Ado'ra, 1 Macc. xiii, 20. Probably the same with Adoraim.

Adora'im, (Map 5,) *two mounds* or *dwellings,* a city of Judah, which Rehoboam fortified, 2 Chron. xi, 9. Doubtless the modern *Dûra,* five miles southwest from Hebron.

Adramyt'tium, (Map 8,) *the court of death, mansion of death,* a sea-port of Mysia, Acts xxvii, 2–5. Now a village of some trade, called variously *Edramit, Adramyt, Adrmyt.* It contains about one thousand houses.

A'dria, (Map 8,) or Adriatic Sea, Acts xxvii, 27; a part of the Mediterranean Sea. The modern Gulf of Venice. In Paul's time it included the whole waters between Greece, Italy, Sicily, and Africa, though sometimes the southern part was distinguished as the Ionian Sea, the northern as Adria. Probably derived its name from Adria, a city in Istria.

Adul'lam, *their testimony, justice of the people* (?) a cave near the Dead Sea, in which David hid, 1 Sam. xxii, 1; 2 Sam. xxiii, 13; 1 Chron. xi, 15. Dr. Thomson describes a cavern at *Khureitun* between Bethlehem and the Dead Sea, where tradition places Adullam.

Adul'lam, (Map 5,) (*id.,*) an ancient city in the plain country of Judah, once the seat of a Canaanitish king, Gen. xxxviii, 1, 12, 20; Josh. xii, 15; 15, 35; Micah i, 15. It was fortified by Rehoboam, 2 Chron. xi, 7. After the captivity it was occupied by the Jews, Neh. xi, 30, and was still a city in the time of the Maccabees, 2 Macc. xii, 38. Probably Adullam was from six to ten miles north-east of Eleutheropolis, but it has not been identified.

Adum'mim, the *red,* or *bloody,* (place,) or, according to some, the *red-haired men.* "The going up," or pass "of Adummim," was a rising ground on the road from Jericho to Jerusalem. It was, and is, the resort of robbers. On the border between Benjamin and Judah, Josh. xv, 7; xviii, 17; compare Luke x, 30–36. It seems to have been on the south face of the gorge of the *Wady el-Kelt.*

Æ'non, *springs,* the place where John baptized, "near to Salim," John iii, 23. Located by some at Salim, near Gerizim; by Dr. Barclay at *Wady Fara!.,* five miles north-east of Jerusalem. A wady is close by, resembling it in name — *Wady Seleim.* The site is still uncertain.

Aha'va, (Map 1,) *water,* a place, or a river, or perhaps a district, where the Jewish exiles assembled who accompanied Ezra to Jerusalem, Ezra viii, 15, 21, 31. Various localities have been suggested; possibly it may be the modern *Hit* on the Euphrates, east of Damascus, anciently called *Ihi* or *Ihi-da-Kira.*

Ah'lab, *fatness, fertility,* a place in the territory of Asher, from which the

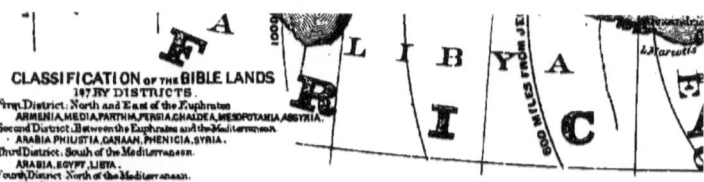

CLASSIFICATION of the BIBLE LANDS BY DISTRICTS.

First District: North and East of the Euphrates
  ARMENIA, MEDIA, PARTHIA, PERSIA, CHALDEA, MESOPOTAMIA, ASSYRIA.
Second District: Between the Euphrates and the Mediterranean.
  ARABIA, PHILISTIA, CANAAN, PHENICIA, SYRIA.
Third District: South of the Mediterranean.
  ARABIA, EGYPT, LIBYA.
Fourth District: North of the Mediterranean.
  SPAIN, ITALY, GREECE, ASIA MINOR.

2ᴅ BY HISTORIC ASSOCIATIONS

1. Lands of the beginning: ARMENIA, CHALDEA, MESOPOTAMIA.
2. Land of Hebrew bondage: EGYPT.
3. Land of Hebrew wandering: ARABIA PETRAEA.
4. The Land of Promise: CANAAN.
5. The Lands of the Jewish wars: PHILISTIA, SYRIA, ARABIA.
6. The Lands of the Captivities: ASSYRIA, BABYLONIA.
7. The Lands of Cyrus the Emancipator: MEDIA PERSIA.
8. The Lands of the Dispersion. See Acts II.

MAP N? 1

MEASUREMENTS.

of SEAS, LAKES & RIVERS		of MOUNTAINS Etc.		of DISTANCES (excluding) The Jerusalem to	
Mediterranean Sea	miles	above Mediterranean			
on Gibraltar to Joppa	2400	Mt Ararat ft. 17320	Cairo	200 Miles
Malta to Alexandria	980	Lebanon	10,051	Thebes	450
Red Sea, the Gulf of Suez	180	Hermon	9,376	Cyrene	740
the Gulf of Akabah	105	Serbal		Malta	1240
the Red Sea proper	1160	Sinai	8,593	Rome	1450
Dead Sea length 47 width 8-9		Olivet	2,665	Athens	780
Sea of Galilee	14 ... 3-7	Zion	2,550	Corinth	630
Black Sea	725 ... 225	Moriah	2,440	Babylon	560
Caspian Sea	630 ... 190	Carmel	1,500	Nineveh	670
Adriatic Sea	460 ... 105	Gilead	5,000	Uz	435
the River Nile	3500	Hor		Mt Sinai	280
Tigris	1150	Baber Mediterranean		Mt Ararat	760
Euphrates	1700	Sea of Galilee	653		
Jordan	257	Dead Sea	1,292		

SCRIPTURE WOR

HUNT & EATON, NEW YORK.

STATUTE MILES
METRES

Canaanites were not driven out, Judg. i, 31. Supposed to be *Gush-Chalab*, or *Giscala*, a place lately identified by Robinson under the name of *el-Jish*, near Safed.

Aho'lah, she has *her own tent*, a symbolical name for Samaria, Ezek. xxiii, 4, 5, 36, 44.

Ahol'ibah, *my tent is in her*, a symbolical name for Jerusalem, Ezek. xxiii, 4, 11, 22, 36, 44.

A'i, (Map 5,) *mass* or *heap of ruins*, a royal city of Palestine, but of no great size. It is mentioned (as Hai) in Abraham's time, Gen. xii, 8; xiii, 3, and was, after repulse before it, destroyed by the Israelites under Joshua, Josh. vii, 2-5; viii, 1-29; ix, 3; x, 2; xii, 9. It must, however, have been afterward rebuilt. Aiath, Isa. x, 28, is probably identical with it; and the men of Ai are said to have returned from Babylon with Zerubbabel, Ezra ii, 28; Neh. vii, 32. Probably it is also the Aija repeopled by the Benjamites, Neh. xi, 31. It lay to the east of Bethel: but its site is still uncertain. Some think it may be at the *Tell el-Haiyeh*, or *Tell el-Hajar*. Captain Wilson identifies it (1869) with *Et-Tell*, "the heap."

2. A town of the Ammonites near Heshbon, Jer. xlix, 3; but *possibly* the word here is not a proper name.

Aij'alon, (Aj-alon.) See AJALON.

A'in, *an eye, a spring, fountain.* A place, or, more probably, a fountain, mentioned as one of the boundary marks of Canaan, Num. xxxiv, 11; to the east of which the line was to run. The *'Ain-el-'Azy*, the main source of the Orontes, is in the position indicated. But its identity with Ain is not fully established.

2. A Levitical city in the territory assigned first to Judah, afterward to Simeon, Josh. xv, 32; xix, 7; xxi, 16; 1 Chron. iv, 32. Ashan in 1 Chron. vi, 59, and possibly En-Rimmon, Neh. xi, 29, may be the same place. The word Ain is joined with many names, as Ain-dor, and implies that there was a great spring at that place. It is then spelt in our version En, as in Endor.

Aj'alon, (Map 5,) *a place of deer*, or *gazelles*, a *deer-field*, a Levitical city of Dan, Josh. xix, 42. A city of refuge, Josh. xxi, 24; 1 Sam. xiv, 31; 1 Chron. vi, 69. The Amorites remained in it, Judg. i, 35; 1 Chron. viii, 13. Taken by Philistines, 2 Chron. xxviii, 18. Fenced by Rehoboam, 2 Chron. xi, 10. The celebrated *valley* must have been just at hand, Josh. x, 12. Ajalon is the modern *Yalo*, on a long hill about fourteen miles from Jerusalem, on the south side of a broad, fertile valley called *Merj Ibn Omeir*.

2. A city in Zebulun where Elon the judge was buried, Judg. xii, 12. Probably the modern *Jalun*.

Ak'aba, (Map 2,) the name of the eastern arm of the Red Sea.

Akrab'bim, *scorpions*, the name of a pass, "Scorpion-pass," forming the southern boundary of the land of Israel, Num. xxxiv, 4; Josh. xv, 3; Judg. i, 36. Near the southern extremity of the Dead Sea. Perhaps it is at the *Wady es-Safieh*.

Al'ameth, 1 Chron. vii, 8. A less correct mode of anglicizing the name Alemeth.

Alam'melech, *king's oak*, a town in the territory of Asher, Josh. xix, 26, mentioned between Achshaph and Amad.

Al'ema, one of the fortified cities of Gilead, 1 Macc. v, 26. Probably the Beer-Elim of Isa. xv, 8.

Al'emeth, or **Ale'meth,** (Map 6,) *covering*, a town of Benjamin allotted to the priests, 1 Chron. vi, 60. In Josh. xxi, 18 it is called Almon. It has been identified with *'Almit* or *'Almuth,* near to *'Anata,* the ancient *Anathoth.*

Alexan'dria, (Map 1,) named from its founder, Alexander the Great. (Alexander=*man-defender.*) A city of Egypt. Men of Alexandria disputed here with Stephen, Acts vi, 9. Its ships, Acts xxvii, 6; xxviii, 11. Birthplace of Apollos, xviii, 24. For a long period it was the greatest of known cities, for Nineveh and Babylon had fallen, and Rome had not yet risen to pre-eminence. It is now an important place, with about sixty thousand inhabitants.

Al'lon, *an oak,* a place on the boundary of Naphtali, Josh. xix, 33. But perhaps a better rendering of the passage would be "the oak at or in Zaanannim." See ZAANANNIM.

Al'lon-Bachuth, *oak of weeping,* the oak-tree under which Deborah, Rebekah's nurse, was buried, Gen. xxxv, 8.

Al'mon. See ALEMETH.

Al'mon-Diblatha'im, (Map 2,) *concealment of the two fig cakes,* the fifty-first station of the Israelites, Num. xxxiii, 46, 47. Probably identical with Beth-diblathaim, Jer. xlviii, 22.

A'loth, perhaps *milk-giving,* a place or district apparently joined with Asher as a commissariat department, 1 Kings iv, 16. Probably it should be Bealoth.

A'lush, (Map 2,) *desolation,* (?) *a crowd of men,* or *a strong fort,* or *a place of wild beasts,* the eleventh station at which the Hebrews rested on their way to Mount Sinai, Num. xxxiii, 13, 14. It is alleged (upon an interpretation of Exod. xvi, 30) that in Alush the Sabbath was instituted, and the first Sabbath kept. But the Sabbath is as old as creation.

A'mad, *people of duration,* a town of Asher, Josh. xix, 26. According to Robinson it may probably be identified with *Shefa 'Omar,* or *Shefa Amar,* a large market town on a ridge of *Haifa.*

Am'alekites, (Map 2,) *a people that licks up,* or *uses ill,* or, perhaps, *dwellers in a valley,* a tribe first mentioned in connection with the expedition of Chedorlaomer, Gen. xiv, 7. We find them occupying the country between Palestine, Idumea, and Mount Sinai, on the elevated plateau (Num. xiv, 25, 40-45) now called *er-Rakhmah;* their seats having been at a very early period probably further eastward. Amalek, the grandson of Esau, was perhaps the progenitor of a clan which was intermingled with an older race, Gen. xxxvi, 12, 15. The period referred to in Gen. xiv, 7, is much more remote than that in xxxvi, 12, 16. They were defeated by Joshua, Exod. xvii, 8-13. They defeat Israel at Hormah, Num. xiv, 45; Deut. i, 44.

A'mam, *meeting place,* or *gathering,* a city in the extreme south of Judah, Josh. xv, 26. The enumeration in the thirty-second verse shows that this name should be joined with the preceding, that is, *Hazor-Amam.* Nothing is known of it. See HAZOR, (4.)

Am'ana, or **Ama'na,** *fixed, a covenant, perennial.* The marginal reading (of many codices and versions) of 2 Kings v, 12; the stream near Damascus, called in the text Abana.

2. A ridge or summit of Anti-Libanus, in which it is presumed the river Amana or Abana has its source, Sol. Song, iv, 8.

Am'athis, or **Amathi'tis,** a district probably identical with Hamath. There Jonathan Maccabeus met the forces of Demetrius, 1 Macc. xii, 25.

Am'mah, *beginning, head, a cubit,* a hill facing Giah, the point to which

BIBLE GEOGRAPHY. 21

Joab pursued Abner after the skirmish near Gibeon, 2 Sam. ii, 24. See METHEG-AMMAH.

Am'monites, (Map 4,) *strong people*, or *son of my kindred*. The nation descended from Ben-Ammi, the son of Lot, born in incest, Gen. xix, 38. Their territory was between the Arnon and the Jabbok, Num. xxi, 24; Deut. ii, 19, 20; Josh. xii, 2; xiii, 10, 25. The Israelites were forbidden to attack them, Deut. ii, 19, 37. Their inhospitality to Israel was punished by their being shut out from the congregation, Deut. xxiii, 3–6; Neh. xiii, 1. They invaded Israel, Judges iii, 13. They oppressed Israel, and were defeated by Jephthah, Judges x, 7–18; xi; xii, 1–3. By Saul, 1 Sam. xi; xiv, 47. By David, 2 Sam. viii, 12; xii, 26–31; xvii, 27; 1 Chron. xviii, 11. By Joab, 2 Sam. x; xi, 1–17; 1 Chron. xx, 1–3. By Jehoshaphat, 2 Chron. xx. By Jotham, and made tributary, 2 Chron. xxvii, 5. Tributary to Uzziah, 2 Chron. xxvi, 8. They invaded Gad, etc., Jer. xlix, 1; Amos i, 13. They assisted Nebuchadnezzar against Jehoiakim, 2 Kings xxiv, 2. They aided in the murder of Gedaliah, Jer. xl, 11, 14; xli, 10, 15. Opposed the building of Jerusalem, Neh. iv, 1–12. Intermarriage with, by Solomon, 1 Kings xi, 1; 2 Chron. xii, 13; Neh. xiii, 26; by Jews, Ezra ix, 1; Neh. xiii, 23.

Notice of their kings: BAALIS, Jer. xl, 14: HANUN, 2 Sam. x; 1 Chron. xix: NAHOSH, 1 Sam. xi; 2 Sam. x, 2; 1 Chron. xix, 1, 2.

For their towns, see HESHBON, MINUITH, RABBAH. They are continually spoken of in conjunction with the kindred people of Moab, and they appear to have worshiped the same God, Chemosh, Num. xxi, 29; Judg. xi, 24; though Moloch or Milcom is specially called their "abomination," 1 Kings xi, 5.

See prophecies concerning the Ammonites in Isa. xi, 14; Jer. ix, 25, 26; xxv, 15–21; xxvii, 1–11; xlix, 1–6; Ezek. xxi, 20, 28–32; xxv, 1–11; Dan. xi, 41; Amos i, 13–15; Zeph. ii, 9–11.

Am'orites, (Map 3,) *mountaineers*, the most powerful of all the nations of Canaan; hence their name often occurs for the Canaanites in general, Gen. xv, 16; Josh. xxiv, 18; Amos ii, 9, 10; Judg. vi, 10. In Gen. x, 16, their origin is traced to *Emori*, an offspring of Canaan. Sometimes we find a city said to be occupied by Amorites, which appears elsewhere assigned to another tribe. Thus Jerusalem is Amorite, Josh. x, 3, 5; Jebusite, xv, 63. More particularly, however, the Amorites occupied the mountains; while the Canaanites dwelt in the lowlands, Num. xiii, 29. They extended themselves to the east of the Jordan, from the Arnon to Hermon, which in their language they called Shenir or Senir. Here they formed two kingdoms under Sihon and Og, including all Gilead and Bashan, which, on Sihon's refusal to let the Israelites pass peaceably, Moses conquered and assigned to the tribes of Reuben and Gad, and to the half-tribe of Manasseh, Deut. ii, 26–30; iii, 8–10. Five kings of the Amorites were destroyed by Joshua; still the nation was by no means exterminated. We find them in the period of the Judges, Judg. i, 34–36; iii, 5; and even to the reign of Solomon, who subjected the remnant of them to bond service, 1 Kings ix, 20, 21. There is also a notice of them as existing after the captivity, Ezra ix, 1.

Mr. Grove (in Smith's Dictionary) argues with great force that the name "Amorite" was a local term, and not the name of a distinct tribe. See also Herzog's *Encyclopedia*, (Philadelphia edition, translated by Dr. Bomberger, vol. i, page 128.)

BIBLE GEOGRAPHY.

Amphip'olis, (Map 8,) a *city* on *both* sides, or *around the city;* a city of Macedonia, on the river Strymon. The Athenians colonized it, and gave it its name because the river flowed on both sides. It was also on the *Via Egnatia*, and under the Romans formed the chief city of *Macedonia prima*. Paul and Silas passed through it on their way from Philippi to Thessalonica, Acts xvii, 1. A village of about one hundred houses, called *Neophorio*, ("New Town," in Turkish *Jeni Kevi*,) now occupies part of its site.

Am'ramite, (from AMRAM, *kindred of the lofty one*, that is, *friend of Jehovah*.) The name given to the family of Amram the Levite, Num. iii, 27; 1 Chron. xxvi, 23.

A'nab, (Map 5,) *place of clusters*, a *grape-town*, a place in the mountains of Judah where once the Anakim dwelt, whom Joshua expelled, Num. xiii, 33; Josh. xi, 21; xv, 50. Now *'Anab*, ten miles south-south-west of Hebron.

Anaha'rath, signification unknown; some render *snorting*, or *burning*, or *gorge*. A city of Issachar, Josh. xix, 19. The site was apparently unknown in the time of Eusebius and Jerome. It was perhaps in the northern part of the tribe, possibly at *Meskarah*, where now are ruins.

An'akim, (Map 3,) (from ANAK, *long-necked*, that is, a *giant;* or perhaps *noble*,) sons of Anak; children of Anak; sons of the Anakim. See Deut. i, 28; ix, 2; Josh. xiv, 15. A gigantic race living in Southern Palestine, among the mountains of Judah and Ephraim, Josh. xi, 21, 22; xiv, 12; and especially in the neighborhood of Hebron. They were the dread of the Israelites, but at length were almost entirely extirpated.

An'amim, signification unknown: perhaps *responding waters*. An Egyptian tribe, descended from Mizraim, whose location is only conjectural, Gen. x, 13; 1 Chron. i, 11.

Anani'ah, one whom *Jehovah covers*, a town where the Benjamites lived after the captivity, Neh. xi, 32. Probably the modern *Beit Hanina*, a small village three miles north of Jerusalem.

An'athoth, (Map 6,) *answers*, that is, to prayers; *echoes*, a priest's city in Benjamin, Josh. xxi, 18; 1 Chron. vi, 60. To this place Abiathar was banished, 1 Kings ii, 26. Jeremiah was born there, Jer. i, 1; xi, 21, 23; xxxii. 7-9. Some of its people returned with Zerubbabel, Ezra ii, 23; Neh. vii, 27. Probably in or near a great road to Jerusalem; for it is mentioned in Isa. x, 30, as on the onward march of the Assyrians, where the Prophet, speaking of it pitifully, says, "O poor Anathoth!" It is the same as the modern *'Anata*, about four miles north-east of Jerusalem. The village is small and poor, but the ruins indicate that the ancient town was walled, and a place of great strength.

A'nem, *two fountains*, a Levitical city in Issachar, 1 Chron. vi, 73; called *En-Gannim* in Josh. xix, 21; xxi, 29; probably the modern *Jenin*. See EN-GANNIM.

A'ner, a *young man,* or perhaps an *exile* or *emigrant*, a Levitical city in the half-tribe of Manasseh west of the Jordan, 1 Chron. vi, 70. Gesenius supposes this to be the same with Taanach of Judg. i, 27, or Tanach, Josh. xxi, 25.

A'nim, *fountains*, a town in the mountains of Judah, Josh. xv, 50. It is supposed to be identified with the modern village of *Ghuwein*, one hour south of Semoa, on the road from Hebron to Moladah.

Anti-Lib'anus, (Map 5,) *opposite Libanus*, Judith i, 7, the eastern of the

ANTAKIA, (ANTIOCH IN SYRIA.)

two great parallel ridges of mountains that inclose the valley of Cœle-Syria proper: "Lebanon toward the sun-rising," Josh. xiii, 5. Now called *Jebel Esh-Shurki.* See LEBANON.

An'tioch, (Maps 1, 8,) (from *Antiochus,*) the name of two places:

1. A very celebrated Syrian city called Antioch the Great, and Antioch Epidaphnes, or "by Daphne," (where were the laurel grove and sanctuary of Apollo and Diana,) in order to distinguish it from other places of the same name. It was founded by Seleucus Nicator three hundred years B. C., and named by him after his father Antiochus. It was on the banks of the Orontes, three hundred miles north of Jerusalem, and about thirty miles from the Mediterranean. It soon became a splendid town. The Syrian kings embellished it. Pompey made it a free city. Herod contributed to its adornment, and the Roman emperors added various structures. Many Jews were settled in Antioch, having been invited thither by Seleucus and granted special privileges. The inhabitants generally were pleasure-seekers and luxurious, and are said to have been fond of inventing nicknames. Hence, possibly, the designation "Christians," given to the disciples of Christ, Acts xi, 26. Antioch is, next to Jerusalem, of the greatest interest and importance in the apostolic history. Here the Gospel was successfully preached, Acts xi, 19-30. Barnabas and Saul were sent thence, Acts xiii, 1-3. Their return is mentioned, Acts xiv, 26-28. To this great city prophets resorte', Acts xi, 27; here the most eminent pastors ministered, xiii, 1; hence w . dispatched that first missionary expedition in which Christianity was planted throughout Asia, xiii, 2-52, and chap. xiv, and from which eventually came the introduction of the Gospel into Europe, xv, 36; xvi, 12; here, too, were fought battles for the fundamental principles of the faith, xv, 1, 2; Gal. ii, 11-14. In the time of Chrysostom the population was computed at 200,000, of whom about one half were professed Christians. Chrysostom states that the Church at Antioch maintained three thousand poor, besides relieving many more. Some stirring notices of this great city may be found in the books of the Maccabees, (especially 1 Macc. iii, 37; xi, 13; 2 Macc. iv, 7-9; v, 21; xi, 36.) The city now bears the name of *Antakiá,* or *Antákieh,* and belongs to the pashalic of Haleb, (Aleppo.) War, pestilence, and earthquakes have reduced it to a mean town with 6,000 inhabitants, among whom are some Jews and a few Christians. The antiquities of Antioch are few and uninteresting, considering the extent and splendor of the ancient city. Its temples, palaces, and colonnades have disappeared. Here and there are traces of ruins; and now and then, amid the gardens, one sees a granite shaft or a marble capital.

2. Antioch of Pisidia, originally founded by the Magnetes on the Meander, was re-established, and named, like the Syrian city, by Seleucus Nicator. It was on a ridge of the Taurus. It became a colony under Augustus, and was named also Cesarea. Paul preached here, but was obliged to flee, Acts xiii, 14-52; 2 Tim. iii, 11. Jews from Antioch persecuted Paul at Lystra; but Paul returned to Antioch, Acts xiv, 19-22, and revisited it, Acts xviii, 22. The site of this city has lately been identified with the modern *Yalobatch,* where a few ruins yet remain.

Antip'atris, (Map 5,) *for his father,* a city built by Herod the Great, in honor of his father, on the site of a former place called *Caphar-Saba.* To this city Paul was brought from Jerusalem by night on his route to Cesarea, Acts xxiii, 31. Probably identical with *Kala'at Ras el 'Ain.*

Anto'nia, (Map 26,) a fortress, or tower built by Herod, and named by him in honor of his friend *Antonius*. It was on the site of the more ancient Baris, on the north-west of the temple. (See JERUSALEM) It was the "castle" of Acts xxi, 34, 37, into which Paul was carried from the temple by the soldiers, and from the stairs of which he made the earnest speech found in Acts xxii. Compare Acts xxi, 40; xxii, 24, 30; xxiii, 10, 16.

Aphar'sachites, Ezra v, 6; vi, 6; and

Aphar'sathchites, Ezra iv, 9, a tribe of Assyrian colonists of Samaria; and

Aphar'sites, Ezra iv, 9, another tribe of Assyrian colonists, about whom nothing is known with certainty. Hiller regards them as the *Parrhasii*, a tribe of eastern Media. Gesenius thinks they are the *Persians*.

A'phek, probably *strength*, the name of several places.

1. A city of the tribe of Asher, Josh. xix, 30, apparently near Phenicia, Josh. xiii, 4; doubtless the same with Aphik, which the Israelites were unable to capture from the Canaanites, Judg. i, 31. This was doubtless the *Aphaca*, celebrated for its temple of Venus, now *Afka* in Lebanon.

2. A city whose king was destroyed by Joshua, Josh. xii, 18. Probably identical with Aphekah, xv, 53.

3. A place in Issachar not far from Jezreel, where the Philistines pitched before the battle in which the ark was taken, 1 Sam. iv, 1. That mentioned in 1 Sam. xxix, 1, may be the same.

4. A town of Syria, in which Ben-Hadad took refuge, on the highway between Damascus and Palestine, 1 Kings xx, 26–30; 2 Kings xiii, 17. It is now called *Fik*, six miles east of the Sea of Galilee. It is remarkable for the great number of inns that it contains.

Aphe'kah, (fem. of Aphek,) *strong place.* A city in the mountains of Judah, Josh. xv, 53. It is considered by most as identical with the Aphek of Josh. xii, 18. It was probably near Hebron, but is unknown.

A'phik, *strong,* or perhaps *water-course,* a city not subdued by Asher, Judg. i, 31. Doubtless the same as APHEK 1.

Aph'rah, *fawn,* or perhaps *dust.* Supposed to be identical with Ophrah, Micah i, 10. See BETH-LE-APHRAH.

Apollo'nia, (Map 8,) *belonging to Apollo,* a name borne by several places in Europe and Asia dedicated to Apollo. The Apollonia through which Paul passed was a city in Macedonia, in the district of Mygdonia, nearly midway between Amphipolis and Thessalonica, Acts xvii, 1. A more noted city by this name was Illyria.

Ap'pii-Fo'rum, (Map 8,) *the market-place of Appius.* A station on the Appian Road, where the disciples met Paul, Acts xxviii, 15. Ancient itineraries fix this place at forty-three miles from Rome; and the forty-third mile-stone, which is still preserved, and some other ruins near Treponti, mark the ancient site.

Ar, (Map 5,) a *city;* in Num. xxi, 28, Ar-Moab; also city of Moab; Rabbah or Rabbath, Rabbath-Moab, and Areopolis. The chief city of Moab, south of the river Arnon, and about seventeen miles east of the Dead Sea. Ar is sometimes taken for the land of Moab, Deut. ii, 9, 18, 29. It was burned by Sihon, Num. xxi, 26–30. Desolation was prophesied, Isa. xv, 1. Ar is "laid waste and brought to silence." A few ruins remain under the name *Rabba,* lying on a low hill about ten miles north of Kerak.

A'rab, *ambush,* a city in the mountains of Judah, Josh. xv, 52, whence possibly the Gentile *Arbite*, 2 Sam. xxiii, 35. Possibly the place known as *Khirbet el 'Arabiyeh* east of Hebron, marks the site.

Ar'abah, (Map 2,) a *sterile region*, the name of a region and of a town. It has usually the definite article—"the Arabah"—and in that case signifies the great Jordan valley. This valley extended from the foot of Anti-Libanus down to the eastern gulf of the Red Sea, a distance of not less than two hundred and fifty miles. The modern Arabs call the upper portion of this valley, or about one hundred and fifty miles of it, *Ghôr*, and the southern part the *Wady el-Arabah*. Arabah occurs but once in our version, (Josh. xviii, 18,) but repeatedly in the original, and is translated in our version "plain," "wilderness," "desert," Deut. i, 1; ii, 8; iii, 17; iv, 49; Josh. iii, 16; xii, 1, 3; 2 Kings xiv, 25; Amos vi, 14. Much light is thrown upon various passages of Scripture by the right understanding of what the Arabah, or "plain," really is. See Josh. viii, 14; 2 Sam. ii, 29; 2 Kings xxv, 4.

2. A city of Benjamin, Josh. xviii, 18; elsewhere called more fully Beth-Arabah, Josh. xv, 61; xviii, 22.

Ar'abatti'ne, 1. A place in Idumea, 1 Macc. v, 3, toward the southern end of the Dead Sea, occupied by the Edomites during the captivity.

2. A toparchy of Judea, extending between Neapolis (Shechem) and Jericho, supposed to have taken its name from MAALEH-ACRABBIM, which see.

Ara'bia, (Maps 1, 12,) 1 Kings x, 15; 2 Chron. ix, 14; Isa. xxi, 13; Jer. xxv, 24; Ezek. xxvii, 21; Gal. i, 17; iv, 23; 2 Esdr. xv, 29; 1 Macc. xi, 16; 2 Macc. xii, 11. The meaning is, *wild, desert place, sterile*. The Hebrew '*Arâb* was applied to nearly the same territory as that called *Kedem*, "the East," (Gen. x, 30; xxv, 6; xxix, 1,) lying to the east of Palestine, but north of the Arabian peninsula. Gradually the appellation obtained a wider scope. The Greek geographers divided the country into *Felix*, *Petræa*, and *Deserta*. A more recent division is as follows: *Arabia Proper*, or *Jezirat el-Arab*, or the great peninsula as far as the northern wastes; *Northern Arabia*, or *El-Badieh*, or the vast Arabian Desert, bounded by the peninsula, the Euphrates, Syria, and the Desert of Petræa; *Western Arabia*, comprising the Peninsula of Sinai and the Desert of Petræa, bounded by the Red Sea, Egypt, Palestine, and Northern Arabia. Arabia Proper may be subdivided into five principal provinces: the Yemen, the districts of Hadramaut, Mahreh, and Oman on the Indian Ocean, and the entrance of the Persian Gulf; El-Bahrein, toward the head of the gulf just named: the great central country of Nejd and Yemameh; and the Hejaz and Tehameh, on the Red Sea. The Arabs also have five divisions: Tehameh, the Hejaz, Nejd, El-Arûd, (the provinces lying toward the head of the Persian Gulf, including Yemameh,) and the Yemen, including Oman and the intervening tracts. They have, however, never agreed either as to the limits or the number of the divisions. The inhabitants of different parts of Arabia, besides being called Arabians, were called Horites, Edomites, Idumeans, Ishmaelites.

Much of the most hallowed portion of Scripture history is connected with this country. Job lived here. Here Moses saw the burning bush unconsumed with fire. Through its wildernesses the Israelites wandered for forty years, witnessing the amazing miracles which God wrought for their deliverance. We have space but for a few Scripture references concerning the country and its inhabitants. The Arabians were descended from Ishmael, Gen xxv, 13, 14; 1 Chron. i, 29–31, with Isa. xxi, 11–17. Their territory,

Gen. xxv. 18. A people who lived in tents, Isa. xiii, 20; Jer. iii, 1. They bring gold to Solomon, 2 Chron. ix, 14; and flocks to Jehoshaphat, 2 Chron. xvii, 11. They invade Judah, and slay Jehoram's sons, 2 Chron. xxi, 16, 17; xxi, 1. Defeated by Uzziah, 2 Chron. xxvi, 7. They oppose the building of Jerusalem, Neh. ii, 19; iv, 7. Their commerce with Tyre, Ezek. xxvii, 21. At Jerusalem on day of Pentecost, Acts ii, 11. Paul visits Arabia, Gal. i, 17. Prophecies of, Isa. xxi, 11-17; xlii, 11; lx, 7; Jer. xxv, 23, 24; xlix, 28, 29.

A'rad, (Map 1,) perhaps *flight*, or *wild ass*, some say *a dragon*, a Canaanitish city north of the wilderness of Judah. The King of Arad resisted the Israelites in their third attempt to enter Canaan, Num. xxi, 1; xxxiii, 40. [Here "King Arad" should be "King of Arad."] The Aradites were subdued by Joshua, Josh. xii, 14; Judg. i, 16. Arad is probably identical with *Tell 'Arâd*, eight hours south of Hebron.

Ar'adus, 1 Macc. xv, 23. See ARVAD, with which it is identical.

A'ram, *high region*, the highland country which lay (with interruptions) between the Tigris and the Mediterranean, Gen. x, 22, 23; xxii, 21; Num. xxiii, 7; 1 Chron. i, 17; ii, 23. Elsewhere translated Syria and Syrians. (See Mesopotamia.) When first the name occurs (Gen. xxiv, 10) it is as Aram-Naharaim, "Aram of the two rivers," (Mesopotamia in our version,) the highland region between the Euphrates and the Tigris. Padan-Aram was also used to denote the same region, Gen. xxv, 20; xxviii, 2. There were a number of small kingdoms comprised in the country of Aram, each distinguished by some special name, as Aram-Zobah, or Zobah, 1 Sam. xiv, 47; 2 Sam. viii, 3; x, 6, 8; 1 Chron. xviii, 5, 9; xix, 6; Aram-Rehob, or Beth-Rehob, 2 Sam. x, 6, 8; Syria-Maachah, 1 Chron. xix, 6; Geshur "in Aram," 2 Sam. xv, 8; compare 1 Chron. ii, 23; Aram-Damascus, 2 Sam. viii, 5, 6; 1 Chron. xviii, 5, 6; and probably many more. All these small States are spoken of collectively under the name of Aram, 2 Sam. x, 13. Damascus was far the most powerful, and its influence gradually extended, till by Aram or Syria was understood that great monarchy of which Damascus was the capital, 1 Kings xi, 25; xv, 18; xx, 1; Isa. vii, 1, 2, 8. This country was peopled by the descendants of Shem. The descent of the Arameans from a son of Shem is confirmed by their language, which was one of the branches of the Semitic family, and nearly allied to the Hebrew.

A'ram-Nahara'im, Judg. iii, 8, marg.; Psa. lx, title. See ARAM.

A'ram-Zo'bah, Psa. lx, title. See ARAM.

Ar'arat, (Map 1,) *sacred* or *holy land*, the name of the mountains in Armenia on which the ark rested after the flood, Gen. viii, 4. This word occurs in 2 Kings xix, 37; Isa. xxxvii, 38; Jer. li, 27; but in the first two passages our version renders it Armenia. In Tobit i, 21, the form is Ararath. The term does not refer to a mountain, but to a country on whose mountains the ark rested. The mountain known to us as Ararat is called by the natives *Massis*, by the Turks *Agri-Dagh*, and by the Persians *Kuh-i-Nuh*, that is, Mountain of Noah. There are two peaks known as "the Mountains of Ararat." The highest is 17,750 feet above the sea, and 14,573 feet above the plain. While, without doubt, the ark rested on the mountains of Armenia, we cannot with certainty fix upon which mountain. Probably it was on some one of the *lower* peaks of the chain. See AB-MENIA.

THE AREOPAGUS (OR MARS' HILL) AND ACROPOLIS.

Ar'arath, Tobit i, 21, another form of Ararat.

Arbat'tis, (but occurring only in dative plural,) a district of the Holy Land mentioned (1 Macc. v, 23) as despoiled by Simon Maccabeus. Probably identical with Arabattine.

Ar'bel. See BETH-ARBEL. Hosea x, 14.

Arbe'la, in Galilee, 1 Macc. ix, 2, probably identical with BETH-ARBEL, and now *Irbid*, on the west side of the sea of Gennesareth.

Arbo'nai, a river between the Euphrates and the Mediterranean. Probably in Mesopotamia, Judith ii, 24. On its banks were several large cities, which Holofernes destroyed.

Ar'chevites, probably the inhabitants of Erech, the city of Nimrod, (Gen. x, 10,) some of whom had been placed as colonists in Samaria, Ezra iv, 9. The name is in the Chaldee form.

Ar'chi, Josh. xvi, 2, and

Ar'chite, a native of a place called Erech, (not the Erech of Babylonia, Gen. x, 10,) not otherwise known, 2 Sam. xv, 32; xvii, 5, 14; 1 Chron xxvii, 33. This city or district was in the neighborhood of Bethel.

Ar'dath, a field mentioned in 2 Esdr. ix, 26, as the scene of the vision of a bereaved woman.

Areop'agus, *the Hill of Mars*, a rocky height in Athens, opposite the western end of the Acropolis. It derived its name from the legend that Mars, (Ares,) the god of war, was tried here by the other gods on a charge of murder. Here was held the noted council of the Areopagus. Its meetings were held on the south-eastern summit of the rock, the Areopagites sitting as judges in the open air. There are still sixteen stone steps cut in the rock, leading up to the hill from the Valley of the Agora below; and immediately above the steps is a bench of stones excavated in the rock, forming three sides of a quadrangle, and facing the south. St. Paul here made his remarkable address, Acts xvii, 19–34. See MARS' HILL.

Ar'gob, (Map 5,) *stony, stone-heap*, a district east of the Jordan, in Bashan, Deut. iii, 4, 13, 14; 1 Kings iv, 13. It was allotted to the half-tribe of Manasseh, and was, in later classical times, called Trachonitis, the *rough*, and has been identified as the modern well-defined *Lejâh*, south of Damascus. This is a very remarkable region. It extends, in the shape of an irregular oval, about twenty-two miles from north to south, by fourteen from east to west, being thickly studded with ruined cities and villages. It is described as an "ocean of basaltic rocks." It is composed of black basalt, which seems to have issued from innumerable pores in the surface of the earth, and thence, in a liquid state, to have flowed out on every side till the plain was covered. A Roman road runs through the district from south to north, probably between Bosra and Damascus. Referring to the remarkable passage in Deut. iii, 4, 5, Mr. Porter says: "Such a statement seems almost incredible. But mysterious, incredible as this seemed, on the spot, with my own eyes, I have seen that this is literally true." "It is literally crowded with towns and large villages, and, though a vast majority of them are deserted, *they are not ruined.* I have more than once entered a deserted city in the evening, taken possession of a comfortable house, and spent the night in peace. Many of the houses in the ancient cities of Bashan are perfect, as if only finished yesterday. The walls are sound, the roofs unbroken, the doors, and even the window-shutters, in their places." "These ancient cities of Bashan contain probably the very oldest specimens of domestic architecture now existing in the world."—Porter's *Giant Cities.* See KENATH; EDREI.

A'riel, *lion of God,* or *hearth* (altar) *of God,* used in Isa. xxix, 1, as a poetical name of Jerusalem.

Arimathe'a, (Map 5,) *the double heights,* a town of Judea, where resided Joseph who begged the body of Jesus, Matt. xxvii, 57; Mark xv, 43; Luke xxiii, 51; John xix, 38. It is supposed by some identical with Ramah, the birth-place of Samuel, and hence identified with the existing *Ramleh,* (ten miles south-east of Joppa,) because of the similarity of the name to that of Ramah, (of which Ramathaim is the dual,) and because it is near Lydda and Diospolis. Possibly Arimathea may be a corruption of Ramathaim, and thus the same as Ramah, (4;) but its identity with Ramleh cannot be sustained. Some identify it with *Renthieh,* ten miles due east from Joppa. See " *The Land and the Book.*" See RAMAH, (4.)

Ark'ites, (Map 3,) *fugitives,* the name of the inhabitants of *Arka,* Gen. x, 17; 1 Chron. i, 15; descendants of the Phenician or Sidonian branch of Canaan. Arka was at the north-west base of Lebanon. Here was a splendid temple for the worship of Astarte. The place was noted as the birthplace of the Emperor Alexander Severus. Ruins of this once splendid city still exist at *Tel 'Arka,* four miles south of the *Nahr-el-Kebir,* and twelve miles north of Tripoli.

Armaged'don, the *mountain,* or perhaps the *city of Megiddo,* a name used emblematically for a place of slaughter and mourning, Rev. xvi, 16. In this passage allusion is made to that great battle-field where Barak and Gideon conquered, Judg. iv; v, 19; vi, 33; vii; where Saul and Josiah fell, 1 Sam. xxix, 1; xxxi; 2 Sam. iv, 4; 2 Chron. xxxv, 20–24—the plain of Esdraelon, on the southern border of which stood Megiddo. See ESDRAELON and MEGIDDO.

Arme'nia, (Map 1,) a country of Western Asia, extending from the Caucasus in the north to the Taurus on the south, triangular in shape. The name of this country does not occur in the Bible under this form. In 2 Kings xix, 37; Isa. xxxvii, 38, our translators have rendered the Hebrew *Ararat* into Armenia, improperly. *Ararat* may be the central region of Armenia round the mountains known by that name. *Minni,* mentioned in Jer. li, 27, (with Ararat and Ashkenaz,) as a kingdom called to arm itself against Babylon, is thought to be a contraction of Armenia. meaning perhaps the district *Minyas.* Then there is Togarmah, Gen. x, 3; Ezek. xxvii, 14; xxxviii, 6, of wider signification, a region which must, from the connection in which it is found, be identified with Armenia. The traditional belief of the Armenians is that they are descended from Thorgomass or Tiorgarmal.

Ar'non, (Map 5,) *noisy,* a *murmur,* a river east of Jordan, the boundary of Moab and the Amorites, Num. xxi, 13, 26; xxii, 36; Deut. ii, 24, 36; iii, 8, 16; Josh. xii, 1. There were fords of Arnon, Isa. xvi, 2; and "high places," Num. xxi, 28, (perhaps mentioned also in Isa. xv, 2.) The Arnon is generally mentioned in connection with the city Aroer, which stood upon its north bank. See passages above, and Josh. xiii, 9, 16; Judg. xi, 13, 18, 22, 26; 2 Kings x, 33. Without doubt the stream now called *el-Mojib* is the ancient Arnon, and the Wady *el-Mojib* is the ravine through which it passed. Where this stream bursts into the Dead Sea it is eighty-two feet wide and four feet deep, flowing through a chasm with perpendicular sides of red, brown, and yellow sandstone, ninety-seven feet wide.

Ar'oer, (Map 5,) *ruins* (?), *heath,* the name of several places:
1. A city on the north bank of the Arnon, assigned, after the conquest of Sihon, to Reuben, Deut. ii, 36; iii, 12; iv, 48; Josh. xii, 2; xiii, 9, 16; Judg. xi, 26; 1 Chron. v, 8. Afterward, with the rest of the trans-Jordanic territory, it was occupied by Hazael, and was subsequently possessed by Moab, 2 Kings x, 32, 33; Jer. xlviii, 19. Ruins called '*Arârah* on the north edge of the ravine of the *Mojib,* mark the site. The valley when viewed from this spot "looks like a deep chasm, formed by some tremendous convulsion of the earth, into which there seems no possibility of descending to the bottom." Difficult and dangerous as is the pass of this ravine, a number of modern travelers have crossed it. Traces of the old Roman road and milestones appear both in descending and ascending. (See Porter's *Hand-Book.*)
2. A town built or rebuilt by the Gadites, Num. xxxii, 34; Josh. xiii, 25; Judg. xi, 33; 2 Sam. xxiv, 5. Perhaps the site is marked by the modern '*Ayra,* two hours south-west of *es-Salt.* (See RAMOTH-GILEAD.) Some consider Aroer mentioned in Isa. xvii, 2, as identical with this place; but this would seem, from its grouping, to be farther north, and dependent on Damascus.
3. A place in Judah, 1 Sam. xxx, 28. Now doubtless '*Ar'arah,* eleven miles west-south-west of *Bir es-Seb'a,* on the road from Gaza to Petræa.

Ar'pad, or **Ar'phad,** *prop, support,* a Syrian city in the neighborhood of Hamath and Damascus; conquered by the Assyrians, 2 Kings xviii, 34, xix, 13; Isa. x, 9; xxxvi, 19; xxxvii, 13; Jer. xlix, 23. Several localities have been suggested as identical with Arpad, the most probable of which is *Arvad,* or Aradus, opposite Hamath. See ARVAD.

Ar'sareth, a region mentioned only in 2 Esd. xiii, 45, and supposed to be beyond the Euphrates.

Ar'uboth, *windows,* a *lattice,* a district possibly on the sea-shore of Judah. It is mentioned only in 1 Kings iv, 10, as one of Solomon's commissariat districts.

Aru'mah, *elevated, exalted,* a town apparently near Shechem, where Abimelech dwelt, Judg. ix, 41. Perhaps it is the same with Rumah of 2 Kings xxiii, 36. Possibly the ruin *el-Ormah,* five miles south-east of *Nablûs,* marks the site.

Ar'vad, (Maps 3, 4,) *wandering, place of fugitives,* a small rocky island off the north coast of Phenicia, about two miles from the shore, called by the Greeks *Aradus.* The inhabitants were called *Arvadites,* Gen. x, 18; 1 Chron. i, 16. In Ezek. xxvii, 8, 11, they are represented as mariners and soldiers aiding in the defense of Tyre. The island has about 3,000 inhabitants, living by fishing and navigation. There is now a village called *Ruad,* with massive Phœnician walls partially preserved.

As'calon, the Greek form of Ashkelon, Judith ii, 28; 1 Macc. x, 86; xi, 60; xii, 33.

A'ser, the Greek form of Hazor, Tobit i, 2; and of Asher, Luke ii, 36; Rev. vii, 6.

A'shan, *smoke,* a Levitical city in the plain, at first assigned to Judah, Josh. xv, 42; afterward to Simeon, xix, 7; 1 Chron. iv, 32. It was given to the priests, 1 Chron. vi, 59. (Compare Josh. xxi, 16, where *Ain* is mentioned instead of Ashan.) In 1 Sam. xxx, 30, *Chor-Ashan* probably is the same. Mr. Grove says: "It has not yet been identified, unless it be the same as Ain; in which case Robinson found it at *Al Ghuweir.*"

Ash'belite, *fires of Baal* (?), or *determination of God*, the descendants of Ashbel, Num. xxvi, 38.

Ash'chenaz, 1 Chron. i, 6; Jer. li, 27, a less correct form of ASHKENAZ, which see.

Ash'dod, (Map 5,) a *stronghold, castle,* one of the five cities of the Philistines, Josh. xiii, 3; 1 Sam. vi, 17. There the worship of Dagon was specially celebrated, 1 Sam. v. It was dismantled by Uzziah, 2 Chron. xxvi, 6; and taken by Tartan, Isa. xx, 1. Jews married women from, Neh. xiii, 23. Language of, xiii, 24. After a long siege Ashdod was taken by Psammetichus, king of Egypt; possibly alluded to in Jer. xxv, 20. Threatened, Amos i, 8; iii, 9; Zeph. ii, 4; Zech. ix, 6; destroyed by the Maccabees, 1 Macc. v, 68; x, 84. It was visited by Philip, Acts viii, 40, (as Azotus.) It was about three miles from the Mediterranean, midway between Joppa and Gaza. It is now an insignificant village called *Esdud*, situated on the eastern declivity of a little flattish hill. The site is beautiful and commanding.

Ash'doth-Pis'gah, *outpourings* (ravines) *of Pisgah*, a ravine or district near the base of Mount Pisgah, Deut. iii, 17. (Compare Deut. iv, 49; Josh. xii, 3; xiii, 20.) Whether *ravine, mountain base,* or *streams poured forth,* be the precise meaning cannot be determined with certainty.

Ash'er, (Map 5,) *happy, blessedness.* 1. The name of the tribe called after the eleventh son of Jacob: so named because Leah thought herself happy at his birth, Gen. xxx, 12, 13. The territory of Asher lay on the shore of the Mediterranean, extending from Carmel to Zidon; bounded by Manasseh, Issachar, Zebulun, and Naphtali. Dr. Thomson reckons the territory at sixty miles in length, with a breadth of ten or twelve miles. It was numbered at Sinai, Num. i, 41; and in the plains of Moab, xxvi, 44–47. Families of, Num. xxvi, 44–47; 1 Chron. vii, 30–40. Encamped north of the Tabernacle, under the standard of Dan, Num. ii, 25, 27. Blessing of Moses upon, Deut. xxxiii, 24. Inheritance in Canaan, Josh. xix, 24–31. Asher did not expel the Canaanites, Judg. i, 31, 32. Their shipping, Judg. v, 17. Reproved for not aiding Barak, Judg. v, 17. Assisted Gideon against Midian, Judg. vi, 35; vii, 23. They joined Ish-Bosheth, 2 Sam. ii, 9. Number of their soldiers in David's time, 1 Chron. vii, 40; xii, 36. They kept Hezekiah's passover, 2 Chron. xxx, 11. The people of this tribe were called Asherites, Judg. i, 32.

2. A place at the east end of the boundary line between Ephraim and Manasseh, Josh. xvii, 7. Now *Yasir*, or *Teyasir*, between *Nablûs* and *Beisan*.

Ash'kelon, As'kelon, (Map 5,) *migration*, one of the five cities of the Philistines. A sea-port between Gaza and Ashdod, lying off the great road from Egypt; it was therefore of little consequence in biblical history. Josh. xiii, 3; 1 Sam. vi, 17; 2 Sam. i, 20. It was taken by Judah, Judg. i, 18. Exploit of Samson there, Judg. xiv, 19. Mentioned by the prophets, Jer. xxv, 20; xlvii, 5, 7; Amos i, 8; Zeph. ii, 4, 7; Zech. ix, 5. In later times it was a place of importance, noted for the worship of Decerto, the Syrian Venus; and it was of some consequence in the Crusades. The place is now a mass of ruins called *El Jore*, or by some *'Askulân*, presenting "such an aspect of utter desolation that it is painful to look upon it."

Ash'kenaz, (Map 12,) (meaning uncertain,) a Japhetic people sprung from Gomer, Gen. x, 3; called also Aschenaz, 1 Chron. i, 6; Jer. li, 27; probably living originally in the neighborhood of Armenia or the Caspian. There are various conjectures as to the precise locality. The Jewish rabbis identify it with Germany; while others find in the name the origin of *As*-ia. Kalisch identifies their city with the ancient city Rhagæ, in the eastern part of Great Media, a day's journey south of the Caspian. The ruins of this city exist at *Rhey*, not far from Teheran.

Ash'nah, *the strong, fortified*, two cities in the maritime low lands of Judah, mentioned in Josh. xv, 33, 43. Their site is not certainly identified.

Ash'taroth, or As'taroth, (Map 3,) (plural of Ashtoreth,) *Statues of Astarte* (?) a city in Bashan, the residence of King Og, Deut. i, 4; Josh. ix, 10; xii, 4; xiii, 12; in the half tribe of Manasseh, xiii, 31; allotted to the Gershomites, 1 Chron. vi, 71. In Josh. xxi, 27, it is called Beesh-terah. Perhaps *Tell 'Ashtere* in *Jaulan* marks the site.

Ash'terathite, 1 Chron. xi, 44. One of David's warriors; probably a native of the following place.

Ash'teroth Kar'naim, (Map 3,) *Ashteroth of the two horns, horned Astarte*, a very ancient city of the Rephaim, Gen. xiv, 5, and probably a distinct place from the preceding. It is doubtless the Carnaim or Carnion of Maccabean history. See 1 Macc. v, 43; 2 Macc. xii, 21, 26. Some think it the modern *Sŭnamein*, thirty miles south of Damascus. Others, with apparently better reasons, identify it with *Mezareib*, where is the first castle on the great pilgrim road from Damascus to Mecca.

Ash'urites, (meaning uncertain, perhaps from a word signifying a *step*,) a tribe mentioned in 2 Sam. ii, 9, as under the authority of Ish-Bosheth. Their history is vague. Some think them the same as the Geshurites. Perhaps they were the Asshurites, or the Asherites; but all such identification is conjectural.

A'sia, (Map 1.) The import of this word in the Old and New Testaments is restricted by the sense in which it was commonly employed in ancient times. Some of the old Greek writers use it for the whole world. Later it was restricted to a continent in contrast with Europe and Africa. In the Roman period it was generally applied only to the single district of Western Asia, known as Asia Minor, although the boundaries of Asia Minor varied at different periods.

In 1 Macc. viii, 6, Antiochus the Great is termed King of Asia, because his dominions included, besides Syria, the greater part of Asia Minor. This title was given to several Syrian kings, xi, 13; xii, 39; xiii, 32; 2 Macc. iii, 3. The term Asia in Acts vi, 9; xix, 10, 22; xx, 4, 16, 18; 1 Cor. xvi, 19; 2 Cor. i, 8; 2 Tim. i, 15; 1 Pet. i, 1; Rev. i, 4, 11, refers to "Asia Proper" or "Proconsular Asia," which comprehended the provinces of Phrygia, Mysia, Caria, and Lydia. Luke, in Acts ii, 9, 10, and xvi, 6, uses the name in a still more restricted sense, counting Phrygia and Mysia as distinct from Asia. The celebrated Seven Churches of the Apocalypse were in Asia, Rev. i, 4.

Asia Minor comprehended Bithynia, Pontus, Galatia, Cappadocia, Cilicia, Pamphylia, Pisidia, Lycaonia, Phrygia, Mysia, Troas, (all being mentioned in the New Testament,) Lydia, Ionia, Æolis, (which are sometimes included under Lydia,) Caria, Doris, and Lycia.

As'kelon, Judg. i, 18. See ASHKELON.

Asmone'ans, (Map 15.) See MACCABEES.

A'sor, 1 Macc. xi, 67; sometimes Nasor. See NASOR and HAZOR.

As'phar, *a pool,* a fountain or cistern in the south or south-east of Palestine, in the wilderness of Thecoe, or Tekoa, 1 Macc. ix, 33.

As'rielites, descendants of Asriel, a son of Manasseh, Josh. xvii, 2; 1 Chron. vii, 14; Num. xxvi, 31.

As'shur, (Map 12,) *a step,* the Hebrew form of Assyria, Gen. x, 11; Num. xxiv, 22, 24; Hosea xiv, 3. See ASSYRIA.

Asshu'rim, *steps,* an Arab tribe said to be descended from Dedan, Gen. xxv, 3; and supposed to be the same with the ASHURITES (which see) in the vicinity of Gilead, 2 Sam. ii, 9.

Asside'ans, probably *saints,* a name given to the more orthodox party among the Jews in Maccabean times. 1 Macc. ii, 42; vii, 13; 2 Macc. xiv, 6.

As'sos, (Map 8,) a sea-port town in Mysia, on the north shore of the gulf of Adramyttium, over against the island of Lesbos, about twenty miles from the town of Troas. On his journey to Jerusalem St. Paul let the vessel go round, while he crossed by land from Troas, and again embarked at Assos, Acts xx, 13, 14. It is now a miserable village, whose neighborhood still bears the name of *Asso.* Many fine ruins remain. The old citadel, above the theater, commands a glorious view.

As'sur, Ezra iv, 2; Psa. lxxxiii, 8; an inaccurate form of Asshur. See ASSYRIA.

Assyr'ia, (Map 1,) *a step,* a kingdom founded by Asshur and Nimrod, Gen. x, 8–12; Micah v, 6. Its extent differed greatly at different periods. The name occurs first in our version as the equivalent of Asshur, Gen. ii, 14; xxv, 18, and may be considered as applying both to a defined region, properly denominated Assyria, and to the empire, enlarged and consolidated by the subjection of neighboring districts, over which the King of Assyria had rule. Probably in the earliest times it was confined to a small tract of low country between the *Jebel Maklûb,* or Taurus range on the north, and the Lesser Zab (*Zab Asful*) toward the south, lying chiefly on the immediate bank of the Tigris. Its limits were gradually extended, until it came to be regarded as comprising the whole region between the Armenian Mountains (lat. 37° 30') upon the north, and upon the south the country about Bagdad, (lat. 33° 30'.) Eastward its boundary was the high range of Zagros, or Mountains of Kurdistan; westward it naturally retained the Tigris as its boundary, although, according to the view of some, it was eventually bounded by the Mesopotamian desert; while, according to others, it reached to the Euphrates. Taking the greatest of these dimensions, Assyria may be said to have extended in a direction from north-east to south-west, a distance of nearly 500 miles, with a width varying from 350 to 100 miles. Its area would thus a little exceed 100,000 square miles, or about equal to that of Italy.

Kings of Assyria: Pul, 2 Kings xv, 19, 20; 1 Chron. v, 26. Tiglath-Pileser or Tilgath-Pilneser, 2 Kings xv, 29; xvi, 10; 1 Chron. v, 26; 2 Chron. xxviii, 16, 20. Shalmaneser, 2 Kings xvii, 3, 6; xviii, 9–12. Sargon, whose general name was Tartan, Isa. xx, 1. Sennacherib, 2 Kings xviii, 13; xix, 37; Isa. xxxvi, xxxvii. Esar-Haddon, 2 Kings xix, 37; Ezra iv, 2; Isa. xxxvii, 38.

Among the prophecies concerning Assyria are the following: Num. xxiv, 22, 24; 2 Kings xix, 21–24; Isa. vii, 17–25; viii, 4–10; x, 5–34; xiv, 24–27;

ATHENS RESTORED, AS SEEN FROM THE PNYX.

xix, 23-25; xx; xxx, 27-33; xxxi, 8, 9; xxxiii, 1-12; xxxvii, 21-38; Ezek. xxxi; Jonah iii, 1-4; Nahum i, ii, iii; Zeph. ii, 13-15; Zech. x, 11. The cities of Assyria built by Nimrod were Babylon, Erech, Accad, Calneh, Gen. x, 9, 10. By Asshur: Nineveh, Calah, Rehoboth, and Resen, Gen. x, 11, 12. Babylon and Nineveh were among the mightiest cities of the earth, and occupy a prominent place in Bible history.

A'tad, *a thorn*, a place called the "threshing floor of Atad," where a solemn mourning was made for Jacob lasting seven days. Gen. i, 10, 11. From this fact it was afterward called ABEL-MIZRAIM, which see.

At'aroth, (Map 5,) *crowns*. A town east of Jordan, in the land of Jazer and Gilead, Num. xxxiii, 3, 34. Identified with *Attarus*, near Machærus.

2. A town on the border of Ephraim, Josh. xvi, 2, 7, and possibly now '*Atara*, south of *Bireh*. This place was also called Ataroth-Addar, or Ataroth-Adar. (Map 6.)

At'aroth-Ad'dar, *crowns of Addar, or greatness;* and AT'AROTH-ADAR, Josh. xvi, 5; xviii, 13. See ATAROTH (2.)

At'aroth, the house of Joab, *crowns of the house of Joab*, 1 Chron. ii, 54. A place in the tribe of Judah. Schwarz may possibly be correct in identifying it with *Latrum*, (for *el-Atron*,) on the road from Jerusalem to *Jaffa*, west of *Saris*.

A'thach, *lodging-place*, a place in the extreme south of Judah, to the inhabitants of which David sent presents, 1 Sam. xxx, 30. Several sites are proposed, but all are merely conjectural.

Ath'arim, *regions*, a place in the south of Palestine, rendered in our version, Num. xxi, 1, "the way of the spies." Perhaps it was a general designation of the region north of Mount Seir. Wilton interprets "the way of the merchants," that is, the caravan road.

Ath'ens, (Map 1,) *Minerva*. The chief city of Attica, about five miles from the sea, the capital of the leading Grecian republic, and the seat of Greek literature in the golden period of the nation, 2 Macc. ix, 15; Acts xvii, 15; xviii, 1; 1 Thess. iii, 1. Athens was one of the most noted cities of the world's history. It was founded by Cecrops, 1856 B. C. It was a very idolatrous city, its idols numbering 30,000. Petronius said it "was easier to find a god in Athens than to find a man."

St. Paul visited Athens on his second missionary journey, Acts xvii, 13-15. In Paul's time Athens was included in the Roman province of Achaia, but it was a free city, retaining some of the forms which belonged to it in its palmy days. The Athenians were curious and superstitious, Acts xvii, 21-23. They disputed with Paul in the *agora*, Acts xvii, 17, 18. Paul went from the *agora*, or market-place, unto *Areopagus*, and stood in the *midst of Mars' Hill*, where he made his famous speech, Acts xvii, 22-31. Some of his audience "mocked;" others said, "We will hear thee again;" while certain "clave unto him," Acts xvii, 32-34. A Christian Church existed in Athens soon after the apostolic times. Tradition makes its first Bishop, Dionysius the Areopagite. See AREOPAGUS.

At'roth, *crowns*, a city of Gad. Num. xxxii, 34, 35. Doubtless this word should be connected with Shophan, thus: Atroth-Shophan, (*the crowns of Shophan*,) to distinguish it from the Ataroth named just before.

Attali'a, (Map 8,) a maritime town of Pamphylia, which derived its name from its founder, Attalus Philadelphus, King of Pergamos. Paul and Barnabas visited it, Acts xiv, 25, on their return to Antioch from the inland parts of Asia Minor. Its name in the twelfth century was Satalia, and it still exists under the name of *Adalia*.

A'va, *ruin, overturning;* also called IVAH, a State conquered by Sennacherib, and from which colonists were sent to Samaria. They worshiped Nibhar and Tartak, 2 Kings xvii, 24, 31; xviii, 34; xix, 13. (Compare Ezra iv, 9.) Some make it a city, the capital of the State. Its site is not certainly identified. Grove thinks it is identical with *Hit* on the Euphrates.

A'ven, *nothingness.* 1. A plain called in the margin Bikath-Aven, Amos i, 5. It seems to be the great plain of Lebanon, in which is Baalbec, still called *El Buka'a.*

2. The name applied to the city elsewhere called On or Heliopolis, Ezek. xxx, 17.

3. A contracted form of Beth-Aven, that is, Bethel, Hos. x, 5, 8.

A'vim, *ruins*, a city of Benjamin, Josh. xviii, 23; mentioned between Bethel and Parah. Some think that a remnant of the people called Avim may have lived there.

A'vim, A'vims, or **A'vites**, (Map 3,) inhabitants of *ruins*, a tribe of early settlers in Palestine, near Gaza, displaced by the Caphtorim, Deut. ii, 23, who drove them northward, where they left a trace of themselves in the hills of Benjamin, Josh. xiii, 3; xviii, 23. See the preceding AVIM.

A'vites, the inhabitants of Ava, 2 Kings xvii, 31. See AVA.

A'vith, *ruins*, a city of the Edomites, where King Hadad reigned, Gen. xxxvi, 35; 1 Chron. i, 46. It was probably situated at the north-east extremity of the range of Mount Seir.

A'zal, *noble; root* or *declivity* of a mountain (?); the place to which, according to Zech. xiv, 5, the cleft in Mount Olivet was to extend.

Aze'kah, *broken up, dug over*, a city of Judah, Josh. xv, 35, where Joshua slew the five kings, Josh. x, 10, 11. Goliath was also slain near it, 1 Sam. xvii, 1. It was fortified by Rehoboam, 2 Chron. xi, 9; besieged and taken by Nebuchadnezzar, Jer. xxxiv, 7; and rebuilt after the captivity, Neh. xi, 30. Its site has not been certainly identified, but Mr. Porter places it at *Tell Zakariya*, in the north-west side of the valley of Elah, not far from *Ain-Shems*.

A'zem, *a bone*, a city allotted first to Judah, then to Simeon, Josh. xv, 29; xix, 3. In 1 Chron. iv, 29 it is "Ezem." According to Wilton "Iim and Azem" designate one place, which he identifies with the modern *el-'Aujeh* of the 'Azâzimeh Arabs.

Az'maveth, *strong as* or *to death*, a village apparently in Benjamm, 1 Chron. xii, 3; Ezra ii, 24; Neh. xii, 29. Some of its inhabitants returned from Babylon with Ezra. It is called Beth-Azmaveth in Neh. vii, 28. It is probably identical with *Hizmeh*, a village north of the site of Anathoth.

Az'mon, *strong*, a place on the south boundary of Palestine, apparently at its west end, Num. xxxiv, 4, 5; Josh. xv, 4. Perhaps the ruins near *Wady es-Shutin* mark the site, about half-way between Elusa and Rehoboth.

Az'noth-Ta'bor, *ears* (summits) *of Tabor*, a place on the borders of Naphtali between Jordan and Hukkok. Josh. xix, 34.

Azo'tus, Acts viii, 40; the Greek form of ASHDOD, which see.

Azo'tus, Mount, 1 Macc. ix, 15. A spot to which Judas Maccabeus pursued the enemy.

Az'zah, *the strong*, a more correct (but unusual) form of the name Gaza. Deut. ii, 23; 1 Kings iv, 24; Jer. xxv, 20; xlvii, 1, marg.

Ba'al, a *lord* or *master,* a city of Simeon, in the vicinity of Ain and Ashan, 1 Chron. iv, 33. It is the same as Baalath-Beer, Josh. xix, 8, and Ramath-Negeb.

Ba'alah, *mistress, one that is governed.* 1. A city in the south of Judah, Josh. xv, 29; apparently the same called Balah, xix, 3; also Bilhah, and assigned to Simeon, 1 Chron. iv, 29. In the first-named passage it forms part of the preceding name, thus: Bizjothjah-Baalah.

2. Another name for Kirjath-Jearim, and therefore in the territory of Judah also, Josh. xv, 9, 10; 1 Chron. xiii, 6; otherwise called Baale of Judah, 2 Sam. vi, 2. In Josh. xv, 60, and xviii, 14, it is called Kirjath-Baal. See KIRJATH-JEARIM.

3. A mountain on the north-west boundary of Judah, between Shicron and Jabneel, Josh. xv, 11.

Ba'alath, *mistress,* (another form of the name Baalah,) a town in the tribe of Dan, Josh. xix, 44. This is thought to be the place fortified or built by Solomon, 1 Kings ix, 18; 2 Chron. viii, 6; but the site and history are not certainly known.

Ba'alath-Be'er, *having a well,* a city of Simeon, Josh. xix, 8; and probably the same with Baal in 1 Chron. iv, 33. Wilton supposes this another form of Bealoth, Josh. xv, 24, and identifies it with the ruined site called *Kurnub,* on the southern declivity of the swell or low ridge which bears the name of *Kubbet el-Baul.* It is doubtless identical with Ramoth-Negeb, or Southern Ramoth, Josh. xix, 8. Compare 1 Sam. xxx, 27.

Baal'bec, (Map 5,) a city of Cœle-Syria, noted for its grand ruins; supposed by many to be the site designated by Solomon's famous "House of the Forest of Lebanon," 1 Kings vii, 2; x, 17; 2 Chron. ix, 16. See BAAL-GAD.

Ba'ale of Ju'dah, *lords* or *cities of Judah,* a name of Kirjath-Jearim or Baalah. See BAALAH (2.)

Ba'al-Gad, (Map 20,) *lord of fortune,* a city in the Valley of Lebanon, under Mount Hermon, the northern boundary of Joshua's conquests, Josh. xi, 17; xii, 7; xiii, 5. Some have supposed this place identical with Baalbec; but the expression of the text, "under Mount Hermon," and the too great distance of Baalbec to the north, are opposed to this supposition. Schwarz and Robinson agree upon *Banias* as the modern representative of Baal-Gad. It also seems to be the same with Baal-Hermon, Judg. iii, 3; 1 Chron. v, 23.

Ba'al-Ha'mon, *place of multitude,* a place where Solomon is said to have had a vineyard, Sol. Song viii, 11. Its location is conjectural. Elsewhere (Judith viii, 3) possibly Balamo; but uncertain.

Ba'al-Ha'zor, *having a village* or *hamlet,* a place near Ephraim, where Absalom had a sheep-farm, and where he murdered Amnon, to avenge his sister, 2 Sam. xiii, 23. Not known.

Ba'al-Her'mon, (Map 5,) *lord of Hermon.* 1. A town, probably identical with Baal-Gad, Josh. xi, 17; 1 Chron. v, 23.

2. A mountain. Probably Mount Hermon. *Jebel es-Sheikh.* See LEBANON.

Ba'al-Me'on, *lord of dwelling,* a Reubenite town, afterward Moabite, Num. xxxii, 38; Josh. xiii, 17; 1 Chron. v, 8; Ezek. xxv, 9. Elsewhere Beth-Baal-Meon, Beth-Meon, and perhaps Beon. About two miles south-east of Heshbon exist ruins thought to be on the site of this place, now called *Miûn* or *Main.*

Ba'al-Per'azim, *burstings forth,* or *having rents,* a place in the valley of

Rephaim, so named by David on defeating the Philistines, 2 Sam. v, 20; 1 Chron. xiv, 11. It is called in Isa. xxviii, 21, MOUNT PERAZIM, which see.

Ba'al-Shal'isha, *lord* or *place of Shalisha*, or *of three*, a place of Ephraim, probably not far from the Gilgal of 2 Kings iv, 38, 42.

Ba'al-Ta'mar, *place of palm-trees*, a place near Gibeah, where the other tribes defeated Benjamin, Judg. xx, 23.

Ba'al-Ze'phon, (Map 2,) *place of Typhon*, or *sacred to Typhon*, a place of Egypt, by the Red Sea, near to which the Israelites crossed the Sea, Exod. xiv, 2; Num. xxxiii, 7. Its site cannot be positively determined.

Ba'bel, *confusion*. The native etymology is *Bab-il*, "the gate of the god *Il*," or, perhaps, simply "the gate of God," Gen. x, 10; xi, 9. The name originally given to the *Tower of Babel;* but afterward in all its other occurrences this word is given in the authorized version, *Babylon*. Finally, (see Ezek. xxiii, 17, marg.,) the term referred to Babylonia.

Bab'ylon, (Map 1,) (the Greek form of BABEL, which see.) The name of several places:

1. The great capital of the Chaldean monarchy. It was situated upon a wide plain on both sides of the Euphrates. This city seems to have grown up around the Tower of Babel, being founded by Nimrod, Gen. x. 10. It rose into great importance and vast dimensions, becoming one of the most splendid cities of history. Semiramis and Nebuchadnezzar are those to whom the city was most indebted for increase in power and magnificence See Isa. xiv, 4; xlv, 1, 2; Jer. li, 58; Dan. iv, 30.

According to Ctesias, the circuit of the city was a little less than forty-two miles. According to Herodotus, an immense double wall surrounded the city, the outer one being fifty-six miles in circumference. Authorities differ as to the dimensions of these walls. The lowest estimate makes them three hundred and fifty feet high and eighty-seven thick; so that two spans of horses, four abreast, could easily pass each other behind the battlements. The wall was built of burnt brick and bitumen, with alternate layers of reeds, and surmounted with two hundred and fifty towers, of which there were more on the east than on the west side, this latter being better protected by bogs. The entire wall was surrounded by a broad, deep trench filled with water from the river. The city was entered by a hundred gates, the posts, wings, and beams of which were of brass, Jer. xlv, 2. It was protected from inundations of the Euphrates by quays, closed in with gates of brass, from which walled steps led down to the river. The two parts of the city were connected by a bridge, built by Nebuchadnezzar, of stone piers, and a movable floor of cedar and palm timber, which was removed at night. The last edifice built by this King was the royal castle, located near his father's palace, (the ruins of which are called *El Kasr*—castle hill.) It was of vast size, and most magnificent in adornments. Its outer wall embraced six miles, within which were two other embattled walls, besides a great tower. Every important gate was of brass. Its greatest boast was the noted hanging gardens, constructed on an artificial hill by a succession of terraces four hundred feet square, and higher than the towers on the city walls, and watered by means of pumps from the river. They were designed to reconcile Queen Artemis to the contrast between the flat plain of Babylon and the beautiful hills of her native Media. These gardens commanded a grand view of the city and circumjacent plain. Walking on the

BABYLON. (restored.)

highest terrace of these magnificent gardens, with such a prospect as he had before him, we may readily imagine how the vanity of his heart would prompt King Nebuchadnezzar to exclaim, "Is not this great Babylon, that I have built for the house of the kingdom by the might of my power, and for the honor of my majesty!" Dan. iv, 30.

While Babylon was the first city of Western Asia in extent, grandeur, wealth, art, cultivation, and learning, it also surpassed all others in wickedness. See Isa. xiv, 11; xlvii, 1; Jer. li, 39; Dan. v, 1. The seat of boundless luxury, its people were addicted to every species of vice. "The rites of hospitality were polluted by the grossest and most shameless lusts. . . . The Babylonians were very greatly given to wine. . . . Women were present at their convivialities, first with some degree of propriety, but, growing worse and worse by degrees, they ended by throwing off at once their modesty and their clothing."—*Q. Curtius.*

In view of the awful wickedness into which this city had fallen, the Divine vengeance came upon city and people with fearful power. Among the terrible and sublime prophecies concerning the fate of Babylon, see Isa. xiv, 4–26; xxi, 1–10; xlvii; xlviii, 14–20; lxvi, 1, 2; Jer. xxi, 4–10; xxvii, 1–11; xxxii, 28, 29; xlix, 28–30; 1; li; Dan. ii, 21–38; iv, 10–26; v, 25–29; vii; Hab. i, 5–11. After a tedious siege the city was taken by Cyrus in 538 or 539 B. C., Isa. xlvii; Dan. v; Jer. l. It was stormed a second time during an insurrection by Darius Hystaspes, after a siege of nineteen months. Darius razed the walls, filled the trenches, and depopulated the city. Xerxes plundered the Temple of Belus. Alexander's thwarted attempt to restore its grandeur only put the disturbed ruins into greater confusion; but the founding of Seleucia blasted all hope of restoring Babylon. Seleucia, Ctesiphon, El Maduin, and Kufa, and even the bridges of Bagdad, fifty miles north, were chiefly built of its bricks, which still continue an article of traffic. It is amazing that after two thousand years so much rubbish remains. No vegetation adorns the soil; wild beasts prowl there; and its ruins are most desolate. Thus most completely have divine prophecies been fulfilled.

"The locality and principal structures of this once famous city are now almost universally admitted to be indicated by the remarkable remains near the modern village of *Hillah,* which lies on the west bank of the Euphrates, about fifty miles directly south of Bagdad. About five miles above *Hillah,* on the opposite bank of the river, occur a series of artificial mounds of enormous size, which have been recognized in all ages as probably indicating the site of the capital of Southern Mesopotamia. They consist chiefly of three great masses of building: the high pile of unbaked brick-work, called by Rich '*Mujellibe,*' but which is known to the Arabs as '*Babil;*' the building denominated the '*Kasr,*' or palace, and a lofty mound upon which stands the modern tomb of *Amran ibn-Alb.* Besides these principal masses, the most remarkable features are two parallel lines of rampart bounding the chief ruins on the east, some similar but inferior remains on the north and west, an embankment along the river-side, a remarkable isolated heap in the middle of a long valley, which seems to have been the ancient bed of the stream, and two long lines of rampart, meeting at a right angle, and with the river forming an irregular triangle, within which all the ruins on this side (except *Babil*) are inclosed. On the west, or right bank, the remains are very slight and scanty. There is the appearance of an inclosure, and of a building of moderate size within it, nearly opposite the great mound of *Amran;* but otherwise, unless at a long distance from the stream, this side of the Euphrates is absolutely bare of ruins." (See Rawlinson's *Herodotus,* ii, 473.)

"Scattered over the country on both sides of the Euphrates, and reducible to no regular plan, are a number of remarkable mounds, usually standing single, which are plainly of the same date with the great mass of ruins upon the river-bank. Of these by far the most striking is the vast ruin called the *Birs Nimrud,* which many regard as the TOWER OF BABEL, situated about six miles to the south-west of *Hillah,* and almost that distance from the Euphrates at the nearest point. This is a pyramidical mound, crowned apparently by the ruins of a tower, rising to the height of one hundred and fifty-three and a half feet above the level of the plain, and in circumference somewhat more than two thousand feet. There is considerable reason to believe, from the inscriptions discovered on the spot, and from other documents of the time of Nebuchadnezzar, that it marks the site of Borsippa, and may thus have been beyond the limits of Babylon."

In regard to the above ruins the following conclusions are considered the most probable: 1. The mass of ruins known as *Babil* is the remnant of the ancient temple of Belus, which was rebuilt by Nebuchadnezzar. 2. The *Kasr* will mark the site of the great palace of Nebuchadnezzar. 3. The mound of *Amran,* thought by some to be the site of the "hanging gardens," most probably represents the ancient palace, coeval with Babylon itself, of which Nebuchadnezzar speaks in his inscriptions as adjoining his own more magnificent residence. It is the only part of the ruins from which bricks have been derived containing the names of kings earlier than Nebuchadnezzar, and is, therefore, entitled to be considered the most ancient of the existing remains. 4. The ruins near each side of the Euphrates, together with all the other remains on the west bank, may be considered to represent the lesser palace of Ctesias, which is said to have been connected with all the other remains by a bridge across the river, as well as by a tunnel under the channel of the stream. 5. The two long parallel lines of embankment on the east may be either the lines of an outer and inner inclosure, of which Nebuchadnezzar speaks as defenses of his palace, or they may represent the embankments of an enormous reservoir, which is often mentioned by that monarch as adjoining his palace toward the east. 6. The southernmost embankment, near the east bank of the river, is composed of bricks marked with the name of Labynetus or Nabunit, and is undoubtedly a portion of the work which Berosus ascribes to the last king. 7. As to *Birs Nimrud,* Rawlinson excludes it (as noted above) from the limits of Babylon, while M. Oppert includes it in the circuit of the city. For full details of this whole subject see Kitto's *Cyclopedia;* Smith's *Bible Dictionary;* Ayre's *Treasury of Bible Knowledge;* Herzog's *Encyclopedia;* M'Clintock and Strong's *Cyclopedia;* Layard's *Nineveh and Babylon.*

2. There was another BABYLON in Egypt, founded by Babylonians who settled along the Nile after the Persian invasions, but it is not alluded to in the Bible.

3. The BABYLON of 1 Pet. v, 13, doubtless refers to ancient Babylon, a portion of whose ruins was long occupied by Jews.

4. The BABYLON of Revelation stands for the city of Rome. Rev. xiv, 8;

BIRS NIMRUD.

xvi, 19; xvii, 5; xviii, 2. In Rev. xvii, 18, "that great city which ruleth over the kings of the earth" could refer to no other city but Rome.

Babylo'nia, (Maps 1 and 16,) the Greek and Roman name of the country called in the Old Testament "*the land of the Chaldeans,*" Jer. xxiv, 5; xxv, 12; Ezek. xii, 13. It designates the territory lying along the Euphrates and Tigris from the point where they approach nearest to each other to the Persian Gulf, having Mesopotamia (Aram) and Assyria on the north and Arabia on the west. Babylon was its chief city. As Babylon became the center of an Asiatic empire, it was all called "Babylonia" in a wider sense. In Hebrew, Babylonia bore the name of Shinar, (the name always found upon native inscriptions,) or "the land of Shinar;" while "Babylon," and the "land of the Chaldeans," seem to signify the empire of Babylon. For names see Isa. xiii, 19; Jer. l, 21; xxv, 26; Dan. i, 2; Job i, 17; Isa. xlvii, 1; Ezek. xii, 13. For division and boundaries see 2 Kings xvii, 24; Isa. xxiii, 12, 13; Dan. iii, 1; Acts vii, 4.

Babylonia is a broad plain of exceeding fertility, yielding in vast abundance grain, palms, and tamarisks, but producing no timber-trees. A dense population once covered this plain, as countless mounds of ruins still existing, and the surviving names of numerous cities, (Erech, Accad, Chalne, Sippara, etc.,) testify; but being infested with Arab robbers it is shunned by travelers. The inhabitants of Shinar belonged to the Shemitic race, spoke a Shemitic dialect—the Aramaic or Chaldaic,—and were called Chasdim, or Chaldeans, after one of the chief and oldest nations of the land. See CHALDEA.

The Babylonians excelled in the manufacture of cloths, garments, etc., Josh. vii, 21. They maintained a very extensive commerce, Josh. vii, 21; Isa. xliii, 14; Ezek. xvi, 29; xvii, 4. With increasing prosperity, luxury and vice also increased. They anointed their bodies with myrrh, and over linen shirt wore a woolen garment, bound round the loins with a girdle, reaching to the ankles, and outside of this a white mantilla. They wore long hair with a band, Ezek. xxiii, 15, *et seq.* They were proficient in astronomy and astrology, Isa. xlvii, 13; Dan. ii, 2. It was the Babylonians who discovered the Zodiac and divided the week into seven days, corresponding with the quarters of the moons. The priests devoted themselves to this science and made it the basis of the religion of the country, 2 Kings xxiii, 5, 7; Dan. iv, 4. Their astronomical observations, recorded on tiles, and long preserved in the Temple of Belus, extend to 2,000 years B. C.

The power of Babylon once ruled the world; but long since have been fulfilled the prophetic words of Isaiah, (xlvii, 1, 5.) "Come down, and sit in the dust. . . . Sit thou silent, and get thee into darkness, O daughter of the Chaldeans: for thou shalt no more be called the lady of kingdoms." The chief city has "become heaps," Jer. li, 37. The system of irrigation, on which the fertility of Babylonia depends, has long been laid aside, and "a drought is upon her waters," l, 39. Her cities are every-where "a desolation," li, 43, and her land a wilderness, the abode of "owls" and "wild beasts of the desert." Isa. xiii, 19, 21, 22; Jer. l. The natives regard the whole site as haunted, and will there neither "pitch tent," nor will "the shepherd fold sheep there," Isa. xiii, 20.

Ba'ca, *lamentation, weeping,* the name of a valley apparently near to Jerusalem, probably dry and sterile. The Psalmist in vision sees the returning pilgrims passing through this valley on their way to Zion, shedding tears of joy so plentifully as to make this barren valley a place of springs, Psa. lxxxiv 6 The plural of this word is rendered "mulberry-trees" in 2 Sam. v, 23. 24; 1 Chron. xiv, 14, 15.

Bahu'rim, *young men,* a village not far from Jerusalem, connected with the flight of David from Absalom. It probably lay on or near the road leading from the Jordan valley to Jerusalem, beyond Olivet to the east, 2 Sam. iii, 16. Here Shimei cursed David, 2 Sam. xvi, 5; and David's two spies hid in a well, xvii, 18. Here Phaltiel bade farewell to his wife on her return to David at Hebron, iii, 16. Besides Shimei, the only other native of Bahurim recorded is Azmaveth "the Barhumite," 2 Sam. xxiii, 31, or "the Baharumite," 1 Chron. xi, 33. It is possibly identical with *Fakhoury,* near Olivet.

Ba'lah, a contraction of the name Baalah or Bilhah, a town of Simeon, Josh. ix, 3. The same as Bilhal, 1 Chron. iv, 29; or Baalal Josh. xv, 29. See also BIZJOTHJAH.

Bal'amo, a place near Dothaim, Judith viii, 3; supposed to be a corruption of Baal-hamon.

Ba'moth, (Map 2,) *heights,* a station of the Israelites in the territory of Moab, Num. xxi, 19, 20; comp. xxviii. It is probably alluded to in Isa. xv, 2, and is doubtless the same with Bamoth-Baal.

Ba'moth-Ba'al, *heights of Baal,* a place in Moab, Josh. xiii, 17 In Num. xxii, 41, it is translated "the high places of Baal." Elsewhere probably Bamoth. The site may be on the present *Jebel Attarus.*

Ban'ias. See CÆSAREA PHILIPPI.

Bas'cama, a place in Gilead, the scene of Judas Maccabeus's death, 1 Macc. xiii, 23.

Ba'shan, (Map 5,) *light* or sandy *soil,* a district east of Jordan. Compare Gen. xiv, 5, with Josh. xiii, 12; Deut. iv, 47. Sometimes it is called "the land of Bashan," 1 Chron. v, 11. See also Num. xxi, 33; xxxii, 33. Also "all Bashan," Deut. iii, 10, 13; Josh. xii, 5; xiii, 12, 30.

It reached from Gilead to Hermon, and from the Jordan Valley to Salchah; embracing the four (later) provinces, Gaulonitis, the modern *Jaulan,* Trachonitis, the ancient Argob, now the *Lejah;* Auranitis, the *Hauran;* and Batanæa, or *Ard-el-Bathanyeh.* It is for the most part a stony, hilly country, made up in the northern part, as far as Jarmuk, of black basalt, and in the southern of limestone, and abounds with rich woodlands and pastures. Hence the Scripture references to fruitfulness and fat pastures, Jer. l, 19; Micah vii, 14; Isa. xxxiii, 9; Nahum i, 4. Its cattle and flocks, Deut xxxii, 14; Psa. xxii, 12; Ezek. xxxix, 18; Amos iv, 1. Its famous oaks, Isa. ii, 13; Ezek. xxvii, 6; Zech. xi, 2. The early inhabitants were Amorites, some of whom were men of gigantic stature, Deut. iii, 11–13; iv, 47. At the time the Israelites entered, Og, King of the Amorites, ruled over the people descended from the old giant races of the land, (Josh. xii, 4,) and who lived in walled cities. Ashtoreth and Edrei were the principal cities, Deut. i, 4; Josh. xii, 4. After defeating the King of Sihon at Jahaz the Israelites turned upon Og, King of Bashan, and defeated him in a great battle at Edrei, and seized his land, assigning it to the half-tribe of Manasseh, Num. xxi, 23. The country east of Jordan continued in the possession of the kingdom of Judah until the time of Jehu, when the Syrian king, Hazael of Damascus, took it from Israel, although it was afterward recovered by Jeroboam II., 2 Kings x, 32, 33; xiv, 25.

The modern examination of this region bears a remarkable testimony to the faithfulness and accuracy of Bible narrative and description. Late travelers tell of vast ruins scattered over a wide extent, revealing the former existence of numerous and splendid cities. (See ARGOB.) Many of these cities still exist in almost perfect condition, yet without an inhabitant. Some of them, however, which Mr. Porter found only a few years ago wholly unoccupied, are beginning now to be inhabited. (See " *The Rob Roy on the Jordan,*" by Macgregor; Porter's *Damascus;* and Porter's *Giant Cities.*)

Ba'shan-Ha'voth-Ja'ir, (Map 13,) *Bashan of the villages of Jair,* the name given by Jair to the region of Argob, conquered by him in Bashan, Deut. iii, 14. It contained sixty cities, with walls and brazen gates, Josh. xiii, 30; 1 Kings iv, 13. In Num. xxxii, 41, it is called HAVOTH-JAIR, which see.

Bath-rab'bim, *daughter of many,* a gate of the city of Heshbon, near which were pools or tanks, Sol. Song. vii, 4.

Bathzachari'as, *House of Zacharias,* a place between Jerusalem and Bethsura, 1 Macc. vi, 32, 33. It is now *Beit Sakâriyeh,* about five miles south of Bethlehem.

Be'aloth, (Map 13,) *corporations,* or *citizens,* (the plur. fem. of Baal,) the name of two places. 1. A town in the extreme south of Judah, Josh. xv, 24, probably the same as the Baalath-Beer of xix, 8. Not certainly known.

2. A district of Asher, of which Baanah ben-Hushai was Solomon's commissariat, 1 Kings iv, 16, (where the authorized version renders incorrectly "in Aloth.")

Bec'tileth, THE PLAIN OF, between Nineveh and Cilicia, Judith ii, 21. Perhaps it is a corruption of "the plain of *Beka'a;*" but quite uncertain.

Be'er, (Map 2,) *a well.* 1. A halting place of the Israelites after they had crossed the Arnon. According to God's command and promise the princes here dug a well, Num. xxi, 16–18. The place is probably identical with Beer-Elim.

2. A town in Judah to which Jotham fled, Judg. ix, 21. The site is not certainly known; but some identify it with Beeroth.

Be'er-E'lim, *well of heroes,* a place on the "border of Moab," Isa. xv, 8. Probably it is the same with Beer, (1.)

Be'er-Lahai'-Roi, (Map 2,) *the well of the living one that sees me,* or *of the living* and *seeing* God. A fountain, between Kadesh and Bered, near which the angel of the Lord found Hagar, Gen. xvi, 7, 14. Isaac dwelt near it, Gen. xxiv, 62; xxv, 11. In these last two passages the authorized version has "the well Lahai-roi." The site is not determined positively.

Bee'roth, (Map 6,) *wells.* One of the four Hivite or Gibeonite cities that made peace with the Israelites, Josh. ix, 17; allotted to Benjamin, Josh. xviii, 25; 2 Sam. iv, 2; Ezek. ii, 25; Neh. vii, 29. In 2 Sam. xxiii, 37, mention is made of Naharai "the Beerothite," (and in 1 Chron. xi, 39, "the Berothite,") one of the "mighty men" of David's guard: It is now identified as *el-Bireh,* ten miles north of Jerusalem, a village of seven hundred inhabitants. According to tradition, it was at this place that Jesus was missed by his parents when returning from Jerusalem, Luke ii, 44. To this day travelers going northward often halt here after the first day's journey from Jerusalem.

Bee'roth-Be'ne-Ja'akan, (Map 2,) *the wells of the sons of Jaakan,* a group of wells in the wilderness; a station of the Israelites, Deut. x, 6. Elsewhere Bene-Ja'akan, Num. xxxiii, 31, 32.

Be'er-She'ba, or **Be-er'-Sheba**, (Map 5,) *well of the oath*, or *of seven*. A city on the south frontier of Palestine. It is first mentioned in the history of Abraham, who planted a grove and dwelt there, Gen. xxi, 31-33; xxii, 19. Abimelech, King of Gerar, came to make a covenant with Abraham, and, either from the oath sworn by the two, or from the seven lambs which he desired Abimelech to receive in token that he (the patriarch) had dug a well the possession of which was disputed, the place was called Beer-Sheba, Gen. xxi, 22-34. Many years later Isaac sojourned in Gerar, but he was obliged to leave it in consequence of the jealousy of the Philistines, who strove with him for the wells which both his father and himself had digged. The then Abimelech, however, followed him to Beer-Sheba, thinking it politic to bind by an oath of friendship so great a chief as Isaac. Isaac entertained him hospitably, the covenant was made, the oath was sworn; and, just after the king's departure, Isaac's servants informed him of the discovery of a fresh well. With the solemn oath which he had sworn fresh in his mind, he called it "the oath-well," Beer-Sheba. The name had existed before, but there was additional propriety in it now; and the town, of which nothing was previously said, from this (perhaps gradually) took the appellation which it ever afterward retained, Gen. xxvi, 12-33. Jacob left Beer-Sheba for Haran, Gen. xxviii, 10; and here also he offered sacrifices on his way to Egypt, xlvi, 1. In Josh. xv, 28, it appears as one of the cities of Judah; and in Josh. xix, 2, and in 1 Chron. iv, 28, as given to Simeon. Samuel's sons were appointed deputy-judges for the southernmost districts of Beer-Sheba, 1 Sam. viii, 2. By the time of the monarchy it had become recognized as the most southerly place of the country. Its position as the place of arrival and departure for the caravans trading between Palestine and the countries lying in that direction would naturally lead to the formation of a town round the wells of the patriarchs, and the great Egyptian trade begun by Solomon must have increased its importance.

Hither Joab's census extended, 2 Sam. xxiv, 7; 1 Chron. xxi, 2; and here Elijah bade farewell to his confidential servant before taking his journey across the desert to Sinai, 1 Kings xix, 3.

"From Dan to Beer-Sheba," Judg. xx, 1, or "from Beer-Sheba to Dan," 1 Chron. xxi, 2, (comp. 2 Sam. xxiv, 2,) now became the formula for the whole of the Promised Land; just as "from Geba to Beer-Sheba," 2 Kings xxiii, 8, or "from Beer-Sheba to Mount Ephraim," 2 Chron. xix, 4, was that for the southern kingdom after the disruption. After the return from the captivity the formula was narrowed still more, and became "from Beer-Sheba to the Valley of Hinnom," Neh. xi, 30. Later it seems to have been a seat of idolatry, Amos v, 5; viii, 14; and it was inhabited after the captivity, Neh. xi, 27, 30.

After Nehemiah no mention is made of it. The site seems to have been almost forgotten till the fourteenth century, when Sir John Maundeville and others recognized the name at a place which they passed on their route from Sinai to Hebron. It was then uninhabited, but some of the churches were still standing. Nothing of consequence was afterward learned until the visit of Dr. Robinson, who found "two deep wells, still called *Bir es-Seba*," the ancient Beer-Sheba. The largest of these wells he found to be twelve and a half feet in diameter, and forty-four and a half feet to the surface of the water, with masonry reaching downward twenty-eight and a half feet. The smaller well was five feet in diameter, and was forty-two feet

BIBLE GEOGRAPHY. 57

to the water. The site is about twenty-seven miles south-east from Gaza. A few ruins suggest the idea of a small straggling city, built over the low hills to the north of the wells, and in the hollows between.

Beesh'-Terah, *house of Astarte.* A city of Bashan, allotted from the district of the half-tribe of Manasseh to the Gershonite Levites, Josh. xxi, 27. Elsewhere Ashtaroth, 1 Chron. vi, 71.

Be'la, *destruction swallowed.* The least of the cities of the plain of Sodom, afterward called Zoar, Gen. xiv, 2, 8. It was spared by Lot's intercession, Gen. xix, 20, 30. See SODOM and ZOAR.

Bel'maim, a place apparently south of Dothaim, Judith vii, 3. It is doubtless the same as Belmen.

Bel'men, a place mentioned as between Bethhoron and Jericho, Judith iv, 4. Doubtless it is the same as Belmaim; but nothing is known of either place.

Ben'e-Be'rak, *sons of lightning,* one of the cities of Dan, Josh. xix, 4, 6. The site is not certainly known.

Be'ne-Ja'akan, *sons of Jaakan,* the name of the tribe of Jaakan or Akan the Horite. It is used as an abbreviation for Beeroth (*the wells of the*) Bene-Jaakan, Num. xxxiii, 31, 32, a halting place of the Israelites.

Ben'jamin, (Map 5,) *son of the right hand,* the name of the tribe called after the youngest son of Jacob. In the first census taken at Sinai, Num. i, 36. 37, the Benjamite males of military age numbered 35,400. Their place was on the west of the tabernacle; their captain was Abidan, the son of Gideoni, Num. ii, 22, 23. Later they had increased to 45,600, Num. xxvi, 41. Their families, Num. xxvi, 38–40; 1 Chron. vii, 6–12; 1 Chron. viii. Moses's blessing upon them, Deut. xxxiii, 12. The allotment of the tribe in Canaan lay between Ephraim and Judah, immediately north of Jerusalem, Josh. xviii, 11–28. It was a compact oblong, about twenty-six miles long by twelve in breadth. It is said to have been a very fertile region, and admirably situated for the development of the characteristics of the tribe. Its passes and its heights were the distinguishing features; the leading events in the fastnesses of the tribe of Benjamin received a special character from the heights or the passes of the territory. The tribe was not able alone to expel the Jebusites, Judg. i, 21. We may mention among the events of note that they assisted Deborah, Judg. v, 14; they were invaded by the Ammonites, x, 9; they had war with the other tribes, Judg. xix, xx; at Shiloh they were provided with wives, Judg. xxi. To Benjamin belongs the honor of giving the first king to Israel, Saul, 1 Psa. ix, 1, 17; x, 20, 21. A band of this tribe was with David at Ziklag, 1 Chron. xii, 1, 2, 16. In the census by Joab, the tribe was not numbered with the rest of Israel, 1 Chron. xxi, 6. The allegiance of the Benjamites was preserved to Ish-Bosheth, 2 Sam. ii, 9, 15, 31; 1 Chron. xii, 29. They returned to David 2 Sam. iii, 19; xix, 16, 17. They adhered to Rehoboam, 1 Kings xii, 21, 2 Chron. xi, 1. For notice of their armies under Asa, see 2 Chron. xiv, 8; under Jehoshaphat. xvii, 17. Their skill as bowmen and slingers, Judg. iii, 15; xx, 16; 1 Chron. viii, 40; xii, 2. On their return from captivity, see Ezra i, 5. The Benjamites at some periods of their history seem to have occupied towns beyond their own boundary, 1 Chron. viii, 12, 13; Neh. xi, 35. Benjamin and Judah were in close alliance, and sometimes a single term included them both, 1 Kings xi, 13; xii, 20. After the death of Solomon Benjamin espoused the cause of Judah, and the two formed a kingdom by themselves. The temple was the common property of both tribes.

It was built by Judah, but the city of "the Jebusite," Josh. xvii, 28, and the whole of the ground north of the Valley of Hinnom, was in the lot of Benjamin. After the exile, also, these two tribes constituted the flower of the new Jewish colony in Palestine. Comp. Ezra iv, 1; x, 9. The individuality of Benjamin was preserved by frequent mention, Ezra ii; Neh. vi; xi. At Jerusalem (doubtless on the north side) was "The High Gate of Benjamin," Zech. xiv, 10; Jer. xx, 2. The genealogy of Saul is carefully preserved in 1 Chron. viii and ix; the name of Kish recurs as the father of Mordecai, the deliverer of the nation, Esth. ii, 5. Again the royal name appears in Rom. xi, 1; Phil. iii, 5, where "Saul, who also is called Paul," has left on record under his own hand that he was "of the stock of Israel, of the tribe of Benjamin."

Be'on, Num. xxxii, 3, probably a contraction of Beth-Meon, Jer. xlviii, 23. A place of pasturage east of Jordan.

Ber'achah, (Map 6,) *blessing*, a valley where Jehoshaphat gained a victory over Ammon, 2 Chron. xx, 26; and where the people assembled to praise God after the battle. It is still called *Wady Bereikut*, near the ruined village of the same name, west of *Tekua*, between Bethlehem and Hebron.

Be'rea, *heavy, weighty*, a place in Judea, near Jerusalem, mentioned in 1 Macc. ix, 4, where Bacchides encamped. Grove says it is now possibly *el-Bireh*, ten miles north of Jerusalem.

Bere'a, (Map 8,) a city of Macedonia, not far from Pella, at the foot of Mt. Bermius. Paul and Silas being persecuted in Thessalonica, retired to this city, being followed thither by their tormentors, Acts xvii, 10, 14, 15. Sopater, one of Paul's companions, was from Berea, Acts xx, 4. The resident Jews of Berea must have been considerable in numbers, while their character is highly commended by the sacred writer, Acts xvii, 11, 12. This was a large and populous city, being afterward called Irenopolis. It is now known as *Verria*, in Roumelia, and has a population of from 15,000 to 20,000.

Be'red, *hail*, a place in the south of Palestine, near the well Lahai-Roi, Gen. xvi, 14. It is supposed by some to be at *el-Khulasah*, twelve miles south of Beer-Sheba.

Berœ'a, (Map 8,) a city spoken of in 2 Macc. xiii, 4, in connection with the invasion of Judea by Antiochus Eupator, as the scene of the miserable death of Menelaus. It was situated about midway between Antioch in Syria and Hieropolis. It is considered the modern *Aleppo*, whose population is about 100,000.

Be'roth. 1 Esdras v, 19. A form of Beeroth, Ezra ii, 25.

Bero'thah and Ber'othai, *my wells*, or, according to some, *place of cypresses*. The first of these two names occurs only in Ezek. xlvii, 16, as forming a part of the northern boundary of Palestine. The other name occurs (but once also) in 2 Sam. viii, 8, being mentioned as a town, from which David took much brass. By some these two places are supposed to be identical. Some have imagined the modern *Beirût* identical with one of the two. But all opinions are merely conjectural.

Be'sor, (Map 5,) *the cool*, a torrent flowing into the Mediterranean near Gaza. It was near this brook that David's men pursued the Amalekites who had burnt the town of Ziklag, not far distant, 1 Sam. xxx, 9, 10, 21.

Be'tah, *confidence*, a Syrian city from which David took much brass,

2 Sam viii, 8. It is called Tibhath in 1 Chron. xviii, 8. Grove says it is now "perhaps *Tuibeh*, between Palmyra and Aleppo; but very uncertain."

Bet'ane, a place mentioned in Judith i, 9, and apparently south of Jerusalem. Unknown.

Be'ten, *belly*, or perhaps *valley*, a place mentioned in Josh. xix, 25 as a border town of Asher. Unknown.

Bethab'ara, (Map 20,) *place* or *house of passage, the ferry*. A place beyond Jordan where John was baptizing, John i, 28. The name is possibly a corruption of Beth-Nimrah, in which case it may be *Nimrin*, on the road from Jericho to *es-Salt*. Possibly it is also identical with Beth-Barah, Judg. vii, 24. Conder suggests that the true site may be farther north, near *Wady Jalûd*, at *Makhâdhet 'Abâra*, the "Ford of the Crossing Over."

Beth'-Anath, *house of response*, a fortified city of Naphtali named with Beth-Shemesh, Josh. xix, 38; Judg. i, 33. Possibly the modern *Ainath*.

Beth-Anoth, *house of response*, a city in the mountains of Judah, Josh. xv, 59. It is probably identified with *Beit-'Ainûn*, about one and a half hours north-east of Hebron, where are extensive ruins.

Beth'any, (Map 5,) *house of dates*, (by some, *house of affliction* or *depression*.)

1. A small town or village on the eastern slope of the Mount of Olives, fifteen furlongs (two Roman miles) from Jerusalem, Mark xi, 1, 11, 12; Luke xix, 29; John xi, 18. It is near the point where the road to Jericho begins to descend more steeply to the Jordan valley. Many fruit and other trees—olives, pomegranates, almonds, oaks, etc.—give the place an air of seclusion and repose. Bethany is endeared to every Christian heart. It was here that our Lord often lodged after the weary toils of the day, Matt. xxi, 17. Here he showed the tenderness of friendship manifested so beautifully toward Lazarus and his sisters. Here Lazarus was raised from the dead, John ii. Jesus was here feasted and anointed, Matt. xxvi, 6-13. The ascension of our Lord took place on his way to Bethany, Luke xxiv, 50. It is now a wretched village of about twenty families, called by the Arabians *el 'Azariyeh*, (from *el 'Azar*, Lazarus.) There remain some relics of antiquity in the form of large beveled stones, probably taken from old buildings. The monks point out various objects of curiosity, as the house of Mary and Martha, and of Simon; the stone on which Jesus sat, (John xi, 20, 28, 30,) and the grave of Lazarus—a deep vault, like a cellar, excavated in the limestone rock in the middle of the village, (contrary to John xi, 31, 38,) in which the Franciscans say mass twice a year. The building which formerly covered the grave, and of which only the stone walls remain, is called the *Castle of Lazarus*, and is said to have been a church built by St. Helena. We have no certain information as to the real age and character of these ruins.

2. In John i, 28, the best MSS. have Bethany for Bethabara.

Beth-Ar'abah, *house of the desert*, one of the six cities enumerated as belonging to Judah in the wilderness, Josh. xv, 6, 61. Elsewhere it is assigned to Benjamin, xviii, 22. It was probably at the north end of the Dead Sea, on the boundary between the two tribes. It is unknown.

Beth-A'ram, *house of the height, mountain-house*, a town of Gad in "the valley," (not the Jordan valley.) Josh. xiii, 27; doubtless also the Beth-Haran of Num. xxxii, 36. In later times it was called Livias, after the Empress Livia. It was probably situated in the *Wady Seir*, which falls into the *Ghôr* opposite Jericho. According to Van de Velde the ruins are still called *Beit-Haran*.

BIBLE GEOGRAPHY.

Beth-Ar'bel, *house of God's court,* or *courts,* (or *ambush.*) A place referred to in Hosea x, 14, as destroyed by Shalman or Shalmaneser. It is probably the same with Arbela, the modern *Irbid,* west of the Lake of Galilee. The place seems to have been famous for its caverns.

Beth-A'ven, *house of nothingness,* (that is, of idols,) a town of Benjamin east of Bethel, Josh. vii, 2; 1 Sam. xiii, 5; xiv, 23. The wilderness (pasture-ground) of Beth-Aven is mentioned in Josh. xviii, 12. The prophet Hosea in sarcasm uses it as a synonym for the neighboring town of Bethel, Hosea iv, 15; v, 8; x, 5, 8, once the "house of God," but then the "house of idols."

Beth-Az'maveth, *house of Azmaveth,* (house strong as death,) a town of Benjamin, whose inhabitants returned with Zerubbabel from Babylon, Neh. vii, 28. It is called Azmaveth in Neh. xii, 29; Ezra ii, 24. It is possibly identical with *Hizmeh,* a village on the hills of Benjamin.

Beth-Ba'al-Me'on, *house of Baal-Meon,* a place in Reuben, on the *Mishor* or Downs, Josh. xiii, 17. Elsewhere Baal-Meon, Beth-Meon, and Beon. Probably the ruins of *Ma'in* mark the site, a short distance south-west of *Hesbân.* See BAAL-MEON.

Beth-Ba'rah, *house of crossing, passages,* a place or ford south of *Beisan,* (Judg. vii, 24,) probably identical with Bethabara.

Beth-Ba'si, a place probably in the Jordan Valley, near Jericho, repaired by Jonathan and Simon Maccabeus, 1 Macc. ix, 62, 64. The more probable form would be Beth-Keziz. See KEZIZ.

Beth-Bir'ei, *house of my creation,* a town of Simeon, 1 Chron. iv, 31. It is probably the same with BETH-LEBAOTH, (which see,) Josh. xix, 6, and ebaoth, Josh. xv, 32.

Beth'-Car, *house of pasture, sheep-house,* a place west of Mizpeh, the site of the stone Ebenezer, 1 Sam. vii, 11. It is unknown.

Beth-Da'gon, (Map 5,) *house* or *temple of Dagon,* the name of several Philistine settlements.

1. A town in the low country of Judah, Josh. xv, 41.
2. A place on the border of Asher, Josh. xix, 27.
3. The temple of Dagon at Azotus, (Ashdod,) 1 Macc. x, 83.

The corresponding modern name *Beit-Dejan* is of frequent occurrence in Palestine; a fact which doubtless proves that the worship of the Philistine god had spread far beyond the Philistine territory.

Beth-Diblatha'im, (Map 2,) *house of Diblathaim,* a city of Moab, denounced by the prophet, Jer. xlviii, 22. Elsewhere Almon-Diblathaim, Num. xxxiii, 46, and DIBLATHAIM, which see.

Beth-E'den, *house of pleasantness,* a name appearing in Amos i, 5, marg. Our version renders it "the house of Eden." It may have been the seat of a petty prince, or, more probably, an occasional residence of the kings of Syria. Some think it was the Paradisus of Ptolemy. There are various conjectures as to its locality, but none are satisfactory. Robinson places it near Damascus on the north, at the ruined village *Jusieh el-Kadîmeh.* Another mere conjecture places it at *Beit-Jenn,* "the house of Paradise," not far to the south-west of Damascus, a short distance from *Medjel.*

Beth-E'ked, *house of binding,* (that is, the sheep.) The name of a place near Samaria, being the "shearing-house" at the pit or well of which the forty-two brethren of Ahaziah were slain by Jehu, 2 Kings x, 12, 14. In verse 12 the form is Beth-Eked-Haroim, for which in the authorized version there is no equivalent. It probably lay between Jezreel and Samaria, in the plain of Esdraelon. Robinson thinks it is *Beit-Kad*, on the edge of "the great plain" east of Jenin.

Beth'el, (Map 5.) *house of God.*

1. A town and sanctuary in central Palestine in the tribe of Benjamin, (though also given to Ephraim,) situated about twelve miles north of Jerusalem. The name was first given by Jacob to the spot close by the city of Luz, where he had his marvelous vision, and where he set up a stone pillar, pouring oil upon it, Gen. xxviii, 11-22. It was here that Abraham pitched his tent, Gen xii, 8; xiii, 3. On Jacob's return from Padan-Aram he again visited the spot, built an altar, and again consecrated a pillar, renewing and confirming the name he had before given it, xxxv. 6-15. The prophet Hosea (Hosea xii, 4, 5) refers to this latter circumstance. Some have thought the original name of Bethel was Luz. But this is a mistake. We find the name in Josh. vii, 2; viii, 9, 12, 17; xii, 9; but the distinction between Bethel, as afterward settled, and Luz is marked, xvi, 1, 2; and when the place was assigned to the tribe of Benjamin, (xviii, 13, 22,) no doubt the new buildings collected round the sacred spot; and whereas there *had been* Luz, there now was Bethel, occupying virtually the position of the old city, and yet not precisely on the original site. The capture of Luz is recorded in Judg. i, 22, 23. Thenceforth Bethel was a holy city; possibly the tabernacle might for awhile have been here. (See Ju..g. xx, 18, 26, 31; xxi, 2, 19, where the word Bethel, generally in our version "the house of God." is perhaps a proper name.) To this place Samuel went in circuit, 1 Sam. vii, 16; and the name often occurs in subsequent history.

Though Bethel belonged to Benjamin, it was occupied by Ephraimites, 1 Chron. vii, 28. Here Jeroboam set up idolatrous calves, 1 Kings xii, 29-33; xiii. It seems to have been recovered by Abijah, 2 Chron. xiii, 19; but the possession of it by Judah was evidently only temporary. Perhaps, however, it belonged to the southern kingdom, when a school of the prophets was at Bethel; but the people were depraved, as is clear from the insult offered to Elisha, 2 Kings ii, 2, 3, 23-25. Calf worship is still mentioned, xv, 29. Probably even more sinful rites were here practiced (Amos iii, 14; iv, 4; v, 5, 6; vii, 10, 13) when the city seems to have become an Israelitish royal residence. One of the priests was stationed at Bethel, who taught the ignorant Samaritans, 2 Kings xvii, 28. Here, also, Josiah, who evidently had authority over the district, fulfilled prophecy by polluting the idolatrous altars, 2 Kings xxiii. 15-18. (For a prophecy against the altar, and account of the withering of Jeroboam's hand, see 1 Kings xiii, 1-6, 32; 2 Kings xxiii, 4, 15-20.) The old prophet was at Bethel, 1 Kings xiii, 11-32. Here the mockers were destroyed by bears, 2 Kings ii, 23, 24. The court of Jeroboam II. was also here. Amos vii, 10-13. Shalmaneser sent thither a priest, 2 Kings xvii, 27, 28. The men of Bethel returned from the Babylonish captivity, Ezra ii. 28; Neh. vii, 32; xi, 31. Bethel is not named in the New Testament, but it is mentioned by Josephus as being taken by Vespasian. The place is now a mass of ruins twelve miles north of Jerusalem, called by the name of *Beitin.* Various stories are told of the stone which was Jacob's pillar.

2. A town in the south of Judah or Simeon, Josh. xii, 16; 1 Sam. xxx, 27 Elsewhere called Chesil, Bethul, and Bethuel, Josh. xv, 30; xix, 4; 1 Chron. v, 29-30.

Beth-E'mek, *house of the valley,* a border town of Asher. Josh. xix, 27 Unknown.

Be'ther, (Map 6,) *dissection, separation.* The name of "mountains" mentioned in Sol. Song ii, 17; viii, 14. Some think it identical with the modern Beitîn. (See BETHEL.) But more probably the site of Bether is the present village of *Bittir,* two hours south-west of Jerusalem.

Bethes'da, (Map 7,) *house of mercy,* or *house of effusion.* A pool at Jerusalem, near the sheep-gate or market, with a cloister of five porches, John v. 2-16. Bethesda is generally supposed to be the pool now called *Birket Israil,* within the wall of the city, close by St. Stephen's Gate, to the northeast of the area of the great mosque. Dr. Robinson, however, is inclined to identify it with the Fountain of the Virgin, (Map 10,) some distance above the Pool of Siloam. The pool, as located in Map 7, measures 360 feet in length, 130 feet in breadth, and 75 in depth, besides the rubbish which has accumulated in it for ages.

Beth-E'zel, *house of firm root,* or *fixed dwelling.* A town mentioned in Micah i, 11, which seems to have been in Philistia. Robinson thinks it is the modern *Beit-Affa,* near Ashdod. See BETH-LEAPHRAH.

Beth-Ga'der, *house of the wall,* a place in Judah, 1 Chron. xi, 51. It is probably the Geder of Josh. xii, 13, and perhaps also identical with Gedor in Josh. xix, 58.

Beth-Ga'mul, *house of the weaned,* or *of the camel,* a town of Moab, Jer. xlviii, 23, in the district of the Mishor or down-country. "It is about forty-five miles south-east of the Sea of Galilee, and, although it has been deserted for centuries, the massive houses look as though the inhabitants had just left them."— *Osborn.* It is now called *Um el-Jemal.*

Beth-Gil'gal, *home of the Gilgal,* a place mentioned in Neh. xii, 29, as "the house of Gilgal," which is probably the same as Gilgal near Bethel. See GILGAL, (2.)

Beth-Hac'cerem, (Map 6,) *house of the vineyard.* A beacon station (a lofty point) near Tekoa, Jer. vi, 1. From Neh. iii, 14, it seems to have been a town having a "ruler." It is possibly identified as the "Frank Mountain," or *Jebel Fureidis,* "Little Paradise hill."

Beth-Hag'gan, *house of the garden.* In 2 Kings ix, 27, our version has "the garden-house"—one of the spots which marked the flight of Ahaziah from Jehu. It is doubtless the same as En-Gannim of Issachar, Josh. xix, 21, and the modern *Jenîn,* on the direct road northward from Samaria. See EN-GANNIM, (2.)

Beth-Ha'nan. See ELON-BETH-HANAN.

Beth-Ha'ran, *house of the height,* a fortified town of Gad east of Jordan, Num. xxxii, 36. Doubtless it is the same as BETH-ARAM, which see.

Beth-Hog'la, or **Hog'lah,** *partridge house,* a town of Benjamin on the border of Judah, Josh. xv, 6; xviii, 19, 21. South-east of Jericho are ruins and a spring called *Kasr-Hajla* and *'Ain-Hajla,* which probably mark the site.

Beth-Ho'ron, (Map 5,) *house of the hollow.* The name of two places, the "upper" and the "nether," Josh. xvi, 3, 5; 1 Chron. vii, 24; 2 Chron. viii, 5. It was on the road from Gibeon to Azekah and the Philistine plain, Josh. x, 10, 11; 1 Sam. xiii, 18; 2 Chron. xxv, 13; Judith iv, 4; 1 Macc. iii, 24. It was on the boundary between Benjamin and Ephraim, Josh. xvi, 3, 5; xviii, 13, 14; counted to Ephraim, Josh. xxi, 22; 1 Chron. vii, 24; and allotted to the Kohathite Levites, 1 Chron. vi, 68. For other notices see also 1 Sam xiii, 18; 1 Kings ix, 17; 2 Chron. viii, 5; xxv, 13; 1 Macc. iii, 13-34; vii, 19; ix, 50. The road from Gibeon, about four miles to the upper Beth

BETHLEHEM.

Horon, is mainly an ascent, just answering to the account given in Josh. x 10; from thence the rugged descent commences, mostly along a kind of r dge, for three miles to the nether village on a lower eminence, and this was "the going down to Beth-Horon," Josh. x, 11; whence there is a short, steep fall to the plain country. The sites of the two towns are undoubtedly occupied by the modern villages of *Beit-Ur el-Foka* (the Upper,) and *Beit-Ur el-Tahta* (the Lower.)

Beth-Jesh'imoth and **Beth-Jes'imoth**, *house of desolations* or *wastes*, a town in Moab, probably in the Jordan Valley, at the north end of the Dead Sea, Num. xxxiii, 49; Josh. xii, 3; xiii, 20; Ezek. xxv, 9. Schwarz states that there are still "the ruins of a *Beth-Jisimuth* situated on the north-east point of the Dead Sea, half a mile from the Jordan."

Beth-Leaph'rah, *house of the fawn*, a place named in Micah i, 10, in connection with other places of the Philistine coast. It is probably identical with the modern village of *Beit-Affa*, six miles south-east of Ashdod.

Beth-Leb'aoth, *house of lionesses*, a place originally allotted to Judah, but afterward transferred to Simeon, Josh. xv, 32; xix, 6. It is called also Lebaoth, and probably Beth-Birei. Possibly the ruin called *El-Beyûdh* marks the site.

Beth'lehem, (Map 5,) *house of bread*. The name of two places in Palestine.
1. A town of Judah, nearly six miles south of Jerusalem. It was an inconsiderable place, hence its name does not occur in the enumeration of cities by Joshua, (chap. 15;) and the prophet Micah (v, 2) styles it "the least among the thousands of Judah." At an earlier date it was called *Ephrath*, or more frequently *Ephratah*, and as such first appears in Gen. xxxv. 19; xlviii, 7, when the death and burial of Rachel are mentioned. Hence Micah (v, 2) uses the title *Bethlehem Ephratah*. The name was afterward applied, it seems, to the whole district; for the inhabitants were called Ephrathites of Bethlehem Judah, Ruth i, 2; 1 Sam. xvii, 12. The same title occurs also in Judges xvii, 7, 9; xix, 1, 2, 18, for the sake probably of distinguishing it from another *Bethlehem* in the tribe of Zebulun, Josh. xix, 15. Bethlehem, although originally of so little consequence, is honored as the birthplace of the most illustrious personage of all history, and as the residence of the three noted characters, Naomi, Ruth, and Boaz, Ruth i, 1, 19; ii, 4; iv. King David was born here, 1 Sam. xvii, 12; xx, 6; and here he was also anointed king by Samuel, xvi, 1–13. Hence Bethlehem was called the "City of David," Luke ii, 4. Many interesting events in David's life are, of course, connected with this place. On the neighboring hills he fed his flocks; from the wild gorges near came the savage beasts that he slew; from here he went to combat the giant, 1 Sam. xvi, xvii; and when a man of war, one day, faint and weary, it was for the water of the well by the gate of Bethlehem that he longed; and three of his mighty men broke through the Philistine host and brought it to him, but he would not drink, 2 Sam. xxiii, 13–17; 1 Chron. xi, 15–19. Here, also, Asahel, Joab's brother, was buried in the sepulcher of his father, 2 Sam. ii, 32; from which we learn that Bethlehem was the native town of the three sons of Zeruiah, the daughter of Jesse, (1 Chron. ii, 16,) Joab, Abishai, and Asahel, as well as of Elhanan, another of David's mighty men of valor, 2 Sam. xxiii, 24. According to 2 Chron. xi. 6. Bethlehem was fortified by Rehoboam; and it was the last resting place of the rebellious remnant that after the destruction of Jerusalem, would go down into Egypt, Jer. xli, 17. The Old Testament

history of Bethlehem closes with the notice that some of its "childrur" returned from the captivity with Zerubbabel, Ezra ii, 1; Neh. vii, 26. But the chief glory of Bethlehem arises from the fact that here was born the Saviour of the world, Matt. ii, 1, 6; Luke ii, 4. Joseph and Mary, as descendants of David, had to repair to Bethlehem, according to the decree or the Roman emperor. There, in the adjoining fields, the angelic host announced the glad tidings of a Saviour's birth; and there, before the great mystery of godliness, God manifest in the flesh, the "wise men from the East," coming from afar, presented their offerings. Here, too, was the slaughter of the little ones by Herod, seeming to awaken again Rachel's lamentation, Matt. ii, 1-18; Luke ii, 1-20.

There has been no doubt or dispute about the site of Bethlehem, as it has always been an inhabited place, and, from its sacred associations, has been visited by an unbroken series of pilgrims and travelers. The crusaders on their approach to Jerusalem first took possession of Bethlehem, at the entreaty of its Christian inhabitants. In A. D. 1110, King Baldwin I. erected it into an episcopal see, a dignity it had never before enjoyed; but, although this was confirmed by Pope Pascal II., and the title long retained in the Romish Church, yet the actual possession of the see appears not to have been of long continuance. In A. D. 1244, Bethlehem, like Jerusalem, was desolated by the wild hordes of the Kharismians. Formerly there was a Mohammedan quarter, but after the rebellion in 1834 this was destroyed by order of Ibrahim Pasha. The modern name of the village is *Beit-Lahm*. It has a population of about three thousand. It is situated on a hill of limestone which runs east and west. The east end of the hill is bold; on the west it slopes gradually to the valley. On the sides of this hill, which is about a mile long, are terraced gardens, with olive-trees, fig-trees, and vines. In the most easterly part of the village is the celebrated Church of the Nativity, which owes its foundation to the Empress Helena, mother of Constantine the Great. It is inclosed within the walls of the convent, which is now parceled out among the Greek, Latin, and Armenian monks. Two spiral staircases lead down to the cave or grotto of the nativity, twenty feet below the floor of the church. This cave is lined with Italian marble; and in a small semi-circular niche, the exact spot marked by a star inlaid in the marble, corresponding to the point in the heavens where the star appeared to the magi, is a Latin inscription stating that Jesus was born *here*. A row of lamps are always burning. Opposite is a large irregular cavity, where it is said the manger stood; a block of white marble being hollowed out in it like a manger. Here, too, is the altar of the magi, and other lamps are suspended. There are also shown the sepulcher of the Innocents, the grotto or crypt where St. Jerome lived and studied, and chapels dedicated to Joseph and other saints. As to the supposition that our Lord was born in a cave, tradition is in its favor, but facts and probabilities are against it. Certainly Christ was born *in* the town; and the place where the magi visited the Saviour was a "house," Matt. ii, 11. The *traditional* scene of the angels' appearance to the shepherds is a plain about a mile away, where is a miserable village called *Beit-Sahur*, while the traditional well of David is half a mile to the north of the town; but, according to Dr. Robinson, there is now "no well of living water" near.

2. A town in Zebulun, Josh. xix, 15; probably the residence of Ibzan, Judges xii, 8 It is now known as *Beit-Lahm*, six miles west of Nazareth,

and is declared by Robinson to be ' a very miserable villege ... without a trace of antiquity except the name."

Beth-Lo'mon, a corruption of Bethlehem, 1 Esdras v, 17.

Beth-Ma'achah, *house of oppression,* (of *Maachah,*) a place named in 2 Sam. xx, 14, 15, and there occurring more as a definition of the position of Abel than for itself; more fully called Abel-Beth-Maachah, 2 Kings xv, 29. It is probably identical with Maachah.

Beth-Mar'caboth, *house of the chariots,* a town of Simeon situated in the extreme south of Judah, with Ziklag and Hormah, Josh. xix, 5; 1 Chron. iv, 31.

Beth-Me'on, *house of habitation,* a place in Reuben, Jer. xlviii, 23; elsewhere rendered Beth-Baal-Meon, Josh. xiii, 17.

Beth-Mil'lo, *wall-house,* the name of two places, Judg. ix, 20; 2 Kings xii, 20. See MILLO.

Beth-Nim'rah, (Maps 5, 20,) *house of limpid water,* a town on the east of Jordan, "in the valley," Josh. xiii, 27; fortified by Gad, Num. xxxii, 36; called Nimrah in Num. xxxii, 3. In Isa. xv, 6, and Jer. xlviii, 34, "the waters of Nimrim" are by some considered in the same locality. This place is said to have been situated about five miles north of Livias. The name still survives in the *Nahr-Nimrin,* the lower end of the *Wady Shoaib,* where the waters of that valley discharge themselves into the Jordan a few miles above Jericho. Heaps of ruins mark the site of the ancient city. This wady runs into the eastern mountains as far as *es-Salt.* There is good reason to suppose that Beth-Nimrah is identical with Bethabara.

Betho'ron, a corruption of Beth-Horon, Judith iv, 4.

Beth-Pa'let, *house of escape,* a town in the south of Judah, Josh. xv, 27; called Beth-Phelet in Neh. xi, 26. Possibly the ruin on *Tell el-Kuseifeh,* near Moladah, may mark the site.

Beth-Paz'zez, *house of dispersion,* a town of Issachar, Josh. xix, 21. The site may possibly be at the ruins *Beit-Jenn,* west of the south end of the Sea of Galilee.

Beth-Pe'or, *house,* or *temple of Peor,* a place east of Jordan, in the district allotted to Reuben, Deut. iii, 29; iv, 46; Josh. xiii, 20. It was in a ravine over against Beth-Peor that Moses was buried, Deut. xxxiv, 6. The place was doubtless dedicated to the god Baal-Peor. It was doubtless one of the summits of *Jebel Siâghah,* where are found extensive ruins of a temple and its surrounding structures.

Beth'phage, (Maps 6, 20,) *house of unripe figs,* a village on the Mount of Olives, on the road from Jerusalem to Jericho, and evidently near to Bethany, Matt. xxi, 1; Mark xi, 1; Luke xix, 29. Jesus lodged there, Matt. xxi, 17. It was possibly west of Bethany, but authorities differ; some even thinking the two names to signify different quarters of the same village.

Beth-Phe'let, Neh. xi, 26. See BETH-PALET.

Beth-Re'hob, *house of the street* or *streets, (house of Rehob,)* a place neai which was the valley in which Laish or Dan was situated, Judg. xviii, 28; called also Rehob, Num. xiii, 21; 2 Sam. x, 8. It was one of the little kingdoms of Aram or Syria. The children of Ammon are said to have hired the Syrians of Beth-Rehob, 2 Sam. x, 6. Being, however, "far from Sidon." it must not be confounded with two towns named Rehob in Asher. This place is supposed to be represented by the modern *Hûnîn,* a fortress overlooking the plain of the *Hûleh,* in which lay the city of Dan.

Beth-sa'ida, (Maps 5, 21,) *house,* or *place of fishing.* 1. A town in Galilee not far from Capernaum, on the western shore of the Sea of Galilee, Matt. xi, 21; Luke x, 13. It was the city of Philip, Andrew, and Peter, John i, 44; xii, 21. It was visited by Christ; the scene of Christ's cure of a blind man; and one of the cities against which Christ prophesied, Mark vi, 45; viii, 22; Luke x, 13. Mr. Porter identifies it with *el-Tabighah;* others with *Khan el-Minyeh.* But this is merely conjectural.

2. According to Pliny and Josephus, another Bethsaida lay east of the lake and the Jordan in Lower Gaulonitis, just above the point where the Jordan flows into the lake. It was built up and enlarged by the Tetrarch Philip not long after the birth of Christ, and received the name of Julias, in honor of Julia, the daughter of the Emperor Augustus. Philip died here, and was buried in a magnificent sepulcher.

The very best authorities disagree as to the existence of *two* places by the name of Bethsaida. After an examination of various writers, we propose an extract from Ayre's *Bible Treasury,* as giving a fair argument for two towns. Ayre says: "We may conclude that there were two places, for the following reasons. The scene of the miracle of multiplying the five loaves was in a desert place belonging to Bethsaida, Luke ix, 10. This place, according to Dr. Thomson, can be exactly identified. There is a bold headland, *Butaiha,* running into the lake; close by is a little cave, and at the foot of the rocky mountain a piece of level greensward. From this spot, near and belonging to Bethsaida-Julias, our Lord, we are told, sent off his disciples by ship to the other side to Bethsaida, Mark vi, 45. And, again, Dalmanutha was on the western side of the lake. But, after being at this place, Jesus crossed to the other side and came to Bethsaida, viii, 10, 13, 22. These reasons seem conclusive for the fact of there being two Bethsaidas. Dr. Thomson, however, imagines there was but one, Bethsaida-Julias; that it was built on both sides of the Jordan, and therefore partly in Galilee; that the desert place being at some little distance, our Lord might well send his disciples thither by boat; that the storm which arose prevented them from making Bethsaida, or even Capernaum; and that, therefore, though they had set out for Bethsaida, they were carried to the land of Gennesaret." (*The Land and the Book,* pp. 372-374. Comp. Ellicott's note, *Hist. Lect.,* p. 207.)

Grove and others locate this Bethsaida "possibly at *et-Tell,* east of Jordan, three miles north of the lake." Others claim a site "corresponding to that of the modern ruined village *el-Araj,* containing some vestiges of antiquity, immediately east of the *debouchure* of the Upper Jordan." See Robinson's *Researches;* Herzog; M'Clintock and Strong.

Beth'samos, 1 Esdras v, 18. Doubtless the Beth-Azmaveth of Neh. vii, 28; the Azmaveth of Ezra ii, 24.

Beth'san, 1 Macc. v, 52; xii, 40, 41. The Greek form of Beth-Shean.

Beth'-Shan, *house of quiet,* 1 Sam. xxxi, 10, 12; 2 Sam. xxi, 12. A variation of Beth-Shean.

Beth'-She'an, (Maps 5, 20,) *house of quiet,* or *security,* a city belonging to Manasseh, 1 Chron. vii, 29, though within the original limits of Issachar, Josh. xvii, 11, and on the west of Jordan, (comp. 1 Macc. v, 52;) called also Bethsan, Beth-Shan, and Scythopolis. The tribes were not able to expel the Canaanites, Josh. xvii, 11, 16; Judg. i, 27; 1 Chron. vii, 28. After the battle on Gilboa, the Philistines fastened the dead body of Saul to the wall of this city, 1 Sam. xxxi, 10, 12; 2 Sam. xxi, 12. In the time of Solomon Beth-Shean seems to have included the neighboring district unto Abel-Meholah; and "all Beth-Shean" was under one of his commissariat officers, 1 Kings iv, 12. Afterward it was called Scythopolis, 2 Macc. xii, 29; a colony being left here from the great Scythian irruption. (See SCYTHIAN.) It is now called *Beisân*, being situated in a very strong natural position, just where the plain of Esdraelon begins to descend to the Jordan valley. It is about three miles west of Jordan, and sixteen from the southern end of the Sea of Galilee. The mountains of Gilboa are a few miles westward, while close on the north runs the water of the *Ain-Jalûd*, whose fountain is in Jezreel, and three other large brooks pass through or by the town. It is a miserable place of about sixty or seventy houses, whose inhabitants are said to be a set of inhospitable and lawless fanatics. Extensive ruins of the old city yet remain.

Beth-She'mesh, (Map 5,) *house of the Sun.* 1. A city on the north boundary of Judah, Josh. xv, 10, toward the land of the Philistines, 1 Sam. vi, 9, 12; and probably in a lowland plain, 2 Kings xiv, 11. It was afterward allotted to the priests, Josh. xxi, 16; 1 Sam. vi, 15; 1 Chron. vi, 59; and was a "suburb city." It is named in one of Solomon's commissariat districts under the charge of Ben-Dekar, 1 Kings iv, 9. Amaziah, king of Judah, was here defeated and made prisoner by Jehoash, king of Israel, 2 Kings xiv, 11, 13; 2 Chron. xxv, 21, 23. In the reign of Ahaz it was captured by the Philistines, 2 Chron. xxviii, 18. It is particularly noted as the scene of the return of the ark from Philistia. Beth-Shemesh was not far from Ekron, and along the road between the two places the Philistines hastened to send back the ark by "milch-kine," 1 Sam. vi, 9, 12. The ark was received with unbounded joy by the Israelites. But by reason of an irreverent curiosity on the part of the people, "fifty thousand and threescore and ten men" were miraculously slain, 1 Sam. vi, 19. Some suppose that a copyist's error has given us this large number of 50,070, instead of 5,070, or 570. Whichever number may be the accurate one, the event was a terrible judgment from the Almighty.

The place is doubtless identical with Ir-Shemesh, Josh. xv, 10; xix, 41, 43; 1 Kings iv, 9; and perhaps with Mount Heres, "Mount of the Sun," Judg. i, 35. It is identified with the modern *Ain-Shems*, fourteen miles west of Jerusalem, a ruined Arab village constructed of ancient materials. Near by are extensive remains.

2. A town of Issachar, Josh. xix, 22. Not known.

3. A town of Naphtali, from which the Canaanites were not expelled, Josh. xix, 38; Judg. i, 33. Not identified.

4. In Jer. xliii, 13, this name refers to *Heliopolis*, or *On*, an idolatrous temple or place in Egypt. The Arabs now call it *Ain-Shems.* See ON.

Beth-Shit'tah, *house of the acacia,* a place to which the Midianites fled from Gideon, Judg. vii, 22. It was probably near the Jordan. Possibly it may be identical with *Shutta*, discovered by Robinson, east of Jezreel, although this is further from Jordan than we should expect.

Bethsu'ra, the form used by the Maccabees for Beth-zur, 1 Macc. iv, 29, 61; vi, 7, 26, 31, 49, 50; ix, 52; x, 14; xi, 65; xiv, 7, 33; 2 Macc. xi, 5; xiii, 19, 22.

Beth-Tap'puah, *house of apples,* a town in the mountains of Judah, near Hebron, Josh. xv, 53. (Comp. 1 Chron. ii, 43.) It is identified with the modern *Teffûh*, about four or five miles west of Hebron, on a ridge of high table land. Olive groves and vineyards still flourish there, and terraces of the ancient cultivation still remain in use.

Bethu'el, perhaps *man of God,* a town of Simeon, 1 Chron. iv, 30; a variation of Bethul, Josh. xix, 4.

Beth'ul, a contraction of Bethuel, Josh. xix, 4. It is called also Chesil, and perhaps Bethel, Josh. xv, 30; 1 Chron. iv, 9; Josh. xii, 16. It was a town of Simeon in the south named with Eltolad and Hormah in Josh. xix, 4. See CHESIL.

Bethu'lia, the site of the events in the book of Judith, where its position is described, Judith iv, 6; vi, 10, 11, 14; vii, 1, 3, 6, 13, 20, etc. In the Middle Ages the name of Bethulia was given to "the Frank Mountain." Frequent attempts fail to identify the site with certainty. One conjecture locates the place at *Sanûr,* about three miles from Dothan, and six or seven from *Jenin,* (Engannim,) which stand on the very edge of the great plain of Esdraelon. Schultz finds Bethulia in the village of *Beit-Ilfa,* a village on the northern declivity of Mount Gilboa, containing rock-graves, and other marks of antiquity.

Beth'-Zur, *house of the rock,* a place in the highlands of Judah, Josh. xv, 58; 1 Chron. ii, 45; elsewhere called Bethsura. It was fortified by Rehoboam, 2 Chron. xi, 7. After the captivity mention is made of its ruler as helping to repair the wall of Jerusalem, Neh. iii, 16; 1 Chron. ii, 45. During the Maccabean wars it was an important place, and of great strength, 1 Macc. iv, 29; vi, 32–47; xi, 65; 2 Macc. xi, 5. It is now known as *Beit-Sûr,* on the main road four miles north of Hebron, where ruins of the ancient town still exist.

Beto'lius, 1 Esdras v, 21. A corruption of Bethel, Ezra ii, 28; Neh. vii, 32.

Betomas'them, or **Betomes'tham,** a place mentioned as near Esdraelon and Dothaim, Judith iv, 6; xv, 4. It is not identified.

Bet'onim, *pistachio-nuts,* a town in Gad, mentioned in connection with Ramath-Mizpeh and Mahanaim, Josh. xiii, 26. Some would identify it with *Batneh,* whose ruins are found on Mt. Gilead, about five miles west of *es-Salt.*

Beu'lah, *married,* a symbolical name applied to the land of Israel, which, when desolate no more, shall again be the delight of the Lord, Isa. lxii, 4. It may refer to the return from Babylon, or to the Jewish Church in her happy union with God.

Be'zek, *lightning.* 1. A city in Judah, the residence of Adoni-Bezek, Judg. i, 3–5. It was probably among the mountains not far from Jerusalem. Not identified.

2. A place within a day's march of Jabesh, where King Saul reviewed his troops previous to the relief of Jabesh-Gilead, 1 Sam. xi, 8, 9. Schwarz thinks it to be *Bezik,* or *Absik,* near Beth-Shean; but this needs confirmation.

Be'zer, IN THE WILDERNESS, *ore of precious metal,* a town of Reuben in the *Mishor,* allotted to the Merarites, and one of the cities of refuge east of the Jordan, Deut. iv, 43; Josh. xx, 8; xxi, 36; 1 Chron. vi, 78. It is barely possible that Bezer corresponds with a village called *Burazin,* twelve miles north of east from Heshbon.

Be'zeth a place near Jerusalem, where Bacchides encamped, 1 Macc. vii, 19. Possibly it may refer to Bezetha. Possibly identical with *Beit Z'ata.*

Bez'etha, (Map 7,) one of the heights on which Jerusalem is built. It was north of Antonia, and separated from it by a deep fosse; but, according to Josephus, not inclosed till the erection of the third wall by Agrippa.

It is undecided whether Bezetha is the eminence north of the present Damascus gate, or that immediately north of the present Haram inclosure. The probability seems in favor of the latter locality, as in our map.

Bil'eam, *foreign*, a place in western Manasseh allotted to the Levites, Chron. vi, 70. It is doubtless identical with Ibleam, Josh. xvii, 17, and Gath-Rimmon, Josh. xxi, 25. Mr. Porter locates Bileam in the plain of Esdraelon, near Megiddo.

Bil'hah, *faltering*, or *bashfulness*, a town in Simeon, 1 Chron. iv, 29, identical with Balah, Josh. xix, 3, and doubtless also with Baalah, xv, 29.

Bith'ron, *the section*, or *the divided place*, a defile in the Arabah, or Jordan valley, 2 Sam. ii, 29. It was between the river and Mahanaim, to which town Abner and his troops returned after crossing the Jordan to the east.

Bithyn'ia, (Map 8,) a district of Asia Minor on the Euxine and the Sea of Marmora, having Mysia on the west, Phrygia and Galatia on the south and east, and Paphlagonia on the east. Bithynia is mentioned only incidentally in the Scriptures, Acts xvi, 7; 1 Pet. i, 1. Its principal cities were Nicomedia, Chalcedon, Heraclea, Nicea, and Prusa, none of which are referred to in the Bible. It was formerly an independent kingdom. Its last sovereign, Nicomedes III., being re-established in his kingdom (of which Mithridates, king of Pontus, had dispossessed him) by Pompey, bequeathed Bithynia to the Romans about 74 B. C. On the death of Mithridates the western part of his kingdom was added to Bithynia, and subsequently the province was again increased by Augustus. Its hills were well wooded, and its valleys productive. Bithynia now forms one of the districts of Turkish Anatolia, and is the nearest province to Turkey in Europe.

Bizjoth'jah, *contempt of Jehovah*, a town in the south of Judah, Josh. xv, 28. It is doubtless identical with Baalah, and with Balah, xix, 2, 3; also with Baalath-beer, xix, 8, and Bilhah, 1 Chron. iv, 29. The signification of the name agrees with the fact that the city was once given up to the worship of Baal.

Bo'chim, *the weepers*, a place where the Israelites wept when rebuked by the angel, Judg. ii, 1, 5. It was near to Gilgal, west of the Jordan near the Dead Sea, and possibly at the present ruins of *Khurbet Jeradeh*.

Bo'han, *a thumb*, a memorial stone in the valley of Achor, on the borders of Judah and Benjamin, set up in honor of Bohan, Josh. xv, 6; xviii, 17. Possibly identical with *Hajar-el-asbah* (stone of the finger) in *Wady Daber*.

Bos'cath, in 2 Kings xxii, 1, inaccurately put for BOZKATH, which see.

Bo'sor, a fortified city east of Jordan, in Gilead, 1 Macc. v, 26, 36. Probably the Bezer of the wilderness mentioned in Deut. iv, 43

Bos'ora, a city in Gilead taken by Judas Maccabeus, 1 Macc. v, 26, 28. Doubtless Bozrah.

Bo'zez, *shining*, or *height*, one of the two "teeth of rock" below Michmash, near Gibeah, 1 Sam. xiv, 4, 5. Dr. Robinson noticed two hills of bluut conical form in the bottom of *Wady Suweinit*, just below *Mukmas*, but Stanley was not able to make them out.

Boz'kath, *strong region*, or *hill*, a town in Judah near Lachish and Eglon, Josh. xv, 39. It is called Boscath in 2 Kings xxii, 1, where it is named as the native place of Adaiah, maternal grandfather of King Josiah.

Boz'rah, (Map 5,) *inclosure* or *fortress*, or *sheep-fold* (?).

1. A city of Edom, the residence of Jobab, one of the early kings, Gen.

xxxvi, 33; 1 Chron. i, 44. Isaiah mentions it in later times in connection with Edom, Isa. xxxiv, 6; lxiii, 1. Other notices occur, Jer. xlix, 13, 22; Amos i, 12; Mic. ii, 12. It is identified as the modern *el-Busaireh*, a village of about fifty houses standing on a height south-east of the Dead Sea, about half-way between the sea and Petra.

2. A place in Moab, mentioned in Jer. xlviii, 24. It is probably the Bosora of 1 Macc. v, 26–28; for Jeremiah's list included cities both "far and near." Porter identifies it with *Busrah*, which lies in the open plain about sixty miles south of Damascus. This site contains extensive ruins. No vineyards remain. The inhabitants number about fifteen families.

Buz, (Map 12,) *contempt*, probably named from the second son of Nahor. Jeremiah mentions the tribe of Buz, and apparently locates their territory in the northern part of Arabia Deserta, Jer. xxv, 23.

Cab'bon, *cake*, or perhaps *bond*, a town in the lowland of Judah. Josh. xv, 40. Possibly it is the modern ruined site *el-Rufeir*, ten miles south-east of Ashkelon.

Ca'bul, (Maps 4, 13,) *bound*, *boundary*, or possibly *as nothing*.
1. A place in the boundary of Asher, Josh. xix, 27. It is probably the modern *Kabûl*, eight or nine miles east of Accho.
2. A district of "twenty cities" given by Solomon to Hiram, King of Tyre, in acknowledgment of the service Hiram had rendered toward the building of the temple, 1 Kings ix, 10–13. Hiram not being pleased with the gift, the district received the name of Cabul—which may mean *as nothing*, or *unpleasing*. Josephus locates this district in the north-west part of Galilee, adjacent to Tyre. After these "cities" were restored by Hiram they were colonized by Israelites, 2 Chron. viii, 2.

Ca'des, 1 Macc. xi, 63, 73. A Grecized form of Kedesh in Naphtali, Josh. xx, 7.

Ca'des-Bar'ne. Judith v, 14. A Grecized form of Kadesh-Barnea.

Cæsare'a, (Map 5,) a noted city of Palestine on the coast of the Mediterranean, on the great road from Tyre to Egypt, about half-way between Joppa and Dora. This city is very frequently alluded to in the Acts of the Apostles. It was the residence of Philip, Acts viii, 40; xxi, 8, 16; and of Cornelius, x, 1, 24; xi, 11. It was the scene of Herod Agrippa's death, xii, 19. It was visited by St. Paul, ix, 30; xviii, 22; xxi, 8, 16; xxiii, 23, 33; xxv, 1. 4, 6, 13; and by Peter, x, 24. The distance of Cæsarea from Jerusalem is given by Josephus as six hundred stadia. The Jerusalem Itinerary gives sixty-eight miles. In a direct line the actual distance is forty-seven English miles. The place was originally called "Strato's Tower." Afterward the city was built by Herod the Great in ten years with the most lavish outlay, calling it Cæsarea Sebaste. It also bore the names of Cæsarea Stratonis, Maritima Cæsarea, and Cæsarea Palestinæ, to distinguish it from Cæsarea Philippi. Josephus tells us it was a most magnificent city. He describes a breakwater built of vast blocks of stone sunk to the depth of twenty fathoms in the sea. Broad landing-wharves surrounded the harbor, and conspicuous from the sea was a temple dedicated to Cæsar and Rome, and containing colossal statues of the emperor and the imperial city. Herod made this city his residence, and thus elevated it to the rank of the civil and military capital of Judea. It was here that Vespasian was first declared emperor. After the destruction of Jerusalem, Cæsarea became the spiritual metropolis of

Palestine; but since the beginning of the fifth century it became the capital of Palestina Prima—one of the three provinces into which the whole land was divided, and subordinate to the Bishopric of Jerusalem. Among the Bishops of Cæsarea, Eusebius is the most celebrated. During the Crusades the city was taken by King Baldwin in 1101, and re-taken by Saladin in 1187 and laid waste. It was subsequently rebuilt, and again devastated, and finally destroyed by Sultan Baibar, who left not one stone upon another. Since that time its extensive ruins have borne the present name of *Kaisariyeh*, and their only inhabitants are wild beasts and reptiles.

Cæsare'a Philip'pi, (Map 5,) a town at the source of the Jordan. It was earlier known by the name of Panium, from the worship of the heathen god Pan. Herod the Great beautified it, and built a temple to Augustus. Later it was enlarged and beautified by Philip the Tetrarch, who gave to it the name of Cæsarea in honor of his emperor, (Tiberius Cæsar,) adding Philippi to distinguish it from Cæsarea on the Mediterranean. Later still Agrippa II. called it Neronias. The oldest name, however, survived, as coins on which Cæsarea Paneas appears sufficiently prove, and it is even now called *Banias*. The site is at the springs of the Jordan, at the southern base of the mighty Hermon, whose towering peaks rise from seven thousand to eight thousand feet above. The distance from Jerusalem is about one hundred and twenty miles, and this appears to be the northern limit of Christ's travels, Matt. xvi, 13; Mark viii, 27. Many think that it was upon one of the near-by spurs of Hermon that our Lord's transfiguration occurred. (See TABOR.) The present village is a mean and destitute place. Many remains of ancient architecture still exist in the vicinity.

Cain, the *lance*, or perhaps *nest*, a city in the lowland of Judah, Josh. xv, 57. Possibly the site is marked by *Yukin*, a short distance south-east of Hebron.

Ca'lah, *vigorous old age*, one of the most ancient of Assyrian cities, Gen. x, 11. It was founded by Asshur or Nimrod. By some the site is believed to have been among the ruins of the modern *Nimrûd*, which have furnished so large a portion of the Assyrian antiquities, and that it was for a long time the royal Assyrian residence, till Sargon built a new city where *Khorsabad* now stands. But Layard is disposed to find Calah at *Kalah Sherghat*, a vast ruin (four thousand six hundred and eighty-five yards around) on the Tigris, about fifty miles below its junction with the Zab, but he does not speak with certainty. A mutilated sitting figure which he found there is now in the British Museum.

Ca'leb, *a dog*, the district allotted to Caleb, probably at or about Carmel of Judah, 1 Sam. xxx, 14.

Cal'neh, (Map 1,) *fortified dwelling*, or probably the *fort* of the god *Ana* or *Anu*. An ancient city of Assyria, of Nimrod's empire, Gen. x, 10; Amos vi, 2. It was probably on the left bank of the Euphrates, south-east of Babylon. Apparently it is the same with Calno, Isa. x, 9; and Canneh, Ezek. xxvii, 23. It is considered identical with modern *Niffer*, about sixty miles south-south-east of Babylon, on the eastern bank of the Euphrates, where extensive ruins remain.

Cal'vary. This word occurs but once, in Luke xxiii, 33, to designate the place where Christ was crucified. The term Calvary is adopted literally from the Latin Vulgate, instead of translating the Greek word by "skull," as in the three other Gospels. "Mount" does not occur in the original. The name has been connected with the fact that executions were performed there, and that skulls were probably left lying around. It is more probable that it was a bare round spot, somewhat skull-shaped. The dispute is very earnest as to whether the spot now venerated as such in the Church of the Holy Sepulcher is really the ancient Calvary. The references in the Scripture are but few. The places of crucifixion and burial were contiguous. Golgotha was outside the city gate, Matt. xxvii, 32; Heb. xiii, 12; yet it was near the city, John xix, 20; it was also close to a public road, for the crowd met Simeon the Cyrenian passing on as he came out of the country, Mark xv, 21; Luke xxiii, 26; and there was a garden just by, John xix, 41. Dr. Barclay mentions a "kind of cape, or promontory of land, projecting south-eastwardly into the Kidron valley, a short distance above Gethsemane." Concerning this he says: "May not this spur of an unnamed ridge be the site of that awful scene, the crucifixion of the Son of God? There is, at this time, no skull-shaped monticule of rock to be found in all the region where, according to Jeremiah, Goath or Gotha was located; but this, of course, is no proof that such a prominence did not once exist." Mr. Fisher Howe, with much force of argument, places the true site of Calvary in the north of Jerusalem, not far from the Damascus gate, above the "Grotto of Jeremiah." There are also strong reasons for locating Calvary on Moriah. See MORIAH; JERUSALEM, pp. 229, 230.

Ca'mon, *full of stalks* or *grain*, the burial place of Jair, the Gileadite, Judg. x, 5. It lay probably east of Jordan; possibly at *Reinum*, near Gerasa.

Ca'na of Galilee, (Map 3.) Cana signifies *reedy, a nest* or *cave*. A village of Galilee about nine miles north of Nazareth. It was the scene of two of Christ's miracles, John ii, 1, 11; iv, 46; xxi, 2; and the native place of Nathanael. Christ began his miracles at Cana by turning water into wine at a wedding. Tradition locates the site at the modern village of *Kefr Kenna*, four and a half miles north-east of Nazareth; but Dr. Robinson locates it at the now deserted village of *Kana el-Jelil*, about nine miles north of Nazareth. De Saulcy, Farrar, and others, with good reason, favor *Kefr Kenna*.

Ca'naan, (Map 3,) *low*, or *lowland*. The country west of the Jordan, called also Chanaan, and the Land of Canaan, after one of the sons of Ham The Greeks applied the term *Cana* to the entire region between the Jordan and the Mediterranean up to Sidon, afterward termed by them Phœnicia, a name which by degrees came to be confined to the northern coast district, or Phœnicia proper. Canaan is generally considered equivalent to the Land of Israel or Palestine.

The Scripture boundary of Canaan represents the sea as its western border from Sidon to Gaza, Gen. x, 19. The southern boundary was a line from Gaza to the southern end of the Dead Sea, including the Judean hills, but excluding the country of the Amalekites, Gen. x, 19; Num. xiii, 29 No part of Canaan lay beyond the Jordan on the east, Num. xxxiii, 51; Exod. xvi, 35; with Josh. v, 12; xxii, 11. On the north, Canaan extended as far as Hamath, which was also the utmost boundary of the "land of promise," Gen. xvii, 8; Num xxxiv, 8. The coast from Sidon northward to Arvad, and the ridge of Lebanon, were inhabited by Canaanites, though they do not appear to have been included in Canaan proper, Gen. x, 15–19. In a few instances, such as Zeph. ii, 5, and Matt. xv, 22, the word Canaan was applied to the low maritime plains of Philistia and Phœnicia. The meaning above given to the word Canaan is disputed by etymologists. In regard to this definition it may be remarked that the land of Canaan contained many

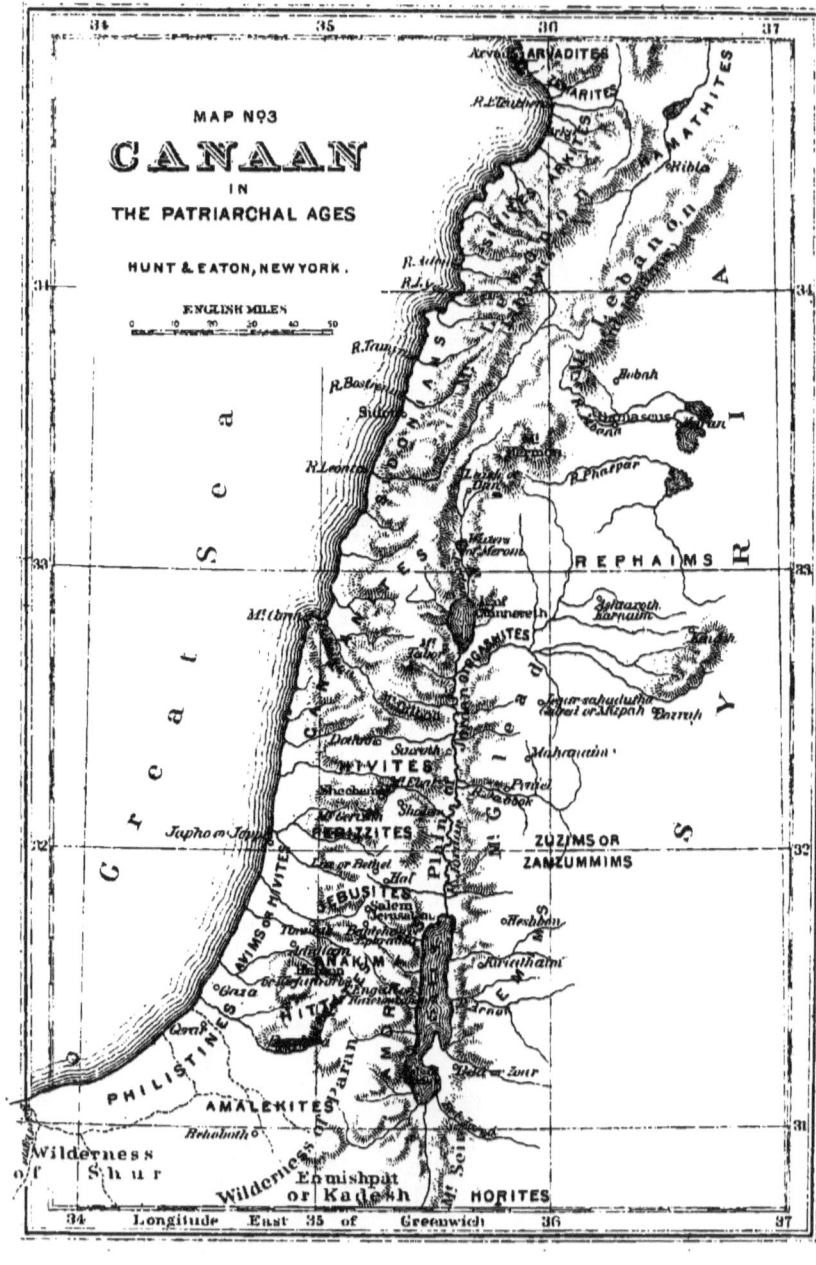

elevated spots, such as Shechem, Hebron, Bethel, Bethlehem, Shiloh. But the term *low* is employed as specially opposed to the "land of Gilead"—the high table-land east of the Jordan. Although Canaan had these heights, yet, as travelers assure us, the land never gives the idea of elevation. For the eye looks continually over the wide maritime plain on the one side, and down into the Jordan valley on the other; and, besides, there is almost always in view the high mountain line beyond the Jordan, in comparison with which the hills of Canaan are dwarfed. See PALESTINE.

Ca'naanite, The, *the zealot*, the designation of the Apostle Simon the Less. Matt. x, 4; Mark iii, 18. This name has no connection with that of the descendants of Canaan.

Ca'naanite and Ca'-naanites, *lowlanders*, the designation of the descendants of Canaan, the son of Ham and grandson of Noah, inhabitants of the land of Canaan and the districts adjoining, Gen. x, 15-18. More precisely, they were a leading people among the early (though not the original) inhabitants of Palestine. They were the lowlanders, and are described as dwelling "by the sea and by the coast of Jordan." Num. xiii, 29. Later the Canaanites are said to be "on the East and on the West," that is, along the sea-coast and in the Jordan valley, while the Amorites and others were "in the mountains," Josh. xi, 3, occupying the central highlands. There were seven nations descended from Canaan, the Canaanites, Hittites,

Amorites, Perizzites, Hivites, Jebusites, and Girgashites, Gen. x, 15-19; Exod. iii, 8; Deut. vii, 1; 1 Chron. i, 13-16. Notices of their territory, Gen. x, 19; xii, 6; Num. xiii, 29; Judg. iv, 2. Jacob was forbidden to marry among them, Gen. xxviii, 1; but Judah's wife was from them, Gen. xxxviii, 2: 1 Chron. ii, 3. Their wickedness and idolatry, Lev. xviii, 28; Deut. xii, 31; Ezra ix, 1; Psa. cvi, 38. Their land given to the Israelites, Gen. xii, 6, 7; xv, 18; xvii, 8; Exod. xxiii, 23; Deut. vii, 1, 3; xxxii, 49; Psa. cxxxv, 11. After the Israelites had possessed themselves of a large part of the country, the Canaanites yet lingered in their ancient seats "in the land of the valley," Josh. xvii, 16, and in the plains of the north, Judg. iv, 2. Still, though the Canaanites had their special location, yet, as being a leading tribe among the inhabitants of the land, their name was sometimes used as including other tribes. Thus Hebron, called Amorite or Hittite when Abraham dwelt there, (Gen. xiii, 18; xiv, 13; xxiii, 2, 3, 5, 7,) is afterward said to be Canaanite, (Judg. i, 10.) This, however, may be partly owing to the change of settlements by conquest or emigration. The Canaanites were a warlike people, and the Israelites found it difficult to expel them, Judg. i, 27-33. Special mention is made of their iron chariots, iv, 2, 3. They had strong and well-built cities, Num. xiii, 28; Deut. vi, 10. Probably also they were a commercial people, for their name came to be synonymous with merchant, Job xli, 6; Prov. xxxi, 24; the original word in both these cases being "Canaanite." The language they spoke, though they were Hamites, was Hebrew, for the patriarchs and their descendants required no interpreter in Canaan as they did in Egypt, Gen. lxii, 23. Possibly the Canaanites adopted the dialect of earlier settlers in the land.

The various cities and nations of Canaan were not all subdued at the same time. Jebus, afterward Jerusalem, was not taken until the time of David, 2 Sam. v, 6; and Sidon seems never to have yielded to the tribe of Asher, to whom it was nominally allotted, Judg. i, 31. Scattered portions of the several nations, escaping, often harassed Israel. The people of Gibeon (Hivites) made peace by stratagem, and thus escaped destruction. The Girgashites seem to have been either wholly destroyed, or absorbed in other tribes. The Anakim were completely destroyed by Joshua, except in three cities, Gaza, Gath, and Ashdod, Josh. xi, 21-23; and the powerful.Amalekites, continually harassing Israel, and frequently defeated, were at last wholly destroyed by the tribe of Simeon, 1 Chron. iv, 43. Individuals among the Canaanites became noted among the Jews; thus Uriah the Hittite was one of King David's captains, 1 Chron. xi, 41. In the height of the Israelitish glory under King Solomon all the remnants of the Canaanitish nations were made tributary, and bond-service was exacted from them, 1 Kings ix, 20.

Can'neh, *a plant* or *shoot* (?), Ezek. xxvii, 23. Doubtless Calneh or Calno.

Caper'naum, (Map 5,) *city of comfort* or *consolation* (?), or perhaps *village of Nahum*. A town in the district of Gennesaret, on the west side of the Sea of Galilee, John vi, 17; Luke iv, 31; Matt. iv, 13. Capernaum was one of the most interesting localities in the Scriptures. In Christ's day it was a flourishing town, Matt. xi, 23. Lying on the great thoroughfare between Damascus and the Mediterranean, it has been suggested that we have here the explanation of "the receipt of custom," Matt. ix, 9. Jesus very frequently visited this city, Matt. iv, 13; ix, 1; it was called "his own city," and it was here that he and his mother's family dwelt after leaving Nazareth, Luke iv 16-31. The house that he

BIBLE GEOGRAPHY. 79

RUINS AT TELL HUM.

occupied (Mark ii, 2) was doubtless the one owned by Peter and Andrew, Mark i, 29; Matt. xvii, 24. At Capernaum Christ chose Matthew or Levi, Matt. ix, 9. Simon Peter and his brother Andrew belonged here, and here probably they heard the call which caused them to leave their nets and follow Jesus, Mark i, 16, 17; compare 29. Christ taught a great deal and performed many mighty works at Capernaum. Here was wrought the miracle on the centurion's servant, Matt. viii, 5; Luke vii, 1; on Simon's wife's mother, Matt. viii, 14; Mark i, 30; Luke iv, 38; on the paralytic, Matt. ix, 1; Mark ii, 1; Luke v, 18; and on the man afflicted with an unclean spirit, Mark i, 33; Luke iv, 33. The son of the nobleman at Capernaum was healed by Jesus' words—spoken probably at Cana, John iv, 41-56. A very beautiful incident occurred here at Christ's home, "in the house," Mark ix, 33; Matt. xviii, 1; compare xvii, 24. In the synagogue of the town Jesus delivered a remarkable discourse, John vi, 59. The people of Capernaum did not appreciate the presence of Jesus, nor his glorious doctrines, nor his "mighty works," hence Christ uttered a most fearful prophecy against the city, Matt. xi. 23; Luke x, 15. This prophecy has been so fulfilled that this once prosperous city is "brought down" to utter ruin, and the very spot wherein it stood is still matter of dispute.

Capernaum must have stood either at *Khan Minyeh* or at *Tell Hûm*. Each of these places presents strong claims as the site. The former place, marked only by a mound of ruins, is situated at the north-eastern extremity of the fertile plain (now called *El Ghuweir*) on the western border of the Lake of Gennesaret, to which the name of "the Land of Gennesareth" is given by Josephus. Dr. Robinson favors *Khan Minyeh*, (see his *Researches*, new edition, ii, 403; iii, 344–358;) so does Mr. Porter; so also Kiepert's map, 1866. Other travelers (among whom is Dr. Thomson) claim *Tell Hûm*, three miles north of *Khan Minyeh*. Extensive ruins are here, consisting of walls and foundations covering a space half a mile long by a quarter wide, on a point of the shore projecting into the lake, and backed by very gently rising ground. The shapeless remains are piled up in confusion all along the shore, and are much more striking than those of any other city on this part of the lake. With two exceptions the houses were all built of basalt, quite black and very compact but rudely cut. Dr. Bartlett (*From Egypt to Palestine*, 1879) thinks the evidence favors this site. For interesting details see Clark's *Bible Atlas*, M'Clintock and Strong's *Cyclopedia*, Thomson's *Land and the Book*, Porter's *Hand-book for Syria and Palestine*, edition 1868. *Our Work in Palestine*, pp. 186, 207.

Capharsal'ama, apparently from the Hebrew, signifying "village of peace." The scene of a battle between Judas and Nicanor, 1 Macc. vii, 31.

Caphen'atha, a place apparently close to Jerusalem on the east, 1 Macc xii, 37. Not known.

Caphi'ra, 1 Esdr. v, 19. Elsewhere Chephirah, Ezra ii, 25.

Caph'thorim. See CAPHTORIM.

Caph'tor, *chaplet, knop*. (The word is probably of Egyptian origin.) The original seat of the Philistines, whence they spread into the country around Gaza and the coasts of Palestine, Deut. ii, 23; Jer. lxvii, 4; Amos ix, 7. Jeremiah calls it an "isle," (marginal reading,) or coast country. In Gen. x, 14 (and consequently in 1 Chron. i, 12) the parenthesis should probably follow Caphtorim. Various opinions have been urged as to the locality of Caphtor. Some authorities claim that it was Cappadocia; some the island of Cyprus; others the isle of Crete; and still others claim the coasts of the Egyptian Delta. The weight of evidence is in favor of Upper Egypt. See Herzog, Ayre, and art. "Philistines" in Kitto.

Caph'torim, the inhabitants of Caphtor. The Philistines, Deut. ii, 23, or connected with them; the descendants of Mizraim. Gen. x, 14; 1 Chron. i, 12. They are called also Caphthorim, and Caphthorims.

Cappado'cia, (Maps 1, 8,) the most eastern province of Asia Minor, but variously extended at different times. Our first knowledge of it is under the Medes and Persians, when it was bounded east by Armenia Minor, north by the Black Sea, west by Paphlagonia and Phrygia, south by Lycaonia and the Taurus, which separated it from Cilicia. Cappadocia was subjugated by the Persians under Cyrus, but after the time of Alexander the Great it had kings of its own, although tributary to the Seleucidæ. Under the Persians the northern part of the country, as above bounded, was a distinct satrapy, and became afterward the independent kingdom of Pontus. The southern part also constituted a kingdom under the name of Cappadocia. This latter kingdom had ten satrapies, to which Rome added the eleventh. The Cappadocians had their own domestic princes until their country was made, in A. D. 17, a Roman province, and placed under Roman

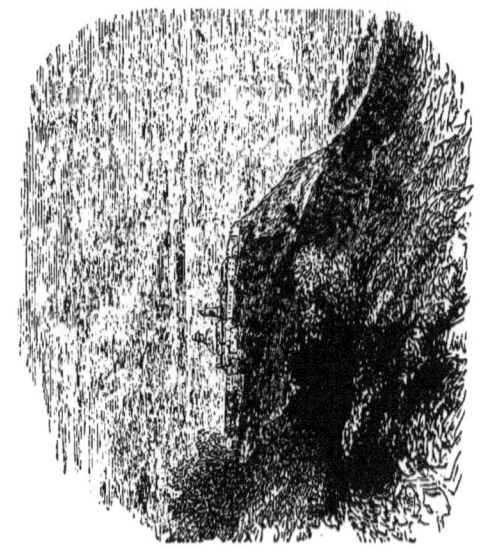

MOUNT CARMEL.

rule. The boundaries of Cappadocia were modified, increased, and diminished several times by the Roman Emperors. In New Testament times the province comprised also Lesser Armenia. Christianity was early propagated in Cappadocia. On the day of Pentecost some of its inhabitants were in Jerusalem, Acts ii, 9. In addressing Christians throughout Asia Minor Peter included the Cappadocians, 1 Pet. i, 1. Cappadocia was easily approached from the direction of Palestine and Syria by means of the pass called the Cilician Gates.

Car'chamis, 1 Esdr. i, 25. See CARCHEMISH.

Car'chemish, (Map 1,) *fortress of Chemosh;* called also Charchemish, 2 Chron. xxxv, 20. A city on the Euphrates, commanding the passage of the river, and therefore the battle-field of Egypt and Assyria, Isa. x, 9; Jer lxvi, 2. Mr. G. Smith identifies it with the ruins of *Kalaat Jerabhis,* on the west bank of the Euphrates, twenty miles below Bir or Biredjuk.

Ca'ria, (Map 8,) the south-western district of Asia Minor. In 1 Macc. xv, 23, it is referred to as the residence of Jews. Caria is not mentioned in the Scriptures. although some of its cities (as Cnidus and Miletus) are spoken of, Acts xx, 15; xxvii, 7.

Carma'nian, a savage people north of the Persian Gulf, 2 Esdr. xv, 30.

Car'mel, (Map 5,) *park, garden.*

1. A noted mountain range, running from the south end of the Bay of Acre inland in a south-east direction. Mt. Carmel consists of several connected hills, with an average height of about 1,500 feet. The highest point is 1,728 feet above the sea. Carmel extends about twenty-eight miles, and connects on the south-east with the mountains of Samaria. It separates the plain of Esdraelon from the great southern plain along the Mediterranean. Carmel first occurs in Josh. xii, 22; xix, 26, as the boundary of the tribe of Asher. It was compared, for its beauty and luxuriant forests, with Bashan, Sol. Song vii, 5; Isa. xxxiii, 9; xxxv, 2; Jer. xlvi, 18; 1, 19; Micah vii, 14; Nahum i, 4; 2 Kings xix, 23. There were caves on the sides toward the sea, Amos ix, 3, and these were used as hiding-places for refugees. Probably Elijah and Elisha during their stay at Carmel occupied one of them, 1 Kings xviii, 19; 2 Kings ii, 25; iv, 25. The wonderful sacrifice on Carmel is detailed in 1 Kings xviii. After the sacrifice Elijah repaired the altar, for it seems that worship had been there offered before. The place can now doubtless be identified with *el-Mukhrakah,* the place of *burning.* There is a natural platform of naked rock, surrounded by a low wall; the sea behind is just visible; the great plain (for it is at the south-eastern extremity of Carmel) lies in front, with Jezreel in the distance, and Kishon just at the mountain's base. There is a well of water near, and from this it has been supposed that the water was obtained which Elijah caused to be poured on his sacrifice and in the trench about the altar. But Dr. Thomson says that he has seen that almost dry; he thinks, therefore, that it could not have continued through the long drought, and that the water was brought from the perennial sources of the Kishon. When, by the prophet's command, the idolatrous priests were seized, they were hurried down the track, still visible to the Kishon, by a knoll, now called *Tell Kussis,* "hill of the priests," and there, according to the law, were put to death. Then Ahab and Elijah very probably returned to the *Mukhrakah,* Elijah to pray for rain, and Ahab to partake of the feast prepared and spread somewhere near at hand, which always formed part of

these sacrifices. From this spot Elijah's servant would have had but a little way to go to command a full view of the sea. And when the cloud like a man's hand was seen, Ahab was bidden to ascend his chariot, and the prophet, tightly girded, preceded him as a runner to Jezreel, twelve miles distant, 1 Kings xviii. Carmel has always been venerated. Pythagoras is said to have visited it; Vespasian offered sacrifices there; and to this day it is held sacred by Jews, Christians, and Moslems alike. There can be no reasonable doubt of the identity of the spot. It has been thought—and it is not un likely—that it was in Carmel that Elijah called down fire upon the two fifties sent by Ahaziah to apprehend him, 2 Kings i. It was frequently visited by Elijah, and frequently alluded to by the prophets, (as above.) Carmel at one time swarmed with monks and hermits, who burrowed in the many caves of the mount. One is called the "Cave of the Sons of the Prophets." In one tract, called the Monks' Cavern, there are as many as four hundred caves adjacent to each other, furnished with windows, and with places for sleeping hewn in the rock. The entrances are so narrow that only a single person can creep in at a time, and the caverns are so crooked that a person is immediately out of sight unless closely followed. See Amos ix. 3. At the present day a cavern is shown called the cave of Elijah, a little below the Monks' Cavern, and which is now a Moslem sanctuary. There is now a convent on Carmel; and the mount is still wooded, and variegated with flowers. Dr. Thomson describes it as very difficult in some parts to force a way through the almost impenetrable jungle. From the summit the view is most impressive. Mr. Tristam (*Land of Israel*, p. 100) says: "We looked down from the giddy height and watched a long caravan of several hundred camels on their way thither, [to Egypt from Phœnicia,] with the attendant crowd of Bedouins and many wild horsemen cantering about them. What pictures of the past rose to the mind's eye! What a gush of historic fancies filled the imagination as we gazed on the strange scene!" Carmel is known by the name of *Jebel Kurmul* in Arabian writers; but it is now generally called *Mar Elyas*.

2. A town in the mountains of Judah, Josh. xv, 55. Here Saul erected a triumphal monument after his expedition against Amalek, 1 Sam. xv, 12. Abigail and Nabal dwelt here, 1 Sam. xxv, 2, 5, 7, 40; hence Abigail was called the Carmelitess, xxvii, 3. Uzziah's husbandmen and vine-dressers were probably here, 2 Chron. xxvi, 10. It is now *Kurmul*, ten miles southeast of Hebron, with a conspicuous fort amid extensive ruins.

Car'melite, a resident of Carmel, (2.) A designation of Nabal, 1 Sam. xxvii, 2; xxx, 5; 2 Sam. ii, 2; of Abigail, ("Carmelitess," A.V.,) 2 Sam. iii, 3; 1 Chr. iii, 1; also of one of David's warriors, 2 Sam. xxiii, 35; 1 Chr. xi, 37.

Car'melitess, 1 Sam. xxvii, 3; 1 Chron. iii, 1. See CARMELITE.

Car'mites, Num. xxvi, 6, a family of Reuben, descended from Carmi.

Car'naim, a fortress in Gilead. 1 Macc. v, 26, 43, 44; also called Carnion, 2 Macc. xii, 21, 26. It is identical with Ashteroth-Karnaim.

Car'nion. See CARNAIM.

Casiph'ia, *silver* (?), a place probably on the route between Babylon and Jerusalem, Ezra viii, 17. Not known.

Cas'luhim, *hopes of life*, or *as pardoned*, or *fortified*. A people related to the Philistines, descended from Mizraim, of the family of Ham, Gen. x, 14; 1 Chron. i, 12. Various localities are conjectured; but the most probable seat of this tribe seems to have been somewhere in Upper Egypt.

BIBLE GEOGRAPHY.

Cas'phon, Cas'phor, or **Cas'pis,** a fortress on the east of Jordan, 1 Macc. v, 26, 36; 2 Macc. xii, 13. Not known.
Ce'dron, a Greek form of KIDRON, which see.
Ce'dron, a fort not far from Jamnia and Azotus, (Ashdod.) 1 Macc. xv, 39, 41; xvi, 9. Perhaps it is the more ancient Gederah and the modern *Kutrah,* south of *Nahr Rubin.*
Celosyr'ia. See CŒLE-SYRIA.
Cen'chrea, or **Cen'chreæ,** (Map 8,) *millet,* the eastern harbor of Corinth on the Saronic Gulf, about nine miles from Corinth. Thence Paul sailed for Ephesus, Acts xviii, 18. In Rom. xvi, 1, we learn that afterward a Church was there organized. The site is occupied by the modern village of *Kikries,* where ruins of ancient buildings remain; as also traces of the moles of the port.
Cesare'a. See CÆSAREA.
Chalde'a, (Map 1,) (Hebrew, *Kasdim, i. e.* "Chaldeans.") The origin of the term *Kasdim* is very doubtful. It has been derived by some from Kesod, the son of Nahor, Gen. xxii, 22; but if Ur was already a city "of the Chaldees" before Abraham quitted it, (Gen. xi, 28,) the name *Kasdim* cannot possibly have been derived from his nephew. On the other hand, the term Chaldea has been connected with the city *Kalwadha,* (Chilmad of Ezekiel xxvii, 23,) and this is possibly correct. Originally Chaldea was a small district in the southern part of Babylonia, lying almost entirely on the right bank of the Euphrates. Chaldea, however, is used in our version for the Hebrew ethnic appellative *Kasdim,* ("Chaldees,") under which term the inhabitants of the entire country are designated, and in this extended sense we here employ it. Thus the Scripture Chaldea must be taken to include the alluvial plain watered by the rivers Euphrates and Tigris, bounded on the east by the last-named stream, but extending across the Euphrates westward to Arabia, and from the Persian Gulf running northward to about the thirty-fourth degree of latitude. This region was probably four hundred miles in length, with an average breadth of one hundred. The cities of Chaldea or Babylonia were very ancient and numerous. "Babel, and Erech, and Accad, and Calneh, in the land of Shinar," are the first towns mentioned in Scripture, Gen. x, 10. Herodotus says there were in that country a "vast number of great cities." The soil was of great fertility, and it is said to have been the only country in the world where wheat grew wild. The ancient Babylonians worshiped nature, particularly the stars. *Bel* was the Supreme God, Isa. xlvi, 1; Jer. l, 2; li, 44; Dan. (*Sept.*) xiv, 3, the Lord of heaven and light, who divided the heaven and the earth and made man. They had many gods, whose images were made of gold, silver, iron, wood, and stone, Jer. l, 38; Dan. v, 4-23. The kingdom was divided into provinces with their proper officers, Dan. ii, 48; iii, 1, 2. The history of Chaldea and Babylon is one of the saddest, yet one of the most profitable in the Bible. Chaldea, once so proud and glorious an empire, has long been "the hindermost of the nations, a wilderness, a dry land, and a desert," a land " wholly desolate;" "a drought is upon her waters, and they are dried up," Jer. l, 12, 13, 38. "The sea has come up upon Babylon, and she is covered with the waves thereof," Jer. li, 42; and she is made "a possession for the bittern and pools of water," Isa. xiv, 23. More than half the country is left dry and waste from the want of a proper system of irrigation, while the remaining half is to a great extent covered with marshes, owing to the same neglect.

The mighty cities are a heap of ruins, and the entire land fulfills the prophecy, "Because of the wrath of the Lord it shall not be inhabited; . . . every one that goeth by Babylon shall be astonished, and hiss at all her plagues," Jer. l, 13. See BABYLONIA.

Chalde'ans, or **Chal'dees.** (For signification see CHALDEA.) The inhabitants of Chaldea, Gen. xi, 28; Job i, 17; Isa. xxiii, 13; Jer. xxi, 4, 9; Ezek. i, 3, etc. Babylon was the capital of this people. It would seem that originally the tribe was located in the southern part of Babylonia, and that the name came by degrees to include other neighboring tribes, till it was commensurate with what was ultimately called Chaldea. Still the whole of the ancient Cushite language was retained as a literary and sacred tongue, so that those who acquired the learning of the Chaldeans studied it in this language, Dan. i, 4. Hence, by a very natural mode of speaking, persons who wore proficients in such studies came to be specially termed Chaldeans; so that we have here a new sense to the term, and thus the name is continually used in the book of Daniel (e. g., ii, 2, 4, 10) as synonymous with Magi, or astrologers; and Daniel himself is called the "Master of the Chaldeans," (ver. 11.) The studies pursued were probably at first astronomy and the kindred sciences, which afterward degenerated into mere sorcery or soothsaying, so that the name of Chaldean was used by way of reproach. They appear to have been gathered into schools or academics, of which the principal seats were Babylon, Ur, Borsippa, etc. See BABYLON, BABYLONIA, CHALDEA.

Cha'naan, Judith v, 3, 9, 10; Baruch iii, 22; 1 Macc. ix, 37; Acts vii, 11; xiii, 19. Another form of Canaan.

Cha'naanite, Judith v, 16, the same as Canaanite.

Char'aca, a place mentioned in 2 Macc. xii, 17, as east of Jordan. Perhaps *Kerak*, south-east of the Dead Sea, marks the site, but very uncertain.

Char'ashim, VALLEY OF, *ravine of craftsmen*, a place perhaps near Lydda, (Lod,) 1 Chron. iv, 14; Neh. xi, 35, "valley of craftsmen." Not definitely known.

Char'chamis, 1 Esdr. i, 25, and

Char'chemish, 2 Chron. xxxv, 20—forms of Carchemish.

Char'ran, Acts vii, 2, 4. Elsewhere Haran.

Che'bar, (Map 1,) *length*, or *strength*, *power*, a river of Babylonia, on the banks of which some of the Jewish captives were located, Ezek. i, 3; iii, 15, 23; x, 15, 20, 22; lxiii, 3. By some it is thought to be the Chaboras, (now *Khabour;*) but more probably it was the *Nahr Malcha*, or royal canal of Nebuchadnezzar, a very extensive work, in cutting which, perhaps, the exiles were employed. See HABOR.

Che'bel. In Josh. ii, 15, the word signifies a *rope* or *cord;* in 1 Sam. x, 5, 10, it means a band, company, or *string* of men; in 1 Kings xxx, 31; Isa xxxiii, 23; Amos vii, 17, "ropes," "tacklings," "line." See also Psa. cxix, 61; Job xviii, 10; Psa. xviii, 4; Jer. xiii, 21, for metaphorical uses. In Psa. xvi, 6, "the *lines* are fallen unto me in pleasant places." Hence it is used as a "portion," an "allotment," a "tract," a "district," and in this sense it is always applied to the region of Argob, as surrounded or girt with a definite boundary like the coast-line. Deut. iii, 4, 13, 14; 1 Kings iv, 13 See ARGOB.

Chel'lian, Judith ii, 23, an inhabitant of Chellus.

BIBLE GEOGRAPHY. 87

Ohel'lus, a place named with Kadesh as west of Jordan, Judith i, 9; ii, 23. Perhaps *Elusa*, south of Palestine, may mark the site.

Che'lod, Judith i, 6. Unknown.

Che'phar-Haam'monai, *village of the Ammonites*. A village of Benjamin, Josh. xviii, 24, probably founded by the Ammonites. Not known.

Chephi'rah, *the village*. In 1 Esdras v, 19, Caphira. One of the Gibeonite towns in Benjamin, Josh. ix, 17; xviii, 26; Ezra ii, 25; Neh. vii, 29. It is now *Kéfir*, two miles east of *Yalo*.

Cher'ethim, perhaps *Cretans*. In Ezek. xxv, 16, and Zeph. ii, 25, the word is rendered "Cherethims" and "Cherethites." See also 1 Sam. xxx, 14. A people named as inhabitants of southern Philistia. See CHERETHITE.

Cher'ethite, a term found alone only in 1 Sam. xxx, 14. Elsewhere the "Cherethites" are named in connection with the "Pelethites." The word, according to Gesenius, means *executioners;* but some think it signifies *those cut off,* that is, *exiles*. The two classes of people here referred to were the life-guards, or body-guard of King David, 2 Sam. viii, 18; xv, 18; xx, 7, 23; 1 Kings i, 38, 44; 1 Chron. xviii, 17; 2 Sam. xxiii, 23. The Gittites, who came after David from Gath, are sometimes mentioned in connection with the above, 2 Sam. xv, 18. See CHERETHIM, and especially PELETHITES.

Che'rith, (Map 5,) *separation, a cutting*, the torrent (brook) where Elijah hid during the early part of the drought, 1 Kings xvii, 3-7. Robinson identifies it with *Wady Kelt*, behind Jericho. Others suppose it to be east of the Jordan. Possibly it is the *Wady Fasail*, farther north than the *Kelt;* but very uncertain.

Che'rub, *strong,* a *warder, as a master, fullness of knowledge,* (the etymology is uncertain.) A place mentioned in Ezra ii, 59; Neh. vii, 61, from which some Jews who could not prove their pedigree returned with Zerubbabel. It is supposed to be in Babylonia.

Ches'alon, (Map 6,) *confidence,* a place on the north-west boundary of Judah, said to be on the side of Mount Jearim, Josh. xv, 10. Probably *Kesla*, eight miles west of Jerusalem, marks the site.

Che'sil, a *fool, ungodly,* a town in the south of Judah, Josh. xv, 30. Probably it is identical with Bethul and Bethuel, Josh. xix, 4; 1 Chron. iv, 30; 1 Sam. xxx, 27.

Chesul'loth, *the hopes,* or *the flank,* a town of Issachar, Josh. xix, 18. Probably it is the same with Chisloth-Tabor of verse 12, and the Tabor of 1 Chron. vi, 77. Some think the modern *Iksal* marks the site.

Chet'tiim, 1 Macc. i, 1. A form of Chittim.

Che'zib, *false,* a town where Judah was when his third son Shelah was born, Gen. xxxviii, 5. It is probably the same with Achzib (2) and Chozeba.

Chi'don, a *javelin, dart,* the name of the threshing-floor where Uzzah put forth his hand to prevent the ark from falling and was struck dead, 1 Chron. xiii, 9. In 2 Sam. vi, 6, it is called the threshing-floor of Nachon. It is not certainly identified, but is supposed to be not far north-west of Jerusalem.

Chil'mad, perhaps *teaching* or *learning;* but the etymology is unknown. A place mentioned with Sheba and Asshur, Ezek. xxvii, 23. Its location is as undefined as the meaning of the name. See CHALDEA.

Chin'nereth, (Deut. iii, 17; Josh. xxi, 35;) or **Chinneroth,** (Josh. xi, 2; xii, 3,) *lyre*. One of the fenced cities of Naphtali. Whether it gave its name to or received it from the lake, which was possibly adjacent, is uncertain. This city was identified by Jerome, but merely on rumor, with the later Tiberias.

M. de Saulcy would identify the site of Chinnereth with the village of *Abu Shushah*, lying on the western edge of the plain *El-ghuweir*, on an eminence about its mid-length, at the entrance of *Wady-Rubuduyeh*.

Chin'nereth, SEA OF, (Num. xxxiv, 11; Josh. xiii, 27;) or **Chinneroth,** Josh. xii, 3. The lake subsequently called Sea of Gennesaret.

Chi'os, (Map 1,) *snow* (?) or *mastic* (?,, a noted island in the Ægean Sea, between Samos and Lesbos, belonging to Ionia in Asia Minor. Anciently it was celebrated for its wine. On his way from Asia to Jerusalem Paul passed this island, Acts xx, 15. It is called now, by the Greeks, *Khio;* by the Italians, *Scio*.

Chis'loth-Ta'bor, *flank of Tabor*, a place on the boundary of Zebulun, Josh. xix, 12. *Iksal*, two and a half miles west of Mount Tabor, may possibly mark the site. See CHESULLOTH.

Chit'tim, (Map 12.) Various significations are given, among which are *Cyprians; those that bruise; gold; staining;* but the primitive meaning is uncertain. Some think the term equivalent to Hittites. The Chittim were a Japhetic people or place remote from Palestine, separated therefrom by the sea, Num. xxiv, 24; Isa. xxiii, 1, 12; Jer. ii, 10; Ezek. xxvii, 6; Dan. xi, 30. In Gen. x, 4, and 1 Chron. i, 7, the name is Kittim. In 1 Macc. viii, 5, we find persons called "King of the Citims," that is, Chittim. In 1 Macc. i, 1, the term is Chettiim, and is applied to the Macedonians under Alexander the Great. Grove says that by Chittim "in the Old Testament no doubt Cyprus is intended; but in the Apocrypha Macedonia." The best summary is given by Kitto: "Chittim seems to be a name of large signification, (such as our Levant,) applied to the islands and coasts of the Mediterranean in a loose sense, without fixing the particular part, though particular and different parts of the whole are probably in most cases to be understood."

Cho'ba and Cho'bai, Judith iv, 4; xv, 4, 5. Two places, probably identical. Perhaps the place is the same with Hobah, near Damascus. See Gen. xiv. 15. Van de Velde suggests that it is probably the modern *Kubatiyeh*, a village one hour and a half south of *Jenin*, on the highway to *Sebustiyeh*.

Chor-A'shan, *smoking furnace*, one of the places which David and his men were "wont to haunt," 1 Sam. xxx, 30, 31. It is probably identical with Ashan of Simeon, Josh. xv, 42; xix, 7.

Chora'zin, (Map 5,) various meanings are given, *district of Zin; the secret; here is a mystery; woody places;* but the signification is uncertain. Chorazin was a town of Galilee, mentioned with Bethsaida and Capernaum as prominent among the places where Christ performed some of his mighty works, Matt. xi, 21; Luke x, 13. The site is disputed by the ablest travelers. Dr. Robinson places it at the ruins *Tell Hûm,* (see CAPERNAUM;) while Dr. Thomson claims *Kerazeh* as the spot, two miles further north. The weight of authority seems to favor the latter place. Macgregor says, however, that if "*Kerazeh* be indeed Chorazin, it must surely be by a stretch of expression that we can say that town was 'upon the lake.' For a great part of the lake is hidden from *Kerazeh*, and its distance from the lake is at least two miles and a half in a straight line." The basaltic relics here "include some beautiful niches of pecten shape, delicately chiseled out of the rough black stone." See *Our Work in Palestine,* p. 206.

Choze'ba, a place whose inhabitants are mentioned in 1 Chron. iv, 22. It is probably identical with Achzib and Chezib, Gen. xxxviii, 6; Josh. xv, 14. Conder identifies it with the ruin *Khirbet Kueizibah*, north of Halhul.

Chub, meaning unknown. A term occurring in Ezek. xxx, 5, as the name of a people in alliance with Egypt. It is variously conjectured to be the name of a tribe in Egypt, or of some other part of Africa.

Chun, *estallishment* (?), *place*. A Syrian city from which David procured brass for building the temple, 1 Chron. xviii, 8. In 2 Sam. viii, 8, it is called BEROTHAI, which see. Its site is not known.

Chu'si, a place mentioned in Judith vii, 18, as near Ekrebel. Some think it may have been at *el-Kawzeh,* six miles west of *Akrabeh.*

Cili'cia, (Map 1.) *from Cylix, the son of Agenor.* The most south-easterly province of Asia Minor, bounded on the west by Pamphylia; separated on the north from Cappadocia by the Taurus range, and on the east by Amanus from Syria, with which it was sometimes coupled, Acts xv, 23, 41; Gal. i, 21. The Mediterranean is on the south. The inhabitants are said to have sprung from the Syrians and the Phœnicians. Its capital was Tarsus, the birthplace of St. Paul. The Jews from Cilicia disputed with Stephen, Acts vi, 9. To its Churches the apostles sent a letter, and Paul visited the Churches, Acts xv, 23, 41; Gal. i, 21. Other notices may be found in Judith i, 7, 12; ii, 21, 25; 1 Macc. xi, 14; 2 Macc. iv, 36; Acts xxi, 39; xxii, 1; xxiii, 34; xxvii, 5. Cilicia, after belonging partially to the Syrian kingdom and to Armenia, became in 63 B.C., when Pompey had subdued the noted pirates, a Roman province, and Cicero was once proconsul of it. The inhabitants of its mountains, however, long maintained their independence.

Cin'neroth, *lyres* or *harps,* 1 Kings xv, 20; probably the district called later the "Lake of Genesareth," and also the "plain of Genesareth." See GENESARETH.

Cir'amah, 1 Esdras v, 20, a place whose people came up with Zorobabel from Babylon. It is probably the same with RAMAH (1,) which see.

Cit'ims, 1 Macc. viii, 5. The Macedonians. Elsewhere CHETTIIMS and CHITTIM, which see.

Clau'da, (Map 8.) an island about seven miles long and three broad, off the south-west end of Crete, passed by St. Paul in his stormy voyage to Rome, Acts xxvii, 16. The modern name is *Gozzo.*

Cni'dus, (Map 8,) a town at the extreme south-west end of Asia Minor, in Caria, on a promontory which projects between the islands of Cos and Rhodes, Acts xxi, 1. In 1 Macc. xv, 23, it is mentioned as one of the Greek cities which contained Jewish residents in the second century B. C.; and in Acts xxvii, 7, as a harbor passed by Paul. Venus was worshiped here, and her famous statue, the work of Praxiteles, stood in one of the three temples dedicated to her. The ruins of Cnidus show it to have been a very magnificent city.

Cœl'e-Syr'ia, (Map 5,) *hollow Syria.* This name (which does not occur in Scripture) was originally given by the Greeks to the valley or hollow between Libanus and Anti-Libanus, a region extending nearly a hundred miles between these mountain ranges. Afterward it included a much wider district, comprising the tracts east of the Jordan down to the very shores of the Red Sea, and the cities of Heliopolis, Abila of Lysanias, Damascus, Gadara, Pella, Philadelphia, etc., and even Scythopolis on the west of the Jordan. In the Apocrypha it is mentioned as Celosyria, apparently as equivalent to Syria, 1 Esdras ii, 17, 24, 27; iv, 48; vi, 29; vii, 1; viii, 67;

1 Macc. x, 69; 2 Macc. iii, 5, 8; iv, 4; viii, 8; x, 11. In 1 Esdras vi, 3, it is called simply "Syria." See SYRIA.

Co'la, a place named in Judith xv, 4, in connection with Chobai, as one of the cities to which Ozias sent orders to expel the enemies of the Jews after the death of Holofernes. Perhaps the name is a corruption of Abelmeholah. Unknown.

Colos'se, Colos'sæ, and **Colas'sæ,** *punishment, correction,* a city of Phrygia on the river Lycus, which empties into the Mæander. Hierapolis and Laodicea were near it, Col. ii, 1; iv, 13, 15, 16. This city was close to the great road which led from Ephesus to the Euphrates. It is spoken of as a city of considerable consequence. But Colossæ was at length overshadowed by the greater cities in its vicinity. It is probable that Paul had not been there when he wrote his Epistle to the Colossians, Col. ii, 1. Among the dwellers at this place were Philemon and his slave Onesimus, also Archippus and Epaphras, the latter of whom was, perhaps, the founder of the Colossian Church, Col. i, 2, 7, 8; iv, 12. Angel worship is referred to in Col. ii, 18; and later a church in honor of the Archangel Michael was erected at the entrance of a chasm, in consequence of some legend connected with an inundation. Colossæ, with the places mentioned above, was destroyed by an earthquake in the ninth year of Nero, but it must have been almost immediately rebuilt. The site of the ancient city was about three miles from the modern village of *Chonas.* The ruins are not extensive.

Co'os, or **Cos,** (Map 8,) *top,* a small island in the Ægean Sea, off the coast of Caria. Its more ancient names were Cea, Staphylus, Nymphœa, and Meropis, the last being the most common. In Maccabean times it was the residence of Jews, 1 Macc. xv, 23. On his voyage from Miletus to Judea Paul passed a night here, Acts xxi, 1. Cos was celebrated for its wines, ointments, and beautiful stuffs, and as the birthplace of Hippocrates. In the chief town of the island (bearing the same name) was a famous temple of Æsculapius. The modern name of the island is *Stanchio.* It has a population of about eight thousand, who mostly profess the Greek religion.

Cor'inth, *satisfied, ornament, beauty.* Ephyre is given by Homer as its earliest name. A noted city of Greece, in the isthmus, which joins Peloponnesus (the Morea) to the Continent. On a vast rock, rising abruptly about two thousand feet above the level of the sea, was the citadel, called the Acrocorinthus. Corinth had two harbors, Cenchreæ, about eight miles distant on the Eastern or Saronic Gulf, (Gulf of Ægina,) and Lechæum on the Western or Corinthian Gulf, (Gulf of Lepanto,) a mile and a half away. Situated thus advantageously, Corinth became wealthy and strong. After suffering various reverses, the city was at length utterly destroyed by the Roman General Mummius, 146 B. C. For a century it lay waste, only some temples and the citadel remaining. In the year 46 B. C. Julius Cesar restored it and made it the Roman capital of the province of Achaia. It was repeopled partly by freedmen from Rome. Its former beauty soon returned. This new city was a regular square of forty stadia on the north side of the citadel, with walls on three sides. Magnificent temples and public buildings, partly raised out of the old ruins, partly new built, adorned it, especially the market-place. The road to the Acropolis, made long by windings, led past temples, altars, and statues, and on the citadel stood the splendid temple of Venus, adorned with a panoplied image of the

CORINTH RESTORED, AS VIEWED FROM THE ACROCORINTHUS.

goddess. The fortress was thought to be the strongest in Greece. Presenting a perpendicular front on the north, its approaches from all other sides were steep and well-fortified. Its situation secured to it extensive commerce, and made it the post and highway of the natural and artistic products of the Orient and Occident. Becoming populous and very rich, Corinth also became luxurious and corrupt to a proverb. Fired by the worship of Venus, sensuality prevailed to a most fearful extent. The arts were cultivated, and its architecture, its sculptures, and its vases have a world-wide renown.

This brief description of the city will greatly assist in a fuller comprehension of Scripture passages. Paul's visit to Corinth is narrated in Acts xviii. Paul founded a Church here, and the Lord had "much people." See 2 Cor. xii, 14; xiii, 1. Apollos visited Corinth, Acts xix, 1. A schism occurred in the Church, 1 Cor. i, 12; iii, 4. The immoralities of the Church, 1 Cor. v; 1 Cor. xi. The Church wrote to Paul, 1 Cor. vii, 1. Its alienation from Paul, 2 Cor. x. Abuse of ordinances, 1 Cor. xi, 22, and xiv. Heresies in Corinth, 1 Cor. xv, 12; 2 Cor. xi. Lawsuits, 1 Cor. vi. Liberality of the Church, ii, 9. Visit of Titus, 2 Cor. viii; xii, 18. Erastus of Corinth, Rom. xvi, 23; 2 Tim. iv, 20. Stephanas, 1 Cor. i, 16; xvi, 15, 17. Crispus, Acts xviii, 8; 1 Cor. i, 14; Caius, Rom. xvi, 23; 1 Cor. i, 14. While it may be seen from 1 Cor. xii, 2, that the Gentiles predominated in the Church, we may infer from Acts xviii, that there were many Jewish converts. The Church was, doubtless, therefore composed of the Roman freedmen, the native Greeks, and the Jews. The Judaizing element was strong, and party spirit struggled for the mastery, with the watch-words Apollos, Peter, and Paul. Paul nobly and wisely reproves these factions in the third and twelfth chapters of 1 Corinthians, adding his magnificent eulogy of charity or love, in the thirteenth chapter.

In the year 268 B. C., Corinth was burned by the Goths, and in 525 it was destroyed by an earthquake. From that time the city endured many reverses, until in 1715 the Turks gained possession of it, and held it until the period of the Greek revolution, when it became the seat of the new government, although taken and retaken more than once during the war. It is still an Episcopal see. The former glory of Corinth has entirely passed away. There remains amid the ancient ruins a miserable village called *Gortho*, composed of wretched houses, whose forlorn occupants "move like shadows along the streets."

Cos. See Co'os.

Crete, (Map 8,) *carnal, fleshly,* a large island in the Mediterranean, about one hundred and sixty miles long, and varying from six to thirty-five miles wide. Acts ii, 11; xxvii, 7, 12, 13, 21. Crete was anciently celebrated for its hundred cities. Although very mountainous, the island has many fruitful valleys. Mount Ida, one of the famous peaks, contained among its remarkable caverns the renowned Labyrinth of antiquity. Many of the fables of mythology laid their scenes in Crete. The inhabitants claimed a very ancient ancestry, and the island was the seat of the most ancient culture, the earliest tribes having sought to secure its possession. The great legislator Minos was from Crete. The Cretans were noted for their patriotism and for their skill in archery; but they also bore a bad reputation for falsehood, deceit, avarice, and licentiousness, Titus i, 12. Titus was left here, i, 5. The prophet quoted by Paul (verse 12) was Epimenides of Gnossus, in whose works Jerome found the passage. In Acts xxvii, 7, 8, 12, we find mention of the following places in Crete: Salmone, Lasea, Phenice; and in 1 Macc. xv, 23, Gortyna. The island now bears the name of Candia, (but the Turks called it *Kirid*,) and has a population of about 300,000, mostly Greeks. The modern Cretans, are said by travelers, to be no better than in the days of Paul—"the worst characters in the Levant." Through very varied fortunes, Crete at length, in 1669, passed under the power of the Turks. The Christians of Crete rose against Turkish despotism in 1866, demanding annexation to Greece. For several years they struggled against their oppressors. The sympathy of Greece with Crete caused a serious and constant irritation between Greece and Turkey. The insurrection of the Christians against the Turkish rule continued until the close of the year 1868, and it was not until the last days of December that the leaders abandoned open resistance as being for the present useless. The people of the United States were in lively sympathy with the Cretans. The Metropolitan of Athens, in a speech addressed to the American minister in Greece, (June 27, 1868,) remarked: " We could hardly stand in our great struggle without the favors of America; but for American kindness many Cretan widows and orphans must have perished of hunger and cold. God bless the Americans, the benefactors of the Christians of the East!"

Cretes and **Cre'tians,** the people of Crete.

Cush, (Map 12,) (derivation uncertain; but some give as signification, *blackness, black, heat.*) The name of a region inhabited by tribes of the Hamite family, Gen. x, 6, 7, 8; 1 Chron. i, 8-10; Isa. xi, 11. If there was (as some think) an antediluvian Cush, (Gen. ii, 13,) it was in Asia; and Cush, the Hamite, may have had his name from a settlement or allotment there. Not to spend time on mere conjectures here, we may notice that the chief habitations of the Cushites were to the south of Egypt, in the extensive tracts called Ethiopia, Ezek. xxix, 10. They also appear to have spread in the Arabian peninsula, where tribes descended from them, Gen. x, 7. Egypt and Cush are associated in the majority of instances in which the word occurs, Psa. lxviii, 31; Isa. xviii, 1; Jer. xlvi, 9, etc.; but in two passages Cush stands in close juxtaposition with Elam and Persia, Isa. xi, 11; Ezek. xxxviii, 5. The terms Cush and Cushites are frequently translated in our version Ethiopia and Ethiopians. In the ancient Egyptian inscriptions Ethiopia above Egypt is termed *Keesh* or *Kesh,* and this territory probably corresponds perfectly with the African Cush of the Bible. (See Wilkinson's *Egypt.*) The Cushites were black, Jer. xiii, 23; robust and large in stature, Isa. xlv, 14, and probably wealthy, xliii, 3. The wife of Moses was a Cushite, Num. xii, 1, (margin.) For valuable information see Smith's, Kitto's, and McClintock and Strong's *Cyclopædias.*

Cu'shan, a name found in Hab. iii. 7, and usually thought to be identical with Cush. Some regard it as the same with the name (of a man) Chushan-Rishathaim. Judg. iii, 8-16.

Cu'shi, that is, the Cushite, the Ethiopian, 2 Sam. xviii, 21-23, 31, 32.

Cuth, (Map 14,) and **Cu'thah,** (signification unknown,) a region whence colonists were brought by the King of Assyria into Samaria, 2 Kings xvii, 24, 30. The locality of this region is extremely uncertain. There are various conjectures. Josephus thought it was a region of inner Persia. Some think that the Cutheans may be identical with a warlike tribe called Cossæi, which occupied the mountain ranges between Media and Persia. Rosen-

Müller and some others favor the Arabian *Irak*, in the district of the Nahr-Malcha, or royal canal, which connected the Euphrates and Tigris to the south of the present Bagdad. Some of the Arabic and Persian writers placed here a town called Kutha. This site has been identified with the ruins of *Towibah*, immediately adjacent to Babylon. Other localities are given, the most of which are essentially in the same quarter. It is also claimed that there may be some historical and etymological connection between Cuth and the Cush of Gen. ii, 13. See CUSH.

Cy'amon, a place mentioned in Judith vii, 3, as lying in the plain over against Esdraelon. Grove inclines to identify it with *Tell Kuimon*, at the eastern end of Carmel. Schultz thinks it the modern *Kumieh*, south-east of Little Hermon. Robinson supposes it may correspond with the present *Fuleh*, on the east side of the plain of Esdraelon.

Cyp'rians, people of Cyprus, 2 Macc. iv, 29.

Cyprus, (Map 8,) the well-known island off the coast of Syria, Acts xxi, 3; xxvii, 4. Its greatest length is one hundred and forty miles, with a width varying from five to fifty miles. It was anciently exceedingly productive. It also yielded precious stones, iron, lead, tin, and copper. The island had very great commercial advantages. It became the chief seat of the rites of Venus. Prominent among its ancient cities were Citium, Salamis, Paphos, Amathos, Arsinœ, and Solœ. Its earliest inhabitants were mainly Phœnicians, who built many of its cities; but Greek colonists settled on its coasts. Cyprus is frequently mentioned in Scripture. Jews very early settled there. The Kittim of Gen. x, 4, and Chittim of Isa. xxiii, 1, are primarily the inhabitants of Citium, and then of the whole island. (See 2 Macc. iv, 29; x, 13; xii, 2.) Cyprians are named in Acts iv, 36; xxi, 16. The first preachers of the Gospel to the Greeks were Cyprians and Cyrenians, Acts xi, 20. The first missionary journey of Paul and Barnabas commenced with Cyprus, Acts xiii, 1–13; and thither Barnabas went again with Mark, Acts xv, 39. In Acts xiii, 5, 6, 7, 13, Salamis and Paphos are named as cities of Cyprus. In 1873 General Cesnola brought to America a large and exceedingly valuable collection of Cypriote curiosities. They consist of articles in brass and glass, of fine pottery and marble statuary.

Cyrene, (Map 8,) a city of Libya, Acts ii, 10. It probably took its name from a neighboring fountain called Cyre. Cyrene was founded by a colony of Greeks from the island Thera in the Ægean, about 632 B. C. The city stood on a table-land, eighteen hundred feet above the level of the sea, in a beautiful and fertile region. It was the capital of a district called Cyrenaica; and, with its port, Apollonia, about ten miles off, and the cities Barca, Teuchira, and Hesperis, (subsequently named Ptolemais, Arsinoe, and Berenice,) it formed the Cyrenaic Pentapolis. It became a dependency of Egypt after the death of Alexander the Great. Then Jews began to frequent it. In 75 B. C. Cyrene became a Roman province; and in 67 B. C., with Crete, it formed a single province, which frequently received the name Creta-Cyrene. Simon, the Cyrenian, was compelled to bear the Saviour's cross, Matt. xxvii, 32; Mark xv, 21; Luke xxiii, 26. Some of the first Christian teachers were from Cyrene, Acts, xi, 20; xiii, 1. Jews from this city were numerous in Jerusalem; hence the designation of a synagogue there, Acts, ii, 10; vi, 9. (See also 1 Macc. xv, 23, and 2 Macc. ii, 23.)

Cyrene was destroyed in the fourth century by Libyans and Saracens, and still the city, together with the surrounding district, is a waste place and a desolation. Wild beasts and wandering Bedouins alternately occupy this region which was once so populous, wealthy, and fertile.

Cyre'nian, a native of Cyrene or Cyrenaica, Mark xv, 21; Luke xxiii, 16; Acts vi, 9.

Dab'areh, Josh. xxi, 28, an inaccurate form for Daberath.

Dab'basheth, *hump* of a camel, a border town of Zebulun, Josh. xix. 11.

Dab'erath, (meaning uncertain,) a town of Zebulun, Josh. xix, 12, or perhaps of Issachar, Josh. xxi, 28; 1 Chron. vi, 72; allotted to the Gershonite Levites. Inaccurately called Dabarch, Josh. xxi, 28. It is probably identical with the small modern village *Deburieh*, at the western foot of Tabor. This is a small, poor, filthy place, containing the bare walls of an old church based upon massive foundations of a still older date.

Dale, THE KING'S, Gen. xiv, 17; 2 Sam. xviii, 18. A valley near Jerusalem, which is probably identical with the southern part of the valley of Jehoshaphat, opening into the plot used for the king's garden, about the well of Joab. See Map 7.

Dalmanu'tha, a place near the Sea of Galilee, into the parts of which our Lord is said to have come, Mark viii, 10. The parallel verse, (Matt. xv, 39,) states that Christ came "into the coasts of Magdala." The two places were therefore contiguous. A mile beyond Magdala (see Map 5) are fields, gardens, copious springs, and ruins. The place is called *'Ain el-Bárideh*, and it is supposed by Porter and others, with great probability, to be the site of Dalmanutha. Dr. Thomson suggests *Dalhamia*, on the river south of the lake; and Schwarz finds it in the "cave of *Teliman*," situated probably in the cliffs above *Mejdel*.

Dalma'tia, (Map 8,) a district in Illyricum, on the east of the Adriatic Sea, visited by Titus, 2 Tim. iv, 10.

Damascenes', people of Damascus, 2 Cor. xi, 32.

Damas'cus, (Map 5,) (in Hebrew, *Dammesek*, *activity* (?) referring probably to its commerce;) but some derive the word from a root which means "to be red," from the color of the earth around Damascus. The etymology is quite uncertain. The city is called by the Syrians *Darmsûk*; by the Arabs, *Dimasckk*, or *Es-Scham* ("the East," the name of the country.)

Damascus is one of the most ancient and important cities of Syria. It lies on the eastern base of Anti-Libanus, in a well-watered, (2 Kings v, 12,) fertile plain, the beauty of which led the Orientals to call it one of the four terrestrial paradises. Julian terms it "the great and sacred Damascus, surpassing every city both in the beauty of its temples and the magnitude of its shrines, as well as the timeliness of its seasons, the limpidness of its fountains, the volume of its waters, and the richness of its soil." Damascus owes all its advantages to its rivers, 2 Kings v, 12. (See ABANA, PHARPAR.) The antiquity of the city may be inferred from Gen. xiv, 15; xv, 2. From the latter passage some think it was built by Abraham or Eliezer.

The first reliable notices of the city are found in 2 Sam. viii, 5, 6; 1 Chron. xviii, 5, 6; 2 Sam. x, 6; 1 Kings xi, 23, etc.; xv, 18, 19; 2 Chron. xvi, 2-7; 1 Kings xx, 1-34; xxii, 1, etc., in connection with accounts of hostilities between the kings of Judah and Israel, and those of Damascus. See also 2 Kings vi, vii, viii, xiii, xiv, xvi. For prophecies concerning this city, see Isa. xvii; Amos i, 3-5; Jer. xlix, 23-27. Damascus

DAMASCUS.

passed afterward into the hands of the Persians, the Greeks, and the Romans—Syria being reduced to a Roman province by Pompey, B. C. 64. Herod the Great erected baths and theaters in Damascus.

Paul was converted on his way to this city, Acts ix; and subsequently the Governor sought to apprehend him, 2 Cor. xi, 32. Many Jews were there, and they had several synagogues, Acts ix, 2; and many of them embraced the Gospel, Acts viii, 1; xi, 19. Christianity was planted in Damascus by Paul, Acts ix, 20; Gal. i, 12. The Gospel spread so rapidly among the population that in the time of Constantine the great temple was converted into a cathedral church, and dedicated to John the Baptist. The city was at length, in A. D. 634, taken from the Christians by the Mohammedans. After various reverses under several masters, in 1516 Selim I. took the city from the Mamelukes and incorporated it with the Turkish Empire. The Mohammedans of Damascus are the greatest fanatics in the East. These fanatics in July, 1860, suddenly rose against the defenceless Christians of the city, massacred about six thousand of them in cold blood, and left their whole quarters in ashes, thus exterminating nearly the whole male population of the Christians.

Damascus is still the largest city in Asiatic Turkey. It is one of the most regular and cleanly of Oriental capitals, containing about 140,000 inhabitants, of whom about 6,000 are Jews. Before the massacre the Christians were reckoned at 15,000. Travelers vie with each other in describing the natural beauties of the site of Damascus. The houses are externally mean, but within many are truly magnificent. Sacred localities are shown the visitor. About a mile and a half east of the city the place is pointed out where Paul was converted. In the city the houses of Judas and Simon, (Acts ix, 11, 17,) and the window from which Paul escaped, (2 Cor. xi, 33,) are shown. A long street running from north-east to south-west, is thought to be that named in Acts ix, 11. The reputed house of Naaman has been converted into a hospital for lepers. But little credit can be given to any of these traditions.

Dam'mesek, 2 Kings xvi, 9, marg. Damascus.

Dam'mim. See EPHES-DAMMIM.

Dan, (Map 5,) *judge.* 1. One of the tribes of Israel, named from Dan, Jacob's first son by Bilhah, Gen. xxx, 6. Their allotment was on the seashore, having Ephraim on the north, Ephraim and Judah on the east, Judah and Simeon on the south. Dan was one of the most numerous of the tribes of Israel, Num. i, 39; xxvi, 41; only Judah and the double tribe of Joseph exceeding it. Although their allotment was very small, it had eminent natural advantages, and was one of the most fertile tracts in all Canaan. So rich a prize was not readily yielded up by the Canaanites. Hence the Amorites "forced the children of Dan into the mountain, for they would not suffer them to come down into the valley," Judg. i, 34; comp. 1 Kings iv, 19. Thus the Amorites seem to have retained portions of Dan until Solomon's time. Of the cities given to Dan (Josh. xix, 40) many, as Ekron and Joppa, never were secured by them; others (like Beth-Shemesh) fell into the hands of Judah, as did also Eshtaol and Zoreah, Josh. xxi, 16; 1 Chron. vi, 59; Josh. xv, 33; Judg. xviii, 1-12. During the expedition against Jabin, under Deborah, Dan "remained in ships," Judg. v., 17, and seems, therefore, in part, at least, to have dwelt along the coast. But soon after a portion of this warlike and enterprising, though greatly diminished tribe, seems to have quit its narrow limits, moved northward, and suddenly taken the rich and flourishing city of Laish; probably a Sidonian colony, situated near the sources of the Little Jordan. They then called this city Dan, and occupied it and the adjacent country, Judg. xx, 1; Josh. xix, 47. On their way to Laish, the Danites robbed one Micah, of Mount Ephraim, of sacred objects, used in an unlawful image-worship of Jehovah, and persuaded a Levite, who had been serving Micah, to join them. At Laish they set up Micah's graven image, and made it the center of their worship, Judg. xviii. This continued until the exile. Some of the tribe remained in the original allotment, near Eshtaol and Zoreah, Judg, xiii, 2, 25; xvi, 31; but they seem to have been overpowered by the Philistines, and then to have merged into the more powerful tribe of Judah; so that the above-named colony was the only distinct representative of the tribe remaining at the time of the exile. This may be the reason why, in Rev. vii, 6, Dan is omitted. In Deut. xxxiii, 22, is the prophetic utterance: "Dan is a lion's whelp; he shall leap from Bashan." In Gen. xlix, 16, 17, is the prophetic blessing of Jacob upon Dan. The above sketch illustrates the fulfillment of the former prophecy, while the administration of the heroic Samson (who was of this tribe) illustrates the meaning of Dan, that is, to judge, and throws some light on the "blessing" of the patriarch. For account of Samson as thus connected with this tribe, see Judges xiii, xiv, xv, xvi.

2. The city of Dan. The original name was Leshem or Laish, Josh. xix, 47. It was located in the extreme north of Palestine—as Beersheba was in the extreme south. Hence the expression "from Dan to Beersheba," (Judg. xx, 1,) meaning throughout the whole land. Laish being captured by the Danites, was called by them Dan. See above under the tribe of Dan. The people of Laish are said to have lived "after the manner of the Zidonians," but far from them. They may have been a colony of Zidon. The Danites brought with them to Laish the graven images stolen from Micah, and there long continued the worship thereof, Josh. xix, 47; Judges xviii. Subsequently Jeroboam here set up one of his calves, 1 Kings xii, 29, 30. Dan is twice mentioned in the Pentateuch, Gen. xiv, 14; Deut. xxxiv, 1. In the last-named place, probably Dan-Laish is meant; as the account of Moses' death must have been supplied by a later writer. As to the former, it is not easy to decide. There might have been another Dan in Abraham's time; but the subject is one of those upon which we can only conjecture. Dan was near Paneas, on the road to Tyre, just by the mound now called *Tell-el-Kady*, ("the Judge's Mound,") close by which rises the *Ledlan*. There is no habitation. A few ruins are found in the vicinity, but so dense is the jungle of briers, thorns, and thistles, that the explorer finds no satisfaction in looking for further ruins.

3 A place associated with Javan in reference to Phœnicia, Ezek. xxvii, 19. See VEDAN.

Dan'ites, members of the tribe of Dan, Judg. xiii, 2; xviii, 1, 11; 1 Chron. xii, 35.

Dan-Ja'an, perhaps *woodland-Dan*. It occurs only in 2 Sam. xxiv, 6. It is generally believed to be identical with Dan, or Laish. Schultz inclines to identify it with an ancient site called *Danian*, or *Danyal*, discovered by him in the mountains above *Khan en-Nakûra*, south of Tyre. Some think it near Gilead.

Dan'nah, perhaps *lowly,* or *lowland,* or *murmuring,* a city among the mountains of Judah, Josh. xv, 49. On the hills west of *Wady el-Khulil* is the modern village of *el-Dhoheriyeh,* consisting of stone hovels, with remains of older structures, which some conjecture to be the site of Dannah. Conder identifies it with *Domeh,* two miles north of *El Dhoherijeh.* See DEBIR.

Daph'ne, the *laurel,* a famous sanctuary of Apollo, with a grove, 2 Macc. iv, 33. The site was one of great natural beauty. It is identified with *Beit el-Mau,* ("the House of the Water,") on the Orontes, five miles southwest of Antioch.

Dath'ema, a fortress in Gilead, 1 Macc. v, 9, 24, 28, 29, 35. It is possibly Ramoth-Gilead—as in the Syriac version.

Da'vid, CITY OF. 1. 2 Sam. v, 7. See ZION.
2. Luke ii, 4, 11. See BETHLEHEM, JERUSALEM.

Dead Sea. See SEA.

De'bir, *sanctuary.* 1. The earlier name was Kirjath-Sepher or Kirjath-Sannah, Josh. xv, 15, 49; Judg. i, 11. A city in the highlands of Judah near Hebron, captured by Joshua, Josh. x, 38, 39; xi, 21; xii, 13; xv, 49. See also Josh. xv, 15-17; Judg. i, 11-13. Afterward it was allotted to the priests, Josh. xxi, 15; 1 Chron. vi, 58. Mr. Grove says: "Perhaps the name may be traced in *Dewîr-ban,* three miles west Hebron." Van de Velde says: "Perhaps at *Dilbeh,* six miles south-west of Hebron. Lieut. Conder identifies it (January, 1875) with *El Dhô'herijeh.* See DANNAH.

2. A place on the north boundary of Judah, between Jericho and Jerusalem, Josh. xv, 7. Unknown.

3. A frontier place of Gad, Josh. xiii, 26, east of Jordan, not far from Mahanaim, and possibly the same with Lodebar in 2 Sam. xvii, 27.

Decap'olis, *the ten cities.* A region containing ten cities, Matt. iv, 25; Mark v, 20; vii, 31. This region lay in the north-eastern part of Palestine, near the lake of Gennesaret, embracing a tract probably on both sides the Jordan. The population of these cities were mostly heathen, (Luke viii, 26, 27, 39,) and the cities themselves, without any special connection, were endowed with certain privileges by the Romans who had authority over them. Probably other neighboring cities had similar privileges. The limits of this territory are not defined with accuracy, and geographers do not all agree as to the names of the cities. Pliny gives the following list: Damascus, Philadelphia, Raphana, Scythopolis, Gadara, Hippos, Dion, Pella, Gerasa, and Canatha—all east of Jordan, except Scythopolis.

This region was exceedingly prosperous and populous in the time of Christ. Now it is as a wilderness, with scarcely an inhabitant. There are many and extensive ruins, those of Gerasa being the most magnificent in Palestine. Of the ten, Damascus alone flourishes. A few wretched families still live among the ruins of Scythopolis, Gadara, and Canatha.

Decision, VALLEY OF, (Joel iii, 14,) a poetical name for the Valley of Jehoshaphat.

De'dan, (Map 12,) (meaning doubtful.) Two tribal names.
1. Cushites, Gen. x, 7; 1 Chron. i, 9; "the sons of Raamah, Sheba, and Dedan." These were on the Persian Gulf.
2. Keturhitea, from a son of Jokshan, Abraham's son by Keturah, Gen. xxv, 3; 1 Chron. i, 32; Jer. xxv, 23; xlix, 8; Ezek. xxv, 13. These were on the borders of Idumea. See Ezek. xxvii, 15, 20; xxxviii, 13; though to which of the two these refer is uncertain. Some have supposed that

two different tribes descended from these two sources, but it is probable that they were a single people, and that the posterity of the Abrahamic intermarried with that of the Hamitic Dedan. The discussion, though very valuable, is too long for our limits. See Smith's *Dictionary*.

Ded'anim, people of Dedan, Isa. xxi, 13.

Deha'vites, *villagers*, a tribe from whom the King of Assyria had sent colonists into Samaria, Ezra iv, 9. They are probably the Daï of Herodotus, (a nomad Persian tribe east of the Caspian Sea,) and perhaps the ancestors of the Danes.

De'lus, *manifest*, 1 Macc. xv, 23. An island in the Ægean, sacred to Apollo. Extensive ruins remain. It, together with an adjoining island, is now called *Dhiles*.

Der'be, (Map 8,) perhaps *juniper tree*, a small city of Lycaonia, coupled with Lystra, Acts xiv, 6, 20; xvi, 1. In Acts xx, 4, (in Greek,) is the term "Derbaean," referring to Gaius, who was born there. It was probably near the pass called the "Cilician gates." Derbe was frequently visited by Paul. The most probable claim for the site seems to be at *Divle*, near the base of Taurus.

Dib'lath, (Hebrew, *Diblah*,) Ezek. vi, 14. Possibly a corruption of Riblah.

Diblatha'im, (Map 2,) *two* or *twin cakes*, a place mentioned in the combined names *Almon-Diblathaim*, and *Beth-Diblathaim*, Num. xxxiii, 46; Jer. xlviii, 22; all referring to the same city of Moab—a station of the Israelites.

Di'bon, (Map 2,) a *pining, wasting*, or perhaps a *river-place*. The name of two cities.

1. A town east of Jordan, assigned to Gad, Num. xxi, 30; xxxii, 3, 34; but afterward assigned to Reuben, Josh. xiii, 9, 17. Later it was held by Moabites, Isa. xv, 2; Jer. xlviii, 18, 22. In Num. xxxiii, 45, it is called Dibon-Gad, and doubtless is the Dimon of Isa. xv, 9. About three miles north of the Arnon exist extensive ruins, bearing the name *Dibân*, which are believed to be the site of Dibon. In 1868 a black basalt stone block was discovered here among the ruins, containing a curious inscription. It contains an historical record of the life and deeds of Mescha, a Moabite king, and of his warfare against Joram, King of Israel, and Josaphat, King of Judah. The language is not purely Hebrew, but shows peculiarities of a Moabitic dialect. See PEREA.

2. A town in the south of Judah, Neh. xi, 25. It is probably the same with the Dimonah of Josh. xv, 22. The site is not certainly known, although several authorities incline to place it at the modern *Ed-Dheib*, a place on the south side of a shallow wady by the same name, a short distance north-east of *Tell-Arad*.

Di'bon-Gad, (Map 2,) *Dibon* or *washing of Gad*, a halting-place of the Israelites, Num, xxxiii, 45, 46, identical with the Dibon (1) of Num. xxi, 30.

Dik'lah, a Joktanite tribe, Gen. x, 27; 1 Chron. i, 21, whose territory cannot certainly be determined. The name in Arabic meaning a *palm-tree*, it is supposed that the descendants of Joktan occupied some region abounding in palms. In Arabia were several such regions. Among many different conjectures, perhaps the most probable one is that the Diklahites settled in Yemen, (in the south-west of Arabia,) occupying a position a little east of the *Hejaz*.

Dil'ean, *gourd-field,* a town in the low-country of Judah, Josh. xv, 38. Van de Velde suggests the modern *Tina* as its site, in the plain south of Ekron.

Dim'nah, *dung-hill,* a Merarite city in Zebulun, Josh. xxi, 34. In 1 Chron. vi, 77. Rimmon is probably substituted for it.

Di'mon, WATERS OF, *pining, wasting,* a city in Moab "with waters," Isa. xv, 9. Doubtless identical with Dibon, (1.)

Dimo'nah, *pining, wasting,* a city in the south of Judah, Josh. xv, 22. Probably the same with the Dibon (2) of Neh. xi, 25.

Di'naites, an Assyrian people, from whom colonists were placed in the cities of Samaria, Ezra iv, 9. Their location and the meaning of the term are unknown.

Din'habah, perhaps *robbers' den* or *place of plundering,* a city of Bela, King of Edom, Gen. xxxvi, 32; 1 Chron. i, 43. The site is not determined.

Di'phath. 1 Chron. i, 6, marg. See RIPHATH.

Diz'ahab, *of gold,* or *possesser of gold,* that is, a place where there is much gold. A place in the Arabian Desert, Deut. i, 1. It is probably the cape now called *Dahab,* on the west side of the Gulf of Akabah, where some ruins exist.

Do'cus, a small fortress near Jericho, where Simon Maccabeus and two of his sons were murdered. It was probably at or near '*Ain Dûk,* near which are traces of ancient foundations.

Do'danim, and **Dod'anim,** *leaders,* (?) the name of a tribe descended from one of the sons of Javan, Gen. x, 4; 1 Chron. i, 7. In the margin and in the text of some copies the word is Rodanim, which is probably an error. As to their place of abode authorities differ. Some think the Dodanim were the Dardani or Trojans; others the Daunians in Italy; and others, with still less probability, the Rhodians. Thus, both their territory and the meaning of the term are involved in obscurity.

Doph'kah, (Map 2,) *knocking,* or perhaps *driving,* (of cattle,) an encampment of the Israelites, between Rephidim and the sea, in the Desert of Sin, Numb. xxxiii, 12, 13. Probably it was at the mouth of *Wady Feirân.*

Dor, (Map 5,) a *dwelling,* an ancient royal city of the Canaanites, Josh. xi, 2; xii, 23, and probably the most southern settlement of the Phoenicians on the Syrian coast. It seems to have been within the territory of Asher, though allotted to Manasseh, Josh. xvii, 11; Judges i, 27. The original inhabitants were not expelled, but it became one of Solomon's commissariat departments, 1 Kings iv, 11. It was besieged and captured by Antiochus Sidetes, 1 Macc. xv, 11, 13, 25, (under the name of Dora.) Its site is identified with the modern village of *Tantûra,* a collection of wretched huts, (wholly constructed of ancient materials,) about nine miles north of Cæsarea.

Do'ra, 1 Macc. xv, 11, 13, 25. See DOR.

Do'thaim, Judith iv, 6; vii, 3, 18; viii, 3; the Greek form of Dothan

Do'than, (Map 5,) *two cisterns,* a place at the southern edge of the plain of Esdraelon, about twelve miles north of Samaria. Here Joseph found his brethren, Gen. xxxvii, 17. It is mentioned as the residence of Elisha, and the scene of a vision of horses and chariots of fire, and where the Syrians were struck with blindness, 2 Kings vi, 13-19. The site is identified with the place still known as Dothan, about five miles south-west of *Jenin.* The great road for caravans from Gilead to Egypt passes near Dothan, Gen. xxxvii, 25-28.

Du'mah, (Map 12,) *silence.* 1. An Ishmaelite place or people in Arabia, (Isa. xxi, 11,) probably so called from the son of Ishmael, whose descendants inhabited that locality, Gen. xxv, 14; 1 Chron. i, 30. The name probably survives in *Doomat el-Jendel,* (" Dumah of the Stones,") a town in the north-western part of the peninsula of Arabia. 2. A town in the mountainous district of Judah, Josh. xv, 42. Ruins exist at a place now called *Ed-Daumeh,* six miles south-west of Hebron, which probably mark the site of Dumah.

Dung-Gate, (Map 7.) See JERUSALEM.

Du'ra, *circle,* the plain in the district of Babylon where Nebuchadnezzar set up his golden image, Dan. iii, 1. M. Oppert places the plain (or, as he calls it, the "valley") of Dura, to the south-east of Babylon, in the vicinity of the mound of *Dowair* or *Dûair.* He has discovered on this site the pedestal of a colossal statue, and regards the modern name as a corruption of the ancient appellation.

East Country. Gen. xxv, 6. Mesopotamia.

East Sea. Numb. xxxiv, 3; Ezek. xlvii, 18; Joel ii, 20; Zech. xiv, 8, margin. The Dead Sea. See SEA.

Ebal, MOUNT, (Map 5,) mountain of *stone, stony.* [Grove says that the name Ebal may, perhaps, like Gerizim, have been derived from an ancient tribe of wanderers—Ebal, son of Shobal, Gen. xxxvi, 23.] A mountain in Palestine opposite Mount Gerizim, in the northern part of Ephraim, on the northern side of the valley of Shechem, Deut. xi, 29; xxvii, 4, 13; Josh. viii, 30, 35. Here was built the first altar erected after the Israelites entered the Promised Land. In the valley between Ebal and Gerizim lies Shechem, the modern *Nablûs.* In Josh. viii, 30-35, we have the account of the curses upon transgressors uttered by half the tribes of Israel standing on Ebal, while the other tribes, standing on Gerizim, pronounced blessings on the people. That the voice is audible from one of these mountains to the other has frequently been proved by actual experiment; the valley at the eastern end being not more than sixty rods wide. Ebal rises about 2,700 feet above the level of the sea, Gerizim 2,600. As the city of *Nablûs* is 1,672 feet above the sea level, Gerizim rises above the city 928 feet, Ebal 1,028. Ebal is not more barren than the other mountain, although the contrary has been maintained by some, owing, probably, to an opinion in regard to the cursing above mentioned. Ruins have been found, and although the mountain has not been fully explored, there is evidence that many more may be yet discovered. The modern name of Ebal is *Sitti Salamiyah,* from a Mohammedan female saint, whose tomb is standing on the eastern part of the ridge, a little before the highest point is reached. Some report the name as *Imâd-ed-Deen,* "the pillar of the religion." This name may come from *Amâd,* the name of another saint's tomb which is shown the traveler. See GERIZIM.

Eb'en-E'zer, *stone of help,* a memorial set up by Samuel to mark his victory over the Philistines, 1 Sam. iv, 1; v, 1; vii, 12. Its position is carefully defined as between Mizpah—"the watch-tower," one of the conspicuous eminences a few miles north of Jerusalem—and Shen, "the tooth" or "crag." Neither point has been identified with certainty—the latter, indeed, not at all.

Ebro'nah, (Map 2,) *passage* of the sea, a station of the Israelites near Ezion-Geber on the Elanitic gulf, Num. xxxiii, 34, 35. Not known.

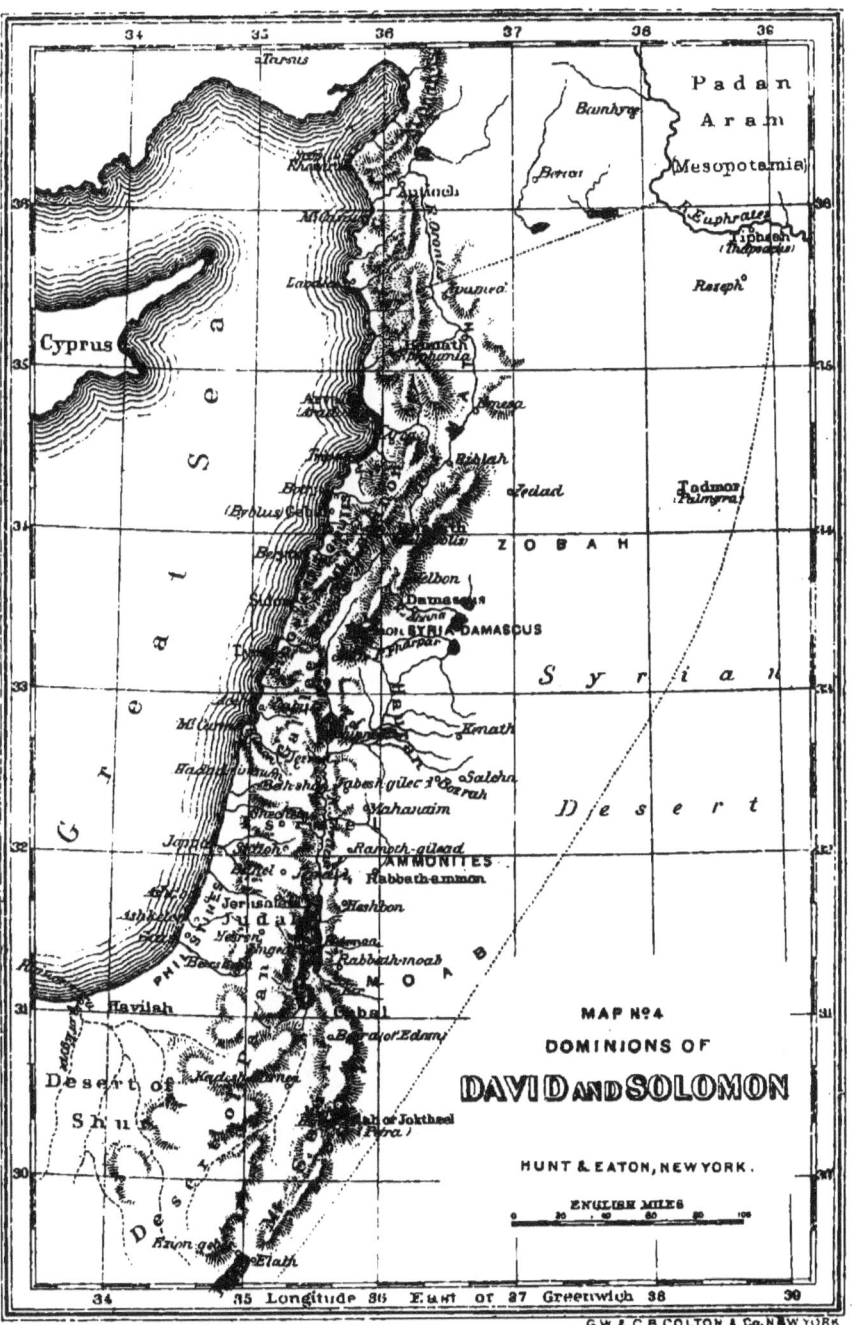

Ecbat'ana, (Maps 1, 14.) This word occurs in the margin of Ezra vi, 2; Achmetha being the word used in the text. Its derivation is uncertain. Rawliuson has left little doubt that the title was applied exclusively to cities having a fortress for the protection of the royal treasures.

1. There were two cities of this name, Ecbatana, the capital of Media Magna, the summer residence of the Persian kings, from Darius Hystaspis, and later of the Parthian monarchs, 2 Macc. ix, 3. This place, situated on the northern flank of the great mountain called formerly Orontes, and now *Elwend,* was, perhaps, as ancient as the other city, and is far better known in history. It is now known by the name of *Hamadan,* and is one of the most important cities of modern Persia, with a population of from 20,000 to 30,000 souls.

2. The northern city, the capital of Northern Media, or Media Atropatene. By the Greeks and Romans it appears to have been known as Gaza, Gazaca, or Canzaca, the "treasure city;" by the Orientals it was termed *Shiz.* When Ecbatana is mentioned, there is generally some difficulty in determining whether the northern or the southern metropolis is intended. Few writers are aware of the existence of the two cities, and they lie sufficiently near to one another for geographical notices, in most cases, to suit either site. The northern city was the "seven-walled town" described by Herodotus, and declared by him to have been the capital of Cyrus; and it was thus most probably there that the roll was found which proved to Darius that Cyrus had really made a decree allowing the Jews to rebuild their temple, Ezra vi, 2. In Tob. iii, 7; xiv, 12, 14; Judith i, 1, 2, the reference is probably to this city. It continued an important place down to the Mogul conquests in the thirteenth century after Christ, and sank ultimately, two or three centuries later, into complete ruin. The present remains are upon and around a conical hill about 150 feet above the contiguous plain. One wall, just at the brow of this hill, may be readily traced, enclosing an oval space of 800 yards by 400. There are no vestiges of other encircling walls. The site of the city is now known by the name of *Takht i-Suleiman.*

Ed, *witness,* a word inserted in the authorized version of Josh. xxii, 34. It is found in some MSS., but is not in the generally received Hebrew text. It is the name of the altar erected by the tribes of Reuben, Gad, and half-Manasseh, on the borders of Jordan in Gilead, to *witness* that they belonged to Israel, although their possessions were separated from those of the other tribes by the Jordan.

E'dar, TOWER OF, tower of a *flock,* a place named only in Gen. xxxv, 21 It was Jacob's first halting place between Bethlehem and Hebron. Jerome located it at one thousand paces from Bethlehem. Its site is unknown.

E den, (Map 1,) *pleasure, delight, mist-rising,* or, the "Garden of Eden," the Bible name of the home of Adam and Eve before their fall, Gen. ii, 8, 15. The LXX., following the Chaldee, calls it "Paradise," a *park, pleasure-garden,* or *orchard of pleasure and fruits,* Neh. ii, 8; Sol. Song iv, 13; Eccles. ii, 5. The record is, (Gen. ii, 8,) "The Lord God planted a garden eastward in Eden." The boundaries both of Eden and of the garden are entirely indefinite. Many theories have been advanced as to the locality of Eden. The dimensions of the garden have been by some writers confined to a circumference of thirty-six or forty miles. Some have made Eden extend over Syria, Arabia, and Mesopotamia. Bush thinks that Eden must have included "the fairest portions of Asia, besides a part of Africa; . . . Cabul, Persia, Armenia,

Kurdistan, Syria, Arabia, Abyssinia, and Egypt." Ephraem Syrus held that it surrounded the whole earth. But all this is mere conjecture. Says Wright, of Trinity College: "The site of Eden will ever rank, with the quadrature of the circle and the interpretation of unfulfilled prophecy, among those unsolved and perhaps insoluble problems which possess so strange a fascination."

The most commonly received conjecture seems to be that which makes the garden, or a *part* of Eden, to be the country through which flow the rivers Euphrates and Tigris, and which claims that the bounds of Eden were by no means narrow. The Hon. I. S. Diehl, who has traversed this whole region, gives us some very strong reasons for locating the "garden" about one hundred miles above the confluence of these two rivers, where the Euphrates, Tigris, and Kerkhan (the ancient Choaspes) unite within a few hundred yards of each other, and form the *Shatt-el-Arab*, or "river of the Arabs;" while about sixty miles below the river *Kharoun* flows in from the east, making "four" important rivers. All along the banks of the *Shatt-el-Arab* for many miles are numerous gardens and groves of the date-tree. The fruit of this tree constitutes the chief article of food of the natives, from which they make some thirty-five different dishes. This fruit is claimed by the natives to have been the identical food of which Adam and Eve did eat in the garden; while the words Eden and Paradise are still used to designate these beautiful fruit gardens. A little north of *Bussorah* is a date grove which pilgrims annually visit as the traditional Paradise. During the year 1869 bricks from *Birs Nimroud* (the supposed Babel) were found, on which are inscriptions which locate the garden of Eden in the tract of country lying between the Persian Gulf and Babylon.

Some authorities locate Eden in Armenia, in the region around Lake Van. This theory seems to us untenable, from the fact that no river flows into Lake Van; and from its altitude and its exceedingly rigorous climate this region would appear entirely unsuitable to have been the "cradle of the human race," or Eden. After all, we must conclude with the author above quoted, Mr. Wright, that, "as every expression of opinion results in a confession of ignorance, it will be more honest to acknowledge the difficulty than to rest satisfied with a fictitious solution." We would refer the reader for a more extended discussion to Kitto's, Smith's, Herzog's, and McClintock and Strong's *Bible Cyclopedias;* and especially to Lange's *Commentary on Genesis.*

E'den, *pleasantness.* A region whose inhabitants had been subdued by the Assyrians, 2 Kings xix, 12; Isa. xxxvii, 12. They had commercial intercourse with Tyre, Ezek. xxvii, 23. Probability locates this region somewhere in the north-west of Mesopotamia.

E'den, THE HOUSE OF, *house of pleasure,* Amos i, 5. See BETH-EDEN.

E'der, *flock,* a town of Judah in the extreme south, on the borders of Edom, Josh. xv, 21. Not known. Schwarz suggests that it may be identical with Arad by a transposition of letters.

E'dom, (Maps 2, 5,) *red,* called also in the Greek form Idumea. The name Edom was given to Esau, the first-born son of Isaac, when he sold nis birthright to his twin brother Jacob for a meal of lentile pottage. The peculiar *red* color of this pottage gave rise to the name Edom. The country afterward given to Esau was called the "field of Edom," Gen. xxxii, 3, or "land of Edom," Gen xxxvi, 6; Num. xxxiii, 37. Edom was previously called

BIBLE GEOGRAPHY. 109

Mount Seir, that is *rugged, bristly,* Gen. xxxii, 3; xxxvi, 8, from Seir the progenitor of the Horites, Gen. xiv, 6; xxxvi, 20-22. The original inhabitants of the country were called Horites from Hori the grandson of Seir, Gen. xxxvi, 20-22, because that name was descriptive of their habits as "dwellers in caves." Esau's eldest son, Eliphaz, was father to Amalek, the progenitor of the Amalekites.

On the death of Isaac, Esau left Canaan and occupied Mount Seir, Gen. xxxv, 28; xxxvi, 6, 7, 8. The descendants of Esau rapidly multiplied, and soon they extirpated the Horites, and adopted their habits as well as their country. Deut. ii, 12; Jer. xlix, 16; Obad. 3, 4.

The country of Edom is the southern continuation of the East Jordan table-land, extending from the southern extremity of the Dead Sea to the north of the Elanitic Gulf, where was situated Elath, the sea-port of the Edomites. It is wholly a mountainous country, called "Mount Seir," "the Mount of Esau," Gen. xiv, 6; xxxvi, 8, 9; Deut. i, 2; ii, 1, 5; Obad. 8, 9, 19, 21. Josephus and later writers call it *Gebalene,* "the mountainous." It extends along the east side of the great valley of Arabah, embracing a narrow tract of about one hundred miles long by twenty broad. Its highest mountains rise about three thousand feet; the best known of which is *Hor,* in the vicinity of Petra, on which Aaron died. Generally the mountain range is bare, especially the western portion; but between the rocky clefts lie valleys with fruitful meadows, fields, and vineyards, and forests are not wanting. The air is pure, the heat is moderated by the cool wind, and the whole region is quite healthy. For towns of Edom see BOZRAH, ELATH, EZION-GEBER, PETRA, SELAH. For mountains see HALAK, HOR, SEIR.

The government of Edom was a union of tribes under dukes, Gen. xxxvi, 15-19, which must early have centralized into a kingdom, since in Genesis xxxvi, 31, already eight succeeding kings are mentioned, who were doubtless elective. The Edomites were warlike, and had a mighty bulwark in their naturally fortified mountain home. They had many gods, 2 Chron. xxv, 14. The prophecies of Isaac (Gen. xxvii, 29; xxxix; xl) are remarkably fulfilled in the later history of the Edomites. Already, in the time of Moses, they conducted themselves in an unbrotherly way toward Israel, in denying to them a free passage through their country, Num. xx, 15, etc.; xxi, 4; Deut. ii, 4, etc. The Israelites were strictly forbidden to oppose the Edomites, Deut. ii, 5; xxiii, 7; but after their more decided hostility to Israel this prohibition was removed. They were received into the congregation at the third generation, Deut. xxiii, 8. They were defeated by Saul, 1 Sam. xiv, 47; and subdued by David, 2 Sam. viii, 14; 1 Kings xi, 16, 1 Chron. viii, 11-13; Psa. lx, (*title;*) Psa. cviii, 9. In the harbors of Edom Solomon equipped a considerable fleet, 1 Kings ix, 26. Hadad, of the seed royal, fled to Egypt, 1 Kings xi; 14-22, 25.

Edom was put under a regent, 1 Kings xxii, 47; Jehoshaphat defeated the tribe, 2 Chron. xx, 22. They joined him in war with Moab, 2 Kings iii, 9, 26. They revolted against Joram, and were defeated, 2 Kings viii, 20-22; 2 Chron. xxi, 8-10. They were also defeated by Amaziah, 2 Kings xiv, 7, 10; 2 Chron. xxv, 11, 12. They invaded Judah, 2 Chron. xxviii, 17. Edom aided Babylon against Israel, Ezek. xxxv, 5; Amos i, 9, 11; Obad. 11-16. Their hatred to Israel was intense, Psa. cxxxvii, 7. Ezek. xxv, 12-14; xxxv, 3-10. The Edomites rejoiced greatly over the fall of Judah, and voluntarily joined the Chaldean conquerors.

Against Edom the prophets spoke with special fervor, Joel iii, 24; Amos i, 11; Isa. xi, 14; xxxiv, 5, sq.; Obad.; Jer. ix, 25; xxv, 21; xxvii; Ezek. xxv, 12; xxxii, 29; xxxvi, 5; Mal. i, 2. The Jews being carried captives to Babylon, the Edomites took easy possession of the country south of Palestine, including Hebron, Ezek. xxxv, 10; 1 Macc. v, 65. Also during the Syrian supremacy they manifested their old hatred toward the Jews, 1 Macc. v, 3, 65; 2 Macc. x, 15; xii, 32; until, subjugated by John Hyrcanus, they were compelled by him to receive circumcision, and were incorporated into the Jewish state. But a fresh triumph awaited Edom. The crafty Idumean, Antipater, obtained the reins of government, and was after a while made by Cæsar procurator of Judea, while Hyrcanus only had the priesthood.

In the year 40 Herod the Great, son of Antipater, was even proclaimed king of Judea by the Roman Senate. After this the Jewish kingdom, with a brief interregnum of Roman governors, was under the rule of Herodian princes. After the destruction of Jerusalem by the Romans under Titus, the names Idumean and Idumea disappear from history. The country from this time was included in the comprehensive name Arabia.

Under the withering influence of Mohammedan rule the great cities fell to ruin, and the country became a desert. God used the followers of the false prophet to fulfill the terrible words of prophecy: "O Mount Seir, I am against thee. . . . I will lay thy cities waste, and when the whole earth rejoiceth, I will make thee desolate. . . . I will make thee perpetual desolations, and thy cities shall not return, and ye shall know that I am the Lord," Ezek. xxxv.

The Crusaders made several expeditions into Edom. They built a strong fortress called Mons Regalis, now *Shôbek*, on a commanding height twelve miles north of Petra. Edom remained unknown from that time till the year 1812, when Buckhardt entered it from the north, and, passing through it, discovered the wonderful ruins of *Petra*. See SELA.

In 1828, Laborde, proceeding northward from *Akabah* also visited Petra, and brought away a portfolio of splendid drawings, which proved that the descriptions of Buckhardt had not been exaggerated. A trip to Petra now forms a necessary part of the eastern traveler's grand tour.

E'domites, Gen. xxxvi, 9, 43; 2 Kings viii, 21; 1 Chron. xviii, 12, 13, 2 Chron. xxi, 8, 9, 10; xxv, 19; 1 Kings xi, 17; 2 Chron. xxv, 14; xxviii, 17; 1 Kings xi, 1. The descendants of Esau or Edom. See EDOM.

Ed'rei, (Map 5,) *strength, stronghold.* 1. One of the two capital cities of Bashan, mentioned in connection with the victory gained by the Israelites over the Amorites under Og, Num. xxi, 33; Deut. i, 4; iii, 10; Josh. xii, 4. It was in the territory of the half-tribe of Manasseh, beyond the Jordan, Num. xxxii, 33. No allusion is made to it in the subsequent Bible history, although it was an important city down to the seventh century of our era. Its ruins bear the name *Edr'a*, and are found on a rocky promontory which projects from the south-west corner of the *Lejah*. These ruins are nearly three miles in circuit, having a strange wild look, rising up in black shattered masses from the midst of a wilderness of black rocks. A number of the old houses remain, being low, massive, gloomy, and some of them half-buried beneath heaps of rubbish. Here a few families make what they call their home. These houses are probably as old as the time of Roman dominion. See Porter's *Handbook for Syria and Palestine*; also Porter's *Five Years in Damascus*.

THE PYRAMIDS.

2. A town in Naphtali, near to Kedesh, Josh. xix, 17. About two miles south of Kedesh is a conical rocky hill called *Tell Khuraibeh*, the "Tell of the ruin," with remains of old buildings, and a rock-hewn tomb. Porter says this may be the site of the long-lost Edrei.

Eg'laim, *two ponds*, or *pools*, a place named in Isa. xv, 8, as apparently one of the most remote points on the boundary of Moab. Possibly the same as En-Eglaim. Mr. Grove says: "With most of the places on the east of the Dead Sea, Eglaim yet awaits further research for its identification."

Eg'lon, (Map 5,) *pertaining to a calf*, a town of the Amorites in the low country. It was about thirty-four miles south-west of Jerusalem, and was formerly Amorite, and its king was Debir, Josh. x, 3–5. For the overthrow of a confederacy which included Eglon, see Josh. x, 23–25; xxxiv, 35; xii, 12. It was afterward allotted to Judah, Josh. xv, 39. The site is doubtless that of modern *'Ajlan*, a shapeless mass of ruins, about ten miles from *Beit Jibrin*, (Eleutheropolis,) and fourteen from Gaza.

E'gypt, (Maps 1, 2, 12.)

NAMES. Among the Hebrews the proper name was *Masor*, (Isa. xix, 6,) more frequently in the dual *Mitsraim*; or, more fully, "the land of Mizraim;" in Greek, *Mestre*, or *Mestraia*. In Homer *Aiguptos* is used, both of the river and the adjacent country. Some have derived the word from a Shemitic root; others from a Sanscrit. But since it is found only among the Greeks and those nations who obtained it from them, its Greek origin seems to be certain. The Coptic name, both Theban and Memphitic, is *Keme*, or *Kem*, (probably pronounced Chem,) and, with the hieroglyphic designation, means BLACK. The name of the country was not derived from the color of the people, which was red, but from that of the soil, which formed a strong contrast with the adjacent countries. In Psa. cv, 23, 27, we have "the land of Ham," (see also lxxviii, 51,) probably referring to Ham the son of Noah. Ham signifies *warmth* or *darkness*. In Isa. xi, 11, it is called Pathros; in Psa. lxxxvii, 4, Rahab. The Arabian name is *masr, urbs, urbs magna*; and Cairo, the present capital, *El Masr*, and the country *Barr Masr*, the land of *Masr*. The dual *Mizraim* can only refer to its division into Upper and Lower Egypt, and not to the two shores of the river; for Egypt was in all times regarded by its inhabitants as a kingdom consisting of two parts, and it is thus described in the hieroglyphics. And this division was not a political one, but rested on an original difference of religion, language, and customs of their population. That *Masr* was in Asia generally the name of Egypt, is now evident from the cuneiform inscriptions. In the Persian, it was *M'udráya*, or *Mudaráya*; in the Median, *Mutsariga*; the Babylonian, *Misir*; the Assyrian, *Musri*.

As to the first of the above list, *Misraim*, perhaps it was originally used not of the country, but of the chief city, and afterward spread as a proper name further northward. Various significations are given: *borders, limits, who is straightened*, or *blocked up*. The modern Arabian name is said to mean *a limit, red earth*, or *mud*. (See *Cyclopedias* of Herzog, and Smith.)

Perhaps "we may with much probability conclude that the names given to this country imply dark—sufficiently appropriate to its black alluvial soil, striking enough after the crops have been gathered in, before the Nile has again covered the surface with its fertilizing flood."—*Ayre*.

SITUATION. Egypt extends from the Mediterranean to the cataracts of the Assouan, "from Migdol to Syene,' Ezek. xxix, 10; xxx, 6, marg., and on the east and west it is bounded by the Arabian and Libyan deserts. Upper Egypt, however, seems really to have comprised nothing more than the narrow winding valley of the Nile, limited on each side by limestone and sandstone hills, which near the river are of no great height, but which, in the eastern desert, are much more lofty; some peaks, as the *Jebel-Gharib*, rising to 6,000 feet. But Lower Egypt is for the most part a vast fertile plain. The Nile divides into several streams, forming a great triangle, of which the limits were the ancient Canopic and Pelusiac branches. The others were the Bolbitine, originally a canal, still open at Rosetta; the Selbenitic, lost in the lake Bourlos; the Phatnitic or Bucolic, open at Damietta, being the eastern extremity of the modern Delta; the Mendesian, and the Tanitic or Saitic. The last two, with the Pelusiac, are absorbed by an extensive lagoon. In early times cultivation reached farther eastward; thus there was a fruitful valley along the canal of the Red Sea. This, the *Wady et-Tumeylat*, is now a sandy wilderness. The principal connection between Egypt and the civilized nations of the North was from Palestine along the coast of the sea toward Pelusium. Along this road the "river of Egypt" (Num. xxxiv, 5; Josh. xv, 4, 47) forms the boundary between Egypt and Palestine. For a long period, however, the Pharaohs also ruled over a large part of Ethiopia and the peninsula of Sinai.

BIBLE ALLUSIONS. Fertility and productions of Egypt, Gen. xiii, 10; Num. xi, 5; Josh. xix, 5-9. Peopled by descendants of Mizraim, Gen. x, 6, 13, 14. Boundaries of, Josh. xv, 4; 2 Kings xxiv, 7; Isa. xxvii, 12; Ezek. xxix, 10. Irrigation of, Deut. xi, 10. Commerce, Gen. xxxvii, 25, 36; 1 Kings x, 28, 29; Ezek. xxvii, 7. Armies, Exod. xiv, 7: Isa. xxxi, 1. The Magi—their learning, Gen. xli, 8; Exod. vii, 11; 1 Kings iv, 30; Acts vii, 22. Priests of, Gen. xli, 45; xlvii, 42. The king's property in the land, Gen. xlvii, 18-26. Embalming practiced, Gen. l, 3. Shepherds abhorred, Gen. xlvi, 34; and sacrifice of cattle, Exod. viii, 26. Egyptians would not eat with Hebrews, Gen. xliii, 32. Not to be hated by Israelites; to be received into the congregation in the third generation, Deut. xxiii, 7, 8. Israelites forbidden alliance with, Isa. xxx, 2; xxxi, 1; xxxvi, 6; Ezek. xvii, 15; xxix, 6. Other interesting allusions, Psa. lxxviii, 12; lxxxi, 5; Zech. x, 10; Heb. viii, 9; Jude 5; Hag. ii, 5; Heb. iii, 16.

Prophecies concerning, Gen. xv, 13, 14; Isa. xix; xx, 2-6; xlv, 14; Jer. ix, 25, 26; xliii, 8-13; xliv, 30; xlvi; Ezek. xxix-xxxii; Joel iii, 19; Zech. x, 11.

Towns and districts of, Ezek. xxx, 13-18.

BIBLE EVENTS. The chief events in connection with Egypt are found in Genesis from chapter xxvii to the end of the book, and in the first fourteen chapters of the book of Exodus. In Matt. ii, 13-20, we have the accounts of the Holy Family's flight into Egypt.

Much light would be thrown on these Bible narratives by an account of Egyptian institutions, religious rites, manners, customs, laws, etc.; but our space does not permit it. We may only say here that the language of ancient Egypt is preserved in the monumental inscriptions which are found in the hieroglyphic mode of writing. These hieroglyphics it was for a long time impossible to decipher; but the first step was taken by means of the famous Rosetta Stone, now in the British Museum, on which were three copies of, as it was presumed, the same inscription. One of these

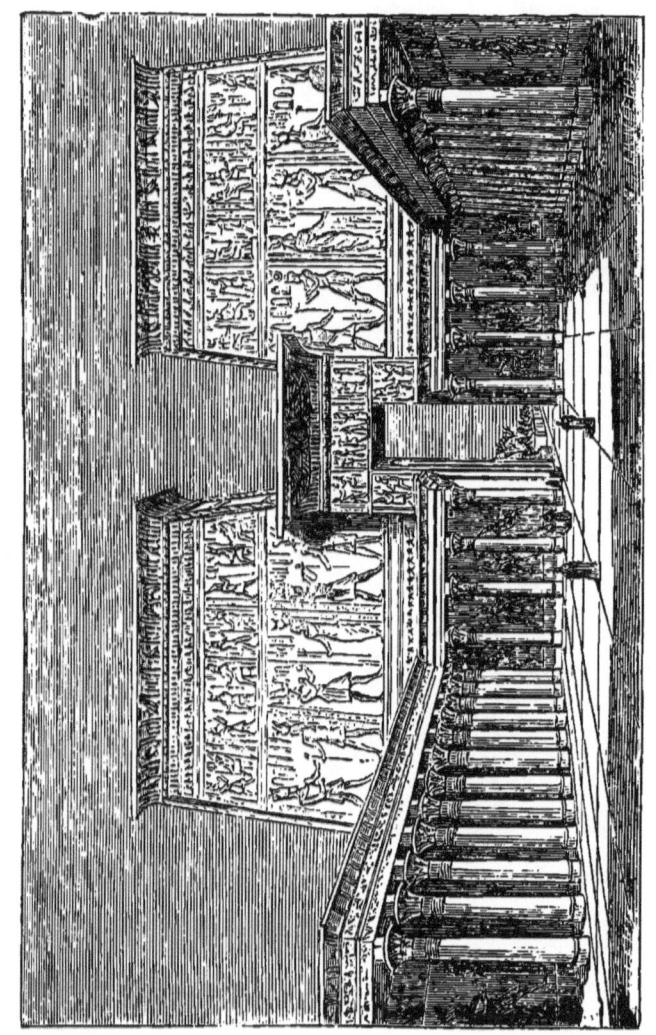

PYLONS AND PORTICO OF A GREAT TEMPLE, (RESTORED ACCORDING TO THE EGYPTIAN COMMISSION.)

was in Greek. A key was therefore obtained to the others; and scholars have since done much to unravel the ancient records.

PRESENT CONDITION, ETC. We have already referred the student to the *prophecies* concerning this country. These have been literally fulfilled. God's judgments have fallen on the land, and the glory of Egypt has long since departed.

Egypt is now a fief, under hereditary rulers, viceroys, of the Turkish Empire. The houses of the wealthier classes in the chief towns are roomy, and substantially built; but the dwellings of the lower orders are many of them but hovels, built of unbaked bricks cemented with mud. The villages stand upon eminences of rubbish, the materials of older buildings, and are thus just above the reach of the inundations. The whole land is crowded with relics of antiquity. The pyramids, the temples, the tombs, speak of a grandeur that has passed away, and these will always attract the curiosity and admiration of the world. The habits of the modern inhabitants illustrate in many respects the narratives of Scripture.

See ALEXANDRIA, AVEN, BAAL-ZEPHON, GOSHEN, MEMPHIS, MIGDOL, NO, NOPH, ON, PATHROS, PITHOM, RAMESES, SUCCOTH, TAHPANHES, ZOAN.

E'gypt, River of, Map 2, (that is, *torrent of Mitzraim.*) See RIVER OF EGYPT.

Egyp'tian, Egyp'tians, (that is, *Mitzraim, Egypt,*) Gen. xliii, 32; xlv, 2; xlvi, 34, and in many other places. A native or natives of Egypt. In Acts xxi, 38, the person so called was no doubt the pretended prophet who posted himself on Olivet, and declared that the walls of Jerusalem would fall down at his word. Felix, however, set upon him, and defeated his followers, while he fled and disappeared.

Ek'rebel, Judith vii, 18; "near to Chusi, which is on the brook Mochmur." Probably now *Akrabih,* about six miles south-east of *Nablûs* in the *Wady Makfuriyeh,* on the road to the Jordan valley.

Ek'ron, (Map 5,) *eradication, emigration,* the most northerly of the five cities of the Philistines, Josh. xiii, 3. In Macc. x, 89, it is called Accaron. It was assigned at first to Judah, Josh. xv, 11, 45, 46; Judg. i, 18; afterward to Dan, xix, 43. It was once taken by Judah, but was always a Philistine place, 1 Sam. v, 10; vi, 17. From Ekron the ark was sent to Israel, 1 Sam. vi, 8. Here was a temple of Baal-Zebub, 2 Kings i, 2, 3, 6, 16. Several of the prophets refer to Ekron, Jer. xxv, 20; Amos i, 8; Zeph. ii, 4; Zech. ix, 5, 7. It is now '*Akir,* five miles south-west of Ramleh; contains about fifty mud houses, without a single remnant of antiquity, except two large wells.

Ek'ronites, inhabitants of Ekron, Josh. xii, 3: 1 Sam. v. 10.

E'la, 1 Esdras ix, 27, a form of Elam, Ezra x, 27.

E'lah, VALLEY OF, (Map 5,) *valley of the Terebinth,* the valley in which David slew Goliath, 1 Sam. xvii, 2, 19; xxi, 9. It is identified now with the *Wady es-Sumt,* or "Acacia Valley," close by *Suweikeh,* the ancient Shocah, which stands on its southern slope, and is about fourteen miles south-west of Jerusalem, on the road to Gaza, and about twelve from Bethlehem. At the junction of *es-Sumt* with two other wadys there is an open space, about a mile wide, with a torrent-bed in the center, strewed with round pebbles, and fringed with acacia bushes. Terebinths also still abound.

E'lam, (Map 1,) *age, eternity,* called Cissia by Herodotus, and by the Greek and Roman geographers Susiana. A country east of Palestine, Gen. xiv, 1, 9;

Isa. xi, 11; peopled by descendants of the sons of Shem, Gen. x, 22. The boundaries of Elam are indefinite. It was a province of Persia, in which was the capital Susa, Ezra iv, 9; Dan. viii, 2. In Greek writers Elymais (Elam) is the province adjacent to Susiana and Media, on the east of Babylonia. In Daniel it seems to include Susiana. The term Elam was at one time used for the whole land of Persia: and it may be here remarked that the word Persia is not found in the Old Testament until the captivity, when the Persian supremacy was commencing. Elam appears as an independent power, Gen. xiv, 1–11. Its independence was in great measure maintained during the Assyrian and Babylonian dominion, but Elamite troops marched under the banner of Sennacherib, Isa. xxii, 6; and ultimately Elam was a province of Babylon, Dan, viii, 1, 2, in fulfillment, as Rawlinson supposes, of the prophecies Jer. xlix, 34–38; Ezek. xxx, 24, 25. Elam is spoken of as supplying part of the army which captured Babylon, Isa. xxi, 2. Captive Israelites were in Elam; their return is predicted, Isa. xi, 11. Elamites were placed in the cities of Samaria, Ezra iv, 9. Jews were still resident there in the apostolic age, Acts ii, 9.

E'lamites, Ezra iv, 9, the original inhabitants of Elam. In Judith i, 6, the Greek form occurs, *Elymæans.* There were Elamites in Jerusalem on the day of Pentecost, Acts ii, 9.

E'lath, E'loth, (Map 4,) *trees, terebinths, a grove,* perhaps a *palm grove.* A town in Edom at the extremity of the eastern gulf of the Red Sea, first mentioned in the accounts of the wandering in the wilderness, Deut. ii, 8. David captured it with Edom, 2 Sam. viii, 14; and it is named in connection with Solomon's navy at the neighboring port of Ezion-Geber, 1 Kings ix, 26; 2 Chron. viii, 17. When Edom revolted it was lost, but was recovered by Uzziah, 2 Kings xiv, 22; and it was finally arrested from Judah by Rezin, King of Syria, who expelled all the Jewish inhabitants, xvi, 6. By the Greeks and Romans it was called Elana, or Ælana, and hence gave name to the eastern gulf of the Red Sea, called the Elanitic Gulf, at present the Gulf of Akabah. (Map 2.) It is now an insignificant place called *Eyleh.*

El-Beth'el, *God of the House of God.* The LXX. omit the "El;" so also Vulgate, *Domus Dei.* Jacob is said to have given this name to the place at which God appeared to him while he was fleeing from Esau, Gen. xxxv, 7. Probably it was the altar which Jacob so named; compare Gen. xxxiii, 20. See BETH-EL.

Elea'leh, *whither God ascends,* a city east of Jordan, allotted to the Reubenites, and which they built or fortified, Num. xxxii, 3, 37. Afterward it was possessed by Moab, Isa. xv, 4; xvi, 9; Jer. xlviii, 34. Its ruins are now called *el-A'al,* close to Heshbon.

Ele'asa, the site of the encampment of Judas Maccabæus before his last battle, 1 Macc. ix, 5. Perhaps it is the same as Adasa and Hadashah.

El-Elo'he-Is'rael, *Almighty, God of Israel,* the name given by Jacob to the altar built by him near Shechem, on the ground where he pitched his tent, and which he afterward bought, Gen. xxxiii, 18–20.

E'leph, *the ox,* a city of Benjamin, Josh. xviii, 28. It may possibly be the ruined site marked *Katamon* on Van de Velde's "Map of the Environs of Jerusalem," about one mile south-west of Jerusalem.

Eleutherop'olis, *the free city.* The original name was Betogabra. This city is not named in Scripture. Eusebius first mentions it, and in his time it was the capital of a large province. It is about twenty-five miles from

Jerusalem on the road to Gaza. It was the seat of a bishop, and so well known was it, that it was made the central point in Southern Palestine from which the position of more than twenty other towns was determined. Its present name is *Beit Jibrin*. It contains some fifty or sixty houses. Ruins of considerable extent exist.

Eleu'therus, *the river,* the northern boundary of the Holy Land, 1 Macc. xi, 7; xii, 30. It is now called the *Nahr el-Kebir*, north of *Tarabulus* (Tripolis).

E'lim, (Map 2,) *trees,* perhaps *palm-trees,* the second station of Israel after crossing the Red Sea, noted for twelve springs and seventy palm-trees, Exod. xv, 27; Num. xxxiii, 9. From the mountain range *et-Tih* several valleys descend toward the sea. Elim is doubtless one of them, but which one is uncertain. Stanley says: "Elim must be [*Wady*] *Gharandel, Useit,* or *Tuiyebeh.*" Trees and shrubs, including wild palms, are said to abound in this vicinity. Palmer inclines to *Gharandel.*

Eli'shah, (Map 12,) (meaning uncertain—some proposing to adopt it from *Elis* or *Hellas*). The name of a maritime people descended from one of the sons of Javan, Gen. x, 4; 1 Chron. i, 7. In Ezek. xxvii, 7, the "isles of Elishah," *maritime regions,* are mentioned. The most probable conjecture makes this people possibly identified with the Æolians, who in early times were settled in various parts of Greece, Thessaly, Bœotia, Ætolia, Locris, Elis, and Messenia. From Greece they emigrated to Asia Minor, and in Ezekiel's age occupied the north-west of that country, named after them Æolis, together with the islands Lesbos and Tenedos.

El'kosh, *God my bow.* The birthplace of the prophet Nahum, Nah. i, 1. Grove says that this place, which is usually identified with *Alkush,* two miles north of *Mosul,* in Assyria, is "more properly somewhere in Galilee." Wright, of Trinity College, says: "The tradition which assigns Elkosh to Galilee is more in accordance with the internal evidence afforded by the prophecy, which gives no sign of having been written in Assyria."

El'lasar, *the oak or heap of Assyria,* the country of which Arioch was king, Gen. xiv, 1, 9. Some confound it with Thelasar, 2 Kings xix, 12. The weight of authority makes it more probably Larsa or Larissa in Lower Babylonia. It is now called *Senkereh,* on the left bank of the Euphrates. Inscriptions found here show the place to have been more ancient than even Babylon.

E'lon, *an oak,* a town in Dan, Josh. xix, 43. Perhaps it is identical with **E'lon-Beth-Ha'nan,** *oak of the house of grace,* 1 Kings iv, 9. One of the places over which Solomon placed a commissariat office. The modern *Beit-Susin* may possibly mark the site. This is a small village looking old and miserable, about half way between the sites of Nicopolis and Zorah.

E'lonites. Descendants of Elon, a family of Zebulun, Num. xxvi, 26.

El'oth. 1 Kings ix, 26; 2 Kings xvi, 6, margin, 2 Chron. viii, 17; xxvi, 2. See ELATH.

El-Pa'ran, *the oak of Paran.* Possibly a tree in the wilderness of Paran, south of the Holy Land, Gen. xiv, 6. Not known. See PARAN.

El'tekeh, *God its fear,* a place in Dan, Josh. xix, 44, allotted to the Kohathite Levites, xxi, 23. Possibly the site may be represented by *El-Mansurah,* a small and miserable village in the plain between Ramleh and Akir.

El'tekon, *God its foundation,* a town in the mountains of Judah, Josh. xv, 59. The modern *Beit-Sahur el-Atikah,* a little south-east of Jerusalem, may possibly mark the site.

Elto'lad, or **El'tolad,** *God its generation,* or *born of God,* (Fürst says, whose *God* is *Mylitta,*) a town in the extreme south of Judah, Josh. xv, 30, allotted to Simeon, xix, 4. Identical with Tolad, 1 Chron. iv, 29. The ruined site, *Tell-Melahu,* may possibly mark the spot. It lies along the north branch of *Wady Sheriah,* which empties into the Mediterranean a little south of Gaza.

Elyma'is, the Greek form of the name Elan., Tobit ii, 10; 1 Macc. vi, 1. See ELAM.

Elyme'ans, Judith i, 6. The Elamites.

E'mim, (Map 3,) *terrors, terrible men,* a tribe of gigantic stature which originally inhabited the region along the eastern side of the Dead Sea. From a comparison of Gen. xiv, 5–7 with Deut. ii, 10–12, 20–23, it seems that the whole country east of the Jordan was, in primitive times, held by a race of giants, all probably of the same stock, comprehending the Rephaim on the north, next the Zuzim, after them the Emim, and then the Horim on the south; and that afterward the kingdom of Bashan embraced the territories of the first; the country of the Ammonites the second; that of the Moabites the third; while Edom took in the mountains of the Horim. The whole of them were attacked and pillaged by the eastern kings who destroyed Sodom and Gomorrah. The Emim were related to the Anakim, and were generally called by the same name; but their conquerors, the Moabites, termed them Emim, (Deut. ii, 11,) very probably on account of their fierce aspect.

Em'maus, or **Emma'us,** (Maps 5, 20,) *hot springs.*

1. A village believed to be about seven and a half miles north-west of Jerusalem, whither were going the disciples whom the Lord met after his resurrection, Luke xxiv, 13. The opinion has prevailed among Christian writers that the Emmaus of Luke was identical with the Emmaus on the border of the plain of Philistia, afterward called Nicopolis, and which was about twenty miles from Jerusalem. But the circumstances of the Scripture narrative are emphatically against this theory, Luke xxiv, 13, 28, 29, 36, 42, 43. Luke says its distance was "threescore furlongs;" and Josephus mentions a village of the same name, at the same distance from Jerusalem.

A tradition of the fourteenth century identifies Emmaus with *Kubeibeh,* about three miles west of ancient Mizpeh, and nine from Jerusalem. Porter says: "There is not a shadow of evidence for this supposition. In fact the site of Emmaus remains yet to be identified." Dr. Thomson (*Land and the Book,* vol. ii, p. 540) is inclined, with others, to locate Emmaus at *Kuriet el-Aineb,* which, he says, "would be the proper distance from Jerusalem, . . . being on the road to *Jaffa.*" Mr. Grove and some others prefer *Kulonieh,* four and a half miles west of Jerusalem. But of this, Clarke (*Bible Atlas,* p. 44) says, "The spot is . . . rather too near to Jerusalem, if we are to accept in a strict sense the distance as stated by St. Luke and Josephus." All is mere conjecture.

2. A town in the Philistine plain, where Judas Maccabeus gained a victory over Georgias, 1 Macc. iii, 40, 57; iv, 3; ix, 50. It lies about twenty-two Roman miles from Jerusalem, and ten from Lydda, at the foot of the mountains of Judah. It was the capital of a toparchy under the Romans. About A. D. 4, it was burned by the Roman general Varus. It was rebuilt (about A. D. 220) by the Christian writer Julius Africanus, when it received the name of Nicopolis. A small miserable village called *Amwâs* still occupies the site of the ancient city.

BIBLE GEOGRAPHY. 121

Em mer. 1 Esdras ix, 21. See IMMER.
Ena'jim. Gen. xxxviii, 14, 21, margin. See ENAM.
E'nam, *the double spring,* a town in the lowland of Judah, Josh. xv, 34. It is possibly alluded to in Gen. xxxviii, 14, (A. V., "an open place.") From its mention with towns which are known to have been near Timnath, this is very probably the place in the "door-way" of which Tamar sat before her interview with her father-in-law. The "open place" is literally "the doorway of Enayim" or Enam. Perhaps the site is marked by *Deir el-Butm* with a well adjoining, laid down by Van de Velde a little beyond *Deir Dubban,* north of Eleutheropolis.

En'-Dor, (Map 5,) *spring* or *fount of the dwelling,* a place in Issachar, but held by Manasseh, Josh. xvii, 11. It was probably the scene of the death of Jabin and Sisera, Psa. lxxxiii, 9, 10. The residence of the witch consulted by Saul, 1 Sam. xxviii, 7. It is now *Endûr,* north of "Little Hermon." Thomson describes it as "a most wretched-looking place."

En-Eg'laim or **En-Egla'im,** *fountain of two calves,* or *of two pools,* a place apparently on the Dead Sea, mentioned in Ezek. xlvii, 10; probably the Eglaim of Isa. xv, 8. M. de Saulcy thinks it identical with *Ain-Ajlah,* situated toward the northern point of the Dead Sea, between Jericho and the Jordan. See EGLAIM.

Engad'di. Ecclesiasticus xxiv, 14. A Greek form of Engedi.
En-Gan'nim, *fountain of gardens.*
1. A place in the low country of Judah, Josh. xv, 34. Not known.
2. A town on the border of Issachar, Josh. xix, 21. It was allotted to Gershonite Levites, xxi, 29. Probably it was the "garden house" (Beth-Gan) of 2 Kings ix, 27. Elsewhere (1 Chron. vi, 73) Anem. It is identified, with scarcely a doubt, in the modern *Jenin,* the first village encountered on the ascent from the great plain of Esdraelon to the hills of the central country. It is still surrounded with "gardens," and a noted "spring" is near by. There are about two thousand inhabitants, who are termed fanatical and unruly.

See BETH-HAG-GAN, with which En-Gannim is probably identical.

Enge'di, (Map 5,) *fountain of the kid,* a place originally called Hazazon-Tamar, 2 Chron. xx, 2. It was in the "wilderness" of Judah, Josh. xv, 62, on the west shore of the Dead Sea, Ezek. xlvii, 10. It was one of David's retreats, 1 Sam. xxiii, 29; xxiv, 1. Saul was found in one of its caves, xxiv, 3. "Camphire in the vineyards of Engedi," Solomon's Song. i, 14. It is now called *Ain-Jidy.* Ruins exist, near which may be found the tents of a few Arabs. Sepulchres and caves abound in the neighboring cliffs. About four hundred feet above the plain is the fountain of *Ain-Jidy,* whose sweet (but warm) water "bursts from the limestone rock, and rushes down the steep descent."

En-Had'dah, *swift fountain,* a place on the boundary of Issachar, near En-Gannim, Josh. xix, 21. Not identified.

En-Hak'kore, or **En-Hakko're,** *fountain of the crier,* the spring of Samson at Lehi—not "the jaw," Judg. xv, 19. "The name is a pun founded on the word in verse 18, *yikera,* 'he called.'" The place has not been identified, although Van de Velde would seem to identify it with the large spring between *Tell-el-Lekiyeh* (which is four miles north of Beersheba) and *Khewelfeh.* But this Tell is some thirty miles from Gaza in a straight line, while Samson's adventures seem to have been confined to a narrow circle.

En-Ha'zor, *spring of the village*, one of the cities of Naphtali, apparently n t far from Kedesh, Josh. xix, 37. Not known.

En-Mish'pat, *fountain of judgment*, the ancient name of Kadesh, Gen. xiv, 7.

En-Rim'mon, *fountain of the pomegranate*, a place inhabited by the men of Judah after the return from the captivity, Neh. xi, 29. It is probably identical with "Ain and Rimmon," Josh. xv, 32; "Ain, Remmon," xix, 7; "Ain, Rimmon," 1 Chron. iv, 32. Possibly the Rimmon of Zech. xiv, 10. Wilton finds En-Rimmon in the modern name *Um er-Rumâmin*. See RIMMON.

En-Ro'gel, (Map 6,) *fountain of the scout*, or *fuller's fountain*, a spring on the boundary between Judah and Benjamin, Josh. xv, 7; xviii, 16. Here, at the time of Absalom's rebellion, Jonathan and Ahimaaz waited for intelligence which they might convey to David, 2 Sam. xvii, 17. Here, too, was the coronation feast of Adonijah, 1 Kings i, 9. The best authorities differ as to the site. Grove says, it is possibly the modern well, *Bir Eyub*, below Siloam; but more probably the *Fount of the Virgin*, a few hundred yards further north. See ZOHELETH.

En-She'mesh, *spring of the sun*, a fountain on the boundary between Judah and Benjamin, Josh. xv, 7; xviii, 17. It was probably east of Jerusalem, beyond the Mount of Olives, and probably identical with the modern fountain about a mile below Bethany, called *Ain el-haud*, or *Ain-Chôt*—the "Well of the Apostles"—the traveler's first halting place on the road to Jericho.

En-Tap'puah, *spring of Tappuah*, or *apple*, or *citron*, a place on the boundary of Manasseh, Josh. xvii, 7. Perhaps identical with TAPPUAH, which see.

E'noch, *initiated*, or *initiating*, that is, dedicated, a city built by Cain, and called after the name of his eldest son, Gen. iv, 17, 18. The site is unknown. See NOD.

E'non. John iii, 23. See ÆNON.

Ephes-Dam'mim, *end*, or *boundary of blood* (?) the place near Azekah where the Philistines were encamped when Goliath was slain, 1 Sam. xvii, 1. In 1 Chron. xi, 13, the form is Pas-Dammim, (which see.) On his way from *Beit-Jibrin* to Jerusalem, Van de Velde came past a ruined site on the high northward-looking brow of *Wady Musur*, about one hour east by south of *Beit-Netif*, called *Khirbet Damun*, which he has no doubt represents the ancient Ephes-Dammim.

Eph'esus, (Map 8.) A city which successively bore also the names of Samorna, Trachea, Ortygia, and Ptelea. Ephesus was one of the twelve Ionian cities in Asia Minor in the mythic times, and said to have been founded by the Amazons, but in later times inhabited by the Carians and Leleges, and taken possession of by the Ionians under Androclus, the son of Codrus. It lay in a fertile alluvial plain south of the river Cayster, not far from the coast of the Icarian Sea, between Smyrna and Miletus, distant from the first-named city three hundred and twenty stadia, or nearly forty miles. Under the Roman government Ephesus was a free city, with its own magistrates and other officers, and legal assemblies. Thus, in Acts xix, 35, 38, we read of "the town-clerk" and "deputies," that is, proconsuls. This city became the great emporium of trade for the Asiatic regions; and, consequently, the inhabitants became luxurious and dissolute. Magic was

TEMPLE OF DIANA (*restored.*)

studied and practiced here. At the head of the harbor of Ephesus stood the magnificent temple of the goddess Diana. This was one of the seven wonders of the world. It was built by the most eminent architects, of the choicest marble, the cost being defrayed by all the Greek cities, aided by Crœsus, King of Lydia. Many years were spent in its erection. It was burned by Herostratus in 355 B. C., on the same night that Alexander the Great was born. It was then rebuilt with still greater magnificence. Its length was four hundred and twenty-five feet by two hundred and twenty broad. The roof, which was of carved cedar, was supported by one hundred and twenty-seven Ionic columns of sixty feet high. The folding doors were of cypress, and the staircase was formed of a single vine from the island of Cyprus. This wonderful temple was made the depository of the wealth of Western Asia. The sacred image of Diana, said to have fallen from heaven, was made of wood, and carved with mystic devices. The silver shrines, of which mention is made in Acts, were probably small models of this image and that part of the temple in which it stood. These shrines were eagerly purchased by visitors, who carried them home and set them up in their houses. There were games held in honor of Diana, and officers called Asiarchs superintended them. In our version these persons have the title of "the chief of Asia," Acts xix, 31.

On his second missionary journey the Apostle Paul visited this important city. Here he found many Jews, in whose synagogue he might preach, and with whom he reasoned. Soon, however, he "sailed from Ephesus," promising to return again. He left Aquila and Priscilla at Ephesus, and they instructed an eloquent Jew of Alexandria, Apollos, who knew only of John's baptism, but preached boldly in the synagogue, Acts xviii, 18-28. Paul, having passed through the upper coasts, came again to Ephesus, Acts xix, 1. The account of his long stay, which "continued by the space of two years;" the "special miracles by the hands of Paul;" his persecution by Demetrius and the worshipers of Diana; the attempt of Sceva's seven sons to expel a demon; the burning of the books concerning the "curious arts;" these are all recorded in Acts xix. Afterward the elders of Ephesus are addressed by Paul at Miletus, on his way to Jerusalem, Acts xx, 16-38. Other references to this city are found in the charge given to Timothy there, 1 Tim. i, 3; the service rendered by Onesiphorus to the Apostle when there, 2 Tim. i, 18; the mission of Tychicus, 2 Tim. iv, 12; and the apocalyptic letter to the Ephesian Church, which had then declined from its first love, Rev. ii, 1-7. Trophimus was an Ephesian, Acts xxi, 29; and the Apostle John is believed to have made Ephesus his residence during the latter part of his life. The site of Ephesus is now occupied by the Turkish village of *Ayosaluk*. Very extensive ruins of the ancient city yet remain. In 1872 a whole cargo of valuable relics from these ruins was shipped for the British Museum.

E'phraim, (Map 5,) *double fruitfulness, double lana, very fruitful* (?), one of the tribes of Israel, sprung from the second son of Joseph, Gen. xli, 50-52. Joseph, when apprised of his father's sickness, was anxious to obtain the recognition of his sons Manasseh and Ephraim, as interested in the covenant blessing. Accordingly, Jacob, outstripping Joseph's anticipation, adopted them as patriarchs, or heads of tribes equally with his own sons. But he placed the younger, Ephraim, before the elder, Manasseh, "guiding his hands wittingly," in spite of Joseph's remonstrance, and prophetically declaring that the posterity of Ephraim should be far greater and more powerful than the posterity of Manasseh, Gen. xlviii. The descendants of any other sons that Joseph might beget were not to be ranked separately, but to be "called after the name of their brethren in their inheritance." Doubtles, Joseph had other sons, and their posterity, perhaps, were sometimes deemed Ephraimites, and sometimes Manassites, according as they chose to locate themselves. This may account for the reproach once thrown upon some Gileadites, as fugitives, belonging justly neither to the one tribe nor to the other, Judg. xii, 5.

At the first census in the wilderness, Ephraim numbered 40,500, Num. i, 33. Their encampment was to be on the west side of the tabernacle, and in the march they were to head the third division, Num. 1, 32, 33; ii, 18, 19. At the second census, in the plain of Moab, their number was only 32,500. Num. xxvi, 37.

Having reached Canaan, Judah, Ephraim, and Manasseh first took their inheritance. The boundaries of Ephraim are given in Josh. xvi, (compare 1 Chron. vii, 28, 29.) We are not able to trace this boundary-line very exactly. But Ephraim occupied the very center of Palestine, embracing an area about forty miles in length, from east to west, and from six to twenty-five in breadth, from north to south. It extended from the Mediterranean on the west to the Jordan on the east: having on the north the half-tribe of Manasseh, and on the south Benjamin and Dan, Josh. xvi, 5, etc.; xvii, 7, etc.; 1 Chron. vii, 28, 29. This fine country included most of what was afterward called Samaria, as distinguished from Judea on the one hand, and Galilee on the other. What was called "Mount Ephraim," (perhaps extending across the border of Benjamin,) consisted of rounded limestone hills, among which were valleys and plains, well-watered, yielding abundantly, as Moses had predicted, "the precious things of the earth and fullness thereof," Deut. xxxiii, 16. The tribes were not at first contented with the size of their allotted portion, but were told, somewhat ironically, by Joshua. that if they were as they called themselves, a great people, they ought to go boldly and occupy the adjacent mountain and woodland country, Josh. xvii, 14-18. The Ephraimites did not fully drive out the Canaanites, Josh. xvi, 10.

The tabernacle was set up in Ephraim, at Shiloh, Josh. xviii, 1. By this circumstance the influence of the tribe was increased, and we find it bearing itself haughtily. We have an example of this in their remonstrance to Gideon after his first victory, which that leader deemed prudent to pacify by a flattering answer, Judg. vii, 24, 25; viii, 1-3. With Jephthah they were still more incensed, because, as they said, he had not solicited their aid. Jephthah, however, boldly attacked and defeated them, and when they fled he intercepted the fugitives at the Jordan, so that there perished in that disastrous quarrel, forty-two thousand men, Judg. xii, 1-6. At first the Ephraimites did not submit to the authority of David, 2 Sam. ii, 8-9; and, though, after the death of Ish-Bosheth, a large body of them went to Hebron to join David and that monarch could speak of Ephraim as the strength of his head, yet the jealousy against Judah sometimes broke out, 1 Chron xii, 30; Psa. lx, 7; 2 Sam. xix, 40-43. David had his ruler in Ephraim, 1 Cl ron. xxvii, 20; and Solomon his commissariat officer, 1 Kings iv, 8. Still, the spirit and weight of the tribe were so great that Rehoboam found it necessary to repair to Shechem, a city within its borders, for his inauguration, 1 Kings xii, 1. And then, on his foolish refusal of their demands, the ten tribes revolted, and established a different mode of worship, 1 Kings xii

VIEW OF THE THEATER AT EPHESUS, (FROM LABORDE.)

After this Ephraim was the main support of the northern kingdom, which came to be designated by its name, and the re-union of which with Judah was the hope of the prophets as the fulfillment of Israel's glory, Isa. vii, 2; xi, 13; Ezek. xxxvii, 15–22; Hos. iv, 17. After the captivity "children of Ephraim" dwelt in Jerusalem, 1 Chron. ix, 3; comp. Neh. xi.

E'phraim, GATE OF, one of the gates at Jerusalem, 2 Kings xiv, 13; 2 Chron. xxv, 23; Neh. viii, 16; xii, 39. Probably in the same direction with the present "Damascus Gate," (*Bab el-Amud.*) See Map 7.

E'phraim, MOUNT, the highland portion of the territory of Ephraim, extending from Bethel and Ramah on the south to the great plain on the north, Josh. xvii, 15; xix, 50; xx, 7; and various other references. Possibly this region included a part, and it may be even the whole of Benjamin. See EPHRAIM.

E'phraim, THE WOOD OF, a forest in which the great battle took place between the forces of Absalom and David, and in which Absalom was killed, 2 Sam. xviii, 6. It lay east of Jordan, not far from Mahanaim, and the name may either have some connection with Manasseh, or be an alteration of Ephron, a place somewhere in that neighborhood.

E'phraimite, Judg. xii, 5; and Ephramites, Josh. xvi, 10. Descendants of Ephraim.

E'phrain, (Hebrew, Ephron,) *the two fawns*, a town of Israel taken by Judah, 2 Chron. xiii, 19. Possibly it is the Ephraim of the New Testament, John xi, 54; or the Ophrah of Benjamin, or connected with Mount Ephron of Judah—but all is conjectural. See OPHRAH.

Eph'ratah, (by some Ephra'tah,) or Eph'rath, *land, region*, or perhaps *fruitful*. The first form occurs in Ruth iv, 11; Psa. cxxxii, 6; the other in Gen. xxxv, 16, 19; xlviii, 7. The original name of Bethlehem. Gesenius and others think the term as used in the Psalm above means Ephraim. If so, the reference may be to the abode of the ark in Shiloh in "Mount Ephraim."

Eph'rathites, 1. A native of Ephrath or Bethlehem, Ruth i, 2; 1 Sam. xvii, 12.

2. Perhaps an Ephraimite, though this is uncertain, 1 Sam. i, 1; 1 Kings xi, 26; also Judg. xii, 5, where "the Ephrathite" is rendered in the Authorized Version "an Ephraimite."

E'phron, a strongly fortified city east of Jordan, apparently between Carnaim and Beth-Shean, 1 Macc. v, 46; 2 Macc. xii, 27. Perhaps it may be connected with the "forest of Ephraim," in which Absalom lost his life. It is not yet identified.

E'phron, MOUNT, *fawn-like mount*, a range of hills on the northern boundary of Judah, between Nephtoah and Kirjath-Jearim, Josh. xv, 9. It is probably the range of hills west of *Wady Beit Hanina;* possibly connected with Ephrain, or the Ephraim of John xi, 54.

E'ranites, THE, Num. xxvi,36, (from Eran, *watchful*) a family of Ephraim, descended from Eran.

E'rech, *length*, one of Nimrod's cities, Gen. x, 10, in Southern Babylonia. In Ezra iv, 9, its people are called Archevites. Some identify Erech with Edessa or Callirhoë, (now *Urfah*,) a town in the north-west of Mesopotamia. The best authorities, however, make Erech the Orchoe of Ptolemy among the marshes formed by the canals of the Euphrates, corresponding with the modern *Warka*, which is eighty-two miles south, and forty-three east from Babylon on the Euphrates. Great numbers of tombs and coffins have been found here, and the place seems to have been the necropolis of the Assyrian kings. A vast mound called *el-Assagah*, (*the place of pebbles*,) or *Irka*, or *Irak*, covers the vicinity. There was another Erech, probably located in Palestine, near Bethel. See ARCHITE.

Esdrae'lon, (Map 5.) the Greek form of Jezreel, Judith iii, 9; iv, 6 (The Hebrew Jezreel being gradually corrupted into the Greek Εσδρηλων. It is also called Esdra-Elom, Judith vii, 3; and Esdre'lom, Judith i. 8, with the addition of "the great plain." In the Old Testament the plain is called the valley of Jezreel, Josh. xvii, 16; by Josephus "the Great Plain " Also in Zech. xii, 11, the valley of Megiddo. The name is derived from the old royal city of Jezreel, which occupied a commanding site near the eastern extremity of the plain, on a spur of Mount Gilboa.

The "great plain of Esdraelon" extends across central Palestine from the Mediterranean to the Jordan, separating the mountain ranges of Carmel and Samaria from those of Galilee. The western section of it is properly the plain of Accho, or Akka. The main body of the plain is a triangle. Its base on the east side extends from *Jenin* (the ancient En-Gannim) to the foot of the hills below Nazareth, and is about fifteen miles long; the north side, formed by the hills of Galilee, is about twelve miles long; and the south side, formed by the Samarian range, is about eighteen miles. The apex on the west is a narrow pass opening into the plain of Akka. This vast expanse has a gently undulating surface—in spring all green with corn where cultivated, and rank with weeds and grass where neglected—dotted with several low gray tells, and near the sides with a few olive groves. This is that *valley of Megiddo* (called from the city of Megiddo, which stood on its southern border,) where Barak triumphed, and where King Josiah was defeated and received his death wound, Judg. v; 2 Chron. xxxv. Probably, too, it was before the mind of the Apostle John when he figuratively described the final conflict between the hosts of good and evil who were gathered to a place called *Armageddon*, (that is, *the city of Megiddo*, Rev. xvi, 16.) The river *Kishon*, "that ancient river" so fatal to the army of Sisera, (Judg. v, 21,) drains the plain, and flows off through the pass westward to the Mediterranean.

From the base of this triangular plain three branches stretch out eastward like fingers from a hand, divided by two bleak, gray ridges—one bearing the familiar name of Mount Gilboa; the other called by Franks Little Hermon, but by natives *Jebel ed-Duhy*. The *northern* branch has Tabor on the one side, and Little Hermon on the other; into it the troops of Barak defiled from the heights of Tabor, Judg. iv, 6; and on its opposite side are the sites of Nain and Endor. The *southern* branch lies between *Jenin* and Gilboa, terminating in a point among the hills to the eastward; it was across it Ahaziah fled from Jehu, 2 Kings ix, 27. The *central* branch is the richest as well as the most celebrated; it descends in green, fertile slopes, to the banks of the Jordan, having Jezreel and Shunem on opposite sides at the western end, and Beth-Shean in its midst toward the east. This is the " valley of Jezreel" proper—the battle-field on which Gideon triumphed, and Saul and Jonathan were overthrown, Judg. vii, 1, etc.; 1 Sam. xxix and xxxi.

Esdraelon was the frontier of Zebulun, Deut. xxxiii, 18. But it was the special portion of Issachar, Gen. xlix, 15.

This plain is one of wonderful richness. Gigantic thistles, luxuriant grass, and the exuberance of the crops on the very few cultivated spots, show its great fertility. But yet it is a plain of desolation, with scarcely a village in it, swept over by the wild Arab tribes in search of plunder.

It has always been a place of insecurity. Chariots and cavalry, of little use in the hill-country, availed in the comparative level of Esdraelon; and Canaanites, Midianites, and Amalekites, those "children of the East," who were "as grasshoppers for multitude," whose "camels were without number," devoured its rich pastures, Judg. iv, 3, 7; vi, 1-6; vii, 1. The Philistines long held it, 1 Sam. xxix, 1; xxxi, 10; and the Syrians frequently swept over it with their armies, 1 Kings xx, 26; 2 Kings xiii, 17. For interesting notices of Issachar in this connection see Gen. xlix, 14, 15; Deut. xxxiii, 18; Judg. v. 15; 1 Chron. xii, 32, 40. The whole borders of this plain are dotted with places of high historic and sacred interest, among which are Nain, Endor, Bethshean, Gilboa, Jezreel, En-Gannim, Taanach, Megiddo, Nazareth, Tabor. It is now called *Merj ibn 'Amer*, "the plain of the son of Amer." See Smith, Herzog, Stanley; and Porter's *Handbook for Syria and Palestine;* and *Our Work in Palestine,* p. 197.

Es'ebon. Judith v, 13. See HESHBON.

E'sek, *strife,* a well dug by Isaac's herdmen in the valley of Gerar, Gen. xxvi, 20, for which the herdmen of Gerar "strove."

Esh'col, THE VALLEY OF, (Map 5,) *a cluster,* a valley of Canaan near Hebron, from which the spies brought a cluster of grapes so large that it was carried on a staff between two men, Num. xiii, 23, 24; xxxii, 9; Deut. i, 24. The name had existed in this neighborhood centuries before from the Amorite chief Eshcol, in Abraham's time.

North of Hebron is a spring of fine water called *Ain el-Khashkali,* which may, perhaps, represent the ancient Eshcol. The name is also written *Ain ei-Rashkala.* Palmer thinks Eshcol lay much further south than Hebron.

E'shean, or **Esh'ean,** *prop, support,* a place in the mountains of Judah, mentioned only in Josh. xv, 52. Van de Velde would locate the site at the ruins of *Khursa,* not far south-west of Hebron. This lacks confirmation.

Esh'kalonites, Josh. xiii, 3, natives of Ashkelon.

Esh'taol, perhaps *retreat, withdrawal,* a place in the low country of Judah, Josh. xv, 33; afterward asigned to Dan, Josh. xix, 41. Samson spent his boyhood in this neighborhood, and here first manifested his wonderful strength, and here too, between Zorah and Eshtaol, he was buried, Judg. xiii, 25; xvi, 31; xviii, 2, 8, 11, 12, (compare 1 Chron. ii, 53, and see DAN.) Several efforts toward identification have been made, but without complete satisfaction. Grove makes the most probable site, "perhaps *Kustul*, east of *Kuriet el-Enab,*" not far from Jerusalem. Mr. Porter thinks Eshtaol may possibly be identical with *Yeshua,* which lies at the eastern extremity of the broad valley which runs up among the hills between Zorah and Beth-Shemesh.

Esh'taulites, THE, 1 Chron. ii, 50. Inhabitants of Eshtaol.

Eshtemo'a, or **Eshtem'oa,** *obedience,* a city in the mountains of Judah, allotted to the priests, Josh. xxi, 14; called Eshtemoh, xv, 50. One of the haunts of David; and to the inhabitants of which he sent presents, 1 Sam. xxx, 28-31. See also 1 Chron. iv, 17, 19; vi, 57. It is probably the modern village of *Semu'a,* seven or eight miles south of Hebron, which contains ancient remains to a considerable extent.

Esh'temoh, Josh. xv, 50. Another form of Eshtemoa.

Esh'ton, *womanish, uxorious, careless,* possibly the name of a place in Judah, but generally considered the name of a person, 1 Chron iv, 11, 12.

Eso'ra, (Properly *Æsora,*) Judith iv, 4, a place fortified by the Jews on the approach of the army of Holofernes. "The Syriac reading suggests Beth-Horon, which is not impossible."—*Smith.*

Es'rom, Matt. i, 3; Luke iii, 33. The Greek form of Hezron.

E'tam, *place of ravenous beasts or birds.*

1. A place in Simeon, 1 Chron. iv, 32. Possibly the site may be marked by *Tell Khewelfeh.* See EN-HAKKORE

2. (Map 5,) a place in Judah, fortified and garrisoned by Rehoboam, 2 Chron xi, 6. It is possibly at or near *Urtas,* not far from Bethlehem. According to Josephus this city was fifty stadia from Jerusalem, and thither Solomon was in the habit of taking a morning drive.

E'tam, THE ROCK, a rock into a cleft of which Samson retired after his slaughter of the Philistines, Judg. xv, 8, 11. It was in Judah, and may probably be identical with *Beit 'Atab.*

E'tham, (Map 2,) *boundary of the sea.* The second station of the Israelites on leaving Egypt, "in the edge of the wilderness," Exod. xiii, 20; Num. xxxiii, 6, 7. Possibly it may be placed at *Seba Biár,* or *Seven Wells,* about three miles from the western side of the ancient head of the gulf. See SHUR.

E'ther, *abundance,* a town of Simeon in the low country of Judah, Josh. xv, 42; xix, 7. In 1 Chron. iv, 32, Tochen is substituted for Ether. It is conjecturally placed at *Beit-Auwa,* a ruined village in the vicinity of the associated localities, south of *Beit-Jibrin* and west of Hebron.

Ethio'pia, (Map 1,) region of *burned faces,* that is, dark-complexioned people. Ethiopia is the Greek name by which the Hebrew *Cush* is generally rendered. [See CUSH.] This country lay to the south of Egypt, and embraced, in its most extended sense, the modern *Nubia, Sennaar, Kordofan,* and northern *Abyssinia,* and, in its more definite sense, the kingdom of *Meroë,* from the junction of the Blue and White branches of the Nile to the border of Egypt. In the Bible, as in classical geography, but one limit of Ethiopia is laid down, its northern frontier, just beyond Syene, the most southern town of Egypt. In other directions the boundaries can only be generally described as the Red Sea on the east, the Libyan desert on the west, and the Abyssinian highlands on the south. See Gen. x, 6; ii, 13; 1 Chron. i, 9; 2 Chron. xxi, 16; Esther i, 1; Isa. xviii, 1; Ezek. xxix, 10; xxx, 5, 6. Anciently the extent assigned to Ethiopia may have been very great, as it was the land of the negroes, and therefore represented all that was known of inner Africa, besides that part of the continent south of Egypt which is washed by the Red Sea. The references in the Bible are, however, generally, if not always, to the territory which was at times under Egyptian rule, a tract watered by the Upper Nile, and extending from Egypt probably as far as a little above the confluence of the White and Blue Rivers.

Besides the above passages there are frequent Scripture references to Ethiopia: the complexion of its people, Jer. xiii, 23; and their warlike character, Jer. xlvi, 9. The merchandise of Ethiopia, Isa. xlv, 14; its precious stones, Job xxviii, 19. Here Moses found a wife, Num. xii, 1. From Ethiopia came part of Shishak's army, 2 Chron. xii, 3. Zerah, King of Ethiopia, was defeated by Asa, 2 Chron. xiv, 9–15; xvi, 8; and another of its kings, Tirhakah, attacked Assyria, 2 Kings xix, 9. The Ethiopian Ebed-Melech showed kindness to Jeremiah, Jer. xxxviii, 7–13; xxxix, 15–18

Some of the prophets mention Ethiopia in their predictions Psa. lxviii. 31; lxxxvii, 4· Isa. xx, 2-6; xlv, 14; Ezek. xxx, 4-9; Dan. xi, 43; Hab. iii, 7; Zeph. ii, 12; Nah. iii, 8-10.

Mention of Ethiopia is made also in the New Testament. There had been dynasties of native sovereigns, and some of these were females, with the official title of Candace. One of the eunuchs "of great authority under Candace, queen of the Ethiopians," was converted by the preaching of Philip, Acts viii, 27-39.

Eth'ma, 1 Esdras ix, 35; apparently a corruption of Nebo in the parallel list of Ezra x, 43.

Euphra'tes, (Map 1,) (Hebrew, *Frath*.) Rawlinson says this word "is probably of Aryan origin, the initial element being '*u*, which is in Sanscrit *su*, in Zend *hu*, and in Greek εὐ; and the second element being *fra*, the particle of abundance. The Euphrates is thus 'the good and abounding river.'" Probably the name was soon shortened to its *modern name* of *Frát*, which is almost exactly what the Hebrew literation expresses. Its most frequent name in Scripture is "the river," 1 Kings iv, 21; Ezra iv, 10, 16, *the* river of Asia in grand contrast to the short-lived torrents of Palestine.

This is the largest, longest, and by far the most important of the rivers of Western Asia. It has two principal sources in the Armenian mountains. The most northern branch, the *Frat*, or *Kara-su*, (Black River,) rises about twenty-five miles north-east of *Erzeroum;* the other, which is the chief, called *Murad-chai*, (River of Desire,) rises on the northern slope of *Ala-tagh*, not far from Ararat. They meet after a course of two hundred and seventy and four hundred miles respectively, at *Kebban Maden*, in 39° east long. The combined stream is here about one hundred and twenty yards wide; its course is at first nearly south; it then turns south-east, pursuing its long course to the sea. Joined by the Tigris at *Kurnah*, it is called *Shat el-Arab*, and ultimately falls into the Persian Gulf. Its entire length is about one thousand seven hundred and eighty miles, more than two-thirds of which are navigable for small steam-vessels. In the latter part of its course from *Hit*, the Euphrates flows through a low alluvial plain, where it often spreads and forms marshes; its width therefore varies, and is said to be greatest about seven hundred or eight hundred miles from its mouth.

Scripture allusions to the Euphrates are frequent. It is first mentioned, as the fourth river of Eden, in Gen. ii, 14. In the covenant with Abraham it is the boundary of Israel, by prophecy, Gen. xv. 18; Exod. xxiii, 31; and the prophecy was remembered at the settlement of Canaan, Deut. i, 7; xi. 24; Josh. i, 4. Reuben extended to the Euphrates anterior to Saul, 1 Chron. v, 9. The prophecy fulfilled to David, 2 Sam. viii, 3-8; 1 Chron. xviii, 3. To Solomon also, 1 Kings iv, 21, (compare 2 Chron. ix, 26.) Upon the disruption of the empire, under Rehoboam, this wide dominion was lost. Egypt's dominion, under Necho, extended to the Euphrates, 2 Chron. xxxv, 20; but this dominion was short-lived, Jer. xlvi, 2; 2 Kings xxiv, 7.

Jeremiah buried his girdle in this river, Jer. xiii, 1-7; and cast his book into it, li, 63, 64. Probably it is included in the reference in Psa. cxxxvii, 1 and Jer l, 38; li, 26. Referred to symbolically in Isa. viii, 7; Rev. ix, 14 xvi, 12.

The shores bordering its central course are uniform, and enriched with tamarinds and poplars; further down it is more fertile, with palm-groves and willows. Its depth, as its width, varies according to locality and season.

Here and there fords are met with; at other places it is crossed on rafts, or, more recently, by bridges, while lower down it is navigable for vessels.

E'zel, THE STONE OF, stone of *departure*, a stone in the neighborhood of Saul's residence, the scene of the parting of Jonathan and David, when the latter finally fled from the court, 1 Sam. xx, 19. It is possibly a corruption of some ancient name not recorded.

E'zem, *bone, strength*, a city of Simeon, 1 Chron. iv, 29; in Josh. xix, 3, called Azem.

E'zion-Ga'ber or Ge'ber, (Map 2,) *the giant's back-bone*, a city on the Red Sea. It was the last station named for the encampment of the Israelites before they came to "the wilderness of Zin, which is Kadesh," Num. xxxiii, 35; Deut. ii, 8; subsequently the station of Solomon's navy, 1 Kings ix, 26; 2 Chron. viii, 17; and of Jehoshaphat's navy, 1 Kings xxii, 48; but the latter ships were "broken, that they were not able to go to Tarshish." It is probably identified with *Ain el-Ghudyân*, about ten miles up what is now the dry bed of the *Arabah*, but (as Kiepert supposed) was then the northern end of the gulf, which may have anciently had, like that of Suez, a further extension.

Fair Ha'vens, (Map 8,) a harbor on the south side of the island of Crete. Recent researches have identified it, and thrown much light on the account of Paul's voyage. It has its old Greek name, *Kalous liniónas*, and is situated four or five miles to the east of Cape Matala, and about the same distance to the west of Cape Leonda. It is a fair winter harbor, but inferior to that of Phenice, about forty miles farther westward. After passing Cape Matala the coast trends to the north; hence the danger, if a northerly gale sprang up, of the vessel's being driven out to sea; and hence the advice given by Paul to lie still at Fair Havens, instead of making for Phenice, Acts xxvii, 8, 9, 10, 21.

Ford, *passage*. Fords of Jordan, Josh. ii, 7; Judg. iii, 28; xii, 5, 6; of Jabbok, Gen. xxxii, 22; of Arnon, Isa. xvi, 2; of the Euphrates, Jer. li, 32. As to the Jordan, anciently its fords were but few in number and well known, but now its fordable places are very numerous. See JORDAN.

Frank Mountain, (Map 6,) Herodium.

Fish Gate, Zech. xiv, 10, one of the gates of Jerusalem.

Fuller's Field, THE, a spot near Jerusalem, 2 Kings xviii, 17; Isa. xxxvi, 2; vii, 3; so close to the walls that a person speaking from there could be heard on them, 2 Kings xviii, 17, 26. It is only accidentally mentioned in these passages, as giving its name to a "highway," which was the "conduit of the upper pool." The "end" of the conduit, whatever that was, appears to have been close to the road, Isa. vii, 3. One resort of the fullers of Jerusalem would seem to have been below the city on the south-east side. [See EN-ROGEL.] The position of this "field" is not fully agreed upon among authorities. Porter says: "There can be little doubt that the 'upper pool' is the cistern now called *Birket el-Mamilla*, at the head of the valley of Hinnom, a short distance west of the Yafa Gate. Hezekiah conveyed the waters from it by a subterranean aqueduct to the west side of the city of David, 2 Chron. xxxii, 30. . . . The fuller's occupation required an abundant supply of water, and an open space for drying the cloths. We may therefore conclude that their 'field' was beside, or, at least, not far distant from, the 'upper pool.'" This seems to us the most probable locality. But see Kitto, and Smith, and Porter's *Handbook for Syria and Palestine*.

Ga'ash, *earthquake,* the name of a hill, a part of the Ephraim range, on the north side of which Joshua was buried, Josh. xxiv, 30; Judg. ii, 9. Mention is made of the brooks of Gaash, 2 Sam. xxiii, 30; 1 Chron. xi, 32. It is not identified.

Ga'ba, *hill,* a city of Benjamin, Josh. xviii, 24; Ezra ii, 26; Neh. vii, 30. The same as GEBA, which see.

Gab'batha, *platform* or *elevated place,* the *bema* or judgment-seat of Pilate, John xix, 13. It was outside of the judgment-hall, where the Jews remained during the Saviour's trial. The "pavement" was probably some mosaic or tessellated work, forming either the bema itself or the flooring of the court immediately round it.

Gab'des, 1 Esdras v, 20. A form of Gaba.

Gad, (Map 5,) The best authorities are divided as to the meaning of Gad. Some claim it to signify a *troop;* while others, (among whom is Gesenius,) make it *fortune,* or *good fortune.* The Septuagint has ἐν τύχῃ, *in fortune;* the Vulgate *feliciter,* (*in felicity,*) Gen. xxx, 11; xlvi, 16; xlix, 19. The tribe of Gad sprang from one of the sons of Jacob by Zilpah, Leah's maid, Gen. xxx, 10, 11. At the first census in the wilderness the descendants of Gad had multiplied to forty-five thousand six hundred and fifty, Num. i, 14, 24, 25. They were attached to the second division of the Israelitish host, following the standard of Reuben, and camping on the south of the tabernacle, their chief being Eliasaph, the son of Deuel, or Reuel, Num. i, 12; ii, 24, 25; iii, 10-16. At the second census, on the plains of Moab, the tribe numbered but forty thousand five hundred, Num. xxvi, 15-18. After the Israelites had subdued the country east of the Jordan, the tribes of Reuben and Gad desired to settle there. It was a land, they said, adapted for cattle, and they had "much cattle." Moses was at first displeased with the request, thinking it might discourage the rest of the people, and perhaps bring upon the nation a fresh judgment from the Lord. But on being assured that the tribes, if their wish were granted, would dispatch their able-bodied men to aid in the conquest of Canaan, Moses gave his consent, and distributed the territories of Og and Sihon among the Reubenites, the Gadites, and half-Manasseh, though the last-named people do not appear to have joined in the request when first made to Moses, Num. xxxii, 1-33. See REUBEN.

The precise limits of Gad are not exactly given. Their territory appears to have lain chiefly about the center of the land east of the Jordan. Reuben's possessions lay on the south. On the east the farthest landmark given is "Aroer, that faces Rabbah," the present Amman, Josh. xiii, 25. Thus the Arabian desert appears to have been the eastern boundary. West was the Jordan, Josh. xiii, 27. The northern boundary is more difficult. Gad possessed the whole Jordan valley as far as the Sea of Galilee, but among the mountains eastward the territory extended no farther north than the river Jabbok. The border seems to have run diagonally from that point across the mountains by Mahanaim, to the southern extremity of the Sea of Galilee, Josh. xii, 1-6; xiii, 26, 30, 31, Deut. iii, 12, 13. Heshbon, though sometimes reckoned to Reuben, (Josh. xiii, 17,) as being on the border of the two contiguous tribes, must really have belonged to Gad, Josh. xxi, 38, 39.

Moses' blessing on Gad is recorded in Deut. xxxiii, 20, 21. After their settlement, faithfully did the trans-Jordanic tribes perform their promise of aiding their brethren in the conquest of Canaan; and when they returned to their own cities with Joshua's blessing, enriched with large spoil. (Num xxxii, 16–32; Josh. i, 12–18; iv, 12, 13; xxii, 1–8;) they built an altar of witness called Ed, Josh. xxii, 10–34. Later, the seat of Ish-Bosheth's sovereignty was established in this territory, for Abner brought him to Mahanaim, and there he reigned, 2 Sam. ii, 8; and there he was assassinated. The Gadites, however, could not have been very enthusiastic in favor of the house of Saul; for many chiefs, bold, enterprising men, expressing very well the general characteristics of the tribe, had joined David while in hold, 1 Chron. xii, 8. And when, a few years later, David was obliged to flee across the Jordan on account of Absalom's rebellion, he found a secure position in Mahanaim, while the country round manifested their attachment to him, and supplied him with abundant stores, 2 Sam. xvii, 24, 27–29. Solomon had commissariat officers in Gad, 1 Kings iv, 13, 14, 19. In 1 Chron. v, the genealogies of the tribe are noted till the days of Jeroboam II., king of Israel, and Jotham King of Judah; and there is an account of a raid made by Reuben, Gad, and Manasseh, with a force of forty-four thousand seven hundred and sixty, upon the Hagarites of Jetur, Nephish, and Nodab, Ishmaelite clans, in which they took a vast deal of booty, and occupied the country they had invaded. In the division of the kingdom, Gad, of course, fell to the northern State, and many of the wars between Syria and Israel must have ravaged its territory, 2 Kings x, 33. Ramoth-Gilead is repeatedly mentioned as the center of engagements, 1 Kings xxii; 2 Kings viii, 28, 29; ix, 14. At last, for the sins of the people, Tiglath-Pileser carried the Gadites and the neighboring tribes away captive into Assyria, 2 Kings xvi, 29; 1 Chron. v, 26; and it is the mournful lament of Jeremiah that Ammon occupied the lost cities of Gad, Jer. xlix, 1.

Gad'ara. See GADARENES.

Gad'arenes'. The inhabitants of the city of Gad'ara. (See Maps 5, 21.) In Mark v, 1, and Luke viii, 26, the term employed is Γαδαρηνῶν, Gadarenes, while in Matt. viii, 28, the word is Γεργεσηνῶν, Gergesenes. The term Γερασηνῶν, Gerasenes, is found in some MSS. A noted miracle was wrought by Christ in their "country," and the Gadarenes asked him to depart. (See the three passages above cited.)

"In consequence of various readings it is uncertain whether it was near this city [Gadara] that the demoniacs were cured; the preponderance of the evidence, however, is in favor of the vicinity of Gadara."—*Herzog*. Porter, (in Kitto) in reference to MS. authorities for the text of Matthew's Gospel, says: "We must implicitly follow the most ancient and credible testimony, which clearly pronounces in favor of Γαδαρηνῶν. [Gadarenes.] This reading is adopted by Tischendorf, Alford, and Tregelles."

Gadara was a large and splendid city, and lay on a hill south of the river Hieromax, (*Yarmûk*,) about six miles south-east of the southern extremity of the Sea of Galilee, and about sixteen miles from Tiberias. Dr. Thomson objects that Gadara is too far from the lake, and thinks the miracle must have been performed at a place called *Kerza* or *Gersa*, which he supposes to be the ancient Gergesa. But it will be noticed that the Gospel narrative does not claim that the *city* of the Gadarenes was near the shore of the lake. Christ crossed the Sea of Galilee "to the *territory* of the Gadarenes," which extended down to the shore. In the time of Christ Gerasa was the capital of northern Peræa, and its province included that of Gadara. It is not stated where the swine were feeding, but the place was near the scene of the miracle, and most probably on the high point of land which separates the ravine of the Hieromax from the lake. From that point there is a long and "steep" descent to the shore, and down into this the swine may have rushed. The site of the city of Gadara is identified with the extensive and remarkable ruins of *Um Keis*, which occupy a circuit of about two miles. The inhabitants are still "dwelling in tombs." While not a house, column, nor wall remains, yet the old pavement of the streets is almost perfect, showing the marks of the chariot wheels in the stones. The tombs are excavated in the limestone rocks, and consist of chambers of various sizes, some above twenty feet square, with deep recesses in the side for bodies. See GERASA. GERGESA. See Kitto and Smith, and Porter's *Hand-book for Syria and Palestine; Our Work in Palestine*, pp. 194, 195.

Gad'ites, persons of the tribe of Gad, Deut. iii, 12, 16; iv, 43; xxix, 8; Josh. i, 12, etc.

Gal'aad, the Greek form of Gilead, 1 Macc. v, 9, 17, 20, 25, 27, 36, 45, 55; xiii, 22; Judith i, 8; xv, 5.

Gala'tia, (Map 8,) a country in Asia Minor. The name is derived from its inhabitants, who originally emigrated from Gallia. From Gallia these people first went into Greece, and after fierce contests with the Greeks, were forced to retire to the shores of the Hellespont. Finding a footing in Asia Minor, their country was called Galatia; and at length, because the prevailing language of the district was Greek, it was also termed Gallo-Græcia. It is not always easy to determine in what sense the word Galatia is used in the New Testament. Sometimes a geographical name is used in a general and popular sense as referring to a region inhabited by a race or tribe of people, and sometimes to define precisely some tract of country marked out for political purposes. Thus, Galatia is used by Luke in Acts xvi, 6, to denote the country inhabited or possessed by the Eastern Galli. In 1 Pet. i, 1, Galatia is mentioned among several Roman provinces; hence, we may conclude that the term is employed to indicate the later Roman province. This province was bounded, according to Ptolemy, on the west by Bithynia and Phrygia; on the south by Pamphylia; on the east by Cappadocia and Pontus; and on the north by the Euxine. The boundaries have not always remained the same; indeed, they were frequently changing. The three capitals were respectively Tavium, Pessinus, and Ancyra. The last of these (the modern *Angora*) was the center of the roads of the district, and may be regarded as the metropolis of the Galatians. These people were fierce, restless, and warlike. Impatient of restraint, they eagerly seized every opportunity to throw off the Roman yoke. They appear to have had little religion of their own, and they readily adopted the superstitions of the Phrygians and the mythology of the Greeks.

Paul introduced the Gospel into Galatia, visiting the "churches" on his second and third missionary tours, Acts xvi, 6; xviii, 23; Gal. i, 6; iv, 13; although his labors are not reported in Acts. The congregations, though chiefly composed of heathen, (Gal. iv, 8, etc.; v, 2; vi. 12,) are mentioned in 1 Cor. xvi, 1; 2 Tim. iv, 10; 1 Pet. i, 1. Disturbances caused by Judaizing teachers called forth Paul's Epistle to the Galatians, after he had failed, during his second visit, (Acts xviii, 2, 3; Gal. iv, 13, 16: i, 9,) fully to allay the strife. The epistle was addressed to the Churches in Galatia proper, not to those in the previously enlarged domains, Acts xiv, 6, 24; xv, 38; compare xvi, 6. See Conybeare and Howson's *Life and Epistles of St. Paul.*

Gala'tians, Gal. iii, 1. Inhabitants of Galatia. The word occurs in the

Ma⸺cabean history, 1 Macc. viii, 20. In the first of these places some suppose that the reference is to the Gauls; but the defeat of the Galatians by the Roman Consul Vulso, 189 B. C., is more likely intended.

Gal'eed, (Map 5,) *heap of witness*, the name given by Jacob to the heap of stones on Mount Gilead, raised as a memorial of the covenant made between Jacob and Laban, Gen. xxxi, 47, 48; compare 23, 25. See GILEAD; JEGAR-SAHADUTHA.

Gal'gala, the Greek form of Gilgal, 1 Macc. ix, 2.

Galile'ans, inhabitants of Galilee. They were partly heathen. This mixture seems to have had a modifying influence upon their religious views, so as to render them more susceptible to the truths proclaimed by Christ, than the more bigoted Israelites of Judea. Josephus describes them as an industrious, spirited, brave people. Though adhering firmly to Judaism, they were less prejudiced than their brethren in Judea, and persevering in whatever they embraced; hence, they were readily incited to insurrections, Acts v, 37; compare Luke xiii, 1. The other Jews despised the Galileans, partly because they were thought not to be Jews of pure blood, partly because they were suspected of holding erroneous doctrines, and partly for their broad dialect, John vii, 52; Acts ii, 7; Matt. xxvi, 73; Mark xiv, 70; Luke xxii 59. It is probable that the contempt in which they were held led the Saviour to regard them with compassion, and to prefer them as the foundation of his kingdom, John ii, 24, 25; Matt. xi, 25, etc. See GALILEE.

Gal'ilee, (Map 5,) *a circle, circuit*. A name given in the Old Testament to a small "circuit" among the mountains of Naphtali, and in the New Testament to a large province embracing the whole of northern Palestine. It is first mentioned by Joshua, Josh. xx, 7. Its limited extent is indicated in 2 Kings xv, 29, where, in detailing the conquests of Tiglath-Pileser, the historian states that "he took Ijon, and Abel-Beth-Maachah, and Janoah, and Kedesh, and Hazor, and Gilead, and *Galilee, all the land of Naphtali.*" Hence, Galilee did not extend beyond the bounds of Naphtali; and a comparison with other passages shows that it embraced only the northern section of that tribe, or, at least, that the name was at first confined to that district, Josh. xx, 7; xxi, 32. The region thus lay on the summit of a broad mountain ridge. At the time that Solomon offered the towns of Galilee to King Hiram, [see CABUL—and compare 1 Kings ix, 11, and 2 Chron. viii, 2,] Galilee, though within the allotted territory of Naphtali, does not appear to have been occupied by the Israelites. It was only after Hiram had declined the towns that Solomon rebuilt and colonized them, (2 Chron. viii, 2, etc.) In Isaiah's time it was still called "Galilee of the Gentiles," Isa. ix, 1. In 1 Macc. v, 21-23, "Galilee of the Gentiles" is said to have had a large heathen population.

In the time of Christ Palestine was divided into three provinces, Judea, Samaria, and Galilee. Josephus divides Galilee into *Upper* and *Lower*, "which are environed by Phœnicia and Syria."

The province of Galilee is about fifty miles long by twenty-five wide. Lower Galilee included the great plain of Esdraelon, with its offshoots, which run down to the Jordan and the Lake of Tiberias, and the whole of the hill country adjoining it on the north to the foot of the mountain-range. On the extreme south it extended as far as the village of Ginea, (modern *Jenin*,) and as both Asbela and Jotopata were in Lower Galilee, we conclude that this lower division included the whole region extending from the plain of

THE SEA OF GALILEE.

BIBLE GEOGRAPHY. 141

Akka in the west, to the shores of the lake on the east. This was one of the richest and most beautiful sections of Palestine.
Upper Galilee embraced the whole mountain range lying between the Upper Jordan and Phœnicia. Its southern border ran along the foot of the *Safed* range, from the north-west angle of the Sea of Galilee to the plain of *Akka*. This was the "Galilee of the Gentiles" above alluded to. For the character of the people (which throws much light on Christ's work in this country) see GALILEANS.
There are many Scripture references to Galilee. To the Bible student the towns, the country, the Sea of Galilee, are full of interest. (See SEA OF GALILEE.) The chief allusions to Galilee: Herod tetrarch of, Luke iii, 1; Mark vi, 21; Luke xxiii, 6, 7. Christ resided in, Matt. xvii, 22; xix, 1; John vii, 1, 9. Christ's teaching and miracles, Matt. iv, 23, 25; xv, 29-31; Mark i, 14, 28, 39; iii, 7; Luke iv, 14, 44; v, 17; xxiii, 5; John i, 43; iv, 3, 43-45; Acts x, 37. The disciples chiefly from Galilee, Acts i, 11; ii, 7. Women from, ministered to Christ, Matt. xxvii, 55, 56; Mark xv, 41; Luke xxii, 49, 55. Christ appeared to his disciples in Galilee after his resurrection, Matt. xxvi, 32; xxviii, 7, 10, 16, 17; Mark xiv, 28; xvi, 7; John xxi. Churches in, Acts ix, 31. Dialect of, Mark xiv, 70.
The first three Gospels are chiefly taken up with Christ's works in Galilee, while John dwells more upon those in Judea. The vineyard, the fig-tree, the shepherd, the desert, in the parable of the Good Samaritan, were all appropriate in Judea; while the corn-fields, the fisheries, the merchants and flowers, (all referred to in above passages,) were equally appropriate in Galilee. Galilee was very populous; Josephus, who knew the province so well, speaks of "two hundred and four towns and villages, the smallest of them containing above fifteen thousand inhabitants." The population of this whole district, it is thought, must have been at least three millions. There was doubtless more life and bustle in Galilee than in Judea, and hence it was a more hopeful field for the labors of Jesus, who spent so great a part of his ministry there. See Dr. Hanna's *Life of our Lord*.
After the destruction of Jerusalem Galilee became the chief seat of Jewish schools of learning, and the residence of their most celebrated Rabbins. Remains of splendid synagogues still exist in many of the old towns and villages, showing that from the second to the seventh century the Jews were as prosperous as they were numerous. See Porter's *Hand-book*.
Gal'ilee, SEA OF, (Maps 5, 21.) NAMES. The Hebrew word *Galil*, which is the origin of the later "Galilee," signifies a *circuit* or *circle*. This body of water is known by several other names: "Sea of Tiberias," John vi, 1; xxi, 1, from the celebrated city on its shores of that name; "Sea" or "Lake of Gennesareth," or "Gennesaret," Luke v, 1; (in 1 Macc. xi, 67, the "Water of Gennesar,") from the beautiful and fertile plain of Gennesaret, adjoining the lake. In Matt. iv, 15, emphatically "The Sea." In the Old Testament the "Sea of Chinnereth," Num. xxxiv, 11; Deut. iii, 17; or "Cinneroth," Josh. xii, 3, from a town of that name which stood on or near its shore, Josh. xix, 35.
SITUATION. This lake, or sea, lies in the northern part of Palestine, in the province of Galilee. In shape it is oval, being about fourteen miles long and seven miles wide in the widest part. The river Jordan enters it at its northern end, and passes out at its southern end, the bed of the lake being simply a lower section of the great Jordan valley. Its level is six

hundred and fifty-three feet below the level of the Mediterranean. It occupies the bottom of a great volcanic basin. The banks on the east are nearly two thousand feet high, deeply furrowed by ravines, but quite flat along the summit, forming, in fact, the supporting wall of the table-land of Bashan. On the north from this table-land the descent is gradual down to the valley of the Jordan, and then a gradual rise to a plateau of nearly equal elevation, skirting the mountains of Upper Galilee. On the west the banks are less regular, but present the same general features, plateaus of different altitudes breaking down abruptly to the shore.

BIBLE ALLUSIONS. In Num. xxxiv, 11, in describing the borders of Israel, "the border shall descend, and reach unto the side of the Sea of Chinnereth eastward;" in Deut. iii, 17, "from Chinnereth even unto the Sea of the Plain, even the Salt Sea." In describing the bounds of God's inheritance, "even unto the edge of the Sea of Chinnereth," Josh. xiii, 27. Reference to Sihon's territory, Josh. xii, 3. The place where "Jonathan and his host" pitched, 1 Macc. xi, 67. In the Old Testament the allusions are but few, and only incidental. Those of the New Testament are many, and in connection with important events.

BIBLE EVENTS. Our blessed Lord spent the most of his public life near the Sea of Galilee. "His own city" stood on its shores, Matt. iv, 13; here he called his first disciples, Luke v, 1-11; Matt. iv, 18-22; Mark i, 16-20. From a ship on its waters he "spoke many things" in parables to the multitude, Matt. xiii, 1-3. Mighty miracles were wrought here, Matt. viii, 24-32; xiv, 22-33; xvii, 27; Mark vii, 31-35; John xxi, 6. One of the most touching incidents of Gospel history, recorded in John xxi, 9-25, occurred on the shores of the Sea of Tiberias soon after Christ's resurrection. Not less than nine cities stood on the borders of this lake, most of which are intimately related to the works of Jesus as he went to and fro from one side to the other. Chief among these were Capernaum, Chorazin, Tiberias, Magdala, and the two Bethsaidas. The deep interest of the Christian in this place is beautifully expressed in a poem by M'Cheyne. We give a few stanzas:

> "How pleasant to me thy deep blue wave,
>   O Sea of Galilee!
> For the Glorious One who came to save
>   Hath often stood by thee.

> "Fair are the lakes in the land I love,
>   Where pine and heather grow;
> But thou hast loveliness above
>   What nature can bestow.

> * * * * *

> "Graceful around thee the mountains meet,
>   Thou calm reposing sea;
> But ah, far more! the beautiful feet
>   Of Jesus walked o'er thee.

> "Those days are past—Bethsaida where?
>   Chorasin, where art thou?
> His tent the wild Arab pitches there,
>   The wild reeds shade thy brow.

> * * * * *

> "O Saviour, gone to God's right hand,
>   Yet the same Saviour still,
> Graved on thy heart is this lovely strand,
>   And every fragrant hill."

BIBLE GEOGRAPHY. 143

PRESENT CONDITION, etc. The modern name is *Bahr Tubariyeh*. Although the Jordan rushes into its northern end, a turbid, muddy torrent, and many warm and brackish springs flow into it, nevertheless the water of the lake is sweet, cool, and transparent, and has a beautiful sparkling look on the beach, which is every-where pebbly. It still abounds in fish, as anciently. Often, as with mountain lakes generally, it is suddenly and violently agitated by winds, Matt. viii, 22-27. The scenery around is destitute of grandeur, beauty, and variety. The shores are singularly uniform, having neither bold cliffs juttting outward, nor bays winding inward. During the summer months the heat is intense. There is no frost, and snow rarely falls. The fishing is greatly neglected, yet the privilege of fishing is considerable sum for the privilege of fishing. In 1858 "the Sea of Galilee could just boast of one small boat," and that was rotten and leaky. All around the sea silence and desolation reign. A recent traveler says: "It seems as if all nature had gone to rest, languishing under that scorching heat. How different it was in the days of our Lord! . . . The cities are in ruins. . . . Tiberias and Magdala are the only inhabited spots. . . . The few inhabitants that remain in the shattered houses of Tiberias and the mud hovels of Magdala, and the black tents of the wandering Bedouin, seem worn and wasted by poverty and sickness."

Gal'lim, *heaps*, or, perhaps, *fountains*. A little village, the native place of Phalti, to whom David's wife, Michal, had been given, 1 Sam. xxv. 44. From Isa. x, 30, we may infer that it was in Benjamin, north of Jerusalem. Porter says it must have been situated on the brow of one of those rocky glens which run down into the wilderness east of Gibeah and north of Anathoth. But it has not been identified.

Ga'reb, THE HILL, a hill near Jerusalem, Jer. xxxi, 39. The signification is *scabby*, from the root meaning *to scratch*. Hence some have supposed this hill to be the place to which *lepers* were sent out of the city. Dr. Barclay makes it "the ridge running from the north-west corner of the city in the direction of Wely Kamat."

Gar'izim, the Greek form of Gerizim, 2 Macc. v, 23 ; vi, 2.

Ga'tam. Gesenius gives the meaning, *one puny* or *thin ;* Fürst translates it *burnt* or *parched vale*. The name of an Edomite tribe descended from one of Esau's sons, Gen. xxxvi, 11, 16 ; 1 Chron. i, 36. Their locality is not known.

Gath, (Map 5,) a *wine-press*, one of the five chief cities of the Philistines, Josh. xiii, 3 ; 1 Sam. vi, 17 ; Amos vi, 2 ; Micah i, 10. Its site has been a subject of much dispute among geographers. Mr. Porter says that one object of his visit to Philistia was to identify, if possible, the site of this ancient city. He concluded that Gath stood upon the hill called by the Crusaders *Alba Specula*, and now *Tell es-Safieh*. It is about seven miles from Bethshemesh, eight from Shochoh, toward Ekron, and six north of Eleutheropolis. The site is a most commanding one, and would form when fortified the key of Philistia. It is close to the mountains of Judah. Most of the best authorities are inclined to agree with Mr. Porter, (see Grove's *Index*, and Herzog ;) but Thomson seeks to show that Gath was the ancient name of Eleutheropolis. The Anakim were ancient inhabitants of Gath, Josh. xi, 22. Goliath and his sons dwelt there, 1 Sam. xvii, 4 ; 1 Chron. xx, 5-8. Thither the ark was taken, 1 Sam. v, 8.

David took refuge there with Achish, the king, 1 Sam. xxi, 10-15 ; xvii,

2-7. A band of Gittites, under Ittai, joined David here, 2 Sam. xv, 18-22; xviii, 2. Taken by David, 1 Chron. xviii, 1. Shimei brought his servants from, 1 Kings ii, 39-41. Fortified by Rehoboam, 2 Chron. xi, 8. Taken by Hazael, 2 Kings xii, 17. Recovered by Jehoash, 2 Kings xiii, 25. Besieged by Uzziah, 2 Chron. xxvi, 6.

The hill or Tell upon which Mr. Porter claims to have found Gath is about two hundred feet high, with steep sides, now in part terraced for vineyards. On the summit are the foundations of an old castle, probably that built, or rebuilt, by the Crusaders; and all round the hill are great quantities of old building stones. On the north-east is a projecting shoulder, and the declivities below it appear to have been scarped. Here stands the modern village. Its houses are all composed of ancient materials, and around are ruins and fragments of columns. Many cisterns are found in the sides of the hill, excavated in the limestone rock. See Porter's *Hand-book*.

Gath-He′pher, *the wine-press of the well,* (in Josh. xix, 13, called Gittah-Hepher,) a town on the border of Zebulun, celebrated as the native place of the Prophet Jonah, 2 Kings xiv, 25. About two miles east of *Sefûrieh,* (Sepphoris, Map 20,) on the top of a rocky hill, now stands the little village of *el-Meshhad,* in which is a tomb which tradition declares to be the *tomb of Jonah.* This village, very probably, marks the site of Gath-Hepher.

Gath-Rim′mon, *wine-press of the pomegranate.* 1. A city of Dan given to the Levites, Josh. xxi, 24; 1 Chron. vi, 69; situated on the plain of Philistia, apparently not far from Joppa, Josh. xix, 45. On Kiepert's map it is placed a short distance south-east from Ekron; but the site has not been identified.

2. A town of the half-tribe of Manasseh, west of the Jordan, assigned to the Levites, Josh. xxi, 25. In the parallel passage in 1 Chron. vi, 70, this place is called BILEAM, which see.

Gauloni′tis. See GOLAN.

Ga′za, (Hebrew, *Azzah,*) (Map 5,) the *strong,* the capital and stronghold of the Philistines, and among the most ancient cities of Palestine, Josh. xiii, 3; Jer. xxv, 20; Gen. x, 19; and one of the oldest in the world. It is on the southern frontier of Palestine, in a sandy plain three miles from the sea. Gaza was an important city before the time of Abraham, Gen. x. It was inhabited by the Avims, Deut. ii, 23; and the Anakims, Josh. xi, 22. Gaza fell to the lot of Judah, Josh. xv, 47; and was taken by him, Judges i, 18; but its inhabitants were not exterminated, Judges iii, 3.

For the interesting and remarkable narrative concerning Samson, his feats of strength, his imprisonment, and his destruction of himself and the people of Gaza, see Judges xvi. Gaza was possessed by Solomon, 1 Kings iv, 24. Taken by Pharaoh, Jer. xlvii, 1, 5. Prophecies against it, Amos i, 6, 7; Zeph. ii, 4; Zech. ix, 5; Jer. xlvii, 5.

The passage in Acts viii, 26, probably refers to *the road* on which Philip should find the eunuch. Several roads led to Gaza. The angel directs Philip to take the way "which is desert," that is, having no towns, uninhabited. Dr. Robinson found "*water*" on the most "southern" road to Gaza, in the midst of the country now without any fixed habitations.

The time of the conquest of Gaza by the Philistines is not known, but it must have been long before the time of Abraham. The terrible prophecies against this city have been remarkably fulfilled. Pharaoh-Necho smote it; Alexander the Great took it after a five-months' siege. It still continued, however, a strong city, and is frequently mentioned in the Maccabean wars, 1 Macc. xi, 61; xiii, 43. It was destroyed by Alexander Jannæus, 96 B. C.; but it was shortly rebuilt. It was given by Augustus to Herod, and after his death included in the province of Syria. About A. D. 65 Gaza was laid in ruins by the Jews, in revenge for the massacre of their brethren in Cæsarea. Recovering soon again, it was one of the chief cities of Syria during the reigns of Titus and Adrian.

This city long remained a stronghold of idolatry, although Christianity was there early introduced. In the beginning of the fifth century its bishop received authority to demolish its temples and build a large Christian Church. In A. D. 634 Gaza was taken by the Moslems, and its splendid church turned into a mosque. From this period it gradually declined, and the Crusaders found it deserted. They built a castle on the hill, which became the nucleus of a new town. The hill seems to be composed in a great measure of rubbish, the *debris* of ancient structures, among which are found broken arches, pieces of walls, and heavy masses of masonry.

The modern name of the place is *Ghuzzeh*. It contains about fifteen thousand inhabitants, of whom two hundred to three hundred are Christians and the rest Mohammedans. The town has no gates, no fortifications, no defenses of any kind. Tradition still points out the position of one of the ancient gates whose doors, posts, and bars Samson carried off.

Gaza'ra, or **Gaz'ara,** 1 Macc. ix, 52; xiii, 53; xiv, 7, 34; xv, 28. Elsewhere Gazera, or both probably identical with Gazer or Gezer.

Ga'zathites, Josh. xiii, 3. Natives of Gaza.

Ga'zer, 2 Sam. v, 25; 1 Chron. xiv, 16. The same as Gezer.

Gaze'ra, 1 Macc. iv, 15; vii, 45. Elsewhere Gazara. See GEZER.

Gaz'ites, or **Ga'zites,** Judges xvi, 2. Natives of Gaza.

Ge'ba, (Map 6,) *hill.* 1. A city of Benjamin (also called Gaba) given to the priests, Josh. xviii, 24; xxi, 17; 1 Chron. vi, 60. It was held for a time by the Philistines; but Jonathan, the son of Saul, took it, and the Philistines soon afterward assembled in great force at Michmash, 1 Sam. xiii, 3, 16. The Israelites, under Saul, took up a strong position at Geba. The two armies were separated by the deep ravine called the "passage of Michmash." A singular contest ensued, and the Philistines fled in confusion, and were driven from the mountains, 1 Sam. xiii, 17; xiv, 5-23. (In the fifth verse, just referred to, the A. V. has Gibeah, but the original is Geba.) Geba was fortified by Asa, 2 Kings xxiii, 8; 1 Kings xv, 22. It is referred to by Isaiah in describing Sennacherib's march to Jerusalem, Isa. x. The place was occupied by Benjamites after the captivity, Ezra ii, 26.

Geba is identified with the modern small village of *Jeba*, which is found on the top of a rocky ridge about six miles north of Jerusalem, and a mile south of Michmash. The latter occupies another ridge, and the wild glen of *Suweinit* separates it from Jeba. Most of the houses of Jeba are half ruinous. A few remains of antiquity can be traced in the large hewn stones that appear in the foundations and walls of the modern houses. See GIBEAH.

2. Judith iii, 10. Probably the site is marked by modern *Jeba,* a large village, with evident traces of antiquity, on the brow of the hill, three or four miles north-east of the city of Samaria, (*Sebastiyeh.*)

Ge'bal, *mountain.* 1. A name occurring in Psalm lxxxiii, 7, as confederate with many enemies of Israel. It is generally supposed to indicate the mountainous tract extending from the Dead Sea southward to Petra, still named *Jebâl*. But some of the best writers identify it with No. 2, as mentioned in conjunction with Tyre. The confederacy referred to was probably that against Jehoshaphat, 2 Chron. xx, 1, 2. The psalm might have been composed on that occasion: it is ascribed to Asaph; and one of the family of Asaph was inspired to encourage the Jewish king with the assurance of victory, (14–17.)

2. A place spoken of in connection with Tyre, Ezek. xxvii, 9. Most probably the residence of the Giblites, and therefore to the north of Palestine, Josh. xiii, 5. The Giblites were employed by Hiram, king of Tyre, in preparing materials for Solomon's Temple, 1 Kings v, 18, margin.

The Greek name of this place was Byblus. The town is now called *Jebeil*, and has a population of about six hundred. It is about seventeen miles north of Beyroot. The ancient ruins are very extensive. Immense numbers of granite columns are strewn about in the village and over the surrounding fields. These columns are mostly small, varying from one foot to two feet in diameter. Some of the stones measure nearly twenty feet in length. The citadel is the most remarkable ruin. The port is nearly choked up with sand and ruins.

Ge'bim, *the ditches,* or *wells,* a place in the neighborhood of Jerusalem, mentioned only in Isa. x, 31. It is supposed to have been between Arathoth and Nob.

Ge'der, *a wall,* a city of Palestine whose king was one of those overcome by Joshua, Josh. xii, 13. It may be identical with GEDOR No. 2, which see.

Gede'rah, *the sheep-cot,* a town in the low country of Judah, Josh. xv, 36; 1 Chron. xii, 4. Probably it was between Diospolis (Lydda) and Eleutheropolis, but there is no identification. Grove says it is possibly now *Kutiah,* a place found on Murray's *Hand-book* map, not far from Ekron.

Gede'roth, *sheep-folds,* a city in the plain country of Judah, Josh. xv, 41, and one of those which the Philistines took from King Ahaz, 2 Chron. xxviii, 18. Possibly the site may be marked by the modern *Beit-Tima,* shown on Van de Velde's map as six miles east of Askelon.

Gederotha'im, *two sheep-folds,* a town in the low land of Judah, Josh xv, 36, named next in order to Gederah. Not known.

Ge'dor, *wall,* 1. A town in the mountains of Judah, Josh. xv, 58, grouped with Halhul and Bethzur. Probably *Jedûr,* on the crest of a high ridge, eight miles north of Hebron, and about two west of the road leading to Jerusalem, may mark the site.

2. A town, apparently in Benjamin, to which belonged "Jeroham of Gedor," whose sons joined David, 1 Chron. xii, 7. It was probably the same as the Geder of Josh. xii, 13. The site is not known.

3. A place in the south of Judah, 1 Chron. iv, 39. It may have been in the direction of Mount Seir. But some read Gerar, as the Septuagint (both MSS.) has Gerar for Gedor.

Gehen'na. See HINNOM, VALLEY OF.

Gel'iloth, *circles, circuits,* or *borders.* A place mentioned in describing the boundary of Benjamin, Josh. xviii, 17. But when the same frontier is elsewhere described we find Gilgal, xv, 7. Geliloth was therefore either another name for Gilgal, or it appears by a transcriber's error.

Genne'sar, THE WATER OF, 1 Macc. xi, 67. See GALILEE, SEA OF.

Genes'areth, or **Gennes'aret,** SEA OF, Mark vi, 53; Luke v, 1. See GALILEE, SEA OF.

BIBLE GEOGRAPHY.

Gennes'aret, or **Genes'areth, LAND OF,** Matt. xiv, 34; Mark vi, 54. Concerning the meaning of the name, the two conjectures most commonly received are, 1. *Valley of flowers;* 2. (and perhaps, with more probability,) *The gardens of the prince.* This "land" was a small district of Galilee lying on the western shore of the lake, near Capernaum, John vi, 15-25; Mark vi, 45-56; Matt. xiv, 34. Mr. Porter says it is a green crescent-shaped plain extending along the shore for three miles, its greatest breadth being about one mile. It is now called *el Ghuweir,* "the Little Ghôr." The soil is extremely fertile, but only small patches are cultivated.

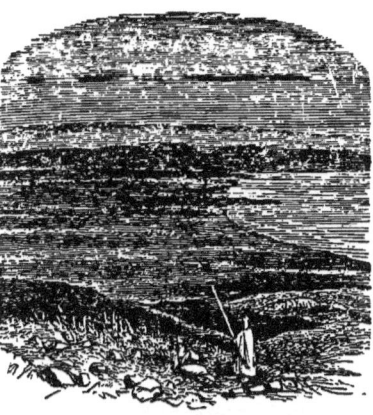

THE LAND OF GENNESARET.

The melons and cucumbers grown here are still the best and earliest in Palestine, and are always first in the markets of Damascus, Acre, and Beyroot.

Ge'on, the Greek form of Gihon, the river, Ecclesiasticus. xxiv, 27.

Ge'rar, (Map 5,) *a lodging-place,* or *region,* or perhaps *water-pots;* a city and district on the southernmost borders of Palestine, in the country of the Philistines, and not far from Gaza, Gen. x, 19. It was visited by Abraham after the destruction of Sodom, Gen. xx, 1, and by Isaac when there was a dearth in the rest of Canaan, Gen. xxvi, 1. It was here that these two patriarchs both committed the sin of falsehood. The Valley of Gerar is mentioned in Gen. xxvi, 17. Gerar was the seat of the first Philistine kingdom that we read of, and gave name to it. It was still an important place in later times, 2 Chron. xiv, 13, 14.

Eusebius and Jerome place Gerar twenty-five Roman miles southward from Eleutheropolis. Dr. Robinson was unable to find any traces of it. The Valley of Gerar has been thought to be the modern *Wady es-Sheriah.* Mr. Wilton, however, believes this valley, to which Isaac retired at the suggestion of Abimelech, to be the *Wady el-Jerûr,* much more to the south. Porter (*Hand-book,* 1868, p. 250) says of Gerar: "It appears that the site of this ancient city has been found, but unfortunately its discoverer has given a very meager account of it. It lies in a shallow wady three hours south-southeast of Gaza, and is called *Khirbet el-Gerar,* 'the ruins of Gerar.' At the spot are 'traces of an ancient city.' This is all the information given by the Rev. J. Rowlands, who, so far as I know, is the only person who has yet visited it."

Ger'asa, (Map 20,) the name of a city (which does not occur in the Bible) in the Decapolis. It formed the eastern boundary of Perea. The ruins of Gerasa are the most extensive and beautiful east of the Jordan. Three gateways still stand, and within the city upward of two hundred and thirty columns remain on their pedestals. Its main street, once lined with colonnades, is still magnificent in decay. Here are found also extensive ruins of the forum, temples, theater, and baths. The present name is *Jerash.* See **GADARENES.**

Ger'gesa, (Map 21.) Origen says a city called Gergesa anciently stood on the eastern shore of the Sea of Galilee, and that beside it was shown the precipice down which the swine rushed. Mr. Porter thinks this "looks like a bold hypothesis to get over a difficulty." Gergesa, however, is also mentioned by Eusebius and Jerome. Clark's *Bible Atlas* (1868) puts it down, as located in our Maps 5 and 21, on the *Wady Semakh;* and Clark says: "But the surveyors of the recent exploring expedition have visited the ruins of a place previously noticed by Thomson, between that spot and the wady which is immediately opposite Tiberias, (W. Fik,) now called *Khersa,* or *Gersa,* and it is most likely that this is the true Gergesa. In Matt. viii, 28, the healing of the two demoniacs is said to have taken place in the country of the Gergesenes, or, according to some MSS., Gerasenes."

The Report of the expedition just referred to claims that this *Khersa* is the most suitable spot for the scene of the miracle, because " at this particular point, and only at this, a spur runs out to the shore." Macgregor, in " Rob Roy," speaking of the miracle as occurring at one of the " several steeps" near the sea at *Khersa,* says: "The place which I regard as most likely for the site of the event is at the end of the short plain under some rocks, and near the green *plateau,* where the swine could feed. Here, for a full half-mile, the beach is of a form different from any other round the lake, and from any other I have noticed in any lake or sea before. It is flat until close to the edge. There, a hedge of oleanders fringes the end of the plain, and immediately below these is a gravel beach, inclined so steep that when my boat was at the shore I could not see over the top even by standing up; while the water alongside is so deep that it covered my paddle (seven feet long) when dipped in vertically a few feet from the shore."

Concerning Gadara, Gerasa, Gergesa, and Gersa, and the "various readings," very much difficulty exists in reference to the place where the demoniacs were healed, and where the swine rushed into the sea. The best and latest authorities differ. See GADARENES, where very high authorities claim GADARA as the city within whose *territory* the miracle was wrought.

Gergese'nes, or **Ger'gesenes,** Matt. viii, 28. See GADARENES.

Ger'gesites, Judith v, 16. The Greek form of Girgashites.

Ger'izim, MOUNT, (Map 5,) that is, mountain of *the Gerizzites,* dwellers in a *shorn* (desert) land. See GERZITES.

A mountain of Ephraim opposite to Mount Ebal, in close proximity to Shechem. It became very important in the history of Israel, because from it the blessing was pronounced upon the people after the entrance into the promised land, Deut. xi, 29; xxvii, 1-13; while from the opposite mountain, Ebal, the curse was thundered against all transgressors, Josh. viii, 30-34. At Ebal a copy of the law, engraved on limestone tables, was erected in the valley, and an altar raised to commemorate the renewal of the covenant between Jehovah and Israel, and to receive the first thank-offering for the occupation of the land of promise. The priests stood at the altar with their faces toward the East; on the left of these, at Ebal, six of the tribes; on the right, at Gerizim, the other six, and these evidently the most important and favored; these last, as standing on the favored *right* side of the altar, responded to the blessings spoken from the altar with amen, while the first six tribes answered and affirmed the curses. That a greater holiness did not at this time already attach to Gerizim above Ebal is evident from this, that the altar was erected at Ebal and not at Gerizim, Deut. xxvii, 4;

and the curse was not pronounced upon the mountain, nor upon those standing upon it, but upon transgressors of the law. In Judg. ix, 7-21, we have the noted parable which Jotham addressed to the men of Shechem from "the top of Mount Gerizim."

After the exile the Samaritans obtained leave from Darius Nothus to erect a temple on Gerizim, and here they worshiped till the temple was destroyed by Hyrcanus. Still, however, they had here an altar, and cherished a determined hatred against the Jews, John iv, 20, 21. At the present day the few remnants of this people still living at Nablûs visit the holy mountain at the four yearly festivals, when not prevented by Turkish fanaticism.

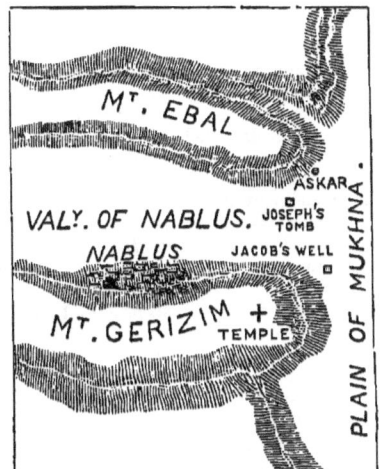

The valley between Ebal and Gerizim is very narrow, being but from two hundred to three hundred paces wide, with a length of about three miles. Ebal rises on the right, and Gerizim on the left hand of the valley, as a person approaches Shechem from Jerusalem. Several modern travelers have by experiment established the fact that it was very easy for the tribes to hear each other pronounce the blessings and the curses.

Very extensive ruins remain on Gerizim. There is a large stone structure which M. De Saulcy and others suppose to be the remains of the Samaritan temple. Dr. Robinson and others equally eminent suppose it to be the ruins of the fortress of Justinian, but in either case occupying the site of the ancient temple. The prospect from this site is not surpassed by any in Palestine both for vastness and variety. Gerizim is still to the Samaritans what Jerusalem is to the Jews, and Mecca to the Mohammadans.

A tradition of the Samaritans claims that it was in Gerizim that Abraham was called to offer up his son Isaac. This claim cannot be sustained. See MORIAH. Another tradition declares that Melchizedek met Abraham in Gerizim. The only shadow of a claim in favor of it is that there is said to be a Shalem or Salem near Shechem, but the Salem of which Melchizedek was king was far more probably Jerusalem. See SALEM.

Gerrhe′nians, 2 Macc. xiii, 24. Possibly the people of Gerar, or Gaza. Grotius and Winer locate them as probably between Pelusium and Rhinocolura, (Map 2.)

Ger′shonites, THE, from Gershon, *expulsion*, the family descended from Gershon or Gershom, the son of Levi, Num. iii, 21, 23, 24; iv, 24, 27; xxvi, 57; Josh. xxi, 33; 1 Chron. xxiii, 7; 2 Chron. xxix, 12. "The Gershonite" was applied to individuals, 1 Chron. xxvi, 21; xxix, 8. During the marches in the wilderness the Gershonites carried the vails and curtains belonging to the tabernacle, on the western side of which they encamped See LEVITES.

Ger'zites, THE, 1 Sam. xxvii, 8, margin. See GEZRITES.
Ge'sem, THE LAND OF. Judith i, 9, the Greek form of Goshen.
Ge'shur, (Map 3,) *a bridge*, a small principality of Syria, forming a part of Bashan, in its north-eastern corner, adjoining the province of Argob, and bordering on the territory of Damascus, Deut. iii, 14; 2 Sam. xv, 8; compare 1 Chron. ii, 23. It was in the territory of Manasseh, but its inhabitants were never expelled, Josh. xiii, 13; compare 1 Chron. ii, 23. King David married "the daughter of Talmai, King of Geshur," 2 Sam. iii, 3; and her son Absalom sought refuge in Geshur, and there remained until taken back to Jerusalem by Joab, 2 Sam. xiii, 37; xv, 8. Geshur was wasted by David, 1 Sam. xxvii, 8. Some writers (among whom are Reland and Pressel) think that Geshur of Bashan (Josh. xii, 5) was distinct from the Geshur of Aram, 2 Sam. xv, 8. But the whole tenor of the Scripture narrative seems against them. See Kitto, Herzog, Grove's *Index*.

Gesh'uri and **Gesh'urites,** 1. The inhabitants of Geshur, Deut. iii, 14; Josh. xii, 5; xiii, 11.

2. An ancient tribe of the desert between Arabia and Philistia, Josh. xiii, 2; 1 Sam. xxvii, 8. See GESHUR.

Ge'ther, *dregs*, a name occurring in Gen. x, 23, and 1 Chron. i, 17. It refers to the tribe of Gether, for whom no locality can be assigned. Kalisch thinks it may be but an Aramæan form of *Geshur*, an identification already proposed by Dr. Thomson.

Gethsem'ane, (Map 7,) the best authorities unite on *oil-press* as the signification. Probably the place contained a press for the manufacture of oil from the olives found there. In John xviii, 1, it is called "a garden;" in Matt. xxvi, 36, "a place" (or field) "called Gethsemane." Luke (xxii, 40) says, "the place," referring to the fact that Jesus was accustomed to pray there. John (xviii, 2) says that Judas "knew the place, for Jesus ofttimes resorted thither with his disciples." Hence the Garden of Gethsemane was, doubtless, a retired spot, at a sufficient distance from public thoroughfares to secure privacy, and yet easy of access.

A tradition which reaches back to the time of Helena locates it on the west side of Olivet, where, near the first bridge crossing the Kidron, on the way from St. Stephen's Gate to the mountain, is an almost square piece of land inclosed by a common stone wall, within which stand eight very old olive-trees. From this gate a zigzag path descends the steep bank, and crossing the valley-bed by the bridge, it branches at the angle of the inclosed garden. One branch leads up a depression in the mount to the village on the top. Another branch keeps more to the right, and also leads to the village. A third runs below the garden, and, ascending the hill diagonally, passes round to Bethany. (This is the road of Christ's triumphal entry.) Another path follows the valley down to Siloam. The spot thus indicated as the reputed site of the garden is about one half to three quarters of a mile (English) from the walls of Jerusalem. Our interest in Gethsemane clusters about that single and wonderful event—the agony of our Saviour on the night before his crucifixion, Matt. xxvi, 36-50; Mark xiv, 32-46; Luke xxii, 39-49; John xviii, 1-14.

Pilgrims to this garden are shown, by the relic-loving guides, the rocky bank where the apostles fell asleep, and the very impressions of their bodies still remaining in the hard stone! A cave of some depth is claimed as the "Grotto of the Agony," where Jesus prayed. Also the place where Judas betrayed his master with a kiss is pointed out. "The garden belongs to the Latins; and the Greeks, enraged at the monopoly, have actually got up and inclosed an opposition one of their own beside the Virgin's tomb. They do not often exhibit it as yet to Franks, because, as I was told, they wish to wait a few years till the trees grow. One would have imagined that the very name of Gethsemane would have been sufficient to check every thought of deception, and to inspire every man claiming the name of *Christian* with love to God and good-will to his fellows."—Porter's *Hand-book*. Dr. Thomson (with others) places the site of the garden in the secluded vale several hundred yards to the north-east of the present Gethsemane.

Ge'zer, *a place,* probably *a precipice,* (called also Gazer, Gazara, Gazera, and Gob,) a Canaanitish royal city between Beth-Horon and the Mediterranean, on the south-western border of Ephraim, Josh. xvi, 3; 1 Chron. vii, 28. The King of Gezer was defeated by Joshua, Josh. x, 33; xii, 12. Gezer, with its suburbs, was allotted to the Kohathite Levites, Josh. xxi, 21; 1 Chron. vi, 67; but the original inhabitants were not dispossessed, Judg. i, 29. and the city remained a frontier fortress of the Philistines for some centuries. . It was the scene of many a fierce contest between its people and the Israelites, 2 Sam. v, 25; 1 Chron. xx, 4; 2 Sam. xxi, 18, (here called Gob.) It was invaded by David, 1 Sam. xxvii, 8. Pharaoh captured and burned the city, and gave it "for a present to his daughter, Solomon's wife," 1 Kings ix, 15-17. Solomon rebuilt it. Gezer is often referred to in the wars of the Maccabees, 1 Macc. xv, 28, 35. The "Journal of the Paris Geographical Society" (1873) claims that M. Clermont-Ganneau has identified Gezer with the ruins of a large and ancient city occupying an extensive plateau on the summit of *Tell el Gezer,* four Roman miles from Emmaus, (Nicopolis.) This identification is one of great importance.

Gez'rites, probably *dwellers in a dry, barren country,* an ancient correction, in 1 Sam. xxvii, 8, of Gerzites, that is, Gerizites, a wandering tribe who may have given its name to Mount Gerizim.

Gi'ah, *breaking forth,* (of a fountain,) a place mentioned in 2 Sam. ii, 24, to designate the position of the hill of Ammah. Not known.

Gib'bethon, *a height,* a town allotted to the tribe of Dan, and afterward, with its suburbs, given to the Kohathite Levites, Josh. xix, 44; xxi, 23. It was besieged by Israel while held by the Philistines, 1 Kings xv, 27; xvi, 15, 17. Possibly the site may be marked by *Saidon,* a large village lying a short distance beyond the well south-east of Ramleh.

Gib'ea, *a hill,* 1 Chron. ii, 49. Possibly the same as Gibeah of Judah. See GIBEAH, (1.)

Gib'eah, (Maps 5, 6,) *a hill,* the name of several towns in Palestine, generally on or near a hill.

1. GIBEAH OF JUDAH. A city mentioned only in Josh. xv, 57; named with Maon, and the southern Carmel. Porter (*Hand-book,* 1868) says it is identified with *Jeb'ah,* on a conical hill in Wady Musurr. Grove (in *Index,* 1868) objects, and says "the site is yet to seek."

2. GIBEAH OF SAUL, also called GIBEAH OF BENJAMIN. The siege of Gibeah, and the painful story of the Levite, are recorded in Judg. xix to xxi. The native place of Saul, the first king of Israel, 1 Sam. x, 26; xi, 4; the seat of his government during the greater part of his reign, 1 Sam. xiv, 2; xxii, 6; xxiii, 19; hence its name, xv, 34. The Amorites here hanged the seven descendants of Saul, 2 Sam. xxi, 6. Isaiah refers to this place in his

BIBLE GEOGRAPHY.

vision of the approach of the Assyrian army to Jerusalem, Isa. x, 29. See Hosea v, 8; ix, 9; x, 9. In 1 Sam. xiii, 16; xiv, 5, "Gibeah" should be Geba. Dr. Robinson at first identified Gibeah with *Jeba*, a half-ruined place about five miles north by east of Jerusalem; but he afterward assigned *Jeba* as the sight of GEBA, and located Gibeah at *Tell-el-Ful*, ("hill of the bean,") about four miles north by west of Jerusalem. Lieut. Conder makes the names Gibeah, Geba, and their variations pertain to one locality, and, with good reason, identifies Gibeah with *Jeba*. See GEBA.

3. In Josh. xviii, 28, another *Gibeah*, in Benjamin, is mentioned. It is joined in the enumeration with Kirjath-Jearim in referring to the ark. It is also referred to in 1 Sam. vii, 1, in the same connection. Kirjath stood on the slope of a hill, and probably on the summit was a suburb called Gibeah.

4. GIBEAH-IN-THE-FIELD, named in Judg. xx, 31, as the place to which one of the "highways" led from Gibeah-of-Benjamin. Probably it is identical with *Jeba* on the *Wady Suweinit*. See GEBA. See Smith's *Dictionary*.

Gib'eah-Haara'loth, *hill of the foreskins,* Josh. v, 3, marg. See GILGAL.
Gib'eath, *hill,* Josh. xviii, 28. Possibly identical with Gibeah No. 3.
Gib'eathite, 1 Chron. xii, 3. An inhabitant of Gibeah.

Gib'eon, (Map 6,) *belonging to a hill,* that is, a hill city. One of the most important cities inhabited by the Hivites, Josh. ix, 7; x, 2; xi, 19. It lay within the territory of Benjamin, Josh. xviii, 25. To its jurisdiction originally belonged Beeroth, Chephirah, and Kirjath-Jearim, Josh. ix, 17. For having obtained through craft a league with Israel, its inhabitants were condemned to be hewers of wood and drawers of water, Josh. ix, 3-15, 27. But when the Gibeonites were besieged by the five kings, Joshua came to their defense, and it was in the great battle which ensued that the

GIBEON.

"sun stood still upon Gibeon," Josh. x, 12, 1-14. The place afterward fell to the lot of Benjamin, and became a Levitical city, Josh. xviii, 25; xxi, 17; where the tabernacle was set up for many years under David and Solomon, 1 Chron. xvi, 39; xxi, 29; 2 Chron. i, 2; the ark being at the same time at Jerusalem, 2 Chron. i, 4. Here it was that Solomon offered a thousand burnt-offerings, and was rewarded by the vision that made him the wisest of men, 1 Kings iii, 4-15; 2 Chron. i, 3-13. This was the place, too, where

Abner's challenge to Joab brought defeat upon himself, and death upon his brother, Asahel, 2 Sam. ii, 12-32. (See HELKATH-HAZZURIM.) Here Amasa was afterward slain by Joab, 2 Sam. xx, 8-12. And it was here Joab met his death while clinging for refuge to the horns of the brazen altar, 1 Kings ii, 28-30, 34; compare 1 Chron. xvi, 39, 40.

The false prophet Hananiah was of Gibeon, Jer. xxviii, 1; and it was there that Johanan overtook Ishmael after the murder of Gedaliah, xli, 12. Men of Gibeon returned from the Babylonish captivity, Neh. iii, 7; vii, 25. In Ezra ii, 20, Gibbar means Gibeon.

The site of the ancient city is clearly identified with the modern village of *el-Jib*, which occupies an imposing spot on the top of a low isolated hill about six miles north-west of Jerusalem. The lofty height of *Neby Samwil* towers immediately over the town. Ruins of considerable extent remain. The place is well supplied with water. In the vale south-east of the village is a copious fountain; and, in the wet season, in the plain below is a pond of considerable extent. This was probably the "Pool of Gibeon" referred to in 2 Sam. ii, 12-17; and here, or at the fountain, were the "great waters of Gibeon," Jer. xli, 12.

Gib'eonites, the people of Gibeon, 2 Sam. xxi, 1-4, 9; 1 Chron. xii, 4; Neh. iii, 7; compare Jer. xxviii, 1. Although cursed and reduced to servitude, this was eventually of a sacred cast, as they were employed about the sanctuary. Hence probably the crime of slaying them was the more aggravated.

Gib'lites, (Map 13,) the people of Gebal, in the north of Palestine, Josh. xiii, 5; 1 Kings v, 18, marg. See GEBAL, (2.)

Gi'dom, *a cutting down*, a place to which the pursuit of the Benjamites extended after the battle of Gibeah, Judg. xx, 45. It was probably in the plain lying north-east of Michmash.

Gi'hon, *a stream* as *breaking forth from fountains*.

1. The second of the four rivers of Paradise, Gen. ii, 13, that "compasseth the whole land of Ethiopia." In the Septuagint, in Jer. ii, 18, it is used as an equivalent for the word Sichor or Sihor, that is, the Nile; and in Ecclesiasticus xxiv, 37, the Nile is intended by the term "Geon." There are various conjectures as to the locality of this river, but, like the boundaries of Paradise, it cannot be determined. See EDEN.

2. (Maps 7, 9.) A place, probably a spring, near Jerusalem, memorable as the scene of the anointing and proclamation of Solomon as king, 1 Kings i, 33, 38, 45. See also 2 Chron. xxxii, 30; xxxiii, 14. It is not easy to locate Gihon. Grove says it is possibly identical with Siloam. See JERUSALEM.

Gilbo'a or **Gil'boa**, (Map 5,) *bubbling fountain*, a ridge of hills rising at Jezreel in the eastern end of the plain of Esdraelon, and extending to the brow of the Jordan valley. The name seems to have been derived from a *well* at its northern base, half a mile from the ruins of Jezreel. Saul was here defeated by the Philistines, and he and his three sons slain; 1 Sam. xxviii, 4, 5, 19; xxxi, 1, 3. David on hearing the news gave expression to his grief in one of the most impressive, beautiful, and pathetic odes in the Bible, 2 Sam. i. Brave men from Jabesh-Gilead rescued and buried the bodies of the royal slain, 1 Sam. xxxi; 2 Sam. xxi, 12-14; 1 Chron. x.

The range of Gilboa extends about ten miles from west to east. The sides are bleak, white, and barren. The modern local name is *Jebel Fukuah*, and upon its top is the modern village of *Jelbûn*. There is a lofty promontory called *el-Mazar*, on which Dr. Thomson thinks Saul and his sons fell.

Gil'ead, (Map 5,) *a hard rocky region; heap of witness.*

1. A mountainous region east of the Jordan, bounded on the north by Bashan, on the east by the Arabian plateau, on the south by Moab and Ammon, Gen. xxxi, 21; Deut. iii, 12–17. It extends from nearly the south end of the Sea of Galilee to the north end of the Dead Sea—about sixty miles; and its average breadth is about twenty. The Jordan is the western boundary, 1 Sam. xiii, 7; 2 Kings x, 33. Sometimes it is called "Mount Gilead," Gen. xxxi, 25; sometimes "land of Gilead," Num. xxxii, 1; and sometimes simply Gilead, Psa. lx, 7; Gen. xxxvii, 25. It is first referred to in connection with the history of Jacob, Gen. xxxi, 21. It was the territory of Sihon and Og, Josh. xii, 2, 5. Falling into the hands of Israel, (Deut. iii, 8, 10,) it was afterward possessed by the two and a half tribes, Deut. iii, 12, 13; compare Josh. xvii, 1. Sometimes, however, by Gilead is to be understood more loosely the whole of the Israelitish trans-Jordanic territory, Deut. xxxiv, 1; Josh. xxii, 9; Judg. xx, 1. It was a place for cattle, Num. xxxii, 1. Balsams or gums seem to have been here produced, Jer. viii, 22; xlvi, 11. Bold chieftains in the country, Judg. xi, 1. Ish-Bosheth was conveyed by Abner to Gilead, being sure of support among such people, 2 Sam. ii, 8, 9. David took refuge there in Absalom's rebellion, 2 Sam. xvii, 22, 24. Elijah a Gileadite, 1 Kings xvii, 1. With Gileadites Pekah rebelled against and slew Pekahiah, and not long after Gilead was overrun by the Assyrian king Tiglath, 2 Kings xv, 25, 29. The "city" in Hosea vi, 8, probably refers to the whole land of Gilead.

The section of Gilead lying between the Hieromax and the Jabbok is now called *Jebel Ajlûn*, while that to the south of the Jabbok constitutes the modern province of *Belka*. One of the most conspicuous peaks in the mountain range still retains the ancient name, being called *Jebél Jil'ad*, "Mount Gilead." It is probably the site of Ramath-Mizpeh of Josh. xiii, 26, and the "Mizpeh-Gilead" from which Jephthah "passed over unto the children of Ammon," Judg. xi, 29. The neighboring village of *es-Salt* occupies the site of the old "city of refuge" in Gad, Ramoth-Gilead.

In the New Testament and in Josephus Gilead is referred to under the terms "Peræa" and "beyond Jordan," Matt. iv, 15; John i, 28.

Under Mohammedan rule this country is semi-barbarian. The whole population of Gilead is composed of a few fierce wandering tribes, and a few inhabitants of villages scattered amid the fastnesses of *Jebel Ajlûn*. "In passing through the country one can hardly get over the impression that he is roaming through an English park. The graceful hills, the rich vales, the luxuriant herbage, the bright wild flowers, the plantations of evergreen oak, pine, arbutus; now a tangled thicket, and now a grove scattered over the gentle slope, as if intended to reveal its beauty; the little rivulets fringed with oleanders, at one place running lazily between alluvial banks, at another. dashing madly down rocky ravines—such are the features of the mountains of Gilead."—*Porter*.

2. In Judg. vii, 3, the name of Mount Gilead is thought by some to be a copyist's mistake for Gilboa; for Gideon was encamped at the "well (spring) of Harod." The spring is now called *Jalood* near *Zerin*. The solution of Schwarz is that the northernmost spur of Mount Gilboa was also called Gilead, where still the name *Jalood* exists.

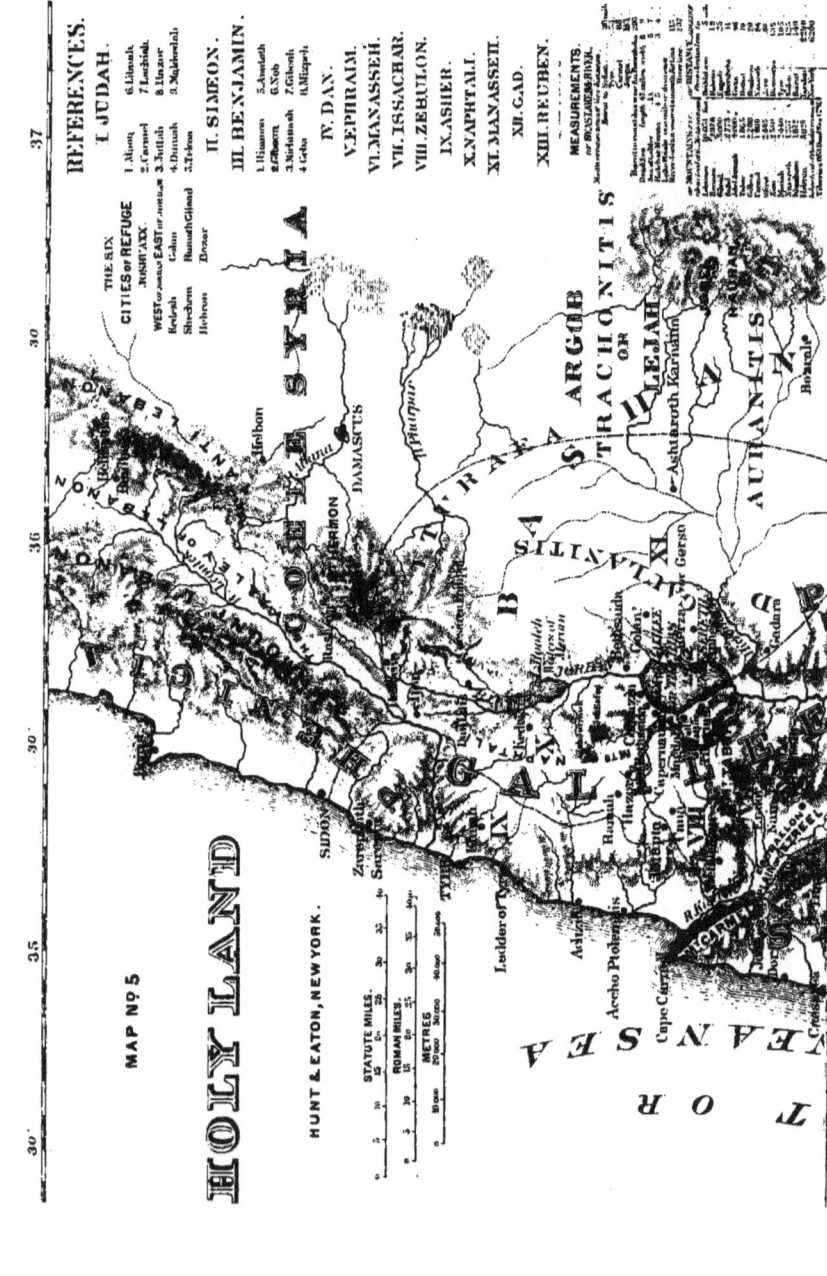

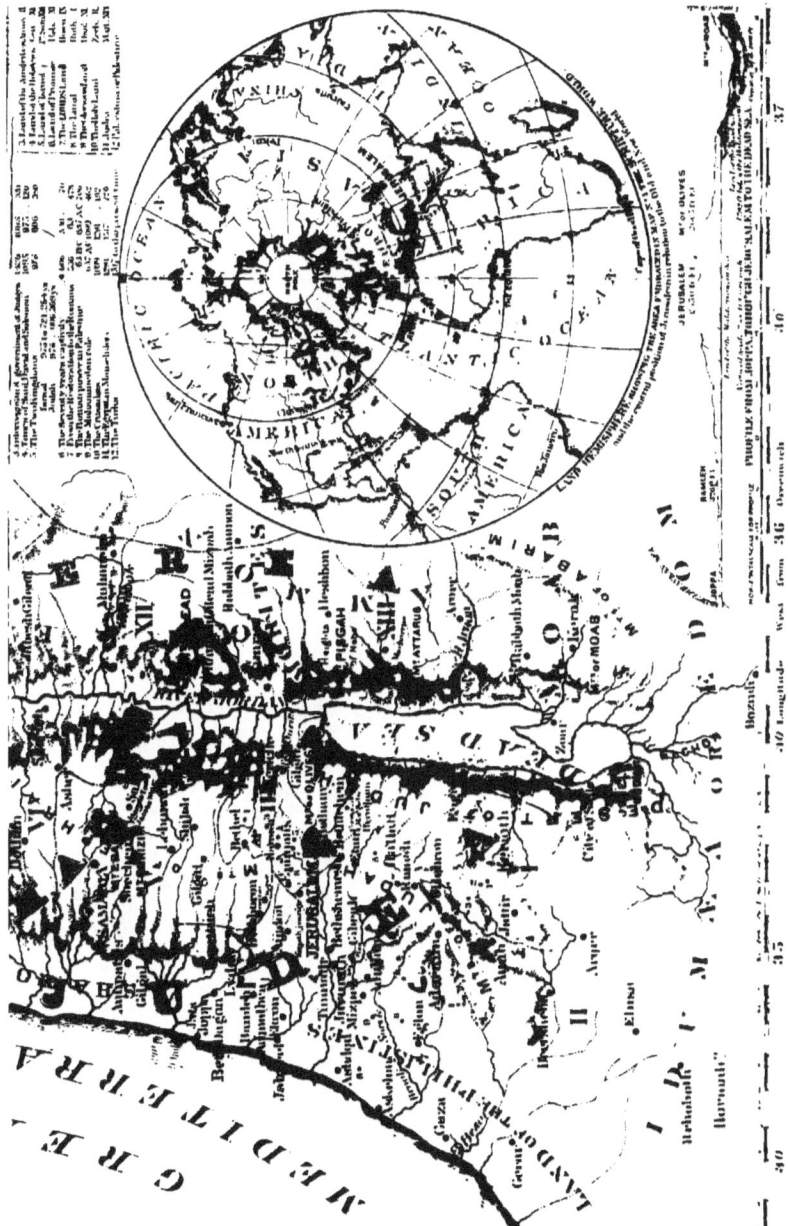

BIBLE GEOGRAPHY. 159

Gil'eadite, a family of Manasseh, descendants of Gilead; also inhabitants of the land of Gilead, Num. xxvi, 29; Judg. x, 3; xi, 1, 40; xii, 7; 2 Sam. xvii, 27; xix, 31; 1 Kings ii, 7; 2 Kings xv, 25; Ezra ii, 61; Neh. vii, 63.

Gil'gal, (Map 5,) *a rolling away.*

1. A place in the Jordan valley near Jericho, the site of the first camp of the Israelites west of the Jordan, where the twelve stones were set up which had been taken from the bed of the stream, Josh. iv, 19, 20; compare iii; Deut. xi, 30. Here was kept the first passover in the land of Canaan, and the Israelites who had been born on the march through the wilderness were here circumcised, Josh. v, 9, 10. The camp remained at Gilgal during the early part of the conquest, Josh. ix, 6; x, 6, 7, 9, 15, 43; and from one narrative we may probably infer that Joshua retired thither at the conclusion of his labors, Josh. xiv, 6; compare xv. Samuel judged here, 1 Sam. vii, 6. In its sacred groves were celebrated the solemn assemblies of Samuel and Saul, and of David on his return from exile, 1 Sam. x, 8; xi, 14; xiii, 4, etc.; xv, 12, etc.; 2 Sam. xix, 15, 40. Agag slain here, 1 Sam. xv, 33. Gilgal was denounced by the prophets for its idolatry, Hosea iv, 15; ix, 15; xii, 11; Amos iv, 4; v, 5. In Josh. xv, 7, a Gilgal is mentioned in describing the north boundary of Judah. In the parallel list of Josh. xviii, 17, it is given as Geliloth, and this Gilgal near Jericho is doubtless intended. See GELILOTH.

The exact site of Gilgal has not been identified. The best authorities conjecture it to have been near the present little village of *Riha.*

2. In 2 Kings ii, 1, 2; iv, 38, is named a Gilgal visited by Elijah and Elisha. This could not be the Gilgal of the low plain of the Jordan, for the prophets are said to have gone *down* to Bethel, which is three thousand feet above the plain. There is a *Jiljilieh* about four miles from Bethel and Shiloh respectively, situated high up on the brow of the central mountain tract: perhaps that is the site of the place in question. Winer suggests that this may be the Gilgal of Deut. xi, 30. Perhaps, also, it is that of Neh. xii, 29. But the place of this latter is referred by some to No. 1 above.

3. In Josh. xii, 23, occurs the name of a royal Canaanitish Gilgal. Possibly the site of this place is marked by the modern village of *Jiljûleh,* about four miles south of Antipatris. But another Gilgal, under the slightly different form of *Kilkilieh,* lies about two miles east of Antipatris, (*Kefr-Saba.*)

Gi'loh, *exile,* a town in the mountains of Judah, Josh. xv, 51; the native place of Ahithophel, 2 Sam. xv, 12; who resided here when Absalom sent for him to Hebron. Giloh was also the scene of Ahithophel's miserable death, 2 Sam. xvii, 23. It is not identified; but *Rafat,* a village with extensive ruins one hour and twenty minutes south of Hebron, has been suggested as the site.

Gi'lonite, a native of Giloh; the designation of Ahithophel, 2 Sam. xv, 12; xxiii, 34.

Gim'zo, *place fertile in sycamores,* a town in the low country of Judah, captured by the Philistines, with Ajalon and other places, in the reign of Ahaz, 2 Chron. xxviii, 18. It is identified with *Jimzu,* a rather large village on an eminence about three miles south-west from Lydda. Here are found many thrashing-floors, and ancient cisterns used as magazines for grain.

Gir'gashites and **Gir'gasites,** *dwelling in clayey or loamy soil,* one of the nations in possession of Canaan before the time of Joshua, Gen. x, 16; xv, 21; Deut. vii, 1; Josh. iii, 10; xxiv, 11; 1 Chron. i, 14; Neh. ix, 8. The name has no connection with the Gergesenes; but nothing is known as to their locality. From Josh. xxiv, 11, we may infer that their territory was on the west of Jordan, near central Palestine.

Git'tah-He'pher, Josh. xix, 13. See GATH-HEPHER.

Git'taim, *two wine-presses,* a town probably of Benjamin. From 2 Sam. iv, 3, it would seem that the ancient Gibeonites were expelled from Beeroth, and either built or colonized Gittaim. In Neh. xi, 33, this town is connected with Rameh, as inhabited after the captivity. The site is unknown.

Git'tites, the inhabitants of Gath, Josh. xiii, 3; 2 Sam. xxi, 19; 1 Chron. xx, 5. The six hundred men from Gath who followed David under Ittai, and who probably acted as a body-guard, are also called Gittites, 2 Sam. xv, 18, 19. Some of these six hundred may have been Hebrews, 1 Sam. xxiii, 13; xxv, 13; xxvii, 2. Obed-Edom, in whose house the ark was placed, is called a Gittite, 2 Sam. vi, 10, 11; 1 Chron. xiii, 13. But because it seems improbable that the sacred ark should be in charge of a Philistine, it has been suggested that Obed-Edom belonged to Gittaim, or to Gath-Rimmon, which was a Levite city.

Gi'zonite. "The sons of Hashem the Gizonite" are named among the warriors of David's guard, 1 Chron. xi, 34. In the parallel list of 2 Sam. xxiii, the word is omitted. Nothing is known of this term.

Go'ath, *lowing,* a place named in Jer. xxxi, 39, in connection with the hill Gareb, and apparently near Jerusalem. See CALVARY.

Gob, *a pit, ditch, cistern,* a place mentioned in 2 Sam. xxi, 18, 19, as the scene of two encounters between David's warriors and the Philistines. In 1 Chron. xx, 4, in referring to one of these battles, the name is given as Gezer, which see. The LXX in some copies has Gath in one verse, a name which in Hebrew much resembles Gob.

Go'lan, (Map 5,) *exile,* by some *circle,* a city of Bashan, in the half-tribe of Manasseh, assigned to the Levites, and appointed one of the refuge cities, Deut. iv, 43; Josh. xxi, 27; 1 Chron. vi, 71. No further mention is made of Golan in Scripture. Its site is not known; but it doubtless gave its name to the district east of Jordan called Gaulonitis. This district extended from the Yarmuk (Hieromax) in the south to the fountains of the Jordan, or the confines of Dan and Cesarea Philippi in the north. On the west it was bounded by the Jordan and the two upper lakes; on the east it reached to the Hauran. Gaulonitis was anciently very populous. Mr. Porter speaks of a list of a hundred and twenty-seven cities and villages; but nearly all of these are now only masses of ruins.

The greater part of this region is a flat and fertile table-land, well watered, and clothed with luxuriant grass. The western side, along the Sea of Galilee, is steep, rugged, and bare.

Gol'gotha, *a skull,* the Hebrew name of the spot at which our Lord was crucified, Matt. xxvii, 33; Mark xv, 22; John xix, 17. See CALVARY.

Go'mer, (Map 12,) *perfection, complete,* a people descended from Gomer, the eldest son of Japheth, Gen. x, 2, 3; 1 Chron. i, 5, 6; Ezek. xxxviii, 6. Gomer is generally recognized as the progenitor of the early Cimmerians, of the later Cimbri and the other branches of the Celtic family, and of the modern Gael and Cymry, the latter preserving, with very slight deviation, the original name.

Gomor'rah, probably *submersion,* one of the five "cities of the plain" or "Vale of Siddim," that, under their respective kings, joined battle there with Chedorlaomer and his allies, by whom they were discomfited till Abram came to the rescue, Gen. xiv, 2–14. Four of the five cities were afterward destroyed by the Lord with fire from heaven, Gen. xix, 23–29. Zoar was spared at Lot's request.

Gomorrah was next to Sodom in importance as well as in wickedness, Gen. xix, 4–8. The miserable fate of these cities is held up as a warning to Israel, Deut. xxix, 23; as a precedent for the destruction of Babylon, Isa. xiii, 19; Jer. l, 40; of Edom, Jer. xlix, 18; of Moab, Zeph. ii, 9; and even of Israel, Amos iv, 11. In 2 Pet. ii, 6, and in Jude 4–7 their fate is "an ensample" to the ungodly. The fearful wickedness of these cities "rings as a proverb" through the prophecies; see Deut. xxxii, 32; Isa. i, 9, 10; Jer. xxii, 14, where Jerusalem is called Sodom, and her people Gomorrah. And yet, according to New Testament teaching, Tyre, Sidon, Capernaum, Chorazin, and Bethsaida were guilty of greater sin when they "repented not," in spite of the "mighty works" which they had seen, Matt. x, 15; compare Mark vi, 11. The site of Gomorrah is not known. A valley of the same name (*Wady 'Amorah*) exists on the south-west side of the Dead Sea, but Mr. Grove and others hold to the opinion that the five cities were probably at the north end of the lake. See SODOM and SEA SALT, where this point is considered.

Gomor'rha, the Greek form of Gomorrah, 2 Esdras ii, 8; Matt. x, 15; Mark vi, 11; Rom. ix, 29; Jude 7; 2 Pet. ii, 6.

Gorty'na, a city of Crete, in which were Jewish residents, 1 Macc. xv, 23. It was near Fair Havens, and possibly Paul may have preached there when on his voyage to Rome, Acts xxvii, 8, 9.

Go'shen, (Map 2,) *frontier,* (?), (meaning very uncertain.)

1. Goshen is the name of a part of Egypt where the Israelites dwelt for the whole period of their sojourn in that country, Gen. xlv, 5, 10; xlvi, 28; xlvii, 27; l, 8; Exod. viii, 22; ix, 26. It is called usually the "land of Goshen," and simply also Goshen. It appears to have borne the name of "the land of Rameses," Gen. xlvii, 11, unless this be the name of a district of Goshen. The Bible does not definitely locate this region. It is probable, however, that it lay east of the Nile, as Jacob is not reported to have crossed that river; nor does it appear that the Israelites did so in their flight from Egypt.

Mr. Poole (in Smith's *Dictionary*) claims that the land of Goshen lay between the eastern part of the ancient Delta and the western border of Palestine, that it was scarcely a part of Egypt Proper, was inhabited by other foreigners besides the Israelites, and was in its geographical name rather Semitic than Egyptian, and that it was probably identical with the modern *Wady Tumeylat,* the valley along which ran the canal of the Red Sea. Dr. Kalisch does not exactly agree with this identification. Goshen did not reach to the wilderness, (Exod. xiii, 20,) and was not, he thinks, a frontier province. Such passages as Exod. viii, 21–23; ix, 25, 26, show, he thinks, that it was surrounded by other Egyptian districts, and properly belonged to Egypt. He supposes it impossible, therefore, to define its boundaries, and concludes that we must be satisfied with a general idea of its position. Mr. Poole remarks concerning the conclusions of another: "If, with Lepsius, we place Goshen below Heliopolis, near Bubastis and *Bilbeys,* the distance from the Red Sea, of three days' journey of the Israelites, and the separate character of the country, are violently set aside."

Goshen was fertile, and abounded in excellent pasture-land, Gen. xlvii, 6, 11; xlvi, 34; xlvii, 4. Fish abundant there, Num. xi, 5; hence, probably, the land bordered on the Nile or some branch of it. The royal residence, doubtless, was not far from Goshen, Gen. xlv, 10; xlvi, 29; xlviii, 1, 2; Exod. v, 20. The Israelites were not all confined to the land of Goshen, for the parents of Moses evidently lived at the capital, Exod. ii, 3, 5, 8. Nor were the inhabitants of Goshen exclusively Israelites, for Egyptians are described as their neighbors, Exod. iii, 22; xi, 2; xii, 35, 36; and that the houses of the two peoples were intermixed, may be inferred from the marking of those of Israel with the blood of the paschal lamb, Exod. xii, 23. Pharaoh's flocks and herds seem to have been pastured in Goshen, Gen. xlvii, 6. Foreigners also probably lived there, for a "mixed multitude" accompanied the Israelites on their march, Exod. xii, 38. The territory was anciently of extraordinary fertility. Travelers represent the land as now needing only the waters of the Nile to render it again fertile. Laborde represents the vicinity of Heliopolis as still covered with palm-trees, and having an inclosure, comprehending a considerable space of ground, which is covered every year by the inundation of the Nile to the height of five feet. A few hours' journey to the north-east of Cairo are large heaps of ruins which the Arabs call *Tell el Jhud,* (Jews' hills,) or *Turbeh el Jhud,* (Jews' graves.) Some claim these as mounds of the Jews, and built by them during their sojourn in Egypt. Dr. Robinson emphatically rejects this claim, and says, "These mounds can only be referred back to the period of the Ptolemies, in the centuries immediately before the Christian era, when great numbers of Jews resorted to Egypt and erected a temple at Leontopolis."

2. A district of Palestine, apparently lying between Gaza and Gibeon, Josh. x, 41; xi, 16. Probably it included some of the rich low country of Judah, and the Israelites may hence have given it its name. It is possible that the name may have been much older, implying intercourse with Egypt. For such implied intercourse, see 1 Chron. vii, 21.

3. A town in the mountains of Judah, Josh. xv, 51, of which no identification has yet been made. Some conjecture that it may have given its name to the district above mentioned, (No. 2.)

Go'zan, (Maps 1, 14,) perhaps *quarry*, a district of Mesopotamia through which the Habor (the modern *Khabour*) flowed, 2 Kings xvii, 6; xviii, 11; xix, 12; 1 Chron. v, 26; Isa. xxxvii, 12. The Israelites were carried captives to this region by Pul, Tiglath-Pileser, and Shalmanezer, or possibly Sargon. In 1 Chron. v, 26, the "river" means the river flowing through Gozan. This tract is probably identical with the Gauzanitis of Ptolemy, and may be regarded as the Mygdonia of other writers. Mr. Layard describes the region lying immediately along the river as one of remarkable fertility.

Greece, or **Hellas,** (Maps 1, 17,) a country in the south-east of Europe, Zech. ix, 13; 1 Macc. i, 1; Acts xx, 2, called also Grecia, Dan. viii, 21; x, 20; xi, 2. The Hebrew is Javan, (the signification of which may be *mud* or *clay,*) Dan. viii, 21, and Joel iii, 6, (see both the A. V. and the Hebrew text.) The term Javan is sometimes given in the A. V., Isa. lxvi, 19; Ezek. xxvii, 13. The descendants of Japheth, in the line of Javan, peopled Greece, Gen. x, 2, 4, 5. The name Javan may be traced in Ionia, the western region of Asia Minor. (See the Septuagint in Gen. x, 2.)

Greece was bounded on the north by Illyricum and Macedonia, from which a range of mountains separated it. On the other sides it was washed by the sea. There were numerous islands off the coasts inhabited by the Greek race, who had also established colonies elsewhere. In after-times the word was applied in a larger sense, and under the Roman dominion Greece was considered as comprehending the provinces of Macedonia and Achaia. So they are mentioned together in the New Testament, Acts xviii, 21; Rom. xv, 26. In Acts xx, 2, however, the term "Grecia" is used in its more restricted and proper sense as distinguished from Macedonia. Sometimes Greece or Grecia is used to designate the Macedonian kingdom of Alexander, as in the passages in Daniel above referred to. In Zech. ix, 13, the term means the Græco-Syrian kingdom, which arose after Alexander's death.

There was little early communication or connection between Palestine and Greece. The Greeks and Hebrews met first in the slave-market, Joel iii, 6. In Maccabean times we find a correspondence of the Jews and the Lacedæmonians, with a reference to a yet earlier document in which the last-named people professed to discover that they were descendants of Abraham, 1 Macc. xii, 2–23. After the complete subjugation of the Greeks by the Romans, and the absorption into the Roman empire of the kingdoms which were formed out of the dominions of Alexander, the political connection between the Greeks and Jews as two independent nations no longer existed. See ACHAIA, ATHENS, CORINTH.

Gre'cia. See GREECE.

Gre'cian, Gre'cians. In the books of the Maccabees *Greeks* and *Grecians* seem to be used indifferently. Compare 1 Macc. i, 10; vi, 2; also 2 Macc. iv, 10, *Greekish.* In the New Testament the terms "Greek" and "Grecian" in the English do not sufficiently convey the difference of meanings. *Hellēnes,* "Greeks," it may be said, generally, were Greeks by race, (for example, Acts xvi, 1, 3; xviii, 17;) or Gentiles as opposed to Jews, (for example, Rom. ii, 9, 10, margin.) *Hellenistai,* "Grecians," were foreign Jews, as opposed to Palestine Jews, Acts vi, 1; xi, 20. *Hellēnikos* is used to denote the Greek language, Luke xxiii, 38; Rev. ix, 11.

Gud'godah, or **Gudgo'dah,** perhaps *thunder,* a station of the Israelites in the wilderness, Deut. x, 7. See HOR-HAGIDGAD.

Gul'loth, *fountains, springs,* a name used to denote the springs added by the great Caleb to the south land in the neighborhood of Debir, which formed the dowry of his daughter Achsah, Josh. xv, 19; Judg. i, 15. These springs are described as "upper" and "lower." An attempt has been lately made by Dr. Rosen to identify them with *Ain Nunkur* and *Dewir-Ban,* spots in a beautiful valley one hour south-west of Hebron, and in this Dean Stanley coincides; but the identification cannot yet be considered certain. See Stanley's *Jewish Church,* vol. i, p. 293, note.

Gu'nites, THE, *colored, dyed,* the name of the "family" which sprang from Guni, son of Naphtali, Num. xxvi, 48.

Gur, *a whelp, lion's cub,* or *dwelling,* the place where it is said that Ahaziah received his mortal wound when flying from Jehu, 2 Kings ix, 27. "The going up to Gur" was probably some steep ascent from the plain of Esdraelon. The place is not identified, but conjecture locates it below *Jenīn.*

Gur-Ba'al, *sojourn of Baal,* a place or district in which dwelt Arabians, against whom God helped Uzziah, 2 Chron. xxvi, 7. This place was probably between Palestine and the Arabian peninsula. Some have supposed it to be identical with Gerar, but the site is wholly unknown. In the passage above cited the Mehunim are mentioned with the Arabians. See MEHUNIM.

Ha'bor, (Map 1,) *joining together,* a river of Mesopotamia which must be distinguished from the Chebar of Ezekiel, 2 Kings xvii, 6; xviii, 11; 1 Chron. v, 26. See CHEBAR and GOZAN. The district through which the Habor runs was one of the countries into which the ten tribes were carried captive. It is identified beyond reasonable doubt with the river Chaboras, now called the *Khabour.* It has several sources, the principal of which is said to be west of *Mardin.* It runs in a winding course, but generally south-south-west, through a rich country, till, having been augmented by tributaries, it empties into the Euphrates at *Karkesia,* the ancient Circesium.

According to Benjamin of Tudela (*Early Travels in Palestine,* p. 93) there were large Jewish communities on the banks of the Khabour.

Mr. Layard represents both sides of the river as covered with mounds, the remains of cities belonging to the Assyrian period.

Hach'ilah, HILL OF, *the darksome hill,* a hill in the highlands of Judah, in the neighborhood of Ziph, in the fastnesses or passes of which David and his six hundred followers were hiding when twice the Ziphites informed Saul of his whereabouts, 1 Sam. xxiii, 19; comp. xiv, 15, 18; xxvi, 1. Saul was diverted from the pursuit in the first case by the intelligence of an incursion of the Philistines; in the second, David and Abishai stole into Saul's camp by night and carried off the king's spear and cruse of water. The probable site of Hachilah is the high hill bounded by deep valleys north and south, on which the ruin of *Yekin* now stands.

Ha'dad-Rim'mon, (Map 4,) a place probably named from Hadad and Rimmon, two Syrian idols. The term *Hadad* was originally the indigenous appellation of the Sun among the Syrians. *Rimmon* may signify *most high,* or perhaps *pomegranate,* a fruit sacred to Venus.

This place was in the Valley of Megiddo, and is named in Zech. xii, 11 as the scene of a great lamentation over the death of some noted person, as the type of the greatest of all lamentations in Jerusalem over its dead. The reference is most probably to the mourning for the death of King Josiah, who fell in battle against Pharaoh-Necho, 2 Kings xxiii, 29; 2 Chron. xxxv, 20–23.

About four miles south of *Lejjûn* is a small village called *Rummaneh,* which Van de Velde identifies with Hadad-Rimmon; but this identification is uncertain.

Had'ashah, or **Hada'shah,** *new,* a town in the lower country of Judah, named between Zenan and Migdal-Gad, in the second group, Josh. xv, 37. Probably identical with Adasa, (1 Macc. vii, 40, 45.) Both Eusebius and Jerome seem to have known the place, but it cannot now be identified.

Hadat'tah, *new,* a town named as in the extreme south of Judah, Josh. xv, 25. The pointing of the Hebrew would seem to indicate that it is to be taken as an adjective qualifying *Hazor,* as if it were Hazor-Chadattah, that is, New Hazor, in distinction from the place of the same name in verse 23. It is not known, although Mr. Wilton seeks to identify it with *Kusr el-Adadeh,* a ruin of imposing appearance on the summit of a hill. (The *Negeb,* pp. 98, 99.)

Ha'did, *sharp,* a place named, with Lod (Lydda) and Ono, only in the later books of the history, but yet so as to imply its earlier existence, Ezra ii, 33; Neh. vii, 37; xi, 34. Its site is probably that of the modern village *El-Hadítheh*, three miles east of Lydda. See ADIDA.

Ha'drach, perhaps *inclosure*, a country of Syria mentioned but once, Zech. ix, 1, 2. The *land of Hadrach* is conjectured by some to be the region of Damascus; but Mr. Porter (in Kitto) says: "The words of the passage do not connect it more closely with Damascus than with Hamath. . . . There is no town or province near Damascus or Hamath bearing a name at all resembling Hadrach. Yet this does not prove that there never was such a name. Many ancient names have disappeared, as it seems to be the case with this."

Ha'garenes', or **Ha'garites**, from Hagar, which signifies *flight*, a people dwelling east of the Jordan, with whom the Reubenites, Gadites, and Eastern Manassites had wars, 1 Chron. v, 10, 19, 20; xxvii, 31. Possibly these people were descended from Hagar, although they seem to be distinguished from the Ishmaelites, Psa. lxxxiii, 6. Some authorities incline to identify them with the Agræi in North-eastern Arabia, on the borders of the Persian Gulf, where are now the town and district of *Hejer*. But nothing is certainly known concerning this tribe.

Ha'i, *heap of ruins*, Gen. xii, 8; xiii, 3. The same as AI.

Ha'lah, (Map 1,) the meaning is uncertain; but the name is probably derived from the very ancient city of Calah, signifying *old age*. A place in Assyria to which the ten tribes were carried captive, 2 Kings xvii, 6; xviii, 11; 1 Chron. v, 26. Halah may with some confidence be identified with the Chalcitis of Ptolemy. It is probably now the modern *Gla*, a mound on the upper *Khabour*, above its junction with the *Jerujer*.

Ha'lak, THE MOUNT, *the smooth mountain*, the name of a mountain twice named as the southern limit of Joshua's conquests, Josh. xi, 17; xii, 7. It was in the direction of Seir, but it has not been identified.

Hal'hul, (Map 5,) *trembling*, a town in the highlands of Judah, Josh. xv, 58. Its ruined site with the name of *Halhul* is found on the eastern slope of a hill four miles north of Hebron, encompassed by fields and fine vineyards. On the top of the hill is an old mosque dedicated to *Neby Yunus*, (Prophet Jonah.)

Ha'li, *necklace, trinket*, a town on the boundary of Asher, Josh. xix, 25, of whose situation nothing is known.

Hal'icarnas'sus, a renowned city of Caria, the birth-place of Herodotus and of Dionysius, the historians. Here was the famous mausoleum erected by Artemisia. It was the residence of a Jewish population in the periods between the Old and New Testament histories, 1 Macc. xv, 23. According to Josephus, these Jews had permission to hold service for prayer by the sea-side. Compare Acts xvi, 13. The modern name is *Budrûm*.

Ha'math, (Maps 1, 13,) *fortress, citadel*, one of the most important cities of Syria from very early times, and ranking among the oldest in the world. Under the Macedonians it was called Epiphaneia, from Antiochus Epiphanes. It was situated at the foot of Anti-Libanus on the Orontes, near Damascus (that is, the limits of the two were contiguous) and Zobah, Josh. xiii, 5; Judges iii, 3; Zech. ix, 2; Jer. xlix, 23; 1 Chron. xviii, 3, 9; 2 Chron. viii, 3. It was the chief city on the highway from Phœnicia to the Euphrates. Originally it was a Phœnician or Canaanite colony, Gen. x, 18, but afterward it was taken by the Syrians, and became the metropolis of a kingdom which included a considerable district of surrounding country, 2 Kings xxiii, 33; xxv, 21. Its king sustained amicable relations with David, 2 Sam viii, 9. etc.; 1 Chron. xviii, 9. It maintained its independence until near Hezekiah's time, when the Assyrians took it, Isa. xxxvii, 12, etc.; compare 2 Kings xv, 19; xviii, 34; xix, 13; Isa. x, 9; Amos vi, 2; though its territory may have been previously curtailed, Num. xiii, 22; xxxiv, 8; Amos vi, 14; 1 Chron. xiii, 5; 2 Chron. vii, 8; viii, 3; Ezek. xlvii, 16; xlviii, 1.

The Assyrians transplanted "people from Hamath" into the depopulated country of the ten tribes, who brought their native deity, Ashima, (probably the Phœnician *Esmun-Esculapius*,) with them. In the Middle Ages Hamath was the capital of a small State, among whose princes was the renowned historian and geographer Abulfeda.

The present name of the city is *Hamah*, and it is still a place of considerable importance, with a population of about thirty thousand, including two thousand five hundred Christians of the Greek Church. Four bridges span the river, (the Orontes, now the *Nahr el-'Asy*,) and a number of huge wheels, turned by the current, raise the water into aqueducts, which convey it to the houses and mosques of the town. Although the houses of the city are plain and poor externally, some of them are splendid within. Some ancient inscriptions on stones have been discovered, but they have not yet been deciphered.

Ha'math the Great, Amos vi, 2; the same as Hamath.

Ha'math-Zo'bah, *fortress of Zobah*, a city which Solomon subdued, 2 Chron. viii, 3. The best authorities consider this as probably a different place from Hamath, but it is not identified.

Ham'math, *warm springs*, one of the fortified cities in the territory allotted to Naphtali, Josh. xix, 35. It doubtless lay about one mile south of Tiberias. Josephus mentions it, under the name of Emmaus, as "a village not far from Tiberias." Josephus also names the hot springs or baths of Hammath, and mentions the fact that the waters were medicinal.

The place is probably identical with the *Hammam*, or *springs*, near Tiberias, which still send up hot and sulphurous waters. The water, too nauseous to be drank, is yet used for bathing, and has a high reputation for medicinal qualities. Possibly Hammath is the same as Hammon, (2,) or Hammoth-Dor.

Ham'mon, *warm, sunny.*
1. A place in Asher, near Zidon, Josh. xix, 28. Not yet identified.
2. A Gershonite city in Naphtali, 1 Chron. vi, 76. Possibly the same as Hammath and Hammoth-Dor.

Ham'moth-Dor, *warm springs' dwelling*, a town of Gershonite Levites, and of refuge in Naphtali. It is possibly the same as Hammon (2,) and Hammath.

Hamo'nah or **Ham'onah,** *multitude*, a city mentioned in a very obscure passage, Ezek. xxxix, 16, apparently as the place in or near which the multitudes of Gog shall be buried after their great slaughter by the Almighty, and which is to derive its name—"multitude"—from that circumstance.

Ha'mon-Gog, THE VALLEY OF, *ravine of Gog's multitude*, the prophetical name to be bestowed on the valley in which Gog and his multitude shall be buried, Ezek. xxxix, 11, 15. See HAMONAH.

Hanan'eel, (Map 9,) *God has graciously given.* The name of a tower which formed part of the wall of Jerusalem, Neh. iii, 1; xii, 39; Jer. xxxi, 38; Zech. xiv, 10. It was between the Sheep Gate and the Fish Gate, and not far from the corner. Dr. Barclay says: "It is probable in the highest degree that in the projection at the north-east corner of the Haram incloure we have the remains of the Tower of Hananeel." Some think it was the same as the Tower of Meah, which see.

Ha'nes. This term and the passage in which it occurs (Isa. xxx, 4) are obscure. It is the name of a city in Egypt which has generally been identified with the Heracleopolis, *Hercules city*, of the Greeks, in Middle Egypt, on the west of the Nile, called in Coptic *Hnes*, or *Ehnes*. But the Chaldee paraphrase reads Tahpanhes. Grotius thinks Hanes a contraction of Tahpanhes. This latter was situated in the eastern part of the Delta, and may possibly be identical with Hanes. See TAHPANHES.

Han'nathon, *graciously regarded*, a town on the northern border of Zebulun, Josh. xix, 14. It is not identified.

Haphra'im, (properly CHAPHARAIM,) *two pits*, a city of Issachar, probably near Shunem, Josh. xix, 19. Eusebius and Jerome place it six miles north from Legio, under the names of Aphraim and Affarea. About six miles north-east of *Lejjun* and two miles west of *Solam* (the ancient Shunem) stands the modern village of *el-'Afûleh*, which is possibly identical with Haphraim.

Ha'ra, *mountainous land*, a place in Assyria, mentioned only in 1 Chron. v, 26, whither some of the Israelitish captives were carried. The Septuagint omits it. Mr. Rawlinson (in Smith's *Dictionary*) says it "is either a place utterly unknown, or it must be regarded as identical with Haran or Charran, the Mesopotamian city to which Abram came from Ur." Mr. Grove thinks it is "possibly a variation of Haran." Rosenmüller and Gesenius suppose that the Persian mountain district *Irak* is meant. Mr. Porter (in Kitto) says: "Hara is joined with Hala, Habor, and the river Gozan. These were all situated in western Assyria, between the Tigris and Euphrates, and along the banks of the *Khabûr*. We may safely conclude, therefore, that Hara could not have been far distant from that region. . . . The conjecture that Hara and Haran are identical cannot be sustained, though the situation of the latter might suit the requirements of the biblical narrative, and its Greek classical name resembles Hara. . . . Hara may perhaps have been a local name applied to the mountainous region north of Gozan, called by Strabo and Ptolemy Mons Masius, and now *Karja Baghlar*."

Har'adah, (Map 2,) *fear*, a desert station of the Israelites, Num. xxxiii, 24, 25. Possibly identical with *Jebel 'Arâdeh* in *Wâdy el 'Ain*.

Ha'ran, (Map 1,) *parched, dry;* called also Charran, Acts vii, 2, 4 The name of the place to which Abraham and his family migrated from Ur of the Chaldees, and where the descendants of his brother Nahor established themselves. It is called "the city of Nahor." Compare Gen. xxiv, 10; with xxvii, 43. It is said to be in Mesopotamia, Gen. xxiv, 10; or, more definitely, in Padan-Aram, xxv, 20. At Haran Abraham dwelt awhile, Gen. xi, 31; xii, 4, 5. Terah died there, Gen. xi, 32. Abraham left Haran to go to Canaan by divine command. Jacob resided at Haran with Laban, Gen. xxvii, 43; xxviii, 7; xxix; xxxi, 18. It was conquered by the Assyrians, 2 Kings xix, 12; being mentioned in connection with Gozan in Mesopotamia. Its merchants are mentioned in Ezek. xxvii, 23, and its idolatry in Josh. xxiv, 14; Isa. xxxvii, 12.

Haran has been generally identified with the Carræ of the Greeks and Romans, and the *Harrân* of the Arabs.

This *Harrân*, of whose identification with Haran there is no reasonable doubt, stands on the banks of a small river called *Belik*, which flows into the Euphrates about fifty miles south of the town. The village is inhabited only by a few Arab families.

A little east of Damascus is a modern village called *Harrân el-Awamîd*, (Map 3,) which Dr. Beke claims as the Haran of Abraham and Laban. But Dr. Beke stands almost alone in this claim; yet his arguments seem plausible. But as the distance traveled over by Jacob and Laban (Gen. xxxi, 17-25) was, according to the common theory, upward of three hundred miles, and as the meaning of Gilead is *hard, stony region*, it is highly probable that the Gilead here referred to must have meant some *rough region* further to the north-east than the Mount Gilead near the Jordan.

Ha'reth, probably *thicket*, a forest in Judah, to which David fled from Saul, 1 Sam. xxii, 5. Probably identical with *Kharith*.

Ha'rod, WELL OF, *spring of trembling, terror*. A spring by which Gideon and his great army encamped on the morning of the day which ended in the rout of the Midianites, and where the trial of the people by their mode of drinking apparently took place, Judges vii, 1.

It is possibly identical with the fountain now called *Ain Jâlûd*, nearly opposite Shunem, about a mile east of Jezreel. *Jalûd* may be a corruption of Harod.

Haro'sheth of the Gentiles. Harosheth signifies *wood-cuttings*, or *carving* in wood, stone, etc. A town of northern Palestine, the home of Sisera, Judges iv, 2, 13, 16. From the fact that this town was the gathering-place of Jabin's army, it would seem that it could not have been far from Hazor.

Dr. Thomson, who makes "the authority of Jabin extend very far," says: "About eight miles from Megiddo, at the entrance of the pass to Esdraelon from the plain of Acre, is an enormous double mound called *Harothieh*, which is the Arabic form of the Hebrew Harosheth, the signification of the word being the same in both languages. This tell is situated just below the point where the Kishon in one of its turns beats against the rocky base of Carmel, leaving no room even for a footpath. A castle there effectually commands the pass up the vale of the Kishon into Esdraelon, and such a castle there was on this immense double tell of *Harothieh*. It is still covered with the remains of old walls and buildings. The village of the same name is now on the other side of the river, a short distance higher up, and, of course, nearer the battle-field. I have not the slightest doubt of this identification. It was probably called Harosheth of the *Gentiles* or *nations*, because it belonged to those Gentiles of Acre and the neighboring plains which we know from Judges i, 31, the Hebrews could not subdue, and, by the way, I believe that Sisera pitched between Taanach and Megiddo, because, as stated in the passage from Judges, those towns were still in the hands of the Canaanites."—*The Land and the Book*, ii, p. 143.

Hashmo'nah, *fatness, fat soil*, a station of the Israelites in the wilderness, mentioned Num xxxiii, 29, as next before Moseroth, which, from xx, 28, and Deut. x, 6, was near Mount Hor. It is not known; but Mr. Wilton inclines to identify it with Heshmon, Josh. xv, 27.

Hassena'ah, *the thorny*, the name probably of a town, Senaah, (see Ezra ii, 35; Neh. vii, 38,) with the (Hebrew) definite article prefixed. The men of this place built the Fish Gate at Jerusalem, Neh. iii, 3. Its site is unknown.

Hau'ran, (Map 5,) *caves, cave-land*, a province of Palestine, east of the Jordan, embracing a portion of the ancient kingdom of Bashan. Ezekiel mentions it in defining the north-eastern boundary of the Holy Land, xlvii, 16, 18. There can be but little doubt that this region is identical with the well-known Greek province of Auranitis and the modern *Haurán.* This province is bounded on the west by Gaulonitis, on the north by the wild and rocky district of Trachonitis, on the east by the mountainous region of Bataniea, and on the south by the great plain of Moab. The surface is perfectly flat, and the soil is among the richest in Syria. The whole district abounds in caves. It contains upward of a hundred towns and villages, most of them now deserted, though not ruined. The buildings in many of these are remarkable, the walls of great thickness, the roofs, doors, and even the window-shutters, are of stone, and they are evidently of very remote antiquity. See ARGOB; BASHAN.

The name of this region is applied by those at a distance to the whole country east of *Jaulán,* but the inhabitants themselves define it as above. See Porter's *Giant Cities of Bashan,* and his *Hand-book of Syria and Palestine.*

Hav'ilah or **Havi'lah,** perhaps *terror; that suffers pain.* A country so named is described in the account of Eden as producing gold, bdellium, and the onyx stone, Gen. ii, 11. It is also said to border on the east toward Assyria, on the Ishmaelite and on the Amalekite territory, xxv, 18; 1 Sam. xv, 7. It is reckoned among the Cushite countries, together with districts on the Arabian Gulf, Gen. x, 7; and among Joktanite countries with districts contiguous to the Persian Gulf, xxix. There is, however, an intermixture in both the places referred to—in the first, of regions on the Persian, in the second, of regions on the Arabian Gulf. "It follows, therefore," says Kalisch, "that in both instances Havilah designates the same country, extending at least from the Persian to the Arabian Gulf, and, on account of its vast extent, easily divided into two distinct parts. Where these two centers of the people of Havilah were it is at present impossible to decide. We have no means of ascertaining whether they were in the land of the Chaulotæi, near the Nabatæi, on the Persian Gulf, or in the territory of the Avalitæ, on the African coast, near the Bab-el-Mandeb, the present *Zeyla.*" (*Com. on the Old Test., Gen.*) Some writers, however, imagine that more than one Havilah is spoken of in Scripture, and some find the name in *Khawlan,* a district of the *Yemen,* and there are still other conjectural localities. The *Khawlan* referred to is a fertile territory, embracing a large part of myrrhiferous Arabia.

Ha'voth-Ja'ir, (Map 13,) *villages of Jair,* the name applied to certain villages on the east of the Jordan, in Gilead or Bashan, which Jair took and possessed, Num. xxxii, 41; Judges x, 4. In the original, references are found in Deut. iii, 14, Josh. xiii, 30; 1 Kings iv, 13; 1 Chron. ii, 23. All these towns, both in Gilead and Bashan, formed one of Solomon's commissariat districts. See JAIR; BASHAN-HAVOTH-JAIR.

Ha'zar-Ad'dar, *village of Addar,* or *of greatness,* a place on the southern boundary of the Holy Land, Num. xxxiv, 4. It is called Adar in Josh. xv, 3. Possibly it is *'Ain el-Kudeirât,* or *Adeirât,* to the west of Kadesh-Barnea; but this is only conjecture.

Ha'zar-E'nan, *village of fountains,* the junction of the north and east boundaries of the Promised Land, Num. xxxiv, 9, 10. It is mentioned as a boundary place also in Ezek, xlvii, 17; xlviii, 1.

Mr. Porter supposes this place to be identical with the modern village of

Kuryetein, which is more than sixty miles east-north-east of Damascus. Here are large fountains, the only ones in that vast region; and here are found fragments of columns, with other ruins; but this identification may be considered as doubtful, chiefly on account of the great distance of the place from Damascus and the body of Palestine.

Ha'zar-Gad'dah, *village of fortune*, or, perhaps, *of the kid*, a town in the extreme south of Judah, Josh. xv, 27. Conder identifies this site with *El Ghurra*. The ruins include three reservoirs, two caves, buildings of blocks of flint—the entire site being inclosed by a wall of blocks of flint.

Ha'zar-Hat'ticon, *middle village*, a place probably east of Damascus named in Ezekiel's prophecy of the ultimate boundaries of the land, Ezek. xlvii, 16, and specified as being on the boundary of Hauran. It is not identified.

Ha'zarma'veth, *the court of death*, the name of one of the sons of Joktan, Gen. x, 26; 1 Chron. i, 20. This name is preserved, almost literally, in the Arabic *Hadramäwt*, the appellation of a province in southern Arabia, east of the modern *Yemen*. The inhabitants carry on a considerable trade in frankincense, myrrh, gum, and other products. Their language is a dialect materially differing from that spoken in *Yemen*.

Ha'zar-Shu'al, *fox village*, or *village of jackals*, a town in the south of Palestine, originally in the territory of Judah, afterward allotted to Simeon, Josh. xv, 28; xix, 3; 1 Chron. iv, 28. It is mentioned as inhabited after the captivity, Neh. xi, 27.

Mr. Wilton inclines to identify it with *Beni-Shail*, not far from Gaza. Van de Velde's map places it at the ruins of *Saweh*, between Beersheba and Moladah. Conder (1875) coincides with Van de Velde.

Ha'zar-Su'sah, and **Ha'zar-Su'sim**, *horse village*, and *village of horses*, one of the cities allotted to Simeon in the extreme south of the territory of Judah, Josh. xix, 5; 1 Chron. iv, 31.

Stanley (*Sinai and Palestine*) thinks this might be, like Beth-Marcaboth, the "chariot-station," a depot for horses, such as those which in Solomon's time went to and fro between Egypt and Palestine. It is doubtful whether there were any such communication between those countries as early as the time of Joshua; but may not the rich grassy plains around Beersheba (Robinson, *B. R.*, i, 203) have been used at certain seasons by the ancient tribes of Southern Palestine for pasturing their war and chariot horses, just as the grassy plains of *Jaulân* are used at the present day by the Druze chiefs of Lebanon, and the Turkish cavalry and artillery at Damascus? (Porter in Kitto, ii, 243.)

This place may possibly be identical with Sansannah, which Wilton believes to have been in the modern *Wady es-Suny* or *Sunieh*, not far from Gaza, on the caravan road between that place and Sinai, (*The Negeb*, pp. 212-215.)

Haze'rim, *the villages*, the plural form of Hazer, which latter is the same with Hazar, occurring in composition with other words, as above.

In Deut. ii, 28 the Avims are said to have lived in "Hazerim," that is, in the villages, as far as Gaza, before their expulsion by the Caphtorim.

Mr. Grove says: "As far as we can now appreciate the meaning of the term, it implies that the Avim were a wandering tribe who had retained in their new locality the transitory form of encampment of their original desert life."

Haze'roth, (Map 2.) *villages,* a station of the Israelites in the desert, mentioned next to Kibroth-Hattaavah, Num. xi, 35; xii, 16; xxxiii, 17; Deut. i, 1. It is doubtless identical with *Hudhera,* which lies about eighteen hours' distance from Sinai on the road to Akabah.

Haz'e'zon-Ta'mar, and **Haz'a'zon-Ta'mar,** *pruning* or *felling of the palm,* the ancient name of Engedi, Gen. xiv, 7; 2 Chron. xx, 2. See EN-GEDI.

Ha'zor, (Map 5,) *inclosure, castle.* 1. A fortified city, which, on the occupation of the country, was allotted to Naphtali, Josh. xix, 36. It was also called Asor and Nasor, 1 Macc. xi, 67. Its position was apparently between Ramah and Kedesh, (Josh. xii, 19,) on the high ground overlooking the Lake of Merom. There is no reason for supposing it a different place from that of which Jabin was king (Josh. xi, 1) both when Joshua gained his signal victory over the northern confederation, and when Deborah and Barak routed his general, Sisera, Judg. iv, 2, 17; 1 Sam. xii, 9. It was the chief city of the whole of northern Palestine, Josh. xi, 10. It stood on an eminence, but the district around must have been on the whole flat, and suitable for the maneuvers of the "very many" chariots and horses which formed part of the forces of the King of Hazor and his confederates, Josh. xi, 4, 6, 9; Judg iv, 3. Hazor was the only one of those northern cities which was burned by Joshua, it being doubtless too strong and important to leave standing in his rear. Whether it was rebuilt by the men of Naphtali, or by the second Jabin, (Judg. iv,) we are not told; but Solomon did not overlook so important a post, and the fortification of Hazor, Megiddo, and Gezer, the points of defense for the entrance from Syria and Assyria, the plain of Esdraelon, and the great maritime lowland, respectively, was one of the chief pretexts for his levy of taxes, 1 Kings ix, 15. Later still it is mentioned in the list of the towns and districts whose inhabitants were carried to Assyria by Tiglath-Pileser, 2 Kings xv, 29. The site is quite uncertain. Dr. Robinson suggests *Tell Khuraibeh* as the spot, a rocky peak a few miles south of Kedesh; of which Mr. Grove says, "We may accept it until a better is discovered." Mr. Porter suggests as a more probable site some ruins which he found occupying a commanding spot on the south bank of *Wady Hendáj,* about six miles south of Kedesh. Captains Wilson and Anderson identify Hazor with *Tel Hara,* a little to the south-east of Kedesh, a place of great strength, with many ruins.

2. One of the cities of Judah in the extreme south, named next in order to Kedesh, Josh. xv, 23. It is not known.

3. Hazor-Hadattah ("new Hazor,") also in the south of Judah, Josh. xv, 25. Also not known.

4. "Hezron, which is Hazor," Josh. xv, 25. What Hazor is intended cannot now be determined.

5. A place in which the Benjamites resided after their return from the captivity, Neh. xi, 33. It seems to have been not very far north of Jerusalem. Mr. Grove thinks it may possibly be identical with *Tell 'Asûr,* north of *Taiyibeh.*

He'brew, He'brews. A name applied to the Israelites, Gen. xiv, 13. The meaning of the term is not agreed upon by critics. Four derivations have been proposed: 1. Patronymic from Abram. 2. Appellative from *ábar,* to pass over, because Abraham crossed over the Euphrates to Canaan. 3. Appellative from *éber,* beyond, because the patriarch had once dwelt beyond that river. 4. Patronymic from Eber, Gen. x, 21, 24, 25; xi, 14-17. Dr. Alexander, editor of Kitto's *Encyclopedia*, says: "On the whole the derivation of *Ibri* (Hebrew) from Eber (the ancestor of Abraham) seems to have most in its favor and least against it." Mr. T. E. Brown (in Smith's *Dictionary*) says: "It seems almost impossible for the defenders of the patronymic Eber theory to get over the difficulty arising from the circumstance that no special prominence is in genealogy assigned to Eber, such as might entitle him to the position of head or founder of the race. . . . There is nothing to distinguish Eber above Arphaxad, Peleg, or Serug." Each of these writers presents a strong array of learned names in support of his theory. The appellative derivation from *'éber*, beyond, seems entitled to especial attention from the fact that, while the Jews used the patronymic term *Israelites* in speaking of themselves among themselves, the term *Hebrews* was the name by which they were known to foreigners. Thus the latter is the word used when foreigners are introduced as speaking, Gen. xxxix, 14, 17; xli, 12; Exod. i, 16; ii, 6; 1 Sam. iv, 6, 9; xiii, 19; xiv, 11; xxix, 33; or, where they are opposed to foreign nations, Gen. xliii, 32; Exod. i, 15; ii, 11; Deut. xv, 12; 1 Sam. xiii, 3, 7. In Greek and Roman writers we find the name *Hebrews*, or, in later times, *Jews*. The same contrast is found in the New Testament between Hebrews and foreigners, Acts vi, 1; Phil. 3-5. The Hebrew language is distinguished from all others, Luke xxiii, 38; John v, 2; xix, 13; Acts xxi, 40; xxvi, 14; Rev. ix, 11. In 2 Cor. xi, 22, the word is used as only second to *Israelite* in the expression of national peculiarity. See ISRAEL.

He'bron, (Map 5,) *alliance, friendship,* the oldest town of Palestine. Its original name was Kirjath-Arba, Judg. i, 10, so called from Arba, the father of Anak, and progenitor of the giant Anakim, Josh. xxi, 11; xv, 13, 14. It was sometimes called Mamre, doubtless from Abraham's friend and ally, Mamre the Amorite, Gen. xxxiii, 19; xxxv, 27; but the "oak of Mamre," where the patriarch so often pitched his tent, appears to have been not in but near Hebron. Hebron is situated among the mountains of Judah, twenty Roman miles south of Jerusalem, and the same distance north of Beersheba, Josh. xv, 54; xx, 7. Not only was Hebron the oldest town in Palestine, but it also occupied the most lofty position, being two thousand eight hundred feet above the Mediterranean. It was "built seven years before Zoan," Num. xiii, 22; that is, Tanis in Egypt, and when Josephus wrote it was two thousand three hundred years old. In the time of the patriarchs we find Amorites or Hittites settled there, Gen. xiii, 18; xiv, 13; xxiii, 2, etc., 17, etc.; xxxvii, 14. The Anakim, an old Semitic nation, must then have spread into that country and taken possession of the town, Gen. xxiii, 2; xxxv, 27; Josh. xiv, 15; xv, 13; Judg. i, 10. At the time the country was conquered by the Israelites we find Canaanites and Anakim there. Joshua took Hebron, utterly destroying its inhabitants, Josh. x, 36, 37; xii, 10. But the Anakim must soon have recovered, and established themselves there again, xi, 21. Hebron was then given to Caleb, who, with Judah's aid, took it a second time, and finally expelled the Anakim, Josh. xiv, 12; xvi, 13, 54; Judg. i, 10. It became a city of refuge and was assigned to the priests, Josh. xx, 7; xxi, 11. Hence it is placed under the descendants of Caleb, 1 Chron. ii, 42, etc., and those of Levi, Exod. vi, 18; Num. iii, 27; 1 Chron. v, 28. In Judg. xvi, 3, a hill is named, near Hebron, to which Samson carried the gates of Gaza. While David reigned over Judah alone (seven and a half years)

MOSQUE AT HEBRON (MACHPELAH) AND PART OF THE TOWN.

Hebron was his residence, 2 Sam. ii, 1; iii, 3; v, 1–5. Absalom went thither to conceal his treasonable project under cover of performing a vow, but more probably because some malcontents there would favor his plot, and there he raised the banner of rebellion, 2 Sam. xv, 7, etc. Rehoboam fortified Hebron as an important frontier post, 2 Chron. xi, 10, and after the exile it was still called Arba, Neh. xi, 25. When the Edomites took Palestine Hebron fell into their hands; but Judas Maccabeus retook it, tore down its fortresses, and burned its towers, 1 Macc. v, 65. Afterward the Romans stormed and burned it, but, being favorably located on the road from Jerusalem to Beersheba, it recovered again.

The modern name of Hebron is *el-Khulîl,* "the friend," that is, of God. The city lies in the narrow "Valley of Eshcol," whose sides are clothed with vineyards, groves of olives, and other fruit-trees. Its population is estimated at from five thousand to ten thousand, including about sixty families of Jews. The houses are all of stone, solidly built, flat-roofed, each having one or two small cupolas. Among the buildings the *Haram* is most prominent. As it contains the sepulchers of the patriarchs, it has long been regarded with veneration, and visited by Jews, Christians, and Moslems; it is, perhaps, the most remarkable remaining architectural relic in Palestine. For an account of the *Haram* see MACHPELAH. See ESHCOL.

A mile up the valley is a vast oak-tree, popularly said to be the tree of Mamre, under which Abraham pitched his tent. See MAMRE. Two ancient pools remain, the lower one one hundred and thirty-three feet square and twenty-two feet deep, the upper eighty-five feet by fifty-five feet, and nineteen feet deep. It might be over one of these that David hanged the murderers of Ish-Bosheth, 2 Sam. iv, 12.

He'bron, perhaps *passage,* a city of Asher, apparently near Zidon, Josh. xix, 28. It is not identified. It may probably be the same as Abdon.

He'lam, *stronghold,* a place between the Jordan and the Euphrates, where David gained a victory over the Syrians, 2 Sam. x, 16, 17. Many conjectures have been made as to the locality of Helam, but to none of them does any certainty attach. The most probable, perhaps, is, that it is identical with Alamatha, a town named by Ptolemy, and located by him on the west of the Euphrates near Nicephorium.

Hel'bah, *fatness, fertile region,* a town of Asher, probably on the plain of Phœnicia, not far from Sidon, Judg. i, 31.

Hel'bon, (Map 5,) *fat, fertile,* a place noted for excellent wines, which were conveyed to Tyre from Damascus, Ezek. xxvii, 18. Helbon has usually been thought to be the modern Aleppo; but Mr. Porter thinks that the modern *Helbûn,* in Anti-Lebanon, near Damascus, is without doubt identical with the place in question. Considerable ruins remain around the village, indicating ancient wealth and splendor.

He'leph, *exchange,* a place on the boundary of Naphtali, Josh. xix, 33. Van de Velde would identify it with *Beitlif,* an ancient site nearly due east of *Ras Abyad,* and west of *Kades;* but this identification is doubtful.

Hel'kath, *a portion,* (in 1 Chron. vi, 75, called Hukok,) a border city of Asher, Josh. xix, 25, afterward allotted to the Gershonite Levites, xxi, 31. It is not identified.

Hel'kath-Haz'zurim, *the field of heroes,* or *of swords,* a spot near Gibeon, where twelve of Joab's men encountered twelve of Abner's, the whole of the combatants falling, 2 Sam. ii, 16.

He'math, *fortress,* 1 Chron. xiii, 5; Amos vi, 14. An incorrect form of Hamath.

Hem'dan, *pleasant,* one of the descendants of Seir the Horite, (Ge x. xxxvi, 26,) whose posterity probably were some of the tribes of Arabia Petræa. The name is Amram in 1 Chron. i, 41.

He'na, perhaps *a troubling,* or *low ground,* a city conquered by some king of Assyria shortly before Sennacherib, 2 Kings xviii, 34; xix, 13; Isa. xxxvii, 13. It was probably on the Euphrates, where now stands *Anah,* or *Ana,* near *Mosaib.*

He'pher, *a pit, a well,* a territory in Palestine, whose petty chief was destroyed by Joshua, Josh. xii, 17. It was part of one of Solomon's commissariat districts, 1 Kings iv, 10. It is not identified.

Heph'zibah, *my delight is in her,* a name which is to be borne by the restored Jerusalem, Isa. lxii, 4.

He'res, 1. A mount, Judg. i, 35; perhaps identical with IR-SHEMESH, which see.

2. Isa. xix, 18, marg. See IR-HAHERES.

Her'mon, MOUNT, (Map 5,) *lofty* or *prominent peak,* so called doubtless because it was visible from a very great distance. The Sidonians called it *Sirion,* from the root signifying "to glitter," and the Amorites *Shenir,* ("to clatter,") both words meaning "breastplate," and suggested by its rounded, glittering top when the sun's rays were reflected by the snow that covered it, Deut. iii, 9; Sol. Song iv, 8; Ezek. xxvii, 5. It was also named *Sion,* "the elevated," towering over all its compeers, Deut. iv, 48.

Mount Hermon was on the north-eastern border of Palestine, Deut. iii, 8; Josh. xii, 1; over against Lebanon, Josh. xi, 17, adjoining the plateau of Bashan, 1 Chron. v, 23.

It was the great landmark of the Israelites. It was associated with their northern border almost as intimately as the sea was with their western. Hermon rises boldly at the southern end of Anti-Libanus to the height of about ten thousand feet above the level of the sea. Its summit (or rather summits, for there are three) is a truncated cone, elevated two thousand or three thousand feet above the more continuous chain. Dr. Thomson describes it as seen from Sarepta, from Tyre, and from the Dead Sea.

The modern name of Hermon is *Jebel esh-Sheikh,* "the chief mountain," and sometimes *Jebel eth-Thelj,* "the snowy mountain." Through the spring till the earlier part of summer the top is covered with snow; but as the weather becomes hotter large masses melt, and the snow remains only in the streaks in the ravines. On one of the summits are the remains of a circular wall inclosing a small, ruined temple. Probably this marks the site of one of the "high places," where worship was paid to idols. "The dew of Hermon" (Psa. cxxiii, 3) was very likely the distillation of the vapors condensed by the snowy crown of the mountain; and "Zion," in the same passage, is no doubt used as being one of the various names of Hermon. It may be added that the ridge *Jebel Ed-Duhy,* on the north of the valley of Jezreel, has been called the "Little Hermon." See LEBANON; TABOR.

Her'monites, Psa. xlii, 7. Inaccurate. It is correctly "Hermons," that is, probably the range of Hermon.

Hesh'bon, (Map 5,) *reason, device,* a city of the Amorites, originally belonging to Moab, east of Jordan, on the boundary of Reuben and Gad; rebuilt by Reuben and allotted to the Levites, Num. xxi. 25-34; xxxii, 3, 37;

BIBLE GEOGRAPHY. 177

Deut. i, 4; ii, 24–30; iii, 2, 6; iv, 46; xxix, 7; Josh. ix, 10; xii, 2. 5; xiii, 10–27; xxi, 39; Judg. xi, 19, 26; 1 Chron. vi, 81. In later times the Moabites regained possession of Heshbon, so that it is mentioned as a Moabitish town in the prophetic denunciations against that people, Isa. xv, 4; xvi, 8, 9; Jer. xlviii, 2, 34, 45; xlix, 3. The ruins of this city still exist twenty miles east of the point where the Jordan falls into the Dead Sea. They are called *Hesbân*, and occupy a low hill in the great plain. There are some remarkable remains among them, and cisterns are still to be seen, with an ancient reservoir, Sol. Song vii, 4.

Hesh'mon, *fatness, fat soil,* a town in the extreme south of Judah, Josh. xv, 27, probably near the Edomitish border. Wilton would connect it with the Edomite king, Husham, Gen. xxxvi, 34, 35; and he identifies it with *'Ain Hasb*. He also thinks it to be the same with Hashmonah, one of the stations in the wanderings of Israel, Num. xxxiii, 29, 30. See Ayre's *Treasury*. Mr. Grove says it is perhaps identical with Azmon, but very doubtful. Conder identifies it with *El Meshash*.

Heth, THE SONS OF, or CHILDREN OF. See HITTITES.

Heth'lon, *wrapped up, hiding place,* a place in the extreme north of the Holy Land, Ezek. xlvii, 15; xlviii, 1. Probably the "way of Hethlon" is the pass at the northern end of Lebanon from the sea-coast of the Mediterranean to the great plain of Hamath, and is thus identical with "the entrance of Hamath" in Num. xxxiv, 8, etc.

Hez'ron, Josh. xv, 25. See HAZOR, (4.)

Hid'dekel, (Map 1,) *the rapid Tigris,* Tigris itself signifying *velocity* or *an arrow*. One of the rivers of Eden, Gen. ii, 14; Dan. x, 4. There can be no reasonable doubt that the Tigris is intended, the Arabic name of which is *Dijleh*. The whole length of the Tigris is estimated at one thousand one hundred and fifty miles. Between *Diarbekram* and *Mosul*, about three hundred miles, it is navigable for rafts in seasons of flood.

In 1838 the steamer "Euphrates" ascended the stream to within twenty miles of *Mosul*. See TIGRIS.

Hierap'olis, (Map 8,) *sacred city,* a city of Phrygia Magna, east of Colosse, and about six Roman miles north of Laodicea. Christianity was probably introduced here at the same time as at Colosse, Col. iv, 13. Its modern name is *Pambouk-Kalessi*. The situation of the city is extremely beautiful, and its ruins are considerable, the theater and gymnasium being the most conspicuous. The hot calcareous springs of the neighborhood have deposited the vast and singular incrustations noticed by travelers.

Hi'len, perhaps *place of caves,* a priests' city in Judah, 1 Chron. vi, 58 It is called Holon in Josh. xv, 51; xxi, 15.

Hin'nom, VALLEY OF, (Map 7.) Hinnom may perhaps signify *lamentation,* but its origin is unknown; it may have been derived from some of its ancient possessors. It was also called "the valley of the son" or "children of Hinnom." The later Jews termed it *Ge Hinnom, Gehenna,* to denote the place of eternal torment. See Josh. xviii, 16; 2 Chron. xxviii, 3; xxxiii, 6; Jer. xix, 2, 6. In Jer. ii, 23 it is called "the valley," and perhaps "the valley of dead bodies," xxxi, 40, and "the valley of vision," Isa. xxii, 1, 5.

Hinnom is a deep and narrow ravine, with steep, rocky sides, to the south and west of Jerusalem, separating Mount Zion to the north from the "Hill of Evil Counsel" and the sloping, rocky plateau of the "plain of Rephaim" to the south. It is first mentioned in Josh. xv, 8; xviii, 16, where the boundary line between Judah and Benjamin is accurately described as passing along the bed of the ravine.

On the southern brow, overlooking the valley at its eastern extremity, Solomon erected high places for Moloch, (1 Kings xi, 7,) whose horrid rites were revived from time to time in the same vicinity by later idolatrous kings. Ahaz and Manasseh made their children "pass through the fire" in this valley, (2 Kings xvi, 3; 2 Chron. xxviii, 3; xxxiii, 6,) and the fiendish cus tom of infant sacrifice to the fire gods seems to have been kept up in Tophet at its south-east extremity for a considerable period, Jer. vii, 31; 2 Kings xxiii, 10. To put an end to these abominations the place was polluted by Josiah, who rendered it ceremonially unclean by spreading over it human bones and other corruptions, (2 Kings xxiii, 10, 13, 14; 2 Chron. xxxiv, 4, 5,) from which time it appears to have become the common cess-pool of the city, into which its sewage was conducted to be carried off by the waters of the Kidron, as well as a laystall where all its solid filth was collected. Most commentators follow Buxtorf, Lightfoot, and others, in asserting that perpetual fires were here kept up for the consumption of bodies of criminals, carcasses of animals, and whatever else was combustible; but the Rabbinical authorities usually brought forward in support of this idea appear insufficient, and Robinson declares (i, 274) that "there is no evidence of any other fires than those of Moloch having been kept up in this valley."

The name by which the valley is now known is (in ignorance of the initial syllable) *Wâdy Jehennam*, or *Wâdy er Rubêb*, though in Mohammedan traditions the Gehenna is applied to the valley of Kidron. Mr. Bartlett (*Walks about Jerusalem*, pp. 62, 63,) says: "There is something in the scenery of this valley and the hill above; its tombs hewn in the rock, long since tenantless; the gray gloom of its old fig and olive trees starting from the fissures of the crags; the overhanging wall of Zion, desolate almost as in the time of her captivity, that forcibly recalls the wild and mournful grandeur of the prophetic writings. Within it, too, is the traditional 'Aceldama,' or Field of Blood, of the traitor Judas, a small plot of ground, overhung with one precipice and looking down another into the glen below, on which is a deep charnel-house, into which it was formerly the custom to throw the bodies of the dead, as the earth was supposed to have the power of rapidly consuming them. The place was selected as the burial-place of pilgrims who died at Jerusalem in the Middle Ages. Such are the scenes that have passed in Hinnom; it is like the scroll of the prophet, 'written within and without with mourning, lamentation, and woe.'"

Hit'tite and **Hit'tites**, (Map 3,) from Heth, *fear*. A tribe of Canaan, called also "children of Heth," whose location was in the southern part of the land, Gen. x, 15; 1 Chron. i, 13; Gen. xv, 10; xxiii, 3-18. Abraham purchased from them the field and cave of Machpelah, Gen. xxiii. Esau's wives were from this people, Gen. xxvi, 34; xxxvi, 2. Notices of their territory are found in Gen. xxiii, 17-20; Num. xiii, 29; Josh. i, 4; Judg. i, 26. It was given to the Israelites, Exod. iii, 8; Deut. vii, 1; Josh. i, 4. Conquered by Joshua, Josh. ix, 1, 2; x-xii; xxiv, 11. Imperfectly conquered, Judg. iii, 5. Intermarriages with the Israelites, Judg. iii, 6, 7; Ezra ix, 1; with Solomon, 1 Kings xi, 1. They were tributary to Solomon, 1 Kings ix, 20, 21; 1 Chron. viii, 7, 8. Had kings in his reign, 1 Kings x, 29; 2 Chron. i, 17; and in Joram's, 2 Kings vii, 6. Uriah and Abimelech, David's captains, were Hittites, 1 Sam. xxvi, 6; 2 Sam. xi, 3; xxiii, 39.

The sacred record says nothing concerning the religion or worship of the Hittites. Even in the enumeration of Solomon's idolatrous worship of the gods of his wives—among whom were Hittite women (1 Kings xi, 1)—no Hittite deity is alluded to. See 1 Kings xi, 5, 7; 2 Kings xxiii, 13.

Among the customs of the Hittites was the very peculiar one of shaving a square place just above the ear, leaving the hair on the side of the face and whiskers hanging down in a long plaited lock. This frightful custom, and other eccentric dealings of the nations with their hair, throw some light upon the injunctions to avoid such customs, which we find in the books of the .aw. See, for instance, Lev. xix, 27.

Hi'vite and **Hi'vites**, (Map 3,) variously defined as *midlanders, villagers, serpents*. One of the ancient peoples of Canaan, who appear to have gathered round two principal centers in the middle of Palestine, and toward the north, Gen. x, 17; 1 Chron. i, 15. The Shechemites belonged to this tribe, Gen. xxxiv, 2; and also the Gibeonites, Josh. ix, 7; xi, 19. One of Esau's wives a Hivite, Gen. xxxvi, 2. Reference to their territory, Josh. xi, 3; Judg. iii, 3; 2 Sam. xxiv, 7. Given to the Israelites, Exod. xxiii, 28; Deut. xx, 17. Conquered by Joshua, Josh. ix, 1; xii, 8; xxiv, 11. Imperfectly conquered, Judg. iii, 5. Tributary to Solomon, 1 Kings ix, 20; 2 Chron. viii, 7.

Ho'bah, *hidden, hiding place*, the place to which Abraham pursued the confederate kings, Gen. xiv, 15. It lay north of Damascus. The village of *Jôbar*, where the Jews have a synagogue dedicated to Elijah, is claimed by the Jews of Damascus as the Hobah of Scripture. Others claim as the site *Burzeh*, three miles north of Damascus. Here is shown a cleft in the rock, in which tradition represents Abraham as *taking refuge* on one occasion from the giant Nimrod. Delitzch (on Genesis) claims that Hobah is identified with a fountain called *Hoba*, near Karjeten, in the "land of Menadnir."

Ho'lon, *sandy*.
1. A town in the mountains of Judah, named between Goshen and Giloh, Josh. xv, 51. It was allotted with its "suburbs" to the priests, xxi, 15. In 1 Chron. vi, 58, it is called Hilen.
2. A city of Moab, Jer. xlviii, 21, in the *Mishor*, east of Jordan. There is no identification of either place.

Ho'mam, *destruction*. A descendant of Seir the Horite, 1 Chron. i, 39. In Gen. xxxvi, 32, the name is Heman. There is a town bearing the name of *El-Homaimeh* south from Petra, and on the hill *Sherah*, which the Arabic geographers describe as the native place of the Abassides. (Robinson, *Bib. Res.*, ii, 572.) With this Knobel compares Homam. (Kitto.)

Hor, Mount, (Map 2,) *the mountain, the mountain of mountains*.
1. A mountain on the boundary line or "at the edge" of the land of Edom, Num. xx, 23; xxxiii, 37. It was the next halting place of the people after Kadesh, (xx, 22; xxxiii, 37,) and they quitted it for Zalmonah, (xxxiii, 41,) in the road to the Red Sea, (xxi, 4.) It was while Israel was encamped by Hor that the divine command was issued for Aaron (who, on account of his disobedience at the water of Meribah, was not to enter Canaan) to go up and die there. Moses and Eleazar accompanied the aged priest to his death, the eyes of the congregation being fixed on them as they ascended. The sacerdotal garments were taken from him and put upon Eleazar his son. So Aaron died; and Moses and Eleazar returned, and the people mourned for him thirty days, Num. xx, 24–29; xxxiii, 38, 39; Deut. xxxii, 50. It is

true that Mosera is elsewhere (x, 6) named as the place of Aaron's death; but Mosera was close by the mountain.

Mount Hor is the highest and most conspicuous of the whole range of the sandstone mountains of Edom, having close beneath it on its eastern side the mysterious city of Petra. Its height, according to the latest measurements, is four thousand eight hundred feet above the Mediterranean, that is to say, about one thousand seven hundred feet above the town of Petra, four thousand above the level of the Arabah, and more than six thousand above the Dead Sea. The mountain is marked far and near by its double top, which rises like a huge castellated building from a lower base, and is surmounted by the circular dome of the tomb of Aaron, a distinct white spot on the dark red surface of the mountain. This lower base is the "plain of Aaron," beyond which Buckhardt, after all his toils, was prevented from ascending. The chapel or mosque of Aaron's tomb is a small square building, measuring inside about twenty-eight feet by thirty-three, with its door in the south-west angle. It is built of rude stones, in part broken columns, all of sandstone; but fragments of granite and marble lie all about. Steps lead to the flat roof of the chapel. The interior of the chapel consists of two chambers, one below the other. Between the two peaks is a little plain, marked by a white cypress. The tomb of Aaron is on the northern-most peak. According to travelers the impression received on the spot is that Aaron's death took place in the small basin between the peaks, and that the people were stationed either on the plain at the base of the peaks, or at that part of the *Wady Abu-Kusheybeh* from which the top is commanded.

Owing to the natural difficulties of the locality and the caprices of the Arabs, Mount Hor and Petra are more difficult of access than any other places which Christian travelers usually attempt to visit. The modern name of *Hor* is *Jebel Nebi Harûn*. Mr. Wilton (*The Negeb*. pp. 126-134) rejects this traditional site of Hor, and suggests *Jebel Moderah*, on the opposite side of the Arabah, some distance to the north-east. No force in the suggestion.

2. A mountain named only in Num. xxxiv, 7, 8, as one of the marks of the northern boundary of the land which the children of Israel were about to conquer. The great range of Lebanon is so clearly the natural northern boundary of the country that there seems no reason to doubt that the whole range is intended by the term Hor.

Ho'reb, (Map 1,) *dry, desert*, probably another name for the whole or part of Sinai, Exod. iii, 1; xvii, 6; xxxiii, 6; Deut. i, 2, 6, 19; iv, 10, 15; v, 2; ix, 8; xviii, 16; xxix, 1; 1 Kings viii, 9; xix, 8; 2 Chron. v, 10; Psalm cvi, 19; Mal. iv, 4; Ecclesiasticus xlviii, 7. See SINAI.

Ho'rem, *devoted*, a city of Naphtali, named with Iron and Migdal-el Josh. xix, 38. Van de Velde suggests *Hurah* as the site of Horem, in the center of the country, half way between the *Ras en-Nakhura* and Lake Merom, on a *tell* at the southern end of the *Wady el-Ain*.

Hor-Hagid'gad, (Map 2,) possibly the *mount of thunder*, or the *conspicuous mountain*, a station of the Israelites in the desert, Num. xxxiii, 32; probably the same as Gudgodah, Deut. x, 7. As the order in both passages is not strictly preserved, Hengstenberg has sought to account for this by supposing that they were, in Deut. x, 7, going the opposite way to that in Num. xxxiii, 32. (*Genuineness of the Pentateuch* ii, 356.) Mr. Wilton is inclined to regard the visit to Hor-Hagidgad as distinct from the journey to Gudgodah;

so that thus the two places would not be absolutely identical. He considers Gudgodah the wady or valley, and Hor-Hagidgad a mountain near. Dr. Robinson describes here "a lone conical mountain," which "forms a conspicuous landmark for the traveler." This, now called *Jebel Aráif en-Náhah*, may be Hor-Hagidgad. (*The Negeb*, pp. 131, 132.) See Smith and Ayre.

Ho'ri, Ho'rites, and **Ho'rims,** (Map 3,) *dwellers in caverns*, the original inhabitants of Mount Seir, probably dwellers in holes and caves, Gen. xiv, 6. They were smitten by Chedorlaomer and his confederates, and afterward entirely dispossessed by the descendants of Esau, Deut. ii, 12, 22. Their genealogy is given in Gen. xxxvi, 20-30; 1 Chron. i, 38-42; but nothing further is recorded of them. Their excavated dwellings are still found in hundreds in the sandstone cliffs and mountains of Edom, and especially in Petra. They seem to have been designated more according to their mode of life than to their specific race.

Hor'mah, (Map 5,) *place desolated*, the city of a Canaanitish king who attacked the Israelites; on which they vowed that if they succeeded in defeating their assailants they would utterly destroy the city. It had before been called Zephath; but it had at once, as a doomed place, the name Hormah given it, though the vow does not seem to have been accomplished till a later period, Num. xiv, 45; xxi, 1-3; Deut. i, 44. The king is enumerated among those that were destroyed in the general war, Josh. xii, 14; and the town was allotted first to Judah, afterward to Simeon, xv, 30; xix, 4. It was Judah, therefore, and Simeon, who sacked Hormah; but it seems to have been subsequently rebuilt, 1 Sam. xxx, 30; 1 Chron. iv, 30. Hormah is doubtless identical with *Sebaita*, near the well of Rehoboth. The ruins are both considerable and imposing. The name Sebaita is etymologically identical with Zephath. The town contains three large church edifices, built of massive masonry, presenting the appearance of fortresses. They may probably be referred to the fourth or fifth century. (See *Desert of the Exodus*.)

Hor'ona'im, *two caverns,* a Moabitish town near Nimrim and Luhith, possibly upon an eminence, Isa. xv, 5; Jer. xlviii, 3, 5, 34. Unknown.

Hor'onite, the name applied to Sanballat, who was one of the principal opponents of Nehemiah's works of restoration, Neh. ii, 10, 19; xiii, 28. He was probably a native of Horonaim, although *Fürst* says of Horon—that is, Beth-Horon.

Ho'sah, *a refuge*, a city of Asher, the next landmark on the boundary to Tyre, Josh. xix, 29. Unknown.

Huk'kok, *decreed*, according to some, *scribe, moat*, a border place of Naphtali, Josh. xix, 34. It is probably identical with *Yakuk*, seven miles south of *Safed*.

Hu'kok, (*id.*,) a Levitical city of Asher, 1 Chron. vi, 75. In Josh. xxi, 31, it is Helkath.

Hul, *circle*, the name of a son of Aram, and grandson of Shem, Gen. x, 23; 1 Chron. i, 17. The position occupied by his descendants is not accurately determined. The most probable opinion locates them in the district to the north of Lake Merom, now *Hûleh*.

Hum'tah, *a place of lizards*, or possibly *a bulwark*, a city in the hill country of Judah, Josh. xv, 54. It is unknown.

Hu'shah, *haste*, a name in the genealogies of the tribe of Judah, 1 Chron iv, 4, which may designate a person, and very possibly a place, we cannot determine which.

Huz'zab, Nahum ii, 9. The margin reads, "Or, *that which was established,* or, *there was a stand made.*" The meaning is uncertain. Ewald supposes it the name of the queen of Nineveh. Rawlinson suggests the *Zab* country, that is, the district watered by the two *Zab* rivers in Assyria. Mr. Grove also inclines to this opinion. Gesenius, uniting the word to the preceding verse, translates, "the palace is dissolved and made to flow down;" while Henderson, (*Minor Prophets,* p 282,) preferring an exactly opposite meaning, reads, "the palace is dissolved, though firmly established."

Hydas'pes, a river mentioned in Judith i, 6. It is not the Hydaspes of India, but it is uncertain what river is intended. Mr. Bevan (in Smith's *Dictionary*) says that it may perhaps be identical with the Choaspes of Susiana.

Ib'leam, *he consumes the people,* a city of Manasseh, but territorially belonging to another tribe, either of Issachar or Asher, Josh. xvii, 11; Judges i, 27; 2 Kings ix, 27. It is doubtless identical with Bileam, 1 Chron. vi, 70. Probably the village *Jelama,* north of *Jenin,* marks the site.

Ico'nium, (Map 8,) a considerable city of Asia Minor, generally considered as belonging to Lycaonia, though Xenophon calls it the last city of Phrygia, and Ammianus Marcellinus places it in Pisidia. It was on the great line of communication between Ephesus and the western coast of the peninsula on one side, and Tarsus, Antioch, and the Euphrates on the other. Iconium was well chosen for missionary operations. St. Paul first visited Iconium with Barnabas from Antioch in Pisidia. Their preaching and miracles were made effectual to the conversion of many; but, a persecution being stirred up by the Jews, the apostles fled to Lystra and Derbe. They visited Iconium again, however, before returning to the Syrian Antioch, Acts xiii, 50, 51; xiv; 2 Tim. iii, 11. Paul must have been at Iconium in his next journey with Silas, Acts xvi, 1–6, and very possibly at a later period, xviii, 23. It is now called *Konieh.* Its population is about thirty thousand. Imposing ruins of Saracenic architecture remain.

Ida'lah, or **Id'alah,** *what God exalts, memorial stone of God,* or *he goes softly.* A city of Zebulun, Josh. xix, 15, probably not far from Bethlehem, west of Nazareth.

Idumæ'a, or **Idume'a,** (Map 5,) the Greek form of the name EDOM, which see, Isa. xxxiv, 5, 6; Ezek. xxxv, 15; xxxvi, 5; 1 Macc. iv, 15, 29, 61; v, 3; vi, 31; 2 Macc. xii, 32; Mark iii, 8.

I'im, *ruins, rubbish.* 1. Num. xxxiii, 45. The contracted form of Ije-Abarim, a station of the Israelites.

2. A town in the extreme south of Judah, Josh. xv, 29.

Wilton connects it with Azem, which follows, and supposes the real place to be Ije-Azem, and identifies it with the ruins of *El-'Aujeh* (or *'Abdeh*) of the 'Azâzimeh Arabs.

Ij'e-Ab'arim, (Map 2,) *ruins of Abarim,* or *of the further regions,* a station of the Israelites, Num. xxi, 11; xxxiii, 44, called also (in 45) Iim. It was next to the torrent Zared, and on the south border of Moab. The site is unknown.

I'jon, (Map 5,) *a ruin,* a town in the north of Palestine belonging to Naphtali. It was taken and plundered by Ben-Hadad, 1 King xv, 20; 2 Chron. xvi, 4. Again it was plundered by Tiglath-Pileser, 2 Kings xv. 29. Its ruins are possibly those on *Tell Dibbin,* a noble site on the fertile and beautiful little plain called *Merj 'Ayûn*, a few miles north-west of the site of Dan, where traces of a strong and ancient city exist.

Illyr'icum, (Map 8,) an extensive district lying along the eastern coast of the Adriatic from the boundary of Italy on the north to Epirus on the south, and contiguous to Mœsia and Macedonia on the east. It was divided into two portions—Illyris Barbara, the northern, and Illyris Græca, the southern. Within these limits was included Dalmatia, which appears to have been used indifferently with Illyricum for a portion, and ultimately for the whole of the district. St. Paul records that he preached the Gospel "round about unto Illyricum," Rom. xv, 19. He probably uses the term in its most extensive sense, and the part visited (if, indeed, he crossed the boundary at all) would have been about Dyrrachium.

Im'mer, *talkative,* the name of a place apparently in Babylonia, Ezra ii, 59; Neh. vii, 61.

In'dia, (Map 5.) This word occurs first in Esther i, 1; viii, 9, as the limit of the territories of Ahasuerus in the East, as Ethiopia was in the West. The Hebrew form *Hoddu* is an abbreviation of *Honadu,* which is identical with the indigenous names of the river Indus, " Hindu," or " Sindhu," and again with the ancient name of the country as it appears in the Vendîdad, " Hapta Hendu." It is evident that India, as here mentioned, did not include the peninsula of Hindostan, but the districts around the Indus—the Punjab, and, it may be, Scinde. India, in the same sense, occurs in the Apocrypha, 1 Esdras iii, 2; Rest of Esther xiii, 1; xvi, 1. It is also mentioned (but by mistake probably for Ionia) in 1 Macc. viii, 8. Though, however, India proper is not named in Scripture, yet it is very likely that Solomon and the Tyrians carried on an Indian trade, and, at a later period, natives of that country seem to have been employed in guiding the elephants which were used in war, 1 Macc. vi, 37.

Ir-Hahe'res. In Isa. xix, 18, the Hebrew is rendered " City of Destruction," though, as is suggested in the margin of the Authorized Version, the original might be taken as the proper name of a city of Egypt. The meaning of the verse is very obscure, and has been variously interpreted. A number of ancient manuscripts warrant the signification, "City of the Sun," in which case it might be identical with Heliopolis, the famous city of Lower Egypt, called On in Gen. xli, 45, and Beth-Shemesh (" City of the Sun ") in Jer. xliii, 13.

Other opinions have been given, but they are generally too fanciful to record.

Calvin uses the word as a descriptive title, and not as a proper name. The prophecy of the whole verse would thus express the idea that for *one* town of Egypt which should perish in unbelief *five* should profess the true faith, and swear fealty to the Lord.

Mr. Poole (in Smith's *Dict.*) says: "If the prophecy is to be understood in a proper sense, we can, however, see no other time to which it applies, and must suppose that Ir-Haheres was one of the cities partly or wholly inhabited by the Jews in Egypt. Of these Onion (Onias) was the most important, and to it the rendering, ' One shall be called a city of destruction,' would apply, since it was destroyed by Titus, while Alexandria, and perhaps the other cities, yet stand. If the prophecy is to be taken tropically, the best reading and rendering can only be determined by verbal criticism." See Kitto.

Ir-Na'hash, *serpent city,* a name occurring among the genealogies of Judah, 1 Chron. iv, 12. The margin reads "the city of Nahash." No trace of this name is found.

I'ron, *piety, pious,* a city of Naphtali named between En-hazor and Migdal-el, Josh. xix, 38. Mr. Grove thinks it possibly *Yarûn.*

Ir'peel, *God restores,* or *heals,* an ancient town of Benjamin, apparently situated on the mountain ridge north of Jerusalem, Josh. xviii, 27. The site is unknown.

Ir-She'mesh, *City of the Sun,* a city of Dan, near Zorah and Eshtaol, Josh. xix, 41. It is doubtless identical with BETH-SHEMESH, (1,) which see.

Ish'maelites, from Ishmael, *whom God hears.* Sometimes the actual descendants of Ishmael, the son of Abraham and Hagar, are meant by this term, and sometimes it seems to comprehend more generally the neighboring Abrahamic tribes, Judges viii, 24; 1 Chron. xxvii, 30; Psa. liii, 6. Nearly four thousand years have passed since the Ishmaelites became a nation, and yet in disposition, in manners, in habits, in government, in occupation, and even in dress, they are the same as they were at the first. Since the days of Abraham the tents of the Ishmaelites have been studded along the whole eastern confines of Palestine, and they have been scattered over Arabia from the borders of Egypt to the banks of the Euphrates.

Ish'meelites, Gen. xxxvii, 25, 27, 28; xxxix, 1; 1 Chron. ii, 17. The same as Ishmaelites.

Ish'tob, *men of Tob,* apparently one of the small kingdoms or states that formed part of the general country of Aram, 2 Sam. x, 6, 8. Although in the ancient versions the name is given as one word, yet it is probable that the real signification is the "men of Tob," a district mentioned also in connection with Ammon in the records of Jephthah, and again, perhaps, under the shape of *Tobie* or *Tubieni,* in the history of the Maccabees. See TOB.

Is'rael, *warrior, prince, contender,* or *wrestler with God.* The name received from God by the patriarch Jacob on the occasion of the mysterious interview on Peniel. Geographically considered, it is the designation of the people descended from Jacob, Gen. xlviii, 20; Exod. v, 2; Num. xxi, 1; Josh. iv, 22; Rom. ix, 6, etc. Sometimes the fuller expression, "children of Israel," occurs. It is also employed to designate the ten tribes which separated from Judah and formed THE KINGDOM OF ISRAEL, 2 Sam. ii, 9; 1 Kings xii, 1, etc. (See Map 14.)

This separation occurred after the death of Solomon, under Jeroboam, the leader of the revolt. Shechem was fixed upon and fortified as the capital of the new kingdom, 1 Kings xii, 25. The beauty of Tirzah led the king to make that city his second capital, 1 Kings xiv, 17. Tirzah continued to be the chief city of Israel until Omri built Samaria as his capital. This city occupied a magnificent site, and was very strongly fortified. It was repeatedly besieged; but it held out against the Assyrians for three years, 2 Kings xvii, 5, while Jerusalem itself was reduced by Nebuchadnezzar in a year and a half, xxv, 1–3. Frequently the dynasties of Israel were broken, and repeatedly did the Syrian power impose the most humbling terms on Israel. Occasionally Israel was the victor, but the monarchy gradually grew weaker until at length the Assyrians captured Samaria, (B. C. 721,) and the tribes of Israel were carried away captive, and their country was occupied by colonists from the East. See 1 Kings xv, 20; xx, 1–4; 2 Kings xiii. 3–7. 22–25 · xiv. 25–28; xv, 29; xvii, 6, 24.

Subsequently a mixed population inhabited the land. Although after the fall of Babylon many persons of the various tribes returned, and although the name Israel was applied to the whole people as settled again in Palestine, (Ezra ii, 70; x, 5; Neh. xii, 47,) yet Israel existed no longer as a nation. See JUDAH, JERUSALEM, WILDERNESS.

Is'sachar, (Map 5,) *there is reward*, or *he brings reward* or *wages*. The tribe called after Issachar, a son of Jacob and Leah. On the journey to Canaan Issachar's place was east of the tabernacle, with his brothers Judah and Zebulun, Num. ii, 5, the group moving foremost in the march, x, 15. The number of the fighting men of Issachar, when taken in the census at Sinai, was 54,400. During the journey they seem to have steadily increased, and after the mortality at Peor they amounted to 64,300, being inferior to none but Judah and Dan; to the latter by only 100, Num. i, 29; xxvi, 25. The numbers given in 1 Chron. vii, 2, 4, 5, probably the census of Joab, amount in all to 145,600.

The territory of Issachar in the Holy Land comprehended the most of the plain of Esdraelon and the neighboring districts—the granary of Palestine. Among its towns were Megiddo, Taanach, Shunem, Jezreel, Bethshan, and the villages of Endor, Aphek, and Ibleam, all historical names. The mountains of Tabor and Gilboa, and the valley of Jezreel, were in the territory of this tribe, and the course of the Kishon lay through it. Manasseh had towns in its borders, Josh. xix, 17–23; xvii, 10, 11. With so fertile a territory this tribe devoted itself to agriculture, taking little interest in the affairs of the nation. But still there is no evidence that the tribe ever declined any military service to which it was called. Deborah commends it for its promptitude in the war with Jabin, Judg. v, 15; and in the days of David it received honorable mention, 1 Chron. xii, 32. Issachar took part in the passover with which Hezekiah sanctified the opening of his reign, 2 Chron. xxx, 18; xxxi, 1. Within five years from this date Shalmaneser, King of Assyria, had invaded the north of Palestine, and, after three years' siege, had taken Samaria, and, with the rest of Israel, had carried Issachar away to his distant dominions. "There," says Mr. Grove, "we must be content to leave them, until, with the rest of their brethren of all the tribes of the children of Israel, (Dan only excepted,) the twelve thousand of the tribe of Issachar shall be sealed in their foreheads, Rev. vii, 7."

It'aly, (Map 8,) the whole natural peninsula between the Alps and the Straits of Messina. At first, the name was applied only to the southern part of the peninsula, but in the New Testament it is used as we now employ it. The "Italian band" mentioned in Acts x, 1, doubtless consisted of men recruited in Italy. The expulsion of Priscilla and Aquila with their compatriots "from Italy," (Acts xviii, 2,) suggests the large Jewish population which Italy is claimed to have contained. Much trade doubtless subsisted between Italy and other parts of the Mediterranean. Acts xxvii, 1; Heb. xiii, 24, etc. See ROME.

Ith'nan, *bestowed*, a city in the extreme south of Judah, Josh. xv, 23. In the Septuagint the name is corrupted by being attached to that next to it. Mr. Wilton would connect Ithnan with Hazor preceding it, and supposes that Hazor-Ithnan was originally a Horite settlement, perhaps occupied by Ithnan, and this settlement he identifies with *el-Ilhora*, a little east of Beersheba. (*The Negeb*, pp. 81–85.) But this identification is uncertain.

It'tah-Ka'zin, *time of a judge*, a landmark of the boundary of Zebulun, named next to Gath-Hepher, Josh. xix, 13. The name is probably more accurately Eth-Kazin, with the Hebrew particle of motion added. It is not identified.

Ituræ'a, or Iture'a, (Map 5,) a small province of Syria on the northern border of Bashan, which formed part of the tetrarchy of Philip the brother of Herod, Luke iii, 1. It appears to have derived its name from *Jetur*, one of the sons of Ishmael, whose descendants settled in this locality, Gen. xxv, 15. After the people of Israel had received their inheritance the trans-Jordanic tribes attacked the Hagarites, on what ground is not stated, clearly, however, with the divine sanction, and overcame them, and their country was possessed by the half-tribe of Manasseh, 1 Chron. v, 18–23. For their own apostasy the Israelites were afterward carried into captivity, and their land became a part of the Assyrian empire, xxv, 26. The Ishmaelites were not entirely rooted out of Iturea. In the second century B. C. Aristobulus, the King of the Jews, reconquered it. The inhabitants being allowed to choose between exile and Judaism, many preferred the first. Iturea was subsequently made a part of the dominions of Herod the Great, who bequeathed it with some adjoining territories to his son Philip. It is now known as *Jedûr*, lying south of Damascus, and north of the *Hauran*. It consists of table-land with an undulating surface, the northern part covered with jagged basaltic rocks, as if molten lava had been forced up through the ground, had spread itself around, and been torn and dislocated in cooling. The southern district is rich and well-watered. The towns and villages of the province are poor and desolate.

I'vah, *overturning, ruin*, or possibly the name of a Babylonian God, *Iva*, representing the sky or ether. A city in Babylon, mentioned as having been subdued, in spite of its gods, by the Assyrian power, 2 Kings xviii, 34; xix, 13; Isa. xxxvii, 13. It appears to be the same with Ava, from which colonists were brought into Samaria, 2 Kings xvii, 24; and probably with the Ahava of Ezra viii, 15, 21, 31. The modern *Hit*, on the Euphrates, noted for bitumen springs, probably marks the site

Ja'akan. See BENE-JAAKAN.

Ja-a'zer, and Ja'zer, whom *he* (God) *helps*, a city of the Amorites east of Jordan, in or near Gilead, Num. xxi, 32. It was conquered and assigned to Gad, and afterward allotted to the Merarite Levites, Num. xxxii, 35; Josh. xxi, 39. In David's reign it seems to have been occupied by Kohathites, 1 Chron. xxvi, 31, Hebron being a son of Kohath. In later times Jazer had fallen into the hands of the Moabites, and is repeatedly mentioned in the prophetic denunciations against Moab, (Isa. xvi, 8, 9; Jer. xlviii, 32,) in connection with the vine of Sibmah. A sea of Jaazer, too, is spoken of; this may be some lake or pool in the neighborhood, or it may be the not distant Dead Sea. The site of Jaazer is not fully identified, but is probably at *Seir* or *Sir*, eight miles west of *Ammân*, and ten north of *Hesbân*.

Jab'bok, (Map 5,) *a pouring out*, a stream falling into the Jordan about midway between the Sea of Galilee and the Dead Sea. It was after Jacob had passed to the south bank of the Jabbok that his brother Esau met him, the mysterious wrestling with God having just occurred, Gen. xxxii, 22, 23. Jabbok is subsequently spoken of as the border of the children of Ammon, Num. xxi, 24; Deut. ii, 37; iii, 16; Josh. xii, 2; Judg. xi, 13, 22. It would seem that the territory of Ammon once extended as far north as this stream, but that Sihon drove them beyond the Arnon; and then, when Israel conquered Sihon, they also took possession of the territory between the two rivers; Jabbok, however, still retaining the name of the Ammonite border. And the Ammonites had lingered in the neighborhood, for, on Sihon's defeat, some of them retreated to the mountains where the Jabbok rises, and were established in their strong defiles; these places Israel did not touch, and here was their capital, Rabbath-Ammon, 2 Sam. xi.

The present name of Jabbok is *Zurka*, or Blue River. The Zurka cuts through Gilead in a deep narrow defile; throughout the lower part of its course it is fringed with thickets of cane and oleander, and the banks above are clothed with oak forests. Toward its mouth the stream is perennial, and in winter often impassable.

Ja'besh-Gil'ead, (Map 5,) *dry* land *in Gilead.* A city of Gilead, situated on a mountain east of the Jordan. Because its inhabitants would not join in the crusade against Benjamin, the whole male population was destroyed, and virgins to the number of four hundred were seized, to be given in marriage to the remnant of the Benjamites, Judg. xxi, 8-14. However, the city survived and regained its importance. Being subsequently besieged by Nahash the Ammonite, the Israelites under Saul rose to rescue it, 1 Sam. xi, 1-11. Saul's kindness was not forgotten by the people of Jabesh. A bold troop of them stole down by night and took the bodies of Saul and his sons from the wall of Bethshan, (where, after the fatal field of Gilboa, they were exposed,) and buried them, 1 Sam. xxxi, 11-13; 1 Chron. x, 11, 12. This service David thankfully acknowledged, 2 Sam. ii, 4-6; though he afterward removed the bones to the sepulcher of Kish, xxi, 12-14. Probably the site is at the present ruin *ed-Deir*, on the south side of the *Wady Yabes*, which enters the Jordan below Bethshan or Scythopolis.

Ja'bez, he *causes pain*, apparently a place in Judah at which the families of the scribes resided who belonged to the families of the Kenites, 1 Chron. ii, 55.

Jab'neel, (Map 5,) *God causeth to be built.*
1. A town on the border of Judah, Josh. xv, 11. It appears afterward to have been occupied by the Philistines, for (under the name of Jabneh) it was one of the places which Uzziah dismantled, 2 Chron. xxvi, 6. In Maccabean history it was known as Jamnia, 1 Macc. iv, 15; and noted as a school of learning after the fall of Jerusalem. According to Jewish tradition Gamaliel was here buried. It is now called *Yebna*, on a hill two miles from the sea and eleven south of Jaffa. It contains about three thousand people, all agriculturists. There are thrashing-floors ranged all round the town. Remains of old buildings are found—possibly relics of the fortress called *Ibelin*, built there by the crusaders.

2. A town of Naphtali, Josh. xix, 33. Mr. Grove says, " We should be disposed to look for its traces at the north-west part of the Sea of Galilee, in the hill country."

Jab'neh, *he lets build.* 2 Chron. xxvi, 6. See JABNEEL, (1.)

Ja'gur, *lodging-place*, a city on the extreme south-eastern border of Judah toward Edom, Josh. xv, 21. Its name might indicate that it was one of the fortified camping grounds of the border Arabs. Nothing is known of it.

Ja'haz, *a place trodden down.* It is called also Jahaza, Josh. xiii, 18; Jahazah, Josh. xxi, 36; Jer. xlviii, 21; and Jahzah, 1 Chron. vi, 78. A place where the decisive battle was fought between the Israelites and Sihon, which resulted in the occupation of the district between the Arnon and the Jabbok, Num. xxi, 23, 24; Deut. ii, 32; Judg. xi, 20. It was allotted to the tribe of Reuben, and afterward assigned to the Levites of the family of Merari; but at a later period it seems to have been in the possession of Moab, Isa. xv, 4; Jer. xlviii, 34. Jahaz seems to have been just north of the Arnon; but no identification has yet been made.

Jaha'za, Jaha'zah, Jah'zah. See JAHAZ.

Jam'nia or **Jamni'a.** 1 Macc. iv, 15. See JABNEEL and JABNEH.

Jano'ah, *rest,* a town in northern Palestine seized by Tiglath-Pileser, 2 Kings xv, 29. Its site is unknown.

Jano'hah, *rest,* a place on the boundary of Ephraim, named between Taanath-Shiloh and Ataroth, the enumeration proceeding from west to east, Josh. xvi, 6, 7. It is doubtless identical with the modern village of *Yanûn,* about eleven miles south-east of *Nablûs.* Here are extensive ruins. Van de Velde says: "Entire houses and walls exist, covered with immense heaps of earth." On the hill north-east of *Yanûn* are also ruins called *Khirbet Yanûn.*

Ja'num, *slumber,* (in the margin, Janus, *flight,*) a town in the mountains of Judah, apparently not far from Hebron, Josh. xv, 53.

Japhi'a, *splendid,* a place on the boundary of Zebulun, Josh. xix, 12. It is probably identical with *Yafa,* situated in a retired valley among the rocky hills about two miles south-west of Nazareth. It contains about thirty houses and the ruins of a church. The Italian monks of Nazareth call it *San Giacamo,* believing it to be the native place of Zebedee and his sons James and John.

Japh'leti, or **Japhle'ti,** *the Japhletite,* a landmark on the southern frontier of Ephraim, west of Beth-Horon the lower, and between it and Ataroth, Josh. xvi, 3. This name probably preserves the memory of some ancient tribe of which we have no knowledge.

Ja'pho, *beauty.* Josh. xix, 46. Elsewhere JOPPE and JOPPA, which see.

Ja'reb, *an adversary.* A term which is supposed by some to be the name of a king; by others that of the place where Jareb was king; while others regard the word as one appellative of the king, Hosea v, 13; x, 6. All are agreed that the king meant is the king of Assyria. Each theory has its able advocates. To consider it as an appellative seems the most probable explanation. See Henderson on the *Minor Prophets,* note on Hosea v, 13.

Jar'muth, (Map 5,) *height.*

1. A town in the low country of Judah, Josh. xv, 35. Its king joined in the confederacy against Gibeon, but was defeated and destroyed, Josh. x, 3-5, 22-26; xii, 11. After the return from the captivity it was inhabited by some of the children of Judah, Neh. xi, 29. The site is doubtless the modern *Yarmûk,* a small and poor village situated on the crest of a rugged hill about eight miles from Eleutheropolis. In the hewn stones and ruins remain a few traces of past strength and greatness.

2. A town in Issachar allotted to the Gershonites, Josh. xxi, 29; identical with the Remeth of Josh. xix, 21, and the Ramoth of 1 Chron. vi, 73. See RAMOTH.

Jash'ubi-Le'hem, *returner to Bethlehem,* the name of a person or a place— more probably the latter. We should infer that it lay on the western side of Judah, in or near the *Shefelah,* the low country, 1 Chron. iv, 22.

Jat'tir, (Map 5,) *pre-eminent, height,* a town in the mountains of Judah, allotted to the priests, Josh. xv, 48; xxi, 14; 1 Chron. vi, 57. To its inhabitants David sent presents, 1 Sam. xxx, 27. The two Ithrite heroes of David's guard were probably from Jattir. The site is doubtless identical with the ruins called '*Attir*, lying on a hill six miles north of *Molada*, and ten south of Hebron.

Ja'van, *mud, clay.*
1. A name used sometimes more specially for Ionia, Isa. lxvi, 19; Ezek. xxvii, 13; for the Macedonian empire, Dan. viii, 21; x, 20; xi, 2; for the Græco-Syrian empire, Zech. ix, 13. (See also Gen. x, 2, 4; 1 Chron. i, 5, 7.) Thus it signifies Grecia, Greece, or the Greek race generally.
2. A town in southern Arabia whence the Phœnicians brought swordblades, etc., Ezek. xxvii, 19. The reference in Joel iii, 6, is probably to this place, which Tuch supposes to have been a Greek colony. It is probably identical with *Uzal* in *Yemen.*

Ja'zar. 1 Macc. v, 8. See JAAZER.

Ja'zer. Num. xxxii, 1, 3. See JAAZER.

Je'arim or **Jea'rim,** MOUNT, *mount of forests,* a place named in specifying the northern boundary of Judah, Josh. xv, 10. It is said to be Chesalon; perhaps Chesalon stood upon the mountain-ridge. The modern *Kesla* stands on what doubtless was Mount Jearim. There are still woods in the vicinity, and Kirjath-Jearim (if that be *Kuriet el-Enab*) is not far off to the northward, separated by the deep and wide hollow of *Wady Ghurab.* See CHESALON.

Je'bus, *place trodden down, thrashing-floor,* the ancient name of Jerusalem, the capital and stronghold of the Jebusites, Judg. xix, 10, 11; 1 Chron. xi, 4, 5. See JERUSALEM.

Jebu'si, the name used for the city of Jebus in describing the landmarks and the towns of the allotment of Judah and Benjamin, Josh. xv, 8; xviii, 16, 28.

Jeb'usite, The, the name of a highland tribe having its chief seat at Jebus, afterward Jerusalem, Gen. x, 16; 1 Chron. i, 14. This tribe was one of the seven nations of Canaan whom the Israelites were commanded to exterminate, Deut. vii, 1; xx, 17. Notices of their territory, Num. xiii, 29; Josh. xi, 3; xv, 8, 63; xviii, 16; Judges i, 21. Their land was given to Israel, Gen. xv, 21; Exod. iii, 8; 17; xxiii, 23. They were defeated by Joshua, Josh. ix, 1; x-xii; xxiv, 11. Adonizedek, king of Jebus, was slain by Joshua, Josh. x. See also Josh. xviii, 28; Judg. xix, 10; 1 Chron. xi, 4. Conquered by David, and Jerusalem taken, 2 Sam. v, 6-9. Araunah was a Jebusite, 2 Sam. xxiv, 16-24. Tributary to Solomon, 1 Kings ix, 20. Intermarried with Israelites, Judges iii, 5, 6; Ezra ix, 12. See JERUSALEM.

Je'gar-Sa'hadu'tha, (Map 3,) *the heap of witness,* the Aramæan name given by Laban to the heap of stones which he set up on Mount Gilead, Gen. xxxi, 47. There appear to have been both a pillar and a pile—the pillar set up by Jacob, and the pile or heap gathered by Laban and his sons. Then was there a solemn feast, and a sacrifice, and a covenant entered into, that neither the one nor the other should pass that pillar and heap to his brother's harm. See GALEED and GILEAD.

Jehosh'aphat, VALLEY OF, (Map 7,) *the valley where Jehovah judgeth,* a valley mentioned only by Joel as the spot in which, after the return of Judah and Jerusalem from captivity, Jehovah would gather all the heathen, and would there sit to judge them for their misdeeds to Israel, Joel iii, 2, 12.

By reference to these passages and their connection, it will be seen that the valley appears to have been intended to symbolize those bloody battle-fields where the hostile nations contiguous to Judea had signal vengeance inflicted on them. Many think a definite place is referred to; and some say it is the "Valley of Berachah," where King Jehoshaphat obtained the signal victory over Ammon and Moab, 2 Chron. xx, 26. Some claim that the valley of the Kidron is meant; and this is the traditional interpretation both among Jews and Christians. Thus for many years the valley of the Kidron has borne the name in question. The reference of the Prophet Joel has given rise to the current belief among Christians, Jews, and Mohammedans, that the Last Judgment will take place there. The Moslems show—as they have shown for certainly two centuries—the place on which Mohammed is to be seated at the Last Judgment, a stone jutting out from the east wall of the Haram area near the south corner, one of the pillars which once adorned the churches of Helena or Justinian, and of which multitudes are now embedded in the rude masonry of the more modern walls of Jerusalem.

But for this traditional identification there is not the slightest ground, either in the Scripture or in Josephus. The name universally given to the glen is Kidron, 2 Sam. xv, 23; 1 Kings ii, 38; John xviii, 1; Joseph, *Bell. Jud.* v, 2, 3, etc. Also, the word translated "valley" is wholly inapplicable to the Kidron; it signifies a low tract of land of wide extent, such as suited a battle-field, Job xxxix, 10, 21; Josh. xv, 8. The Kidron is always termed "torrent valley," or "glen." The Kidron is a narrow rocky ravine, and wholly unsuitable for such an event as is referred to by Joel; and even though we could believe that the prophet referred to a specific valley, this could not be the true one. See KIDRON.

Jeho'vah-Ji'reh, *Jehovah will see, or provide,* the name given by Abraham to the place where the angel of the Lord appeared to him when about to offer up his son Isaac, Gen. xxii, 14. This name seems to have given place to Moriah, which was also probably the earlier name, (verse 2.) The circumstance gave rise to a proverb, "In the mountain of Jehovah it will be seen," that is, foreseen, provided for; so that it became a belief among the Jews that in the place which God had pointed out as his holy mountain, the place where he would be worshiped, there should be provision for the guidance of his people; the place of worship should be the place of revelation. Mount Moriah became in after times the site of the Temple, 2 Chron. iii, 1; and then did these earlier intimations receive their full accomplishment.

Jeho'vah-Nis'si, *Jehovah my banner,* the name given by Moses to an altar erected by him in celebration of the great victory obtained by the Israelites over the Amalekites, Exod. xvii, 15. It was erected either upon the hill overlooking the battle-field, upon which Moses sat with the staff of God in his hand, or upon the battle-field itself. According to Aben Ezra, it was on Horeb. Probably the allusion of the text is to the sacred rod which Moses held in his hand during the battle as a kind of banner, and which, as it was raised or lowered, influenced the result of the fight.

Jeho'vah-Sha'lom, *Jehovah is peace,* the name given by Gideon to the altar erected by him at Ophrah of the Abi-Ezrites, to commemorate the salutation of the angel of the Lord, Judges vi, 24.

Jeho'vah-Sham'mah, *Jehovah is there,* the name of the future Jerusalem, the Church of God, Ezek. xlviii, 35, margin.

Je'hud, *praised,* a city allotted to the tribe of Dan, Josh. xix, 45. It is probably identical with the village *el Yehudijeh*, about seven miles east of Jaffa.

Jekab'zeel, which *God gathers*, Neh. xi, 25, a fuller form of KABZEEL, which see.

Jem'naan, Judith ii, 28. Probably Jabneel or Jamnia.

Je'rah, *month*, (from the same root as *the moon*,) a son of Joktan, Gen. x, 26; 1 Chron. i, 20. As he is placed next in succession to Hazarmaveth, we may conclude that the region colonized by him was in or near the province of Hadhramaut. In this neighborhood is a "moon-mountain," and also a "moon-coast." (See HAZARMAVETH.) To precisely determine the locality requires a more accurate knowledge of Arabia than we now possess.

Jerah'meelites, from Jerahmeel, *on whom God has mercy*. A tribe or clan descended from Jerahmeel, 1 Sam. xxvii, 10; xxx, 29. They inhabited the southern border of Judah.

Jer'echus, 1 Esdr. v, 22. The Greek form of Jericho.

Jer'icho, (Map 5,) *city of the moon*, or *place of fragrance*. Called also the "City of Palm-trees," Deut. xxxiv, 3; 2 Chron. xxviii, 15; and Jerechus, 1 Esdr. v, 22.

SITUATION. Jericho was the largest city in the valley of the Jordan. It lay about twenty miles north-east from Jerusalem, on the west side of the river Jordan, and north of its entrance into the Dead Sea. Between this city and Jerusalem was a fearful wilderness, which is still the haunt of robbers. The city stood upon a plain, whose fertility (as of an oasis in the desert) may be attributed to the fountain of Elisha referred to in 2 Kings ii, 19–22. Very near the city, on the west, is Mount Quarantania, a high desolate hill in the wilderness, with which tradition connects the fasting and

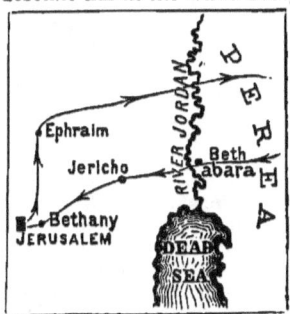

the temptation of Christ, and from whose top Satan showed the Saviour "all the kingdoms of the world, and the glory of them." The peculiar situation of Jericho in the valley of the Jordan, and on the great commercial thoroughfare from Damascus or Assyria to Arabia or Egypt, made it the great port of entry and the chief city of ancient Canaan.

BIBLE ALLUSIONS. The city is first mentioned in the Old Testament, Num. xxii, 1; xxvi, 3, in defining the position of the Israelites, who, when encamped in the plains of Moab, were over against it. A strongly fortified place, with thick walls, Josh. ii, 15. Had much treasure, Josh. vi, 24; vii, 21. Its territory of considerable extent, Josh. iv, 19. It was one of the oldest cities of Palestine, and a royal residence before it was taken by the Israelites, Josh. ii, 2, 3; viii, 2; x, 1, 28.

BIBLE EVENTS. Jericho was the first town of Canaan attacked by the Israelites after their forty years' wandering. The history of its siege and capture is very remarkable. Two spies were sent to the city, and received by Rahab, Josh. ii; Heb. xi, 31. It was near Jericho that Joshua saw the "Captain of the Lord's host," Josh. v, 13–15. After being besieged and encompassed seven days its walls miraculously fell, and the city was utterly destroyed, Josh. iii, 16; iv, 12; vi, 1; xxiv, 11. Rahab and family alone were spared, Josh. ii, 14; vi, 25. Joshua pronounced a curse upon any who should attempt to rebuild it, vi, 26. The site was assigned to Benjamin, xvi, 7; xviii, 21, and was the boundary of Ephraim, xvi, 1. Soon after it was occupied by Israelites, Judges iii, 13. Compare 2 Sam. x, 5; 1 Chron. xix, 5. But it was not *fortified*, and perhaps the curse of Joshua had reference merely to its being refortified. The Kenites dwelt there, Judges i, 16; compare iv, 11. In Judges iii, 13, we find this "City of Palm Trees" "possessed" by Eglon, king of Moab. Thither David sent his embassadors, 2 Sam. x, 5. Hiel, the Bethelite, was signally punished for an attempt to restore it, 1 Kings xvi, 34. Here Elijah spent his last days, and here was a school of prophets, 2 Kings ii, 4, 5, 15. Elisha miraculously healed its waters, 2 Kings ii, 19-22. To "the plains of Jericho" the Chaldeans took King Zedekiah, 2 Kings xxv, 4; Jer. xxxix, 5. After the exile the inhabitants returned thither, Ezra iii, 34; Neh. vii, 36, and the men of Jericho helped them to build the walls of Jerusalem, Neh. iii, 2. Subsequently the Syrian, Bacchides, fortified the city, 1 Macc. ix, 50, over which was placed one Ptolemeus, who had abundance of silver and gold. Afterward it was enlarged and adorned by Herod the Great, and also by Archelaus. In the time of Christ Jericho was wealthy and flourishing, which may be inferred from the fact that a chief and rich publican or tax-gatherer was there stationed, Luke xix, 2. Christ tarried with this publican, and brought salvation to his house, Luke xix, 5, 9. Near this city Jesus healed two or three blind men, Matt. xx, 29-34; Mark x, 46-52; Luke xviii, 35-43. It was on the fearful road between Jericho and Jerusalem that Christ laid the scene of the beautiful parable of the good Samaritan, Luke x, 30-37. Under Roman authority Jericho was the chief city of a toparchy, and was visited by Vespasian. When Titus besieged Jerusalem it is said that he also overthrew Jericho, and that it was afterward rebuilt.

PRESENT CONDITION. Although Josephus gives a glowing account of the region of Jericho, calling it an earthly paradise, modern travelers find nothing but wretchedness and ruin. The present inhabitants pay no attention to the fertile soil. The fountain of Elisha, now called *Ain es-Sultan*, still sends forth its "beautifully transparent, sweet and cool waters," only to make the site of ancient Jericho seem more thoroughly desolate. The palm-trees have disappeared; the plain is intensely hot; and instead of the mighty city, there stands on this once lovely plain only a little mean, filthy village of about forty huts, called *Riha* or *Eriha*, with two hundred inhabitants. North of the village is a castle or tower, about thirty feet square and forty feet high, almost in ruins, which tradition calls the house of Zaccheus. Robinson supposes it was built in the twelfth century. Remnants of water-courses, and traces near the village, indicate the site of ancient Jericho. The location of the earlier city, and that rebuilt by Herod, or during the Byzantine period, cannot be ascertained without further researches.

Jer'uel, or **Jeru'el,** *founded of God.* The scene of the discomfiture of the Ammonites, Moabites, and other Arab tribes who invaded Judea in the reign of Jehoshaphat, 2 Chron. xx, 16. It was probably between Eugedi and Tekoa, and distant by a short march from Berachah, now *Bereikut.*

Jeru'salem, (Maps 5-11,) *foundation* or *habitation of peace,* the Jewish capital of Palestine.

I. NAMES. This renowned city is mentioned in Scripture under the following names: Salem, ("peace,") Gen. xiv, 18; Jehovah-Jireh, ("the Lord

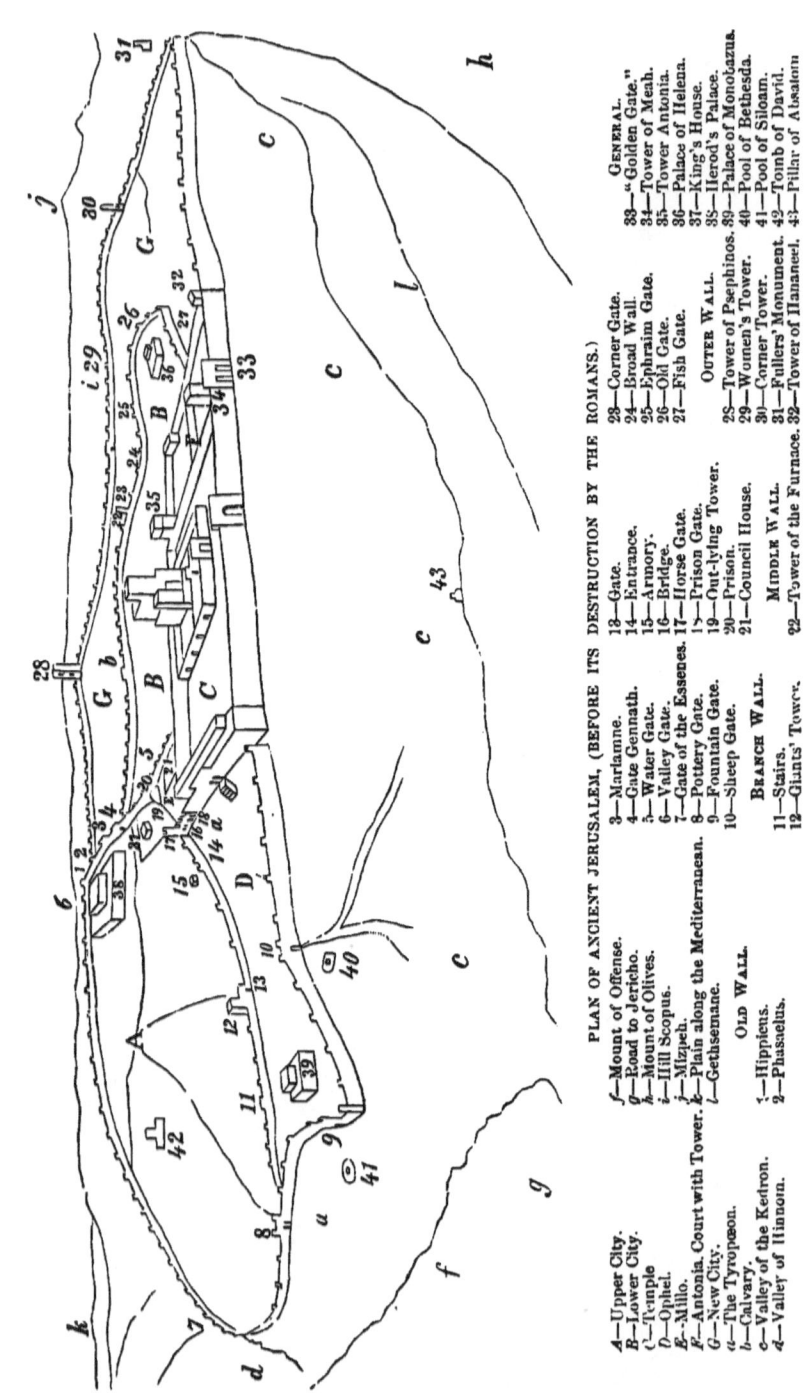

PLAN OF ANCIENT JERUSALEM, (BEFORE ITS DESTRUCTION BY THE ROMANS.)

A—Upper City.
B—Lower City.
C—Temple
D—Ophel.
E—Millo.
F—Antonia Court with Tower.
G—New City.
a—The Tyropœon.
b—Calvary.
c—Valley of the Kedron.
d—Valley of Hinnom.

f—Mount of Offense.
g—Road to Jericho.
h—Mount of Olives.
i—Hill Scopus.
j—Mizpeh.
k—Plain along the Mediterranean.
l—Gethsemane.

OLD WALL

1—Hippicus.
2—Phasaelus.

3—Mariamne.
4—Gate Gennath.
5—Water Gate.
6—Valley Gate.
7—Gate of the Essenes.
8—Pottery Gate.
9—Fountain Gate.
10—Sheep Gate.

BRANCH WALL

11—Stairs.
12—Giants' Tower.

13—Gate.
14—Entrance.
15—Armory.
16—Bridge.
17—Horse Gate.
18—Prison Gate.
19—Out-lying Tower.
20—Prison.
21—Council House.

MIDDLE WALL

22—Tower of the Furnace.

23—Corner Gate.
24—Broad Wall.
25—Ephraim Gate.
26—Old Gate.
27—Fish Gate.

OUTER WALL

28—Tower of Psephinos.
29—Women's Tower.
30—Corner Tower.
31—Fullers' Monument.
32—Tower of Hananeel.

GENERAL.

33—"Golden Gate."
34—Tower of Meah.
35—Tower Antonia.
36—Palace of Helena.
37—King's House.
38—Herod's Palace.
39—Palace of Monobazus.
40—Pool of Bethesda.
41—Pool of Siloam.
42—Tomb of David.
43—Pillar of Absalom.

BIBLE GEOGRAPHY. 195

will provide,") Gen. xxii, 14; Jebus, or Jebusi, ("the city of the Jebusite,") Josh. xviii, 28; Judg. xix, 10; 2 Sam. v, 6; Jerusalem, 2 Sam. v, 5; [The use of the name Jerusalem in Josh. x, 1, was probably in anticipation of the name which it afterward received;] Zion, 1 Kings viii, 1; City of David, Psa. xlvi, 4; Ariel, Isa. xxix, 1; City of God, Psa. xlvi, 4; City of the Great King, Psa. xlviii, 2; City of Judah, 2 Chron. xxv, 28; Holy City, Neh. xi, 1-18; City of Solemnities, Isa. xxxiii, 20. In Gal. iv, 25, 26, and in Heb xii, 22, Jerusalem is used symbolically. "New Jerusalem," Rev. iii, 12; xxi, 2.

In the Vulgate the city is called Hierosolyma. The Greek historian Herodotus styles it Kadytis. After it was rebuilt by the Roman Emperor Hadrian he called it Ælia Capitolina, from his own name Publius Ælius, and that of Jupiter Capitolinus. By the Arabs, Turks, Persians, and other Mussulmans, the place is known as *el-Khuds*, ("the Holy,") or *Beit-el-Makhuddis*, ("the Holy House," or "House of the Sanctuary.")

Prophecy declares that the Holy City shall receive "a new name." "Thou shalt be called Hephzibah . . . for the Lord delighteth in thee . . . and thou shalt be called Sought Out, a city not forsaken," Isa. lxii, 2, 4, 12. "Under the general name of Jerusalem the Holy City has now occupied a prominent position on the page of history for nearly thirty-eight long centuries, which shows it to be at least one thousand one hundred and sixty-eight years older than Rome, the self-yclept 'Eternal City,' and 'mistress of the world.' If any city on earth deserves the appellation of 'eternal,' it is Jerusalem. It shall become 'an eternal excellency.' God has chosen it as his dwelling-place forever."—*City of the Great King*, p. 45.

II. SITUATION. Jerusalem is situated on the central chain of limestone mountains running north and south through Palestine. Its latitude is that of the northern end of the Dead Sea. It is distant from the Dead Sea and Jordan Valley fifteen miles, and from the Mediterranean thirty-one miles. (The topography of the site will be given below.)

III. BIBLE ALLUSIONS. "The name Jerusalem is used eight hundred and eighteen times in the Scriptures of the Old and New Testaments."—*Osborn.*

SITUATION AND APPEARANCE. Psa. cxxii, 3; Psa. cxxv, 2; Sol. Song vi, 4; Micah iv, 8.

GATES. These were very numerous in the ancient city. The following list of allusions to them is taken from Smith's *Dictionary:*

(1.) Gate of Ephraim, 2 Chron. xxv, 23; Neh. viii, 16; xii, 39. This is probably the same as the (2.) Gate of Benjamin, Jer. xx, 2; xxxvii, 13; Zech. xiv, 10. If so, it was four hundred cubits distant from the (3.) Corner Gate, 2 Chron. xxv, 23; xxvi, 9; Jer. xxxi, 38; Zech. xiv, 10. (4.) Gate of Joshua, governor of the city, 2 Kings xxiii, 8. (5.) Gate between the two walls, 2 Kings xxv, 4; Jer. xxxix, 4. (6.) Horse Gate, Neh. iii, 38; 2 Chron. xxiii, 15; Jer. xxxi, 40. (7.) Ravine Gate, (that is, opening on ravine of Hinnom,) 2 Chron. xxvi, 9; Neh. ii, 13, 15; iii, 13. (8.) Fish Gate, 1 Chron. xxxiii, 14; Neh. iii, 1; Zeph. i, 16. (9.) Dung Gate, Neh. ii, 13; iii, 13. (10.) Sheep Gate, Neh. iii, 1, 32; xii, 39. (11.) East Gate, Neh. iii, 29. (12.) Miphkad, Neh. iii, 31. (13.) Fountain Gate, (Siloam?) Neh. xii, 37. (14.) Water Gate, Neh. xii, 37. (15.) Old Gate, Neh. iii, 39. (16.) Prison Gate, Neh. xii, 39. (17.) Gate Harsith, (perhaps the sun; A. V. East Gate,) Jer. xix, 2. (18.) First Gate, Zech. xiv, 10. (The two following are from Josephus:) (19.) Gate Gennath, (Gardens.) (20.) Essenes' Gate.

To these should be added the following gates of the temple: Gate Sur, 2 Kings xi, 6, called also Gate of Foundation, 2 Chron. xxiii, 5. Gate of the Guard, or behind the Guard, 2 Kings xi, 6, 19. Called the High Gate, 2 Chron. xxiii, 20; xxvii, 3; 2 Kings xv, 35. Gate Shallecheth, 1 Chron. xxvi, 16.

STREETS. East-street, 2 Chron. xxix, 4. Street of the house of God, Ezra x, 9. Street before the water gate, Neh. viii, 1. Street of the gate of Ephraim, Neh. viii, 16. Bakers'-street, Jer. xxxvii, 21.

BUILDINGS. High-priest's palace, John xviii, 15. Castle, Acts xxi, 34. Stairs, Neh. iii, 15. Temple, 1 Kings v–vii; ix, 8; 2 Kings xii, 4; 2 Chron. ii–iv; xxiv, 4; Jer. lii, 12; Ezra i, iii–vi; Ezek. xl, xliii; Hag. ii, 9; Matt. xxi, 12, 13; Mark xii, 41–44; Luke xxi, 5, 6; John ii, 13–17; Acts iii, 2, 11, etc. Gabbatha, John xix, 13. See PRETORIUM.

TOWERS. See HANANEEL, MEAH, MILLO, OPHEL, SILOAM.

PLACES IN AND AROUND Christ's Sepulcher, John xix, 41. Gareb, Jer. xxxi, 39. See ACELDAMA, CALVARY, GETHSEMANE, HINNOM, VALLEY OF JEHOSHAPHAT, MAKTESH, MORIAH, OLIVES, MOUNT OF, TOPHET.

POOLS, FOUNTAINS, AND BROOKS. See BETHESDA, EN-ROGEL, GIHON, KIDRON, SILOAM.

IV. BIBLE EVENTS. Jerusalem is first brought to our notice under the name of Salem, when its king, Melchizedek, "brought forth bread and wine" for Abram, after the return of the latter "from the slaughter of Chedorlaomer," Gen. xiv, 18. A little later, when Abraham was about to offer up his son Isaac on the eastern portion of the site of the city, [see MORIAH,] God provided another sacrifice, and the patriarch "called the name of that place Jehovah-Jireh," Gen. xxii, 14.

When the Israelites crossed the Jordan into Canaan they found the city and adjacent country in possession of a people called Jebusites, whence the name by which the city was then known, Jebus, or Jebusi, Josh. xviii, 28; Judg. xix, 10; comp. Ezek. xvi, 3. Jebusi is then mentioned as just upon the frontier line of Judah and Benjamin, but being itself actually within the Benjamite border, Josh. xv, 8; xviii, 16, 28.

The position of Jerusalem was such as to make it a place of leading importance at the time of the invasion of the land of Joshua. Hence we find its "king," Adonizedek, summoning four neighboring chieftains to assist him in the punishment of Gibeon for having made peace with Israel. Then occurred the famous battle, during which the sun stood still upon Gibeon, and the moon in the Valley of Ajalon, Josh. x. Although in this battle the five kings were slain, and their armies "consumed" "with a very great slaughter," yet so strong was the city of the Jebusites that these people retained possession of the citadel, or stronghold of Zion, for a long period. We are told in Joshua (xv, 63) that the children of Judah could not, and in Judges, (i, 21,) after an account of the taking and burning of Jerusalem by the children of Judah, that the children of Benjamin did not drive out the Jebusites; and it is added in the former verse, "but the Jebusites dwell with the children of Judah," and in the latter, "but the Jebusites dwell with the children of Benjamin in Jerusalem unto this day."

This stronghold was retained by the Jebusites for several hundred years, during the whole of the troubled times of the Judges and the early days of the kingdom of Israel. Thus we do not hear of Jerusalem again until the time of David. When David had finally triumphed over the house of Saul,

FRONT VIEW.

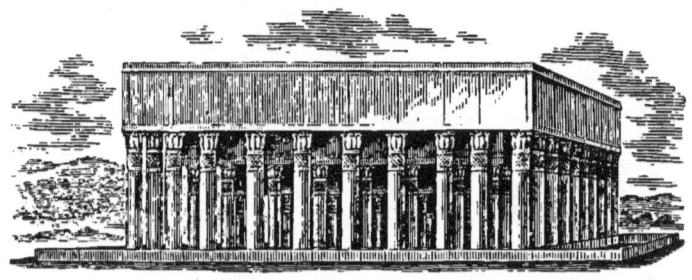

WEST END.

INTERIOR.
SOLOMON'S TEMPLE ACCORDING TO PAINE.

and had become firmly established on the throne of all Israel, as well as Judah, (B. C. 1048,) in Hebron, which had been the chief city of the tribe of Judah ever since its first ineffectual attempt on the citadel of Zion, one of his first expeditions was against this fortress of Jebusi.

The Jebusites were exceedingly confident of their ability to withstand King David. Deriding his efforts, they either placed literally the weakest of their population upon their ramparts, or they set there in array the images of their gods, and then from the walls the inhabitants insultingly shouted to the Hebrew armies, "Except thou take away the blind and the lame thou shalt not come in hither," 2 Sam. v, 6. Taunted thus, with their indignation fully aroused, and divinely assisted, the warriors of Israel "took the stronghold of Zion: the same is the city of David," 2 Sam. v, 7; comp 1 Chron. xi, 4–9.

Jerusalem now became the capital of the united kingdoms of Israel and Judah, and Zion was made the site of the royal residence. For the erection of the king's palace "Hiram, King of Tyre, sent messengers to David, and cedar-trees, and carpenters, and masons," 2 Sam. v, 11. The achievements of the Hebrew king produced a profound impression upon the neighboring powers. The Philistines "came up to seek David," "and spread themselves in the Valley of Rephaim," but were repulsed. Coming again to the same valley, David smote them "from Geba until thou come to Gazer," 2 Sam. v, 17–25; 1 Chron. xiv, 8–17.

Jerusalem was designed to be not only the civil capital of the kingdom, but also the spiritual center to which the tribes should yearly go up to the worship of the Lord. Hence David resolved to bring up to Jerusalem the ark of the covenant from Kirjath-Jearim, where it had remained ever since the high-priesthood of Eli. The progress of the ark was arrested by a fearful catastrophe; but after a short delay it was "brought into the city of David with gladness," and placed "in the midst of the tabernacle that David had pitched for it" on Mount Zion, 2 Sam. vi, 2–17.

In the midst of the splendor and prosperity of his reign David was moved to make a census of the people of Israel and Judah. This he did either for the purpose of taxation, or to ascertain the number of fighting men whom he could summon for war. The divine displeasure being incurred by this act, God sent a pestilence of three days' continuance, and "there died of the people from Dan even to Beer-sheba seventy thousand men. David himself saw the destroying angel standing over Jerusalem, on Mount Moriah, near the thrashing-floor of Araunah the Jebusite. According to Jewish tradition. this was the same place where Abraham had stood ready to slay his son when the Lord provided a sacrifice. David bought this thrashing-floor, and upon it erected an altar unto the Lord and offered sacrifices, humbly confessing his sinfulness. This spot, rendered thus memorable, was selected by God as the site of that wondrous temple, for the building of which King David spent the remainder of his life in accumulating the materials, 2 Sam. xxiv; 1 Chron. xxi; xxii, 2–4, 14–16; xxviii, 11–18; xxix, 2–9.

David was succeeded by his son Solomon, B. C. 1015. The magnificent temple which Solomon erected occupied seven years and a half in building, being completed and dedicated B. C. 1004, 1 Kings vi–viii. With most imposing ceremonies the ark of the Lord was brought from Zion and placed in the temple beneath the wings of the cherubim in the Holy of Holies. The tabernacle also, and all its sacred vessels, were conveyed thither from

Gibeon, and probably deposited as sacred memorials within the temple walls, 1 Kings viii, 4; 2 Chron. v, 5.

Having finished the temple, Solomon turned his attention to the enlargement of his kingdom and power. He surrounded Jerusalem with strong walls and towers, and filled it with magnificent structures. There was his own palace, which must have been of vast size to accommodate the many women of his harem; there was also the immense establishment for his chariots and horses; the palace which he built for Pharaoh's daughter; and the palace of the forest of Lebanon; together with the costly aqueduct by which the city was supplied with water, 1 Kings vii, 1, 2, 8; iv, 26; x, 26. Solomon also built other cities in different parts of his dominions, 1 Kings ix, 17–19. He formed alliances with powerful princes, and carried on a lucrative commerce with Egypt by land, with eastern Africa and India by the Red Sea, and with Spain and western Africa by the Mediterranean, 1 Kings ix, 26–28; x, 22, 28; 2 Chron. ix, 21, 23, 28. By his wealth and influence and the prestige of his power he extended the range of his dominion from the Euphrates to the Nile, 1 Kings iv, 21; 2 Chron. ix, 26. The wealth that thus flowed into this magnificent city was vast indeed. Gold was exceedingly abundant, and "the king made silver to be in Jerusalem as stones," 1 Kings x, 27; 2 Chron. ix, 27.

"But King Solomon loved many strange women, together with the daughter of Pharaoh, women of the Moabites, Ammonites, Edomites, Zidonians, and Hittites." "He had seven hundred wives, princesses, and three hundred concubines; and his wives turned away his heart." 1 Kings xi, 1, 3.

Hence we find this wonderful man, who in his youth received so many testimonies of God's favor, at last in his old age building heathen temples for Ashteroth, Chemosh, and Milcom on the right hand (that is, the south side) of the Mount of Corruption, east of Jerusalem, 1 Kings xi, 7; 2 Kings xxiii, 13. The worship of Moloch was also established in the Valley of Hinnom, south of the city, 2 Kings xxiii, 10. These temples of dishonor long continued to give a character of unholiness to the sacred city.

For the very heinous sins of Solomon God visited him with sore punishments. He was succeeded by his son Rehoboam, through whose weakness and folly the kingdoms of Judah and Israel were separated by the revolt of the ten tribes, 1 Kings xii.

In the fifth year of Rehoboam's reign Jerusalem was besieged by Shishak, King of Egypt, and plundered of all its treasures, 1 Kings xiv, 25–28.

In the reign of Asa much was done toward banishing idolatry from Jerusalem. Asa repelled an Ethiopian host which invaded his kingdom, and enriched himself with its spoils, devoting much of the same to the service of the temple, 1 Kings xv, 9–15; 2 Chron. xiv, 9–15. But he employed these same treasures in purchasing the aid of the King of Syria against Baasha, King of Israel, 1 Kings xv, 16–19. Asa's son, Jehoshaphat, was an upright and powerful monarch. His reign gave to Jerusalem great influence over the surrounding nations. He took away the "high places and groves" from Judah, 2 Chron. xvii, 1–6. But unfortunately he made an alliance with Ahab and Ahaziah, the wicked kings of Israel, and married his son Joram to Athaliah, Ahab's daughter, 2 Chron. xviii, 1; 2 Kings viii, 25, 26. The evil results of this marriage pervaded the three following reigns of Joram, Ahaziah, his son by Athaliah, and Athaliah herself. During Joram's reign Jerusalem was plundered by the Philistines and Arabians, 2 Chron. xxi, 16, 17.

Athaliah made her way to the throne by the destruction of all the princes of the house of Judah, except the infant Joash, her own grandchild, who was snatched out of her hands, and educated in the temple till he was seven years old. She and her sons partially destroyed the temple, and took from it the holy things, which they dedicated to the service of Baal. The wicked queen was put to death by the high-priest Jehoiada, guardian of young Joash, B. C. 878, 2 Chron. xxi-xxiii.

While Jehoiada lived Jerusalem was free from idolatry, but on his death the weak prince Joash put to death Jehoiada's son, Zechariah, on account of his testimony against idolatry.

Hazael was hindered from invading Jerusalem by the gift of the treasures from the temple at the hands of Joash, 2 Chron. xxiv.

During the reign of Amaziah, who succeeded Joash, the King of Israel defeated and took prisoner the King of Judah, breaking down four hundred cubits of the wall of Jerusalem, and plundering the temple, 2 Kings xiv, 11-14; 2 Chron. xxv, 21-24.

The break was repaired by the next king, Uzziah, who also erected towers and strengthened generally the fortifications, furnishing engines for throwing great stones and arrows, 2 Chron. xxvi, 9-15. During this reign occurred three fearful judgments—an earthquake, a plague of locusts, caterpillars, and canker-worms, and an extreme drought.

Jotham built a gate to the temple, repaired the walls, and added to their strength, 2 Kings xv, 35; 2 Chron. xxvii, 3.

Ahaz, the son and successor of Jotham, was an idolater. By trying to gain the aid of the Assyrians against Israel and Syria he gave the former a footing in Jerusalem, 2 Kings xvi, 2-18.

Hezekiah succeeded Ahaz. Under his godly reign Jerusalem was exceedingly prosperous. Every trace of idolatry was destroyed. The temple and its sacred worship were fully restored, 2 Kings xviii, 1-8. But again the holy city was threatened by heathen foes. Assyria, now at the height of her glory, having already possessed Samaria, and carried away the ten tribes of Israel into captivity, now sought to subjugate Egypt. On his triumphal march toward Egypt, Sennacherib, the Assyrian monarch, stopped to re-assert his supremacy over Jerusalem. Hezekiah, who had already rebelled against his authority, alarmed at this new demand, stripped the temple of its treasures, and sent them to avert, if possible, the wrath of Sennacherib; but, so far from being appeased, this monarch sent Rabshakeh to threaten the city with destruction unless the people should be willing to fully submit to his demands, 2 Kings xviii, 9-37.

It was at this time that Hezekiah took care to divert the water-courses, by the construction of his famous works for drawing the waters of the Gihon from their source into the city, to supply the people, and to distress the enemy in case of a siege. (See GIHON.) He strengthened the ramparts, and built additional towers and a new wall; he also constructed works in the citadel, and provided abundance of weapons, 2 Kings xx, 20; 2 Chron. xxxii, 4-30; Isa. xxii, 9-11. Through the prophet Isaiah divine aid was promised to the king and people of Jerusalem, and while the opposing host lay encamped on the west of the city, "it came to pass that night, that the angel of the Lord went out, and smote in the camp of the Assyrians a hundred fourscore and five thousand," 2 Kings xix, 35.

Manasseh, the son of Hezekiah, in the early part of his reign filled Jerusalem with idols and their shrines. He was carried captive to Babylon by the Assyrians, where he remained for twelve years. On his return, however, having repented of his sins, he endeavored to restore the true worship of God, and greatly strengthened the fortifications of the city, 2 Chron. xxxiii, 1-16. The ungodly Amon next reigned for two years.

Josiah, one of the best of Judah's kings, succeeded to the throne. He made a thorough reformation in the kingdom, and before he was eighteen he had completely destroyed the idols and places of idolatrous worship throughout all the land of Israel, as well as of Judah. The high-priest, Hilkiah, having discovered the books of the law, Josiah ordered the strict observance of the passover, after a neglect of centuries, 2 Kings xxii, xxiii.

At this time mighty struggles were agitating the thrones of the East. Nineveh was besieged by the Medes and Babylonians. Necho, the Egyptian Pharaoh, taking advantage of Assyria's distress, made an attempt against Carchemish, one of its important posts on the Euphrates. As Necho was advancing from the sea-coast, through the valley of Esdraelon, Josiah met him at Megiddo, and there received a fatal wound. He was, however, carried to die at Jerusalem, 2 Chron. xxxv, 20-24. One of his three sons, Jehoahaz, was elected king by the people. Necho, on returning from the capture of Carchemish, (B. C. 608,) deposed the new king, and carried him captive into Egypt, leaving upon the throne his elder brother Eliakim, whose name the conqueror changed to Jehoiakim, (whom *Jehovah sets up*,) 2 Chron. xxxvi, 1-4.

"The next visit paid to Jerusalem was that of Nebuchadnezzar. It is doubtful at what time, but probably after the victory which he in his turn obtained over Pharaoh-Necho at Carchemish (B. C. 605) in the fourth year of Jehoiakim. He obliged Jehoiakim to acknowledge himself his subject, and took some treasure and captives to Babylon—among the rest Daniel and the 'three Hebrew children.' But Jehoiakim rebelling three years afterward, Jerusalem was beset by the tributaries of Nebuchadnezzar, who carried on a harassing warfare against it until his death, in the eleventh year of his reign. His son Jehoiachin succeeded him, and Jerusalem being now besieged by Nebuchadnezzar in person, he came out with his mother, servants, princes, and officers, and delivered himself into his hands. Then it was that Nebuchadnezzar took possession of all the treasures of the king's house and of the temple, and carried away from Jerusalem all the princes and chief men, as well as all the ingenious craftsmen and artificers, and all that were strong and apt for war, leaving only the poorest of the people; and over these he set an uncle of Jehoiachin, to whom he gave the name of Zedekiah, and 'made him swear by God' that he would remain his subject, Ezek. xvii, 14. This oath Zedekiah (2 Chron. xxxvi, 13) broke, trusting in the help of Pharaoh Hophra, King of Egypt, and thereby not only provoked the vengeance of Nebuchadnezzar, but incurred the anger of God. Nebuchadnezzar invested Jerusalem on the tenth day of the tenth month, (B. C. 588,) in the ninth year of Zedekiah. Engines of war raised on heights about the walls hurled weighty missiles into the city, the walls were battered with rams, and famine and pestilence prevailed within them. There was a temporary lull in the siege, during which the Chaldean army went to meet the Egyptians, who were coming to the relief of Jerusalem; but the Egyptians turned back without an encounter, and the siege was resumed. The wall was broken on the ninth day of the fourth month of the second year of the siege, and Zedekiah secretly took flight, passing over the Mount of Olives toward the Jordan; but he was taken near Jericho, and conveyed to Riblah in Cœle-Syria, in the extreme north of Palestine, where Nebuchadnezzar was watching from afar the siege of Tyre. There his two sons were slain before his eyes, and he was deprived of sight and carried to Babylon. There also were slain Seraiah, the chief priest, and Zephaniah, the second priest, three door-keepers of the temple, five officers of the court, two of the army, and sixty persons of note who were found in Jerusalem. The rest of the people, with the remaining treasure of the temple—some of it broken in pieces for facility of removal, including the great brazen sea and the two pillars Jachin and Boaz—were carried away. This was the third great deportation of captives from Jerusalem to Babylon. It was effected by Nebuchadnezzar about a month after the siege. He completed his work by burning the temple and the city, and razing the walls to the ground. From this time the land 'enjoyed her Sabbaths' till the end of the seventy years."—Kitto. 2 Kings xxv, 1-10; 2 Chron. xxxvi, 11-19; Jer. xxxii, 24; xxxviii; xxxix, 1-8; lii, 1-15, 28-30. Besides the vast numbers that were thus carried away to Babylon, many others went into Egypt. Jer. xliii, 4-7.

With such a history before us, how forcible are the sad words of the tearful prophet as he beholds the desolations of Jerusalem: "How doth the city sit solitary, that was full of people! how is she become as a widow! she that was great among the nations, and princess among the provinces, how is she become tributary! She weepeth sore in the night, and her tears are on her cheeks . . . she dwelleth among the heathen, she findeth no rest . . . and from the daughter of Zion all her beauty is departed . . . Zion spreadeth forth her hands and there is none to comfort her," Lam. i, 1, 3, 6.

"It was not till Babylon had been itself humbled and taken by Cyrus that Jerusalem revived. The Persian conqueror gave leave (536 B. C.) for the Jews to return to their own country. A large caravan accordingly proceeded to Judea under Zerubbabel and the high priest Joshua, and on the first day of the seventh month they set up, in a solemn assembly at Jerusalem, the altar of burnt-offering. And in the second year after their return, on the first of the second month, they laid the foundation of a new temple. It was a day of gladness and yet of bitter sorrow—of glad hope that the presence of the Lord might again be there, of grief when the old men among them, who remembered Solomon's glorious structure, surveyed the ruins around, and thought how little their feeble means could do to raise a temple like the one destroyed, Ezra iii. And soon there was the busy malice of adversaries at work; and it was not till the reign of Darius Hystaspis that the building was effectually carried on, nor till the twenty-first year after the decree of Cyrus that the new house was dedicated, Ezra vi. All the while, and for much longer, Jerusalem lay without walls and gates, till about 446 B. C., Nehemiah, the cup-bearer of Artaxerxes Longimanus, obtained leave to go to the city of his fathers. Sad was the spectacle as he viewed it—the ramparts broken down, and the marks of fire yet upon the gates. Neh. ii. By his exertions, however, under the king's commission, in spite of opposition, the walls were rebuilt, and there was a solemn day of rejoicing after the completion of the work, Neh. iii; iv; vi; xii, 27-43. Still there were kept many vacant spaces in the city, and the population was small; it was agreed, therefore, that one tenth part of the whole people should dwell in the capital, (vii, 4; xi, 1, 2.) Thus was the holy city re-established."—Ayre.

Here the Old Testament record leaves us. About 320 B. C. Ptolemy Soter, King of Egypt, made an incursion into Syria and took Jerusalem. Multitudes of the Jews were afterward carried captive to Egypt and northern Africa. In 301 B. C. Jerusalem was secured to the Ptolemies, by the defeat of Antigonus at Ipsus, and they retained possession of the city for more than one hundred years. Under the high priest Simon the Just, about 300 B. C., the temple was adorned, the foundations were extended and deepened, and the walls of the city strengthened. During the sway of the Ptolemies the Holy City enjoyed great prosperity. Yet from time to time serious calamities occurred. At length the Egyptian king Ptolemy Philopator entered Jerusalem, B. C. 221. He made a sacrifice in the Temple Court, and would have entered the Holy Place but for the earnest opposition of the high priest.

Jerusalem was wrested from the kings of Egypt by Antiochus the Great, King of Syria, B. C. 203. Then it was retaken, four years later, by the Alexandrian general, Scopas, but it was very soon re-occupied by Antiochus. In 2 Macc. iii, may be found an account of the unsuccessful attempt of Heliodorus, who was sent to rob the temple of its treasures. Josephus, however, does not mention this incident. Antiochus the Great was succeeded by his son, Seleucus Philopator, and the latter by his brother, the execrable Antiochus Epiphanes, B. C. 175. This Syrian king used his utmost efforts to introduce into Jerusalem the customs of the Greek cities. Various evil practices were thus established, whence ensued party riots and fearful massacres. Several times was the temple robbed of its treasures; captives were carried off to Antioch; fires occurred in the city; the worship of God was prohibited, and the temple profaned by idolatrous rites. 1 Macc. i; 2 Macc. v–vii.

Finally occurred an insurrection, which was begun at some distance from Jerusalem by an aged man of priestly family—the father of five sons. He died in the first year of the war thus incited, 166 B. C. His son Judas was victorious over the Syrians, and gained the surname of Maccabeus for himself and his race. (See MACCABEES.) Under the Maccabean princes Jerusalem was greatly strengthened, and enjoyed more or less prosperity; but even during a considerable period of their power a Syrian garrison still held possession of the citadel of Acra. So strong was this garrison that it was not till 142 B. C. that it was forced by famine to capitulate. This was the first year of Jewish freedom, the liberty of the nation being established under Simon, the high priest. Simon built a very strong tower—the Baris, afterward called Antonia, in which with his followers he resided. Under his son and successor, John Hyrcanus, another attempt to regain Jerusalem was made by Antiochus VII. After the investment of the city, negotiations led to an honorable peace. Hyrcanus repaired the walls, which had been disma tled, and he ruled in prosperity for many years. He was succeeded by his son Aristobulus, 107 B. C. This prince assumed the title of king, which was also borne by his successors. He was succeeded by Alexander Jannæus, 105 B. C., during whose reign occurred a fierce strife between the Pharisees and Sadducees, resulting in the death of more than six thousand citizens. Queen Alexandra next held the throne in peaceable possession for nine years, from 79 B. C. Hyrcanus II. claimed the crown at her death, but yielded it to his brother, Aristobulus, after a few months' possession. By the conquest of Syria under the Roman general Pompey, 65 B C.,

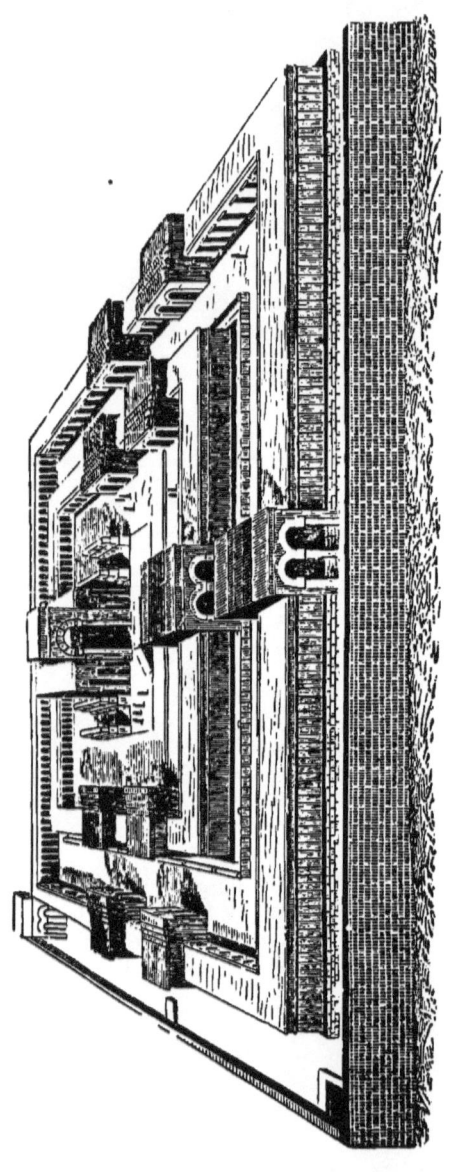

HEROD'S TEMPLE, (ACCORDING TO REV. T. O. PAINE.)

Aristobulus became a prisoner, and Hyrcanus was restored. The latter received Pompey with open arms. The temple, however, was occupied by the friends of Aristobulus, who sustained a severe siege for three months. Pompey having captured the temple, was greatly surprised not to find any image of a Deity in the Holy of Holies. Leaving the sacred treasures untouched, he demolished the walls of the city, and, imposing a tribute upon the people, he still allowed Hyrcanus to govern, not, however, as king, but as high-priest. About 47 B. C. Hyrcanus received from Julius Cæsar the title of ethnarch, while Cæsar also made Antipater procurator of Judea, and allowed the walls of Jerusalem to be rebuilt. Meanwhile Crassus had rifled the temple of its treasures on his way to Parthia, and Gabinius, who had been made proconsul of Syria, had established in Jerusalem one of the five Sanhedrims, or Senates, by which the country was to be governed. Soon Antipater was poisoned by Malichus, and the latter was in turn assassinated by order of Herod, son of Antipater. This young Herod had been made governor of Galilee when his father was made procurator of Judea. Antigonus, the only surviving son of Aristobulus, now claimed the throne, and, with the aid of a Parthian army just then invading Syria, forced Herod to fly, and made himself king, B. C. 40.

Herod, having obtained from the Roman Senate a decree appointing him King of Judea, appeared with an army before Jerusalem, and after a protracted siege captured the temple and the city. He put to death all the chief of the Maccabean party, including the whole Sanhedrim, except the eminent Hebrew doctors, Hillel and Shammai. About B. C. 31 a fearful earthquake destroyed ten or twenty thousand persons, and a great part of Jerusalem. Herod proceeded soon to rebuild and beautify the city. He erected a theater; he enlarged and strengthened the Baris, naming it Antonia, after Anthony. He also built a new palace, and, after two years' preparation, laid the foundation of his magnificent temple, the principal buildings of which were completed B. C. 9. He also erected towers of immense strength and size.

It was "in the days of Herod the king" that Jesus was born, Matt. ii, 1; but Herod lived but a few months after the Saviour's birth. It was probably on his death-bed that this wicked king ordered the murder of the infants, Matt. ii, 16-18. Archelaus succeeded Herod, Matt. ii, 22. Judea now became a Roman province under the governor of Syria, and was administered by a procurator or lieutenant-governor of its own. The procurator resided at Cæsarea, leaving the affairs of Jerusalem to be managed by the highpriest and Sanhedrim.

Jesus was very often in Jerusalem, and its people were witnesses of his wonderful words. We can only refer to some of these, together with his discourses in the streets of the city. He went up to the feasts, John v, 1; vii, 1-14. His triumphal entry is recorded in Matt. xxi, 1-11. He wept over the city, Luke xiii, 34. The miracles of Christ, John ii, 23; iii, 2; iv, 25; v, 1-9; ix. His discourses, Matt. xxi-xxv; John v, 10-47; vii, 14-23; viii-x; xii-xvii.

At the time of Christ's trial and crucifixion Pontius Pilate was procurator of Judea, Matt. xxvii. He was removed from office, A. D. 36, on account of his tyrannical conduct. Herod Agrippa, (grandson of Herod the Great,) who had already received from the Emperor several of the Syrian tetrarchies, succeeded to the entire kingdom of his grandfather, A. D. 41, and he often resided at Jerusalem. After the death of Christ Jerusalem continued to be the scene of many interesting events connected with the history of the early Church. These events can only be referred to.

At Jerusalem the Gospel was first proclaimed, Luke xxiv, 47; Acts ii, 14. Here the disciples were commanded to remain till the descent of the Holy Ghost, Acts i, 4. Here they met to pray, Acts i, 12–14. Here Matthias was elected as an apostle, Acts i, 15–26. Here occurred the descent of the Holy Ghost on the day of Pentecost, with its wondrous results, Acts ii,1–47. Miracle of Peter and John; Peter's discourse, Acts iii. Peter and John imprisoned and released; thanksgiving of the Church, Acts iv, 1–30. Disciples filled with the Holy Ghost, Acts iv, 31. They sold their property and had all things in common, Acts ii, 44, 45; iv, 32–37. The falsehood of Ananias and Sapphira, and their death, Acts v, 1–11. Miracles of the apostles; increase of the Church, Acts v, 12–16. Apostles imprisoned; delivered by an angel; brought before the council; Gamaliel's address; their preaching, Acts v, 17–42. Increase of the Church; disputes between Grecians and Hebrews; disciples appointed to distribute the funds, Acts vi, 1–7.

Stephen's disputes in the synagogue; accusation before the council; defense and death, Acts vi, 8–15; vii. Persecution by Saul; dispersion of disciples, who preach to the Jews of Phenice, Antioch, and Cyprus, Acts viii, 1–5; xi, 19–21. The apostles remain in Jerusalem; Jewish Christians blame Peter for his intercourse with Gentiles; his defense, Acts viii; xiv; xi, 1–18.

Persecution by Herod; James killed; Peter delivered in answer to the prayers of the Church; progress of the Gospel, Acts xii, 1–17, 24. Collections for the poor saints in Jerusalem made by Gentile Churches, Acts xi, 29, 30; Rom. xv, 25, 26; 1 Cor. xvi, 1–3. Decree of Council in reference to circumcision, etc., Acts xv, 1–29.

Paul was here taught by Gamaliel, Acts xxii, 3. Paul's visits to Jerusalem, Acts ix, 26–28; xi, 29, 30; xv, 2–6; Gal. ii, 1–7. A great tumult, and Paul taken to Cæsarea, Acts xxi–xxiii.

Herod Agrippa, whose accession to power (A. D. 41) has been already noticed, added greatly to the outward magnificence of Jerusalem. But an evil fame attends him for his treatment of the Christians. In the midst of his infamous career he was stopped by Divine interposition. His fearful death, which occurred A. D. 44, is recorded in Acts xii.

Herod's son being too young to govern in such troublous times, Cuspius Fadus was made procurator of Judea, while upon Herod, King of Chalcis, was conferred the right of appointing the high-priest, and the superintendence of the temple. About A. D. 46 Tiberius Alexander became procurator, and in A. D. 48 he was followed by Ventidius Cumanus. In this last named year Herod, King of Chalcis, died, and a year or two later the younger Agrippa succeeded to his office and title, Acts xxv, 13. Cumanus, being unable or unwilling to check the disturbances which had been growing in Jerusalem for some time, was removed from power, A. D. 52, and Felix was appointed his successor. Felix aggravated rather than repressed these disorders, and he was superseded by Porcius Festus, A. D. 60. Festus died in 61 or 62, and Albinus was appointed his successor. The latter on arriving in Jerusalem found the city in fearful disorder by reason of quarrels among the priesthood, each leader of the same having his party of banditti at command. Albinus was soon superseded by Gessius Florus, whose cruelty and rapacity roused the Jews in defense of the temple and its treasures. The slaughter of thousands of persons in the contests that followed against Florus brought Agrippa to Jerusalem with the hope of restoring quiet. Agrippa's proposal that the Jews should submit to Florus until another procurator should be appointed was received with such violence and fury that the king was obliged to leave the city.

The jealousy and prejudices which had long existed not only between the Jews and Romans, but also among the Jews themselves, and which had frequently been manifest in the various disorders which had already afflicted Jerusalem, now at length broke forth in direct hostility to the Roman power. Scarcely had Agrippa left the city when Eleazer, the son of Ananias the high-priest, raised the standard of revolt by refusing to offer the customary sacrifice for the Emperor and the Roman people. The insurgents were now masters of the temple and the city. Agrippa sent three thousand horse. Fierce contests ensued in which the rebels were the victors. At length Cestius Gallus, the Governor of Syria, interposed, but without success. With the loss of his engines of war and the slaughter of five thousand of his troops, he was obliged to withdraw from the city, November A. D. 66.

The Jews now felt themselves strong enough to make organized resistance to the Emperor. The most important posts in Palestine were assigned to their bravest citizens. Cestius Gallus and Florus being both dead, the government of Syria was assigned by Nero to his general, Vespasian; while the latter desired his son Titus to come to him from Egypt with his legions.

During A. D. 67, various important places of the country fell into the hands of Vespasian, who had occupied himself in Galilee. On his reducing Giscala, John, the chief personage there, escaped to Jerusalem, where he became one of the famous leaders. By the summer of 68 the Roman army had approached Jerusalem, when Vespasian, hearing of Nero's death, awaited orders from the new Emperor, Galba. Meanwhile the state of affairs within the city was extremely deplorable. In the middle of the year following Vespasian was made Emperor, and his son Titus headed the forces in the ever-memorable siege of Jerusalem in the beginning of A. D. 70, "The city was crowded with strangers who had gone up to the Passover; and two hostile parties formed, if it may be so called, the garrison. Eleazer and John of Giscala held the temple and Antonia, while Simon Ben Gioras occupied Phasælus, the upper and lower city, and Akra; there was also a body of Idumeans. The outer wall was first gained by the besiegers, and then the second wall. Both the city and the temple were next attacked; but the Romans made at first little way. Then, as the southern and western parts had not been invested, and the inhabitants could go out and supplies be brought in, Titus determined to surround the whole of Jerusalem with a wall; it was thirty-nine furlongs (nearly five miles) in extent, and was completed in three days. Now the people were penned up, in awful fulfillment of Christ's words, (Luke xix, 43, 44,) as sheep for the slaughter. And there were dismal omens of coming ruin. A man traversed the streets crying, 'Woe, woe to Jerusalem!' and the priests are said to have heard a deep voice, 'Let us depart!' as if the Divine presence were quitting its hallowed abode. Fresh assaults were delivered; at length, on the tenth day of the fifth month, the anniversary of the burning of the temple by Nebuchadnezzar, contrary to Titus's command, the temple was fired, and but the bare walls of the sanctuary remained. Still the upper city held out;

and Titus, standing on the bridge that joined it to the temple, offered terms. It was in vain; and in other desperate assaults the last defenses were overcome, and the leaders, Simon and John, ultimately taken; and all was demolished save the west wall of the upper city and Herod's three towers, left as memorials of what Jerusalem had been; and so thoroughly was the site leveled and dug up that Josephus declares none would have imagined that it ever had been inhabited. [See *Josephus, Bell. Jud.*, Lib. VII, i, § 1.]

"The number of persons who perished in this siege was enormous. Josephus reckons two millions and a half assembled at the passover when Cestius was governor, and declares that 1,200,000 were shut in the city by the arms of Titus, of whom 1,100,000 were destroyed. Doubtless these numbers are exaggerated; and Mr. Ferguson, in Smith's *Dict. of the Bible*, vol. i, pp. 1025, 1026, denies that the city could ever have contained more than 50,000 ordinary inhabitants, and supposes that, at the festivals, these might be increased to 60,000 or 70,000. Dr. Thomson, well qualified to judge, deems this estimate far too low. He believes that 100,000 could find homes even now within the circuit of modern Jerusalem, and that, allowing for the greater extent of the ancient town, twice as many may have dwelt comfortably there. He also reminds us that, at their sacred solemnities, the Jews were able to camp out, and that doubtless multitudes located themselves in the gardens, and on the slopes around. Vast, therefore, must have been, after every allowance, the multitudes assembled at the fatal siege, and dreadful was the slaughter. It was a fearful retribution when thus their accumulated sins, crowned by that worst deed, the slaughter of their king, were visited upon the nation. Proud, too, was the triumphal procession which swept through the streets of Rome when the treasures of the temple and the sacred vessels were borne as trophies by the victor, the iron entering, indeed, now into the souls of the vanquished. The representation of these trophies may be seen on the yet existing Arch of Titus, and a medal is preserved which commemorates the subjugation of the sons of Jacob. [See ROME.]

"The cup of retribution was even yet not full. There was a Roman garrison on the spot, and some inhabitants returned, and a kind of town gradually gathered around. At length the Emperor Adrian placed a military colony there. But the Jews rose in violent rebellion under Bar-Chochebas, possessed themselves of the restored city, and it required all the might of the empire again to subdue it, 135 A. D. Then Adrian carried out his design. The site was occupied by a colony of soldiers. Foreigners alone might dwell in it, and Jews were forbidden to approach. Temples to the heathen deities were erected, and the name was changed to Ælia Capitolina.

"When the empire became Christian [313 A. D.] the ancient designation revived, though the name Ælia was not obsolete for many centuries. Helena, mother of Constantine the Great, made a pilgrimage thither, and tried to identify the holy places. Churches were erected, and Jerusalem became a Christian city. Julian, in his hatred of the Gospel, allowed the Jews to rebuild the temple, [363 A. D.] But the design was frustrated. The work was, there can be no question, interrupted by fire, which was attributed to supernatural causes. For a long while afterward Jerusalem appears to have been unmolested; but the Persian Chosroes II took it in 614 A. D. It was re-occupied by the Emperor Heraclius in 628, but surrendered to the Caliph Omar in 637."—Ayre.

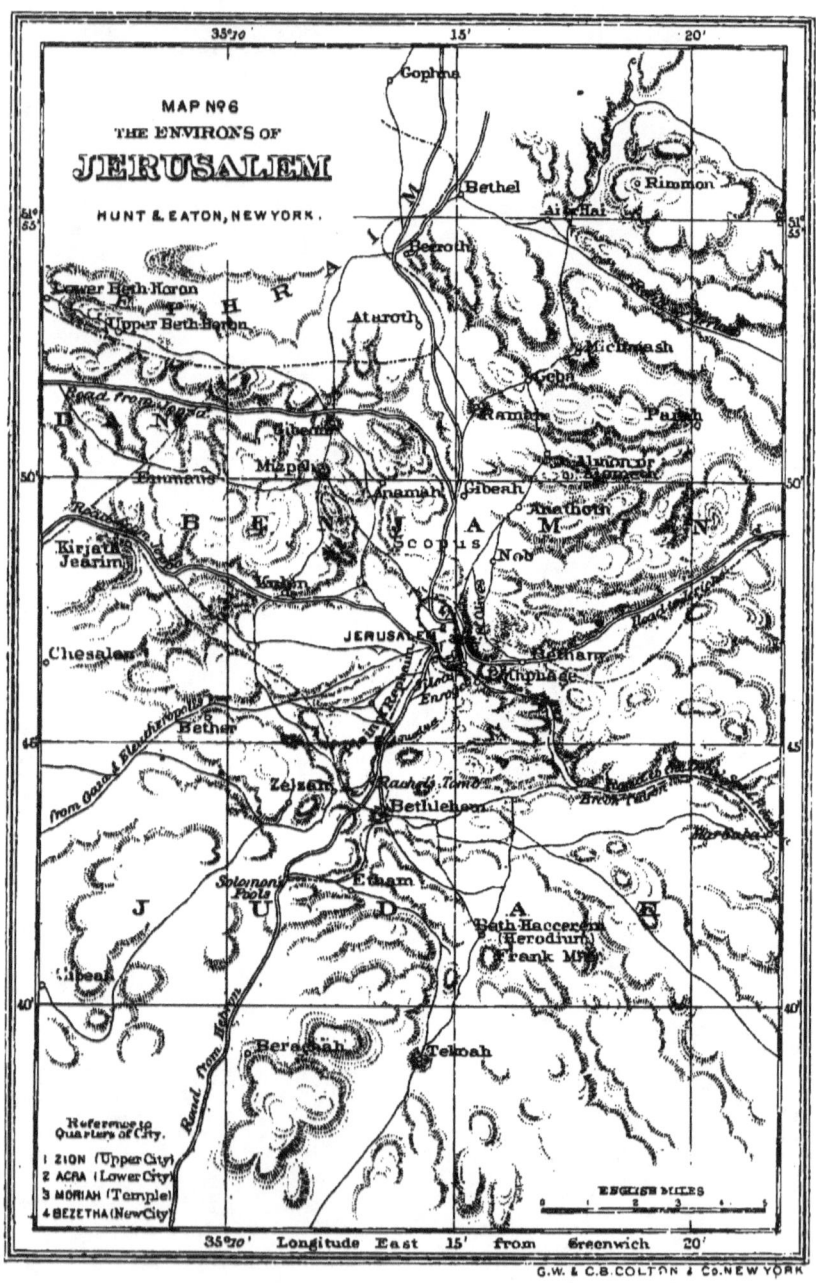

Jerusalem now became one of the sacred cities of the Mohammedans. The splendid Mosque of Omar, built on Mount Moriah, is an enduring monument of this caliph's desire to raise a temple to the honor of the true God upon a spot equally venerated by Jew and Christian.

The Holy City successively passed now into the power of Arabs and now under Turkish rule, until it was wrested from the Fatimite Arabs in 1076 by the race of the Seljouk Turks. These barbarous masters practiced such infamous wrongs upon the Christians that all Christendom was roused with indignation to repossess the sacred site of the ancient temple and city. Then followed the famous Crusades, and Jerusalem was taken by the first Crusaders, 1099 A.D., from the Fatimites of Egypt, who had already dispossessed the Seljouks eleven months before. Godfrey of Bouillon, who was then elected king, was the first of a dynasty of thirteen Latin kings, nino of whom reigned successively in Jerusalem, until it was taken in 1187 by Saladin. The third Crusade was then projected, but without success, and the remaining kings of the dynasty were only titular, and resided at Tyre, Acre, or elsewhere in Palestine. In 1229 the Emperor Frederic II., of Germany, by virtue of a treaty with the Sultan of Egypt, seized Jerusalem, but through neglect it fell again under Mohammedan rule. In 1241 the Sultan of Damascus gave up the city to the Christians, to induce them to aid him against Egypt. Three years afterward it was taken by the Kharismians, a Tartar horde, after a two days' battle, and in 1247 these new masters of the city were dispossessed by the Mohammedans of Syria.

In 1517 the Ottoman Sultan Selim I. took Jerusalem with the rest of Syria and Egypt; and in 1542 the present walls of the city were built by Soliman the Magnificent. The Pasha of Egypt, Mohammed Ali, occupied Jerusalem in 1832; but by European interference he was deprived of his Syrian possessions, and in 1841 Jerusalem once more passed under the Turkish scepter.

V. PRESENT CONDITION, ETC.—In 1864–65 the Royal Engineers made the "Ordnance Survey of Jerusalem," and published the result of their labors in two folio volumes. The success of this expedition led to the effort, by the society known as the "Palestine Exploration Fund," to further explore the Holy City by means of *excavations*. The work was begun in February, 1867, under the direction of Lieutenant Warren, R. E. The exceedingly valuable results of this difficult work are published in the Society's *Quarterly Statements*. From these *Statements*, from the *Survey*, and from the *Hand-book for Syria and Palestine*, by the Rev. J. L. Porter, LL. D., the following details are chiefly derived:

1. GENERAL TOPOGRAPHY.—Jerusalem stands on a broad mountain ridge, the summit of which is broken up into a wilderness of bleak limestone crowns separated by deep ravines. White rocks project from the scanty soil, and the soil itself is almost as white as the rocks, save where a little fountain trickles, or a vine stretches out its long green branches, or a dusky olive lifts up its rounded top and casts its dark shadow.

In the midst of these crowns commence two valleys. At first they are only gentle depressions in a rocky plateau. They both run eastward for a short distance; that on the north continues in this direction about one mile and a half, and then makes a sweep to the south, descends rapidly, and becomes deep and narrow, with precipitous sides. This is the *Valley of the Kidron*. The other, after running about three fourths of a mile east by south, turns suddenly southward, but in less than three fourths of a mile more it er counters a rocky hill-side, which forces it again into an eastern course. It now descends between broken cliffs on the right and shelving banks on the left until in half a mile farther it unites with the Kidron. This is the *Valley of Hinnom.* On the broad ridge between Hinnom and the Kidron stands Jerusalem. This ridge is itself divided by another valley, the *Tyrcpœon,* which runs with a slight curve from the north-west to the south-east, and falls into the Kidron a little above its junction with the Valley of Hinnom. Of the portions into which the ridge is thus divided that on the west is the larger and loftier, and is the Mount Zion of Scripture; that on the east is Moriah. All around the site are loftier summits—nothing approaching to mountains, but rounded, irregular ridges—overtopping the buildings from fifty to two hundred feet, with openings here and there, through which glimpses at the more distant country are obtained. On the east is the triple-topped Mount of Olives, its terraced sides rising steeply from the Kidron. On the south is the so-called Hill of Evil Counsel, overhanging the ravine of Hinnom. On the west the ground ascends to the brow of *Wady Beit Hanina,* about two miles distant. On the north is the hill Scopus, a western projection of the ridge of Olivet. It was while the inspired penman looked upon the "mountains round about Jerusalem" that he compared the righteous to "Mount Zion, which cannot be removed, but abideth forever," Psa. cxxv, 1, 2.

The elevations of the various points within the city are given in Map 7, which will repay careful study. For a fuller account of the "heights" or "crowns" on which the city stands, see ZION, MORIAH, OPHEL, BEZETHA, ACRA.

THE CASTLE OF DAVID, AND YAFA GATE.

2. THE MODERN WALLS.—These were erected, as has been stated, by Sultan Soliman, in 1542. They appear to occupy the site of the walls of

the Middle Ages, from the ruins of which they are mostly constructed. Although high and of imposing appearance, they are far from strong. They are, however, sufficient to keep in check the roving Arab tribes and the turbulent peasantry. The section of the wall on the eastern side, south of St. Stephen's gate, is of far earlier date, being constructed in part of massive beveled stones. Of a similar character is the south-eastern section: these parts form the inclosure of *Haram-esh-Sherif*, "the Noble Sanctuary." The circuit of the walls is nearly two and an eighth geographical miles. The form of the city is irregular, the walls having many projections and indentations; but four sides can easily be made out, and these nearly face the cardinal points. The eastern wall runs in nearly a straight line along the brow of the Valley of Jehoshaphat, (Kidron.) The northern runs nearly west for about six hundred yards over two ridges of rock, which have been excavated to a considerable depth on the outside, thus giving the battlements an imposing and picturesque appearance. Turning then south-west, the wall crosses the valley in which is the Damascus Gate, and ascends the ridge to the north-west angle, where there is a projection. This is the highest point in the city, and commands a fine panoramic view. On the outside the rock has been cut away to some depth, while on the inside are massive foundations of an ancient tower, now called *Kul'at el-Jâlûd*—"Goliath's Castle." The western wall runs south-east to the Yâfa Gate, and then south along the brow of the Valley of Hinnom. Adjoining the Yâfa Gate on the south are the massive towers and deep moats of the old citadel, the "Castle of David." See ZION. The southern wall is carried eastward over the level summit of Zion, and then east by north in a series of zigzags, down the declivity and across the Tyropœon, till it joins the southern wall of the *Haram*.

3. GATES.—At present there are five *open* gates in the walls—two on the south, and one near the center of each of the other sides. They seem to occupy ancient sites. They are as follows: 1. *Bâb el-Khulil*, "the Hebron Gate," usually called by Franks "the Yâfa Gate." It is on the west side of the city, close to the north-western angle of the citadel. It consists of a massive square tower, the entrance to which from without is on the northern side, and the exit within on the eastern. All the roads from the country south and west converge to this gate. 2. *Bâb el-'Amûd*, "the Gate of the Column," better known as "the Damascus Gate." This is on the north, in the center of the valley between the two ridges on which the city stands. It is the most ornamental of the gates, and presents an imposing appearance with its turrets, battlements, and machicolations. From it runs the great north road, past the tombs of the kings and over the ridge of Scopus, to Samaria and Damascus. 3. *Bâb el-Asbât*, "the Gate of the Tribes," called by native Christians *Bâb Sitty Mariam*, "the Gate of my Lady Mary," and by Franks "St. Stephen's Gate," is on the east side, about two hundred feet north of the *Haram* wall. It is a plain portal, with lions sculptured over it. A road leads from it down to the bottom of the Kidron, and thence over Olivet to Bethany and Jericho. 4. *Bâb el-Mughâribeh*, "the Gate of the Western Africans," called by the Franks "the Dung Gate," is a small obscure portal on the south side of the city, near the center of the Tyropœon. It appears to have been but little used, though from it a path leads down to the village of *Silwân*. 5. *Bâb en-Neby Dâûd*, "the Gate of the Prophet David," "Zion Gate," is on the summit of the ridge of Zion, and has in

front of it a small Armenian convent, and a group of buildings clustering round the tomb of David.

Besides these there are two gates now walled up. One is on the north side, about half way between the Damascus Gate and the north-east angle of the city. It is a small portal in a tower, and has been shut since 1834. Natives call it *Bâb ez-Zahery*—"the Gate of Flowers," but it is better known as "the Gate of Herod." The other is "the Golden Gate," in the eastern wall of the *Haram*. The Arab name is *Bâb ed-Dahariyeh*, "the Eternal Gate;" and it is sometimes called *Bab et-Taubeh*, "Gate of Repentance."

The *Golden Gate* is one of the most striking features in the eastern wall. It is in the center of a projection fifty-five feet long, and standing out six feet. The portal is double, with semicircular arches profusely ornamented. The architecture of the interior is very peculiar. In the center is a range of columns, some Corinthian, some debased Ionic, with exaggerated capitals; and at the sides are corresponding pilasters. From these spring groined arches supporting the roof. Although the external ornaments and arches and the interior columns and vaulting are comparatively modern, M. de Vogüé on a close inspection discovered that the gate itself is ancient. Colossal monolithic jambs, one about twelve and the other fourteen feet high, corresponding in form and position to those in the southern gates, remain in position, and are the sole vestiges existing above ground of a massive portal long anterior in date to that now standing.

INTERIOR OF THE GOLDEN GATE.

4. STREETS.—The streets of Jerusalem are only dark and narrow lanes, wretchedly paved, where paved at all, and slippery with filth. A few of the leading thoroughfares run in what Easterns would probably call straight lines, and they serve as a key to the rest. One street, called the "Street of David,"—that generally the first trodden by the Western pilgrims—leads from the Yâfa Gate eastward past the open space beside the citadel, then down the side of the ridge and across the valley to the principal entrance of the *Haram, Bâb es-Silsilah*. Another main street commences at the Damascus Gate, traverses the city from north to south, passing near the eastern end of the Church of the Holy Sepulcher and through the principal bazaar, and terminating a little eastward of the Zion Gate. The northern

section of it is called "the Street of the Gate of the Column," and the southern "the Street of the Gate of the Prophet David." Two other streets may here be noticed. The first is "Christian Street." It runs northward from the Street of David, passing between the Church of the Sepulcher and the Greek Convent. It contains a number of Frank shops. About the center of it a narrow lane leads down eastward to the door of the Church of the Sepulcher, and also to the fine old gateway

A STREET IN JERUSALEM.

of the palace of the Knights of St. John. Another street begins at the Latin Convent, passes down through gloomy archways to the bed of the Tyropœon, and then, after two sharp turns, strikes across in front of the Serai (or "palace ") to St. Stephen's Gate. This is the *Via Dolorosa* of the monks; but called by residents "the Street of the Palace." This street is full of traditional sites concerning the Crucifixion. The monks point out the spot where Pilate showed the Saviour to the crowd, saying, "Behold the Man!" Here the street is spanned by the *Ecce Homo Arch.* If this was the Saviour's route to Calvary, little do these monks seem to know that the accumulated rubbish of centuries covers the true Dolorosa. The student will find other streets indicated on Map 10.

5. VALLEYS WITHIN THE CITY.—The *Tyropœon* Valley, (Map 11,) according to Josephus, separated Zion from Akra on the north, and from Moriah and Ophel on the east. Thus it swept round two sides of the "Upper City," or Zion. The exact position of the head of the Tyropœon is one of the vexed questions of Jerusalem topography. This question involves the position of Zion, concerning which there has been much controversy. For this we have not space. See ZION. The simple interpretation of certain passages in Josephus (see *B. J.*, v, 4, 1; *Ant.*, xv, 11, 5) leads us to look for the *head* of this valley *immediately* along the northern brow of Zion. There a depression still exists; but recent explorations have demonstrated that the valley was originally much deeper than it is now. Another valley is mentioned by Josephus as a "broad valley." Josephus says: "Over against this (Akra) was a third hill, naturally lower than Akra, and formerly separated from it by another *broad valley.* But afterward, during the sovereignty of the Asmonæans, they threw earth into this valley, desiring to connect the city with the temple; and leveling the summit of Akra, they made it lower, so that the temple might appear above it." From these and other passages in

11

Josephus, it seems clear that the Tyropœon Valley began at the Yâfa Gate. From this gate it runs eastward for about five hundred yards, and then, sweeping round the north-east corner of Zion, it turns southward and continues about eight hundred yards farther, till it joins the Kidron. At its mouth is a pool still called Siloam.

JEWS' WAILING PLACE.

The Jews' Wailing Place is in the Tyropœon Valley, at the base of the wall which supports the west side of the temple area. There is here a small quadrangular paved area between low houses and the *Haram*. In the wall are five courses of large beveled stones in a fine state of preservation, though the joints in the lower courses are in some places much worn, and here and there displaced. Here the Jews have been permitted for many centuries to approach the precincts of the temple of their fathers, and bathe its hallowed stones with their tears. On each Friday at this retired spot Jews of both sexes, of all ages, and from every quarter of the East, are there raising up a united voice of wailing over a desolated and dishonored sanctuary. Compare Psa. lxxix, 1, 4, 5.

Anciently there was on the western side of the Tyropœon a place called the "Xystus." It was a kind of Forum, or place of public assembly, attached to the east side of the palace on Zion, and having colonnades and cloisters. From various notices in the writings of Josephus we learn that the Xystus was connected at its southern end with the temple court by a bridge. The position of this bridge has been discovered within the past few years: an account of it will be found on page 232.

6. QUARTERS OF THE CITY.—The first two streets above named divide the city into four quarters. The north-east is the Mohammedan quarter, the north-west the Christian, the south-west the Armenian, the south-east the Jewish. Until within the past few years the lanes and houses in the Jewish quarter were in a wretched state of squalor and dilapidation, but a great change for the better has taken place, chiefly owing to the enlightened efforts and princely generosity of Sir Moses Montefiore. The *Haram* constitutes a "quarter" of itself, almost equal in extent to one fourth of the city. See pages 227, 228.

7. GENERAL APPEARANCE.—As seen from some commanding eminence, the walls of the city seem much too large for it; the buildings do not nearly fill up the space inclosed. There is a group of gardens at the north-eastern angle, and there is another group at the north-western; at the south-western angle is the large garden of the Armenian convent, while an extensive tract

of waste ground—partly covered with heaps of rubbish, partly overgrown with prickly pear—extends along the southern wall from Zion Gate to the *Haram*. And the site of the once splendid palace of the Knights of St. John, in the very center of the city, is at present bare and desolate.

8. THE POPULATION of Jerusalem is variously estimated at from 10,000 to 30,000. The nearest approximation that can be made seems to be about as follows: Moslems, 4,000; Jews, 8,000; Greeks, 1,800; Latins, 1,300; other sects, 900—Total, 16,000.

The *Mohammedans*, as a body, are natives. Connected with the *Haram*, and living in idleness on its ample revenues, is a large number of *Dervishes*. These make the city a hot-bed of fanaticism, so that one cannot approach the precincts of their den without being assailed with abuse.

The *Jews* are divided into two sects, the *Sephardim* and the *Askenazim*. The Sephardim are of Spanish origin, having been driven out of Spain in 1497. At first they were scattered among the great cities of the Turkish Empire, but they gradually congregated in Jerusalem. Though long resident in the Holy City, comparatively few of them speak Arabic; their language is a corrupt Spanish. They are subjects of the Sultan, but are permitted to have their own rabbinical laws. Their chief rabbi is called by the Turks *Khakham Bashi;* his Hebrew title is " the Head in Zion." His principal interpreter has a seat in the *Mejlis*, or "council" of the city. The Askenazim are chiefly of German and Polish origin, and their numbers are continually augmented by fresh arrivals. They are all foreigners, and subject only to the consular agents of their native country. They were readmitted into Palestine in the beginning of the present century under the wing of the Sephardim. The Askenazim have a chief rabbi, but the only authority acknowledged by the government is the Khakham Bashi above named. They are divided into several sects: the *Perushin*, or Pharisees, who are the most numerous; the *Khasdim*, or "Pious," characterized by intense fanaticism, and the *Khabaad*. The *Karaites* form a small but distinct community. They reject the Talmud, and receive the Old Testament; but they are few in number and weak in influence.

The whole Jewish community, being mainly supported by contributions from Europe, and being taught to regard those contributions as a debt owing to them, spend their time in idleness. A few study the Talmud and controversial works in the reading-rooms, of which they have thirty-six, with a large paid staff of readers. The news of the funds collected for them by their brethren in other countries, and of the large sums occasionally contributed for their relief by benevolent friends in England, attract numbers of the needy and idle to the Holy City.

The *Greeks*, or members of the " Holy Orthodox Church of the East," are all native Arabs, speaking the language of the country, and having their own *secular* married clergy. The Patriarch of Jerusalem is their head. He has subject to him fourteen sees, but some of them have now neither bishops nor flocks. The patriarch was long an absentee, residing at Constantinople, but since 1845 he has taken up his abode in the convent beside the Church of the Sepulcher. The patriarch, the superior clergy, and all the monks, are foreigners, generally from the Greek islands, and speaking only the Greek language.

The *Armenians* are a branch of that Church and nation whose members are spread so widely over the various provinces of the Turkish Empire.

The community here numbers about three hundred, who are all foreigners, generally engaged in commerce and trade. Their spiritual ruler is styled Patriarch of Jerusalem.

The *Georgians* were at one time among the wealthiest and most influential of the Christian sects in the city, but they have gradually declined. Gradually the Greeks and Armenians bought up their convents and property, and now they are dependent upon the former for hospitality when they visit any of the sacred shrines. The *Copts* and *Abyssinians* possess two convents. The *Syrians* are under the protection of the Armenians, and have a small convent in Zion, called the "House of Mark."

The *Latins* are principally seceders from the Greek Church. They are mostly natives of Syria, and speak the Arabic language. Some of them get a scanty subsistence by carving beads, crosses, and other trinkets for pilgrims, while a few more have their wants supplied from the alms of the great convent. When the monastic system was introduced into Syria in the fourth century, hundreds of pilgrims began to crowd to the hallowed scenes of Bible history, and cluster round them in cells and grots. Many came from countries in which the authority of Rome was paramount. The most celebrated of these was *St. Jerome*, who settled at Bethlehem in 386. During subsequent centuries others were added, but it was in the time of the Crusades that the Church of Rome was enabled to establish an active and wide-spread ecclesiastical agency in this land. The head-quarters were at first in the "Hospital of the Knights of St. John." From this they were driven, on the capture of the city by Saladin, and took up their abode on Zion around the spot where the tomb of David now stands. This also being wrested from them, they then bought the present Convent of *St. Salvador*, to which they removed in 1561. The remains of the Latin ecclesiastical establishments are now well known by the name of *Terra Santa* convents. They are all in the hands of that class of the Franciscans called *Fratres Minores ab Observantia*, and are under the superintendence of a "warden," having the rank of abbot, and styled "Guardian of Mount Zion and Keeper of the Holy Land." In 1847 a Latin Patriarch was appointed for Jerusalem, and he has spiritual oversight of the country, though not of the convents. There are at present fourteen convents in Syria subject to the warden, namely, Jerusalem, St. John in the Desert, Ramleh, Bethlehem, Yâfa, 'Akka, Nazareth, Sidon, Beyroot, Tripoli, Larissa, Aleppo, Damascus, and Mount Lebanon.

Protestants.—The little community of Protestants was organized mainly by the "London Society for Promoting Christianity among the Jews." A mission of inquiry was sent to Palestine in 1820. The first missionary, Dr. Dalton, took up his residence in Jerusalem in 1824. Many difficulties were encountered before ground could be bought for the erection of a church. Some temporary buildings were commenced, but the death of the architect and the breaking out of a war with Egypt prevented further progress. In 1841 an agreement was made between the English and Prussian governments to establish a bishopric of the Anglican Church at Jerusalem, with a diocese embracing Mesopotamia, Chaldæa, Syria, Palestine, Egypt, and Abyssinia. It was stipulated that the bishop should be nominated alternately by the crowns of England and Prussia, the Archbishop of Canterbury having the right of *veto* with respect to those nominated by the latter. In 1842 the foundation-stone of the new church was laid. The work advanced

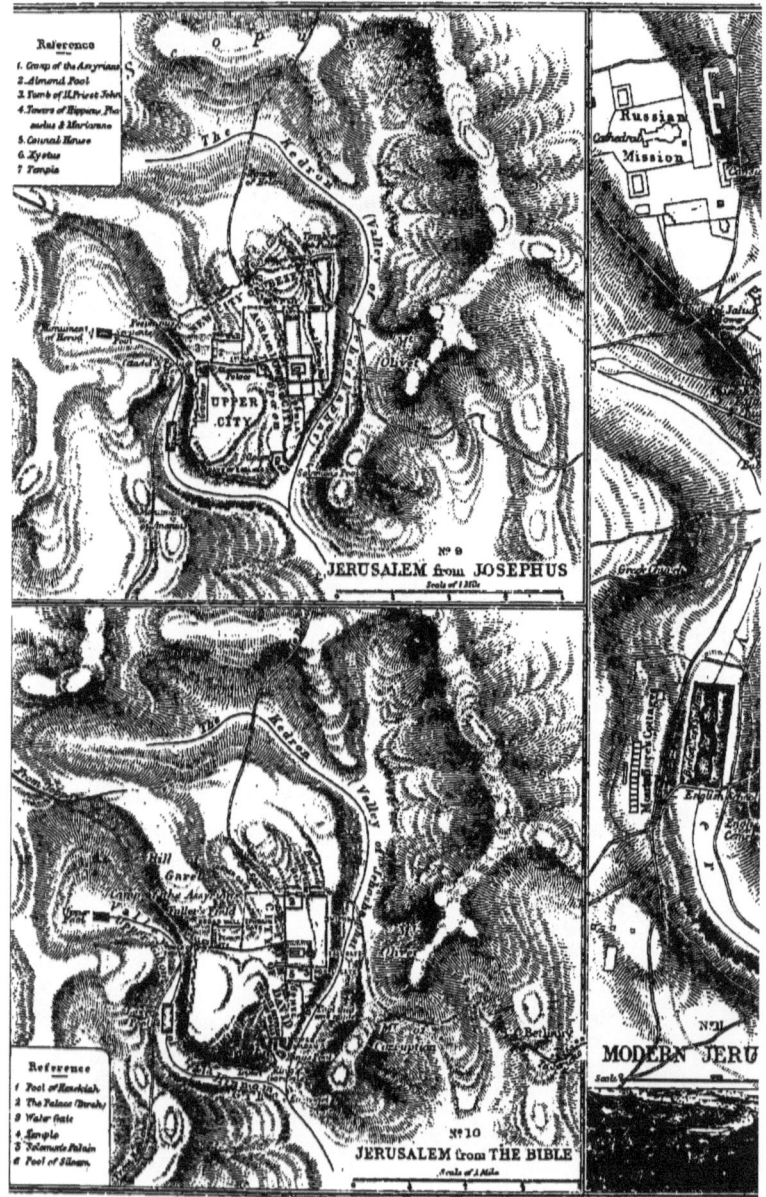

HREE EPOCHS

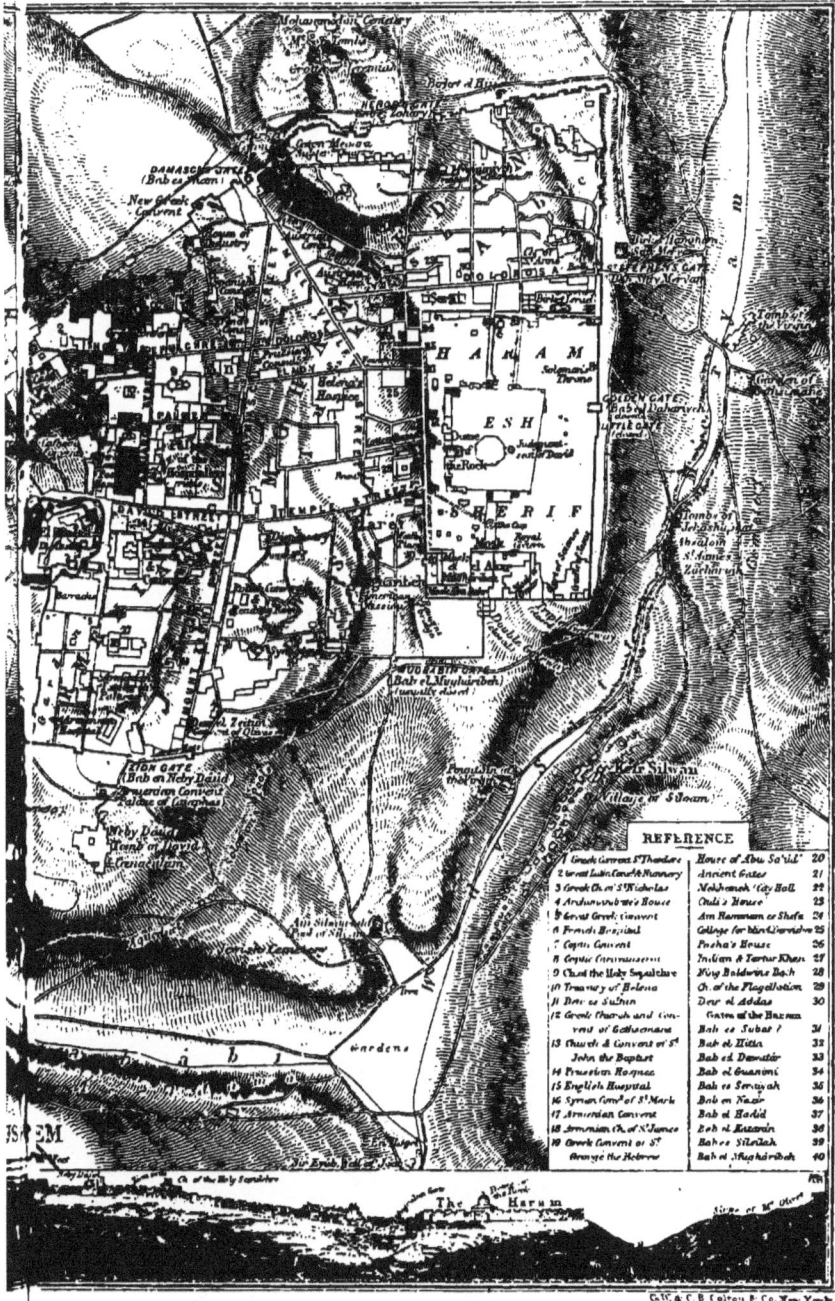

MOSQUES IN THE HARAM INCLOSURE AT JERUSALEM, (FROM THE ROOF OF THE GOVERNOR'S HOUSE ON THE NORTH.)

till January, 1843, when the Turkish authorities interfered, insisting that if a church were erected at all it must be attached to and dependent on a consulate.

9. PRINCIPAL STRUCTURES.—The most prominent building is the Mosque of Omar, called also "The Dome of the Rock," or *Kubbet es-Sukrah*. It occupies a part of the spacious area known as the *Haram esh-Sherif*, "the Noble Sanctuary," (Map 10.) "The massive and lofty walls by which this area is surrounded, the green grass of the inclosure, dotted with olives and cypresses, and ornamented by marble fountains and *mihrabs*; the broad, elevated platform, encircled by graceful arches, and diversified by carved pulpits, prayer niches, and cupolas; and the great mosque itself, with its noble dome rising up in the center of all, bright and gorgeous as a vision of fairy-land, its enameled tiles glittering in the sunbeams and exhibiting all the hues of the rainbow wrought into patterns of wondrous intricacy and grace—these together form a picture such as is scarcely surpassed in the world. . . . It is so secluded, so still and solemn, that the very sight impresses one with a sense of its sacredness."—*Porter.*

Common tradition says that after the Caliph Omar took the city he inquired where the Jewish temple had stood. After some search he was conducted to the celebrated rock *es-Sukrah*, then covered over with filth and rubbish. This rock he himself helped to cleanse, and then built over it the mosque still existing. But Arab historians inform us that the Caliph Abd el-Melek rebuilt the mosque after a design of his own; that it was commenced in A. D. 686; that it was magnificently decorated, and that the outside of the dome was covered with plates of gold. Their accounts are much confused, but doubtless the mosque of Abd el-Melek was built over the sacred rock, and was identical to a great extent with that now existing. The *Kubbet es-Sukrah* is octagonal, each side measuring sixty-seven feet. The lower part of the wall is composed of various-colored marbles, arranged in intricate patterns. The upper part is pierced with fifty-six pointed windows, filled with stained glass of a brilliancy equal to some of the finest specimens in European cathedrals. The whole interior of the walls and dome is ornamented in gilt stucco in the arabesque style. The dome is of wood, and directly under it is the celebrated *rock* from which the mosque takes its name.

The "Sacred Rock" is thus described by Captain Wilson: "The rock stands four feet nine and a half inches above the marble pavement at its highest point, and one foot at its lowest; it is one of the 'missæ' strata, and has a dip of 12° in a direction of 85° east of north. The surface of the rock bears the marks of hard treatment and rough chiseling; on the western side it is cut down in three steps, and on the northern side in an irregular shape, the object of which could not be discovered. Near, and a little to the east of the door leading to the chamber below, are a number of small rectangular holes cut in the rock, as if to receive the foot of a railing or screen, and at the same place is a circular opening communicating with the cave. The entrance to the cave is by a flight of steps on the south-east, passing under a door-way with a pointed arch, which looks like an addition of the Crusaders; the chamber is not very large, with an average height of six feet; its sides are so covered with plaster and whitewash that it is impossible to see any chisel marks, but the surface appears to be rough and irregular." Concerning this rock the Moslems relate a number of absurd traditions.

Within the *Haram* inclosure are many other structures. Facing *Báb es-Silsileh*, "the Gate of the Chain," (which is in the west wall of the inclosure,) is a small but richly ornamented cupola called the "Dome of Moses," (not the lawgiver.) On the left of the gate are cloisters. Near these are buildings occupied as colleges of dervishes and public schools. To the northward are several prayer-stations, and at the northern end is a section of the massive ancient wall, and also the scarped rock on which stood the citadel of Antonia. In the north-east corner there is nothing worthy of notice. Along the eastern wall is a little building called the Throne of Solomon. A little south of this is the Golden Gate, projecting far into the grassy court. Just in front of the great mosque on the east is the beautiful little cupola *Kubbet es-Silsileh*, "the Dome of the Chain." It is sometimes called "the Dome of Judgment," from the belief that the judgment-seat of King David occupied the spot. At the north-west corner of the platform of the great mosque is *Kubbet el-Arwáh*, "the Dome of Spirits," with a cistern or cave beneath it. South of this (on the platform) is the cupola *Kubbet en-Neby*, "the Dome of the Prophet," which claims to mark the spot from which the prophet began his ascent to Paradise; and close to it on the south is a *Masjud*, where the angels gave him the necessary instructions for his journey.

On the southern line of the inclosure is the Mosque *El-Aksa*. A little north of the Gothic porch of the mosque is a marble fountain called *El-Kas*, "the Cup." Beneath this is a very large subterraneous reservoir, into which the water from the pools of Solomon was once conveyed. It is nearly fifty feet deep, and interspersed with little islands of rock, upon which similar-shaped tapering rock-work has been raised to support the ground above. Some distance farther, and within a few feet of the great door of *El-Aksa*, is the entrance to the passage leading to the southern gateway of the ancient temple. Concerning the Mosque *El-Aksa*, authorities differ as to the date of its erection. Some claim it to be, at least in site and outline, identical with the magnificent basilica built about the middle of the sixth century by the Emperor Justinian in honor of the Virgin. De Vogüé affirms that the present structure is entirely Arab; but that its form of a basilica, its cruciform plan, and the existence of certain ancient remains, prove that it was preceded by a Christian church whose ruins served as the kernel of the mosque. Mr. Fergusson, on the other hand, most emphatically denies that this is the Mary Church of Justinian. He maintains that *El-Aksa* is wholly a Mohammedan structure; that it was built by the Caliph Abd el-Melek at the close of the seventh century; and that Justinian's church was erected in the south-east corner of the *Harum* area. The Mosque *El-Aksa* has the form of a basilica of seven aisles. It is 272 feet long by 184 wide, over all thus covering about 50,000 square feet. Captain Wilson says that a great part of the mosque is covered with whitewash; but the interior of the dome, and the portion immediately under it, is richly decorated with mosaic work and marble casing. The arabesques and mosaics are similar in character, though of different design, to those in the "Dome of the Rock."

In the south-east corner of the *Haram* is the *Mosque of Isa*, (Jesus.) Through this is the entrance to the vaults which sustain this section of the area. These vaults will be described below.

On the west of *Aksa* is the building generally called the Mosque of *Abu-Bekr*. But Captain Wilson says that the Sheikh of the *Haram* and the educated Moslems in Jerusalem know nothing of this name; and that they invariably call it *Al-Baka'at-al-Baidha*, (the white corner or place,) sometimes adding "of Solomon."

In the "Christian Quarter," in a narrow, crooked street, sometimes called Palmer Street, stands the renowned church of "the Holy Sepulcher." Dean Stanley says this is "the most sacred of all the Holy Places, in comparison with which, if genuine, all the rest sink into insignificance; the interest of which, even if not genuine, stands absolutely alone in the world." This "church" comprises a group of buildings 350 feet long by 280 wide, "including seventy sacred localities, presided over by seventeen different sects in separate chapels inside the edifice." We give the names of some of these "chapels:" "Chapel of Adam;" "Church of the Ointment-bearers," or "Church of the Forty Martyrs;" "The Greek Church;" "Chapel of the Division of the Vestments;" "Chapel of Helena;" "Chapel of the Invention of the Cross;" "Chapel of the Mocking;" "Chapel of Golgotha;" "Chapel of the Elevation of the Cross;" "Chapel of the Crucifixion." The entrance from Palmer Street leads into an open court which is about ninety feet long by seventy wide. Certain parts of the church seem to be ancient, that is, anterior to the Crusades. The whole, however, is much dilapidated.

The *Holy Sepulcher* itself occupies the center of the grand rotunda. Dr. Thomson thus speaks of the Sepulcher: "Externally it looks very much like a small marble house. All the world knows that it is twenty-six feet long and about eighteen broad, and, I should think, something more than twenty feet high. It stands quite alone, directly under the aperture in the center of the dome. I went into the Chapel of the Angel by its low door, saw the stone on which the angel sat, crept into the proper sepulcher room, and looked at the raised, altar-like recess on the north side, whose fine *marble* slab is said to cover the real rock couch where the body of our Lord was laid. I did not measure these rooms, nor count the silver lamps which crowd the little apartment overhead. A thousand pilgrims have counted and measured, and given very various results."

For centuries the sacred site of Christ's sepulcher attracted the enthusiasm of all Christendom. And although this enthusiasm of late years has sensibly abated, yet the traditional interest which still gathers about the Holy Sepulcher is considerable. It is not certain that the present church covers the sepulcher "hewn out of the rock" (Mark xv, 46) in which was laid the body of Jesus. We know that Christ was crucified "without the gate," (Heb. xiii, 12,) "nigh to the city," (John xix, 20,) at a place called *Golgotha*, "the place of a skull," (Matt. xxvii, 33,) and apparently near or beside some public thoroughfare, (Matt. xxvii, 39.) Therefore if the present "church" in question be *outside* the old walls, it *may* cover the ancient sepulcher. If it prove to be *inside* those walls, then the site must be abandoned. This topographical aspect of the question can be determined only by the plan adopted by the *Exploration Fund*—by digging until the foundations of the ancient walls are fully revealed.

We find no reference in *history* to the site of the Holy Sepulcher until about 300 years after the Crucifixion. Speaking of this tomb, Eusebius declares that "impious men, or rather the whole race of demons through the agency of impious men, had labored to deliver over that illustrious monument of immortality to darkness and oblivion." Hence it appears that the sepulcher had been covered with earth, and over it had been erected a temple of Venus. In the fourth century, when the Emperor Constantine and his mother Helena had become Christian, she had a dream by which she was impelled to go to Jerusalem. It is said that, having searched diligently for the sepulcher in which Christ was buried, they found it. On this site Constantine built a group of edifices, which was begun A. D. 326, and dedicated in 335. To the building which stood on the place of our Saviour's passion was given the name *Martyrion*, and the chapel at the sepulcher was called the *Anastasis*, or "Resurrection." The Martyrion was destroyed by the Persians in 614, but was rebuilt about sixteen years later. The buildings were now erected on a different plan, partly from want of funds, and partly to accommodate the additional "Holy Places" that were springing up about the sepulcher. Bishop Arculf, who visited Jerusalem in the end of the seventh century, gives a full account of these edifices.

These buildings were again destroyed by the Caliph Hâkim in 1010, and they were not rebuilt until 1048. The Crusaders took Jerusalem in 1099. They remodeled the old structures and added many new shrines. These numerous buildings, as they appeared in 1103, are fully described by Sæwulf, an English monk who followed the Crusaders to Palestine. See *Early Travels*, pp. 37, 38. With the exception of some slight repairs, the buildings remained as the Crusaders left them till the year 1808, when they were partly destroyed by fire. The roof of the rotunda fell in upon the sepulcher, but the latter, though crushed without, was uninjured within. The marble columns which supported the great dome were calcined, and the walls injured. It is difficult to determine precisely how much damage was done, owing to the different statements of the various sects. After much difficulty and long negotiations permission was granted by the Porte to rebuild the church. The new church, as it now stands, was consecrated in 1810.

Some earnest and able writers have recently maintained that the Sepulcher of Christ was on Mount Moriah, and that the church of the *Anastasis* built by Constantine is the "Dome of the Rock," (Mosque of Omar.) See CALVARY; MORIAH. See Mr. Fergusson's article on JERUSALEM in Smith's *Dictionary*, and an Essay by S. Smith, M. A., on *The Temple and the Sepulcher*.

The *Cœnaculum*. On the southern brow of Zion, without the walls, stands the *Mosque of David*. This is said to occupy the site of the tombs of David, Solomon, and other kings. A description of it will be found under ZION. We notice here a "large upper room" of the Mosque, called the *Cœnaculum*. It is a "vaulted gothic chamber," which Stanley says "contains within its four walls a greater confluence of traditions than any other place of like dimensions in Palestine." The room is fifty feet long by thirty wide, and is manifestly ancient. Tradition claims this place as the scene of the Last Supper, of the meeting after the resurrection, of the miracle of Pentecost, of the residence and death of the Virgin, the martyrdom of Stephen, etc.

The *Palace of Caiaphas* is a building which stands between the Cœnaculum and the Zion gate. There are many other structures of note in the city, but we have not space for a description of them. The student will find a list of some of them, and their location indicated in Map 10.

10. CHIEF POINTS OF INTEREST IN THE VICINITY. See, under BIBLE ALLUSIONS, (in the present article,) "PLACES IN AND AROUND;" and "POOLS, FOUNTAINS, AND BROOKS."

11. CLIMATE OF JERUSALEM. The general temperature of the mountainous region on which the city stands does not differ much from the south of France; but in other respects there is a wide difference. The variations of

rain, sunshine, and shade, which in a greater or less degree ex st during the summer in most parts of Europe, are here unknown. From May to September is one uninterrupted blaze of sunshine. There is generally a breeze; but, as during the day it is wafted across white sterile hills by which the sun's rays are strongly reflected, it becomes like the " breath of a furnace." The rains begin about the middle of October. Snow often falls in January and February, and ice occasionally appears on the surface of the pools. The rains usually cease in April, though showers sometimes fall in May. The sirocco wind, which blows at intervals in spring and the early part of summer, is the most oppressive. This wind always comes from the south, and illustrates our Lord's words in Luke xii, 55. While on the whole the climate of Jerusalem is salubrious, it would be much improved by a proper attention to cleanliness throughout the streets, courts, and waste places of the city.

12. GENERAL RESULTS OF EXCAVATIONS IN AND AROUND THE CITY.—The modern city stands on the accumulated ruins of two thousand years. Within historical knowledge Jerusalem has sustained more than twenty sieges; and again and again the city has "become heaps," Micah iii, 3. Through these heaps of rubbish the tool of the explorer has pierced to a depth, in some places, of more than one hundred feet. In reading the following details compare Maps 7, 10, and 11 with the plans as shown in the frontispiece and on page 194.

The Bezetha Quarry.—Not far from the Damascus Gate is the entrance to the vast cavern from which it is probable the huge stones were quarried for the magnificent structures of Jerusalem. The quarry is six hundred feet long, and extends in a southeasterly direction. The roof of rock is about thirty feet high, even above the great heaps of rubbish on the bottom. The niches in the wall from which the stone blocks have been taken are not only of the same form and size with the stones in the south-east corner of the *Haram* area, but also of the same material. Chisel-marks are yet everywhere to be seen. Here, doubtless, is the place where the stone was "made ready," so that on the temple site ' there was neither hammer nor ax, nor any tool of iron, heard in the house while it was in building," 1 Kings vi, 7 At the end of the cave are blocks of stone half-quarried, with the marks of the chisel still fresh upon them.

The Haram Elevation.—Moriah was originally of such a shape that it would have been impossible to build the temple on the natural ridge. Solomon therefore raised massive walls from the valley on each side, and thus secured a level platform. Hence between the walls and the hill-slopes there were vast hollows. These, however, were in great measure utilized for the temple service by forming vaults, tanks, avenues, etc. Figure 1 (facing page 232) will illustrate the plan of the platform. K is the ridge of Moriah; A A is the natural rock; B B is the accumulated *débris;* C is the present surface at the south-west end of the *Haram*, the Tyropœon Valley; D is the present surface at the east end, the Kidron Valley; E is the wall below the ground. F is the *Haram* wall above ground. At G, at the south-west end, a shaft has been sunk to the depth of eighty-seven feet, where the true bed of the Tyropœon was found. See dark patch under E. The south *Haram* wall below the ground (E) has been exposed in many places, and practically traced through the whole length of about 1,000 feet, and it is, without doubt, the wall of Solomon's temple. When Jesus declared "there shall not be left one stone upon another that shall not be thrown down," he referred to the temple, not to the inclosure, Mark xiii, 1, 2. In the west wall at the Jews' Wailing-Place, and also at the south-east corner, (H,) are many courses of huge beveled stones in a fine state of preservation. These stones have remained in their present position since the days of our Lord. If the accumulated rubbish were removed, this wall would rise grandly one hundred and fifty feet above the Hinnom Valley. Upon the old temple walls Herod's cloister, the Stoa Basilica, rose to an additional height of fifty feet. See Map 31. It has been discovered also that the wall at the north-east angle rose to a height as great as that of the south wall. The deepest shaft yet sunk at the northeast angle is one hundred and ten feet below the surface, and it "found the rock still sloping downward, and revealed the existence of a valley, suspected before, but not certainly known, across the north-east angle. The surface of the *Haram*, therefore, in some part of which the temple, without any doubt, stood, is like the lid of an oblong box, three of whose angles are about one hundred and twenty feet above the rock."

Captain Warren has made a most important discovery at the south-east angle. He found certain peculiar characters inscribed on the stones in the very lowest course, where they lie on the living rock. The eminent Semitic scholar, M. Deutsch, decides that the marks are "partly letters, partly numerals, and partly special masons' or quarry signs;" that they "were on the stones when they were first laid in their present places;" and, most important of all, "they are Phenician." It will be remembered that Phenician workmen were furnished to Solomon by the king of Tyre, 1 Kings v-vii.

Robinson's Arch.—A few rods south of the Jews' Wailing-Place, and at a distance of thirty-nine feet from the south-west angle of the *Haram* wall, are three courses of stone, extending fifty-two feet, and projecting from its surface. It was believed by Dr. Robinson that these stones formed the segment of an arch, corresponding in position to a bridge, which, according to Josephus, connected the temple with the "Upper City." The excavations by Captain Warren have established this theory. This officer, by sinking a shaft at this place, found the western pier which supported the other end of the arch. This pier is of the same length with the segment on the *Haram* wall. From the base of the pier to the *Haram* wall a limestone pavement extends, and on this pavement were found the *voussoirs* of the wedge-shaped arch-stones of the bridge, lying in rows north and south, just as they had been cast down centuries ago—probably at the siege of Titus. Warren made a still more important discovery by sinking a shaft through the pavement to the depth of twenty-three feet. Here was found a conduit cut out of the solid rock, and running north-west along the bed of the Tyropœon. Across this water-course the explorers saw the *voussoirs* of another, and therefore still more ancient arch. Probably this was the bridge destroyed by Aristobulus for the purpose of cutting off the temple from communication with the city when it was besieged by Pompey. In the conduit a square hole was also discovered, which indicates that it was the opening of a cistern. Thus the passage was not a cistern, but a conduit for pure water. "Scandals whispered at the mouth of this well may have echoed round its rocky sides as far back as the time when the Jebusites and Canaanites ruled in the land."

The bridge of which Robinson's Arch formed a part extended from the temple to Zion. It was 52 feet wide and 350 long, and rested upon several arches. Figure 2 will illustrate the discoveries made at the bridge. A is

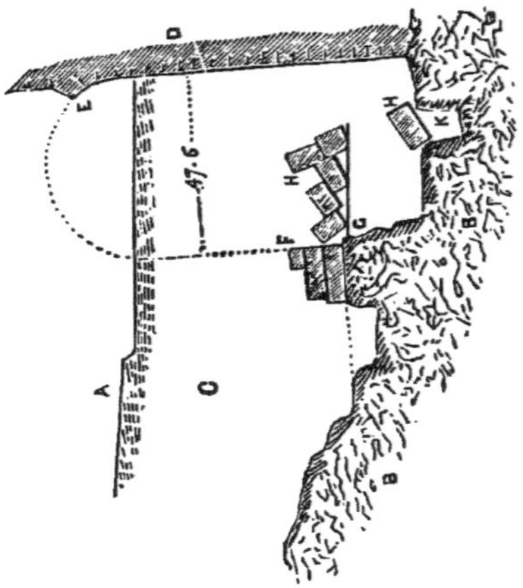

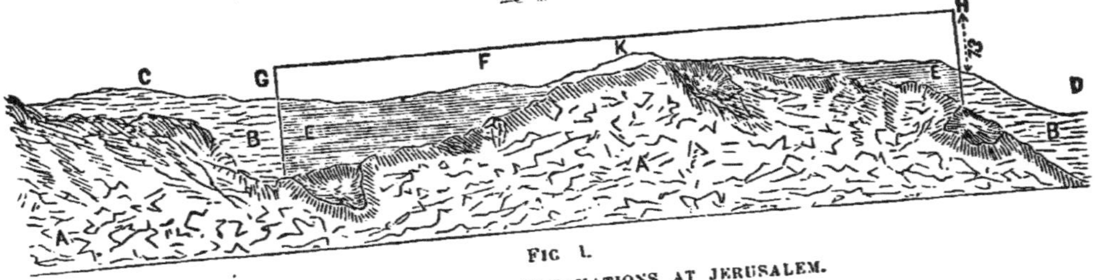

FIG. 1.
PLANS ILLUSTRATING EXCAVATIONS AT JERUSALEM.

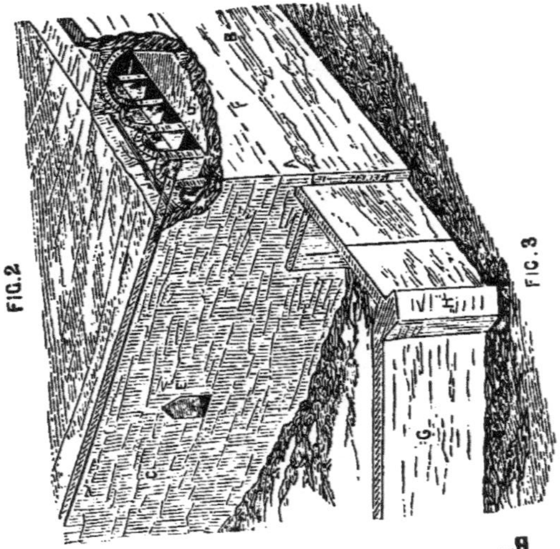

FIG. 2.

FIG. 3.

the present surface; BB is the natural rock; C, the accumulated rubbish; D, the *Haram* wall; E, the segment of Robinson's Arch; F, the pier of the arch; G, the pavement; HH, the fallen *voussoirs;* K, the water-course.

It was upon this magnificent bridge, and upon the stupendous walls adjacent, that the Queen of Sheba looked in such amazement that "there was no more spirit in her," 2 Chron. ix, 4. The "ascent" by which Solomon "went up into the house of the Lord" may have been the massive flight of steps which rose up on each side of the valley. These stairs have not yet been discovered.

ROBINSON'S ARCH.

At the *south-east corner* of the *Haram* wall the spring of *another arch* is visible: all that is to be seen is one course formed of two stones. Its distance from the corner is the same as Robinson's Arch; hence a line or path would lead straight from one to the other. The spring course of this second bridge would indicate a much slighter structure than the one above described. The Kidron Valley here is also much broader and deeper than the Tyropœon. Concerning the design of this bridge there are two theories: one is, that it was for the scapegoat to pass over on its way to the Dead Sea and the desert; the other, that it was an aqueduct by which the waters from the temple could "issue out toward the east country, and go down into the desert, and go into the sea," Ezek. xlvii, 8. The great accumulation of *débris* at this point shows that the ancient bed of the Kidron is about fifty feet deeper than the present valley, and probably a hundred feet nearer the temple area.

The Vaults.—Under the south-east corner of the *Haram* area are the immense sub-structures called "Solomon's Stables" by the Franks, and *Al Masjed al-Kadim* (the old mosque) by the Moslems. The entrance to the vaults is described by Captain Wilson as "through a hole, broken in the crown of one of the arches, near the south wall of the *Haram*, between the *Aksa* mosque and the cradle of Jesus. . . . In the masonry of the piers may still be seen the holes by which the Crusaders fastened their horses when the place was used as a stable." In their *present form* these vaults are comparatively modern; but yet "there are distinct traces of somewhat similar vaults of a far more remote age—coeval, in fact, with the massive foundations of the encircling wall."—*Porter.* Concerning these sub-structures De Vogüé says: "It appears to me evident that at the epoch of the first system of masonry a net-work of gigantic caves, arched like the fragments which we have now before our eyes, occupied the whole artificial section of the platform of the temple; the Arab substructions which we now describe are a later and feeble imitation of that splendid arrangement. It may be that some well-preserved portions of these vaults still exist under the southwestern corner of the *Haram* and under the Mosque *el-Aksa.*" The vaults of the temple are incidentally mentioned by Josephus, *B. J.*, v, 3, 1.

The Wall of Ophel.—Southward of the vaults just described Captain Warren has found the ancient wall of Ophel. Figure 3 (facing page 232) illustrates both this important discovery and also the vaults: A is the southeast corner of the *Haram* area; B is the east wall; C is the south wall; D "Solomon's Stables," laid open in the plan for inspection; E is a gate to the vaults; F is the line of the present surface of the ground; G is the ancient wall of Ophel, disentombed for inspection; H is one of the towers. This wall has been traced for 700 feet south-south-west of this tower. While we may not determine its date, it seems probable that this wall is at least on the site of the old wall built by Manasseh, and mentioned in Nehemiah. This discovery shows how the suburb of Ophel lay under the temple wall. See 2 Chron. xxvii, 3; xxxiii, 14; Neh. iii, 26, 27. See OPHEL.

Barclay's Gate.—About 270 feet from the south-western angle of the west *Haram* wall is an enormous lintel, which rests over a gateway named after Dr. Barclay. In 1866 Captain Wilson excavated to a depth of about 25 feet in front of the north jamb of the gate without reaching the sill. He also explored a cistern in the *Haram* area, which proved to be the continuation of the Mosque *el-Burak*, the two together forming the passage leading from Barclay's Gate to the *Haram* area above. In March, 1869, Captain Warren made an excavation not far from the former shaft. At 5 feet below the surface a lamp and pieces of broken pottery were found. At about 23 feet from the surface the sill course of stones was met with. The top of this course is 28 feet 9¼ inches below the lintel, and the bottom is 32 feet 1¼ inches below it. Nine inches below the bottom of the sill course the explorers came upon a stone flagging forming the flat roof to a drain running along the *Haram* wall toward the south-west angle. This conduit is 2 feet 4 inches wide, and 5 feet 6 inches high. It is the same drain with that found *above* the pavement at Robinson's Arch. Sinking through this drain, the top of a wall appeared, perpendicular to and abutting on the *Haram* wall, at 31 feet below the surface. The excavation continued until at 73 feet 7 inches the rock was struck. This is cut horizontally, and the bottom stone of the *Haram* wall is let into it. Of the mode of access to this gate Warren says: "It appears that the road to Barclay's Gate from the Tyropœon Valley may have been by means of a causeway, raised 46 feet above the rock. Whether it may have been solid or supported on arches is not apparent."

Wilson's Arch.—A few rods north of the Wailing Place, and just beneath *Bab es-Silsileh*, Captain Wilson, descending into a cistern called *el-Burâk*, found a section of the old *Haram* wall in a fine state of preservation. Beyond it is an arch, having a width of 43 feet and a span of 42, built of massive stones from 7 to 13 feet in length. On the west side of this arch Captain Warren discovered, in 1868, a vast system of vaults and subterranean chambers. The road to *Bab es-Silsileh* passes over the arch, and thus we have proof that here was one of the ancient entrances to the temple.

The valley from Jaffa Gate to Bab es-Silsileh.—Captain Warren says: "During the past year (1869) many tanks have been examined in the city, and the level surface of rock ascertained from them, so that we have now an approximate contour plan showing the surface of rock in the city.... At each tank are petty difficulties.... One result, however, is the certainty of a valley running down from the Jaffa Gate to the *Bab es-Silsileh*."

Gennath Gate, (so called).—Referring to the result of the excavations made up to December, 1869, Warren remarks: "The jambs of the gate do not rest on the rock, but on made earth mixed with pottery, similar to what we found at lowest point south-east angle of *Haram* area.... No walls of any kind were found near the rock, and no signs of any wall older than the Gennath Gate within thirteen feet to the east, and twenty feet to the south; if the first wall of the city was built up from the rock, and was not totally destroyed, it was not within the above-mentioned distance of this gate."

Damascus Gate.—Recent excavations at and around the Damascus Gate show that it occupies the site of one of the ancient gates of the city, but whether of the *second* or the *third* wall is still undetermined.

Golden Gate.—A shaft and gallery outside the Golden Gate, excavated with great labor, were crossed and stopped by a thick wall which the explorers could not get through.

Excavations at the north-east angle of the Haram Area.—At this angle several points of much interest have been settled by Captain Warren. Under date of August, 1869, he writes: "1. We find that the tower (so-called Tower of Antonia) at the north-east angle of the *Haram* area forms part of the main east wall, and at near its base the wall and tower are flush, or in one line. 2. The wall is built up of beveled stones from the rock, but up to a certain height (nearly the same as at Robinson's Arch) the stones have rough faces. 3. The rock, which is only 20 feet below the surface at the St. Stephen's Gate, falls rapidly past the tower, so that at the southern angle the wall is covered up with *débris* to a depth of no less than 110 feet, and the total height of the wall is over 150 feet. 4. There is now no doubt that the valley at the *Bab az-Zahiré* passes down through the *Birket Israil* (the so-called Pool of Bethesda) into the *Haram* area, and thence out to the east between the north-east tower and the Golden Gate. . . . 5. Some characters in red paint have been found on the bottom of the stones of the *Haram* wall under the southern end of this tower. . . . 6. It appears probable that the four courses of beveled stones of this tower, which appear above ground, are *in situ*, and also in the wall south of the tower, but of this latter it does not seem so certain. 7. The faces of the stones below a certain line are described as rough, (in paragraph 2,) but they are quite unlike the roughly-faced stones at the south-west angle. The faces project from two to *twenty* inches or more, presenting a very curious appearance. 8. The stone used does not seem to be so compact and hard as that used at the south-east angle, and the chisel working is not so carefully done." In November, 1869, Warren adds: "The gallery has been driven 40 feet south of southern angle of the north-east tower, and a shaft sunk facing five courses of the wall. . . . It is highly probable that the *Haram* wall at this end is, from the present surface to the rock, (over 110 feet,) composed of stones with well-dressed marginal drafts, and with faces projecting considerably; while the tower forming part of the wall is composed of stones with projecting faces up to a certain height, and after that with the well-known type of beveled stones."

The Water Supply of Jerusalem.—Notwithstanding the natural disadvantage of position, the Holy City seems always to have had an abundant supply of water. At present the city is well supplied by cisterns. Every house of any size has one or more of them. Many of these are ancient. Attached to the Convent of the Copts, east of the Holy Sepulcher, is a cistern of great extent, and excavated wholly in the rock. Large cisterns are also found in the Latin Convent, in the Church of the Flagellation, among the olive-groves north of the city, and in every quarter within the circuit of the ancient walls. There are also many large open reservoirs in and around the city. The water of the *Birket el-Mamilla* (Upper Pool of Gihon?) is conducted by a subterranean conduit to the Pool of Hezekiah, within the city, and also to the cisterns of the citadel. This conduit passes underneath the city well near the Jaffa Gate. Compare Isa. vii, 3; xxxvi, 2; with 2 Kings xx, 20; 2 Chron. xxxii, 30. The Pool of Hezekiah is about 240 feet long by 144 wide. It has no great depth. This reservoir originally extended 60 feet farther north, and the stones of its boundary wall are found to be of high antiquity. One of the largest pools around Jerusalem is found on the west side of the great north road not far from the tombs of the kings. It seems to have been connected by subterranean channels with the *Birket Israil*, and also with *Birket Sitti Mariam*, and probably with other cisterns in the vicinity.

The work of Hezekiah (compare 2 Chron. xxxii, 3, 4, 30, with Ecclus. xlviii, 17) in bringing water into the city was one of vast magnitude and labor, as the aqueducts and reservoirs were mostly excavated in the rock. It is probably to these works of Hezekiah that Josephus refers when he mentions a gate near the tower of Hippicus through which water was brought into the city, and also an aqueduct connected with the royal palace on Zion. In sinking the foundation for the English Church, which occupies a part of the site of the palace, the architect discovered, at a depth of more than 20 feet beneath the surface, "a vaulted chamber of fine masonry in perfect repair, resting on the rock. Within it were steps leading down to a solid mass of stone-work covering an immense conduit, partly hewn out of the solid rock, and partly built with even courses of masonry, and lined with cement an inch thick." This conduit was traced eastward for more than 200 feet. Apertures from above open into it at intervals, and these were evidently made to enable people to draw water by means of bucket and line.

The cisterns or fountains beneath the *Haram* have already been referred to, (page 228.) A fuller description is here given. A vast supply of water was needed not only for the ordinary use of the large population of Jerusalem, but for the great demand made by the Temple service. The cisterns under the Temple area formerly furnished an almost inexhaustible supply. At least forty-three well-mouths now lead to reservoirs below the *Haram* area. One of them, described in Ecclesiasticus l, 3, as "in compass as the sea," is referred to by Aristeas, the embassador of Ptolemy Philadelphus. It contains at least 1,000,000 gallons. The tank under *El-Aksa* holds 700,000 gallons, and Warren computes the capacity of the cisterns under the *Haram* area at 5,000,000 gallons. Strabo describes Jerusalem as "within truly well-watered, but without altogether dry." Tacitus speaks of it as "a fountain of perennial water, mountains hollowed out underneath, also fishpools and cisterns, rain-water being preserved." The ancient aqueduct from Solomon's Pools still supplies the city with water. See SOLOMON'S POOLS.

About 300 yards south of the *Haram* is the "Fountain of the Virgin." This fountain is connected by a subterranean conduit with the interior of the hill beneath Ophel, which it thus supplied with water.

Near the southern end of Ophel, in the Tyropœon, is the "Pool of Siloam." This pool is connected with the Fountain of the Virgin. See SILOAM.

In the bottom of the Kidron, a little below its junction with the Valley of Hinnom, is "The Well of Joab," the *Bir Eyûb* of the Arabs. The Franks call it the "Well of Nehemiah." Some identify "En-Rogel" with this well. See EN-ROGEL; ZOHELETH. *Bir Eyûb* is 125 feet deep, walled up with large hewn stones terminating in an arch above, apparently of high antiquity.

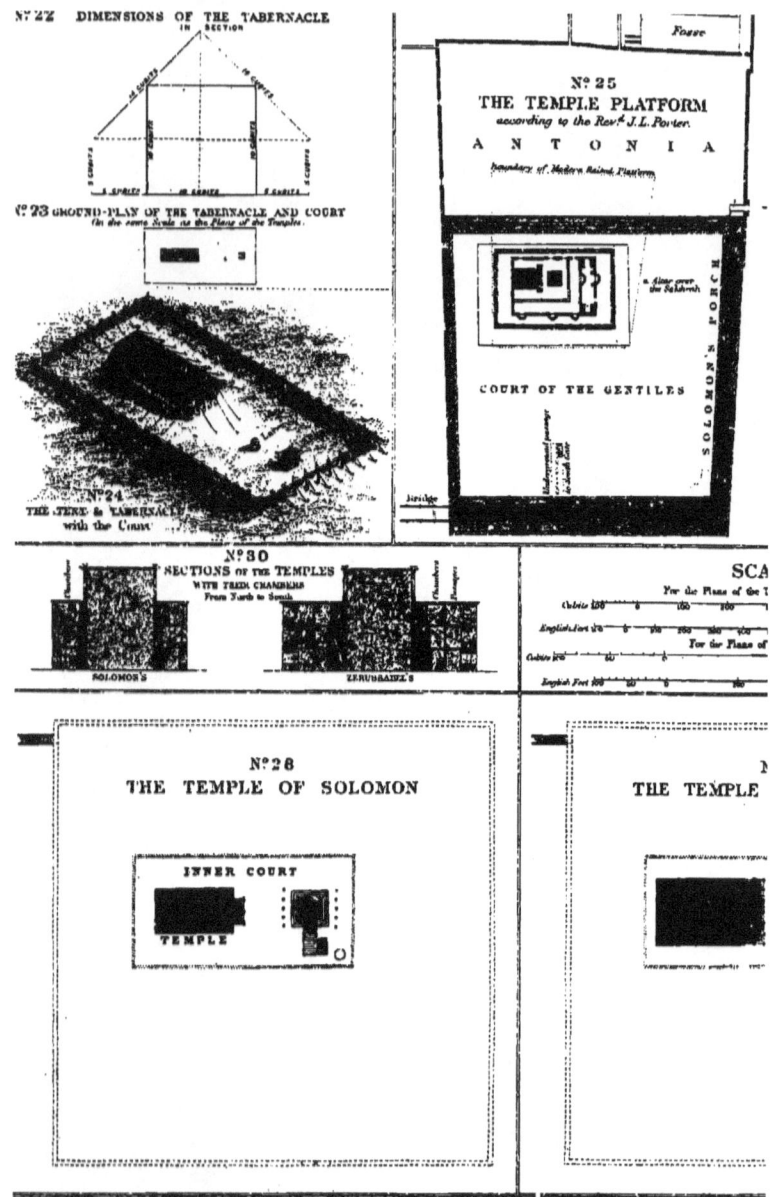

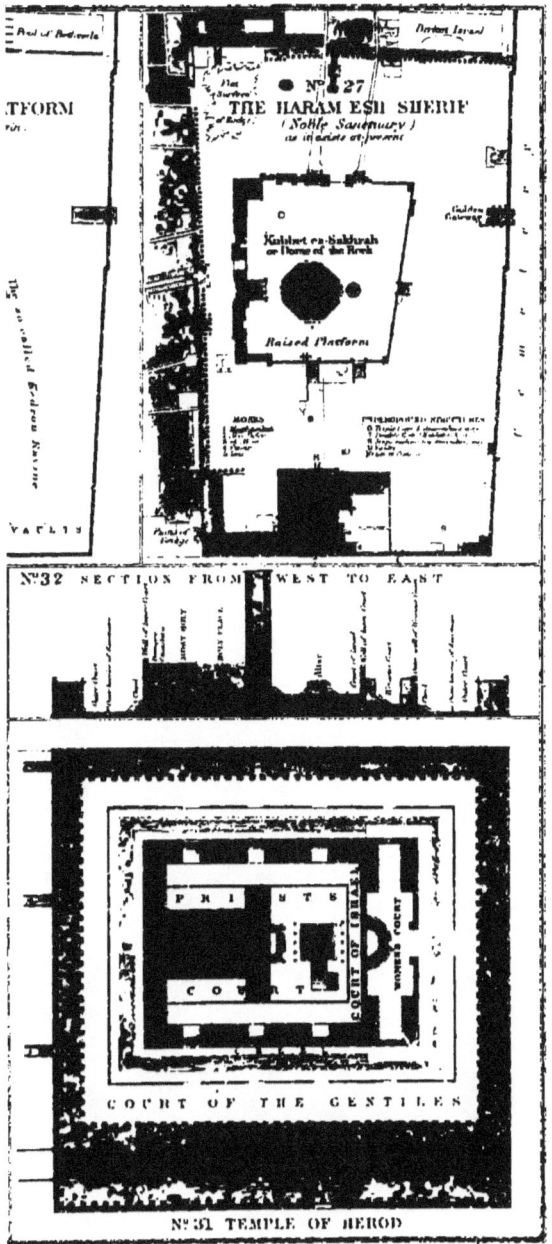

One of the most interesting excavations is that made by Captain Warren, in connection with *the Great Rock-cut Aqueduct in the Kidron Valley.* This aqueduct, which is a splendid piece of engineering, lies from 70 to 90 feet under the surface of the rock. It extends from near *Bir Eyûb* to a point over 1,800 feet down the valley, where it "stops unfinished and suddenly." It is not determined whether this great tunnel comes down the Kidron Valley, the Tyropœon, or by the valley from the Jaffa Gate. Nor is the purpose for which it was used yet discovered; but "we have the chance of its being a clue to the Altar of the Temple, and—which is of more practical value to the inhabitants of Jerusalem—to the hidden springs of Hezekiah, which, if found, might again supply the city with living water."

The site of the Temple, the ancient Walls and Gates.—Modern writers disagree concerning the exact *site of the Temple* and the extent of its courts. All, however, seem to admit that the Temple stood somewhere within the present *Haram* inclosure. Williams makes the Temple area identical with the northern section of the *Haram,* and claims that the southern was added at a later age. He places the high altar on the Sacred Rock, and the *Naos* or fane on the platform a little to the west. Others, among whom are Catherwood and De Vogüé, assert that the whole *Haram* was included in Herod's Temple. Fergusson maintains that the whole Temple area occupied a section of the south-west corner of the *Haram,* measuring about 600 feet square. He locates the *Naos* a short distance east of the Wailing-Place. All the rest of the *Haram* was outside the ancient city until Agrippa built the wall which now incloses the *Haram* on the east. Robinson, Porter, and others, identify the Temple platform with the lower section of the *Haram,* reaching northward as far as the Golden Gate. See Maps 25, 26, 27. (See an able dissertation on the Temple in Strong's *Harmony of the Gospels.*)

The *ancient walls* were built at different periods. The *first* or old wall encircled Zion; the *second* Akra; the *third* Bezetha. There seems also to have been another wall—a strong rampart which extended along the eastern brow of Zion. Josephus gives us the general course of the three walls, (*Wars,* v, 4, 2.) The walls built by Nehemiah after the captivity, as well as the sites of the gates, were substantially the same as those described by Josephus, Neh. iii. We have not space to describe the course of these walls. The conjectural plan is given on page 194, and the list of gates on page 195. The first or old wall was made exceedingly strong by David, Solomon, and their successors. An account of excavations made along the northern line of this wall may be found under Zion. The second wall was built for the defense of Akra. The third wall, or Wall of Bezetha, was commenced by the elder Agrippa about A. D. 43, under the Emperor Claudius, in a style of great strength, but was left off through fear of offending the emperor. The Jews afterward completed it, though on a more humble scale. Much difference of opinion has existed concerning the course of these walls and the sites of the gates and towers; the course of the *second* wall being the chief subject of controversy, as it involves the genuineness of the Holy Sepulcher.

The topography of ancient Jerusalem can be determined only by the process of excavation. The general results of this method, as given in the preceding pages of this article, afford the strongest grounds for believing that the officers now prosecuting the work with so much zeal and ability will be able to settle most, if not all, of the vexed questions concerning the ancient sites in and around the Holy City.

Jesh'anah, or **Jesha'nah,** *old,* a town taken by Abijah from Jeroboam, 2 Chron. xiii, 19. Schwarz places it at "*Al-Sanim,* a village two miles west of Bethel," but this identification is not confirmed.

Jesh'imon, or **Jeshi'mon,** *the waste,* a name used to designate the position of Pisgah and Peor, both described as "facing the Jeshimon," Num. xxii, 20; xxiii, 28. Again, the hill of Hachilah is described as being to the south of Jeshimon, 1 Sam. xxiii, 19; and before it, xxvi, 1, 3. Also when David and his men were in the wilderness of Maon they were in the plain, that is, the *Ghor,* the sunken district of the Dead Sea, 'south of Jeshimon,' xxiii, 24. Mr. Grove says that Jeshimon was probably on the west of the Dead Sea. Some suppose it a high waste land east of the Dead Sea, in view of the hill country on the west. Mr. Porter thinks there may have been two Jeshimons: one east of the Jordan, connected with Pisgah and Peor; the other west of the Jordan, and connected with Hachilah and Maon, and he is inclined to believe that the term Jeshimon (sometimes elsewhere translated *desert, wilderness*) here means in the one instance the "wilderness of Arabia," and in the other the "wilderness of Judea." But perhaps it is unsafe to lay much stress on the Hebrew sense of the name.

Jesh'ua, *Jehovah the salvation,* the name of a town occupied by the children of Judah after their return from exile, Neh. xi, 26. It probably lay in the extreme south of Judah, near Moladah, but its site is unknown.

Je'tur, *nomadic camp,* Gen. xxv, 15. See ITURÆA.

Jeth'lah, *high, may he exalt* him, a city of Dan, named with Ajalon and Thimnathah, Josh. xix, 42. Unknown.

Jew, Jews. The term "Jew" seems to have come into use first as the designation of a subject of the kingdom of Judah, 2 Kings xvi, 6; xxv, 25; Jer. xxxii, 12; xxxviii, 19; xl, 11; xliii, 9; although in some of these passages it is probably used in a wider sense, as applicable to all who were of the seed of Abraham, and such is undoubtedly its meaning in Jer. xxxiv, 9. After the return from the captivity it became the designation of the whole Israelitish people, a consequence, probably, of the predominance of the members of the kingdom of Judah among those who returned. In the later books of the Old Testament we find the term frequently thus used, and even extended to those who still remained dispersed among the Gentiles, Ezra iv, 12, 23; v, 5; vi, 8; Neh. i, 2; ii, 16, etc. In the New Testament the term is used to indicate a descendant of Jacob, a member of the Jewish community as distinguished from one of Gentile birth, Mark vii, 3; Luke xxiii, 51; John iv, 9, etc. It is also employed to designate one who adhered to the Jewish religion and modes of worship, especially as distinguished from the followers of Jesus Christ, Rom. ii, 17; iii, 1; 1 Cor. ix, 20, etc. Then, again, it was used to denote one who truly came up to the spiritual idea of the Jewish institute, who was a true son of the covenant in its higher, its spiritual aspect, Rom. ii, 28, 29; Rev. ii, 9. The phrase, "the Jews," sometimes occurs, with an implied allusion to the antagonism between those who adhered to the Mosaic institute and those who embraced Christianity, to describe those who came forth as the active enemies of Christ and his cause. In this sense it is used especially in St. John's Gospel; and thus also it appears to be employed in Matt. xxviii, 15; Acts xii, 3; xx, 3.

By the classical writers the term "Jews" is used as the proper designation of the Hebrew people; but the references they make usually show utter ignorance both of the history and character of the people.

Jew'ry, the district or province of Judea, Dan. v, 13. This term occurs in several passages of the Apocrypha, being retained from the older translations, and the Greek is so translated in two passages of the New Testament, Luke xxiii, 5; John vii, 1.

Jez'reel, (Map 5,) *what God planteth* or *scattereth.*
1. A city in the south of Judah, Josh. xv, 56. In his wanderings David took a wife from this town, Ahinoam the Jezreelitess, 1 Sam. xxv, 43; xxvii, 3; xxx, 5. The site is lost.

2. An ancient city of Canaan, situated on the western declivity of Mount Gilboa, overlooking the great plain to which it gave the name *Esdraelon.* On the northern side of the city, between the parallel ridges of Gilboa and Moreh, lies a rich valley, an offshoot of Esdraelon, running down eastward to the Jordan. This was called the Valley of Jezreel; and Bethshan, with the other towns in and around the valley, was originally inhabited by a fierce and warlike race who had "chariots of iron," Josh. xvii, 16; Judg. vi, 33; Hosea i, 5. The region fell to the lot of Issachar, but neither this tribe nor its more powerful neighbor Ephraim were able to drive out the ancient people, Josh. xix, 18. In David's time Jezreel was one of the important towns that remained true to the house of Saul until Ish-Bosheth's death, 2 Sam. ii, 8, etc. Ahab chose it as the royal residence, 1 Kings xviii, 45; xxi, 1. Here Jehu put Jehoram and Jezebel and Ahaziah to death, 2 Kings ix, 15-26, 30-37. See also 2 Kings x, 11. In the valley of Jezreel occurred that memorable victory of Gideon over the Midianites, Judg. vi, 33; also the melancholy defeat of Israel by the Philistines by the "fountain of Jezreel," 1 Sam. xxix, 1-11; xxxi, 1-6; 2 Sam. iv, 4. In Ahab's time the city gained its greatest pre-eminence. That monarch had a palace here, which probably stood in the eastern quarters of the town; for it was just as Jehu entered the gate that Jezebel looked out upon him, 2 Kings ix, 31. The vineyard of Naboth must have been outside of the walls to the east, near the fountain, since it was into that portion that Joram's body was cast before Jehu entered the city, 24-26.

In the Middle Ages this town was known as *Stradela;* and during the Crusades as *Parvum Gerinum,* or *Gerin.* Its modern name is *Zerin.* It occupies a noble site on the western point of Mount Gilboa, about one hundred feet above the plain. It overlooks the whole expanse of Esdraelon to Carmel and the hills of Galilee; and from it one can look down the broad and fertile vale of Jezreel to the tell of Bethshan, and away beyond it and beyond the Jordan to the hills of Gilead. The line of the old road along which Jehu drove can be traced; it descends the steep slope, and enters the valley near a fountain. *Zerin* is now a wretched village. Mr. Porter says it contained, when he recently visited it, about twenty miserable houses. The only sightly building is a square tower, now used as a *meddfeh,* or inn, where travelers are treated to bare walls, and a supper at the public expense. Round the village are heaps of rubbish, and more than three hundred cisterns or subterraneous granaries for storing corn and preserving it from the plundering Bedouin. There are also several sarcophagi, some with sculptured ornaments.

Jez'reelite and **Jez'reelitess,** an inhabitant of Jezreel, 1 Kings xxi, 1, 4, etc.

Jiph'tah, *he opens,* one of the towns allotted to Judah, in the plain of Philistia, and was probably near to Eleutheropolis, Josh. xv, 43. It is not identified.

Jiph'thah-el, *God opens,* a valley which formed part of the boundary between Asher and Zebulun, Josh. xix, 14, 27. According to Dr. Robinson this place was identical with Jotapata, the city which so long withstood Vespasian, (see Josephus, *B. J.*, iii, 7;) and it survives in the modern *Jefat,* a village in the mountains of Galilee, half way between the Bay of Acre and the Lake of Genesareth.

Jog'behah, *lofty, elevated,* a town in the territory of Gad, east of the Jordan, Num. xxxii, 35. Gideon surprised Zeba and Zalmunna at Karkor, near this place, Judges viii, 10, 11. It is possibly *El-Jebeiha,* between *Ammân* and *Es-Salt.*

Jok'deam, *possessed by the people* (?), a town in the south of Judah, near Juttah and Carmel, Josh. xv, 56. Unknown.

Jok'meam, *gathered of the people,* one of the cities given to the Kohathites out of the tribe of Ephraim, 1 Chron. vi, 68; 1 Kings iv, 12, (though in the A. V. inaccurately Jokneam, probably by a printer's error.) It was probably in the eastern part of the tribe, and identical with Kibzaim, Josh. xxi, 22. Mr. Porter and others think that the Jokmeam of the Hebrew text of 1 Kings iv, 12, was at the western extremity of Esdraelon, and that it was no doubt identical with Jokneam, as the translators of our A. V. seem to have thought. But in this passage the town in question is named with places which we know to have been in the Jordan valley, at the extreme east boundary of the tribe. See Robinson's *Biblical Researches,* and also Kitto's *Cyclopedia.*

Jok'neam, (Map 5,) *possessed by the people,* an ancient royal Canaanitish city situated at the base of Mount Carmel, whence its name, *Jokneam of Carmel,* Josh. xii, 22; xix, 11. In Judith vii, 3, it is Cyamon. It was allotted to the Merarite Levites, Josh. xxi, 34. Its king was one of those destroyed by Joshua. The site is probably identical with *Tell Kaimon,* a hill below the eastern end of Carmel, with the Kishon about a mile distant. Jokneam is found in 1 Kings iv, 12; but it is an error. See JOKMEAM.

Jok'tan, (Map 1,) *small,* a Hebrew Shemite, the progenitor of thirteen nations in Arabia, whither his tribe emigrated before Abraham's time, Gen. x, 25; 1 Chron. i, 19; Gen. x, 26–30. The Arabs call their progenitor *Kachtan* (=Joktan.) They unanimously pronounce the Joktan Arabs the true aborigines of Arabia, who occupied the southern peninsula, and possessed *Yemen* and Arabia Felix. In *Yemen,* south of Mecca, on the Red Sea, there is a district still called *Kachtan,* in which Edrisi, the early Arabian geographer, locates a town called *Beischat-Jaktan.* Even the sepulcher of Joktan is still pointed out near *Keschin.* Northern Arabs are thought of less pure Arab blood, the Ishmaelites excepted. Were the tribes of Arabia better known, the tribes mentioned in Gen. x, 26–29, might still be found there, for their different clans set great store upon keeping distinct.

Jok'theel, *subdued of God.*
1. A town of Judah, situated in the plain of Philistia, (*Shephelah,*) and apparently not far distant from Lachish, Josh. xv, 38. Not identified.
2. The name given by Amaziah, King of Judah, to *Selah,* a stronghold of Edom, to show that he had captured it, 2 Kings xiv, 7; 2 Chron. xxv, 11–13. The date of this victory was about B. C. 830. This stronghold, or cliff, is asserted by Eusebius to be a "city of Edom, also called by the Assyrians Rekem," by which undoubtedly he intends the city of Petra, which see.

JAFFA, (ANCIENT JAPHO OR JOPPA.)

BIBLE GEOGRAPHY. 249

Jop'pa, (Map 5.) Some derive this name from the Hebrew, signifying *beautiful;* others from Japhet, the son of Noah; classic authors from "Iopa," the daughter of Æolus. Some interpret it as "the watch-tower of joy," perhaps from its lofty situation. In Josh. xix, 46, it is Japho. In the Apocrypha it has the form Joppe, 1 Esdras v, 55, etc.

Joppa was one of the most ancient and important sea-port towns of Palestine, situated on the Mediterranean coast, about thirty geographical miles from Jerusalem, and nearly midway between Gaza and the promontory of Carmel. It was on a hill so high, says Strabo, that people affirmed (but incorrectly) that Jerusalem was visible from its summit. Having a harbor—though always a dangerous one—it became the port of Jerusalem when Jerusalem became the metropolis of the kingdom of the house of David; and certainly never did port and metropolis more strikingly resemble each other in difficulty of approach both by sea and land. Hence, except in journeys to and from Jerusalem, it was not much used.

The first mention of Japho is in the description given by Joshua of the boundaries of Dan, of which it was one of the marks, Josh. xix, 46. We hear of it no more till the time of Solomon. By that king, probably, Joppa was made the port of the Jewish capital, and the western outlet of its trade, as Ezion-Geber was the eastern. The cedar and pine wood from Mount Lebanon was landed by the servants of Hiram, King of Tyre, at Joppa, whence it was carried to Jerusalem for the great temple, 2 Chron. ii, 16. Also by the same port materials from Lebanon were, by permission of Cyrus, conveyed for the rebuilding of the second temple under Zerubbabel, 1 Kings v, 9; Ezra iii, 17. At Joppa Jonah embarked for Tarshish, in attempting to escape a mission to Nineveh, Jonah i, 3. During the captivity the situation of the city and its commercial importance seem to have saved it from ruin.

After the close of Old Testament history Joppa rose in importance. It being the only port in Palestine proper at which foreign ships could touch, it was not only the shipping capital, but the key of the whole country and the sea-board. During the Maccabean wars it was one of the principal strongholds of Palestine, 1 Macc. x, 75; xiv, 5, 34. It would seem that Jews then constituted only a minority of the population, and the foreign residents—Greeks, Egyptians, and Syrians—were so rich and powerful, and so aided by the fleets of their own nations, as to be able to rule the city. On one occasion they enticed two hundred Jews on board ships and threw them into the sea. For this cruelty Judas Maccabeus attacked the town by night, and burned all the shipping, with every human being on board, 2 Macc. xii, 3-7. The Maccabean princes subsequently strengthened the fortifications, placed a garrison in the citadel, and retained Joppa in their hands as the chief port of their little kingdom, 1 Macc. xii, 34; xiii, 11; xiv, 5. Joppa was among the first cities captured by the invading Romans, B C. 63, when it was annexed to the Roman province of Syria. Afterward Cæsar gave Joppa (with other cities) to Herod the Great. After Herod's death, the city passed into the hands of Archelaus; but on his deposition, in A. D. 6, the whole of Palestine was annexed to the Roman province of Syria, and placed under the immediate rule of a deputy.

In the apostles' time Joppa had a mixed population of Greeks, Syrians, Phœnicians, and Egyptians, with a few Roman officials, and a large Jewish community. When Peter visited Lydda, ten miles distant, the Christians of Joppa sent for him, hoping that he could raise the dead Tabitha. He came and raised her, and, while staying there with "one Simon a tanner, whose house was by the sea-side," and while praying on the house-top, he had that remarkable vision which showed him that the distinction between Jew and Gentile was forever removed by the Gospel, Acts ix, 36–43; x, 9–18. Joppa had its history in the time of the Crusades; it is said to have been the see of a Christian bishop.

The modern name of the city is *Yafa*, or Jaffa. Its population is estimated variously at from four thousand to fifteen thousand. Mr. Porter says it contains "about five thousand inhabitants, of whom one thousand are Christians, about one hundred and fifty Jews, and the rest Moslems." The little rounded hill on which the city stands is encompassed on the land side by orchards of orange, lemon, apricot, and other trees, which for luxuriance and beauty are not surpassed in the world. They extend for several miles across the plain. The houses are huddled together without order, the streets are narrow, crooked, and filthy; the town is so crowded along the steep sides of the hill that the rickety dwellings in the upper part seem to be toppling over on the flat roofs of those below. Very few remains of antiquity are found, except a few broken columns scattered about the streets, and through the gardens on the southern slope of the hill, and the large stones in the foundations of the castle. The monks pretend to show the "house of Simon the tanner." M. Clermont-Ganneau has discovered near Jaffa a tomb of the first century, containing inscriptions which reproduce Bible names. The harbor and landing are miserable, yet the town has still considerable trade as the port of Jerusalem, and its fruits are considered the best in Syria. Among its population are fugitives and vagabonds from all countries.

Jop'pe, 1 Esdras v, 55; 1 Macc. x, 75, 76. See JOPPA.

Jor'dan, (Map 5,) *flowing down*, or *the descender*, the great river of Palestine. This celebrated stream is "without any parallel, historical or physical, in the whole world."

The first Scripture notice of the Jordan occurs in the story of the separation of Abraham and Lot, "before the Lord destroyed Sodom and Gomorrah." The sacred writer tells us that "all the plain of Jordan" was "well watered every-where . . . as the garden of the Lord," Gen. xiii, 10. At the destruction of the "cities of the plain" some great physical change must have been produced in the valley of the Jordan, Gen. xix.

Another great epoch in the Jordan's history was the passage of the Israelites after their forty years' wandering; Josh. iii; iv; v, 1; Psa. cxiv, 3. It was in harvest-time—the beginning of April—when the rains were still falling heavily in Hermon, and the winter snows were melting under the rays of the warm sun, and when a thousand mountain torrents thus fed swept into the Jordan, and made it "overflow all its banks;" or, as the Hebrew literally signifies, made it "full up to all its banks." Doubtless the Jordan rose higher anciently than now. Thus the circumstances under which the crossing occurred rendered the miracle the greater, and the power of God more striking. The "overflow" of Jordan is noticed also in Jer. xii, 5; 1 Chron. xii, 15.

The Jordan was also crossed by Jacob, Gen. xxxii, 10; by Gideon, Judg. viii, 4; by the Ammonites, Judg. x, 9; by Abner, 2 Sam. ii, 29; by David, 2 Sam. xvii, 22; xix, 15, 31; 1 Chron. xix, 17; by Absalom, 2 Sam. xvii, 24; by Elijah, 2 Kings ii, 6–8; by Elisha, 2 Kings ii, 14. There were various "fords" of the Jordan, see Josh. ii, 7; Judg. iii, 28; vii, 24; xii, 5, 6. Jeremiah speaks of lions coming up from "the swelling of Jordan," Jer. xlix, 19. The original literally signifies "pride," "beauty," or "glory," and refers to the dense jungles and verdant foliage of the banks; these jungles are impenetrable except to the wild beasts that dwell there. In 2 Kings vi, 2-7, is mention of the miracle by which iron was made to swim in the Jordan.

Naaman was cured of his leprosy in the waters of the Jordan after his indignant depreciation of this river as compared with the rivers of Damascus. "The rivers of Damascus water its great plain, converting a desert into a paradise; the Jordan rolls on in its deep, deep bed, useless, to the Sea of Death."—*Porter.*

This river was the scene in later times of John's baptism, when there "went out to him Jerusalem, and all Judea, and all the region round about Jordan," Matt. iii, 5, 6; Mark i, 5; John i, 28. But the great event of the New Testament history enacted at Jordan was the baptism of our Lord himself, thus making this the "queen of rivers," the "sacred river." In commemoration of this baptism the Christian pilgrims who assemble at Jerusalem at Easter visit the Jordan in a body and bathe at the spot which tradition has rendered sacred. The exact locality where our Lord was baptized cannot be determined, but it would seem that the baptism took place toward the mouth of the river, in the confines of Judea. An interesting account of these pilgrim bathers is given by Stanley in *Sinai and Palestine*, pp. 308-310.

The sources of the Jordan are on the slopes of Anti-Libanus. The principal of these are (1) the *Hasbány*, which rises in the great Fountain of *Fuarr*, near *Hashbeiya;* (2) the *Bániásy*, which bursts just outside a cave at *Bániás;* (3) the *Leddan*, from the west base of a hill (*Tell el-Kady*) on which stood ancient Dan; (4) the *Esh-shar.* Of these "the *Hasbány* is longest by forty miles; the *Leddan* is much the largest, and the *Bániásy* the most beautiful."— *Thomson.* Various eminent travelers have investigated the sources and course of this great river; but the most thorough and valuable exploration of the sources is that made in 1869 by Mr. J. Macgregor, M. A. Speaking of the *Hasbány* source, Macgregor (*The Rob Roy on the Jordan*, pp. 195-203) says: "Young Jordan is like the prettiest tiny stream in Scotland, with white hollowed rocks and weird caverns; but the gravel is prettier here than in my own land, pebbles of yellow and bright blue, banked in by fruitful loam of a deep rich red, and all so silent and unaffected. So it winds until steeper rocks gird the water, narrowing where wild beasts' paws have marked the sand. Farther down a bold cliff dips into a pool of deepest green. Here I launched the 'Rob Roy,' certainly the first boat that ever floated on the pool. The few natives round us stopped in wonder, sitting—that is their posture for lost astonishment. They assured us this pool of *Fuarr* is 1,000 feet deep, and, being entirely unapproachable for sounding from the cliff overhead, imagination has full sway to fancy it fathomless. The cold matter-of-fact sounding-line stopped short at *eleven* feet. I was astonished at the illusion, for the water here looked any depth you please. Of course the people did not believe my word for it, but nevertheless it is a sturdy fact that less than two fathoms measures this abyss. . . . Just opposite the cliff, and a few yards away, is a three-cornered island of sand and small gravel, with many low bushes on it, and luxuriant spotted clover, and under and from out these there bubbles, gurgles, and ascends the first undoubted subterranean source of the Jordan. There are about twenty of these curious fountains on this islet, and the water runs from them in all directions. That which pours out toward the north runs a few feet *up the stream*, being at first a foot higher in level. The island and the rocks near it are formed into a weir, for the terribly practical purpose of supplying a mill. Perish all the mills and millstones that spoil the birthplace of such a stream! . . .

"Camp struck and all things packed, we floated the canoe again just below the falls, to begin our descent of the river. In front was the bridge, with two pointed arches of eighteen feet span. . . . The stream was swift and shallow here, but it occupied only one arch of the bridge. . . . The river bends below the bridge with all the waywardness of a trout stream in the Highlands. Thick trees hang over its clear surging waters, and reeds fill the bays twenty feet high; while rocks, and a thousand hanging, straggling creepers on them, tangle together over silent pools. Who had seen these before the Rob Roy? It can scarcely be supposed that any other boat had been here, from which a man could look upon these earliest beauties of the hallowed stream." After a heavy fall of rain, this adventurer returned to the waterfall and found that the current had doubled in force and volume. Then he visited the curious bitumen pits found in the vicinity. "The people live beside them in very simple huts, and they go down fifty feet into the earth to fill baskets with the black shining treasure which 'grows,' they say, however much they may dig." The *Esh Shar* is only a minor tributary one or two yards broad. The *Leddan* source issues from *Tell el Kady*, "from the deeps of the earth in a noble spring said to be the largest single source in the world." Of this hidden source, which defies every effort to enter its retreat, Macgregor goes on to say that one "can just hear the smothered murmuring of pent-up secret waters; and on the west side of the embankment, beneath a mass of fig-trees, reeds, and strongest creepers, the water issues free into the day, filling up to the brim the circular basin a hundred feet wide. Here the new-born Jordan turns and bubbles, and seems to breathe for a while in the light, and then it dashes off at once a river, with a noisy burst, but soon it hides its foam and waves in another thicket, and then its loud rushing is shrouded in darkness as it hurries away to the mysterious plain. . . . They told me this pool also was bottomless. . . . Behold the abyss of the Dan source of Jordan—it is only five feet deep!"—P. 217. About an hour's ride from *Tell el-Kady* eastward is the most interesting source of the Jordan—at *Banias*. Of this the same author remarks: "The head of all is in front of a steep-faced cliff about eighty feet high, of white and pink stone, much scathed by weather and cut about by man. . . . A lofty and wide cavern opens deep in the rock, and just in front of this, outside, but apparently from at least the level of the cavern's present floor, a copious flood of sparkling water wells up and forward through rough shingle, and in a few yards it hides its noisy dashings in a dense jungle."—P. 226. The *Husbany* and the *Banias* unite near the spot marked by Van de Velde as *Tell Sheikh Yusuf*, "the Mount of the Lord Joseph," and thus it is here that the Jordan is for the first time really formed. Each river at their confluence seems to be about seventy feet wide and seven or eight feet deep. Here the united stream is about one hundred feet broad. Its banks are perfectly steep, and are from twelve to twenty feet high. After a short distance the stream encounters a marsh, with which the banks are level. Here much of the river's volume is lost by flooding aside into branches, while the main stream

BATHING PLACE OF PILGRIMS ON THE JORDAN.

turns and twists exceedingly, and becomes very narrow. At this point the river forks out into six different channels. Of these the canoeist says, "Every one was hopelessly bad, and . . . the Rob Roy became firmly entangled in a maze of bushes eight feet high." Leaving this impassable spot, Macgregor, by a circuitous route, passed southward to the north end of Lake *Hûleh*, (Merom,) to find the Jordan as it enters the lake. The result was "the complete and novel discovery of the hitherto unknown channel of Jordan." Eminent geographers have stated that the Jordan enters Lake *Hûleh* "close to the eastern end of the upper side." But Macgregor's more sure mode of investigation as a canoeist has determined that the channel enters the lake nearly midway on the northern shore. The mouth of the Jordan "here is one hundred feet wide, and it is entirely concealed from both shores by a bend it makes to the east. The river thus enters the lake at the *end* of a promontory of papyrus. . . . Once round the corner, and entering the actual river, it is a wonderful sight indeed, as the graceful channel winds in ample sweeps or long straight reaches in perfect repose and loneliness, with a soft, silent beauty all its own."—*Ibid.*, p. 288. Proceeding northward, Rob Roy "entered a beautiful little lake. . . . The general contour of it was round, but the edges were curved into deep bays, with dark alleys and bright projecting corners, and islets dotted the middle. . . . The breadth of this east and west was estimated at half a mile."—P. 293. After the most careful inspection Macgregor was convinced that this lake is "*the earliest flow of the Jordan as one river*," after it dives into the barrier whither he had traced it a few days before. The north end of this lake he computes at less than three miles and a half from the mouth of the channel. He estimates the breadth of the barrier above noted at about half a mile. Lake *Hûleh* was sounded by this indomitable boatman in every direction, and it shows an average depth (in the winter time) of about eleven feet. In one place it was seventeen feet deep, but in no part of the lake did he find three fathoms of water. Leaving Lake *Hûleh* at its southern extremity, the Jordan runs on with the very rapid descent of about seven hundred feet in the next ten miles, when it empties into the sea of Galilee. Flowing out from the southern end of this sea, the stream descends with great speed, more rapidly in some places than in others, until it is lost in the Dead Sea. From the *Hasbany* source to the Dead Sea the direct distance is about 120 miles; but the crooked line of the Jordan is about 200 miles. The source at *Hasbeiya* "is 1,700 feet above the Mediterranean, and the Dead Sea is 1,300 feet below the Mediterranean; so that the total fall of Jordan is 3,000 feet, which would be 15 feet per mile of its channel, or 25 feet per mile of its direct distance."—*Rob Roy*, p. 316. See SALT SEA. See also a view of the Jordan line on page 354. The velocity of the current is retarded by the number of rapids. Says Lieut. Lynch: "We have plunged down twenty-seven threatening rapids, besides a great many of lesser magnitude." The river varies in width from eighty to one hundred and fifty feet, and in depth from five to twelve feet. At its mouth it is one hundred and eighty feet wide, and three feet deep. There are two sets of banks, or "terraces," through the lower of which the river flows. "From the stream, above the immediate banks, there is on each side a singular terrace of low hills, like truncated cones, which is the bluff terminus of an extended table-land reaching quite to the base of the mountains of the *Hauran* on the east, and the high hills on the western side."—*Lynch*.

The present Arab name of Jordan is *Esh-Sheriah*, (the watering place,) with tne added appellation *El-Kebir*, (the great.) The eloquent words of Macgregor concerning this queen of rivers will be read with interest:

"Jordan is the sacred stream not only of the Jew, who has 'Moses and the prophets;' of the Christian, who treasures the memories of his Master's life upon earth; of the cast-out Ishmaelite, who has dipped his wandering bloody foot in this river since the days of Hagar; but of the Moslem faithful also, wide scattered over the world, who deeply reverence the Jordan. No other river's name is known so long ago and so far away as this, which calls up a host of past memories from the Mohammedan on the plains of India, from the latest Christian settler in the Rocky Mountains of America, and from the Jew in every part of the globe. Nor is it only of the past that the name of Jordan tells, for in the more thoughtful hours of not a few they hear it whispering to them before strange shadowy truths of that future, happier land that lies over the stream of death."—*The Rob Roy and the Jordan*, p. 212.

Jot'bah, *goodness, pleasantness*, the residence of Haruz, the father of Meshullemeth, queen of Manasseh, and mother of Amon, King of Judah, 2 Kings xxi, 19. Probably it is the same with the following:

Jot'bath and **Jot'bathah**, (Map 2,) *goodness, pleasantness*, a station of Israel in the wilderness, described as "a land of torrents of waters." Num. xxxiii, 33; Deut. x, 7. On the western side of the Arabah there are several spots where the wadys converge, and one of these is probably the locality indicated.

Ju'da, a Greek form of Judah, Matt. ii, 6, etc. For the Juda of Luke i, 39, see JUTTAH.

Judæ'a and **Jude'a**, (Map 5,) the Greek form of Judah, though with a larger signification; the province rather than the mere tribe. Ezra employs the Chaldee word *Yehûd* to denote the whole country in which the Jews settled after the return from captivity, Ezra v, 1, and he calls it the "province of Judea," v, 8. Daniel uses the word in the same sense, to denote the land of the Jews generally, Dan. ii, 25; v, 13, where it is rendered in the A. V. both *Judah* and *Jewry*. In Arabic the word *Yehûd* is applied exclusively to the Jews as a people. As applied to the country, this term derived its name from the imperial tribe of Judah; and it seems to have comprised the territory occupied by those who returned from Babylon, the mass of these exiles having been of the tribe or of the kingdom of Judah, as distinguished from Israel. It is true that the remnants of many other tribes returned also. Thus the sacrifices were for the twelve, Ezra vi, 17; viii, 35; and we have special mention of Ephraim and Manasseh, 1 Chron. ix, 3; of Benjamin and the Levites, Ezra i, 5; and of others whose pedigrees were lost, ii, 59, 60. We know also that so multifarious were those that came back that it is said, "all Israel dwelt in their cities," (70,) and that later in the sacred history the descent of individuals not of Judah is specified, Luke ii, 36; yet as Jerusalem was now again the general metropolis, it was natural that the name of the great tribe which settled around it should prevail above the rest. And, indeed, before the captivity the kings of Judah seem to have recovered in a measure their authority over the rest of the land, 2 Kings xxiii, 19, 20; 2 Chron. xxxiv, 6, 7, 9. In the Apocrypha "Judea" or "the country of Judea" frequently occurs; for example, 1 Esdr. iv, 45; vi, 8; Tobit i, 18, though the distinctive name of Israel is by no means abandoned, 1 Macc. i, 20, 25; vi, 18, 21. After the disgrace of Archelaus, Judea was attached to the Roman province of Syria; the procurator, subordinate to the governor of Syria, residing at Cæsarea. Before the commencement of our era Palestine was divided into three distinct provinces—Galilee, Samaria, and Judea, John iv, 3-5. Judea lay on the south, and extended from the Jordan and Dead Sea on the east to the Mediterranean on the west; and from about the parallel of Shiloh on the north, to the wilderness in the south; and also included, apparently, a strip of coast running as far north as Ptolemais. This was the province usually meant by the term *Judea* in the N. T., Luke v, 17; Matt. iv, 25; John iv, 47, 54; but sometimes the word is used in a wider sense. Thus in Luke i, 5, Herod is called King of Judea; that is, the general name Judea is given to his whole kingdom, which included all Palestine both east and west of the Jordan. The trans-Jordanic provinces are referred to as belonging to Judea in Matt. xix, 1; Mark x, 1; Luke xxiii, 5. Josephus says that part of Idumea was embraced in Judea. The southern part of Palestine, between Hebron, Beersheba, and Gaza, was then called Idumea, and thus formed part of the proper province of Judea.

The "hill-country" of Judea (Luke i, 65) embraced the crown of the mountain ridge around Jerusalem and southward. This was the native country of the Baptist, Luke i, 39. The "Wilderness of Judea," or, emphatically, "*The* Wilderness," as it is termed, Matt. iv, 1, is that wild and desolate region along the whole eastern slope of the mountains, from the brow of the ridge at Bethany, Bethlehem, and Tekoa, down to the shore of the Dead Sea.

In the time of Christ that section of Judea which formed the scene of a part of our Lord's teachings, labors, and sufferings was a land of vineyards, olive groves, and fig orchards, which flourished luxuriantly in the deep glens and along the terraced sides of the limestone hills. But now the glory and the beauty of the land are departed. Here and there is a deep glen bordered with belts of olives, and its banks above are green with the foliage of the oak, but the noble forests are gone; the vegetation that resulted from careful irrigation is gone, the terraces that supported the soil on the hill-sides are broken, and, instead of spreading vine and fig-tree, we have now naked rocks and confused heaps of stones. One may wander for miles together without seeing a vestige of *present* habitation, save the little goat-pen on the hill-side, and the groups of sheep and goats round the fountains; but there is scarcely a hill-top that is not crowned with ruins, and there is scarcely a fountain where fragments of walls and scattered heaps of stones do not indicate the sites of former dwellings.

Ju'dah, (Map 5,) *praised, celebrated,* a tribe of the children of Israel named from the fourth son of Jacob and Leah. At the first census of the tribe in the wilderness they numbered 74,600 adult males, being 11,900 more than the largest of the other tribes, Num. i, 26, 27; ii, 4. Judah always had the foremost place, the post of honor, on the east of the tabernacle, and was chief of the first of the four grand divisions of the host, leading the van while marching, Num. ii, 3, 9; x, 14. In the second census in the plain of Moab Judah had multiplied to 76,500, Num. xxvi, 19-22. Moses's blessing on the tribe is recorded in Deut. xxxiii, 7.

Judah was the first tribe which received its allotted possessions west of the Jordan, and this territory included fully one third of the whole land; but only about one third of the inheritance was available for actual settlement. Joshua, in the fifteenth chapter, gives the boundaries and the principal towns of Judah. Its eastern boundary was the Dead Sea and the

Arabah, and its western the Mediterranean Sea. On the north the border ran from the mouth of the Jordan, by Jericho, Jerusalem, Kirjath-jearim, Beth-Shemesh, Ekron, and Jabneel, to the coast. The southern border cannot now be so accurately defined, because the region through which it ran is to a great extent unexplored, and the sites of the places named are unknown. It is said to begin at "the shore of the Salt Sea, and from the bay that looks southward;" but it is clear from what follows that the line ran *due south* from that point, through the Arabah, as far as Kadesh-Barnea, (35 miles,) where it turned westward, and extended, apparently in nearly a straight line, to the river of Egypt, now *Wady-el-Arish,* 50 miles south-west from Gaza. The country thus defined was sixty-five miles long, and averaged about fifty in breadth. On the east, extending along the Dead Sea and the Arabah from north to south, was "the Wilderness," Josh. xv, 6, averaging fifteen miles in breadth, a wild, barren, uninhabitable region. Different sections of it were called by different names, as "Wilderness of Engedi," 1 Sam. xxiv, 1; "Wilderness of Judah," Judg. i, 16; Wilderness of Maon," 1 Sam. xxiii, 24. On the west of Judah's allotted territory was the Plain of Philistia, called the Shephelah, or "low country," in the Bible, Josh. xv, 33, etc. It extended from Joppa to Gaza, and embraced the whole of that noble plain which constituted far the richest portion of the land. But the people of Judah not being able to withstand the war chariots of the Philistines in the open plain, the Shephelah was thus worse than useless to the tribe. They never completely conquered it. The real possessions of Judah, therefore, consisted only of the central mountain range, the hill country, with its terraced slopes and peaks, all clothed in the rich foliage of the vine, and its long winding glens, running down between rocky ridges into the Shephelah, their sides covered with olives and figs, and their winter brooks running through cornfields below, and its southern declivities, breaking into undulating downs and broad steppes of pasture-land, out toward Beersheba. A portion of Judah's territory was afterward taken for Simeon; perhaps not a compact district, but certain cities with their villages "within the inheritance" of Judah. Josh. xix, 1-9. Dan, too, got a section of the very best of the western declivities. (Compare verses 40-48.)

But the position and power of Judah were greatly strengthened by this division of its territory, for Dan defended Judah from the Philistines, and Simeon from the Edomites. Joshua captured some of the towns in the hill country, and, at first, some portions of the Shephelah, Josh. x, 28-35, 38-40; xi, 21; and after his death Judah and Simeon together destroyed the chief Philistine cities and sacked Jerusalem, Judg. i, 1-20.

During the rule of the Judges the tribe of Judah was mainly occupied in completing the conquest of the territory. A few strongholds in the mountains still remained in the hands of the Canaanites; these they took, and they also made a successful expedition into Philistia, capturing Gaza, Askelon, and Ekron, though they were unable to establish permanent settlements there. In all these expeditions they were aided by Simeon, Judg. i. Judah maintained an independent spirit toward the other tribes; and while they acquiesced in the Benjamite Saul's appointment as king, it could hardly have been with a very good grace, as may be inferred from the very small contingent they supplied to that monarch's army when proceeding against Amalek, 1 Sam. xv, 4. Gladly, therefore, did they embrace the opportunity of Saul's death to anoint their own tribesman, David, king in Hebron;

and for some years they maintained a separate monarchy, 2 Sam. ii, 1-11. When the nation was reunited under David's scepter, the haughty men of Judah thought little of and cared little for the rest of the tribes, 2 Sam. xix, 40-48; xx, 2, 4; an omen of the entire separation which occurred after Solomon's death.

In anointing David king, Judah had no consultation with the other tribes; this was the first step toward an independent kingdom. Ephraim was the rival of Judah, and was the only tribe which showed any disposition to dispute its supremacy. The sanctuary, so long at Ephraimite Shiloh, was now transferred to Jerusalem, locally Benjamite, but actually appropriated by the house of Judah. Thus Judah exulted, and Ephraim was proportionately dissatisfied. Probably the division of Israel into two kingdoms may thus be traced to the rivalry of these powerful tribes. When the kingdom was divided under Rehoboam and Jeroboam the history of Judah as a tribe lapsed into that of *Judah as a kingdom.* See Map 14. To the kingdom of Judah adhered the single tribe of Benjamin, 1 Kings xii, 16, 17, 19, 21. The remaining ten tribes constituted the *kingdom of Israel.* Rehoboam fortified fifteen cities, not as a result of strength, but as a mark of weakness, 2 Chron. xi, 5-11. By his foolish disobedience the king provoked the anger of the Lord, and Shishak, king of Egypt, swept like a storm from the desert over his dominions, plundered Jerusalem, carried off the wealth of the temple, and left the king of Judah humiliated and impoverished, 2 Chron. xii, 1-10.

Judah in the first three reigns was generally in an attitude of hostility to Israel. Rehoboam had, indeed, been checked, 2 Chron. xi, 1-4; but Jeroboam had been defeated by Abijah in a great battle, 2 Chron. xiii. Asa was successful against an Ethiopian host, 2 Chron. xiv; and the kingdom was populous and prosperous. Jehoshaphat's reign was happy and successful, 2 Chron. xvii; xix; xx; but he made the mistake of forming an alliance with the wicked king of Israel, Ahab, by taking Ahab's daughter for a wife to his son, 1 Kings xxii; 2 Chron. xviii. A series of calamities followed. Weak and wicked princes sat on the throne. Edom revolted, and the royal family were almost extirpated. Athaliah (Ahab's daughter) usurped the crown; and when the right heir was restored, he ruled justly only so long as the priest Jehoiada lived, and then saw his kingdom desolated, and was slain by conspirators, 2 Chron. xxi-xxiv. Under the reign of Amaziah, Jerusalem was taken and plundered by the king of Israel, Jehoash, 2 Chron. xxv. The power of Judah now rapidly declined. If the decline was stayed for awhile by the early prudence of Uzziah, by the efforts of the godly Hezekiah, and the reforms of the lamented Josiah, it went on with accelerated pace under the rule of the headstrong Ahaz, the ferocious Manasseh, and Josiah's miserable children, 2 Chron. xxvi-xxxvi. Syria became confederated with Israel to destroy Judah. And then a mightier power stepped forward: Assyria, which was gradually absorbing all the neighboring States. The kingdom of Israel fell. And though Judah seems to have had some authority afterward over the country of the ten tribes, it could have been only delegated. Her king was only a vassal to a foreign power. She was dependent now on Egypt, now on Babylon. Finally the country was ravaged by the king of Babylon; Jerusalem was burnt with fire, and the holy temple of the Lord, where his glory had dwelt, was laid in ashes; and then Judah was no more, 2 Kings xxiv, xxv; Jer. xxxix-xli. For subsequent events see JERUSALEM.

Ju'dah, THE CITY OF. 2 Chron. xxv, 28. Probably the "city of David" at Jerusalem.

Ju'dah upon Jor'dan. Josh. xix, 34. Possibly a corruption of some other name. See NAPHTALI.

Jut'tah, *extended,* an ancient town in the mountains of Judah, mentioned in the group with Maon and Carmel, Josh. xv, 55. It was allotted to the priests, xxi, 16. Reland conjectures that the Juda of Luke i, 39, in which Zacharias resided, may be identical with Juttah. For this there is no evidence. See JUDA. Juttah is doubtless identical with *Yutta,* a large village situated on the declivity of a hill about five miles south of Hebron.

Kab'zeel, *God gathers,* a city of Judah, the first named in the enumeration of those next to Edom, and apparently further south, Josh. xv, 21. It was the native place of the hero Benaiah-ben-Jehoiada, 2 Sam. xxiii, 20; 1 Chron. xi, 22. There is a Jekabzeel mentioned by Nehemiah among the villages of Judah re-occupied after the captivity, which is considered identical with this place, Neh. xi, 25. Mr. Wilton (*The Negeb,* pp. 69-72) would place it at *'Ain el-'Arûs,* at the confluence of the *Wady el-Kuseib* and other streams in the *Sabkhah.* But this lacks confirmation.

Ka'des, the Greek form of Kadesh, Judith i, 9.

Ka'desh, (Map 2,) *sacred;* or **Ka'desh-Bar'nea,** probably *sacred places,* or *deserts.* Originally the name of this place was *En-Mishpat,* (*fountain of judgment,*) Gen. xiv, 7. It is probably also the Kedesh of Josh. xv, 23. Kadesh was a station of the Israelites, and the only station called a city, Num. xx, 16. It lay on the southern border of Canaan, Num. xxxiv, 4; Josh. x, 41, in the desert of Zin, Num. xx, 1; xxvii, 14; xxxiii, 36; Deut. xxxii, 51, on the border of Edom, Num. xx, 16. The term Kadesh, though applied to signify a "city," yet had also a wider application to a region in which Kadesh-Meribah certainly, and Kadesh-Barnea probably, indicate a precise spot. See Gen. xx, 1.

The first notice of Kadesh occurs in the story of the capture of Sodom by the eastern kings, Gen. xiv. It continued to be a place of note during the whole period of the patriarchs, Gen. xvi, 14; xx, 1. From Kadesh Moses sent the spies to traverse the land of Canaan; and thither they returned, bringing an evil report of it, Num. xiii, 3, 26; xxxii, 8. Then from Kadesh the Israelites were compelled to turn back disheartened to the desert again. After an interval of thirty-eight years' wandering they again returned to Kadesh, Num. xiv, 29-33; Deut. i, 40; ii, 14. There Miriam died, Num. xx, 1. It was at Kadesh, too, that the waters of *Meribah* flowed when the children of Israel, toward the end of their wanderings, strove with the Lord, and Moses and Aaron did not sanctify him, and were consequently excluded from the promised land, Num. xx, 1, 13. The Israelites were unquestionably twice at Kadesh, remaining there on each occasion for a considerable length of time. They came about July of the *second* year of the Exodus, and again about the same time of the *fortieth* year, Num. xii, 16; xiii, 26; xx, 1, etc. As to the site of Kadesh, very great diversity of opinion exists among the best authorities. Some affirm that Kadesh and Kadesh-Barnea are different places. Of those who consider that there is but one place, Mr. Rowlands, followed by Mr. Williams and Professor Tuch, places the site of Kadesh in the midst of the *Desert of Tîh,* about forty-five miles south of Beersheba, Raumer places it at *Ain Hasb,* in the Arabah, twenty miles south of the

WILDERNESS OF KADESH.

Dead Sea; Stanley at *Petra;* Rohinson and Porter at *'Ain el-Weibêh,* northwest of Petra. Delitzch locates it at *Kadus,* between Hebron and the southern end of the Dead Sea. Professor E. H. Palmer, with strong arguments, claims that Kadesh must be identified with *'Ain Gadis,* as originally suggested by Mr. Rowlands. (See Map 2.) 'Ain Gadis is in meaning and etymology identical with Kadesh. Kadesh is the most important site in the whole region indicated, as it forms the key to the movements of the Israelites during their many years' wanderings in the great Desert of *Et-Tih.* (See *Desert of the Exodus.*)

Kad'monites, *eastern,* or *orientals,* one of the tribes which inhabited the country given in covenant promise to Abraham, Gen. xv, 19. Perhaps they comprise the nations generally, "children of the East," who extended from Canaan to the Euphrates. See Gen. xxix, 1; Judg. vi, 3.

Ka'nah, *a reed,* or *place of reeds.*
1. A town in the territory of Asher, near Zidon, Josh. xix, 28. It is not clearly identified. Dr. Robinson, Mr. Porter, and some others propose as the site the modern village of *Kâna,* which is six miles inland, not from Zidon, but from Tyre, nearly twenty miles south thereof. It has about three hundred families, with no traces of ruins. About one mile north of it are very considerable ruins; and in a ravine near by are some singular figures of men, women, and children sculptured on the face of the rocks. But Mr. Grove (in Smith's Dictionary) says: "An *Ain Kana* is marked in the map of Van de Velde, about eight miles south-east of *Saida,* (Zidon,) close to the conspicuous village *Jurjûa,* at which latter place Zidon lies full in view. This at least answers more nearly the requirements of the text. But it is put forward as a mere conjecture."
2. A torrent which divided Ephraim from Manasseh, Josh. xvi, 8; xvii, 9. Dr. Robinson identifies it with a *Wady Kanah* which rises in the plain of Mukhna, south of Nablus, and runs south-west till it joins *Nahr el-Aujeh,* and falls into the sea about four miles north of Joppa. But this seems much too far south. Mr. Porter proposes the *Nahr el-Akhdar,* which flows into the sea about two miles south of the ruins of Cæsarea. Mr. Grove inclines to agree with the conjecture of Schwartz, that Kanah is a wady which commences west of and close to *Nablûs* at *Ain el-Khassab,* and falls into the sea at *Nahr Falaik,* and which bears also the name of *Wady el-Khassub*—the reedy stream. The name *Khassab* is borne by a large tract of the maritime plain at this part. See Stanley's *Sinai and Palestine,* and Clark's *Bible Atlas.*

Kar'kaa or **Karka'a,** *a foundation, bottom, floor,* a place on the southern border of Judah, situated on the high table-land west of Kadesh-Barnea, Josh. xv, 3. It is not again mentioned, and the site is unknown.

Kar'kor, *foundation, level ground,* a place on the east side of Jordan to which Zeba and Zalmunna fled with their army when defeated by Gideon, Judg. viii, 10. It was doubtless somewhere on the level plateau of the Mishor, near the eastern border of Moab. The site is unknown

Kar'naim. See ASHTEROTH-KARNAIM.

Kar'tah, *city,* a city of Zebulun, assigned to the Merarite Levites together with Jokneam, Josh. xxi, 34. Van de Velde (*Memoir,* p. 327) suggests that it may be identical with *el-Harti,* a village with traces of antiquity on the banks of the Kishon at the base of Carmel, and only a few miles north-west of the site of Jokneam. The names, however, are radically different.

Kar'tan, *two towns, double city,* one of the three cities assigned to the

Levites out of the tribe of Naphtali, Josh. xxi, 32. It is probably the same with Kirjathaim, 1 Chron. vi, 76. Nothing is known of its history or site.

Kat'tath, *small,* a town of Zebulun, Josh. xix, 15. Some suggest that this town is the same as Kitron, Judg. i, 30; but there is no evidence for this. The site of Kattath is unknown.

Ke'dar, (Map 12,) *black, black-skinned,* an Arabian tribe descended from Kedar, one of the sons of Ishmael, Gen. xxv, 13–16. They inhabited the north of Arabia east of the Holy Land. The tents of all the nomad tribes of Arabia are black, and the color of their skin is uniformly of a light bronze hue. Some think their name was given them because of the color of their tents; others because of the darkness of their complexion. As to their complexion, the name Kedar was no more applicable to one tribe than another. The "children of Kedar" (Isa. xxi, 17) are more frequently spoken of in Scripture than any of the other Arab tribes. They dwelt chiefly in tents, though some occupied cities and villages. They were rich in flocks, and they were also celebrated as warriors, 1 Chron. i, 29; Psa. cxx, 5; Sol. Song i, 5; Isa. xxi, 16, 17; xlii, 11; xlix, 28; lx, 7; Jer. ii, 10; Ezek. xxvii, 21. A very ancient Arab tradition states that Kedar settled in the *Hedjaz,* the country round Mecca and Medina, and that his descendants have ever since ruled there. It is a remarkable fact that at the present time the inhabitants of the *Hedjaz* are composed of the powerful and warlike tribe called *Beni Harb,* "children of *war,*" some of whom live in villages and towns, but most of them in tents. They are still rich in flocks and herds, and they still dwell in safety among their native hills, as did their forefathers, Jer. xlix, 31, 32. See also in this the fulfillment of the promise concerning Ishmael, Gen. xvi, 12.

Ked'emoth, *antiquities,* or perhaps *eastern,* a city on the eastern side of Moab, near Arnon, encircled by a "wilderness" or "pasture-land" of the same name, Deut. ii, 24–26. It was allotted to Reuben and the Merarite Levites, Josh. xiii, 18; 1 Chron. vi, 79. This district has not been explored.

Ke'desh, (Map 5,) *sanctuary.*

1. A town on the south-eastern border of Judah, near the confines of Edom, Josh. xv, 23. Possibly identical with KADESH, (Kadesh-Barnea,) which see.

2. A royal Canaanite city taken by Joshua, (Josh. xii, 22,) in Issachar, and allotted to Gershonite Levites, 1 Chron. vi, 72. In Josh. xxi, 28, it is called Kishon. See KISHION.

3. Kedesh, Josh. xix, 37, called also Kedesh in Galilee, Josh. xxi, 32; and, in Judg. iv, 6, Kedesh-Naphtali. An ancient Canaanitish town allotted to the tribe of Naphtali, and subsequently assigned to the Gershonite Levites, and made one of the three cities of refuge west of the Jordan, Josh. xxi, 32. It seems to have been a "sanctuary" of the old Canaanites; and the Israelites, while they retained the name denoting its character, made it in some respect their sanctuary also. It was "the holy place of Naphtali," and the asylum of all northern Palestine. Barak lived there, and there he assembled his army, Judg. iv, 6, 9. Heber the Kenite resided there, Judg. iv, 11. It was captured by Tiglath-Pileser, and its inhabitants carried away to Assyria, 2 Kings xv, 29. In 1 Macc. xi, 63, (as Cades,) it is reckoned a town of Galilee. Josephus speaks of Kedesh as situated on the confines of the country of Tyre in Upper Galilee. Dr. Robinson has doubtless identified the site of this town at *Kedes,* a village situated on the western edge of the

basin of the *Ard-el-Huleh,* the great depressed basin or tract through which the Jordan makes its way into the Sea of Merom. *Kedes* is ten English miles north of *Safed,* and four to the north-west of the upper part of the Sea of Merom. The site is a splendid one, well watered and surrounded by fertile plains. There are numerous sarcophagi and other ancient remains.

Ke'dron. See KIDRON.

Kehel'athah, (Map 2,) *assembly,* a desert encampment of the Israelites, Num. xxxiii, 22, between Sinai and Kadesh. Its history is unknown.

Kei'lah, *fortress,* a city of Judah, situated in the Shephelah or plain of Philistia, near Mareshah and Nezib, Josh. xv, 33, 44. It was besieged by the Philistines, and relieved by David, 1 Sam. xxiii, 1–5. David and his six hundred settled for a time in the town, but when threatened by an attack from Saul he discovered that the ungrateful inhabitants were resolved to betray him, so "David and his men . . . arose and departed out of Ke'iah," verses 6–13. Keilah was re-occupied after the captivity, Neh. iii, 17, 18. In 1 Chron. iv, 19, it is not clear whether a person or a place is meant. Keilah is doubtless identical with *Kila,* a large ruined tower or castle on a projecting cliff eight miles from *Beit Jibrin* (Eleutheropolis) on the way to Hebron, and in the neighborhood of *Beit Nûsib* (Nezib) and *Maresa,* (Mareshah.)

Ke'nath, (Map 4,) *possession,* a strong city of Bashan, in the province of Argob, Num. xxxii, 42; 1 Chron. ii, 23; compare Deut. iii, 14. It appears to have been one of the "threescore great cities, fenced with high walls, gates, and bars," which Jair captured, Deut. iii, 3, 4. Nobah, a Manassite, headed a separate expedition against Kenath, took it, and called it Nobah, Num. xxxii, 42. From the chronology of Judg. viii, 11, it would appear that it retained this last name at least two hundred years. Eusebius speaks of Kanatha as "a village of Arabia . . . near Bozra." Its site is doubtless that of the modern *Kenawât,* a ruined town at the southern extremity of the *Lejah,* about twenty miles north of *Busrah.* The ruins cover a space about one mile long by half a mile wide. Mr. Porter says that days may be spent in sketching, exploring, and copying inscriptions. Some of the ruins are among the most splendid of the *Haurân.*

Ke'naz, *hunting,* Gen. xxxvi, 11; 1 Chron. i, 36, 53. One of the dukes of Edom, whose descendants are probably represented in the modern Arab tribe, the *Aenezes,* who extend from the Euphrates to Syria, and from Aleppo to the mountains of *Nejd.* They are said to be able to bring ninety thousand camel riders into the field, and ten thousand horsemen.

Ken'ezite, or **Ken'izzite,** *hunter,* an Edomitish tribe whose land was promised to Abraham, Gen. xv, 19. They probably inhabited some part of the Arabian desert on the confines of Syria, to which the expeditions of Joshua did not reach In Num. xxxii, 12; Josh. xiv, 6, 14, the term is a patronymic of Caleb, derived from Kenaz, mentioned in Judg. i, 13.

Ken'ite, Ken'ites, *smiths,* or *dwellers in a nest,* a tribe who originally inhabited the rocky and desert region lying between southern Palestine and the mountains of Sinai, adjoining—and even partly intermingling with—the Amalekites, Num. xxiv, 21; 1 Sam. xv, 6. Their land was promised to Abraham, Gen. xv, 19. Jethro was a Kenite, Judg. i, 16; and it was when Moses kept his flocks on Horeb that the Lord appeared to him in a burning bush, Exod. iii, 1, 2. Jethro is also said to have been "priest of Midian," and a "Midianite," Num. x, 29; hence we conclude that the Midianites and Kenites were identical. The Midianites were descended from Abraham's son by Keturah, while we may fairly infer that the Kenites were a branch of the larger nation of Midian. The Kenites were very friendly to the Israelites. They seem to have accompanied the Hebrews in their wanderings. At any rate they were with them on their entrance into the Promised Land. Their encampment was within Balaam's view when he delivered his prophecy, Num. xxiv, 21, 22, and we may infer that they assisted in the capture of Jericho, the "city of palm-trees," Judg. i, 16; compare 2 Chron. xxviii, 15. Some of their descendants were also found in the north of Palestine, Judg. iv, 11. When Saul marched against the Amalekites he carefully avoided any injury to the Kenites, 1 Sam. xv, 6. David maintained the same friendly relations with them, 1 Sam. xxx, 29. The house of the Rechabites was of this tribe, traced to the original ancestor, Hemath, 1 Chron. ii, 55.

Ke'rioth, (Map 5,) *cities.*
1. A town in the south of Judah. Some have supposed this the birthplace of Judas Iscariot. Probably Kerioth-Hezron is one name, Josh. xv, 25. See HEZRON. The site of Kerioth is possibly identical with *Kuryetein,* ("the two cities,") a ruin about ten miles south of Hebron, and three from *Main,* (Maon.)
2. A city of Moab mentioned by Jeremiah in connection with Beth-Gamul and Bozrah, Jer. xlviii, 24. It is also called Kirioth, Amos ii, 2. But perhaps in this last passage, and in Jer. xlviii, 41, the word is not a proper name, and should be translated "the cities." Ancient interpreters appear to give no clue to the position of this place; but Mr. Porter identifies it with *Kureiyeh,* a ruined town of some extent lying between *Busrah* and *Sulkhad,* in the southern part of the *Haurán.* Mr. Grove thinks a more plausible identification would be *Kureiyat,* at the western foot of *Jebel Attarus,* and but a short distance from either Dibon, Beth-Meon, or Heshbon.

Ke'ziz, VALLEY OF, *valley of the end,* or, perhaps, *of destruction,* (from a root signifying "to cut off,") a place mentioned among the cities of Benjamin, Josh. xviii, 21. The name does not re-appear in the O. T., but it is possibly intended under the corrupted form Beth-Basi in 1 Macc. ix, 62, 64. Some conclude that the Hebrew *Emek* (valley) should not be here translated as *Beth* (house) is not translated in the preceding proper name. Therefore the name of the town would be *Emek-Keziz,* as it is rendered in the Septuagint. It must have stood in the Jordan valley, near Jericho.

Kib'roth-Hatta'avah, (Map 2,) *graves of lust,* or *longing,* a station of the Israelites in the wilderness. Here the people, craving flesh to eat, murmured. The Lord sent them vast numbers of quails, and "while the flesh was yet between their teeth, ere it was chewed, ... the Lord smote the people with a very great plague," and many were there buried, Num. xi, 31–35; xxxiii, 16, 17; Deut. ix, 22. Professor E. H. Palmer identifies this station with *Erweis el Ebeirig,* not far from *'Ain Hudherah,* (HAZEROTH.) Here he found many "inclosures of stone." Arab tradition declares these to be relics of a huge pilgrim caravan that was lately lost in the desert.

Kib'zaim, or **Kibza'im,** *two heaps,* a city of Ephraim assigned to the Levites, Josh. xxi, 22. In 1 Chron. vi, 68, Jokmeam is probably another name for this place. The site is unknown.

Ki'dron, (Map 7,) *turbid.* The Hebrew word *nachal* is in the Old Testament, with one single exception, (2 Kings xxiii, 4—the "fields of Kidron,") attached to the name of Kidron. This term *nachal* appears to be exactly

THE MONASTERY OF MAR SABA—GORGE OF THE KIDRON.

equivalent to the Arabic *wady*, which signifies a *valley*, or *ravine*, either with or without a river. Some derive Kidron from the root signifying "to be black," but the cause of this name is not assigned. Possibly it may arise from the gloominess of the glen, or from the turbid stream; or from the blood and refuse of the temple running into it. Others think it was so called from *cedar*-trees which grew in it. In John xviii, 1, it is *Cedron*.

Kidron is a valley and torrent between Jerusalem and the Mount of Olives, 1 Kings ii, 37; Neh. ii, 15; Jer. xxxi, 40. This mountain ravine is in most places narrow, with precipitous banks of limestone; but here and there its banks have an easy slope, and along its bottom are strips of land capable of cultivation. When fleeing from Absalom David crossed the Kidron, 2 Sam. xv, 23. In Kidron idols were destroyed and burned by Asa, Josiah, and the Levites, 1 Kings xv, 13; 2 Kings xxiii, 6, 12; 2 Chron. xxix, 16. See also 2 Kings xi, 16. The source of the Kidron was sealed by Hezekiah, 2 Chron. xxxii, 4. Jesus crossed this valley on that memorable night of the agony in Gethsemane, John xviii, 1.

TOMBS IN THE VALLEY OF THE KIDRON.

In reference to the passage in 2 Chron. xxxii, 4, Mr. Grove (in Smith's *Dictionary*) inclines to think that the Kidron was "the brook that ran through the midst of the land," the spring-head of which Hezekiah stopped so effectually that the ancient bed has since been generally dry.

This ravine is now known as *Wady Sitti-Maryam*, and the VALLEY OF JEHOSHAPHAT, (which see.) Mr. Porter describes the head of the Kidron as in a slight depression on the broad summit of the mountain ridge of Judea, a mile and a quarter north-west of Jerusalem. The sides of the depression and the elevated ground around it are whitened by the broad jagged tops of limestone rocks, and almost every rock is excavated, partly as a quarry, and partly to form the façade of a tomb. The valley, or depression, runs for about half a mile toward the city; it is shallow and broad, dotted with corn-fields, and sprinkled with a few old olives. It then bends eastward, and in another half-mile is crossed by the great northern road coming down from the hill Scopus. On the east side of the road, and south bank of the Kidron, are the celebrated *Tombs of the Kings*. The bed of the valley is here about half a mile due north of the city gate. As it advances southward the right bank, forming the side of the hill Bezetha, becomes higher and steeper, with occasional precipices of rock, on which may be seen a few fragments of the city wall; while on the left the base of Olivet projects, greatly narrowing the valley. Opposite St. Stephen's gate the depth is fully one hundred feet, and the breadth not more than four hundred feet. Soon the Kidron becomes narrower still, and traces of a torrent bed first begin to appear. Further down, three hundred yards, the hills on each side rise precipitously from this torrent bed, which is here spanned by a single arch. The ravine continues, narrow and rugged, five hundred yards more, to the Fountain of the Virgin, situated in a deep cave to the right. The village of *Silwân*, the ancient Siloam, is now seen on the left, its houses clinging to the cliff. About four hundred yards below the fountain the Tyropœon comes in on the right, descending in graceful terraced slopes, fresh and green, from the waters of the "Pool of Siloam." The valley is now wider, affording a level tract for cultivation. Here of old were the "King's Gardens," (Neh. iii, 15,) extending down to the mouth of Hinnom; and about a hundred yards below this point is the *Well of Joab*, the ancient En-Rogel, Josh. xv, 7. The total length of the Kidron from its head to this fountain is two and three quarter miles. From hence it runs in a winding course through scenery of the wildest character, past the convent of St. Sâba, where it is called *Wady er-Râheb*, the "Monk's Valley." Mar Sâba is one of the most remarkable buildings in Palestine, founded A.D. 439 by the saint whose name it bears. The name "Monk's Valley" was given to this part of Kidron, doubtless, because of the many caves and grottoes in the sides of the chasm, both above and below the convent, which were once the abode of monks and hermits. Below the convent Kidron takes the name *Wady en-Nâr*, "the Valley of Fire," from its bare and scorched aspect, and it runs in a deep, narrow, wild chasm until it falls into the Dead Sea, not far from its north-west corner, about fourteen miles from Jerusalem.

Ki'nah, *lamentation*, or *song of mourning*, a place mentioned only in Josh. xv, 22, as on the southern border of Judah. Mr. Wilton, (*The Negeb*, pp. 74–76,) proposing an emendation of the text, reads Hazar-Kinah, "the Kenite inclosure," or "settlement," and identifies it with the ruined site *el-Hudhairah*, the main encampment of the *Jehâlin*, an Arabian tribe. (See *Ayre*.) Prof. Stanley (*S. and P.*) ingeniously connects Kinah with the Kenites who settled in this district, Judges i, 16. These theories lack confirmation.

King's Dale, Gen. xiv, 17; compare 2 Sam. xviii, 18. These two passages of Scripture give us no information as to the position of the dale; nor does any ancient author locate it. It has been variously located—in the Valley of Jehoshaphat or Kidron, at Beersheba, at Lebanon, and near the Jordan. Mr. Porter, (*Kitto*, vol. ii, p. 45, ed. 1865,) showing that the original words signify a "plain" or "broad valley," and not a *ravine*, claims that in the immediate neighborhood of Jerusalem there is one place, and only one, which appears to answer to these indications, and that is the *Plain of Rephaim*. It is on the direct route from the north to Hebron; a practicable road leads down from it through the wilderness to the shore of the Dead Sea; and it is so close to Jerusalem that Melchizedek from the heights of Zion could both see and hear the joyous meeting of the princes of Sodom with the victorious band of Abraham and the reclaimed captives. Mr. Stanley thinks the context shows that the place was somewhere near the Valley of the Jordan, probably on its eastern side, where the death of Absalom occurred, and where it would therefore be mentioned as a singular coincidence that he had erected his monument near the scene of his death. (See *Sinai and Palestine*, p 247.)

Kir, *a wall, a walled place*, the place to which the inhabitants of Damascus were carried captive by the king of Assyria, 2 Kings xvi, 9; Amos i, 5. Kir is also named with Elam, Isa. xxii, 6; and the Syrians are said to have been brought from Kir, Amos ix, 7. A difference of opinion exists in regard to the position of Kir. Some suppose it to be identical with the *Curna* of Ptolemy, a city of Media on the river Mardus. Others think that Kir was a province or district along the banks of the river Cyrus, which is on the extreme northern frontier of ancient Assyria. Isaiah mentions Elam and Kir together, and hence Keil (on 2 Kings xvi, 9) thinks it more natural to identify the latter with Curna or with Carinæ, also a city of Media, now called *Kerend*. Mr. Porter (in Kitto) says: "It is now impossible satisfactorily to settle the question; we cannot even state with certainty whether the Kir of 2 Kings is identical with that of Isaiah; the latter may perhaps have been in Media near Elam, and the former on the banks of the Cyrus."

Kir-Har'aseth, (Maps 4, 5, 13,) *city of the hill*, 2 Kings iii, 25; **Kir-Ha'resh,** Isa. xvi, 11; **Kir-Har'eseth,** Isa. xvi, 7; and **Kir-He'res,** Jer. xlviii, 31, 36. A city and important fortress of Moab, called *Kir of Moab* in Isa. xv, 1. It is now *Kerak*, a town of about three thousand inhabitants. It stands on the top of a rocky hill about ten miles from the south-east corner of the Dead Sea, and near the southern frontier of Moab. The city was at one time strongly fortified, and is still inclosed by a half-ruinous wall, flanked by seven massive towers. In the time of the Crusades it was an important place. On the western side of the town stands the citadel, a strong building, separated from the town by a deep moat hewn in the rock. It appears to have been built by the Crusaders. In 1869 a Semitic monument was discovered in this region, containing a very ancient Phœnician inscription concerning the deeds of a Moabitish king. See DIBON, (1.)

Kiriatha'im, *double city*, a place in Moab, Jer. xlviii, 1, 28; Ezek. xxv, 9. See KIRJATHAIM.

Kiriathia'rius. 1 Esdras v, 19; a corruption of Kirjath-Jearim.

Kir'ioth, *cities*. Amos ii, 2. See KERIOTH.

Kir'jath, *city*, a city of Benjamin, Josh. xviii, 28. Probably Kirjath-Jearim.

Kirjatha'im, *double city.*

1. A city on the east of the Jordan in Reuben, Num. xxxii, 37; Josh. xiii, 19. In later times it was in the possession of the Moabites, Jer. xlviii, 1, 23; Ezek. xxv, 9, in which places it is called *Kiriathaim*. It is possibly the modern *Kureiyat*, under the southern side of *Jebel Attarus*.

2. A place in Naphtali, allotted to the Gershonite Levites, 1 Chron. vi, 76. See KARTAN.

Kir'jath-Ar'ba, *city of Arba*, or, according to the Jews, *city of four*, because Adam, Abraham, Isaac, and Jacob were buried there. It was an early name of Hebron, Josh. xiv, 15; Judg. i, 10; Gen. xxiii, 2; xxxv, 27; Josh. xv, 13, 54; xx, 7; xxi, 11. In Neh. xi, 25, the name occurs without explanation. See HEBRON.

Kir'jath-A'rim, an abbreviation of Kirjath-Jearim, Ezra ii, 25.

Kir'jath-Ba'al, *city of Baal*, another name for Kirjath-Jearim, Josh. xv, 60; xviii, 14. Also Baalah, and Baale-of-Judah.

Kir'jath-Hu'zoth, probably *city of streets*, a city of Moab, Num. xxii, 39; perhaps regarded as a place of sanctity. It is not identified.

Kir'jath-Je'arim, or **Kirjath-Jea'rim,** (Map 5,) *city of woods*. Called also Baalah, Josh. xv, 9, 10; Baale-of-Judah, 2 Sam. vi, 2; Kirjath-Baal, xviii, 14; Kirjath-Arim, Ezra ii, 25; Kiriathiarius, 1 Esdras v, 19. It was one of the four cities of the Gibeonites, Josh. ix, 17, on the north boundary of Judah, xv, 9; and the southern one of Benjamin, xviii, 14, 15. The ark was brought from Beth-Shemesh to this place, after it had been removed from the land of the Philistines, and here it remained till removed to Jerusalem by David, 1 Sam. vii; 1 Chron. xiii. It was the native place of the prophet Urijah, Jer. xxvi, 20; see also 1 Chron. ii, 50, 52, 53. This was also one of the ancient sites which were again inhabited after the exile, Ezra ii, 25; Neh. vii, 29. The term "wood" in Psa. cxxxii, 6, is perhaps an allusion to this city. The place is probably identical with *Kuriet el-Enab*, (city of grapes,) now usually know as *Abû Gosh*, (father of lies,) from the robber chief whose headquarters it was, at the eastern end of the *Wady Aly* on the road from *Jaffa* to Jerusalem. It is now a poor village, its finished buildings being an old convent and a Latin church. The latter is now deserted, but not in ruins, and is said to be one of the largest and most solidly constructed churches in Palestine. Some scholars locate Emmaus (Luke xxiv, 13–35) at this place. See EMMAUS, (1.)

Kir'jath-San'nah, *palm city*, another name for Debir, Josh. xv, 49. Called also Kirjath-Sepher.

Kir'jath-Se'pher, *book city*, the early name of Debir, which had also the name of Kirjath-Sannah, Josh. xv, 15, 16; x, 38, 39; xi, 21; xii, 13; xxi, 15; 1 Chron. vi, 58; Judg. i, 11, 12. This city has been considered by some as originally a seat of learning. It was taken by Othniel, for which he obtained Achsah, Caleb's daughter, in marriage.

Kir of Moab, (Maps 4, 5,) *fortress of Moab*. Isa. xv, 1. See KIR-HARASETH.

Kish'ion, *hardness*, a town of Issachar, apparently situated in the great plain of Esdraelon, where most of those with which it is grouped also stood, Josh. xix, 20. It was one of four allotted to the Levites, xxi, 28. In 1 Chron. vi, 72, it is called Kedesh. Its site is unknown.

Ki'shon, *hardness*, an incorrect form of Kishion, Josh. xxi, 28.

Ki'shon, THE RIVER, (Map 5,) *tortuous, winding stream*, a noted river of Palestine, which drains nearly the whole plain of Esdraelon, and falls into the Mediterranean near the northern base of Mount Carmel. This stream was the scene of two of the grandest achievements of Israelitish history— the defeat of Sisera and the destruction of the prophets of Baal by Elijah, Judg. iv, 7, 13; v, 21; 1 Kings xviii, 40; Psa. lxxxiii, 9—here inaccurately "Kison." The Kishon has a vast number of little tributaries from the hills on the north and south sides of the plain. During the summer all the water-courses are perfectly dry, but when the heavy rains of winter and early spring fall large torrents rush down from Tabor and the hills of Galilee, speedily filling the deep miry beds in the alluvial plain below, and rendering the passage of them both difficult and dangerous. This explains Judg. v, 4, 20, 21. The modern name of Kishon is *Nahr Mukutta*, which some think means "the river of slaughter." It may also signify "river of the ford."

Ki'son, Psa. lxxxiii, 9, an incorrect rendering of Kishon.

Kith'lish, probably *a man's wall*, a town of Judah, in the Shephelah or plain of Philistia, and grouped with Lachish and Eglon, Josh. xv, 33–40. Unknown.

Kit'ron, *knotty*, a town of Zebulun from which the Canaanites were not expelled, Judg. i, 30. Perhaps it may be a corruption of Kattath, Josh. xix, 15. In the Talmud it is identified with Zippori, (Sepphoris,) now *Seffurieh*.

Kit'tim. Gen. x, 4; 1 Chron. i, 7. See CHITTIM.

Ko'a, *stallion*, *he-camel*, hence *prince* or *nobleman*, Ezek. xxiii, 23. It probably designates a city or district of Babylonia.

Ko'hathites. See LEVITES.

La'ban, *white*, one of the stations of the Israelites after crossing the Red Sea, Deut. i, 1. Some have regarded it as identical with Libnah, (Num. xxxiii, 20,) which was the second station from Hazeroth. But this is uncertain.

Lacedæmo'nians, the inhabitants of Sparta or Lacedæmon, with whom the Jews claimed kindred, 1 Macc. xii, 2, 5; 6, 20, 21; xiv, 20, 23; xv, 23; 2 Macc. v, 9. See SPARTA.

La'chish, (Map 5,) probably *obstinate, tenacious, impregnable*, an ancient royal city of the Canaanites, situated in the Shephelah or plain of Philistia, bordering on the mountains of Judah, Josh. xv, 33 ; and allotted, with Eglon and other places, to the tribe of Judah, xxxix. It was captured by Joshua, Josh. x, 3, 5, 23, 31–35; xii, 11. Fortified by Rehoboam, 2 Chron. xi, 9. King Amaziah was killed there, 2 Kings xiv, 19; 2 Chron. xxv, 27. The city was besieged and probably taken by Sennacherib, 2 Kings xviii, 13–17; xix, 8; 2 Chron. xxxii, 9; Isa. xxxvi, 2; xxxvii, 8. Lachish is mentioned in Jer. xxxiv, 7; Micah i, 13; and it was inhabited after the return from Babylon, Neh. xi, 30.

On the tablets and sculptures discovered by Mr. Layard in the palace of Sennacherib at Nineveh, there is a description of the siege of Lachish. Above the king's head is the following inscription in cuneiform characters: "Sennacherib, the mighty king, king of the country of Assyria, sitting on the throne of judgment before, the city of Lachish—I give permission for its slaughter." Modern research presents this as one of the most important confirmations of Scripture history.

Eusebius describes Lachish as in his day a village "seven miles distant from Eleutheropolis, southward as you go to Darom." Darom was a small province south of Gaza, near the coast. Between Gaza and *Beit-Jibrin*, and about eleven miles from the latter, are the ruins of the modern *Um Lâkis*. This name suggests the royal city of Lachish, and Mr. Porter says, "There can scarcely be a doubt that in the desolate ruin of *Um Lâkis* we have all that remains of the Canaanitish city and Jewish stronghold." These ruins consist of heaps of stones and mounds of rubbish, with here and there a few broken fragments of marble and granite columns, strewn over a low hill in the midst of a great undulating plain.

Lad'der of Tyre, (Map 5,) a mountain north of Acre, rising immediately from the sea, 1 Macc. xi, 59. It is a natural barrier between Palestine and Phœnicia. In ancient times a road was carried, by a series of zigzags and *staircases*, over the summit, to connect the plain of Ptolemais with Tyre. It was the southern pass into Phœnicia proper. The road still remains, and is the only one along the coast. A short distance from it is a little village called *Nakûrah*, and the pass is known as *Râs en-Nakûrah*, "the excavated cape."

Lahai'-Roi, THE WELL, Gen. xxiv, 62; xxv, 11. See BEER-LAHAI-ROI.

Lah'mam, *provisions*, a town of Judah situated in the Shephelah, and apparently not far from Eglon, Josh. xv, 40. Lahmas may be the true form of the word. The site is unknown.

La'isa, 1 Macc. ix, 5. A place where Judas encamped. Possibly the same as the Laish of Isa. x, 30, but very uncertain.

La'ish, (Map 5,) *strong,* or *a lion,* Judg. xviii, 7, 14, 27, 29. In Josh. xix, 47, Leshem. The original name of the city of Dan. See DAN.

La'ish, (Hebrew, Laishah,) *a lion,* apparently a village of Benjamin, near Jerusalem, Isa. x, 30; possibly the same as Eleasa and Adasa. See LAISA.

La'kum, *way-stopper,* that is, *a fortress,* a town of Naphtali, near the Jordan, Josh. xix, 33. Unknown.

Laodice'a, (Map 8.) There were six Greek cities by this name in Asia. The one mentioned in Scripture lay on the confines of Phrygia and Lydia, about forty miles east of Ephesus, on the small river Lycus. It was originally called Diospolis, afterward Rhoas. Being rebuilt and beautified by Antiochus II., King of Syria, it was named after the king's wife, Laodice. Its trade was considerable. From Rev. iii, 17, we infer it to have been a place of great wealth. St. John delivered to Laodicea the fearful warning found in Rev. iii, 14–19. It is referred to in Col. iv, 13, 15, 16. We have good reason for believing that when, in writing from Rome to the Christians of Colossæ, Paul sent a greeting to those of Laodicea, he had not personally visited either place. But the preaching of the Gospel at Ephesus (Acts xviii, 19) must inevitably have resulted in the formation of Churches in the neighboring cities, especially where Jews were settled, and there were Jews in Laodicea. Later this place became a Christian city of eminence, the see of a bishop, and a meeting-place of councils. The Mohammedan invaders destroyed it, and it is now a scene of utter desolation. Amid the ruins is a little village called by the Turks *Eski-Hissar,* (*old castle.*) The ruins indicate that the city was situated on six or seven hills, covering a large extent of ground.

Lase'a, (Map 8,) a city of Crete "nigh" to Fair Havens, Acts xxvii, 8. Until recently the site of this town was altogether unknown. Rev. G. Brown discovered it in 1856. It lies about the middle of the southern coast of Crete, about five miles east of Fair Havens, and close to Cape Leonda. Masses of masonry are found along the beach. There are the ruins of two temples. Many shafts, and a few capitals of Grecian pillars, all of marble, lie scattered about, and a gully, worn by a torrent, lays bare the substructions down to the rock. The place still bears the ancient name.

La'sha, *fissure,* a place which marked the utmost border of the ancient Canaanites, Gen. x, 19. It probably lay east or north-east of the Cities of

THE GRAND RANGE OF LEBANON.

the Plain, and consequently beyond the Dead Sea. It probably derives its name from the breaking forth of the hot springs which are believed to identify the place.

Mr. Bevan says: "We can neither absolutely accept nor reject the opinion of Jerome and other writers who identify it with Callirhoë, a spot famous for hot springs near the eastern shore of the Dead Sea." There is no proof that a town ever existed at this point, yet remains of pottery, tiles, and coins, show that there must have been some habitations, perhaps for the accommodation of invalids resorting thither. According to Josephus, Herod, during his last illness, visited the springs of Callirhoë. The spot in question is situated in a narrow wild ravine, the scenery of which is very romantic.

Lasha'ron, *the plain*, one of the Canaanitish towns whose kings were killed by Joshua, Josh. xii, 18. Some have supposed the place identical with the district of Sharon, but this is very doubtful.

Leb'anon, (Map 5.) NAMES.—In Hebrew prose it occurs constantly without the article, as in 1 Kings v, 20; in poetry sometimes with, sometimes without the article, as in Isa. xiv, 8, and Psa. xxix, 5, 6. In Greek, both in the Septuagint and classic authors, the name is Libanus. Sometimes the Septuagint has Anti-Libanus, the reason for which does not appear, Deut. i, 7; iii, 25; Josh. i, 4; ix, 1. The classic Latin name, as well as the reading of the Vulgate, is Libanus; Arab geographers call the range *Jebel Libnân;* but when the Syrians use the term (which is seldom) it refers to the western range. The northern section is called *Jebel Akkâr*, the central *Sunnin*, and the southern *Jebel ed-Druze*. There are also other modern local names. In Josh. i, 4, (as elsewhere,) *Lebanon* includes both the eastern and western mountain ranges, while in Josh. xiii, 5, the eastern range is appropriately distinguished as "Lebanon toward the sun-rising." Latin writers always designate the eastern range by the name *Anti-Libanus*, which signifies opposite, or "over against Lebanon." The southern section of this range is known to the sacred writers as Hermon, ("the lofty peak.") The Sidonians called it Sirion; the Amorites Shenir, or Senir, (the glittering "breastplate" of ice,) and Sion, ("the upraised,") Deut. iii, 8, 9; iv, 48; Josh. xi, 17; xii, 1, 5; 1 Chron. v, 23; Sol. Song iv, 8; Ezek. xxvii, 5. Anti-Libanus is now called by native geographers *Jebel esh-Shurky*, "East Mountain," while Lebanon proper is sometimes termed *Jebel el-Ghurby*, "West Mountain."

Lebanon signifies "white;" "the White Mountain" of Syria in ancient times; the mountain of the "Old White-Headed Man," or the "Mountain of Ice," in modern times. The term *white* is employed either because of the whitish limestone rock which composes the great body of the whole range, or, more probably, because snow covers the peaks most of the year. In Jer. xxviii, 14, mention is made of the "snow of Lebanon;" and in the Chaldee paraphrase the name of Lebanon is "snow mountain," which is synonymous with a modern Arabic appellation sometimes used, *Jebel eth-Thelj*. The highest mountains in all parts of the world have a similar signification.

SITUATION.—The Bible represents Lebanon as lying on the northern border of the Promised Land, Deut. i, 7; iii, 25; xi, 24; Josh. i, 4; ix, 1 The two distinct ranges both begin in latitude 33° 20', and run in parallel lines from south-west to north-east for about one hundred miles, with an average base breadth of about twenty miles. At the northernmost termination of the chain the plain of Emesa opens out, which is "the entering in of Hamath," so often mentioned as "the extreme limit, in this direction, of the widest possible inheritance of Israel," Num. xiii, 21; 2 Kings xiv, 25; 2 Chron. vii, 8, etc. Between these two ranges is the long, narrow valley, from five to eight miles in width, called *Cœle-Syria*, ("Hollow Syria,") termed in Scripture "the Valley of Lebanon," Josh. ii, 17. The modern name is *el-Buka'a*, "the valley." This is a northern prolongation of the Jordan valley, and a southern prolongation of that of the Orontes.

SCRIPTURAL REFERENCES.—Besides the above passages, which mainly refer to the name and situation, there are many other Bible allusions to this vast mountain range. Lebanon and its inhabitants, the Giblites and Hivites, were promised to Israel; but a great part of the region was not conquered, Josh. xiii, 2–6; Judges iii, 1–4. In Deut. iii, 25, it is called "that goodly mountain," which Moses desired to see; in Judges iii, 3, "Mount Lebanon;" in 2 Chron. ii, 2, "the mountain;" "the tower of Lebanon," Sol. Song vii, 4. This goodly mountain was famous for cedars, Psa. xxix, 5; xcii, 12; Isa. xiv, 8; for flowers, Nahum i, 4; for fragrance, Sol. Song iv, 11; Hosea xiv, 6; for wine, Hosea xiv, 7; for appearance, "the glory of Lebanon," Isa. xxxv, 2. Lebanon was covered with snow, Jer. xviii, 14; some of it was barren, Isa. xxix, 17; a place for wild beasts, for "lions' dens," "the mountains of the leopards," Isa. xl, 16; Heb. ii, 17; Sol. Song iv, 8. It was the source of many streams, Sol. Song iv, 15. The groves and forests of goodly cedar and fir on Lebanon, and also its stones, were the chosen material with which King Solomon built the royal palace and the splendid temple of the Holy City, 1 Kings v, 5, 6, 8–10, 13–18; vii, 2–12. Solomon had "stores" in Lebanon, 1 Kings ix, 19. From the grand heights of this "tower of Lebanon" (Sol. Song vii, 4) the old Assyrian conquerors looked down upon the Holy Land, 2 Kings xix, 23. When the second temple was built the people "gave money . . . to bring cedar trees from Lebanon," Ezra iii, 7. The snows, the streams, the verdant forests, the richness and the grandeur of Lebanon, made it always to the Hebrews the emblem of wealth, of majesty, and of glory. See Psalm lxxii, 16; cxxxiii, 3; Sol. Song v, 15; Isa. xxxv, 2; lx, 13; Hosea xiv, 5, 6. Compare also Isa. x, 33, 34; xxix, 17; Jer. xx, 6, 23; Ezek. xxxi, 15.

PRESENT ASPECT, ETC.—Dean Stanley says: "From the moment that the traveler reaches the plain of Shechem in the interior, nay, even from the depths of the Jordan valley by the Dead Sea, the snowy heights of Hermon are visible."—*S. and P.*, page 395. Mr. Porter says that the view of Lebanon from the Mediterranean is "exceedingly grand," and that from the shores of Cyprus he saw its "glittering summits."—*Hand-book for Syria and Palestine.* "I have traveled in no part of the world where I have seen such a variety of glorious mountain scenes within so narrow a compass."—*Van de Velde.* The chief summits of Lebanon are, *Sunnin*, about 9,000 feet high, and *Jebel Mukhmel*, nearly 10,200 feet, which is the highest peak in Syria. The average height of the chain is 6,000 to 8,000 feet. The loftiest peak of Anti-Libanus is Hermon, boldly rising 10,000 feet. The average height of this range is about 5,000 feet. The valley of Cœle-Syria is drained by the river Litany, (or Leontes,) which has cut through Lebanon a most beautiful gorge. In the latter part of its course this stream passes through a wild chasm, whose banks in some places are more than a thousand feet high, "of naked rock, and almost perpendicular." "In wild grandeur this chasm has no equal in Syria, and few in the world." Anti-Lebanon is still a "well of living water," the four great rivers of Syria having here their source. The renowned cedars are found in a vast recess in the central ridge of Lebanon, about eight miles in diameter. They stand alone, with not another tree in sight, at an elevation of at least 6,000 feet above the Mediterranean. "The grove is now scarcely half a mile in circuit, and contains about four hundred trees of all sizes, the young ones mostly on the outskirts, and the oldest in the center. Only a few, perhaps a dozen, very ancient trees remain. There are, however, thirty or forty others of very considerable dimensions, some of them three, four, and five feet in diameter. One or two of the oldest are upward of forty feet in girth, but the trunks are short and irregular."—*Hand-book*, 1868. These trees grow less in number continually; and some travelers do not count so many as above stated. Dr. Thomson says: "I counted four hundred and forty-three; and this cannot be far from the true number." Cedars have been recently found also in other parts of the range. The western slopes of Lebanon are very beautiful, with "evergreen oaks and pines clothing the mountain's side, while fig-trees, vines, mulberry and olive trees abound on terraced heights or in picturesque glens. Corn is cultivated in every possible nook; villages nestle amid the cliffs; and convents crown the summits of wellnigh perpendicular rocks."—*Ayre*. Wild

beasts are, as always, numerous in the recesses of the range. Fossils abound in the rocks. Iron and coal have also been found. Compare Deut. viii, 9; xxxiii, 25. In the northern parts the mountain is peopled with Maronite Christians, numbering about 150,000, whose chief occupation is in rearing the silk-worm. Druses occupy the southern parts, and between these tribes there have been serious outbreaks. Anti-Libanus is more barren and more thinly peopled than the western range. The ruins of this region are very extensive, and full of interest. One of the most reliable and earnest explorers tells us that he has visited more than thirty temples in Lebanon and Anti-Lebanon; that "Greece itself cannot surpass in grandeur the temples of Ba'albek and Chalcis." (See Porter's *Damascus*.) The Pasha of Damascus holds this whole range under his authority.

Leb'aoth, *lionesses,* a town on the southern border of Judah, Josh. xv, 32. See BETH-BIREI and BETH-LEBAOTH.

Lebo'nah, (Map 5,) *frankincense,* a place mentioned in Judges xxi, 19 as a landmark to determine the position of Shiloh, which lay south of it. About three miles west of Shiloh is the small village of *Lubbân,* which is doubtless identical with Lebonah. Above its old gray houses are numbers of sepulchral caves, showing that it was a place of wealth and importance in the days of Israel's glory.

Le'cah, *a going, journey,* a term mentioned in 1 Chron. iv, 21, apparently as the name of a town. It appears to have been near Mareshah, but nothing is known of it.

Le'habim, or **Leha'bim,** *flames,* a Mizraite people, Gen. x, 13; 1 Chron. i, 11. They were probably identical with the ancient Lubim or Libyans, who perhaps first settled on the borders of the Nile, among or beside the Mizraim, but afterward occupied the vast territory known to classic geographers as Libya. See LUBIM.

Le'hi, *cheek,* or *jaw-bone,* a place in Judah, on the confines of Philistia, near the cliff Etam, where Samson slew a thousand Philistines with the jawbone of an ass, Judges xv, 9, 14, 19; in verse 19, "in the jaw " should be, "in Lehi." Samson having dispersed the Philistines, "cast away the jawbone, and called that place *Ramath-Lehi,*" which may be rendered "the casting away of the jaw-bone." This place is probably named in 2 Sam. xxiii, 11, though in the A. V. rendered "in a troop." The site of Lehi is unknown, although several attempts have been made to identify it.

Le'shem, a *precious stone,* perhaps *opal* or *jacinth,* a variation in the form of Laish, Josh. xix, 47.

Letu'shim, (Map 12,) *the hammered, sharpened,* the name of the second of the sons of Dedan, son of Jokshan, Gen. xxv, 3. He founded a tribe who dwelt in Arabia east of Edom.

Leum'mim, (Map 12,) *peoples,* the name of the third of the descendants of Dedan, son of Jokshan, Gen. xxv, 3. Ptolemy mentions a tribe in Arabia Felix called Allumœoti, which appears to be a corruption of the old Hebrew Leummim with the Arabic article prefixed. In Arabia Deserta was a city called Lama, which possibly, may have been an ancient settlement of this tribe.

Le'vites, (from Levi, *a joining,*) the descendants of the patriarch Levi. They were chosen by God (Num. iii, 6-13; xvi, 9; Deut. x, 8; 1 Chron. xv, 2) as a reward for their zeal, Exod. xxxii, 26-28; Deut. xxxiii, 9, 10; Mal. ii, 4, 5. They were taken instead of the children of Israel, Num. iii, 12, 41-45; viii, 14, 16-18; xviii, 6. The cattle of the Levites were taken instead of the firstlings of Israel, Num. iii, 41, 45.

Moses was ordered to take the Levites from among the children of Israel and cleanse them by purification, Num. viii, 6, 7, 21; by sacrifices, Num. viii, 8, 12; by imposition of the elders' hands, and being presented to God as an offering by the high-priest for the people, Num. viii, 9-20. Their punishment for encroaching on the priestly office, Num iv, 19, 20; xvi, 1-35, 40; xviii, 3. They were governed by chiefs, 2 Chron. xxxv, 9; Ezra viii, 29; Neh. xi, 22. They entered upon their service at twenty-five years of age, Num. viii, 24; at twenty years, after David's time, 1 Chron. xxiii, 24, 27; Ezra iii, 8; upon full service at thirty years, Num. iv, 3, 30, 47; 1 Chron. xxiii, 3; superannuated at fifty years, Num. iv, 47; viii, 25, 26. The tribe of Levi was composed of three great families, the Kohathites, the Gershonites, and the Merarites. The first were to have charge of the sacred vessels; the second, of the hangings and curtains of the Tabernacle;

while the last had the care and custody of the boards and pillars thereof. Such division of work suited a movable camp, but it would not suit a settled nation. Hence Moses made other assignments of duty to the Levites. See Deut. xvii, 8–12; comp. xxvii, 14; xxxi, 9, 26.

In the march of Israel the Levites were in the center, Num. ii, 17; they encamped round the tabernacle, Num. i, 50–53; iii, 23, 35. They lodged round the temple while in attendance, 1 Chron. ix, 27, 33; and the nightwatch employed Psalm cxxxiv as a song. They were at liberty to reside and minister at the temple instead of in their cities, and provision was made for them, Deut. xviii, 6–8.

The name Levite was used for a particular class, Ezra x, 23, 24; Neh. vii, 1, 73. The Levites led the exalted strain of praise after the captivity, Neh. ix, 6–38. Mention is made of them in the prophecies, Isa. lxvi, 21; Jer. xxxiii, 18; Ezek. xliv, 10–14; Mal. iii, 3. Brief mention is made of the Levites in the New Testament, Luke x, 32; John i, 19; Acts iv, 36.

Lib'anus, the Greek form of Lebanon, Esdras iv, 48; v, 55; 2 Esdras xv, 20; Judith i, 7; Ecclus. xxiv, 13; l, 12.

Lib'nah, (Map 2,) *whiteness.*

1. A station of the Israelites in the desert, Num. xxxiii, 20. The site is unknown.

2. A city in the lowlands of Judah, apparently between Makkedah and Lachish, which was one of the cities captured by Joshua after the defeat of the confederate kings at Gibeon, Josh. x, 29, 31, 32, 39; xii, 15; xv, 42. It was allotted to the priests, Josh. xxi, 13; 1 Chron. vi, 57. In the days of King Joram Libnah revolted, 2 Kings viii, 22; 2 Chron. xxi, 10. This city was besieged by Sennacherib; and it was while his army was encamped before it that the angel of the Lord smote of the Assyrians a hundred fourscore and five thousand, 2 Kings xix, 35; Isa. xxxvii, 8–36. Zedekiah's mother was of Libnah, Jer. lii, 1. It is suggested by Van de Velde and others that Libnah may have stood on the conspicuous isolated hill called *Arak el-Menshieh,* five miles west of Eleutherpolis, and on the direct route from Makkedah to Eglon. On this hill is a village with a few ruins.

Lib'ya, (Map 1,) (Hebrew, Phut, *affected,* or perhaps *a bow,*) the part of Africa north-west of Egypt, Jer. xlvi, 9; Ezek. xxxviii, 5; Acts ii, 10. For Libya of the O. T. see PHUT; for Libya of the N. T. see LUBIM.

Lib'yans, Dan. xi, 43, inaccurately for LUBIM.

Lod, (Map 5,) *strife* (?) a town of Benjamin, 1 Chron. viii, 12; Ezra ii, 33; Neh. vii, 37; xi, 35. Now *Ludd.* See LYDDA.

Lo-De'bar, *without pasture,* a town of Gilead beyond Jordan, 2 Sam. ix, 5; xvii, 27. It was probably near Mahanaim; possibly "of Debir," Josh. xiii, 26, signifies Lodebar. The site is unknown.

Lu'bim, and **Lu'bims,** *dwellers in a scorched land,* (in Dan. xi, 43, Libyans,) an African people named with Cushites and Sukkiim, 2 Chron. xii, 3; xvi, 8; Nahum iii, 9. They are probably the same as the LEHABIM, (which see,) and located north-west of Egypt, the inhabitants of the great province of Libya. Early geographers used the name Libya in a somewhat vague sense, making it sometimes include all Africa, sometimes all except Egypt, and sometimes that region lying immediately on the west side of Egypt. The Greeks knew the boundaries of Egypt, and they gave the name Libya vaguely to the rest of the continent, just as they called the whole of Southern Syria, Palestine, from the Philistines. Herodotus classes the Ethiopians and Libyans together as do the sacred writers. In Acts ii, 10, Luke mentions some of these people as "dwellers in the parts of Libya about Cyrene." See CYRENE; PHUT.

Lud, perhaps *strife* or *inhabitants of the desert*, a people in Asia Minor called Ludi or Lydians, descended from a son of Shem named Lud, Gen. x, 22 ; 1 Chron. i, 17. Their original settlements were probably in Armenia, but they seem to have migrated westward and driven out the Mæonians, who inhabited the tract between the rivers Hermus and Mæander; which was from this eastern race denominated Lydia. They were brave and warlike, and their service was sought by the Tyrians, Isa. lxvi, 19; Ezek. xxvii, 10. In Judith ii, 23, though the word is coupled with Phud, (that is, Phut,) the Lydians are probably meant.

Lu'dim, (Map 12,) a people descended from Mizraim, the second son of Ham, Gen. x, 13; 1 Chron. i, 11. They are distinct from the Shemite tribe of Lud, which is noticed in the preceding article. The country of Ludim is not satisfactorily identified. This people seem to have been an African nation, and were probably settled in Lower Egypt, north of Memphis. They probably retained, to some extent, a distinct name, and certain distinctive peculiarities in laws and mode of life, like the Maronites or Druzes in Northern Syria.

Lu'hith, THE ASCENT OF. Luhith signifies *made of boards or posts*. This place seems to have been some famous pass, either on the way up to Moab from the great valley of the Arabah, or across some of its deep and wild ravines, probably the latter, Isa. xv, 5; Jer. xlviii, 5.

Luz, *almond-tree* or *hazel?*
1. A town near to which Jacob rested and had a prophetic vision. It was close to or identical with Bethel, Gen. xxviii, 29; xxxv, 6; xlviii, 3; Josh. xvi, 2; xviii, 13; Judg. i, 23. See BETHEL.
2. A city in the "land of the Hittites," Judg. i, 26. It was built by the man who had betrayed the ancient Luz to the Ephraimites. There is much conjecture concerning the locality both of Luz and the Hittites. Mr. Porter says, (in *Kitto,*) "The Hittites appear to have retired before the Israelites to Northern Syria and settled in the mountains and on the banks of the Orontes; Probably Luz was situated somewhere in that region."

Lycao'nia, (Map 8,) a province of Asia Minor. Its length was about twenty geographical miles from east to west, and its breadth about thirteen. When visited by Paul it was a Roman province, Acts xiv, 6; xvi, 1–6; xviii, 23; xix, 1. Its chief towns were Iconium, the capital, Lystra, and Derbe. "The speech of the Lycaonians" (Acts xiv, 11) is supposed by some to have been the ancient Assyrian language, also spoken by the Cappadocians; but it is more usually conceived to have been a corrupt Greek, intermingled with many Syriac words.

Lyc'ia, (Map 8,) a province in the south-west of Asia Minor, opposite tne island of Rhodes. Phrygia lay on the north, Pamphylia on the east, Caria on the west, and the Mediterranean on the south. Lycia is named in 1 Macc. xv, 23, as one of the countries to which the Roman Senate sent its missive in favor of the Jews. Two of the towns of Lycia are mentioned in the New Testament, Patara, Acts xxi, 1, 2; Myra, Acts xxvii, 5. The Lycians were a warlike people, powerful on the sea, and attached to their independence, which they successfully maintained against Crœsus, king of Lydia, and were afterward allowed by the Persians to retain their own kings as satraps. The victory of the Romans over Antiochus (B. C. 189) gave Lycia rank as a free state, which rank it maintained till the time of Claudius, when it was made a

LUDD, (ANCIENT LYDDA.) RUINS OF THE CHURCH OF ST. GEORGE.

province of the Roman empire. At first it was combined with Pamphylia, but at a later period of the empire it was a separate province, with Myra for its capital. Curious and very ancient architectural remains have been found in this province, many specimens of which have been placed in the British Museum.

Lyd'da, (Maps 5, 20,) the Greek form of LOD, which see. It was called by the Romans Diospolis. Lod was one of the ancient cities of Palestine, 1 Chron. viii, 12. It was twelve miles from Joppa, on the road to Jerusalem. The place was occupied again immediately after the captivity, Ezra ii, 33; Neh. viii, 37. About 145 B. C. the district of Lydda, with two others adjoining, was separated from Samaria and annexed to Judea. See 1 Macc. xi, 30-34. After the death of Julius Cæsar, Cassius Longinus, who commanded in Palestine, sold the whole people of Lydda into slavery. Antony, however, a short time afterward set them at liberty and restored them to their homes. Its chief interest to us is in its New Testament history. Here it was that Peter wrought the great miracle of healing upon the paralytic Eneas, by reason of which great multitudes, both in Lydda and the neighborhood, were converted to the faith, Acts ix, 32-38. Under the Romans the city became wealthy, and it was a seat of Jewish learning.

The modern name is *Ludd*. The village contains about one thousand inhabitants. Although the houses are small and poor, and its lanes dirty, yet there is an air of thrift about the place not often seen in Palestine. It is said that St. George was born and buried here, and the traveler finds the remains of a splendid church dedicated to his memory.

Lyd'ia, (Map 8,) a maritime province in the west of Asia Minor, 1 Macc. viii, 12. In Ezek. xxx, 5, it is incorrectly put for Lud, with which it has no connection. Lydia was the center of that dominion of which Crœsus was the last king. In later times Antiochus the Great, King of Syria, was compelled by the Romans to yield it to Eumenes, King of Pergamos; and after the death of Attalus III. it came under the immediate authority of Rome, and was made part of the province of Asia. See LUD and LUDIM. For its towns see PHILADELPHIA, SARDIS, THYATIRA.

Lyd'ians, an inaccurate rendering of Ludim, Jer. xlvi, 9.

Lys'tra, (Map 8,) a city in Lycaonia, in Asia Minor, near to Derbe. Lystra and Derbe stood on the great road leading from Cilicia to Iconium. When Paul and Barnabas were persecuted at Iconium "they fled unto Lystra and Derbe, and unto the region that lieth round about," Acts xiv, 6. At Lystra Paul healed a cripple; and this occurrence produced such an impression on the superstitious people that they offered divine honors to the apostles, Acts xiv, 8-16. Here also Paul was stoned and left for dead, verse 19. On his recovery he withdrew with Barnabas to Derbe, but soon retraced his steps through Lystra, encouraging the new disciples to be steadfast, verses 20. 21. Lystra was the home of Timotheus, 1 Tim. iii, 10, 11.

This city is mentioned by Strabo and Ptolemy, but its position is not defined. Yet there are strong reasons for identifying its site with the ruins called *Bin-bir-Kilissi*, (*the thousand and one churches*,) on the eastern declivity of a lofty mountain south-east from Iconium. Here are the remains of a great number of churches.

Ma'acah, *oppression*, a small kingdom east of Argob and Bashan, Deut. iii, 14; Josh. xii, 5; 2 Sam. x, 6, 8; called also Maachah and Syria-Maachah,

1 Chron. xix, 6, 7. The people were descended from Nahor, Gen. xxii, 24. It is not clear whether any connection subsisted between this kingdom and Abel-Beth-Maachah.

Maach'athi and **Maach'athites,** the people of the preceding place, Deut. iii, 14; Josh. xii, 5; xiii, 11, 13; 2 Sam. xxiii, 34; 2 Kings xxv, 23; 1 Chron. iv, 19; Jer. xl, 8.

Maal'eh-Acrab'bim, *the ascent of scorpions,* Josh. xv, 3. See AKRABBIM.

Ma'arath, *a naked* or *open place,* a town in the highlands of Judah, Josh. xv, 58. Lieut. Conder identifies it (1875) with an ancient site south of *Beit Ain'um* (Beth Anoth.)

Mac'alon, 1 Esdras v, 21, a corruption of Michmash, Ezra ii, 27.

Mac'cabees, THE, (Map 15,) from Maccabeus, which probably signifies *a hammer.* This was the surname of Judas, the son of Mattathias, who gave his name to the heroic family of which he was one of the noblest representatives, 1 Macc. ii, 4. The Maccabees were also called Asmonæans or Hasmonæans, doubtless from Chasmon, the great-grandfather of Mattathias; but some derive the term from a Hebrew word signifying *fat,* that is, nobles or princes, Psa. lxviii, 31. The title Maccabees was also applied to the Palestinian martyrs in the persecution of Antiochus Epiphanes, and even to the Alexandrine Jews who suffered for their faith at an earlier period.

In the general persecution of the Jews by the Syrians, God raised up for them a deliverer in the noble family of the Asmonæans. The standard of independence was first raised by Mattathias, and the noble war for the rights of opinion was carried on for twenty-six years by his illustrious sons—counting from the first stroke at Modin—with five successive kings of Syria. Judas Maccabeus succeeded his father in the year 166 B. C., and soon gained a victory over the Syrians which made him master of Judea. The war was still waged, and it was not till the year 142 B. C. that Jewish freedom was established, under Simon the brother of Judas. Simon transmitted his power and the pontifical dignity to his son Hyrcanus, whose son and successor, Aristobulus, assumed the title of king. His brother, Alexander Jannæus, succeeded, and after his death a civil war was waged between his sons Hyrcanus and Aristobulus—the last named of whom was defeated by the Romans under Pompey—and with Antigonus, his son, the dynasty ended, in the year 40 B. C. The last two members of the family were Aristobulus and Mariamne, grandchildren of Aristobulus II.; and with the death of Mariamne the Maccabean race may be said to be extinguished. The first and second books of Maccabees are full of interest in reference to these princes and the wars above noted. See JERUSALEM.

Macedo'nia, (Map 8,) the well-known country on the north of Greece. In the Apocrypha it is denoted by Chittim, 1 Macc. i, 1. Its boundaries varied at different periods. After the time of Philip it reached on the east to the Ægean Sea and the frontiers of Thrace; on the north it was separated from Mœsia by a mountain chain, and similarly from Illyricum on the north-west and west; on the south it bordered on Thessaly and the Ægean. Under Philip it rose to great power. His son Alexander subdued the chief part of the then known world. Daniel describes his empire, Dan. viii, 5–8, 21. Coins still exist representing Macedonia under the symbol denoted by the prophet. The Romans conquered this province in 167 B. C., and it was at first declared free; but after being divided into four districts, of which Amphipolis, Thessalonica, Pella, and Pelagonia were the chief towns it became, 142 B. C., a single Roman proconsular province, and so remained till the reign of Tiberius. Afterward a change was made, and from the time of Claudius Macedonia and Achaia comprehended the whole of Greece, Rom. xv, 26; 2 Cor. ix, 2; 1 Thess. i, 8.

In Acts xvi, 9-12, is recorded Paul's vision concerning Macedonia. Paul afterward made several visits to that country in his missionary journeys, Acts xx. 1, 3; 2 Cor. ii, 13; vii, 5; 1 Tim. i, 3. The Macedonians were commended for their liberality to the saints of Jerusalem, and to Paul. Rom. xv, 26; 2 Cor. viii, 1-5; xi, 9. See also Acts xix, 22, 29; xxvii, 2. For other details see the cities above named, and APOLLONIA, BEREA, NEAPOLIS, PHILIPPI.

Macedo'nian, Acts xxvii, 2, an inhabitant of Macedonia.

Machæ'rus, (Map 5,) the place where John the Baptist was imprisoned and beheaded, nine miles east of the northern part of the Dead Sea, Mark vi 21-29. Tristram identifies it among extensive ruins at *M'Khuar*.

Mach'benah, *a cloak*, probably a town of Judah, of which Sheva was the "father," that is, the founder, 1 Chron. ii, 49. Its site is wholly unknown.

Ma'chirites THE, from Machir, *sold*. The descendants of Machir, the father of Gilead, Num. xxiv, 29.

Mach'mas, 1 Macc. ix, 73, the Greek form of Michmash.

Machpe'lah, *portion, lot*, or, probably, *double cave*, the spot in Hebron containing the field in which was the cave purchased by Abraham from the sons of Heth. This cave became the burial-place of Sarah, Abraham, Isaac, Rebekah, Leah, and Jacob, Gen. xxiii, 19; xlix, 29-32; l, 12, 13 It still exists, but very few besides Mohammedans are permitted to visit it. It is inclosed by a very ancient structure called *El Haram*, standing on the declivity of a hill, the town of Hebron lying for the most part below to the south and west. The whole building is about two hundred feet long, one hundred and fifteen broad, and fifty high. Within the exterior edifice is a large mosque, once perhaps a Christian church, and beneath the dome is the cave. In this mosque are the six tombs, possibly over the places where the actual sarcophagi lie in the cave below. The interior of the mosque was described about sixty years ago by a Spanish renegade who assumed the named of Ali Bey. A fuller account of it has recently been given by Dr. Stanley who accompanied the Prince of Wales in his visit to the *Haram* in 1862. See Stanley's *Sermons in the East*, and *Lectures on the Jewish Church*. His account has been supplemented by Mr. Ferguson, and more recently by the Marquis of Bute, who was conducted through the building in 1866. In the inner porticoes and inside the mosque are chapels or shrines containing the tombs of the patriarchs, these tombs being the monuments or cenotaphs in honor of the dead who lie beneath. Thus are shown in the outer portico the shrines of Abraham and Sarah, which are guarded by massive silver gates. Within the mosque are the tombs of Isaac and Rebekah, guarded by gates grated with iron bars. The shrines of Jacob and Leah are shown in recesses, corresponding to those of Abraham and Sarah, but in a separate cloister opposite the entrance of the mosque.

As to the cave itself all attempts to enter it have been thus far successfully resisted by Moslem prejudices. It is considered highly probable that some remains of the patriarchs, especially of the embalmed body of Jacob, still lie in the cave. This tomb is undoubtedly accessible to the guards of the mosque, but whether even they venture to enter it is very doubtful

Time will yet, doubtless, throw open mosque and cave alike to all. See HEBRON.

Mad'ai, (Map 12,) *middle land*, the name of one of the sons of Japheth, Gen. x, 2; 1 Chron. i, 5. It is extremely probable that the nation of the Medes is intended. See MEDES, MEDIA.

Ma'dian, Judg. ii, 26; Acts vii, 29. The Greek form of MIDIAN.

Madman'nah, *a dunghill*, one of the towns in the south of Judah, Josh. xv, 31; 1 Chron. ii, 49. In the time of Eusebius and Jerome it was called Menoïs. Probably it is identical with the modern *el-Minydy*, a town about fifteen miles south-south-west of Gaza.

Mad'men, *a dunghill*, a place in Moab, threatened with destruction in the denunciations of Jeremiah, Jer. xlviii, 2. Of its history or site nothing is known. In Isa. xxv, 10, margin, the term is used as an appellative.

Madme'nah, *a dunghill*, a place in Benjamin, north of Jerusalem, the inhabitants of which were frightened away by the approach of Sennacherib's army, Isa. x, 31. In Isa. xxv, 10, margin, this term is employed, while the text translates it as an appellative. If the prophet refers to a place, possibly he alludes to Madmen, the preceding town, in Moab.

Ma'don, *contention*, a Canaanite city, probably in the north of Palestine, captured by Joshua, Josh. xi, 1; xii, 19. Nothing is known of it.

Mag'bish, *a gathering* or *freezing*. In Ezra ii, 30, it is stated that the children of Magbish returned from captivity. In the corresponding list in Neh. vii, the name is wanting. Whether Magbish is the name of a man or of a place is uncertain, but it more probably refers to a place—apparently in the tribe of Benjamin.

Mag'dala, (Map 5,) *a tower*, accurately Magadan, according to the chief MSS. and versions. Syrian villages often have two names, and sometimes the same name has different forms. Magdala appears to have been substituted for the original and more accurate form. In Matt. xv, 39, it is said that Christ took ship and came into the "coast of Magdala." The parallel passage in Mark viii, 10, has the "ports of Dalmanutha." Magdala was situated on the western shore of the Sea of Galilee, and Dalmanutha was probably a village near it. Mary called Magdalene was probably a native of Magdala.

The small village of *Mejdel*, which stands on the shore, three miles north of Tiberias, is doubtless identical with Magdala. It now contains about twenty miserable huts, standing amid low, shapeless mounds, which apparently cover the remains of the ancient houses.

Ma'ged, 1 Macc. v, 36. See MAKED.

Magid'do, 1 Esdras i, 29, the Greek form of Megiddo

Ma'gog, (Map 12,) perhaps *the place*, or *region of Gog*; or, it may be, *great mountain*. Magog was a tribe of the sons of Japheth, Gen. x, 2; 1 Chron. i, 5. In the prophecies of Ezekiel we may gather some notion of the greatness of this people, Ezek. xxxviii, xxxix. From the Apocalypse we learn that Gog and Magog represent the entire antichristian powers of the whole earth, Rev. xx, 8, 9. A wide-spread tradition of the Jews made these two terms synonymous with the aggregate powers of evil as opposed to the kingdom of God. Magog was used by Ezekiel undoubtedly as referring to the more modern Scythians—those numerous tribes living north of the Caucasus. Ancient writers speak of their extended conquests. They made their name a terror to the whole Eastern World. Although they pressed through Palestine (in the seventh century B. C.) toward Egypt, God preserved the Jews from their fury. They were bribed off by the Egyptian king, and at last driven back about 596 B. C.

Mahana'im, (Map 5,) *camps* or *double camp,* a town east of the Jordan and on the north bank of the Jabbok, lying in the territory of Gad. It was the scene of the wrestling of Jacob, Gen. xxxii, 2. The place was afterward assigned to the Levites, Josh. xiii, 26, 30; xxi, 38; 1 Chron. vi, 80. Abner established Ish-Bosheth at Mahanaim, 2 Sam. ii, 8, 12, 29. Here David had his headquarters during Absalom's rebellion, and here he made his lamentation, 2 Sam. xvii, 24, 27; xix, 39; 1 Kings ii, 8. Solomon had a commissariat officer here, 1 Kings iv, 14. In Sol. Song vi, 13, allusion is made to Mahanaim as if still a place of repute for sanctity.

Its site is thought by some high authorities to be identical with a ruin called *Mahneh* in the *Jebel Ajlân,* north of the Yarmûk. But the distance of this ruin from the Jordan and from the *Yarmûk* (Jabbok) does not seem to accord with the Bible narrative. Some of the passages above referred to show that the town was walled, and large enough to contain the "thousands" who followed David thither. According to Josephus Mahanaim was a strong and beautiful city, and anciently one of the most important cities east of the Jordan. Says Mr. Porter: "It would seem strange that a holy place and a strongly fortified city, such as Mahanaim, should have abruptly disappeared from history, and have left no trace behind except a poor village. May it not be, therefore, that the ruins of *Gerasa* occupy the site of Mahanaim? (Map 20.) The situation would suit the Scripture narrative. The ancient history of Gerasa is unknown. . . . The ruins of Gerasa are the most splendid east of the Jordan."

Ma'haneh-Dan, *camp of Dan,* the place where the Danites assembled and encamped before going against Laish. It was "behind Kirjath-Jearim," Judg. xviii, 12; and "between Zorah and Eshtaol," xiii, 25. Possibly this last reference may be to another camp of Dan. Kirjath-Jearim is identified with tolerable certainty in *Kuriet-el-Enab,* and Zorah in *Sur'a,* about seven miles south-west of it. But no site has yet been suggested for Eshtaol which would be compatible with the above conditions, and no satisfactory site for Mahaneh-Dan has been found.

Mah'lites, THE, from Mahli, *sickly.* The descendants of Mahli the son of Merari, Num. iii, 33; xxvi, 58.

Ma'kaz, *end,* a place mentioned in describing the district allotted to the second of Solomon's purveyors, 1 Kings iv, 9. It seems to have been situated on the western slopes of the mountains of Judah, but it is not identified.

Ma'ked a city in Gilead into which the Jews were driven by the Ammonites, and from which they were delivered by Judas Maccabeus, 1 Macc. v, 26, 36. In verse 36 it is written Maged. The site is unknown.

Makhe'loth, *assemblies, choirs,* one of the encampments in the wilderness, Num. xxxiii, 25. Unknown.

Makke'dah, or **Mak'kedah,** probably *place of shepherds,* a city in the low country of Judah, whither the defeated Canaanites were pursued by the Israelites in the battle of Beth-Horon. Here was a cave in which the five confederate fugitive kings hid themselves. Stones were rolled on the mouth of the cave, and the pursuit of the multitude continued until they that remained "entered into fenced cities." Then Joshua returned to the cave, opened it, slew the kings, and 'hanged them on five trees," Josh. x, 10, 16, 17, 20, 21, 26, 28, 29; xii, 16; xv, 41. Eusebius and Jerome locate this city about eight miles from Eleutheropolis toward the east. Mr. Porter, in 1857, found, about eight miles north-east of Eleutheropolis, a small village called *el-Kledinh*, not far from Jarmuth, in the hill-side near which were numerous large caves. This, Porter thinks, may mark the site of Makkedah; yet its distance of twenty miles from Beth-Horon he admits may be an objection. (See *Kitto*.) Captain Warren (*Our Work in Palestine*, 1873) suggests that the village of *El Mughár*, (the cave,) lying less than eight miles from Ramleh, has the modern name of the ancient Makkedah, and he proposes that further researches be made at this place.

Mak'tesh, *a mortar,* a quarter or suburb of Jerusalem specially denounced by the prophet, Zeph. i, 11. It seems to have been a valley somewhat in the shape of a "mortar." The Targum refers it to the valley of Kidron. The best modern authorities generally concur in supposing Maktesh to mean the Tyropœon, a deep valley in the center of the city, where the shops and principal places of business were and still are situated.

Mal'los, a place in Cilicia, twenty miles from Tarsus. Its inhabitants revolted from Antiochus Epiphanes because he had given them to his concubine Antiochis, 2 Macc. iv, 30.

Mam're, perhaps *fruitfulness, fat.* This term occurs as the name of a man; but also, and first, as the name of a place, the "plain of Mamre which is in Hebron," Gen. xiii, 18; "the oak grove of Mamre the Amorite," Gen. xiv, 13. Mamre was one of Abraham's favorite places of residence, and it was here that he entertained the three angels, and here that he received the first distinct promise of a son, Gen. xviii, 1, 10, 14. Five times Moses states that Machpelah lay "before Mamre," see Gen. xxiii, 17, 19; xxv, 9; xlix, 30; l, 13. '[See MACHPELAH.] If the field and cave where the patriarchs were buried were on the hill which forms the north-eastern side of the Valley of Hebron—of which there is no doubt—then Mamre must have been within sight of, or "facing," the cave of Machpelah, which is now covered by the great *Haram*, and so near the town of Hebron that it could be described as *at* it. See HEBRON.

Man'ahath, *rest,* a Benjamite place mentioned only in 1 Chron. viii, 6. The passage in which the name occurs is very obscure, and the site of the place is wholly unknown.

Mana'hethites, THE, a people mentioned in two obscure passages giving the descendants of Caleb of the tribe of Judah, 1 Chron. ii, 52, 54. The preceding town of Manahath would naturally suggest itself as the home of this tribe; but that was of Benjamin. No satisfactory location can be assigned the tribe or their city.

Manas'seh, (Map 5,) *forgetting,* or, who *makes forget.* (In Rev. vii, 6, Manasses.) One of the tribes of Israel sprung from the elder son of Joseph, Gen. xli, 51; xlvi, 20. For the course pursued by Joseph in his anxiety to obtain the recognition of his sons, Manasseh and Ephraim, as interested in the covenant blessing, see EPHRAIM, and compare Gen. xlviii. In spite of Joseph's efforts Manasseh, although the elder son, was degraded into the second place. The same inferiority is reiterated in the last words of Moses; "They are the ten thousands of Ephraim, and they are the thousands of Manasseh," Deut. xxxiii, 17.

During the march from Egypt to Canaan the position of the tribe of

Manasseh was, with Ephraim and Benjamin, on the west of the Tabernacle, Num. ii, 18, 20; x, 22, 23. At the census at Sinai it numbered 32,200, Num. i, 34, 35. Forty years later, on the banks of the Jordan, the tribe had increased to 52,700. On this occasion it is remarkable that Manasseh resumes his position in the catalogue as the eldest son of Joseph. Possibly this is due to the prowess which the tribe had shown in the conquest of Gilead, for Manasseh was certainly at this time the most distinguished of all the tribes.

As the Israelites drew near the end of their wanderings, and when the districts east of the Jordan, ruled over by Sihon and Og, were being subdued, the tribes of Reuben and Gad, who possessed much cattle and saw that the land of Gilead was a place for cattle, desired that Moses would there assign them their inheritance, engaging to aid by a large auxiliary force in the conquest of western Canaan, Num. xxxii, 1–32. Part of the tribe of Manasseh were joined with them. They seem to have been bold, warlike men, delighting in adventure, who attacked and conquered the difficult country to the north, with the singular region of Argob, Num. xxxii, 33, 39–42; Deut. iii, 13–15; Josh. xvii, 1. This then was the territory of trans-Jordanic Manasseh; it extended from Mahanaim northward, including half Gilead, and the kingdom of Bashan, Josh. xiii, 29–31. This region is described by travelers as for the most part beautiful in its aspect, diversified by mountains, hills, and valleys, and fertile for the subsistence of those who were settled in it. It was, indeed, the richest tract of all Palestine, it being to this day the granary of a great part of Syria. Of the cities belonging to it, Golan, Ashtaroth, and Edrei are particularly mentioned, of which the two former were made Levitical cities, Golan being also a city of refuge, Josh. xx, 8; xxi, 27; 1 Chron. vi, 71. See ARGOB. The inheritance of the other half of the tribe was on the west of the Jordan. Their allotment is not very accurately defined in the Bible. It lay on the north side of Ephraim, and included the northern section of the hills of Samaria. The border between Ephraim and Manasseh could not have been far to the north of the city of Samaria, as Michmethah, one of its landmarks, is said to lie before Shechem, Josh. xvii, 7. Farther west, the tribes were separated by the river Kanah. Manasseh's lot extended across the whole country, from the Mediterranean to the Jordan, as is stated by Josephus, and as may be inferred from Josh. xvii, 9, 11. Manasseh and Ephraim appear to have been almost joined together as one tribe; and they complained to Joshua that though they were "a great people" yet only "one portion" had been allotted to them, Josh. xvii, 14. It was true that the great cities of Beth-Shean, Taanach, Megiddo, and Dor, with their rich environs, had been assigned to them out of Issachar, yet they pleaded that these cities were strong, their inhabitants warlike, and that they had chariots of iron; but Joshua tells them that it is for this very reason the cities were assigned to them, and that the extension of their territory depended on their own valor, Josh. xvii, 17, 18. When the Israelites were fully established in Palestine, these towns were made tributary, and the land attached to them was probably taken possession of, though the old inhabitants were never completely expelled, Judg. i, 27. Dor became one of the cities of Phœnicia, and Beth-Shean was an independent fortress in the time of David, 1 Sam. xxxi, 10. The home of the western Manassites was in the rich valleys of Mount Ephraim, and along the wooded heights of Carmel, Josh. xvii, 15.

This section of the tribe of Manasseh almost disappears from history immediately after its settlement. Subsequent notices of it are brief and unimportant, 1 Chron. xxvii, 20, 21; 2 Chron. xv, 9; xxx, 11. This may be accounted for by its close connection with Ephraim, which soon became the dominant tribe in the northern division of Palestine. Ephraim and Manasseh are usually grouped together, 2 Chron. xxxi, 1; xxxiv, 6, 9; and seem to have been regarded in later times as forming one people.

The Manassites east of the Jordan were for a long period the guardians of the eastern frontier of Israel, keeping in check the border tribes; and when, in consequence of national sin, the whole land groaned under the iron yoke of the Midianites and the Amorites, two warriors of Manasseh—Gideon and Jephthah—drove back with terrible slaughter the cruel tyrants, and freed Israel, Judges vi; xi. Located on the north-eastern border, the Manassites suffered severely from the growing power and ambition of the monarchs of Damascus; and they were among the first who were subdued and led captive by the Assyrians. With the Reubenites and Gadites they were taken away to Hela, Habor, and the river Gozan, 1 Chron. v, 26. After the captivity some of them seem to have settled in Jerusalem, 1 Chron. ix, 3.

Manas'ses, the Greek form of Manasseh, Rev. vii, 6.

Manas'sites, the members of the tribe of Manasseh, Deut. iv, 43; Judg. xii, 4; 2 Kings x, 33.

Ma'on, *habitation,* a town in Judah which gave name to a wilderness where David hid himself from Saul, and around which Nabal had great possessions, Josh. xv, 55; 1 Sam. xxiii, 24, 25; xxv, 2. Dr. Robinson identifies the site with the present village of *Main,* which is about seven miles south of Hebron. A few ruins are found on the top of a conical hill.

Ma'onites, THE, (Hebrew, Maon,) an Arabian tribe mentioned with the Amalekites, Judg. x, 12. They are identical with the Mehunims noticed in 2 Chron. xxvi, 7. They are also probably intended in the term translated "habitations" in 1 Chron. iv, 41. The Maonites may possibly be traced to a residence in Maon, now *Main,* in Judah. But, leaving their name at this place, these Maonites migrated eastward, probably making their head-quarters at Beth-Meon, on the plateau of Moab; and also at the large modern village of *Ma'ân,* on the eastern border of Edom, about fifteen miles east of Petra. This village is one of the most important stations on the route from Damascus to Mecca. Remains of antiquity are found among the modern houses.

Ma'rah, (Map 2,) *bitterness,* a station three days' journey from the place where the Israelites crossed the Red Sea. Here was a well whose waters were exceedingly bitter. The Lord showed Moses a tree, "which when he had cast into the waters, the waters were made sweet." Exod. xv, 22–25; Num. xxxiii, 8, 9. Palmer identifies Marah with *'Ain Hawwarah,* a spring of bitter water three days from *Ayûn Mûsa.* (See SHUR.) *Hawwarah* signifies "a small pool, the water of which sinks into the soil little by little, leaving the residue unfit to drink." Between the two stations noted above an unvaried desert plain extends, entirely without water. Palmer says: "The soil about this part of the country, being strongly impregnated with *natrûn,* produces none but bitter or brackish water; and it is worth observing that the first of these springs with which we meet . . . is reached on the third day of our desert journey to Sinai." See *Desert of the Exodus.*

Mar'alah, *trembling,* a landmark on the boundary of Zebulun, Josh. xix, 11. Mr. Porter rejects Keil's attempt to locate Maralah on Carmel as entirely against the plain indications of Scripture, and conjectures that its site may be identical with the little village of *M'alûl*, on the top of a hill about four miles south-west of Nazareth. The ruins of a temple, with other vestiges of antiquity, are here found.

Mare'shah, *place at the top* or *head*, or perhaps *possession*, a city in the low country of Judah, Josh. xv, 44. It was fortified by Rehoboam, 2 Chron. xi, 8. Asa defeated the Ethiopian king, Zerah, near this place, 2 Chron. xiv, 9, 10; see also 1 Chron. ii, 42; iv, 21, where possibly this town may be intended. This was the native place of Eliezer the prophet, 2 Chron. xx, 37. The prophet Micah includes this city among the towns which he attempts to rouse to a sense of their danger, Micah i, 15. It was laid desolate by Judas Maccabeus on his march from Hebron to Ashdod, 1 Macc. v, 65–68. Josephus mentions Mareshah among the places possessed by Alexander Jannæus, which had been in the hands of the Syrians; but by Pompey it was restored to the former inhabitants and attached to the province of Syria. It was rebuilt by Gabinius, but was again destroyed by the Parthians in their irruption against Herod. About a mile and a half south of Eleutheropolis Dr. Robinson found a remarkable tell, or artificial hill, on which were the foundations of some buildings, and these, he believes, may mark the site of Mareshah.

Mar'isa, the Greek form of Mareshah, 2 Macc. xii, 35.

Ma'roth, *bitterness*, *bitter fountains*, one of the towns in the western lowlands of Judah, Micah i, 12. Unknown.

Mars' Hill. Acts xvii, 19, margin, 22. See AREOPAGUS.

Mar Sab'a, (Map 6,) a noted convent on the road from Jerusalem to the Dead Sea. See KIDRON.

Mas'aloth, mentioned in 1 Macc. ix, 2, as a place in Arbela besieged and captured by Bacchides and Alcimus on their way from the north to Gilgal. Arbela is probably the modern *Irbid*, about three miles north-west of Tiberias. Dr. Robinson suggests that the name Masaloth may have originally signified "steps" or "terraces." In that case it was probably a name given to the remarkable caverns still existing on the northern side of the *Wady el-Hûmâm*, and now called *Kula'at Ibn Ma'an*, that is, caverns, which, according to Josephus, actually stood a remarkable siege of some length by the forces of Herod.

Mash, *drawn out*, (?) a Shemite Aramean people, Gen. x, 23. In 1 Chron. i, 17, called Meshech. It seems probable that the name Mash is represented by the Mons Masius of classical writers, a range forming the northern boundary of Mesopotamia, between the Tigris and Euphrates, below which lay Nisibis, and by the river Masche which flowed past that city.

Ma'shal, *entreaty*. 1 Chron. vi, 74; Mishal in Josh. xxi, 30; and Misheal in Josh. xix, 26. A town in Asher, afterward assigned to the Gershonite Levites. The form Mashal suggests its identity with the Masaloth of later history; but as Mr. Grove says, "there is nothing to remark for or against this identification."

Mas'pha. 1. Opposite Jerusalem, 1 Macc. iii, 46. The ancient MIZPEH of Benjamin.

2. On the east of Jordan, 1 Macc. v, 35. Probably the ancient MIZPEH of Gilead.

Mas'rekah, *vineyard of noble vines*, the seat of one of the early kings of Edom, Gen. xxxvi, 36; 1 Chron. i, 47. The site is unknown.

Mas'sa, *a lifting up, a gift* (?), *patience* (?), a son of Ishmael, and also apparently the name of the place in which his descendants settled, Gen. xxv, 14, 16; 1 Chron. i, 30. Some identify Massa with the Masani of Ptolemy, a people of Eastern Arabia, bordering on Babylonia, and doubtless the same as the Masei of Pliny, a nomad tribe of Mesopotamia.

Mas'sah, *temptation,* a name given to the place where the Israelites encamped in Rephidim. Here the people, having no water to drink, "tempted Jehovah, saying, Is Jehovah among us, or not?" Exod. xvii, 7. Moses "called the name of the place Massah and Meribah." (See MERIBAH.) The events at Massah are frequently afterward referred to, Deut. vi, 16; ix, 22· xxxiii, 8. The site is unknown. See REPHIDIM.

Mat'tanah, (Map 2,) *a gift*, a station of the Israelites, lying on the border between Moab and the Amorites, on the north side of the Arnon, and eastward toward the wilderness of Arabia, Num. xxi, 11, 13-19. The passage is somewhat obscure, but by Mattanah allusion is probably made to some great *gift* from God—perhaps the "well" mentioned in Num. xxi, 16-18. The Targumists treat Mattanah as if a synonym for Beer, the well which was "given" to the people.

Me'ah, THE TOWER OF, (Map 9,) *the tower of the hundred,* one of the towers in the wall of Jerusalem, as rebuilt after the return from the captivity, Neh. iii, 1; xii, 39. It stood between the Sheep Gate and the tower of Hananeel, but the site of each of these is disputed. According to Mr. Porter, "The most probable theory appears to be that the Sheep Gate adjoined the temple on the north, and that Meah was only a short distance from it, thus occupying the position on which the great fortress of Antonia was afterward built. Those who adopt this view, however, are not agreed as to the size of the temple-courts, and consequently they differ as to the real site of Meah." Dr. Barclay locates this tower east of the temple on the very brink of the Kidron; while Ferguson would place it near the north-western angle of the ancient city. See HANANEEL.

Mea'ni, a corrupt Greek form of Mehunim, 1 Esdras v, 31; compare Ezra ii, 50.

Mea'rah, *a cave,* a place mentioned only in Josh. xiii, 4, in describing the land which at that time still remained unsubdued. It was apparently near Zidon. Some think it was simply a cave, but more probably it was a city or district. "About half way between Tyre and Sidon, close to the shore, are the ruins of an ancient town; and in the neighboring cliffs are large numbers of caves and grottoes hewn in the rock, and formerly used as tombs. Dr. Robinson suggested that this may be 'Mearah of the Sidonians,' (ii, 474.) The ruins are now called *Adlân;* but perhaps take their name from the village on the mountain-side."—Porter in *Kitto.*

Med'aba, the Greek form of Medeba, 1 Macc. ix, 36.

Me'dan, *strife, contention,* one of the sons of Abraham and Keturah, Gen. xxv, 3; 1 Chron. i, 32. All Keturah's sons seem to have become the heads of Arab tribes. On the Euphrates is a village called *Madan,* and in *Hejaz,* Arabia, is a city called *Maadan;* both of which are conjecturally traced to Medan.

Med'eba, *waters of quiet,* or *rest,* a city of Moab, Num. xxi, 27-30. In the allotment to the trans-Jordanic tribes this place fell within the territory of Reuben, Josh. xiii, 16; but while the whole plain was occupied by the Reubenites, the city of Medeba itself, being doubtless strongly fortified, was probably suffered to remain, like many in Western Palestine, in the hands of its old inhabitants. Thus it is not found in the list of cities assigned to Reuben. It gave its name to a district of level downs called "the Mishor of Medeba," or, "the Mishor on Medeba," verse 9. In David's time Medeba appears to have passed into the hands of the Ammonites, for they concentrated their forces and allies to resist an attack which their own insolence and folly led them to anticipate. They were totally defeated by Joab, and the allies were dispersed; but the Ammonites found refuge in Medeba, 1 Chron. xix, 1–15. In the prophetic curse upon Moab Medeba is mentioned as one of its chief cities, Isa. xv, 2; compare 1 Macc. ix, 36. The Moabites had then recovered their ancient country. Medeba is mentioned by Ptolemy. It was known to Eusebius and Jerome. The ruins of Medeba still exist under the Arabic name *Madeba*. They lie about four miles south-east of Heshbon, with which they are connected by an ancient paved road. Not a building remains standing. Among the ruins are a large cistern, and the remains of a massive temple of the Doric order.

Medes, (Map 12,) the inhabitants of Media, 2 Kings xvii, 6; Ezra vi, 2; Esther i, 19; Isa. xiii, 17; Dan. v, 28, 31; 2 Esdras i, 3; Acts ii, 9, etc. See MEDIA.

Me'dia, (Map 1,) a large country in Asia. The name is the same as Madai, (*middle land,*) one of Japheth's sons, Gen. x, 2. The Hebrew word thus translated Madai, is also rendered Medes, 2 Kings xvii, 6, etc.; and Media, Esther i, 3, etc.; and also Mede, Dan. xi, 1. In the period of which Herodotus writes the people of Media were called Arians.

Media was separated from Persia on the south by a desert; on the west the boundary was the mountains of Zagros, and the chain proceeding thence to Ararat, the Araxes limited it northward; while on the east it reached to the desert, the Caspian gates, and the mountains south of the sea. Anciently Media was divided into Media Magna, and Media Atropatene. The former included the Nisæan plain, famous for a breed of horses, and corresponded with the modern *Irak Ajemi*, with parts of *Kurdistan* and *Luristan*. Media Atropatene, named from the satrap Atropates, who established himself there when Alexander overthrew the Persian Empire, corresponded to *Azerbijan*, and perhaps *Talish* and *Ghilan*. In each of the two divisions of Media was a chief city called ECBATANA, which see. According to Rawlinson the entire length of the kingdom of Media might be five hundred and fifty miles from north to south, and its breadth from two hundred and fifty to three hundred.

After the notice in Gen. x, 2, of Madai, who must be considered their founder, the Medes are not again mentioned in Scripture during a period of fifteen centuries, until Isaiah, in his prophetic threat against the Babylonians, (about B. C. 720,) declares, "I will stir up the Medes against them," Isa. xiii, 17. In very ancient times doubtless the Medes were powerful, and they are said to have conquered Babylonia; but later they appear to have been oppressed and plundered by the Assyrians, who planted military colonies among them.

About B. C. 625, the Medes, under their king, Cyaxares, took Nineveh, and Media now became the most powerful monarchy in Western Asia. Cyaxares ruled over Assyria, Persia, Media, Armenia, and other countries, from the Halys to the Caspian Gates, and from the Caspian and Black Seas to the Persian Gulf. But the power of Media was short-lived. On the death of Cyaxares the throne was left to Astyages. In a war between the Medes and Persians the latter under Cyrus were victorious, and the two kingdoms were united under one scepter B. C. 558. Not only was the life of Astyages spared, but he was allowed to retain his title of king. Doubtless these two nations were branches of the same great Arian family, and this fact would account for the honorable position which the Medes still occupied in the Persian court and realm. This also would illustrate the predictions which represent the Medes as the chief agents in the overthrow of Babylon, while they acted in conjunction with the Persians, Isa. xiii, 17; Jer. li, 11, 28.

The earliest Scripture mention of Median territory refers to the removal of some of the Israelites into Median cities by Assyrian kings, 2 Kings xvii, 6; xviii, 11. The predictions of Median conquest afterward made by the prophets above alluded to were completely accomplished, Dan. v, 28, 31. The union of the Medes and Persians as a Medo-Persian kingdom is frequently referred to, Esther i, 3, 14, 18, 19; x, 2; Dan. vi, 8, 12. Achmetha or Ecbatana, in Media, is alluded to as being the royal residence, Ezra vi, 2.

But the lofty Median spirit was not satisfied in holding the first rank among the Persian satrapies. In the third year of Darius Hystaspes the Medes elected a king and joined the Assyrians and Armenians against the Persians. Darius defeated their army, captured the usurper at Rhages, and put him to death at Ecbatana. During the reign of Darius Nothus they made another unsuccessful revolt. With the rest of the Persian Empire Media was conquered by Alexander the Great, and eventually the whole country passed over to the Parthian monarchy. At the present time Media is included under the dominions of the Shah of Persia.

The religion of the ancient Medes, which was identical with that of the Persians, consisted of the adoration of two great beings—Ormazd, the principle of *Good*, and Ahriman, the principle of *Evil*. With this was connected the worship of the heavenly bodies, and at a later period was added the worship of the elements, and of fire as the chief. Their priesthood, called *Magi*, claimed power to interpret dreams and foretell events.

Me'dian, THE, the designation of Darius, also called the Mede, Dan. v, 31; xi, 1.

Mediterra'nean Sea, (Maps 5, 8.) This name does not occur in Scripture. It is called the "Great Sea," Num. xxxiv, 6, 7; Josh. i, 4; ix, 1; xv, 12, 47; xxiii, 4; Ezek. xlvii, 10, 15, 20; xlviii, 28; the "Sea of the Philistines," Exod. xxiii, 31; "Sea of Joppa," Ezra iii, 7; "The Sea," Josh. xv, 4, 46; Acts xvii, 14; the "hinder sea," Zech. xiv, 8; the "utmost sea," Deut. xi, 24; xxxiv, 2; Joel ii, 20.

Megid'do, (Map 5,) *place of troops*. In Zech. xii, 11, Megiddon. Sometimes Magiddo, 1 Esdr. i, 25, 31. Perhaps also ARMAGEDDON, which see. Megiddo was an ancient royal city of the Canaanites enumerated among those whose kings were slain by Joshua, Josh. xii, 21. It lay on the southern edge of the plain of Esdraelon. Though within the allotted territory of Issachar, it, with several other cities in the plain, was assigned to Manasseh, Josh. xvii, 11; 1 Chron. vii, 29. The Manassites were not able to expel the old inhabitants; but when the power of Israel was fully established the Canaanites were reduced to slavery, Josh. xvii, 13-18; Judges i, 27, 28. The plain by which this city stood is sometimes called the Valley of Megiddo, 1 Chron. xxxv, 22. See ESDRAELON. It was the battle-field of Palestine, where the Israelites gained some of their most glorious victo-

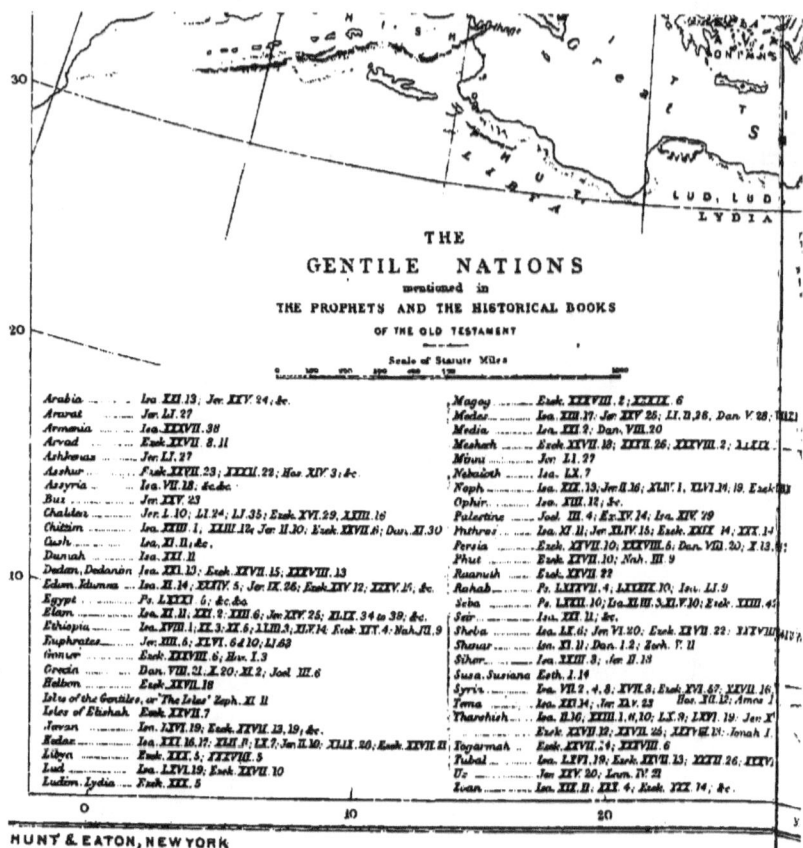

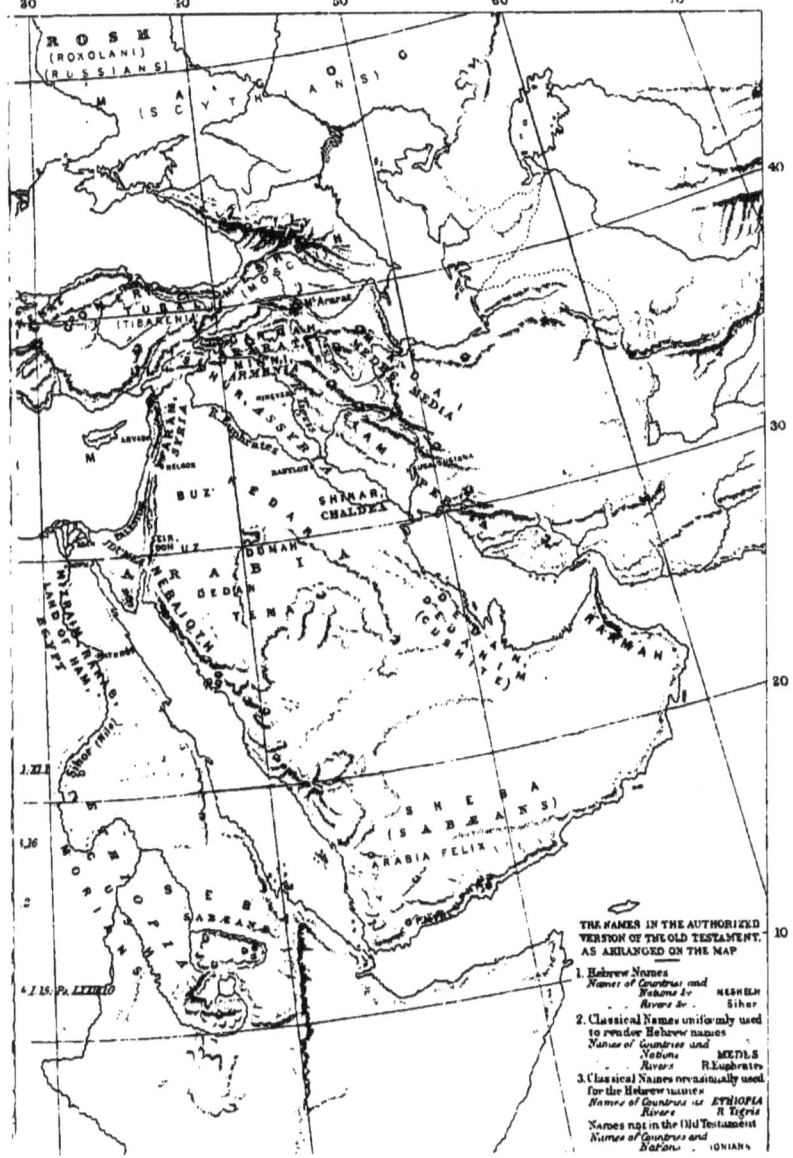

ries and sustained some of their most terrible defeats. Megiddo has derived its chief celebrity from two of these battles. The first was the victory of Barak, a spirited account of which is in Judges iv; v. Solomon fortified this place, and the region round was one of his commissariat districts, 1 Kings ix, 15; iv, 12. Hither Ahaziah, King of Judah, fled, 2 Kings ix, 27. The second battle ended in a fearful defeat to Israel. Pharaoh-Necho, marching against the King of Assyria, passed up the plains of Philistia and Sharon. King Josiah foolishly attempted to stop him while defiling through the glens of Carmel into the plain of Megiddo. He was defeated, and as he fled the Egyptian archers shot him in his chariot. He was taken to Jerusalem, but appears to have died on the road, 2 Kings xxiii, 29; 2 Chron. xxxv, 20-24. See also Zech. xii, 11.

Among the Roman historians the name of a city called Legio is often found. The position of Legio in that part of the plain where Megiddo must have been situated, and its proximity to Taanach—with which Megiddo is almost uniformly joined in Scripture—lead to the belief that Legio was the Roman name of the Hebrew Megiddo. The ruins of Legio are now called *El-Lejjûn*. These consist of some heavy foundations and heaps of hewn stones, intermixed with columns of granite, marble, and limestone. There are also traces of a large *Khan*. Mr. Porter (*Hand-book*, p. 365) says of this place and its ruins: "Megiddo is situated in a nook of the hills, on the border of the plain. About half a mile north of the ruins a large green mound called *Tell el-Mutsellim*, 'The Governor's Tell,' terminates a low projecting ridge.... It is a most commanding site, affording a view of the whole plain of the ancient cities of Shunem, Jezreel, and Taanach." Although this hill has been for ages under cultivation, a few faint traces of old buildings are seen; and some are inclined to believe that on this tell stood the stronghold of Megiddo. In a deep bed near the base of the tell flows the stream which passes *Lejjûn*. This is considered by some of the best authorities as "the waters of Megiddo," mentioned in Judges v, 19; but Dr. Stanley (*S. and P.*, p. 339) supposes these "waters" rather to be "the pools in the bed of the Kishon" itself.

Mehu'nim, Ezra ii, 50. Called also Maon, Meani, Meunim, Mehunims.

Mehu'nims, *habitations*, 2 Chron. xxvi, 7. See MAONITES.

Me-jar'kon, *the waters of yellowness*, a town of Dan, mentioned only in Josh. xix, 46, and apparently situated in the plain near Joppa. Unknown.

Mek'onah, or **Meko'nah,** *a place*, or *base* of a pillar, that is, foundation, a town, apparently situated near Ziklag, on the southern border of Palestine, Neh. xi, 28. It was inhabited by the men of Judah after the captivity, and seems to have been a place of some magnitude.

Mel'ita, (Map 8,) an island in the Mediterranean, on which was wrecked the ship which was conveying St. Paul to Rome as a prisoner, and which was the scene of the interesting circumstances recorded in Acts xxvii, xxviii. Melita was the ancient name of Malta, and also of a small island in the Adriatic, now called Meleda. Each of these has been earnestly advocated as the Melita of Scripture. The received and well-established opinion is in favor of Malta. The chief argument for Meleda is mainly based on the statement that the ship of St. Paul was "driven up and down in (the sea of) Adria," when wrecked on Melita. But this claim is completely refuted. From various ancient writers it is proved that the name of Adria was not, in its ancient acceptation, limited to the present Adriatic Sea, but comprehended the seas

BIBLE GEOGRAPHY.

of Greece and Sicily, and extended even to Africa. See ADRIA. Moreover, ample memorials of St. Paul's visit exist in Malta, while in Meleda there is an utter absence of such memorials. Dr. Kitto well says: "There is, perhaps, no piece of land of the same extent in the world which is made to contain reference so diversified and so numerous to any one person as the island of Malta to St. Paul, who is, in fact, the tutelary saint of the island." To the place where it is supposed the shipwreck took place, the name of St. Paul's Bay has been given, and this bay exactly answers the description given in the Scripture narrative. There is also a creek with a sandy beach and a place of two seas, Acts xxvii, 39, 41.

The apostle tarried on the island three months, during which the "barbarous people" showed him much kindness, while Paul in turn performed some miraculous cures, Acts xxviii, 1-11. The term "barbarous," applied to the islanders, it is claimed, would not be given to the civilized people of Malta, especially by a Jew. But the use of this term merely intimates that they were not of Greek or Roman origin. This appellation accurately describes the ancient inhabitants of Malta; but it could not apply to the inhabitants of Meleda, who were Greeks.

Malta lies south of Sicily, from the nearest point of which it is fifty-eight miles distant. Its circumference is about sixty miles, its length twenty, and its breadth twelve. Malta has no mountains or high hills, and makes no figure from the sea. It was colonized by the Phœnicians, from whom it was taken by the Greek colonists in Sicily about 736 B. C. The Carthagenians obtained possession of it 402, and the Romans 242 B. C. In Acts xxviii, 7, notice is made of the chief Roman officer. On the division of the Roman empire Melita belonged to the western portion, but it was afterward attached to the Empire of the East. About the end of the ninth century the island was taken from the Greeks by the Arabs, who made it a dependency upon Sicily, which was also in their possession. In A. D. 1090 it was wrested from the Arabs by the Normans, and it went through other changes afterward till A. D. 1530, when Charles V., who had annexed it to his empire, transferred it to the knights of St. John of Jerusalem, whom the Turks had recently dispossessed of Rhodes. This Order of St. John, commonly called Knights of Malta, gradually fell into decay, and the island was surrendered to the French in 1798. The English gained possession of it in 1800, and held it by military power till 1814, when it was formally acknowledged a British dependency, in which condition it still remains. The population is about one hundred and twenty thousand.

Mem'phis, (Map 1,) Hos. ix, 6; in Hebrew, Moph. In Isa. xix, 13, and elsewhere, the form is Noph. Various interpretations are given of the meaning of this name. The Hebrew forms are contractions of the ancient Egyptian *Men-Nufr* or *Men-Nefru,* "the pyramid city." The sacred name of Memphis was *Ha-Ptah, Pa-Ptah,* or *Ha-Ptah-Ka,* or *Ha-Ka-Ptah,* "the abode of Ptah," or "of the being of Ptah." The ancient Egyptian common name signifies either "the good abode," or "the abode of the good one," that is, Osiris, or "the gate of the blessed." Some trace in the name of the city a connection with Menes, its founder. Memphis was a very ancient and celebrated city of Egypt. It lay on the left bank of the Nile. According to tradition, Menes, the founder, obtained a site for his city by damming up a branch of the Nile and restraining the water to a new channel which he dug. The era of Menes is not satisfactorily determined. Wilkinson dates it B. C. 2690 ; Poole, B. C. 2717 ; Bunsen, B. C. 3643 ; Brugsch, B. C. 4455 ; and Lepsius, B. C. 3892. All agree that the city belongs to the earliest periods of authentic history.

Memphis was surrounded with mounds and embankments to protect it against the inundations of the river, and these served also for security against hostile attacks. It would seem to have been the capital of those Pharaohs who reigned in Lower Egypt in the times of the patriarchs, and it was their territory in which Abraham, Jacob, and the Israelitish tribes sojourned. Under Psammetichus this city became the metropolis of all Egypt, and it grew and flourished as the southern Thebes declined. Under Persian rule and the government of the Ptolemies Memphis (the center of the Memphitic nome or province) continued the chief city, but the foundation of Alexandria was fatal to its prosperity. Even in Strabo's time, though still large and populous, many of its great buildings were falling into decay. And when at length Cairo rose in its neighborhood, Memphis rapidly declined.

According to Diodorus Siculus the city had a circumference of about nineteen miles, and the houses or inhabited quarters, as was usual in the great cities of antiquity, were interspersed with numerous gardens and public areas. Temples, palaces, magnificent gateways and colonnades, colossal statues, catacombs for the sacred bulls, a paved road lined with colossal lions, beautiful and richly ornamented " inclosures," the grand and wonderful pyramids of the adjacent Necropolis—all these united to give Memphis the pre-eminence which it enjoyed as "the haven of the blessed." But its glory long ago departed. Jeremiah (xlvi, 19) declares that "*Noph* shall be waste and desolate without an inhabitant." See also Isa. xix, 13 ; Jer. ii, 16; xlvi, 14 ; Ezek. xxx, 16.

Abd-el-Latif, the Arabian physician, who visited the place in the thirteenth century, describes its ruins as then marvelous beyond description. Abulfeda, in the fourteenth century, speaks of the remains of Memphis as immense, but for the most part in a state of decay. So complete was the ruin of Memphis that for a long time its very site was lost. Recent explorations have brought to light many of its antiquities, which have been distributed among the museums of Europe and America. A very large number of relics may be seen at the Abbott Museum in New York. The Necropolis, adjacent to the city, gave to Memphis the title of "City of the Pyramids." The principal seat of the Pyramids, the Memphitic Necropolis, was in a range of about fifteen miles from *Sakkara* to *Gizeh*, and in the groups here remaining nearly thirty are probably tombs of the imperial sovereigns of Memphis.

The site of this once magnificent city is marked by the insignificant village of *Mcet Raheeneh*, or *Mitraheny*.

Meon'enim, THE PLAIN OF, *the oak of the sorcerers.* A celebrated oak (not a plain) near Shechem, Judg. ix, 37. It is probable that under or near this tree divination had been practiced.

Meph'aath, *splendor,* perhaps a *lofty, conspicuous place,* a city in Reuben, situated in the plain country, or Mishor, near Heshbon, assigned to the sons of Merari, and subsequently in the possession of the Moabites, Josh. xiii, 18 xxi, 37; 1 Chron. vi, 79; Jer. xlviii, 21. Its site is lost.

Me′ran, a place mentioned with Theman as famous for its merchants and wise men, Bar. iii, 23. The locality is very uncertain. Probably it was some district in Arabia. Some think it a corruption of Medan or Midian. There are other opinions, but all are mere conjecture.

Mer′arites. See LEVITES.

Meratha′im, THE LAND OF, *the land of double rebellion*, probally a poetical name for Chaldea, Jer. 1, 1. The term may be intended to express the double captivity—that of Israel and that of Judah, or the land in which first the Assyrians and then the Babylonians oppressed God's people.

Mer′ibah, (Map 2,) *chiding, strife.*

1. The name given to the place where the rock was struck and the people murmured. It was in the Desert of Sin, on the western gulf of the Red Sea, Exod. xvii, 1–7. See MASSAH.

2. Another fountain produced in the same manner, and under similar circumstances, in the Desert of Zin, (*Wady Arabah*,) near Kadesh, Num. xx, 13, 24. In Deut. xxxiii, 8, this place is mentioned with the preceding Meribah, which is called Massah, to prevent the confusion of the two Meribahs. This Meribah, near Kadesh, is almost always indicated by the addition of "waters," that is, "waters of Meribah," as if further to distinguish it from the other, Psa. lxxxi, 7; cvi, 32; and still more distinctly, "waters of Meribah in Kadesh," Num. xxvii, 14; Deut. xxxii, 51; Ezek. xlvii, 19. Only once is it called simply Meribah, Psa. xcv, 8.

Me′rom, THE WATERS OF, (Map 5,) *the waters of height*, or, *the upper waters*, the name of a lake situated in the northern part of the Holy Land. By the "waters of Merom" Joshua encountered and crushed the confederacy of the northern tribes of Canaan, under the leadership of Jabin, King of Hazor, Josh. xi, 5, 7. This is the only passage in Scripture in which the lake is mentioned, and we have no clear indication of its precise geographical position. Nor is the name of Merom found in Josephus. In his account of the battle the confederate kings encamp "near Beroth, a city of Galilee not far from Kedes;" nor does he mention any water. Josephus, in speaking of the second Jabin, says that he "belonged to the city Asor, (Hazor,) which lay above the Lake of *Samachonitis*." Inasmuch as the Hazor of the first and the Hazor of the second Jabin were, doubtless, one and the same place, and as the waters of Merom are named in connection with the former, most geographers have inferred that the waters of Merom are identical with the *Samachonitis* of Josephus, and that both are identical with the modern *Bahr el-Hûleh*. But some high authorities are opposed to this threefold identification. Speaking of Merom, Mr. Grove says: "The name is usually given to the Lake of *Hûleh*, but without any sufficient reason." (Grove's *Index* in Clark's *Atlas*.) Says Keil, (on Josh. xi, 6–9): "The traditional opinion that 'waters of Merom' is the Old Testament name for Lake of Samachonitis or Hûleh, is not founded upon any historical evidence, but is simply an inference of Reland (1) from the statement made by Josephus (Antiq., V, 5, 1) that Hazor was above the Lake of Samachonitis, it being taken for granted without further reason that the battle occurred at Hazor, and (2) from the supposed similarity in the meaning of the name, namely, that *Samachonitis* is derived from an Arabic word signifying to be high, and therefore means the same as *Merom*, (height,) though here again the *Zere* is disregarded, and *Merom* is arbitrarily identified with *Marom*."

Meron'othite, perhaps *rejoicing*, a native of some place called Meronoth, probably in Benjamin, 1 Chron. xxvii, 30; Neh. iii, 7.

Me'roz, perhaps *secret*, or *refuge*, a place in the north of Palestine whose inhabitants were rebuked for not aiding Barak against Sisera, Judg. v, 23. It must have been in the neighborhood of Kishon. Mr. Grove inclines to the conjecture of Schwarz, that Meroz is to be found at *el-Murûssus*, a ruined site about four miles north-west of *Beisan*, on the southern slopes of the hills which are the continuation of the so-called "Little Hermon."

Me'ruth. 1 Esdras v, 24. A corruption of IMMER, which see.

Me'sech and **Me'shech**, (Map 12,) *a drawing out, possession.*
1. A Japhetic people, Gen. x, 2; 1 Chron. i, 5; Psa. cxx, 5; Ezek. xxvii, 13, etc. They were probably the progenitors of the Moschi and Muscovites. On the Assyrian monuments their name is written *Muskai*. In the above passages this people appear as the ally of Gog, and as supplying the Tyrians with copper and slaves, and are considered as one of the remotest, and at the same time rudest, nations of the world. Although the Moschi were a comparatively unimportant race in classical times, they had previously been one of the most powerful nations of Western Asia. The Assyrian monarchs were engaged in frequent wars with them, and it is not improbable that they had occupied the whole of the district afterward named Cappadocia.
2. A Shemite people, 1 Chron. i, 17. See MASH.

Me'sha, *retreat*, or *middle district*, a place in the possessions of the Joktanites, whose "dwelling was from Mesha, as thou goest unto Sephar, a mount of the east," Gen. x, 30. The situation of Mesha has been a subject of much controversy among geographers. So, also, have been the boundaries of the Joktanites. See JOKTAN. Mesha was probably the western limit of Joktan, and if so, should be sought for in north-western *Yemen*. The most probable site seems to be *Moosa*, a port on the Red Sea. It is mentioned by Ptolemy, Pliny, and others. In classical times it was a place of note, but it has fallen into decay if the modern *Moosa* be the same place. Gesenius would identify Mesha with *Mesene*, once an island now a portion of the delta at the mouth of the Tigris in the Persian Gulf, and which is frequently mentioned by classic and ecclesiastical writers. Kalisch adopts this view. But it is very doubtful whether this island was in existence in the days of Moses. Mr. Forster identifies Mesha with a mountain range called *Zames* by Ptolemy, which commences near the Persian Gulf, and runs in a south-westerly direction nearly across the peninsula. No site can be agreed upon.

Mesopota'mia, (Map 1,) *in the midst of rivers; Syria of the two rivers*, the district lying between the rivers Tigris and Euphrates, and deriving its name from this circumstance. This tract, "between the two rivers," is nearly seven hundred miles long, and from twenty to two hundred and fifty miles broad. Its limits seem to have varied at different periods, or the name was vaguely used so as to be applied to different extents of territory by different writers. Thus, while Strabo draws a line between it and Babylonia, Pliny assigns it to Assyria, and extends it southward as far as the Persian Gulf. The Mesopotamia of Scripture is the north-western part of the district above described. It consists of the mountain country extending from *Birehjik* to *Jezireh-ibn-Omar* upon the north; and, upon the south, of the great undulating Mesopotamian plain, as far as the *Sinjar* hills and the river *Khabour*. A part of this tract is the district called Padan-Aram.

Nahor and his family, quitting Ur of the Chaldees, settled in Mesopotamia, Gen. xxiv, 10; and here resided Bethuel and Laban; and to this place Abram sent his servant to fetch Isaac a wife "of his own kindred," Gen. xxiv, 15, 29, 38; xxv, 20. Hither, also, a century later, came Jacob on the same errand, Gen. xxviii, 5, 7; xxix, 4; xlvi, 15; and thence he returned with his two wives after an absence of twenty-one years, xxxi, 17, 18; xxxiii, 18; xlviii, 7. See also Acts vii, 2, and Gen. xi, 28–31. At the close of the wanderings in the wilderness, Balak, the king of Moab, sent for Balaam "to Pethor of Mesopotamia," (Deut. xxiii, 4,) which was situated among "the mountains of the East," (Num. xxiii, 7,) by a river, (xxii, 5,) probably the Euphrates. About half a century later we find, for the first and last time, Mesopotamia the seat of a powerful monarchy. Chushan-Rishathaim, King of Mesopotamia, establishes his dominion over Israel shortly after the death of Joshua, Judges iii, 8; and he maintains his authority for the space of eight years, when his yoke is broken by Othniel, Caleb's nephew, Judges iii, 9, 10. Finally, the children of Ammon, having provoked a war with David, "sent a thousand talents of silver to hire them chariots and horsemen out of Mesopotamia, and out of Syria-Maachah, and out of Zobah," 1 Chron. xix, 6; compare Psa. lx, title. See also Acts ii, 9. This country became afterward part of the Assyrian and then of the Babylonian Empire. It was subject to the Persian kings, conquered by Alexander, and subsequently ruled by the Syrian monarchs. In later times it was alternately under Roman and Parthian sway, till ultimately relinquished to Parthian or Persian rule. Of the chief cities of modern Mesopotamia, *Orfa* and *Harran* are believed to be the ancient Ur and Haran; *Nisibin* and *Diarbekr*, the ancient Nisibis and Amida.

Dr. Tilstone Beke has suggested that the Haran of the Bible is not in the district as above described, but is identical with a village four hours east of Damascus. But Dr. Beke seems to be almost alone in this opinion. See HARAN.

Me'theg-Am'mah, *bridle of the metropolis,* or *bridle of Ammah.* In 2 Sam. viii, 1, the passage reads, "David took Metheg-Ammah out of the hand of the Philistines;" but the margin has "the bridle of Ammah," instead of Metheg-Ammah. In the parallel passage, (1 Chron. xviii, 1,) "Gath and her daughter towns" is substituted for Metheg-Ammah. Possibly the sacred writer may mean that when David took the bridle of the mother-city (probably Gath) out of the hand of the Philistines he subdued the metropolis of the Philistines.

Meu'nim, *habitations,* Neh. vii, 52. See MEHUNIM.

Mich'mash, and **Mich'mas,** *something hidden,* a town of Benjamin, Ezra ii, 27; Neh. vii, 31; xi, 31; east of Beth-Aven, 1 Sam. xiii, 5; and south from Migron, on the road to Jerusalem, Isa. x, 28. It is also called Macalon, 1 Esdr. v, 21. At Michmash was a pass where the progress of a military body might readily be impeded, and it was doubtless a place of considerable military importance. From the chivalrous exploit of Saul's son, Jonathan, the place is chiefly celebrated, 1 Sam. xiii; xiv, 4–16. Here Jonathan Maccabeus fixed his abode, 1 Macc. ix, 73. It has been identified, with great probability, in the modern village of *Mukhmas,* which lies about seven miles north of Jerusalem, on the northern edge of the great *Wady Suweinit.* The village is almost desolate. There are many foundations of hown stones, among which are a few columns. Some travelers believe that they have recognized the rocks Bozez and Sen<h, the scene of Jonathan's exploit.

Mich'methah, *hiding-place,* a place on the boundary of Ephraim and Manasseh, facing Shechem, Josh. xvi, 6; xvii, 7.

MICHMASH.

With our present data it is impossible to decide whether the two passages indicate two towns or one. If one only, then it must have been near Shechem, but the site is unknown.

Mid'din, *measures,* a town in the "wilderness" of Judah, mentioned only in Josh. xv, 61. It probably lay close to the Dead Sea; but its site is unknown.

Mid'ian, (Map 2,) *strife.* In Judith ii, 26, and Acts vii, 29, Madian. The name of Abraham's fourth son by Keturah, and of a powerful and celebrated nation of Arabia that sprung from him, Gen. xxv, 2; Num. xxii; 1 Chron. i, 32, 33. The plural form, Midianites, is used a few times, Gen. xxxvii, 28; Num. xxv, 17; xxxi, 20. Midian, though not the oldest, was the most celebrated son of Keturah. What Judah became among the tribes of Israel, Midian became among the tribes of Arabia. For a long period the Midianites appear to have been the virtual rulers of Arabia, combining into a grand confederacy, and then guiding or controlling, as circumstances required, all the Arabian branches of the Hebrew race. One of the early kings of Edom, Hadad, "smote Midian in the field of Moab," Gen. xxxvi, 35. From this fact we may conclude that the Midianites were at that time settled on the eastern borders of Moab and Edom. Being an enterprising people, the Midianites were not satisfied with the dull routine of pastoral and agricultural life. Some districts of Arabia, Eastern Palestine, and Lebanon yielded valuable spices and perfumes, which were in great demand in Egypt, not merely for the luxuries of the living, but for the embalming of the dead. In this profitable trade the Midianites engaged. It was to one of their caravans passing through Palestine from Gilead to Egypt that Joseph was sold by his brethren, Gen. xxxvii, 25, etc. The historian calls these traders both *Ishmaelites* and *Midianites,* the two names being used synonymously. But the merchants in this caravan were, it seems, true Midianites, though they may have been accompanied by Ishmaelites, verses 28, 36; but compare 25, 27 Midian is next mentioned in the history of Moses, when, having killed the Egyptian, he fled to the "land of Midian," Exod. ii, 15, and married a daughter of a priest of Midian, 21. The portion of Midian here referred to was probably the peninsula of Sinai, for we read (Exod. iii, 1) that Moses led the flock of Jethro, his father-in-law, "to the back side of the desert, and came to the mountain of God, even Horeb;" and this agrees with a natural supposition that he did not flee far beyond the frontier of Egypt. It should, however, be remembered that the name of Midian was perhaps often applied, as that of the most powerful of the northern Arab tribes, to the northern Arabs generally, that is, those of the Abrahamic descent; just as *Bene-Kedem* embraced all those people, and, with a wider signification, other Eastern tribes. If this reading of the name be correct, "Midian" would correspond very nearly with our modern word "Arab;" limiting, however, the modern word to the Arabs of the Northern and Egyptian deserts. All the Ishmaelite tribes of those deserts would thus be Midianites, as we call them Arabs, the desert being their "land." We may suppose that the bulk of this nation inhabited the region extending from the eastward of Moab and Edom, perhaps along the frontier of Palestine, down to the shores of the eastern gulf of the Red Sea, and that some of the wandering branches of it were occasionally found in the Sinaitic peninsula. On the shores of this Eastern gulf the Arabian geographers have placed the ruins of a town called *Madyan*.

The Midianites joined with Moab in inviting Balaam to curse the tribe of Israel, Num. xxii, 4–7. They did this because when the Israelites in their journeyings passed round the southern end of Edom they entered the proper territory of Midian. Balaam came; but the Lord turned the intended curse into a blessing. But the prophet adopted another and effectual mode of injuring the Israelites. He persuaded the women of Moab and Midian to work upon the passions of the Israelites, and entice them to the licentious festival of their idols, and thus bring upon them the curse of heaven, Num. xxv. Terrible vengeance then fell upon Midian. Their cities and castles were burned; all the males that fell into the hands of the conquerors were put to death, and with them all the married females; and the young women and children were reduced to slavery. Moses' account of this war, as found in Num. xxxi, shows us that the Midianites had much wealth and many cities. They were governed, it would seem, by several chiefs, heads, perhaps, of separate clans; and they were apparently under some sort of vassalage to the Amoritish King Sihon, Josh. xiii, 21, their settlements extending into his country. In later times, when they overran Palestine in conjunction with the Amalekites, penetrating to the Philistine plain, and coming with their cattle and their tents, as if to establish themselves there, they were also commanded by a number of chiefs or kings. Seven years they prevailed against Israel, till Gideon was raised up as a deliverer. Then so entirely were they defeated that we read little more of them in the sacred history, Judg. vi, vii, viii. See also Psa. lxxxiii, 9; Isa. ix, 4; lx, 6; Judith ii, 26. They seem henceforth to be comprehended under the general name of Arabian.

Recent investigations have shown that the whole desert east of Edom and Moab is thickly studded with the ruins of ancient cities and castles.

Every-where there are evidences of partial cultivation in former days, and also traces of a comparatively dense population.

Mid'ianites. See MIDIAN.

Mig'dal-E'dar. See EDAR, TOWER OF.

Mig'dal-El, *tower of God,* one of the fenced cities of Naphtali, Josh. xix, 38. The name Migdal was, and still is, very common in Palestine. Concerning the site of the Migdal in question there are several conjectures. Three miles north of Tiberias, on the sea-shore, is a small village, with ancient ruins, called *Mejdel,* the Arabic representative of Migdal, and now identified with the Magdala of the N. T. Dr. Robinson considers this as probably identical with Migdal-El. In Van de Velde's map a village called *Mejdel Selim* is placed near the northern extremity of the mountains of Naphtali, the position of which, Mr. Porter thinks, would seem to agree with that of Migdal-El. Mr. Grove mentions a place called *Mujeidel* on the *Wady Kerkerah,* near *Yarûn,* which he conjectures may mark the site of the town in question.

Mig'dal-Gad, *tower of Gad,* that is, the ancient idol. A town of Judah situated in the plain of Philistia, apparently to the north-west of Lachish, mentioned only in Josh. xv, 37–39. Although apparently mentioned by Eusebius and Jerome as "Magdala," it seems to have been unknown by them. About two miles east of Ascalon is a large and prosperous village called *Mejdel,* surrounded by orchards and cultivated fields. This may mark the site of Migdal-Gad. Many traces of antiquity are found among the houses, such as large hewn stones and broken columns.

Mig'dol, (Map 2,) *a tower,* the name of one or two places on the eastern frontier of Egypt.

1. A place near the head of the western arm of the Red Sea, Exod. xiv, 2; Num. xxxiii, 7, 8.

2. A city on the north-eastern border of Lower Egypt. Although thought by some identical with No. 1, it seems highly probable that it was a different place. A colony of Jews settled here after the destruction of Jerusalem, Jer. xliv, 1; xlvi, 14. It seems to have been an important town, and not merely a fort or military settlement. Ezekiel, in prophesying the desolation of Egypt, couples Migdol with Syene in the extreme south, "from Migdol to Syene," Ezek. xxix, 10, margin; xxx, 6, margin. Probably this Migdol is the Magdol mentioned in the Itinerary of Antoninus as a town in Egypt about twelve Roman miles southward of Pelusium.

Mig'ron, *precipice.* This name occurs in 1 Sam. xiv, 2, in the description of the successful attack of Jonathan upon the Philistines at Michmash; "Saul tarried . . . under a pomegranate-tree, *which is in Migron.*" In Isa. x, 28, the prophet, giving the route of the Assyrian army toward Jerusalem, says, "He is come to Aiath, he is passed to Migron; at Michmash he hath laid up his carriages." Whether Migron was a rock or a town is not determined. Some suppose that two places are indicated by these two Scripture passages. The Migron of Isaiah seems a little further north than that noted in 1 Samuel. Mr. Porter thinks that Migron may possibly lie in or close to the southern brow of the ravine now called *Wady Suweinit.* There are many commanding cliffs and several ruined villages in the region round Geba and Michmash; but no identification of the site of Migron can be had.

Mile'tum, 2 Tim. iv, 20. The same as the following.

Mile'tus, (Map 8,) a city and sea-port of Ionia in Asia Minor, about thirty miles south of Ephesus. St. Paul touched here on his voyage from Greece to Syria, and delivered to the elders of Ephesus, who had come to meet him there, a remarkable and affecting address, Acts xx, 15–38. In 2 Tim. iv, 20, it is stated that Paul left Trophimus sick at Miletum. In Acts xxi, 29, we find Trophimus with the apostle at Jerusalem at the close of the journey above mentioned. To solve this apparent contradiction, some think there was a Miletum in Crete; but the difficulty is settled in the supposition of a journey made by the apostle after his first imprisonment at Rome. Various combinations are possible. See Conybeare and Howson's *Life and Epistles of St. Paul.*

Miletus was the old capital of Ionia, though Ptolemy assigns it to Caria. It is said to have had four havens, one of which was capable of holding a fleet. Several men of renown were natives of this place—Thales, Timotheus, Anaximander, Anaximenes, Democritus. The city had an evil reputation for licentiousness and luxury. The remains of Miletus were probably absorbed in the swamp formed by the silting up of the Meander; so that the site of the city, which was once on the coast, is now ten miles inland. The ruined site bears the name of Melas. An insignificant village stands near it, and there are yet visible the ruins of the once magnificent temple of Apollo.

Mil'lo, (Map 7,) *fullness* or *filling in, rampart, fortress.* The definite article (in Hebrew) is always prefixed, "The Millo." It is the name given to part of the citadel of Jerusalem, probably the rampart. It seems to have been in existence when David took the city from the Jebusites, see 2 Sam. v, 9; 1 Chron. xi, 8. Its repair or restoration was one of the great works for which Solomon raised his levy, 1 Kings ix, 15, 24; xi, 27; and it formed a prominent part of the fortifications by which Hezekiah prepared for the approach of the Assyrians, 2 Chron. xxxii, 5. In this last text the Septuagint has "the fortifications of the city of David." Sepp places this fort at the extreme north of the city, near the Damascus gate. Grove says Millo was "possibly the citadel, the *akra* or fortress on Mount Zion, but very doubtful."

Mil'lo, THE HOUSE OF.

1. Perhaps a clan at Shechem, mentioned only in Judg. ix, 6, 20. Nothing is known of it.

2. The spot at which King Joash was murdered by his slaves, 2 Kings xii, 20; probably the Millo of the preceding article.

Min'ni, perhaps *division,* a portion of Armenia, Jer. li, 27; perhaps the region of the *Manavasæi,* near the center of Armenia.

Min'nith, (Map 5,) probably *allotment,* a place east of the Jordan, probably between Heshbon and Rabbath-Ammon. It is named as the point to which Jephthah's slaughter of the Ammonites extended, Judg. xi, 33. In Ezek. xxvii, 17, the "wheat of Minnith" is mentioned as being supplied by Judah and Israel to Tyre, but it is not absolutely certain that the same Minnith is intended. Minnith still existed in the time of Eusebius, four Roman miles from Heshbon, on the road to Philadelphia. It is thus put down on Keipert's map, but its site is not yet established.

Miph'kad, (Map 9,) *appointed place, number,* one of the gates of Jerusalem, probably in the city of David, on the north side, Neh. iii, 31.

Mis'gab, *the high place,* a name occurring in Jer. xlviii, 1, where the prophet in pronouncing the doom of Moab says, "Kiriathaim is confounded and taken; *Misgab* is confounded and dismayed." Some suppose that the

BIBLE GEOGRAPHY.   315

word should here be translated "the high place," and that thus it would be synonymous with and descriptive of Kiriathaim. The words "fortress of the high fort," in Isa. xxv, 12, may perhaps refer to Misgab. Possibly Misgab is identical with *Mizpeh of Moab* named only in 1 Sam. xxiii, 3.

Mi'shal and **Mi'sheal,** *entreaty,* a place in Asher allotted to the Gershonite Levites, Josh. xix, 26; xxi, 30. It is not known. See MASHAL.

Mish'raites, from a root which may signify *slippery place,* natives of a town colonized from Kirjath-Jearim, 1 Chron. ii, 53. Nothing is certainly known of them. Probably they founded the towns of Zorah and Eshtaol.

Mis'rephoth-Ma'im, (Map 5,) *burnings of water* or *burnings by the water,* a place near Zidon, Josh. xi, 8; xiii, 6. Drs. Thomson and Schultz attempt to identify it with a ruin called *Musheirefeh,* on the northern border of the plain of Akka, near *Ras en-Nakûra.* This seems too far south. Grove thinks it "not impossibly Zarephath." But the site, as well as the meaning of the name, are as yet only conjectural.

Mith'cah, probably *place of sweetness,* or *sweet fountain,* one of the unknown encampments in the desert, Num. xxxiii, 28, 29.

Mith'nite, a native of an unknown place called Methen, 1 Chron. xi, 43.

Mityle'ne, (Map 8,) the capital of the Isle of Lesbos, in the Ægean Sea, about seven miles and a half from the opposite point on the coast of Asia Minor. St. Paul touched at Mitylene in his voyage from Corinth to Judea, Acts xx, 14, 15. It was noted for its beauty, riches, and literary renown. Among the natives were Sappho, Alcæus, Pittacus, and Theophrastus. Mitylene still exists, and has given its name to the whole island. The modern town, a place of little importance, is called sometimes *Mitylen,* and sometimes *Castro.*

Mi'zar, *smallness;* "the hill Mizar," or "the little hill," a hill mentioned only in Psa. xlii, 6. It is apparently in the north part of trans-Jordanic Palestine.

Miz'pah and **Miz'peh,** (Map 5,) *watch-tower, lofty place.* A name borne by several places in ancient Palestine. Every Mizpah was a station of observation, commanding a wide view, from which friend or foe could be seen and signaled.

1. On Mount Gilead; also called Mizpeh of Gilead, Judg. xi, 29; and elsewhere probably Ramoth-Mizpah and Ramath-Gilead. It was named by Laban from the heap of stones set up by him and Jacob to serve as a witness of their covenant, and as a landmark of the boundary between them, Gen. xxxi, 23, 25, 48, 52. Here also the armies of Israel and the Ammonites encamped, Judg. x, 17; xi, 11, 29; and Jephthah dwelt here, verse 34. Mention is made of Mizpah in Judg. xx, 1, 3; xxi, 1, 5, 8, concerning the gathering there of Israel. With the other cities of Gilead, Mizpah was taken by the Maccabees, 1 Macc. v, 35. Mr. Porter (in *Kitto*) says: "About three miles north-west of *Es-Salt* [Ramoth-Gilead] is the highest peak east of the Jordan. . . . Its top is broad and flat, and would form a fine gathering-place for a nation of warriors. . . . The peak is now called *Jebel Osh'a,* 'the hill of Hosea,' because upon its top is a gigantic tomb said to be that of the prophet. It is probable that this is the true site of 'Mizpeh of Gilead,' the gathering-place of the Eastern tribes." See *Hand-book.* But there are strong reasons for believing the place mentioned in the passages in Judges last referred to to be the Mizpeh No. 6, below.

2. Mizpeh of Moab, where the king of that nation was living when David

committed his parents to his care, 1 Sam. xxii, 3. The site is unknown, but possibly at Kir-Moab, now *Kerak.*

3. The Land of Mizpeh, somewhere in the north of Palestine, the residence of the Hivites who joined the northern confederacy against Israel, Josh. xi, 3. Possibly this may be identical with

4. The Valley of Mizpeh, Josh. xi, 3, 8, to which the discomfited hosts of the same confederacy were pursued by Joshua. This is, perhaps, the modern *Buka'a,* that enormous tract, the great country of Cœle-Syria, between the ranges of Lebanon and Anti-Lebanon.

5. A city in the lowland of Judah, Josh. xv, 38. This possibly is identical with the modern *Tell es-Sâfiyeh.* But the southern part of this plain abounds in little tells, to any one of which the name of Mizpeh might be applicable.

6. A city in Benjamin, Josh. xviii, 26. Here Israel assembled, 1 Sam. vii, 5-7, 11, 12, 16. See also Mizpeh, (1,) above, in connection with Judg. xx, 1, 3; xxi, 1, 5, 8. Here Saul was elected king, 1 Sam. xi, 17-21. Asa fortified Mizpeh, 1 Kings xv, 22; 2 Chron. xvi, 6; and it was the place where Gedaliah was assassinated, 2 Kings xxv, 23, 25; Jer. xl, 6-15; xli, 1-16. Nehemiah states that the men of Gibeon and Mizpah were joined in rebuilding a part of the wall of Jerusalem, Neh. iii, 7, 15, 19. The Massepha of 1 Macc. iii, 46, which is probably identical with this place, and which was "over against Jerusalem," indicates that Mizpeh was in sight of Jerusalem. About four or five miles west of north from Jerusalem is the modern village of *Neby Samwil,* standing on a peak which rises about six hundred feet above the plain of Gibeon, and which is the most conspicuous object in the whole region. This village is claimed as the most probable site for Mizpeh by Robinson, Porter, and others. See Map 6. Eusebius and Jerome locate Mizpeh near Kirjath-Jearim. But Mr. Grove, agreeing with Professor Stanley and Dr. Bonar, presents strong reasons for putting Mizpeh on the Scopus of Josephus, one of the summits of the ridge north of Jerusalem. It is the "broad ridge which forms the continuation of the Mount of Olives to the north and east, from which the traveler gains, like Titus, his first view, and takes his last farewell of the domes, walls, and towers of the Holy City." Speaking of the term "over against," Mr. Porter says: "Any scholar who visits Jerusalem and studies the narrative in 1 Macc. iii, will admit that it is as applicable to *Neby Samwil* as to Scopus." See an interesting discussion by Mr. Grove in Smith's *Dictionary,* and by Mr. Porter in Kitto's *Cyclopædia.* Also Stanley's *Sinai and Palestine,* p. 222.

In 2 Chron. xx, 24, mention is made of a "watch-tower (Mizpeh) in the wilderness" of Judah, in connection with the miraculous destruction of the Ammonites and Moabites who invaded Judah in the reign of Jehoshaphat. It was probably a noted tower or castle between Tekoa and Engedi, but nothing is known concerning it. The Mizpah of Hosea v, 1, may be either that of Gilead or of Benjamin, it is wholly uncertain which.

Miz'raim, (Maps 2, 12,) *the two Egypts,* or **Land of Mizraim,** the name by which Egypt is generally designated in Scripture. It is usually employed to designate the whole of Egypt, but in Isa. xi, 11, it designates Lower Egypt as distinct from Pathros or Upper Egypt. See EGYPT.

Mo'ab, (Maps 4, 5,) probably *from father,* or possibly the *desirable land.* The name Moab is applied both to the son of Lot by his eldest daughter,

(Gen. xix, 37,) and to the well-known nation of which Moab was the progenitor. The land of Moab is on the east of the Dead Sea. From the neighborhood of Zoar the children of Lot must have extended themselves: Ammon to the more distant north-east country, previously inhabited by the Zuzim or Zamzummim; Moab in the districts nearer the original seat. Here lived the Emim, a gigantic race, a branch probably of the Rephaim; but the Moabites were successful in expelling them, (Deut. ii, 9, 10,) and occupied at first a considerable region, the uplands east of the Dead Sea and the Jordan as far as the mountains of Gilead, together with the lowlands between their own hills and the river—a region perhaps fifty miles in length and ten or twelve broad—the celebrated *Belka* and *Kerrak* of the modern Arabs, the most fertile on that side of Jordan. It comprised three divisions, the "country" or "field" of Moab to the south of the Arnon, Ruth i, 1, 2, 6; the "land" of Moab, the open country opposite Jericho to the Gileadite hills, Deut. i, 5; and the "plains," or more properly the arid district in the Jordan sunk valley, Num. xxii, 1. Of the valuable district of the highlands they were not allowed to retain entire possession. The warlike Amorites, crossing the Jordan from the west, overran the richer portion of the territory on the north, driving Moab back to his original position behind the Arnon. The plain of the Jordan valley appears to have remained in the power of Moab. When Israel reached the boundary of the country this contest had only very recently occurred. Sihon, the Amorite king, under whose command Heshbon had been taken, was still reigning there—the ballads commemorating the event being still fresh in the popular mouth, Num. xxi, 27–30. After such losses Moab might well dread the advancing hosts of the Israelites. "Moab was sore afraid of the people," Num. xxii, 3, 4. Their country, though now very much smaller, was yet more secure than formerly. It was now bounded north by the vast chasm of the Arnon, Num. xxi, 13; Judg. xi, 18; on the west by the precipices or cliffs, descending almost perpendicularly to the sea, and intersected only by one or two steep and narrow passes; and on the east and south by a circle of hills which open only to allow the passage of a branch of the Arnon and another of the torrents which descend to the Dead Sea. It was well watered, with valleys and wide plains among its hills; it was fruitful, and its downs afforded abundant pasture, Ruth i, 1; Isa. xvi, 8, 10; 2 Kings iii, 4. Ar or Rabbath-Moab was the metropolis, and Kir or Kir-Hareseth was one of the strongest fortresses. As the Hebrews advanced in order to take possession of Canaan they did not enter the proper territory of the Moabites, Deut. ii, 9; Judg. xi, 18; but conquered the kingdom of the Amorites (a Canaanitish tribe) which had belonged to Moab, whence the western part, lying along the Jordan, frequently occurs under the name of "land of Moab," Deut. i, 5; xxix, 1. The Moabites, fearing the numbers that were marching around them, showed them at least no kindness; and Balak, King of Moab, in conjunction with the Midianites, hired Balaam to utter prophetic curses against Israel, which, however, the Lord turned into blessings in his mouth, Num. xxii, 2–6; xxiv, 1–10. For this unfriendliness a prohibition was made against admitting a Moabite into the congregation of the Lord to the tenth generation, Deut. xxiii, 3–5. The Moabites (combining with the more guilty Midianites) were more successful in debauching the Israelites, and bringing a heavy retribution upon them for the idolatry and immorality into which they had enticed them, Num. xxv, 1–5. The Gadites now took possession of the northern portion of the territory which the Amorites had wrested from the Moabites, and there established themselves; while the Reubenites settled in the southern part, Num. xxxii, 34. (Compare Josh. xiii, which, however, differs somewhat in the designation of particular towns.)

In Deut. xxix we have the covenant which Moses made with the children of Israel in the land of Moab. From Deut. xxiv we learn that Moses viewed the Promised Land from a Moabite sanctuary, and that he died and was buried in the land of Moab.

After the settlement in Palestine, Moab, in conjunction with Ammon and Amalek, subjected the southern tribes of Israel, and perhaps also part of the trans-Jordanic territory; but Ehud delivered Israel after a servitude of eighteen years, Judg. iii, 12-30. Toward the end of this period, however, peace and friendship were restored, mutual honors were reciprocated, and Moab appears often to have afforded a place of refuge to outcasts and emigrant Hebrews, Ruth i, 1; compare 1 Sam. xxii, 3, 4; Jer. xl, 11; Isa. xvi, 2. Saul waged successful war against Moab, 1 Sam. xiv, 47; and David made it tributary, 2 Sam. viii, 2, 12; xxiii, 20. On the death of Ahab, Moab refused to pay the customary tribute of lambs and rams, 2 Kings i, 1; iii, 4; compare Isa. xvi, 1. Jehoram, though in conjunction with Jehoshaphat and his dependent, the King of Edom, he wasted the country, yet was unable to reconquer it, 2 Kings iii, 6-27. The Moabites and Ammonites had previously attacked Jehoshaphat, but were entirely defeated, 2 Chron. xx, 1-25; and we find them making incursions in the reign of Joash into the kingdom of Israel, 2 Kings xiii, 20, 21; but we may reasonably suppose them to have been brought under by Jeroboam II., 2 Kings xiv, 25-28. After the carrying away of the trans-Jordanic tribes into captivity, the Moabites doubtless occupied their territory, Isa. xv, 2, 4; xvi, 8; Jer. xlviii, 2, 22, 23, and they were then probably in possession of all they had formerly lost to the Amorites. The Moabites joined the Chaldeans against Jehoiakim, 2 Kings xxiv, 2; but encouraged Zedekiah against Nebuchadnezzar, Jer. xxvii, 3. They beheld with malicious satisfaction the destruction of the kindred people of Judah, Ezek. xxv, 8-11; Zeph. ii, 8-10. According to Josephus, Nebuchadnezzar, on his way to Egypt, made war upon them, and subdued them, together with the Ammonites, five years after the destruction of Jerusalem.

After the return from the captivity it was a Moabite, Sanballat, of Horonaim, who took the chief part in annoying and endeavoring to hinder the operations in the rebuilding of Jerusalem, Neh. ii, 19; iv, 1; soon after the captivity, also, Moabites and Ammonites are represented as dwelling in their ancient seats and as obeying the call of the Assyrian general, Judith iv, 3. Thenceforth the name of the Moabites is lost under that of the Arabians, as was also the case with Ammon and Edom.

The form of government in Moab we may suppose was monarchical, the chiefs possessing also considerable influence, Num. xxii, 8, 10, 14; xxiii, 6. The religion was idolatrous, their deities being Baal-Peor and Chemosh, Num. xxv, 1-3; 1 Kings xi, 7.

Several of the prophets predicted the desolation of Moab; and the subjection of Moab finds a place in every ideal description of splendid wars and golden ages predicted for Israel, Isa. xi, 14; xv; xvi; Jer. xxv, 21; Amos ii, 1-3; Zeph. ii, 8-11; Psa. lx, 8. These predictions find their fulfillment in the desolation of the whole region east of the Jordan. Although the sites, the ruins, and the names of many ancient cities of Moab can be traced, not

BIBLE GEOGRAPHY.   319

one of them exists at the present day as tenanted by man. The (American) Palestine Exploration Society have discovered many interesting ruins. See PEREA. For the "Moabite Stone," see DIBON.

Mo'abites, Mo'abitess. Natives of the land of Moab. Gen. xix, 37; Ruth i, 22, etc.

Moch'mur, THE BROOK, a wady, or torrent, mentioned only in Judith vii, 18, as specifying the position of Ekrebel. This "brook" may be either the *Wady Makfuriyeh*, on the northern slopes of which stands *Akrabeh*, southeast of *Nablûs*, or the *Wady Ahmar*, which is the continuation of the former eastward.

Mo'din, the native place of the Maccabees, 1 Macc. ii, 1, 15, 23, 70; ix, 19; xiii, 25, 30; xvi, 4; 2 Macc. xiii, 14. It occupied a distinguished place in Jewish history during the rule of the Asmonæan family. It contained their ancestral sepulcher. Eusebius and Jerome appear to have known the place, locating it near Diospolis, (Lydda.)

Possibly the site of Modin may be at the village called *Latron*, fifteen Roman miles from Jerusalem in the mouth of *Wady 'Aly*, where it opens from the mountains of Judea into the plain. Here is a high conical tell, crowned with the ruins of a large fortress. *Kubâb*, two miles further from Jerusalem, is also claimed as the site; but here no ruins seem to exist.

Mol'adah, *birth, lineage,* a city in the extreme south of Judah, grouped with Kedesh, Beersheba, and other places, Josh. xv, 21-26. With Beersheba it was afterward assigned to the tribe of Simeon, Josh. xix, 2; and occupied by the family of Shimei, 1 Chron. iv, 28. Some of the returned captives settled there, Neh. xi, 26.

About twenty geographical miles south of Hebron, on the road leading to Aila in the Red Sea, and ten east of Beersheba, are the ruins of an ancient fortified town now called *el-Milh*, which probably mark the site of Moladah. Two ancient wells here found make the spot a favorite watering-place.

Mo'rasthite, Jer. xxvi, 18; Mich. i1. A native of MORESHETH, which see.

Mo'reh, *teacher.*

1. The name of an oak, or grove of oaks, near Shechem, the first recorded halting-place of Abram after his entrance into the land of Canaan, Gen. xii, 6. The oak and terebinth seem to have been greatly venerated anciently in Palestine. Many of them were distinguished by proper names, Gen. xxxv, 8; under their shade altars were erected, councils held, and celebrated persons buried. Possibly this oak took its name from some Canaanitish chief by the name of Moreh. Moreh is again mentioned on the entrance of the Israelites into Canaan, Deut. xi, 30.

2. A "hill" in the plain of Jezreel, at whose base the camp of the Midianites was pitched, Judg. vii, 1, 12. It is probably identical with *Jebel ed-Duhy,* or "little Hermon."

More'sheth-Gath, or **Mo'resheth-Gath,** *possession of the wine-press,* a place named with Lachish, Achzib, Mareshah, and other towns of the lowland district of Judah, Micah i, 14. Micah is called "the Morasthite," Micah i, 1; Jer. xxvi, 18; but whether Moresheth-Gath is the Moresheth of which the prophet was a native is not certain; but possibly they are the same. Dr. Thomson inclines to identify this place with Mareshah, which he regarded as a "suburb" of Gath. He says, (*The Land and the Book,* vol. ii, p. 360:) "Micah probably wrote Moresheth-Gath in order to fix the location of the suburb by the name of the main city." But the affix "gath" may possibly refer to vineyards, the signification of "gath" being a winepress. Good authorities differ from Dr. Thomson, but no satisfactory site has been suggested.

Mori'ah, (Map 7,) variously interpreted—*the appearance of Jehovah, the chosen of Jehovah, Jehovah is thine instructor.* See JEHOVAH-JIREH. The name Moriah occurs in two passages only. In Gen. xxii, 2, Abraham is directed to go into the "land of Moriah," and there to offer up his son as a sacrifice. In 2 Chron. iii, 1, it is stated that Solomon began to build the temple at Jerusalem "in Mount Moriah." The Jews, "in uninterrupted succession," declare these two sites to be identical; and with this theory ordinary Christian interpretation agrees. A Samaritan tradition claims that Gerizim was the scene of Abraham's sacrifice, and that the mountains of Gerizim and Ebal, from their neighborhood to *Moreh*, a spot well known to Abraham, were the mountains in the land of Moriah. Dean Stanley, following this tradition, uses some strong arguments in favor of Gerizim as the scene of the event in question. (*Sinai and Palestine*, pp. 246-248.) But this identification cannot be maintained. Moriah was higher in Abraham's time than afterward, when its summit was leveled to receive the Temple; and if that summit could not be seen "afar off," as Stanley alleges it could not be, still the *heights* about Jerusalem could readily be seen from the ridge *Mâr Elias*. And this would fulfill the requirements of the passage which Gesenius translates "the land about Moriah." Besides, the terms "afar off" are evidently not employed to signify any considerable interval, Gen. xxii, 4, 5. Moreover, it is quite improbable that in the specified time the journey could have been made from Beersheba to Gerizim.

Some authorities claim that Moriah was also the place where Christ was crucified and buried. S. Smith, M. A., has written a valuable little treatise on "*The Temple and the Sepulcher,*" (London, 1865,) in which, claiming Calvary and Moriah as identical, the author says: "Nothing is more clear than that, after the resurrection of Christ, the heathen did all they could to desecrate the spot and to hide it from his disciples. For this purpose they covered it with earth, and raised over it a temple to Venus, and made their blood-offerings to her on the altar. And, to crown the indignity, we may well suppose that they pierced through the floor of the sacred cave [the "Cave of Rock"] to discharge the refuse from the altar sacrifices above it. That being the case, I claim the abomination as another proof that what is now the dome of the rock was the church built by Constantino over the Sepulcher of Christ." See CALVARY; JERUSALEM.

Mose'rah and **Mose'roth,** (Map 2,) *bond, bonds.* Mosera in Deut. x, 6, apparently the same as Moseroth, its plural form in Num. xxxiii, 30, 31, is the name of a place near Mount Hor, and the scene of Aaron's death.

Mo'zah, *a going forth, a fountain,* a town of Benjamin, grouped with Mizpeh and Chephireh, Josh. xviii, 26. The site of Mozah is not determined; but possibly it may be at *Kulonieh*, about four miles west of Jerusalem. See EMMAUS.

Myn'dus, (Map 8,) a town of Caria, between Miletus and Halicarnassus, 1 Macc. xv, 23. It seems to have been a place favorable for trade, and many Jews settled there. The modern name is *Mentesche.* Some ancient remains are found.

My'ra, (Map 8,) a sea-port of Lycia, in Asia Minor. It lay about twenty furlongs from the sea, upon a rising ground, at the foot of which flowed a navigable river, with an excellent harbor at its mouth. When Paul was on his voyage from Cæsarea to Rome he and the other prisoners were landed here, and were re-embarked in a ship of Alexandria bound to Rome, Acts xxvii, 5. The town is now called *Dembra* by the Greeks, and is remarkable for its remains of various periods of history.

My'sia, (Map 8,) *criminal,* the north-western province of Asia Minor. Paul passed through Mysia, and embarked at Troas, on his first voyage to Europe, Acts xvi, 7, 8. Troas, though within the same range of country, had a small district of its own, which was viewed as politically separate. Mysia, although now poorly tilled, is one of the finest tracts in Asia Minor.

Na'amah, *pleasant,* a city in the lowland of Judah, grouped with Lachish, Eglon, and Makkedah, Josh. xv, 41. It is not identified.

Na'amathite, *one of Naamah,* one of Job's three friends, Zophar, who evidently lived in a place called Naamah, Job ii, 11, etc. Uz, the country of Job, was in Arabia; Eliphaz, the *Temanite,* and Bildad, the *Shuhite,* Job's other two friends, were Arabians; hence it seems reasonable to conclude that Zophar was also from some place in Arabia. But no identification of Naamah has been made.

Na'aran, *puerile, juvenile,* a town mentioned in 1 Chron. vii, 28, as the eastern limit of Ephraim. It was probably identical with NAARATH, which see.

Na'arath, (Hebrew, *Naarah,*) *a girl, handmaid,* a town named in Josh. xvi, 7, as one of the landmarks on the (southern) boundary of Ephraim. It seems to have been in the Jordan valley, north of Jericho. Eusebius describes it as "a village of Ephraim, now *Oorath,* (Jerome, *Naorath,*) a village of the Jews five miles from Jericho." Kiepert's map locates *Naaratha* at about that distance north of Jericho; but the site of the town is not yet identified.

Na'bathites, 1 Macc. v, 25; ix, 35. See NEBAIOTH.

Na'chon, *prepared,* the threshing-floor by which Uzzah died, between Kirjath-Jearim and Jerusalem, 2 Sam. vi, 6. It is called Chidon in 1 Chron. xiii, 9. After the death of Uzzah it received the name of Perez-Uzzah. The site is unknown.

Nadab'atha, the city from which the children of Jambri were conducting a bride with music and great pomp when attacked and slaughtered by Jonathan and Simon, to avenge the death of their brother John, 1 Macc. ix, 37. It lay, probably, east of the Jordan; but no identification has been made.

Na'halal, Nahal'lal, and **Na'halol,** *pasture,* a town in Zebulun, afterward assigned to the Merarite Levites, Josh. xix, 15; xxi, 35; Judg. i, 30. Schwartz, Van de Velde, and others would identify Nahalal with the modern village and ruins of *Malûl,* four miles west of Nazareth—a theory suggested, probably, from one Hebrew MS. which, in Josh. xxi, 35, reads *Mahalol.* Mr. Porter thinks *Malul* to be more probably the site of the ancient Maralah. See MARALAH.

Naha'liel, (Map 2,) *valley of God,* a station of the Israelites, Num. xxi, 19. It was north of the Arnon, and not far from Pisgah. Possibly the name is preserved in that of the *Wady Enkheileh,* a branch of the *Mojib,* the ancient Arnon. This suggestion, to say the least, may prove of value to future travelers.

Na'in, (Map 5,) *beauty, pleasantness,* a town in Galilee, mentioned only in

NAIN.

Luke vii, 11. One of Christ's greatest miracles occurred here, the raising of the widow's son to life. The place still exists under the name of *Nein*. It is situated on the north-western edge of the "Little Hermon," or *Jebel ed-Dûhy*, where the ground falls into the plain of Esdraelon. Dr. Thomson says, "It took me just an hour to ride from the foot of Tabor to Nain." The site is very beautiful, but the village is a small, poor hamlet of about twenty houses or huts, around which are quite extensive ruins. The most interesting remains are the tombs, hewn in the rock, a short distance east of the village.

Na'ioth, *habitations*, a place in or near Ramah, where Samuel abode with his disciples, and whither David fled to him, 1 Sam. xix, 18, 19, 22, 23; xx, 1. Probably Naioth was the dwelling of a school of prophets, and not a town or village.

Na'phish, *recreated, refreshment*, the name of the tribe and nation which sprang from Ishmael's son, Naphish, Gen. xxv, 15; 1 Chron. i, 31. In 1 Chron. v, 19, Nephish. This seems to have been a numerous tribe, and very rich in cattle. They probably intermarried with other and more powerful nations of Arabia, and thus lost their own individuality as a tribe. Their locality has not yet been determined.

Naph'tali, (Map 5,) *my wrestling*. In the New Testament the form Nephthalim is employed. This was one of the tribes of Israel, sprung from the son of Jacob by Bilhah, Rachel's maid, Gen. xxx, 8; xxxv, 25; Exod. i, 4; 1 Chron. ii, 2.

At the first census after leaving Egypt the tribe numbered fifty-three thousand four hundred, Num. i, 42, 43. Its place on the march was north of the tabernacle, under the standard of Dan, Num. ii, 25, 29; x, 25, 27. At the second census, in the plains of Moab, the number had diminished to forty-five thousand four hundred, Num. xxvi, 48-50.

The blessing which Jacob pronounced upon Naphtali (Gen. xlix, 21) was intended to shadow forth under poetic imagery the future character and history of the tribe: "Naphtali is a hind let loose: he giveth goodly words." The qualities shown by the tribe were those of a "hind"—timid and distrustful of its own powers, swift of foot to elude its enemies, but when brought to bay, fierce and strong to defend its life. They left several of their cities in the hands of the Canaanites, Judg. i, 33; they had not confidence to fight alone, but when assailed they made a noble defense, and united with others in pursuit of a flying foe, Judg. v, 18; vi, 35. Their want of self-confidence was chiefly shown in the case of Barak, and then, too, they displayed in the end heroic devotion and unwearied alacrity, Judg. iv, 6-10; v, 18. "He giveth goodly words," indicated that the tribe was to be famous for the beauty of its language. Probably there were poets and writers among them whose names have not come down to us. We have one noble ode ascribed in part at least to a Naphtalite, Judg. v, 1.

The blessing of Moses had reference to the nature of the territory occupied by Naphtali: "O Naphtali, satisfied with favor, and full with the blessing of the Lord, possess thou the west and the south," Deut. xxxiii, 33. A more literal and accurate rendering of the Hebrew would be, "Naphtali, replete with favors, and full of the blessings of Jehovah, possess thou the sea and Darom." "The sea and Darom" would signify the region by the Sea of Galilee, and the mountains to the north of it.

The possessions allotted to Naphtali are described in Josh. xix, 32-39. They lay at the northern angle of Palestine. On the east they were bounded by the Jordan and the lakes of Merom and Galilee; on the south by Zebulun; on the west by Asher; and on the north apparently by the river Leontes. Naphtali possessed a greater variety of soil, scenery, and climate than any of the other tribes. Its northern portions are the highlands of Palestine. The grand ravine of the Leontes separates its mountains from the chain of Lebanon, of which, however, they may be regarded as a prolongation. The southern section of Naphtali was the garden of Palestine. Josephus described the plain on the shore of the lake, then called Gennesaret, as an earthly paradise, where the choicest fruits grew luxuriantly, and where eternal spring reigned. And even now, though more a wilderness than a paradise, its surpassing richness is evident. The glowing accounts which modern travelers give of the fertility of this territory show that Naphtali was surely "satisfied with favor, and full with the blessing of the Lord."

On account of its position Naphtali was in a great measure isolated from the Israelitish kingdom. The powerful Syrian expeditions usually passed along the east base of Hermon, and across the Jordan at Jacob's bridge. Hence the Naphtalites in their mountain fastnesses escaped their devastations. But whenever the enemy marched through the Valley of Cœle-Syria, then Naphtali bore the first brunt of the onset, and its chief cities, Ijon, Abel, Kadesh, and Hazor, were the first that fell, 1 Kings xv, 20; 2 Chron. xvi, 4. Naphtali was also the first tribe captured by the Assyrians, under Tiglath-Pileser, 2 Kings xv, 29; Isa. ix, 1. After the captivity the Israelites again settled largely in Naphtali, and its southern section became the most densely populated district in Palestine. It became the principal scene also of our Lord's public labors. After his brethren at Nazareth rejected and sought to kill him he came and dwelt in "Capernaum, which is upon the sea-coast, in the borders of Zebulun and Nephthalim," Matt. iv, 13. The new capital of Galilee had recently been built by Antipas, and called after the emperor Tiberias. Other towns—Magdala, Capernaum, Chorazin, and the two Bethsaidas—dotted the shore, which teemed with life and industry. Vast multitudes followed Jesus wherever he went, Mark ii, 1-12 · Matt. xiii,

1-23, etc. Here were spoken the greater number of Christ's beautiful parables, and here, too, was the scene of most of his miracles. Thus the beautiful prophecy of Isaiah, as quoted and applied by Matthew, (iv, 15, 16,) was literally fulfilled. See TIBERIAS; GALILEE, SEA OF.

Naph'tuhim, *border-people*, an Egyptian tribe, descendants of Mizraim, Gen. x, 13; 1 Chron. i, 11. Kalisch and some others seek to identify this people with the city of Naphata or Napata, the capital of an ancient Ethiopian kingdom, and one of the most splendid cities in Africa. This city and its territory lay on the southern frontier of Mizraim, in the north of the province of Meroë, at the great bend of the Nile, and having the desert of Bahiuda on the south. Extensive and splendid ruins remain—pyramids, temples, sphinxes, and sculptures. Two lions, sculptured in red granite, have been brought from these ruins and are now in the British Museum.

Na'sor, THE PLAIN OF, the scene of an engagement between Jonathan Maccabeus and Demetrius, 1 Macc. xi, 67. It is doubtless identical with the ancient Hazor, in Galilee.

Naz'areth, (Map 5,) perhaps *separated, branch, sanctified*, but the signification is very doubtful. A town in Galilee, the residence of Joseph and Mary, Luke i, 26, 27, 56; ii, 4, 39; but chiefly celebrated as the home of our blessed Lord after the return from Egypt. This was the place of Christ's boyhood, the scene of his domestic relations, his private life, his mental development, his prayers and communion with the Father, and his early labors, Matt. ii, 23; Luke ii, 39, 51; Matt. iv, 13. When entering on his public life Jesus came from Nazareth, Mark i, 9; Matt. iii, 13. Nazareth was now no longer his home, yet he returned thither, (Luke iv, 16,) and his fellow-townsmen sought to kill him. After this he made Capernaum his residence,

"his own city," Luke iv, 16-31; Matt. iv, 13-16; ix, 1. But again Christ visited Nazareth, and still "they were offended at him," Matt. xiii, 54-58; Mark vi, 1-6. For other interesting allusions to this city see John i, 45, 46; Acts ii, 22; iii, 6; iv, 10; x, 38; xxii, 8; xxvi, 9.

Nazareth is not mentioned in the Old Testament, nor in any writer before the birth of Christ, nor is it found in any classic author; yet its name has become a household word throughout Christendom. Splendid structures have been built to commemorate it, and thousands of pilgrimages have been made in honor of it. Not until the time of Constantine did it attract much attention, nor does it seem to have been visited by any pilgrims till about the sixth century. In the seventh century it contained two churches—one built over "the fountain," the other over the house of Mary, now occupied by the Latin convent. During the Crusades its great church was rebuilt and richly endowed, and the town was made the seat of a bishop.

The place still exists under the modern name of *en-Násirah*. It stands in an upland vale amid the hills of Galilee, two miles from the plain of Esdraelon and six west of Tabor. A girdle of rounded hills encircles it, giving that air of quiet, peaceful seclusion which constitutes its chief charm. "The narrow

NAZARETH.

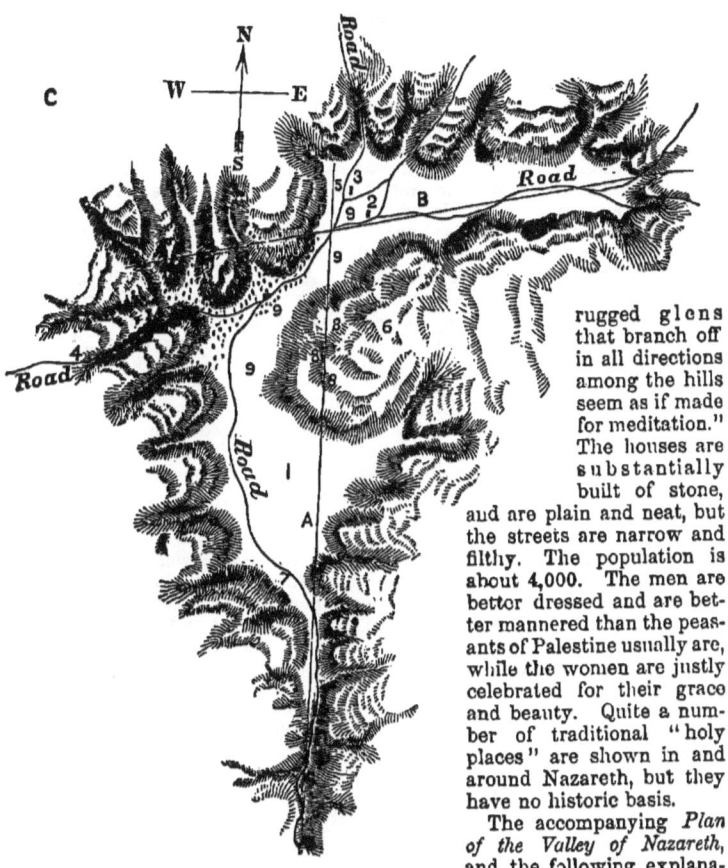

rugged glens that branch off in all directions among the hills seem as if made for meditation." The houses are substantially built of stone, and are plain and neat, but the streets are narrow and filthy. The population is about 4,000. The men are better dressed and are better mannered than the peasants of Palestine usually are, while the women are justly celebrated for their grace and beauty. Quite a number of traditional "holy places" are shown in and around Nazareth, but they have no historic basis.

The accompanying *Plan of the Valley of Nazareth*, and the following explanation, are from the pen of Dr. J. S. Jewell, in an article contributed to the "Sunday-School Journal." Concerning two visits made by him (in 1869) to this valley, "or basin, as it may truly be called," Dr. Jewell says: "My first approach was made by the western road, marked 4; my next by one of the roads which descend into the eastern end of the valley. The usual camping place is indicated by number 5. Its length along the line A is about one mile and two fifths. It will be observed, as you follow the valley northward from its narrow, rocky south end, it expands and soon widens at figure 1 many hundred feet. This part is not very rocky, and has some scattering olive and fig-trees on it, and some low, rude stone walls, dividing it into little patches sown in wheat, barley, etc. The hills on either hand are bare, rocky, and treeless, and rather steep. Many small valleys or ravines, hardly worthy the name, descend the hill-sides into the basin. From the time you first enter the valley at No. 7 you can see some of the houses of the town. You soon have to your right hand a rocky point or ridge coming down into the basin. The limestone here, as elsewhere, projects through the scanty soil. At the places marked 8 are several artificial caves, probably once occupied as dwellings, now choked with rubbish. In that part of the valley (a few hundred feet wide) marked 9 are many hedges of the largest specimens of cactus I have ever met with anywhere, save in Galilee. Here are also many old olive and fig trees. The position of the town, as will be seen, is on the west side of the valley, on the slopes of that part of it where, as you follow northward, it turns eastward. At No. 2, just out of the village to the north-east, is the Fountain of the Virgin, or Fountain of the Annunciation. At No. 3 is the little chapel of the Annunciation. The line B, drawn along the upper or eastern part of the valley, may represent its axis, and is somewhat less than a mile in length. The hills standing about this basin are highest in the direction of C, beyond which, on the highest point, is a small *wely*, or tomb of a *sheik*. From this a most extensive prospect is had of the surrounding country, especially south, west, and north. It has been well described by Dr. Robinson."

Ne'ah, *the shaking*, a town on the eastern border of Zebulun, Josh. xix, 13. It lay between the valley of Jiphthah-el and Japhia. About three miles north-west of Nazareth is a little village called '*Ain*, the position of which might answer to Neah.

Neap'olis, (Map 8,) *new city*.

1. The place in Northern Greece where St. Paul first landed in Europe, Acts xvi, 11. Doubtless he landed here also on his second visit to Macedonia, Acts xx, 1. The site is now occupied by the Turkish village of *Kavalla*, situated on a rocky promontory. It has a population of about five thousand or six thousand, nine tenths of whom are Mussulmans and the rest Greeks. The remains of Neapolis are extensive. Besides an aqueduct nearly ten miles in length, there are Ionic columns and hewn stones, sculptured stones, and marble sarcophagi.

2. The name of Neapolis was given to Shechem during the Roman age. Josephus usually called the city Sichem; but he has Neapolis in *Bell. Jud.*, iv, 8..1. See SHECHEM.

Neba'ioth and Neba'joth, (Maps 12, 13,) *heights*, the chief and oldest of the Ishmaelite tribes, Gen. xxv, 13; xxviii, 9, etc. In 1 Macc. v, 25; ix, 35, Nabathites. This tribe is considered identical with the Nabatheans of classic authors, and the *Beni Nabat* of the Arabs. Their territory, at first, appears to have been on the south-east of Palestine, in and around the mountains of Edom. There Esau became allied with them; and soon they went more to the south and east, to secure pasture for their rapidly increasing flocks. Afterward they built towns, especially the magnificent Petra, whose splendid rock temples and tombs have been the wonder of the world for the last half century. (See SELA.) They surpassed all other Arab tribes in refinement and commercial enterprise. They were celebrated for their astronomy, magic, medicine, and agriculture. Their government was monarchical, but the power of their kings was limited. Plundered by Sennacherib, contending in war with various kings, they became at length little better than a nation of robbers. But the Syrian wars curbed and reformed them; and they had the confidence of some of the Maccabean princes. The kingdom of the

Nabatheans was overthrown by Cornelius Palma, governor of Syria, in A. D. 105, and annexed to the Roman Empire. Their enterprise and wealth soon declined, and when the fierce followers of Mohammed overran Western Asia, the cities of the Nabatheans were ruined, their country laid waste, and the remnant of the people were mingled with the tribes of the desert.

Nebal'lat, *folly in secret,* a town occupied by the Benjamites after the captivity; mentioned only in Neh. xi, 34, and grouped with Lod, (Lydda.) Possibly Neballat is identical with the village of *Beit Nebála,* about four miles north-east of Lydda, which has some few traces of antiquity. Or it may be at another place of nearly the same name, *Bir Nebála,* lying to the east of *el Jib,* (Gibeon,) and within half a mile of it.

Ne'bo, MOUNT, (Map 5.) The name Nebo may come from a root signifying "to project," or "to be high;" hence *a projection.* Or it may be traced to the heathen deity Nebo, the planet Mercury, which the Chaldeans and ancient Arabs worshiped as the celestial scribe or writer; in this sense the signification of Nebo is *interpreter*—that is, of the gods. Some have supposed that there was an ancient high place on Nebo where this deity was worshiped; but there is no proof of this. This was the mount in Moab, "over against Jericho," "up into" which the Lord commanded Moses to go "and behold the land of Canaan," Deut. xxxii, 49. "And Moses went up from the plains of Moab unto the mountain of Nebo, to the top of Pisgah . . . and the Lord showed him all the land of Gilead, unto Dan," etc. Deut. xxxiv. Nebo was a peak of the range called ABARIM, which see.

Several peaks have been suggested as Nebo: *Jebel Attarûs* is one; but it is not opposite Jericho, and lies much too far south to answer the Scripture narrative. *Jebel Jil'ad* is another, but it is about the same distance too far north, being about fifteen miles north of a line drawn eastward from Jericho. The most probable conjecture identifies this peak with *Jebel Nebbah,* south of *Wady Hesban.* See PISGAH.

Ne'bo, (for signification see preceding article.)

1. A city of the Gadites east of the Jordan, grouped with Heshbon, Elealeh, and Baal-Meon, Num. xxxii, 3, 38; xxxiii, 47. Nebo was rebuilt by the Gadites; but from 1 Chron. v, 8, it would seem that both it and Baal-Meon were inhabited by a Reubenite family; or perhaps that family held the country up to the borders of Nebo and Baal-Meon. Later it was captured by the Moabites, and Isaiah joins it with Dibon and Medeba, in the curse pronounced upon that land, Isa. xv, 2. Jeremiah also predicts its fall as a city of Moab, Jer. xlviii, 1, 22. "The ruins of Nebo are on a mamelon, slightly depressed, and projected from the line of the main ridge, which runs north and south from Heshbon to Ma'in, and are about two miles west of its crest."—TRISTRAM: *The Land of Moab,* p. 338.

2. A place in Benjamin where dwelt some who returned from Babylon, Ezra ii, 29; Neh. vii, 33. Seven of them had foreign wives, whom they were compelled to discard, Ezra x, 43. Possibly Nebo is identical with the small modern village of *Beit Nûbah* in the plain of Sharon, about twelve miles north-west of Jerusalem.

Ne'geb, *the south, the south country.* As the term Negeb is occasionally used in this volume, it may not be amiss to here give a few explanatory words. The sacred writers appear to have employed this term and some others not merely as appellations, (as usually rendered in the Authorized Version,) but in a topographical sense, to indicate some specific region or province. In Gen. xii, 9, we read, "And Abram journeyed [from Bethel; going on still *toward the south*," that is, "to the Negeb." In Gen. xiii, 1, "Abram went up out of Egypt . . . *into the South*," that is, "to the Negeb." In 1 Sam. xxx, 14, there is the Negeb of the Cherethites, or Philistines; also in 1 Sam. xxvii, 10; xxx, 14, Negeb of the Kenites, Negeb of the Jerahmeelites, Negeb of Judah, and the Negeb of Caleb.

At the time of the Exodus the Negeb was chiefly inhabited by the Amalekites, Num. xiii, 29. Its northern limit was the *Shephelah* and the mountains of Judah. On the east it bordered on the *Arabah* as far south as the parallel of Kedesh. Its southern border cannot now be defined; but it did not reach either to the peninsula of Sinai nor to Egypt. See a valuable work entitled *The Negeb, or South Country of Scripture*, by Rev. E. Wilton.

Nehel'amite. The margin reads "*dreamer*," Jer. xxix, 24, 31, 32. A false prophet called "Shemaiah." Nothing is known concerning the derivation of this word. It is probably the name of a family; but the locality cannot be determined.

Nei'el, or **Ne'iel,** perhaps *moved*, or *treasured, of God*, a place mentioned as one of the landmarks on the boundary of Asher, Josh. xix, 27. It occurs between Jipthah-el and Cabul. Neiel is not named by any classic or ecclesiastical writer. Mr. Grove thinks the site may possibly be represented by *Mi'ar*, a village conspicuously placed on a lofty mountain brow just half-way between *Jefât* and *Kabûl*—"but very doubtful."

Ne'keb, *the cavern*, a town on the border of Naphthali lying between Adami and Jabneel, Josh. xix, 33. Possibly this name should be connected with the preceding as "Adami-Nekeb," or "Adami-the-Cavern.' The Talmud (separating the two) gives the name of Nekeb as Tziadatha, which is now unknown.

Ne'phish, 1 Chron. v, 19. Incorrectly for Naphish.

Neph'thali, and **Neph'thalim,** variations of Naphtali, Tob. i, 1–5; xii, 3; Matt. iv, 13, 15; Rev. vii, 6.

Neph'toah, THE WATER OF, *water of opening*, a spring or fountain, and apparently a streamlet issuing from it, in the border between Judah and Benjamin, Josh. xv, 9; xviii, 15. Geographers are not well agreed as to the site. Mr. Porter (in *Kitto*) considers the spot probably at *Ain Yalo*, in *Wady-el-Werd*, three miles south-west of Jerusalem; while Mr. Grove, (in Smith's *Dictionary*,) following others, supposes this fountain to be about two miles and a half north-west of the city at *Ain Lifta*, situated a little distance above the village of the same name, in a short valley which runs into the east side of the great *Wady Beit Hanina*.

Neto'phah, a *dropping, distillation*, a place apparently in Judah, and near Bethlehem, mentioned among the towns occupied after the captivity, Ezra ii, 22; Neh. vii, 26; 1 Esdras v, 18, but existing much earlier than this date. See 2 Sam. xxiii, 28, 29; 2 Kings xxv, 23; 1 Chron. ii, 54, etc.; Neh. xii, 38; Jer. xl, 8; in which passages the inhabitants of this place are called Netophathi and Netophathites. The village of *Beit Nettif*, which some suggest as the site of Netophah, is doubtless too far from Bethlehem, being on the brow of the valley of Elah. On Van de Velde's map is the name of a village called *Antûbeh*, lying about two miles north-east of Bethlehem, which Mr. Grove suggests as the site of Netophah. This would seem to agree with the Scripture notices.

Ne'zib, (Map 5,) *a garrison, statue*, or *idol*, a place in the lowland of Judah,

Josh. xv, 43. It is identified with *Beit Nusib*, five miles from *Beit Jibrin*, (Eleutheropolis,) on the road to Hebron. It lies neither in the mountain not in the plain, but in the low hilly ground which connects the two. The ruins are of considerable extent, consisting of massive foundations, broken columns, and large building stones.

Nib'shan, *light, soft soil,* a city in the wilderness of Judah, apparently near Engedi, on the shore of the Dead Sea; mentioned only in Josh. xv, 62. It is wholly unknown.

Nicop'olis, (Map 8,) *city of victory.* There were several ancient cities by this name. Paul refers to one of them in Titus iii, 12. There seems to be no scriptural evidence as to what city is intended. One Nicopolis was in Thrace, near the borders of Macedonia; another in the north-eastern corner of Cilicia; a third was the celebrated Nicopolis in Epirus. Each of these has its advocates as the city referred to by the Apostle, but the one last named seems to be the one indicated. This important city was built by Augustus in commemoration of the battle of Actium. Ruins of considerable extent remain under the name of *Paleoprevesa,* "Old Prevesa." For an interesting account of Nicopolis in Epirus see Wordsworth's *Greece*, and Conybeare and Howson's *Life of St. Paul.* Emmaus was at one time called Nicopolis. See EMMAUS.

Nile, (Map 1,) "the blue," "the dark." The river Nile is frequently mentioned in the Bible, but not under this name. See RIVER OF EGYPT; SHIHOR, and SIHOR.

Nim'rah, *limpid, pure,* (as water) or *panther,* east of Jordan, apparently near Heshbon, Num. xxxii, 3. Perhaps it is identical with BETH-NIMRAH, which see. The name *Nimr* ("*panther*") appears to be a common one east of the Jordan, and until further exploration is possible it will be exceedingly difficult to identify places under this term.

Nim'rim, *limpid, pure,* or *panther.* "The waters of Nimrim," a stream or brook within the country of Moab, mentioned in the denunciations of that nation uttered or quoted by Isaiah and Jeremiah, Isa. xv, 6; Jer. xlviii, 34; (compare Num. xxxii, 3, 36.) Mr. Grove thinks it is "possibly in *Wady Nemeirah,* south of the *Lisan;* but very doubtful." Kiepert's map locates a Nimrim there. Mr. Porter speaks of "copious springs" near the ruins of Beth-Nimrah, which he considers "the waters of Nimrim," on which Isaiah pronounced the curse. See NIMRAH, and BETH-NIMRAH.

Nin'eveh, (Maps 1, 14,) probably *habitation of Ninus;* or perhaps *City of Nin,* from the Assyrian god *Nin.* The ancient capital of Assyria. By the Greeks and Romans it was usually called *Ninus,* after the name of its founder. This once magnificent city stood upon the eastern bank of the Tigris, opposite the place where *Mosul* now stands on the western bank.

In Gen. x, 11, (margin,) we are told that Nineveh was founded by Nimrod. Hence it was one of the oldest cities in the world. The name of Nineveh is on Egyptian monuments of Thothmes III. about 1400 B. C. After the brief allusion in Genesis, Nineveh is not again noticed in Scripture until the time of Jonah, about 800 B. C., when the prophet was commanded by God to go to that "great city and cry against it," Jonah i, 2. Then it was a most powerful monarchy—" an exceeding great city of three days' journey," iii, 3; with a vast population, iv, 11. The preaching of Jonah caused but a temporary repentance in Nineveh, and we find the prophet Nahum uttering fearful predictions against the city. These were terribly fulfilled. See the whole book of Nahum; also Zeph. ii, 13-15; compare Ezek. xxxi. Sennacherib was assassinated in Nineveh, 2 Kings xix, 36, 37; Isa. xxxvii, 37, 38. Christ employed the name of Nineveh as a warning to all transgressors, Matt. xii, 41; Luke xi, 32.

The history of Nineveh, like its rise, is involved in much obscurity. The accounts of its vastness and splendor are only traditional. According to Diodorus Siculus the city had the form of a rectangular parallelogram, being 150 stadia in length by 90 in breadth, the whole circuit being 480 stadia, or, as variously computed, 32, 56, 60, or 74 miles. Strabo says it was larger than Babylon, and Diodorus asserts that the walls were 100 feet high, broad enough for three chariots abreast, and flanked with 1,500 towers, each 200 feet high. We have no ancient description of the buildings of this great city; nor is there any account of Nineveh in the Persian cuneiform inscriptions discovered among its ruins. After a long career of prosperity at length Nineveh fell, and with it also fell the Assyrian Empire. In Jeremiah's catalogue of "all the nations" (Jer. xxv) there is no mention of either the city or the empire. Their fall was complete. The time of their overthrow is variously computed: by some at 585 B. C., by others at 606 B. C., and by others still at 625 B. C., which is the most probable date. The last Scripture notice occurs in Zeph. ii, 13-15, about 630 B. C.

According to Ctesias, (as preserved in Diodorus,) Nineveh was besieged by Cyaxares, the Median monarch, assisted by the Babylonians under Nabopolassar. His efforts were unsuccessful for two years, when, aided by an extraordinary rise of the Tigris, which swept away a part of the walls, he entered the city with his army. The Assyrian monarch, Saracus, in despair, burned himself in his palace, and the barbarous conquerors gave the entire city to the flames.

The once magnificent Nineveh now became "a desolation, a place for beasts to lie down in," Zeph. ii, 15. And two hundred years afterward, when Herodotus passed very near the site, there was no vestige of the city. Nor does Xenophon mention the name of Nineveh, although with his troops he camped by the site, (401 B. C.) The historians of Alexander (with one exception) make no allusion to the place, although that great general won a victory in the immediate vicinity. The site is called Ninos by Tacitus, in recording its capture by Meherdates, near the close of Nero's reign. On the coins of Trajan and Maximin the words *Colonia Ninivia Claudiopolis* seem to show that Claudius had there founded a colony. Among the ruins of the site have been found many remains of the Roman period—terra-cottas, sculptures, vases, coins. In A. D. 627 the name of Nineveh once more occurs, in the mere mention of a battle occurring there, in which Heraclius, the Emperor of the East, triumphed over the Persian Chosroes. And in A. D. 637 we find the Arabs giving the name of *Ninawi* to a fort on the east bank of the Tigris.

Nineveh was for a long period well-nigh forgotten, and its site unknown. Until a very recent period a few shapeless mounds opposite Mosul, a noted city on the western bank of the Tigris, were all that tradition could point out as remaining of Nineveh. That the ruins of so large and important a city should so long have been lost is indeed among the remarkable facts of history. Says Ayre: "It is more than curious, it is the wise providence of Him who uncovereth secret things, that, in our busy, speculative, superficial age, when men are questioning the truth of his revelation, and, wise in their

BIBLE GEOGRAPHY. 335

own conceit, denying his moral government of the worlds he has framed, the earth should, as it were, give forth a voice, reveal the buried palaces of ancient days, and proclaim thereby a fresh attestation to the truths of sacred writ."

In 1820 Mr. Rich, political resident at Bagdad, brought a few relics of ancient Nineveh, obtained from both Koyunjik and Neby Yunus. But we are indebted chiefly to Dr. Layard, who visited the site of the ruins in 1840, and to M. Botta, who was French consul at Mosul in 1841. Concerning these ruins Layard remarks: "If we take the four great mounds of Nimrud, Koyunjik, Khorsabad, and Karamles as the corners of a square, it will be found that its four sides correspond pretty accurately with the 480 stadia, or 60 miles, of the geographer, which make the three days' journey of the prophet."

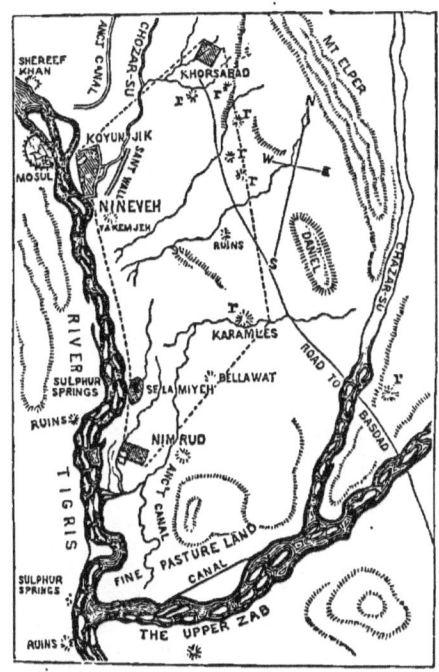

PLAN OF RUINS—MOUNDS AT NINEVEH.

M. Botta met with little success in excavating at Koyunjik, where he began his work; but on changing his labors to Khorsabad he soon discovered slabs and sculptures, and succeeded in laying bare the ground-plan of a magnificent palace. Many relics secured by him are now in the museum of the Louvre, and constitute the national collection of Assyrian monuments in France. The success of M. Botta greatly stimulated Dr. Layard, who directed his attention to the great mound of Nimrud, considerably to the south of Mosul, and about six and a half miles from the point where the Zab falls into the Tigris. Having at length secured aid, by the liberality of Sir Stratford Canning, Mr. Layard succeeded in November, 1845, in excavating a chamber in what is now called the north-west palace of Nimrud. The ruins at Nimrud are of higher antiquity than those at Khorsabad, and evidently assignable to different epochs. More important discoveries were then rapidly made. The fanatical and jealous Moslems, however, offered no little opposition to the great explorer. They often afforded much amusement also in the manifestation of their astonishment at some of the relics exhumed. Dr. Layard gives the following illustrative incident. He says: "One morning I had ridden to the encampment of Sheikh Abd-ur-Rahman, and was returning to the mound, when I saw two Arabs of his tribe urging their mares to the top of their speed. On approaching me they stopped. 'Hasten, O bey!' exclaimed one of them, 'hasten to the diggers, for they have found Nimrod himself. Wallah! it is wonderful, but it is true! we have seen him with our eyes. There is no God but God;' and, both joining in this pious exclamation, they galloped off, without further words, in the direction of their tents. On reaching the ruins I descended into the new trench. . . . The Arabs withdrew the screen they had hastily constructed, and disclosed an enormous human head, sculptured in full out of the alabaster of the country. . . . I saw at once that the head must belong to a winged lion or bull. . . . It was in admirable preservation. The expression was

WINGED LION (IN THE BRITISH MUSEUM) FROM NINEVEH.

calm, yet majestic, and the outline of the features showed a freedom and knowledge of art scarcely to be looked for in works of so remote a period. . . . One of the workmen, catching the first glimpse of the monster, had thrown down his basket, and had run off toward Mosul as fast as his legs could carry him. The neighboring Arab sheikh and half his tribe were soon upon the spot, and confidently pronounced the gigantic head to be the work of no human hands, but one of the idols which Noah had cursed before the flood."

These mounds extend on the eastern bank of the Tigris from Shereef Khan in the north to Nimrud in the south, about twenty-five miles, and from the Tigris to Khorsabad and Karamles on the east, about ten or twelve miles. Traces of ancient structures are to be seen throughout this large extent of country. The western face of the ruins opposite Mosul is about a mile from the Tigris, which probably once ran close to them. These ruins consist of an embankment generally forty or fifty feet high, with Koyunjik and Neby Yunus (the traditional *tomb of Jonah*) on its western face. *Koyunjik* measures about 860 yards by 300; *Neby Yunus* 560 by 400. The entire length of the western wall is about 4,533 yards; the northern side is 2,333 yards; the southern about 1,000; while the eastern, which forms a curve, is 5,300 yards. In many places the towers may still be traced, and it is thought the gate-ways were arched. One was discovered in the center of the northern wall and another in the inner east wall. The former consisted of two halls, 70 feet by 23, which opened on the plain and on the interior of the inclosure by means of gate-ways, which were flanked by colossal man-headed bulls and winged human figures. The ruts of chariot wheels can still be traced on the limestone slabs of the pavement. This gate-way was buried beneath an immense amount of rubbish. On the eastern side are moats and formidable ramparts. The remains at *Koyunjik* indicate structures of greater extent and magnificence than those found elsewhere. As many as seventy-one chambers were uncovered, which are paneled with bas-reliefs for an extent of nearly two miles, and twenty-seven entrances were excavated, which were flanked by colossal winged bulls, or lion-sphinxes, although little more than half was explored. *Nimrud* is similar to the ruins above noted, but its defenses were by no means so important. It consists of an inclosure, indicating ancient walls nearly square, being about 2,331 yards by 2,095. The Tigris ran formerly along the south and western sides; the others were protected by moats. There is a great mound, 700 yards by 400, on the south-west face, with a kind of earthen pyramid, rising to the height of 140 feet in its north-west corner. A group of mounds also exists at the south-east corner, called by the Arabs *Athur*, a name which seems at one time to have been applied to the whole of Nineveh. Athur is said to have been Nimrod's lieutenant. *Khorsabad* is a square of about 2,000 yards. Towers and gate-ways are traced, but there are no indications of moats. On the north-west face of the inclosure rises a great mound, which is divided into two parts, the lower 1,350 feet by 300, the upper 650 feet square and about 30 high. The summit was formerly occupied by an Arab village, and at one corner is a pyramid like that at Nimrud, but much smaller. Throughout all the ruins Mr. Layard and his fellow-laborers continually encountered calcined sculptured alabaster, charcoal, and charred wood buried in masses of brick and earth, slabs and statues split with heat—all indicative of the destruction of the ancient city or cities by fire, as above noted. At Nimrud was discovered the remarkable obelisk of black marble now preserved in the British Museum. This is $6\frac{1}{2}$ feet high, by $17\frac{1}{2}$ inches square at the top, and 2 feet square at the bottom. Upon this obelisk are various inscriptions and figures representing kings, officers, captives, and tribute. These are interpreted as referring to the victorious Assyrians, and to the conquered captive Jews. Other inscriptions among the ruins are deciphered to signify world-wide conquests. Sculptures there are that tell of royal pastimes, of the excitement of the chase, and the luxury of banquets; there are the symbols of strange worship, and much besides, revealing the wealth, the glory, and the grandeur of the place, now "a desolation, and dry like a wilderness."

It is thought by some good authorities that Nineveh could not have included the large territory covered by all these ruins, and that these severally indicate different cities. See Gen. x, 11, 12. Thus it is proposed to identify *Nimrud* with the ancient Calah. But Mr. Fergusson believes Calah is to be identified with *Kalah Sherghat*. (See CALAH.) Thus also he would identify Resen with *Nimrud*, and Nineveh with *Koyunjik* alone. (See RESEN.) Another theory supposes the great mounds to represent vast fortified palaces, erected by different kings, standing in ample parks; and these parks and palaces, it is claimed, comprised in one vast area the magnificent metropolis of the mighty Assyrian Empire. In this respect Nineveh would resemble Ispahan, Damascus, and other modern Oriental cities. Each theory is beset with difficulties, and certainty seems impossible. The last theory, however, appears to us at least as tenable as the former. Within the inclosures above mentioned few traces of buildings are found; hence they may have been parks. For the "much cattle" of Nineveh (Jonah iv, 11; iii, 7) there must have been a great space within the circuit for breeding and pasturage.

Doubtless *Koyunjik* was the grand original center, to which, from time to time, additions were made by the erection of new edifices on the site of old ones, and former quarters might be deserted as new palaces arose. Thus we could somewhat appreciate the passage, "Nineveh was an exceeding great city of three days' journey. And Jonah began to enter into the city a day's journey," Jonah iii, 3, 4. This view seems to be corroborated by the explorations made. The inscriptions tell of the various sovereigns who built or rebuilt various quarters, and recount the deeds of those who dwelt there. The most ancient of the excavated edifices, the north-west palace of Nimrud, was rebuilt or founded by Asshur-Dani-Pal, conjecturally the Sardanapalus of the Greeks, whose reign is approximately placed at 950-920 B. C. The palace at Khorsabad is thought to have been founded by Shalmaneser, but built principally by Sargon about 725. The most magnificent of all the palaces, that of Koyunjik, was the work of Sennacherib, about 700 B. C. He also founded the palace at Shereef Khan, five and a half miles north of Koyunjik, and the one at Neby Yunus, though this last appears to have been finished by Esar-Haddon. On the same platform with Sennacherib's palace was another one, erected by the son of Esar-Haddon. To him also is attributed the south-east palace at Nimrud. It is observed that the sculptures in edifices of different periods show a marked diversity in skill, as well as in manners and dress. Dr. Layard marks the traces of Egyptian taste in the later monuments, which are unknown in the earlier remains.

The Assyrian edifices were built upon artificial platforms, varying from thirty to fifty feet above the ground-level. These were sometimes made of sun-dried bricks, as at Nimrud, and sometimes of earth and rubbish, as at Koyunjik; and they seem to have been faced with stone, the ascent being either by slopes or flights of steps. Large quantities of cedar wood were found in some of the ruins. The prophet refers to this. "He shall uncover the cedar work," Zeph. ii, 14. In these palaces no traces of windows have been discovered. The rooms were probably lighted from above, or through the doors only, as is the case now at Mosul. Probably curtains were hung before the apertures, and a device resorted to similar to the modern *talar*.

In 1849 a portion of the royal library at Nineveh was discovered by Layard. This library consisted of small tablets and cylinders of baked clay, covered with inscriptions. Thousands of these fragments were sent to London. Mr. George Smith, of the British Museum, has succeeded in deciphering some of the inscriptions. One of the tablets contains a history of the flood, and "reads like a new page from the Bible." It gives the account of

VIEW OF THEBES (*restored*) DURING THE INUNDATION.

the flood as told by Sisit, the Xisuthrus of Berosus, and who corresponds to the Noah of Scripture. Although the writing varies from the Mosaic account, there is, however, a striking agreement between the two records in the main points of the story. The tablet in question belonged to the library of Assurbanipal, 660 B. C., and is a translation into the Assyrian from the ancient Accad language of the original Babylonians. It was brought to Nineveh from the older Babylonian city of Erech. The date assigned it reaches back to the seventeenth century before Christ.

The chief sources of information concerning Nineveh are Mr. Layard's two works, *Nineveh*, and *Nineveh and Babylon;* Botta's *Monument de Ninive;* Vaux's *Nineveh and Persepolis;* Fergusson's *Palaces of Nineveh and Persepolis Restored;* Rawlinson's *Herodotus;* and Rawlinson's *The Ancient Monarchies.*

No, and No-A'mon. The most probable meaning of No is *place, portion.* Hence No-Amon=*the portion* or *place of Amon*, that is, the possession of the Egyptian god Amon, the chief seat of his worship. No was a large and celebrated city in Egypt. It is first mentioned in Jeremiah, (xlvi, 25 :) "I will punish the multitude of No;" literally, "the Amon of No," where the reference may be rather to the *deity Amon* than to the *people* of the city. The next passage, in Ezek. xxx, 14, 15, 16, also predicts punishment. The last notice of this city, occurring in Nahum iii, 8, both gives its full name, and describes its position: "Art thou (Nineveh) better than populous No, that was situate among the rivers, that had the waters round about it, whose rampart was the sea, and her wall was from the sea?" Here "populous No" is in the Hebrew No-Amon, that is, "No of Amon."

There can be no doubt that No is identical with Thebes, the Diospolis Magna of the Greeks, the ancient and splendid metropolis of Upper Egypt. Thebes was one hundred and forty stadia in circuit, lying on both sides of the Nile. This agrees with the passage above, "situate among the rivers, that had the waters round about it;" and this was the only city in ancient Egypt which we know to have been built on both sides of the Nile. The expression in Nahum, "whose rampart was the sea," etc., refers to the river Nile, which, to the present day, is usually termed in Egypt *el-Bahr*, "the sea." This city was celebrated for its hundred gates, for the multitude and splendor of its temples, obelisks, statues, etc. But it was "rent asunder," and the "judgments in No" laid this mighty metropolis in ruins, Ezek. xxx, 14–16. About 714 B. C. occurred the Ethiopian conquest of Thebes, and the establishment of an Ethiopian dynasty, when it is probable that the Ethiopians made it their Egyptian capital. Immediately after their rule it was taken twice, at least, by the Assyrians. According to Rawlinson, Esar-Haddon and his son Asshur-Bani-Pal both conquered Egypt, and the latter took Thebes twice; but the exact time of these conquests has not been fixed. The prophet Nahum (iii, 8) doubtless refers to one or both of these events. Possibly the Babylonians inflicted further injuries, although the monuments of Thebes do not seem to have suffered from the Assyrians. The Persians under Cambyses burnt it. Later Egyptian kings still added to its edifices, and the earlier Greek sovereigns followed their example. About 81 B. C., after a siege of three years, Thebes was finally destroyed by Ptolemy X. Lathurus. At the present time there are two villages on the eastern bank of the river, *El-Karnak*, and *El-Uksur;* the former, which is inconsiderable, near the oldest part of ancient Thebes; the latter, which is large, and the most important place on the site, so as to deserve to be called a small town, lying some distance to the south on the river's bank. Opposite *El-Karnak* is the ruined village of *El-Kurneh*, the population of which mainly inhabit sepulchral grottoes; and opposite *El-Uksur* the village of *El-Ba'eerat*, which indeed is almost beyond the circuit of Thebes. The entire ruins of this vast city indicate that it was quadrangular in shape, about four miles by two. Remains of magnificent temples, colossal obelisks, pillars, and statues, lie scattered over this wide space. Says Rosière, in his Description of Egypt, "Thebes, the foremost city of the world in the time of Homer, is still, at the present day, the most surprising. One feels as though he were in a dream while contemplating the immensity of its ruins, the vastness and majesty of its edifices, and the numberless remains of its ancient magnificence." The great hall of the Temple of Karnak is said, to be one hundred and seventy feet long by three hundred and twenty-nine feet wide, supported by one hundred and thirty-four columns, the loftiest of which, forming the central avenue, are nearly seventy feet high, and about twelve feet in diameter. Beyond this great hall are many ruined chambers, and two great obelisks standing in their places amid a heap of ruins. The approach to Karnak from the south is by a series of majestic gate-ways and towers—the appendages of later times to the original structure. Every thing in this vicinity reveals the grandeur of the ancient city. Hieroglyphic inscriptions abound among all the ruins. The full interpretation of these will give us invaluable testimony as to the early history of the Egyptians, and aid in a better understanding of the Scriptures.

Nob, (Map 6,) probably *a high place*, a priests' city in Benjamin, in sight of Jerusalem, 1 Sam. xxii, 19; Isa. x, 32; Neh. xi, 31, 32. The tabernacle and the ark of the covenant were probably here in the time of Saul. David, fleeing from Saul, went "to Nob, to Ahimelech the priest," 1 Sam. xxi, 1, 4. Doeg, the Edomite, informed against Ahimelech, and the priest was summoned before the wrathful king. Saul sent out Doeg, who smote Nob with the edge of the sword, 1 Sam. xxii, 9-19. Some think Nob may be identical with *el-Isawiyeh*, north-east of Jerusalem on the road leading to Anathoth. But Mr. Porter believes he has found the site on a conical rocky tell less than a mile south of *Tuleil el-Ful*, (Gibeah.) Conder (1875) locates Nob at *Neby Samwil*, and inclines to consider Nob and Mizpeh (6) identical; but his argument is inconclusive.

No'bah, (Map 4,) *a barking*, a name at one time borne by Kenath, Num. xxxii, 42. From the chronology of Judg. viii, 11, it appears to have held this name two hundred years. See KENATH.

Nod, *flight, wandering*. In Gen. iv, 16, we read that Cain "went out, and dwelt in the land of Nod, on the east of Eden." While the site of Eden is not fixed, we cannot determine that of Nod. The Hon. I. S. Diehl tells us that he found the inhabitants of *Bussorah* and *Bushire* claiming that the land of Nod and the city of Enoch lay between these two cities, on the north-east coast of the Persian Gulf. In the place thus designated are found vast ruins of cities which are claimed to have been built before the deluge. The inscriptions on many of these ruins are still undeciphered. *Bushire* itself claims to be an antediluvian city of the land of Nod, and the name is a contraction of *Abu-Sheer*, "city of the fathers."

No'dab, *nobility*, an Ishmaelite or Hagarite tribe, mentioned only in 1 Chron. v, 19. So far as known, no Arab tribe now bears this name.

Noph, (Map 1,) Isa. xix, 13; Jer. ii, 16, etc.; Ezek. xxx, 13, 16. See MEMPHIS.

BIBLE GEOGRAPHY. 343

No'phah, *blast*, perhaps *windy place*, a Moabite town, Num. xxi, 30. It seems to have lain between Heshbon and Medaba. Unknown.

O'bal, *stripped*, or *bare of leaves*, a tribe of Arabs, from Obal the seventh son of Joktan, Gen. x, 28. In 1 Chron. i, 22, Ebal. Bochart identifies this tribe with the *Abalites* or *Avalites* of classic geographers, who dwelt beside a gulf of the same name on the eastern coast of Africa, near the Straits of *Bab el-Mandeb*. But this identity is not established.

O'both, (Map 2,) *water-skins, bottles*, a station of the Israelites in the wilderness east of Moab; the first after the setting up of the brazen serpent, Num. xxi, 10, 11; xxxiii, 43, 44. Unknown.

Oc'ina, a place mentioned in Judith ii, 28, among the towns on the sea-coast of Palestine, which were terrified at the approach of Holofernes. It is perhaps a corruption of Accho, now *Akka*.

Odol'lam, 2 Macc. xii, 38. The Greek form of ADULLAM, which see. Possibly the site is at *Bet Dûla*, east of *Beit Jibrin*, (Eleutheropolis.)

Ol'ives, THE MOUNT OF, and Olivet, (Maps 6, 7,) the hills or ridge east of Jerusalem, separated from the city by the Kidron valley, Zech. xiv, 4; Ezek. xi, 23. Its name is derived from the olive-trees which once abounded on its sides, Neh. viii, 5. Some of these trees still remain. This mount or hill is mentioned by the name of Olives but once in the Old Testament, (Zech. xiv, 4,) but it is alluded to in several other passages. Doubtless events occurred here other than those distinctly recorded.

It was up the slopes of Olivet that David went weeping and wearied when fleeing from the Holy City during Absalom's rebellion; and here that he met Hushai and Ziba, 2 Sam. xv, 30, 32; xvi, 4. In 1 Kings xi, 7, it is recorded that Solomon built "a high place for Chemosh *in the hill that is before* Jerusalem," meaning Olivet, which is literally *before* the city, being visible from every part of it. In 2 Kings xxiii, 13, the same hill is called "The Mount of Corruption," doubtless from the idolatrous rites there practiced.

From the New Testament history Olivet derives its chief interest. It appears to have been a favorite resort of Jesus. By the way of Olivet the Saviour entered Jerusalem, Matt. xxi, 1; Mark xi, 1; Luke xix, 29, 37. Here Christ taught his disciples, and here foretold the ruin of the Holy City, Matt. xxiv, 3; Mark xiii. Here "at night he abode in the mount," Luke xxi, 37; John viii, 1. Hither after the passover feast he came on that fearful night of his agony, Luke xxii, 39; Matt. xxvi, 30. And then, when the agony was passed, and he had risen, a victor over death and the grave, our blessed Lord ascended from Olivet up into heaven, Acts i, 12.

The ridge of Olivet is about a mile long from north to south. Its elevation is nearly three hundred feet above the temple site. The Arabs call it *Jebel-et-Tur*. "Its appearance as first seen sadly disappoints the Bible student. Properly speaking it is not a hill. It is only one of a multitude of rounded crowns that form the summit of the broad mountain ridge which runs longitudinally through Central Palestine. Zion, Moriah, Scopus, Gibeah, Ramah, and Mizpeh, are others like Olivet. These bare rocky crowns encircle the Holy city—Olivet being the highest and most conspicuous in the immediate vicinity."—*Porter*.

The several summits of the Mount of Olives are named as follows, beginning at the north: 1. *Viri Galilæi*, (Men of Galilee,) a name given by monks and pilgrims, from the tradition that here the angels said to the apostles, "Ye men of Galilee, why stand ye," etc. An older tradition locates the station of the angels in or beside the Church of the Ascension. The summit is now crowned by a confused heap of ruins, encompassed by vineyards; hence its modern name, "The Sportsman's Vineyard." 2. *Ascension.* The top of Olivet, (about 500 yards south of the preceding.) The traditional site of Christ's ascension, on which stands a modern church or mosque erected in honor of that event.

THE MOUNT OF OLIVES.

" Within the chapel is the rock which has been pointed out to pilgrims, at least since the seventh century, as imprinted with the footsteps of our Saviour. . . . Here there is nothing but a simple cavity in the rock, with no more resemblance to a human foot than to any thing else." —*Stanley.* Dr. Thomson, speaking of his visit to the place, remarks, " We came out of the Church of the Ascension with feelings of utter disgust." The spot thus commemorated by the mosque is not the place whence Christ ascended. Dr. Porter says: " It was not in Bethany, nor was it on such a conspicuous place as the summit of Olivet. The writer carefully examined the whole region. He saw one spot, as far from Jerusalem as Bethany, near the village, but concealed by an intervening cliff, and this he thought in all probability the real scene. The disciples, led by Jesus, would reach it by the path over the top of Olivet, and they would naturally return to the city by the same route." 3. *The Prophets,* a summit about 500 yards to the south of the Church of the Ascension, but not quite so lofty. A large catacomb or group of caves on the declivity of the hill is called "The tombs of the Prophets." 4. *Mount of Offense*—The southernmost elevation of the ridge, being at least 150 feet lower than Olivet proper. The highest point of Olivet, according to Van de Velde, is 2,724 feet above the level of the sea. Extensive views are afforded from its various points. From the one side we may look down into Jerusalem; while from the eastern side the vision extends over the dreary hills toward Jericho, with the northern end of the Dead Sea visible, and the mountains of Moab beyond. Along the Kidron the base of the hill is more rugged than any other part of the western side. "With the exception of *Silwân* at its western base, Bethany at its eastern, and *Kefret-Tûr* on its summit. Olivet is deserted. No man dwells there

There are three or four little towers, one habitable, the others ruinous—
built originally as watch-towers for the vineyards and orchards."—*Porter*.
See GETHSEMANE.

On, (Map 2,) *light*, and, specially, *the sun*. The Septuagint translates On
as Heliopolis, "city of the sun." In Jer. xliii, 13 it bears the name of Beth-
Shemesh, which has a similar meaning. The Arab name of On is '*Ain Shems*,

PLAIN AND OBELISK OF HELIOPOLIS.

that is, "fountain of the sun." This was one of the oldest cities in the world.
It was situated in Lower Egypt, about ten miles north-east of Cairo. On
is first mentioned in the Bible in Gen. xli, 45, where it is said that Pharaoh
gave to Joseph a wife, Asenath, the daughter of Potipherah, priest of On,
(compare verse 50, and xlvi, 20.)

It has been thought that Isaiah speaks of On (Isa. xix, 18, margin) when
he prophesies that one of the five cities of Egypt that should speak the
language of Canaan should be called Ir-Ha-Heres; but see IR-HA-HERES.
The passage in Jeremiah (xliii, 13) predicts the destruction of On under the
name of *Beth-Shemesh*. When Ezekiel (xxx, 17) declares that "the young
men of Aven shall fall by the sword," On is intended. See AVEN.

According to Herodotus, Heliopolis was one of the four great cities that
were rendered famous in Egypt by being the centers of festivals, which were
attended by solemn religious processions and homage to the gods. In Heliopolis the observance was held in honor of the sun. For a long time this
city was the chief seat of Egyptian science; and in Strabo's time were to be

seen the halls in which Eudoxus and Plato had studied under the direction of the priests. Heliopolis suffered greatly from the Persian invasion. It furnished works of art to Augustus for adorning Rome, and to Constantine for adorning Constantinople.

The site of the city is now marked by low mounds, inclosing a space about three fourths of a mile long by half a mile wide, where once stood the famous Temple of the Sun and other buildings. But the only remnant of ancient magnificence is a solitary obelisk of red granite, sixty-eight feet high. In the neighboring village of *Matariyeh* is a fountain called '*Ain Shems*. Near this is a gnarled old sycamore under which tradition says the holy family once rested.

O'no, *strong*, a town of Benjamin built by the sons of Elpaal, 1 Chron. viii, 12. (In 1 Esdr. v, 22, called Onus.) It was re-occupied after the captivity, and grouped with Lod, Ezra ii, 33; Neh. vii, 37. A plain near it bore its name, Neh. vi, 2. Nehemiah also mentions a valley in connection with it, xi, 35; compare 1 Chron. iv, 14. Perhaps the plain and valley were identical. Ono was probably near Lod or Lydda. The village of *Kefr 'Ana*, five miles north of Lydda, which has been suggested as the site of Ono, seems too far; while *Beit Unia*, another village proposed, is much farther from Lydda, lying in the mountains between Bethel and Beth-horon.

O'nus, 1 Esdr. v, 22. The Greek form of Ono.

O'phel, (Map 7,) *the hill, swelling mound*, a part of ancient Jerusalem. It was surrounded and fortified by a separate wall, 2 Chron. xxvii, 3; xxxiii, 14; Neh. iii, 26, 27; xi, 21. After the captivity the Levites (Nethinim) resided here. Ophel probably was the hill or ridge lying on the east of Mount Zion and south of the temple area, between the Tyropœon (the central valley of Jerusalem) and the Valley of Kidron. It is about fifteen hundred and fifty feet long by two hundred and ninety broad, ending in a rocky bluff forty or fifty feet below the pool of Siloam, underneath the southern face of which, in a groove of the solid rock, flows "cool Siloam's shady rill." In the margin of the A. V. the word is rendered "tower." In 2 Kings v, 24, the term "tower," or Ophel, cannot refer to this hill, but possibly to one near Samaria. See JERUSALEM.

O'phir, (Map 12,) perhaps *abundance*, or *red*, or *dust*, (the etymology is very obscure.) Ophir was a celebrated region, abounding in gold, whence the navies of King Solomon and Hiram, sailing from a port on the Red Sea, brought back every three years *gold*, precious stones, and sandal-wood, also silver, ivory, apes, and peacocks; 1 Kings ix, 28; x, 11; 2 Chron. viii, 18; ix, 10. Jehoshaphat attempted to bring gold from Ophir, but his ships were wrecked at Ezion-Geber, 1 Kings xxii, 48. The gold of Ophir, proverbial for its fineness, is frequently mentioned, Job xxii, 24; xxviii, 16; Psa. xlv, 9; Isa. xiii, 12; 1 Chron. xxix, 4; Tob. xiii, 17; Ecclesiasticus vii, 18.

The exact situation of Ophir has long been a subject of doubt and discussion. Many have been the localities assigned it. The following countries among others have been proposed; Armenia, Arabia, India, St. Domingo, Mexico, New Guinea, Urphe in the Red Sea, and Ormuz in the Persian Gulf, Ceylon, Pegu, Malacca, Sumatra, Peru, and various parts of Africa. The best interpreters now hesitate only between *Africa, Arabia*, and *India*.

Ophir first occurs in the Bible as the name of one of Joktan's sons. Many Arabian localities were probably peopled by the Joktanites, the tribes calling the territory after their name, and among others Ophir, Gen. x, 26-29. The argument for locating Ophir in *Arabia* takes it for granted that the author of the tenth chapter of Genesis regarded Ophir the son of Joktan as corresponding to some city, tribe, or region in Arabia. This is undoubtedly a reasonable inference. There is an Arabian town, Aphar, called by Ptolemy Sapphara, now *Zafár* or *Saphar*, which appears to have been the metropolis of the Sabæans, and distant twelve days' journey from the emporium *Muza* on the Red Sea. There are also *Dofir*, a considerable town of Yemen; and Zafar or Zafari, now *Dofar*, a city on the southern coast of Arabia; both of which towns might agree in name with Ophir. Again it can be urged that several ancient writers have represented Arabia as a gold-producing country, and rich also in precious stones. And if gold and some other articles mentioned above are not now found in Arabia, Ophir may, nevertheless, have been an Arabian emporium, or grand market into which were brought those precious commodities from India and Africa, and even from Ethiopia, to which Herodotus ascribes gold, elephants' teeth, and various kinds of trees. Pliny also speaks of the confluence of merchandise in Arabia. Although these are strong grounds for locating Ophir in Arabia, there are, nevertheless, arguments of very considerable weight in favor of India as this land of gold. Max Muller, in endeavoring to identify India with Ophir, says: "The names for apes, peacocks, ivory, and almug-trees (brought by Solomon's fleet from Ophir) are foreign words in Hebrew, as much as gutta-percha or tobacco are in English. Now, if we wished to know from what part of the world gutta-percha was first imported into England, we might safely conclude that it came from that country where the name gutta-percha formed part of the spoken language. If, therefore, we can find a language in which the names for peacocks, apes, ivory, and almug-trees, which are foreign to the Hebrew, are indigenous, we may be certain that the country in which that language was spoken must have been the Ophir of the Bible. That language is no other but Sanscrit, the parent language of the East India languages."

Some few eminent writers locate Ophir on the eastern coast of *Africa*, making it comprise Nigritia and the Sofala of Arabian writers, now Zanguebar and Mozambique, where there is a gold district called *Fura*. Discoveries made by Britton, Merensky, Gruetzner, and Mauch point to Zimabye as the long-lost site. Gold, diamonds, and precious stones abound, and there are ruins of undoubted antiquity.

Oph'ni, *moldy*, a city of the Benjamites, Josh. xviii, 24. Probably it is the *Gophna* of Josephus, and the Gufna, or Beth-Gufnin, of the Talmud, which still survives in the modern *Jifna* or *Jufna*, two or three miles northwest of Bethel.

Oph'rah, *female fawn.*

1. A place in Benjamin, Josh. xviii, 23; 1 Sam. xiii, 17. This is perhaps identical with Ephrain or Ephron, 2 Chron. xiii, 19; and Ephraim, John xi, 54; and Apherema, 1 Macc. xi, 34. Possibly the site of Ophrah may be at the modern *Et-Taiyibeh*, about five Roman miles north-east of Bethel. Here are ancient ruins on a commanding site.

2. A town in Manasseh, west of the Jordan, the native place of Gideon, and the scene of his exploits against Baal, Judg. vi, 11, 24. Here also Gideon resided after his accession to power, and this was the place of his burial, Judg. viii, 32; ix, 5. Ophrah became a place of pilgrimage and public resort, because here was deposited the ephod which was made or enriched

with the ornaments taken from the Ishmaelite followers of Zebah and Zalmunna, Judg. viii, 27. Not identified.

O'reb, 2 Esdr. ii, 33. Mount Horeb.

O'reb, THE ROCK, *the raven's crag,* the place where the men of Ephraim put to death Oreb, a prince of Midian, from whom it derived its name, Judg. vii, 25; Isa. x, 26. It is claimed by Reland and others that Oreb was east of the Jordan, (compare Judg. vii, 25, and viii, 1,) and they suggest that the site of this rock or place may have been '*Orbo,* a place in the neighborhood of Beth-Shean, mentioned by the rabbinical writers. But from Judg. viii, 4, it appears that Gideon crossed the river in his pursuit of the "kings of Midian." May we not infer that Oreb was slain on the *west* side of the river, and that his head was taken to Gideon "on the other side of Jordan."

Pa'dan-A'ram, (Map 1,) *the plain,* or *arable land, of Syria; Aram of the field.* In Gen. xlviii, 7, Padan. (See ARAM.) The name by which the Hebrews designated the tract of country which they otherwise called Aram-Naharaim, "Aram of the two rivers," the Greek Mesopotamia, Gen. xxiv, 10, and "the field (country) of Aram," Hosea xii, 12. The term was perhaps more especially applied to that portion which bordered on the Euphrates, to distinguish it from the mountainous districts in the north and north-east of Mesopotamia. Abraham sent his steward to Padan-Aram, to the "city of Nahor," Gen. xxiv, 10. Only from the family, the offspring of Nahor and Milcah, Abraham's brother and niece, could a wife be sought for Isaac, the heir of promise, Gen. xxv, 20; and Jacob, the inheritor of his blessing, Gen. xxviii, 2, 5, 6, 7; xxxi, 18; xxxiii, 18; xxxv, 9, 26; xlvi, 15; xlviii, 7.

Dr. Tilstone Beke has suggested that we are to seek the Aram-Naharaim and the Padan-Aram of the Bible in those extensive plains of luxuriant pastures which extend for more than three days' journey eastward beyond the Jebel Hauran. (Map 5.) His reasons chiefly rest on the identification of the Haran of the Bible with *Harrán-el-Awamíd,* or *Harrán of the Pillars,* a village four hours east of Damascus, first noticed in Porter's *Five Years in Damascus.* See HARAN.

Pa'i, *a bleating,* 1 Chron. i, 50. See PAU.

Palesti'na, Exod. xv, 14; Isa. xiv, 29, 31. See PALESTINE.

Pal'estine, (Maps 3, 4, 5, 8,) *land of strangers,* or *emigrants.*

I. NAMES.—The Hebrew word is *Pelesheth.* The same term is sometimes translated Philistia. In no part of Scripture does either the Hebrew word, or the English Palestina or Palestine, refer to the whole region in question: they signify simply "Philistia," "the land of the Philistines." (See PHILISTIA.) The Greek writers used the form *Palæstina,* employing it at first in the same limited sense, but afterward including under that name the whole land of Palestine on both sides the Jordan, as allotted to the twelve tribes of Israel. However, ancient classic writers, as also early Christian authors, did not always employ the terms consistently—sometimes referring merely to Philistia, again to all the region west of Jordan, and sometimes to the entire land on both sides the river. Hence only by the context can the student understand in what sense the term is employed. See *Boundaries* below.

This country is known in Scripture by various other names: Canaan, Num. xxxiii, 51; The Land of Promise, Gen. xiii, 15; Heb. xi, 9; The Land of Jehovah, Hosea ix, 3; Land of Israel, 1 Sam. xiii, 19; The Land, Ruth i, 1; Immanuel's Land, Isa. viii, 8; (="thy land, O Immanuel;") Judea.

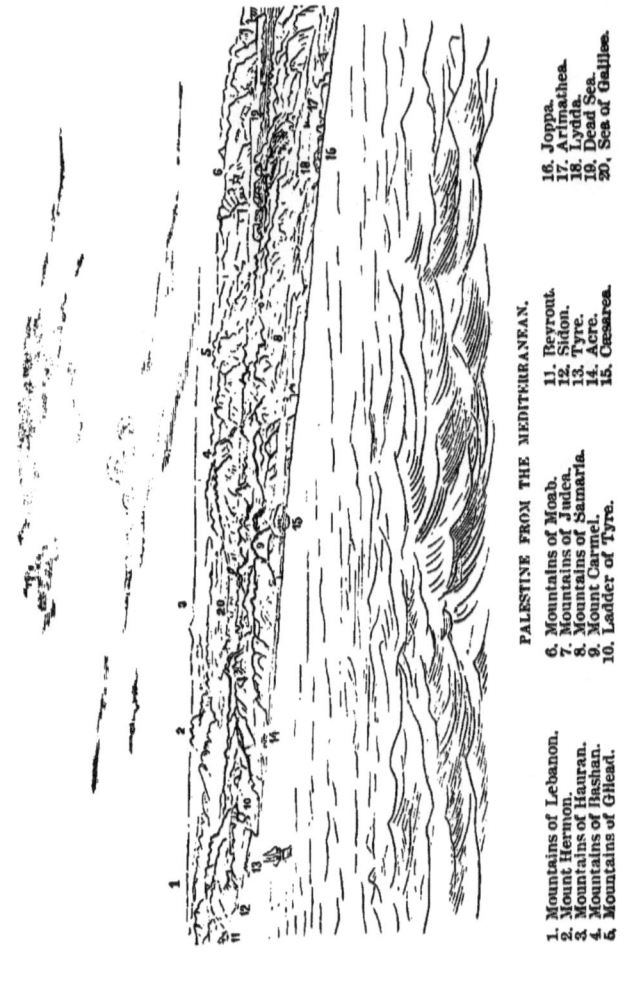

PALESTINE FROM THE MEDITERRANEAN.

1. Mountains of Lebanon.
2. Mount Hermon.
3. Mountains of Hauran.
4. Mountains of Bashan.
5. Mountains of Gilead.
6. Mountains of Moab.
7. Mountains of Judea.
8. Mountains of Samaria.
9. Mount Carmel.
10. Ladder of Tyre.
11. Beyrout.
12. Sidon.
13. Tyre.
14. Acre.
15. Cæsarea.
16. Joppa.
17. Arimathea.
18. Lydda.
19. Dead Sea.
20. Sea of Galilee.

(but at first confined to the inheritance of the tribe of Judah,) 2 Chron. ix, 11; The Holy Land, Zech. ii, 12. During the Middle Ages this last name nearly superseded all others, and it is now adopted, with Palestine, as a geographical term. "The very dust and stones and air of the land are still considered holy by the poor Jews."

II. SITUATION AND BOUNDARIES.—The Jews regarded Palestine as the center of the earth. An absurd tradition, still current in Jerusalem, makes the Church of the Holy Sepulcher the physical center of the world; and under the dome of the Greek church is a spot claimed to be the exact point as indicated by our Lord himself. Aside from empty tradition, it may be truthfully remarked that this wonderful region of country, standing midway between Assyria, Egypt, and Greece, those three greatest ancient empires, was indeed for ages the only center of religious light and knowledge among the nations of the earth.

As to the exact limits of Palestine writers very greatly differ—a fact that has caused much confusion in sacred geography. In the Bible we find several boundaries mentioned: (1.) As promised to Abraham and his seed; (2.) As described by Moses before his death; (3.) As actually allotted to the twelve tribes by Joshua; and (4.) As shown in Ezekiel's vision.

Concerning the *first:* The Lord said to Abraham at Sichem, "Unto thy seed will I give this land," Gen. xii, 7. At Bethel God said, "All the land which thou seest, to thee will I give it, and to thy seed forever," Gen. xiii, 15. This view could not have embraced one fourth of Palestine. But in Gen. xv, 18, the Lord made very definite the patriarch's vast inheritance when he declared: "Unto thy seed have I given this land, from the river of Egypt, (here doubtless meaning the Nile,) unto the great river, the river Euphrates." This promise was renewed just after the Israelites had left Egypt. See Exod. xxiii, 31, where the boundaries are given with still more fullness. The specific conditions of faithfulness (Exod. xxiii, 22, 23) not having been fulfilled by Israel, this whole territory was not given to the people, Josh. xxiii, 13-16; Judg. ii, 20-23. Yet it is recorded of King David that he "went to recover his border at the river Euphrates," and that he conquered the whole country from Egypt to the Euphrates, and from the desert of Arabia to the Mediterranean, 2 Sam. viii, 3-8. But this great area of the "Land of Promise," originally given to Abraham, is not intended under the name of *Palestine.*

The boundaries as *described by Moses* are given with much fullness in Num. xxxiv, 1-12. This territory was much less extended than that promised to Abraham. The southern border extended from Kadesh-Barnea, in a line running a little north of west, (see Map 2,) to the "river of Egypt," (probably the stream known now as *Wady el-Arish.*) The western border was the "great sea," the Mediterranean. The eastern boundary line extended through the Valley of Cœle-Syria, and along the Jordan, and thus excluded all the country east of the Jordan. But Moses regarded the land east of the river as part of the inheritance, for he had already allotted it to three of the tribes, Num. xxxii, 1-33; xxxiii, 50-54. See REUBEN, GAD, MANASSEH. The passage in Num. xxxiv, 7-9, which gives the northern limit, is variously interpreted. Some make the parallel of Antioch the north border; others run the line near the parallel of Sidon, the dispute having reference chiefly to the precise location of "the entrance of Hamath," (verse 8.) The point near Sidon is "the entrance" to Hamath, *going north from central Palestine;* but Moses, in this passage, is speaking of the boundary *going east from the sea-coast*, or *from Mount Hor.* As by "Mount Hor" the great range of Lebanon is doubtless intended, (see HOR, 2,) the sacred writer must have referred to some well-known "pass" from Lebanon into the kingdom of Hamath. Mr. Porter ably maintains this view, and finds such a "pass" not far west of Emesa, (see Map 4,) running from the west between the northern end of Lebanon and the *Nusairîyeh* mountains. The northern boundary line, as fixed by Mr. Porter, began at the sea, apparently at or near the mouth of the river Eleutherus, and "ran eastward to the northern peak of Lebanon; thence it swept round through the pass, and extended north-east to Hamath; then it turned south-east by Ziphron, (*Zifrân*,) and Zedad, (*Sudud*,) to Hazar-Enan, (*Kuryetein.*")

All this territory was never actually possessed by the Israelites, although the conquests of David reached beyond it, and Solomon for a time received tribute from its nations and tribes. From Sidon northward the range of Lebanon was still held by the Giblites and other tribes, Judg. iii, 1–3; the Phœnicians held the coast-plain north of Carmel, while a large portion of the Shephelah, with the southern sea-board, was still retained by the Philistines. The Lord made known to the Jews that these various nations were left in the land "to prove Israel," Judg. iii, 4. It must be remembered that the term Palestine does not include all the territory just indicated.

The land as allotted to the tribes is described in Num. xxxii; Josh. xiii, 8–32; and in Josh. xv–xix. The *south* line was the same as that described by Moses; compare Num. xxxiv, 3–5; Josh. xv, 2–4. The *west* border was also the same; Josh. xv, 11; xvi, 3, 8; xvii, 9, 10; xix, 29. The *north* border began at Sidon on the coast, (Map 5;) thence it ran south-east across Lebanon to Ijon and Dan, Josh. xix, 28; 1 Kings xv, 20; thence over the southern shoulder of Hermon to the northern end of the mountains of Bashan, Num. xxxii, 33; Deut. iii, 8–14; Josh. xii, 4–6. The *east* border is not so clearly defined. Salcah and Bashan are given as eastern limits, Josh. xii, 5; xiii, 11; Deut. iii, 10. From Salcah it appears to have run south-west along the border of the Arabian wilderness (*Midbar*) to the river Arnon, Josh. xii, 1, 2. Thence turning west it followed the river line to the Dead Sea, excluding Moab and Edom. Compare Maps 5 and 14. Some of the territory thus allotted to the tribes was never conquered nor occupied. Thus the Philistines and the Phœnicians still held their possessions along the coast, and some of the northern nations retained their mountain strongholds, as did the Geshurites and Maachathites theirs in Bashan, Judg. i, 19, 31, 33; Josh. xiii, 13.

The borders of the land, according to Ezekiel's vision, are the same as those described by Moses, except on the *east*, and include, in addition to the area given by Moses, the whole kingdom of Damascus, and the possessions of Reuben, Gad, and half-Manasseh, Ezek. xlvii, 13–21.

Modern Palestine does not exactly correspond with any of the preceding boundaries, nor have its limits been precisely fixed by geographers. They are thus given approximately by Mr. Porter: "On the south a line drawn from the lower end of the Dead Sea to Beersheba and Gaza; on the west the Mediterranean; on the north a line drawn from the mouth of the River *Litány* to Dan, and thence across *Jebel el-Hîsh* and the plain of *Haurân* to the northern end of the *Haurân* mountains; on the east, a line running from the north-eastern angle through Salcah to *Kerak* and the Dead Sea." Palestine is therefore about 140 miles long from Dan to Beersheba, about 60

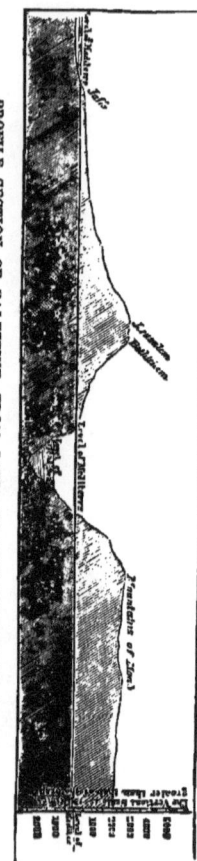

PROFILE SECTION OF PALESTINE, FROM JAFFA TO THE MOUNTAINS OF MOAB.

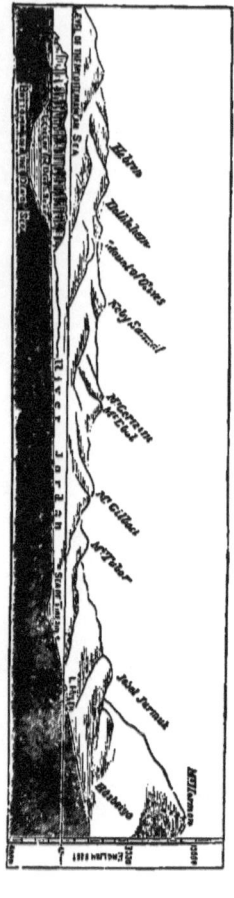

PROFILE OF PALESTINE FROM THE DEAD SEA TO MOUNT HERMON, ALONG THE LINE OF THE JORDAN.

miles wide on its southern line, and about 100 miles on the northern border, having a superficial area of about 12,000 square miles. Speaking of this small area, Dean Stanley says: "In Palestine, as in Greece, every traveler is struck with the smallness of the territory. He is surprised, even after all that he has heard, at passing, in one long day, from the capital of Judea to that of Samaria; or at seeing, within eight hours, three such spots as Hebron, Bethlehem, and Jerusalem.... The time is now gone by when the grandeur of a country is measured by its size, or the diminutive extent of an illustrious people can otherwise than enhance the magnitude of what they have done. The ancient taunt, however, and the facts which suggested it, may still illustrate the feeling which appears in their own records. The contrast between the littleness of Palestine and the vast extent of the empires which hung upon its northern and southern skirts, is rarely absent from the mind of the prophets and Psalmists. It helps them to exalt their sense of the favor of God toward their land by magnifying their little hills and dry torrent-beds into an equality with the giant hills of Lebanon and Hermon, and the sea-like rivers of Mesopotamia.... Nor is it only the smallness, but the narrowness, of the territory which is remarkable. From almost every high point in the country its whole breadth is visible, from the long wall of the Moab hills on the east, to the Mediterranean sea on the west." Compare Psa. lxviii, 15; Isa. ii, 2; Psa. xlvi, 4.

III. DIVISIONS. See CANAAN, PHŒNICIA, PHILISTIA, GILEAD, BASHAN, JUDEA, GALILEE, SAMARIA, and also each of the TWELVE TRIBES OF ISRAEL.

IV. PHYSICAL GEOGRAPHY. The study of the physical geography of Palestine is one of the best keys to its history. This subject cannot here be fully exhibited, as the student will find it presented in the various articles named above under the head of DIVISIONS.

MOUNTAINS. The mountainous nature of Palestine is well illustrated in the cut which opens this article. It is copied from a remarkable painting executed by Professor W. H. Perrine, of Michigan. For its use we are indebted to the "Sunday-School Journal." A mountain range extends through the center of the country, beginning with the grand range of Lebanon on the north, and running in nearly a south line (not parallel with the coast) to the southern end of the land. Near the center this ridge is intersected by a belt of plain called Esdraelon. The northern part of the ridge is picturesque, and often grand. But the aspect of the southern part is in general dull and uniform. But "in traveling down the road which runs along the broad back of the ridge to Jerusalem and Hebron the eye sees an endless succession of rounded hill-tops, thrown confusedly together, each bare and rocky as its neighbor. South of Hebron these sink into low, swelling hills, similar in form, but smaller; and these again gradually melt into the desert plain of *et-Tih.*"—*Porter.* See LEBANON, TABOR, EBAL, GERIZIM, MORIAH, OLIVES, MOUNT OF. From this central ridge at the plain of Esdraelon Carmel shoots off, and terminates at the Mediterranean in a high, bold promontory. See CARMEL.

On the east of the Jordan is also a mountain range. The whole country east of this river is a grand elevated terrace, from which rise the various mountain heights. See HERMON, GILEAD, NEBO, ABARIM, MOAB. The mountain mass of Palestine is Jura limestone, with basaltic and other deposits, and it gives evidence of having been greatly disturbed either by volcanic action or otherwise. East of the Jordan black basalt forms that whole district of Bashan called the *Lejah.* See ARGOB. Basalt also underlies the plain of Esdraelon.

PLAINS.—See PHILISTIA, SHARON, ESDRAELON, HAURAN. "The *Philistine* plain is one vast corn-field."—*Ayre.* (Compare Zeph. ii, 5, 6.) *Sharon's* "wide undulations are sprinkled with Bedouin tents, and vast flocks of sheep."—*Stanley.* (See 1 Chron. xxvii, 29.) "*Esdraelon* is far from being a *dead* level, the western half having a decided dip toward the sea, while its different parts roll up in long swells like gigantic waves. . . . I have seen nothing to compare it with except some of our rolling prairies in the West, and these lack Tabor, and Little Hermon, and Gilboa, and Carmel, and a hundred other natural beauties."—*Thomson.* The *Hauran* is "one uniform plain of surpassing fertility. Not a rock or stone can be seen except on the little conical hills that appear here and there on its surface."—*Porter.*

VALLEYS.—See JORDAN, KIDRON, HINNOM, ACHOR, AJALON, ELAH, JEZREEL, SUCCOTH, REPHAIM. These are the chief valleys. The valley of the Jordan is the most remarkable feature in the physical geography of Palestine. For details concerning it see JORDAN, and compare the profile cut of the Jordan line accompanying the present article.

STREAMS.—There are many streams in Palestine, but in reality only one that is deserving the name of river—the JORDAN. Several of the streams are perennial. See ARNON, JABBOK, KISHON. To this class belong also the *Yarmuk, Belus,* and others not mentioned in Scripture. Among the hills are many fountains, and there are winter-torrents flowing from the mountains. Throughout the land also are wells, cisterns, and aqueducts. These indicate the inconstant supply of water from natural sources, and illustrate the labors of the patriarchs in digging wells and defending them. See Gen. xxvi, 15; Deut. vi, 11; 2 Sam. xxiii, 15; John iv, 6.

LAKES.—See GALILEE, SEA OF; MEROM, WATERS OF; SEA, SALT.

CLIMATE.—Palestine embraces a very great variety of climate and temperature. On the northern border may be found the region of perpetual snow. In the south, by the sultry shores of the Dead Sea, are the heat and vegetation of the tropics; while throughout other portions of the land the various shades of climate produce the vine and the fig-tree; the palm and the banana yield their fruit, and the oak and pine flourish. Snow falls along the higher portions of the land, but is seldom seen below an elevation of two thousand feet. South of Hebron snow is rare, and frost less intense. Along the sea-board of Philistia and Sharon, and in the Jordan Valley, snow and frost are unknown. The summer heat varies much in different localities, being especially oppressive along the shores of the Dead Sea. The dry soil and dry atmosphere render the greater part of the coast salubrious. At Hebron and at Jerusalem, and generally along the summit of the central ridge, the heat is never intense; yet travel becomes exhausting by reason of the cloudless sun and the white soil.

RAIN.—The autumnal rains begin about the last of October. In Lebanon they occur about a month earlier. In October the quantity of rain is small. The rainy season then follows, continuing at intervals during four months. Many of the showers are very heavy. Rain falls at intervals in April, and becomes less frequent in May, by the end of which month it altogether ceases. During the next four months no rain falls, except on occasions so rare as to cause not merely surprise, but alarm; and not a cloud is seen in

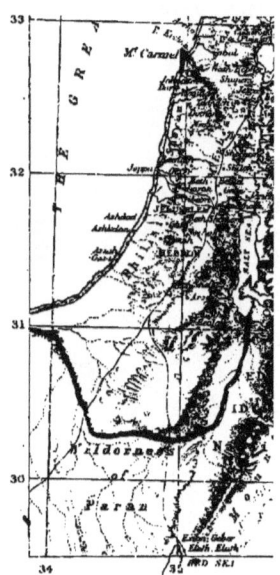

HUNT & EATON, NEW YORK.

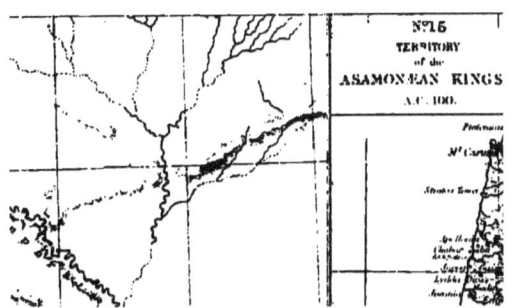

the heavens as large as a man's hand. Compare 1 Sam. xii, 17, 18; Sol. Song ii, 11.

SEASONS.—Seed-time begins in October, after the first rains, and continues till January. Harvest in the lower Valley of the Jordan sometimes begins at the end of March; in the hill country of Judea it is nearly a month later, and in Lebanon it rarely begins before June, and is not completed in the higher regions till the end of July. The young grass shoots up in November, after the heavy falls of rain, and in December the ground is covered with verdure. Oranges, lemons, and citrons are ripe in January; in May, apricots; and in the warm plains by the Sea of Galilee melons are produced in the same month. Figs, cherries, and plums ripen in June; and in the same month are gathered roses from the "Valley of Roses," near Jerusalem, and the gardens at Damascus, for the manufacture of rose-water. The grape, fig, peach, and pomegranate are in perfection in August, the crowning time of fruit. The vintage continues through September. A few weeks pass and the whole country is parched, the soil becomes dust, and all is barrenness, except in the orange-groves of Joppa and those few portions of the soil which are irrigated.

PLANTS.—Only the principal plants of Palestine can here be noticed. The cedar is confined to the higher regions of Lebanon. Among the smaller trees and bushes are the juniper, dwarf elder, sumac, and hawthorn; the ivy, honeysuckle, and some species of rose. The "oak of Bashan" is found also in Gilead and Galilee, and all over Jebel el-Hísh. An oak of another and smaller variety spreads over Carmel, the ridge of Samaria, and the western slopes of the Judean mountains. The arbutus, hawthorn, pistachio, and carob or locust tree are in some places intermixed with the oak. Common brambles are abundant, and also the wild olive. The plane trees, the sycamore, and the palm are found in the lowland, but are not abundant. Along the Dead Sea and in the Jordan Valley are the nubk, papyrus, tamarisk, acacia, retama, (a kind of broom,) sea pink, Dead Sea apple; and on the banks of the rivers several species of willow and reed.

Most conspicuous among the *flowers* are the lily, tulip, anemone, poppy, hyacinth, cyclamen, star of Bethlehem, crocus, and mallow. Large sections of country are in the early spring covered with these and other flowers, presenting the appearance of a vast natural parterre.

The vine is the staple of the hills and mountains. The olive is found in almost every village in Western Palestine; but its chief groves are at Gaza, *Nablûs*, and on the western declivities of Galilee. The chief fruit-bearing trees and shrubs are mentioned above under SEASONS. The principal cereals are Indian corn, wheat, barley, rye, and rice in the marshy plain of the upper Jordan. There are also the pea, the bean, large and small, and the lentil. Among esculent vegetables, the potato, recently introduced, carrots, lettuce, beets, turnips, and the cabbage. In the Jordan Valley and in the sandy plains are raised immense quantities of cucumbers, melons, gourds, and pumpkins. Cotton is produced in large quantities; hemp is abundant, but flax is less common.

ANIMALS.—We can refer only to the principal species and varieties of animals. Some species formerly known have now disappeared. There are now horses, asses, mules, oxen, sheep, goats, buffaloes, dogs, and cats. Among the wild creatures are bears, panthers, jackals, wolves, foxes, hyenas, wild boars, badgers, porcupines, squirrels, hares, rats, and mice. Among the *birds* are eagles, vultures, kites, falcons, owls, ravens, crows, quails, partridges, storks, herons, sea-swallows, gulls, doves, and various birds of song. *Reptiles* exist in great variety. Lizards are almost every-where among the rocks and old ruins. Serpents abound. The scorpion and tarantula are less numerous. There are frogs, toads, and tortoises. Crocodiles are also said to exist in the Crocodile River, in the plain of Sharon. Insects are exceedingly numerous. The common fly and mosquito are found; also the bee, the wasp, and the hornet. There are horse-flies, butterflies, ants, spiders, grasshoppers, beetles, earwigs, with the glow-worm and the fire-fly, and, the most formidable of all, the locust.

V. MODERN DIVISIONS.—These consist of two great pashalics: (1.) *Sidon*, embracing all Western Palestine; and (2,) *Damascus*, all east of the Jordan.

The present inhabitants of Palestine are a mixed race, descendants of the ancient Syrians, and of the Arabs who came in with the armies of Khalifs. There are a few Jews, Armenians, and Turks. The Druses, who reside in *Haurân*, and occupy a few villages in Galilee and on Carmel, are converts from Mohammedanism. Patriotism is unknown. There is scarcely a man in the land who would give a *para* to save it from ruin. "The patriotism of the Syrian is confined to his own house; any thing beyond it does not concern him—selfishness reigns supreme."

For the HISTORY of Palestine see CANAAN; JEWS; ISRAEL; JUDAH; MACCABEES; JERUSALEM.

Palestine is now pre-eminently "a land of ruins." "Every-where, on plain and mountain, in rocky desert and on beetling cliff, are seen the remains of cities and villages. In Western Palestine there are heaps of stones, or white dust and rubbish, strewn over low tells; in Eastern the ruins are often of great extent and magnificence."—*Porter*. "The ruins we now see are of the most diverse ages; Saracenic, Crusading, Roman, Grecian, Jewish, extending perhaps even to the old Canaanitish remains, before the arrival of Joshua. This variety, this accumulation of destruction, is the natural result of the position which has made Palestine for so many ages the thoroughfare and prize of the world."—*Stanley*.

Pamphyl'ia, (Map 8,) *nation made of every tribe* (?), a province of Asia Minor. It is on the southern coast, bending in the form of a crescent round a wide, open bay, Acts xxvii, 5. Round the head of the bay sweeps an undulating plain, shut in in the background by a semicircle of lofty mountains. This plain is nowhere more than twenty miles broad, its total length being about eighty miles. Its surface is furrowed by a series of alternate low rocky ridges and broad picturesque valleys, down which wind rivers and torrents. This narrow strip of land constituted the ancient province or principality of Pamphylia. Later, during the Roman rule in Asia Minor, this province included a large section of Pisidia on the north, and of Lycia on the west; and at one period the pro-consul of Pamphylia ruled all Lycia. Luke distinguishes Lycia from Pamphylia, Acts xxvii, 5. Many Jews settled in Pamphylia, 1 Macc. xv, 23. Strangers from Pamphylia were in Jerusalem on the day of Pentecost, Acts ii, 10. Perga, in Pamphylia, on the river Cestrus, about eight miles from the coast, was the first place in Asia Minor which Paul visited in his first missionary journey, Acts xiii, 13. In the verse just referred to occurs the record, "And John, departing from them, returned to Jerusalem." John's reason for so doing is not intimated. Compare Acts xv, 36–40. From Perga Paul and his companions went north "to

Antioch in Pisidia," (xiii, 14,) doubtless encountering "perils by robbers" over the wild mountain road. "And after they had passed throughout Pisidia they came to Pamphylia. And when they had preached the word in Perga, they went down into Attalia: and thence sailed to Antioch," Acts xiv, 24–26. The province has now a few little towns and villages near the coast, some of which contain remains of former grandeur.

Pa'phos, (Map 8,) *which boils, or is hot*, a city of Cyprus at the western end of the island. It was the seat of the Roman governor. When Paul visited Paphos, the governor, Sergius Paulus, was converted through the apostle's preaching and the miracle performed on Elymas, the sorcerer, Acts xiii, 6–11. Paphos, or "New Paphos," was noted for the worship of Venus, who is fabled to have risen from the sea at this place; hence one of her names, *Paphia*; but her grand temple was at "Old Paphos," which was not far from the harbor and the chief town, "New Paphos." The new city had also a temple. The modern name is *Baffa*, where ruins are found.

Par'adise. See EDEN.

Pa'rah, *the cow, heifer-town*, a town in the territory of Benjamin, grouped between Bethel and Ophrah, Josh. xviii, 23. Possibly the site may be at the ruins called *Khurbet Fürah*, in *Wady Fârah*, about three miles below Michmash, at the junction with *Wady Suweinit*.

Pa'ran, (Map 2,) *a place of caves*, the name of a wilderness and of a mountain.

1. A desert or wilderness, having Palestine on the north, the Valley of Arabah on the east, and the Desert of Sinai on the south. Its western boundary (which is not mentioned in the Bible) appears to have extended to Egypt and the Mediterranean, 1 Kings xi, 18. The first notice of Paran is in connection with the invasion of the confederate kings. This invasion swept over Mount Seir "unto El-Paran, which is by the wilderness," Gen. xiv, 6. Hagar and Ishmael went from Abraham's tent at Beersheba out into "the wilderness of Paran," Gen. xxi, 14, 21. When the Israelites took their journeys out of the wilderness of Sinai, it is recorded that "the cloud rested in the wilderness of Paran," Num. x, 12. A march of several days intervened between Sinai and Paran, Num. x, 11; 3, 34, 35; xii, 16. From Paran the spies were sent out to survey Canaan, Num. xiii, 3; and, after completing their mission, they returned to the camp, "unto the wilderness of Paran to Kadesh," verse 26. The detailed itinerary in Num. xxxiii does not mention Paran, because it was the name of a wide region; but the many stations in Paran are recorded, (17–36,) and probably all the eighteen stations there mentioned between Hazeroth and Kadesh were in Paran. Moses says of Paran, "We went through all that great and terrible wilderness which ye saw by the way of the mountain of the Amorites, and we came to Kadesh-Barnea," Deut. i, 1–19. Through this very wide wilderness, from pasture to pasture, as do the modern Arab tribes, the Israelites wandered in irregular lines of march. And it was when about entering on this toilsome and fearful march that Moses besought his father-in-law, Jethro, not to leave them; because, as a nomad pastoral chief, he knew the best pastures and all the wells and fountains, Num. x, 31. In later times David took refuge in this wilderness after Samuel's death, 1 Sam. xxv, 1. This reference shows that Paran bordered on the southern declivities of the mountains of Judah. Probably its boundary was not very accurately defined, and whatever part of that region lay beyond the limits of

settled habitation was called "the wilderness or pasture-land of Paran," and this included a large section of the NEGEB, (which see.) Josephus mentions a valley of Paran, but it was situated somewhere in the wilderness of Judea. This region, through which the Israelites journeyed so long, is now called by the name it has borne for ages, *Bedu et-Tih*, "the wilderness of wandering." Between the wilderness of Zin and that of Paran there seems to be no distinct boundary line. See ZIN.

Travelers passing through the district of *Et-Tih* corroborate Moses's description in Deut. i, 19. See SINAI; WILDERNESS.

2. MOUNT PARAN. In Deut. xxxiii, 2, Moses says: "The Lord came from Sinai, and rose up from Seir unto them; he shined forth from Mount Paran." In Hab. iii, 3, the prophet, in describing the glory of God, says: "God came from Teman, and the Holy one from Mount Paran." Teman was another name for Edom or Seir, and hence the local allusions of Moses and Habakkuk are identical. Mount Paran was doubtless the ridge or series of ridges lying on the north-east part of the wilderness of *Et-Tih*, and now called *Jebel-Magráh*.

Par'thians, (Maps 1, 17,) occurs only in Acts ii, 9, in the list of the multitudes who were in Jerusalem on the day of Pentecost. The persons here indicated were Jews who had settled in Parthia. Parthia, called also Parthyræa and Parthyene, was originally a small mountainous district lying to the north-east of Media. Ancient Parthia, or Parthia proper, lay between Aria and Hyrcania, and was peopled by a rude and poor tribe of Scythian origin. It formed a part of the great Persian monarchy, being a dependency on the satrapy of Hyrcania. The Parthians were a part of the army of Xerxes, and also of that of the last Darius. They took sides with Eumenes on the breaking up of Alexander's kingdom, and became subject to Antigonus and the Seleucidæ. About 256 B. C., revolting against the Syro-Macedonian power, the Parthians succeeded in establishing their independence under Arsaces I. The sovereigns under this dynasty are known as the Arsacidæ. Here was the beginning of the great Parthian empire, which in the early days of Christianity extended itself over all the provinces of what had been the Persian kingdom, having the Euphrates for its western boundary, by which it was separated from the dominions of Rome. Parthia, as a power, almost rivaled Rome, and indeed it was the only existing power which the Romans could not subjugate. By the defeat and destruction of Crassus near Carrhæ, (the scriptural Harran,) the Parthians acquired that character for military prowess ascribed to them by the best writers of the Roman classical period. Their chief strength was in the vast multitude of their horsemen, whose skill with the bow and arrow was very remarkable. These expert horsemen were specially dreaded by the Romans. With the latter the Parthians frequently contended, sometimes vanquished, sometimes victors, until, in A. D. 226, Artabanus, the last of the Arsacidæ, was forced to yield his kingdom to the revolted Persians, who under Artaxerxes, son of Sassan, succeeded in re-establishing their empire. The rulers of this new Persian empire received the name of Sassanidæ. Thus the Parthian kingdom lasted nearly five centuries. During the Syro-Macedonian period the Parthian and Jewish history kept apart in separate spheres, but under the Romans the Parthians defended the party of Antigonus against Hyrcanus, and even took and plundered Jerusalem, 40 B. C. The Parthians strove to imitate the art and polish of any whom they conquered. Many of their efforts at imitation were ludicrous failures, yet in following the Greek models they had some measure of success. Their architecture was better than their sculpture, and some of the Parthian ruins are among the most remarkable of Oriental remains.

Parva'im, perhaps *eastern regions*, a region mentioned in 2 Chron. iii, 5, as producing the finest gold. Bochart and others would identify this place with Ophir. Some propose *Barbatia* on the Tigris, which is named by Pliny. Hitzig suggests "hill," from the Sanscrit *paru*, as the meaning, and refers Parvaim to Arabia. Wilford, Gesenius, and other good scholars, would derive the word from the Sanscrit *pûrva*, "eastern," a general term corresponding to our Levant; thus, "gold of Parvaim" would signify gold of the eastern regions.

Pas-Dam'mim, *the end* or *cessation of blood*, a place mentioned only in 1 Chron. xi, 13, in describing the scene of a fierce contest with the Philistines. In 1 Sam. xvii, 1, the form is Ephes-Dammim. Which form is the earlier or more correct has not been decided. This place lay on the side of the Valley of Elah, between Shochoh and Azekah. It may have been a little district and not a town. Van de Velde proposes to identify Ephes-Dammim with some ruins called *Dâmûm*, three miles east of Shochoh up the valley. Mr. Porter, who carefully surveyed this region, thinks the camp of the Philistines must have been west of Shochoh.

Pat'ara, (Map 8,) a Lycian city in Asia Minor, situated on the sea-coast. Paul visited it on his journey from Greece to Syria, Acts xxi, 1, 2. Patara was a very ancient city, founded, it is said, by Patarus, a son of Apollo, and devoted to the worship of Apollo. At the time of Paul's visit it doubtless was, as it had long been, a splendid and populous city. Paul remained not more than a few hours, probably, yet Christianity obtained a hold in the city, and it subsequently became the seat of a bishop, and was represented in the Council of Nice. Ruins of great extent and beauty remain, including a theater, some baths, a triple arch which was one of the gates of the city, an old castle, temples, altars, and columns. Traces of the walls are found, but the site of the city is now a desert, and sand hills are gradually concealing the ruins themselves. Over the great city gate-way is the inscription in Greek, "Patara, the metropolis of the Lycians." The ruins bear the old name.

Path'ros, probably *region of the south*, or, perhaps, *the abode of Hat-Her*, (the Egyptian Venus,) a part of Upper Egypt, probably lying about Thebes. In Gen. x, 14, and 1 Chron. i, 12, we have the plural of Pathros, Pathrusim, which is given as the name of a Mizraite tribe. The Mizraim were from Masor, a son of Ham, Gen. x, 6; and the Pathrusim from Pathros, son of Masor, xiii, 14. The tribe gave their name to the country which they settled, and perhaps, too, the name was descriptive of their country. One of the provinces of Thebaïs was called Phaturites, a name which is identical with the word by which the Septuagint renders Pathros. In Isa. xi, 11, the prophet seems to distinguish Pathros from Mizraim, but Jeremiah evidently includes it in the latter, Jer. xliv, 1, 15; while in Ezek. xxix, 14, Pathros seems to be only another name for Mizraim, (Egypt.) See Ezek. xxx, 14. Thus the sacred writers always group Pathros with Egypt. Jerome, in translating the passage in Ezekiel, (xxix, 14,) appears to have thought that Pathros was the earliest seat of the Egyptian nation, an opinion warranted by the passage, and corroborated by traditional records and existing monuments. There can be no doubt that Pathros was the country which by classic geographers is usually called Thebaïs—a strip of fertile valley forming the basin of the Nile. It was shut in on the east and west by deserts, and extended from the Delta on the north to Philæ on the south.

Pathru'sim. Gen. x, 14; 1 Chron. i, 12. The people of PATHROS, which see.

Pat'mos, (Map 8,) the island in the Ægean Sea to which St. John was banished "for the testimony of Jesus," Rev. i, 9. Patmos was about fifteen miles in circuit.

On account of its rocky, barren, and desolate nature, the Roman government used the island as a place to which they might banish the very worst criminals. It is said that these convicts had to work in mines that existed on the island. Among such vicious characters the pure and loving John was obliged to live in exile. Here, on this sterile spot, he was favored with those visions from heaven which have invested Patmos with the deepest interest to the Christian.

The coast of Patmos is high, and consists of a succession of capes, which form so many ports, some of which are excellent. The only one in use is a deep bay, sheltered by high mountains on every side but one, where it is protected by a projecting cape. The only inhabited site of the island is the town attached to this port. It is situated on a high rocky mountain, rising immediately from the sea, and contains about four hundred houses; while the landing place below, *La Scala,* has about fifty, including some shops. In the middle of the town, on the very top of the mountain, is a monastery named after St. John. It was built by the Emperor Alexius Comnenus. The library contains a great many printed books and manuscripts, the latter of which have been examined and described by Dr. Clarke and Professor Carlisle. About half-way up the mountain from *La Scala* to the town is shown a natural grotto in the rock, where St. John is supposed to have witnessed his visions, and to have written the Revelation. A small church is built over the grotto, connected with which is a school or college where the ancient Greek literature is said to be well taught and understood. In the Middle Ages the island bore the name of *Palmosa;* now it is called *Patino.*

Pa'u, *a bleating,* a place probably in Idumæa. In 1 Chron. i, 50, Pai, the "city" of Hadar, King of Edom, Gen. xxxvi, 39. A ruined site in Idumæa called *Phauara* may possibly be identical with Pau, but quite uncertain.

Pe'kod, *visitation, punishment,* or *noble* (?), a name applied to Babylonia, or part of it, Jer. l, 21; and to the inhabitants collectively, Ezek. xxiii, 23. The passage in Jeremiah may be applied to Babylonia and its people as the object of Jehovah's wrath, but the passage in Ezekiel seems to have a different signification. The terms "visit" and "punish" are often used concerning the whole or parts of Babylonia. Compare with the above Jer. l, 18, 27, 31; Psa. cxxxvii, 8. A city called *P'qod,* in Babylonia, where there was a school, is mentioned by the Rabbins.

Pe'lethites, THE, according to Gesenius, *runners, couriers.* With the Cherethites the Pelethites composed the body-guard of King David, 2 Sam. viii, 18; xv, 18; xx, 7, 23; 1 Kings i, 38, 44; 1 Chron. xviii, 17. Mr. Poole, of the British Museum, (in Smith's *Dictionary,*) doubts Gesenius's interpreta-

PATMOS; HARBOR OF LA SCALA—THE TOWN OF PATINO ON THE HEIGHT.

tion of these names, and suggests that the Egyptian monuments throw fresh light on their etymology. He argues that Rameses III. conquered a nation under the name of "Shayretana of the Sea," and that these latter people were probably the Cretans, who were identical with the Cherethim. Egyptian kings of the nineteenth and twentieth dynasties employed the Cherethim as mercenaries. Although the Pelethites have not been similarly traced in Egyptian geography, yet the similarity of the two names, and the fact that they are usually mentioned together, favor the idea that both were of the same stock. The etymology of both names may be connected with the migration of the Philistines. In 1 Sam. xxx, 14; Ezek. xxv, 16; Zeph. ii, 5, the Cherethim are mentioned either as a Philistine tribe or as the Philistines themselves. Mr. Poole, making this body-guard cognate to the Philistines, concludes that the term Cherethites may as well signify "exiles" as "executioners;" and Pelethites might signify "fugitives" as appropriately as "couriers" or "runners."

Pelu'sium. Ezek. xxx, 15, 16, margin. See SIN.

Peni'el and **Penu'el**, (Map 3,) *face of God*, the place where Jacob wrestled in his mysterious conflict, Gen. xxxii, 24–32. It seems to have been on the north bank of the Jabbok, but some locate it on the south. The person with whom the patriarch wrestled declared himself to be God, hence Jacob called the name of the place Peni-el, "for I have seen God face to face." Possibly Penuel was the original, as it is the usual form of this name. The change of form has not been explained by etymologists. Mr. Grove thinks that possibly "the slight change to Peniel was made by Jacob or by the historian to suit his allusion to the circumstance under which the patriarch first saw it." Penuel is the form given in the Samaritan Pentateuch. Probably this spot was marked at the time of this wonderful event simply by some rude stone to serve as a memorial. Five hundred years afterward Gideon, in pursuing the Midianites, finds a city and a tower occupying the site of Penuel, Judg. viii, 8. Returning from the conquest of the Midianites, Gideon "beat down the tower of Penuel, and slew the men of the city," Judg. viii, 17. Possibly the city remained a ruin till the time of Jeroboam, who, after taking up his abode in Shechem, "went out from thence and built Penuel," 1 Kings xii, 25. This region of country has been explored but slightly, and the site of Penuel is yet unknown.

Pe'or, *the cleft, opening*, a mountain in Moab, to the top of which Balak led Balaam that he might see the whole host of Israel and curse them, Num. xxiii, 28. The Israelites were then encamped on the east bank of the Jordan, near the north-east end of the Dead Sea. Peor is described as "looking to the face of Jeshimon," that is, the wilderness of Arabia. Doubtless Peor was connected with the town of Beth-Peor, which is described as "over against" the site of the Israelitish camp, Deut. iii, 29; comp. xxxiv, 6. See BETH-PEOR and PISGAH. In Numbers xxv, 18, and xxxi, 16, the words "the matter of Peor," and "the iniquity of Peor," in Joshua xxii, 17, refer to the Midianitish idol Baal-Peor. Probably the temple of this deity stood on the top of the mountain, while the town Beth-Peor may have been situated on the slope at the base. A village bearing the Greek form of Peor, *Fogor*, is mentioned by Jerome as on the west of the Jordan near Bethlehem. It is doubtless identical with *Beit Fághûr* or *Kirbet Fághûr*, five miles south-west of Bethlehem, barely a mile to the left of the road from Hebron.

Per'azim, Mount, *mountain of breeches,* a mountain mentioned by Isaiah in speaking to the Israelites of the Divine vengeance, Isa. xxviii, 21. The mount is nowhere else mentioned in Scripture, but it is doubtless identical with the Baal-Perazim of 2 Sam. v, 20; and it is probably to David's conquest of the Philistines at Baal-Perazim that Isaiah alludes. Doubtless there was a "high place" of Baal on the top of the mount, and hence the name Baal-Perazim. See BAAL-PERAZIM.

Pere'a, (Map 5,) *beyond,* the region east of the Jordan; specifically the territory of the trans-Jordanic tribes. Jesus occasionally went thither, Matt. xix, 1; Luke xv, 3. Perea is full of interest to the student. It was "the first land conquered, the first lost by the hosts of Israel." The American Palestine Exploration Society have undertaken a thorough scientific exploration of the whole region between Kerak and Damascus as far as the 37th meridian, embracing about 15,000 square miles. Pisgah has been fully identified, and many hitherto unknown ruins in Moab have been marked. See MOAB: PISGAH.

Pe'rez-Uz'za, or **Pe'rez-Uz'zah,** *the breach of Uzzah,* called also Nachon, 2 Sam. vi, 6; and Chidon, 1 Chron. xiii, 9. See NACHON.

Per'ga, (Map 8,) a town of Pamphylia, in Asia Minor, on the river Cestrus, about sixty stadia from its mouth. It was originally the capital of the province; but when Pamphylia was divided, Side became the chief town of the first, and Perga of the second Pamphylia. Perga was noted in antiquity for the worship of Artemis, (Diana,) whose temple stood on a hill outside the town. St. Paul landed at the city on his voyage from Paphos, and here Mark left them, Acts xiii, 13. Returning from the interior of Pamphylia, Paul visited Perga again, and there preached the Gospel, Acts xiv, 25. The site of Perga is marked by extensive remains of vaulted and ruined buildings. The Turks call the place *Eski-Kalesi.*

Per'gamos, and **Per'gamum,** (Map 8,) *height, elevation,* a noted city of the Great Mysia. It was situated about twenty miles from the sea, on the north bank of the river Caicus, in one of the most lovely and fertile valleys in the world. The name was originally given to a high and remarkable hill, which presented a conical appearance when viewed from the plain. The place rose to great importance under the successors of Alexander, and became the capital of a kingdom which the last sovereign, Attalus III., bequeathed (133 B. C.) to the Roman people. The city was noted for its vast library, containing 200,000 volumes. Antony removed this library to Egypt and presented it to Cleopatra. The art of preparing skins for manuscripts was brought to great perfection at Pergamos, hence the name of *pergamena,* or parchment. Under the Romans Pergamos was the capital of the kingdom which they erected into a province under the name of Asia Propria. Here were splendid temples of Zeus or Jupiter, of Athene or Minerva, of Apollo, of Æsculapius and others, all situated in a grove of extreme beauty, called Nicephorium, which was considered the great glory of the city. In this magnificent city was one of "the seven churches in Asia," to which John addressed his Apocalypse, commending it for its fidelity and firmness in the midst of much persecution, and in a city so eminently addicted to idolatry, Rev. i, 11; ii, 12–17. In this passage Pergamos is called "Satan's seat." Some think this phrase refers to the persecutions against the Christians, which of course were Satan's work. Others refer it to the Temple of Æsculapius, where this deity was worshiped under

PERSEPOLIS.

the form of a living serpent. In Rev. xii, 9, the same writer calls Satan "that old serpent." In Rev. xi, 13, a faithful martyr, Antipas, is mentioned as being slain in Pergamos, "where Satan dwelleth."

The modern name of the city is *Bergama*. It is a place of some importance, with a population variously estimated at from 14,000 to 30,000, of whom 3,000 are Greeks, 300 Armenians, and the rest Turks. Ruins of great extent remain, consisting of temples, bridges, theaters, and other structures. The modern houses are mostly small, mean wooden buildings.

Per'izzites, THE, (Map 3,) *villagers*, one of the original tribes inhabiting the Holy Land. The Greek forms Pheresites and Pherezites occur in 1 Esdr. viii, 69; 2 Esdr. i, 21; Judith v, 16. They inhabited Canaan in the time of Abraham, Gen. xiii, 7; and of Jacob, xxxiv, 30. Their land was promised to Abraham's posterity, Gen. xv, 20; Exod. iii, 8; xxiii, 23; Josh. iii, 10; Neh. ix, 8. They are frequently mentioned in connection with the Canaanites, to whom they seem to have been second in importance. They are also grouped with the Hittites and Rephaim, Gen. xv. 20; Joshua locates them in the mountains with the Amorite, Hittite, and Jebusite, Josh. xi, 3. They were a warlike race, like the Rephaim, and had their strongholds among the heights of Judah and Ephraim, xvii, 15. Israel was commanded to destroy them, Deut. xx, 17; and they were defeated by Joshua, Josh. ix, 1, 2; xi, 3; xii, 8; xxiv; xi; and by Simeon and Judah, in Bezek, Judg. i, 3, 4, etc. Bezek, although not identified, was probably within the allotted territory of Judah. The Perizzites were not exterminated, however, and they not only remained in Palestine, but even intermarried with the Israelites, Judg. iii, 5–7. Ezra charged this abomination upon the Israelites, Ezra ix, 1. They were made tributary to Solomon, 1 Kings ix, 20; 2 Chron. viii, 7.

The origin of the Perizzites is involved in obscurity. They are not named in the Canaanitish catalogue of tribes in Gen. x. Kalisch and other able biblical scholars incline to the belief that the names Canaanites and Perizzites designate respectively the inhabitants of the walled towns, and of the open country or unwalled villages. In 1 Sam. vi, 18, and Deut. iii, 5, the expressions "country villages" and "unwalled towns" are understood by the Septuagint to refer to the abodes of the Perizzites, and are thus translated. Mr. Porter says on this point: "This view . . . appears to be plainly opposed to the biblical narrative. The Perizzites are there spoken of in the very same terms in which the other tribes are spoken of. Their habits are nowhere specified, and the word Perizzite is manifestly as much a proper name as Hittite, Canaanite, or Hivite; and we have reason to believe that from whatsoever quarter they came they were among the very earliest inhabitants of Palestine." See *Kitto*.

Persep'olis, (Map 17,) a noted city of Persia, mentioned only in 2 Macc. ix, 2, where it is said that Antiochus Epiphanes, in attempting to burn its temples, provoked a resistance which forced him to an ignominious retreat. Persepolis was the capital of Persia proper, and the frequent residence of Persian monarchs from the time of Darius Hystaspis to the invasion of Alexander the Great. This conqueror wantonly burnt it. The buildings generally were built of cedar-wood, which caused the conflagration to be very rapid and general. The temples, which were of stone, probably escaped. The ruins now existing prove that it must either have been rebuilt, or not totally destroyed by Alexander. It is not identical with Pasargadæ, the ancient capital, as many have supposed. The latter was at *Murgaub*, about forty-two miles due north of Persepolis, where the tomb of Cyrus may still be seen. Persepolis was situated near the plains of *Merdusht*, near the junction of two streams, where now exist extensive and splendid ruins called *Chehl-Minar*, " Forty Pillars."

Per'sia, (Maps 1, 17,) (Heb., Pharas,) *pure, splendid, horse, or horseman* (?). Some conjecture the " Persians " to mean *the Tigers*. The etymology is very obscure, and these conjectures are wholly unsatisfactory. Persia was properly the designation of the province of *Fars* or *Fursistan*, a district bounded on the north by Media and Mount Aprassia, the Parachoathras of the ancients; on the south by *Laristan* and the Persian Gulf, on the west by Susiana, and on the east by Caramania. In Scripture, however, and in the classics, the name more frequently denotes the extensive empire of the Persians, which at one time stretched from India to Thrace and Egypt, and included parts of Europe, Asia, and Africa. In this sense it occurs, 2 Chron. xxxvi, 20, 22; Ezra iv, 5, 7, 24; vi, 14; Esther i, 3, 14, 18; Dan. x, 13, 20; xi, 2. In the more limited sense it is found in Dan. viii, 20; and perhaps also in Ezek. xxvii, 10 and xxxviii, 5, although the combination there of Persia with Lud and Libya seems to render it possible that the reference may be to an African settlement of Persians rather than to those who remained in their primitive seat. Sallust speaks of Persian immigrants into Egypt, and these Pliny identifies with the Pathrusi. The province of Persia proper is very mountainous; there are few plains of any extent in it, but many of the valleys are picturesque and fertile.

The Persians, who inhabited Persia proper, and thence conquered a mighty empire, were doubtless of the same race as the Medes, both being branches of the great Arian stock, which under various names established their sway over the whole tract between Mesopotamia and Burmah. Their name does not occur till the later periods of Bible history, the first reference occurring in 2 Chron. xxxvi, 20, 22. In remote antiquity the nation occupied other settlements to the east of the Caspian. It is said that a certain Achæmenes was their leader, about 700 B. C., into the country called after them. From this leader the royal and noble Achæmenian race derived its name. There is nothing, however, very certain before the reign of the great Cyrus. The Medes seem to have held the Persian princes in vassalage until the elder Cyrus, who (B. C. 558) introduced the Persian dynasty, which held rule over Media as well as Persia. In some of the passages above we have an account of Cyrus's permission to the captive Jews to return to Jerusalem. Thus Isaiah's prophecy (Isa. xliv, 28; xlv, 1-7) was fulfilled, both in the return of these exiles and in the overthrow of the power that had enslaved them. But the Jews were hindered in the work of rebuilding their temple. Their foes hired counselors to oppose them "all the days of Cyrus," Ezra iv, 5. (Compare Dan. x, 13.) It was not till the end of one and twenty years that the temple was completed, Ezra vi, 14, 15. Cyrus died 529 B. C. His tomb is still said to be seen at the ruins of Pasargadæ, the ancient capital. (See PERSEPOLIS.) The successor of Cyrus was his son Cambyses, (probably the Ahasuerus of Ezra iv, 6,) who invaded Egypt. Gomates, the Magian, who pretended to be Smerdis, son of Cyrus, then usurped the throne. He is the Artaxerxes who forbade the rebuilding of the temple, (7-23.) He was slain after a reign of seven months, and was succeeded by Darius Hystaspes. The latter favored the Jews, and permitted them to complete their temple, Ezra iv, 2, 11; v; vi; Hag. i, 1: Zech. i, 1. Darius built palaces at Persepolis and at Susa, (Shushan.) On the death of Darius, B. C. 485, Xerxes (probably the Ahasuerus of Esther and Mordecai) succeeded to the throne. Xerxes, after a reign of twenty years, was assassinated by Artabanus, who enjoyed his power for the short term of seven months. Artaxerxes (I.) Longimanus took the throne B. C. 465, and bore rule for the long period of forty years. He is doubtless the king who stood in such friendly relations toward Ezra and Nehemiah, Ezra vii, 11–28; Neh. ii, 1-9, etc. This is the last of the Persian kings who had any special connection with the Jews, and the last but one mentioned in Scripture. His successors were Xerxes II., Sogdianus, Darius Nothus, Artaxerxes Mnemon, Artaxerxes Ochus, and Darius Codomannus. The last named is probably the "Darius the Persian" of Nehemiah xii, 22. His empire was finally overthrown by Alexander the Great, B. C. 330, thus putting an end to the Persian monarchy after it had existed for over two hundred years. Then followed the Grecian empire. Persia is frequently referred to in the Apocrypha, 1 Esdr. iii, 1; Judith i, 7; Bel i, 1; 1 Macc. iii, 31. In later ages the name and power of Persia revived, and to the present day it has a name among the powerful nations of Asia. See MEDIA.

Per'sians, Esth. i, 19; Dan. v, 28. See PERSIA.

Pe'thor, perhaps a *table,* or, possibly, *soothsayer,* a town mentioned by Moses as the native place of Balaam the prophet, and situated "upon the river," (the Euphrates,) Num. xxii, 5; and also as in "Aram-Naharaim," or Mesopotamia, Deut. xxiii, 4. Some think Pethor was probably in the neighborhood of Bashan; but its site is wholly unknown. See PADAN-ARAM.

Pe'tra. See SELA.

Phar'atho'ni, one of the cities of Judea fortified by Bacchides during his contests with Jonathan Maccabeus, 1 Macc. ix, 50. It probably represents an ancient Pirathon, but hardly that of the Judges.

Phar'par, (Map 5,) *swift, lively,* one of the two "rivers of Damascus" alluded to by Naaman, 2 Kings v, 12. The two chief streams in the district of Damascus are known as the *Barada* and the *Awaj.* The *Barada* is doubtless identical with the ABANA, which see; while the *Awaj* is unquestionably the same with the Pharpar. This identity of the *Awaj* and Pharpar was suggested by Munro in 1833, and confirmed by Dr. Robinson; but its sources, course, and the lake into which it falls, were first explored by Mr. Porter in 1852. The *Awaj* has two principal sources—one high up on the eastern side of Hermon, just beneath the central peak; the other in a wild glen a few miles southward, near the romantic village of *Beit Jann.* The streams unite near *Sasa,* and the river flows eastward in a deep rocky channel, and falls into a lake, or marsh, called *Bahret Hijâneh,* about four miles south of the lake into which the Barada falls. Although eight miles distant from the city, yet the *Awaj* flows across the whole plain of Damascus; and large ancient canals drawn from it irrigate the fields and gardens almost up to the walls. Its total length is about forty miles; its volume about one fourth that of the *Barada.* The latter is evidently much superior to the *Awaj;* for, while the Barada is copious, and also perennial in the hottest seasons, the *Awaj* is described as a small "lively" stream, often dry in the lower part of its course.

In a remote age the mountain range around the sources of the Pharpar was occupied by the warlike Maachathites, 1 Chron. xix, 6, 7; Josh. xii, 5.

Afterward it formed part of the tetrarchy of Abilene, Luke iii, 1. Farther down the river divided the territory of Damascus from Iturea.

The district through which the *Awaj* flows is now called *Wady el-Ajam*, "the Valley of the Persians," extending from the walls of Damascus along the base of Anti-Libanus to the borders of *Jedûr* beyond the *Awaj*. Its extreme length is thirty-two miles, its greatest breadth thirty, but near the lake into which it empties it is but four or five. Some parts of it are extremely fertile, and it contains about fifty villages, with a population of eighteen thousand. See Porter's *Damascus*; Ritter's *Palestine*; *The Rob Roy on the Jordan*.

Phase'lis, a town in Asia Minor, on the borders of Lycia and Pamphylia. Jews were settled here, many having been brought thither as slaves. In 1 Macc. xv, 23, the Romans are represented as demanding of this town that all Jewish exiles who may have taken refuge there should be given up to Simon the high priest. Phaselis was early a place of considerable importance; but later it became a resort of pirates. It is now *Tekrova*.

Pheni'ce.
1. The accurate form of Phenicia, Acts xi, 19; xv, 3, etc. See PHENICIA.
2. (Map 8.) A town and harbor, more properly Phœnix, on the southwest coast of Crete. The name is doubtless derived from the Greek word for the *palm-tree*, which was said to be indigenous to the island. In his journey to Rome, the ship having reached Fair Havens, on the coast of Crete, Paul admonished the officers, telling them that the voyage would be "with hurt and much damage;" and it was in making the attempt to reach Phœnix that they were caught by the gale and driven to Claudia, Acts xxvii, 8–16.

Phœnix is identified with the harbor of *Lutro*, at the narrowest part of the island, and opposite the island of Clauda, where the inhabitants preserve the memory of the ancient name, *Phœniki*. A little way from the shore, on a hill, are found some ruins of the town.

Phenic'ia, and **Phœnic'ia**, (Maps 1, 5, 8.) The name is probably derived from the Greek phœnix, *palm-tree*, a tree found in great numbers in this country. Some, however, derive it from *Phoinos*, "purple;" or from Phœnix, the son of Agenor, and brother of Cadmus, etc. The accurate form is Phenice, and thus it frequently occurs. Phenicia is the name applied to a small country on the coast of Syria, lying along the Mediterranean, with an average breadth of twenty miles, reaching from the river Eleutherus, near Aradus, on the north, one hundred and twenty miles, to the promontory of Carmel, or the town of Dor, on the south. But the limits of the country varied very greatly at different periods. Phenicia proper was very small in area, extending from the Promontorium Album, *Ras el-Abyad*, six miles south of Tyre, to the Bostrenus, *Nahr el-Auly*, two miles north of Sidon, twenty-eight miles in length, with an average breadth of but one mile; but near Sidon the mountains retreat to a distance of two miles, and near Tyre to five miles. The term Phenicia does not occur in the Old Testament, as might be expected from its being a Greek name. It occurs frequently in the Apocrypha. It is found in only three passages in the New Testament, Acts xi, 19; xv, 3; xxi, 2; but none of the passages give the extent of the land in question. We derive its limits from Pliny, Strabo, Ptolemy, Josephus, etc.; and these do not always agree on the boundaries. Phenicia was probably peopled by the descendants of Ham; for Sidon is said to have been the first-born of Canaan; and the Arkite, and probably the Sinite, the Arvadite, and the Zemarite, had their settlements in this region, Gen. x, 15, 17, 18. Opinions concerning this point are various. At the earliest dawn of authentic history these people are found already established along the Mediterranean, and for centuries afterward there is no record of their origin. Herodotus makes them, both on their own statements and by accounts preserved in Persian histories, immigrants from "the Erythrean Sea." This sea is taken by different investigators to stand either for the Arabian or the Persian Gulf. Some have seen in them the Hyksos driven to Syria. Most theories are merely vague speculations. But it appears certain that at different periods, and from different parts, many immigrations of Semitic branches into Phenicia must have taken place, and that these gradually settled into the highly civilized nationality which we find constituted as early as the time of Abraham, Gen. xii, 6. The passage above quoted (Gen. x, 15–18) is probably the most valuable source of information which we possess.

The Greeks professed to have borrowed letters from the Phenicians; and it is unquestionable that the characters they used were of great antiquity, the origin perhaps of the old Hebrew. Inscriptions which have been discovered prove that the language of the Phenicians was nearly akin to Hebrew.

The principal cities of Phenicia were the renowned cities of Sidon and Tyre, with Tripolis, Byblos, and Berytus. This country was admirably situated for commerce. From the countries on the Persian Gulf and the Red Sea, the coasts of Arabia, Africa, and India, the Phenicians brought spice, precious stones, myrrh, frankincense, gold, ivory, ebony, steel, and iron, and from Egypt embroidered linen and corn—giving in exchange not only their own raw produce and manufactures, but gums and resins for embalming, wine and spices. They traded with Syria and Mesopotamia, with Babylon, Aleppo, and Judea, with Armenia, with the Euxine coast and the coast of the Atlantic—with almost all nations, both by sea and by land. Their caravan traffic was great with Egypt and Arabia. Their extensive early commerce with Greece is frequently alluded to in Homer, and is further shown by the remarkable fact of the abundance of Semitic or Phenician words in Greek for such things as precious stones, fine garments, vessels, spices, and eastern plants in general, musical instruments, weights and measures. This people appear to have had an uncommon knowledge both of astronomy and physical geography; they had also practical sense, boldness, shrewdness, vast energy, and a happy genius, all of which united made and kept them the unrivaled masters of ancient commerce and navigation. The prophet Ezekiel gives a most glowing account of Tyre, calling it "a merchant of the people for many isles," and naming some of the many countries or isles, Ezek. xxvii, 1–25. This chapter closes, and the following one opens, with the great and irrecoverable fall of Tyre. In Ezek. xxviii, 20–26, the prophet predicts the overthrow of Sidon.

The religion of the Phenicians in its popular form was that natural but debased and foolish worship paid to the sun, moon, and planets, etc., by the appellations of Baal, Ashtoreth, Asherah, Beelzebub, Chiun, etc. Their worship was a constant temptation to polytheism and idolatry. The sun, moon, and five planets were worshiped under a pantheistical personification of the forces of nature, these objects not being regarded as lifeless globes of matter, obedient to physical laws, but as intelligent animated powers, influencing the human will, and controlling human destinies The influence of the polytheistic religion of the Phenicians upon the Israelites was exceedingly demoralizing. Idol worship and its most cruel rites became common among the Jews. Jer. xix, 5; xxxii, 35. See TYRE; SIDON.

Pher'esites, and **Pher'ezites,** the Greek form of Perizzites, 1 Esdr. viii, 69; 2 Esdr. i, 21; Judith v, 16.

Philadel'phia, (Map 8,) *love of a brother,* or *of brotherhood,* a city of Lydia, situated about twenty-five miles south-east from Sardis, in the plain of Hermus, about midway between the river of that name and the termination of Mount Tmolus. This city contained one of "the seven churches of Asia," to which John addressed his Apocalyptic epistles, Rev. i, 11; iii, 7-13. The town was built by King Attalus Philadelphus, from whom it derived its name. In 133 B. C. it passed, with the dominion in which it lay, into the hands of the Romans. It continued a place of importance and strength down to the Byzantine age; and it withstood the Turks for a longer period than any other town in Asia Minor, being taken at length by Bajazet I. in 1392 A. D. See RABBAH.

The above passage in Revelation is one of entire commendation to the church in Philadelphia, and the city still remains. Mr. Gibbon *(Decline and Fall,* chap. lxiv) says, "Among the Greek colonies and churches of Asia Philadelphia is still erect; a column in a scene of ruins; a pleasing example that the paths of honor and safety may sometimes be the same." The modern name is *Allah Shehr,* "City of God," that is, High-town. It covers a considerable extent of territory, running up the slopes of four hills, or rather of one hill with four flat summits. The country around is exceedingly beautiful. The town, although spacious, is badly built, the dwellings are mean, and the streets filthy. The inhabitants are mostly Turks. A few ruins are found, including remains of a wall and about twenty-five churches. In one place are four strong marble pillars, which once supported the dome of a church. One of the old mosques is believed by the native Christians to have been the church in which assembled the primitive Christians addressed in the Apocalypse. See Trench's *Seven Churches in Asia.*

Philip'pi, (Map 8,) *lover of horses, warlike,* a noted city of Macedonia, situated in a plain, on the banks of a deep and rapid stream called Gangistes, (now *Angista.*) The old name of the city was Krenides, and sometimes Datus. Philip, king of Macedon, having taken it from the Thracians, made it a frontier fortress and gave it his own name. Philip's city stood upon a hill, probably that seen a little to the south of the present ruins, which may have always formed the citadel. The famous battle of Philippi, between Antony and Octavius and Brutus and Cassius, was fought B. C. 42. Augustus made Philippi a Roman colony, in honor of his victory. St. Paul came from Neapolis to Philippi, and there abode "certain days," Acts xvi, 12. In verse 13 the apostle speaks of a place "by a river-side, where prayer was wont to be made." Lydia, a trader from Thyatira, was the first convert made from the effort at the place of prayer, and she and her household were baptized, verses 14, 15. On their way "to prayer" the apostles were met by a damsel who brought her masters much gain by soothsaying. For casting the "spirit of divination" out of the girl, Paul, with Silas, was ordered to be scourged and cast into prison. In this prison occurred one of the most cheering and remarkable scenes in the history of the apostolic Church. The jailer and his whole house were converted; while the magistrates themselves were compelled to make a public apology to the apostles and set them at liberty, Acts xvi, 16-40. Soon after Paul again visited Philippi, and probably he remained in the city and its vicinity a considerable time, Acts xx, 1-6. The Philippian Christians were exceedingly kind to Paul; of all the Churches, they alone sent subsidies to relieve his temporal wants. During his imprisonment at Rome Paul remembered their kindness with much gratitude, and wrote them an epistle, Phil. iv, 10, 15, 18; 2 Cor. xi, 9; 1 Thess. ii, 2.

Philippi is wholly in ruins, and without a name. Remains of walls are found, and "by the river" is the site of a gate through which, doubtless, the apostles passed to the place of prayer. There exist also foundations, tombs, broken columns, heaps of rubbish, the remains of theaters, palaces, and private houses.

Philis'tia, (Maps 1, 5,) *land of strangers* or *sojourners.* The Hebrew word rendered Philistia in Psa. lx, 8; lxxxvii, 4; xcviii, 9, is identical with that elsewhere translated Palestine. The form Philistia does not occur in the Septuagint nor in the Vulgate. Palestine originally meant only the district inhabited by the "Philistines." In Psa. lxxxiii, 7, the word is rendered "Philistines." Josephus calls these people "Palestines." Philistia, or the "land of the Philistines," embraced the coast plain on the south-west of Palestine, extending from Joppa on the north to the Valley of Gerar on the south, a distance of about forty miles, and from the Mediterranean on the west to the foot of the Judean hills. Its breadth at the northern end was ten miles, and at the southern about twenty. It appears to have run as far inland as Beersheba, Gen. xxi, 33, 34; xxvi, 1, 14-18; Exod. xxiii, 31; Josh. xiii, 2, 3. A name very commonly given to it in the Bible is *Shephelah,* that is, a low, flat region, (Deut. i, 7; Josh. ix, 1; x, 40,) in the Hebrew. See PHILISTINES; PALESTINE; SEPHELA.

Philis'tim, Gen. x, 14, and

Philis'tines, (Map 3, 4, 5,) *strangers, sojourners;* but some render it *low-landers,* and some *white ones;* while others connect the word with *Pelasgi.* The Philistines inhabited the district of Palestine or PHILISTIA, (which see.) Their origin is involved in much obscurity. According to the genealogy in Gen. x, 13, 14, they were of the Mizraimite race, (Hamites,) from the Casluhim, probably increased from the Caphtorim. In Amos ix, 7, the prophet speaks of "the Philistines from Caphtor;" and in Jer. xlvii, 4, they are called the "remnant of the country of Caphtor." The passage in Deut. ii, 23, speaks of the "Caphtorim who came forth from Caphtor" as the destroyers of the Avim, the people who held the south-western sea-coast before the Philistines supplanted them. A very earnest effort has been made by some modern critics to show that the Philistines were descendants of Shem, and that they migrated from Crete either directly, or through Egypt into Palestine. This theory, besides being exposed to other formidable objections, is not consistent with Scripture. Overwhelming evidence traces the Philistines to Caphtor. Both the Casluhim and Caphtor must be looked for in Egypt. See CAPHTOR. The date of the first immigration of the Philistines into Palestine, or that part of it held before them by the Avim, is uncertain. It must, however, have taken place after that of the Canaanites, whose possessions at one time extended to Gerar and Gaza, Gen. x, 19. Abraham found the Philistines in the "south country." They were not then a powerful tribe, and evidently were of pastoral habits, Gen. xx. Their chief, Abimelech, seems to have regarded the patriarch with his numerous tribe of dependents as quite equal in power with himself, being glad to make a treaty with Abraham at Beersheba, Gen. xxi, 22, 23. The treaty was renewed with Isaac, Abimelech giving as a reason for pressing his departure from Gerar, "Thou art much mightier than we," Gen. xxvi, 12–23. The Philistines rapidly increased in numbers and in power. In the time of Joshua they were in possession of the fertile plain, the *Shephelah*, lying along the coast between the Mediterranean and the hill-country of Judah and Dan. Perhaps the tribe had naturally increased into a nation, or they may have been re-inforced by fresh settlers from Egypt. Some have thought that Jeremiah (xlvii, 4) and Amos (ix, 7) allude to such an immigration. The subsequent history of the Philistines shows that they were no longer a pastoral people merely, but well skilled in handicrafts, engaged in commercial pursuits, and especially powerful in war, able to contend even with the Sidonians and Egyptians, 1 Sam. vi, 4; xiii, 20; xvii, 5–7; Judg. xvi, 26–29; Joel iii, 3–6; Amos i, 6. The Pelethites, who, with the Cherethites, composed King David's body-guard, are supposed to have been Philistines. See PELETHITES.

The land of the Philistines lay within the limits of the Promised Land, Num. xxxiv, 5, 6; Ezek. xiii, 17; xxiii, 31. It was assigned to Judah and Dan, Josh. xv, 45–47; xix, 41–45; but Joshua never in reality seems to have gone to war with them, and five lords of the Philistines remained in five chief towns, to be a scourge to Israel through almost the whole course of their existence, Josh. xiii, 3; Judg. iii, 3. Not long after Joshua's death we find this people holding the Israelites in bondage, until Shamgar, the son of Anath, "slew of the Philistines six hundred men with an ox-goad, and he also delivered Israel," Judg. iii, 31; x, 7, 11. But Israel's deliverance was of short duration. Under Jephthah, and still more under Samson, the Philistines continued to molest the Israelites, and, in conjunction with the Ammonites, they kept the Israelites in subjection for forty years. The wonderful exploits of Samson against the Philistines, and his successes, are recorded in Judges xiii–xvi. In the battle of Aphek the Philistines carried away the ark of God, and slew thirty thousand Israelites, 1 Sam. iv, 1–11. Samuel first put an end to this period of national humiliation. In the battle of Mizpeh the Philistines not only lost their sway over Israel, but had to yield to them their own territories of Ekron and Gath, 1 Sam. vii, 11, 12, 14. This seems, however, to have been only a partial victory, and of short duration. Saul had to contend with them during his whole reign. The valiant support of Jonathan and David gained for him the battles of Michmash, where the Philistines were routed and pursued to Ajalon, and of Socho, (where Goliath was slain by David,) which ended in the flight of the Philistines and their pursuit to the gates of Gath and Ekron with a loss, according to Josephus, of thirty thousand killed and twice that number wounded, 1 Sam. ix, xii–xiv, xvii, xviii. Subsequently they suffered other defeats, chiefly at the hand of David, until the latter was himself obliged to seek refuge with Achish, King of Gath, 1 Sam. xix, 8; xxiii, 1–5, 27; xxvii, 1–7; xxix; Psa. lvi, title. For the defeat of the Philistines by the Amalekites, see 1 Sam. xxx; 1 Chron. xii, 19. At Gilboa the Israelites suffered from the Philistines one of their heaviest reverses, in which both Saul and his sons were slain, 1 Sam. xxxi; 1 Chron. x, 1. After Ish-Bosheth's death, when all Israel and Judah had submitted to David, the Philistines, who hitherto had left him undisturbed, renewed their hostilities, but were repeatedly beaten—at Baal-Perazim with the loss of their gods, and at Rephaim with immense slaughter. David still had to march against them frequently. His arms were always victorious, and he was able to leave to his son Solomon their territory as a conquered domain, 1 Kings iv, 21; 2 Chron. ix, 26; 2 Sam. v, 17-25; viii, 1, etc. Under Solomon, while retaining some of their petty chiefs, they were tributary, 1 Kings ii, 39, 40; iv, 21, 24. Gezer, at the extremity of the Philistine plain, was given to Solomon by Pharoah, and he deemed it prudent to fortify it and some other bordertowns, 2 Kings ix, 15-17. When the kingdom was divided we find both states from time to time involved in hostilities with the Philistines, 2 Kings x, 27; xvi, 15; 2 Chron. xxi, 16, 17; and although Jehoshaphat and Uzziah obtained advantages over them, it was not till the reign of Hezekiah that they were entirely subdued, 1 Chron. xvii, 11; xxvi, 6; 2 Kings xviii, 8. About the same time Sargon, King of Assyria, took Ashdod, the frontier fortress, after a three years' siege, Isa. xx, 1. Gaza was taken by Pharaoh, Jer. xlvii, 1; and under the invasion of Sennacherib the greater part, if not all of the strongholds fell under Assyrian sway, Isa. xxxvi. At the Babylonish captivity the old hatred against Israel broke out, Ezek. xxv, 15-17; but on the return alliances were made by the Jews with Philistine women, Neh. xiii, 23, 24. The sacred writer calls these "wives of Ashdod," as though the name of Philistine were forgotten or lost, and the corrupt Hebrew spoken by their offspring was Ashdodite, and not Philistine. Alexander the Great traversed their country and took Gaza, and Philistia was involved in the fortunes of the Syrian, Egyptian, Maccabean, and subsequent Jewish wars. Finally it fell under the power of the Romans. Pompey incorporated some of its cities with Roman Syria; farther portions fell to Herod and Salome's share. See 2 Esd. i, 21; 1 Macc. iii, 24, 41, etc.

The chief gods worshiped by the Philistines were Dagon, Judg. xvi, 23; 1 Sam. v, 1-7; 1 Chron. x, 10; Ashtaroth, 1 Sam. xxxi, 10; Baal-Zebub, 2 Kings i, 2, 3, 6, 16; and Decerto, the female counterpart to Dagon, not mentioned in Scripture. They had priests and diviners, and in their campaigns they carried their images with them, 1 Sam. vi, 2; 2 Sam. v, 21. Their government was a kind of federal union. The five principal cities had districts with towns and villages dependent on them, Josh. xv, 45–47; 1 Chron. xviii, 1, but in war they acted in concert. Those called "lords" had much influence in the affairs of state, controlling the "King" of Gath, 1 Sam. xxix, 3-9. The Philistines are said to have been tall and well-proportioned, with regular features, and a complexion lighter than that of the Egyptians. They shaved the beard and whiskers entirely. Their weapons of war consisted of circular shields, javelins, spears, poniards, and long swords. From 1 Sam. xiii, 5, we learn the vast number of chariots which they were able to bring into battle.

For the present condition of the land of the Philistines see ASHDOD, ASKELON, EKRON, GATH, GAZA, GERAR, GIBBETHON, METHEG-AMMA, JABNFEL.

Phi'son, the Greek form of Pison, Ecclesiasticus xxiv, 25.

Phœnic'ia. See PHENICIA.

Phryg'ia, (Map 8,) *dry, barren,* a province of Asia Minor, bounded by Bithynia and Galatia on the north; on the east by Cappadocia and Lycaonia; on the south by Lycia, Pisidia, and Isauria; on the west by Caria, Lydia, and Mysia. Perhaps, however, it may be said that no geographical term of the New Testament is less capable of an exact definition. In early times

Phrygia seems to have comprehended the greater part of Asia Minor. Subsequently it was divided into Phrygia Major on the south, and Phrygia Minor, or Epictetus, (*acquired,*) on the north-west. The Romans divided the province into three districts: Phrygia Salutaris on the east, Phrygia Pacatiana on the west, and Phrygia Katakekaumene (*the burnt*) in the middle, where there are traces of volcanic action. The country was well watered and fertile, and its pastures fed celebrated breeds of cattle and sheep. Jews were found here from the time of the Syrian dominion, Acts ii, 10. In apostolic times Phrygia was not a regularly defined Roman province. By the term, as vaguely used in the New Testament, we are rather to understand a region, portions of which, varying at different periods, were comprehended under different Roman provinces. The cities of Laodicea, Hierapolis, and Colossæ belonged to Phrygia, and Antioch in Pisidia was also within its limits. Paul, in his missionary journeys, twice traversed the province, Acts xvi, 6; xviii, 23.

Phud, Judith ii, 23, another form of Phut.

Phut, (Maps 8, 12,) *afflicted,* or, a *bow* (?), Gen. x, 6; more accurately, Put, 1 Chron. i, 8. Phut was a son of Ham, and progenitor of an African people of the same name, though sometimes the name is rendered Libya, or Libyans, Jer. xlvi, 9; Ezek. xxvii, 10; xxx, 5; xxxviii, 5; Nah. iii, 9. Mr. R. S. Poole (in Smith's *Dictionary*) inclines to identify Phut with Nubia or the Nubians; which identification, he thinks, "would account for the position of Phut after Mizraim in the list in Genesis, notwithstanding the order of the other names." But, according to Josephus, (*Antiq.,* Lib. I, 6, 32,) Phut was the colonizer of Libya; and he confirms his belief by stating that there was a river of that name in the country of the Moors, whence the whole adjoining region was termed Phut by Greek historians. In Coptic, moreover, Libya is called *Faiat,* and the inhabitants of that part which adjoins Egypt bear a corresponding name. The term Libya is given to the country from one of the sons of Mizraim, Libys, the progenitor of the LEHABIM, which see. As indicated above, some Scripture passages render Phut in the A. V. as Libyans, and Libya; so in the Vulgate and Septuagint, Libyes. The identification of Phut with Libya is indorsed by very eminent writers, among whom are Bochart, Rosenmüller, Gesenius, Michaelis, Keil, Kalisch, and Delitzsch. This identification is, however, very vague in reference to the extent of Libya. See LUBIM. As above, in Nah. iii, 9, Phut and Lubim [Lehabim] are associated; probably they were inhabitants together of the same district. Probably the Lehabim touched on the border of Upper Egypt, while Phut was contiguous to Lower Egypt, and extended westward along the north coast of Africa, and into the very interior of the continent. The designation of *Phut* seems to have been generic; of *Lehabim,* etc., specific, and in territory limited. Hitzig supposes that Phut was west of Libya, on the north coast of Africa. Kalisch, on the supposition that the identification dwelt upon above might be untenable, suggests that Phut might have been *Buto,* the capital of the Delta, on the south shore of the Butic lake. But these conjectures seem to have little to support them. See Kalisch's *Commentary on Old Test., Gen.;* and Kitto's *Cyclopedia,* art. HAM.

Pi-be'seth, or **Pib'eseth,** (Map 2,) *the* [city] *of Bubastis,* or *Pascht.* The name is derived from the goddess Bubastis, (Copt. *Pascht,* the goddess of fire,) whom the inhabitants of this city worshiped, and to whose temple here great numbers of people made yearly a festive pilgrimage. This was a city of Lower Egypt, whose destruction, together with the captivity of its people, was predicted by Ezekiel, Ezek. xxx, 17. Bubastis was situated about forty miles north-east from the central part of Memphis. In Egyptian annals few notices of the place are found. It was doubtless a city of great importance when Ezekiel predicted its ruin. Herodotus has described it with unusual minuteness; and Wilkinson (in *Modern Egypt*) assures us that the outlines of his account may still be verified. The Persians took it, and destroyed its walls; but under the Romans the city was still a place of some importance. It was near this city that the canal leading to Arsinoe (*Suez*) opened to the Nile. This ancient city is undoubtedly represented by the modern *Tel-Bustak*, in the eastern part of Lower Egypt. Here are found mounds of great extent, which consist of the crude brick houses of the town, with the usual heaps of broken pottery. Herodotus mentions the temple of the goddess Bubastis as well worthy of description, being more beautiful than any other known to him. This is entirely destroyed; but the remaining stones, which are of the finest red granite, confirm the historian's account.

Pi-Hahi'roth, (Map 2,) *mouth of caverns;* or, more probably, *the grassy places*, a place near the northern end of the Gulf of Suez, east of Baal-Zephon, where the Israelites encamped on their departure from Egypt when Pharaoh's host overtook them, Exod. xiv, 2, 9; Num. xxxiii, 7, 8. In the vicinity indicated travelers have found the name *Ghuweybet-el-boos*, "the bed of reeds." Yet, as doubtless the head of the gulf ran anciently farther to the north than now, no identification can be accurately made.

Pir'athon, perhaps *chief*, a place in Ephraim. Abdon was buried there, Judg. xii, 13, 15. One of David's mighty men was a Pirathonite, 1 Chron. xxvii, 14; xi, 31; 2 Sam. xxiii, 30. Dr. Robinson and others identify it with the little village of *Fer'ata*, lying about six miles west-south-west of *Náblûs*, (Shechem,) on the summit of a tell among low hills.

Pir'athonite. See PIRATHON.

Pis'gah, (Map 5,) *piece, section,* or *the height*, a high ridge on the east of Jordan, opposite Jericho, remarkable as having been the scene of Moses' view of Palestine. Pisgah was a part of the range of mountains called Abarim. It was in the territory afterward assigned to Reuben, and thus was north of the Arnon, Num. xxi, 20; Deut. iii, 27; iv, 49; xxxiv, 1. Pisgah had places on its top with a flat surface, and even cultivated land. Balak brought Baalam "into the *field* of Zophim, to the top of Pisgah," and there he "built seven altars," Num. xxiii, 14. The American Palestine Exploration Society, under Lieut. Stever, have made a thorough survey of this whole region. Assuming that the peak of Nebo is correctly located, (see NEBO,) Professor Paine, accompanying the explorers, claims to have identified Pisgah beyond dispute. It is a summit or "shoulder" a little to the westward of Nebo; and while it is not so lofty as the latter peak, yet the spot commands a much more magnificent sweep of vision than is gained from any other point in the vicinity. See ABARIM; PEREA; ZOPHIM.

Pisid'ia, (Map 8,) *a pitch-tree, pitchy,* a province of Asia Minor, with variable boundaries. It lay north of Pamphylia, and stretched along the Taurus range. On the north it reached to, and was partly in, Phrygia, which was also variable in territory, but far more extensive. "Antioch in Pisidia" was sometimes called a Phrygian town. St. Paul twice visited this region. In company with Barnabas he entered it from Pamphylia on the south, and crossed over the mountains to Antioch. Acts xiii, 14. Although their mission was successful, "and the word of the Lord was published throughout all that region," yet Paul and Barnabas were "expelled out of their coasts," verses 49, 50. After a perilous journey through Lycaonia and Isauria they again returned through Pisidia to Pamphylia, apparently by the same route, Acts xiv, 21-24. Pisidia and its inhabitants were alike wild and rugged; and probably it was among the defiles of Pisidia that Paul encountered some of those "perils of robbers" and "perils of rivers" of which he afterward speaks in 2 Cor. xi, 26. Perhaps fear of Pisidian bandits would account for John's sudden departure from the apostle, Acts xiii, 13, 14.

The scenery of Pisidia is wild and grand. Many of the ravines are singularly grand—bare cliffs rising up more than a thousand feet on each side of the bed of a foaming torrent. The Pisidian tribes maintained their independence against their more powerful neighbors, against the Grecians, and even the Romans. The latter took possession of Antioch, establishing a colony there, and other towns in the plain country; but they were content to receive a scanty tribute from the tribes generally, and to allow them to remain in undisturbed possession of their mountain fastnesses.

Pi'son, *overflowing*, one of the four "heads" into which the stream that watered Eden was parted, Gen. ii, 11. The Pison cannot be identified, although conjectures concerning its location are almost numberless. The most ancient and most universally received opinion identifies it with the Ganges. Among the many other streams proposed by various writers may be mentioned the Nile, the Indus, the Hydaspes, the Danube, the Naharmalca, (a canal which formerly joined the Euphrates with the Tigris,) the Phasis, etc. In the passage in Genesis the river Pison is defined as that which surrounds the whole land of Havilah. See HAVILAH.

Pi'thom, (Map 2,) *the narrow place* (?) or, perhaps, the *abode of Atum*, one of the treasure cities built by the Israelites in the land of Goshen for Pharaoh, Exod. i, 11. Some consider it identical with the Patumos of Herodotus, which appears to have been situated on the east side of the Pelusiac arm of the Nile, not far from the canal which unites the Nile with the Red Sea in the Arabian part of Egypt. Pithom, therefore, may perhaps be placed on the site of the present *Abhaseh*, at the entrance of the *Wady et-Tumeylat*.

Pon'tus, (Map 8,) *the sea*, the north-eastern province of Asia Minor, bordering on the Euxine Sea, (Pontus Euxinus,) from which it took its name. Under the Roman Emperors the name comprised the whole district along the southern bay of the Euxine, from the river Halys to Colchis and Armenia, separated on the south from Cappadocia by lofty mountains. After the defeat of Mithridates, King of Pontus, 66 B. C., a division of it was made, a portion being added to the Roman province of Bithynia, the rest being parceled out among petty provinces. Under Nero, Pontus became a Roman province under one administration with Cappadocia. From Acts ii, 9, we learn that Jews had established themselves in Pontus. Here lived Aquila, Acts xviii, 2. The apostle Peter addresses his Epistle to "the strangers scattered throughout Pontus," and other regions, 1 Pet. i, 1. The principal towns of Pontus were Amasia—the ancient metropolis, and the birthplace of the geographer Strabo—Themiscyra, Cerasus, and Trapezus, which last, under the name of *Trebizond*, is still an important town.

Pools. See BETHESDA; SILOAM; SOLOMON'S POOLS; JERUSALEM.

Pot'ter's Field, THE, Matt. xxvii, 7. See ACELDAMA.

Preto'rium, the head-quarters of the Roman Governor at Jerusalem,

Mark xv, 16. The same Greek word is rendered "common hall," (margin, "governor's house,") Matt. xxvii, 27; "hall of judgment," or "judgment hall," John xviii, 28, 33; xix, 9; Acts xxiii, 35; and in Phil. i, 13, "palace," (margin, "Cæsar's court.") The passage in Acts refers to Herod's palace at Cæsarea. The Roman military commanders usually appropriated to themselves the palaces that they found in provincial cities; thus in Jerusalem Herod's palace was the pretorium of the Procurator, justice being sometimes administered in the open court before it; so also in Cæsarea. Possibly at Jerusalem while a body-guard might remain with the Governor at the "palace," the rest of his troops may have been quartered in the Castle of ANTONIA, which see.

Ptolema'is, (Map 5,) the city called Accho in the earliest Jewish annals, and Ptolemais under Macedonian and Roman power. It is often mentioned in the Apocrypha, 1 Macc. v, 15, 22, 55; 2 Macc. xiii, 24, 25, etc. Paul on returning from his third missionary tour visited Ptolemais and "saluted the brethren, and abode with them one day," Acts xxi, 7. The place is now called *Akka,* or *St. Jean d'Acre.* See ACCHO.

Pul, a region mentioned only once, Isa. lxvi, 19. Much difficulty exists both in defining and locating Pul. The name is the same as that of Pul, king of Assyria, which signifies *elephant,* or *lord, king.* Pul is spoken of with Tarshish and Lud, Tubal, Javan, and "the isles afar off." Bochart, Henderson, Michaelis, and others, suppose it to be the island of Philæ, and the surrounding regions on the Nile to the south of Elephantine. Porter, Grove, Poole, and other good authorities, make it some distant *province* of Africa, Philæ being a very small island. Mr. Poole says, "The balance of evidence is almost decisive in favor of the African Phut or Put." See PHUT.

Pu'non, (Map 2,) *darkness,* one of the stations of the Israelites, Num. xxxiii, 42, 43. It lay between Zalmonah and Oboth. According to Jerome it is identical with *Phenon,* celebrated for its copper mines in which convicts were sentenced to labor, between Petra and Zoar. Possibly it was here that Moses set up the brazen (copper) serpent, Num. xxi, 9, 10. This identification would agree with the requirements of the wanderings; but modern explorers have found no trace of the name.

Put, 1 Chron. i, 8; Nah. iii, 9; elsewhere PHUT, PHUD, LIBYA, which see.

Pute'oli, (Map 8,) *sulphurous wells,* or *springs,* a seaport of Campania in Italy, in the most sheltered part of the Bay of Naples. Its ancient Greek name was Dicæarchia. It was a favorite watering-place of the Romans, its hot-springs being considered efficacious for the cure of various diseases. Here also ships usually discharged their passengers and cargoes, partly to avoid doubling the promontory of Circeium, and partly because there was no commodious harbor nearer to Rome. Hence the ship in which Paul was conveyed from Melita landed the prisoners at this place, where the apostle stayed a week, Acts xxviii, 13, 14. Puteoli is connected with many historical personages. Scipio sailed hence to Spain. Cicero had a villa near the city. Here Nero planned the murder of his mother. Vespasian gave to this city peculiar privileges, and here Hadrian was buried. It was ravaged by Alaric and Genseric in the fifth century. Puteoli is now an ordinary town called *Pozzuoli.* There are considerable remains, consisting of the aqueduct, the reservoirs, portions of baths, (probably,) the great amphitheater, the building called the Temple of Serapis, and particularly the ruins of the celebrated ancient mole, sixteen piers of which are still to be seen.

Quaranta'nia, *forty days*. A mountain very near Jericho on the west, with which tradition connects the fasting and the temptation of Christ, and from whose top Satan showed the Saviour "all the kingdoms of the world, and the glory of them." The mountain received this traditional name about the time of the Crusades in commemoration of the *forty days'* fast. The Arabs have adopted the name under the form of *Jebel Kuruntul.* Quarantania rises precipitously, an almost perpendicular wall of rock, twelve or fifteen hundred feet above the plain, crowned with the ruins of a chapel on its highest point. The eastern front is full of grots and caverns, where hermits are said to have once dwelt in great numbers.

Ra'amah, (Map 12,) *a trembling,* the fourth son of Cush, and the father of Sheba and Dedan, Gen. x, 7; 1 Chron. i, 9. Sheba and Dedan became nations of greater importance and notoriety than Raamah, but the latter is mentioned among the distinguished merchants that traded with Tyre, Ezek. xxvii, 22. There can be no doubt that the original settlements of the descendants of Raamah were upon the south-western shore of the Persian Gulf. The town of Regma, situated on the Arabian shore of the Persian Gulf, on the northern side of the long promontory which separates it from the ocean, is possibly the original seat of the tribe. According to Forster (*Geography of Arabia*) the nation migrated from Regma along the eastern shores of Arabia to the mountains of Yemen, where he finds them in conjunction with the family of Sheba.

Raam'ses, Exod. i, 11. See RAMESES.

Rab'bah, (Maps 5, 20,) a *great* city, or metropolis.

1. The capital of the Ammonites, Josh. xiii, 25. The full name is Rabbath-beni-Ammon, Deut. iii, 11. In Ezek. xxi, 20, it is termed Rabbath of the Ammonites. By the Greek and Roman writers it is often mentioned as Philadelphia. Here was the bed or sarcophagus of the giant Og, Deut. iii, 11. The city was besieged and taken by David for the ill treatment of his embassadors by the Ammonites, Joab having previously, after a long siege, stormed one of the divisions of it, probably the lower town, in which was the spring whence a stream of water, yet existing, flowed, 2 Sam. xi, 1; xii, 26–29; xvii, 27; 1 Chron. xx, 1–3. Afterward the Ammonites regained their independence, Jer. xlix, 2, 3; Ezek. xxi, 20; xxv, 5; Amos i, 14. Some centuries later, when these parts were subject to Egypt, Rabbah was restored or rebuilt by Ptolemy Philadelphus, who called it Philadelphia; but the old name was not entirely superseded. It was one of the cities of the Decapolis, and as far down as the fourth century was considered a very strong and remarkable city. In the early centuries of our era it was the seat of a bishopric, and remained a prosperous city until the conquest of Syria by the Saracens. The modern name is *Ammán.* Its ruins lie about twenty-two miles east of the Jordan, and about fourteen north-east of Hoshbon. "The aspect of the whole place is desolate in the extreme. . . . The abundant waters attract the vast flocks that roam over the neighboring plains, and the deserted palaces and temples afford shelter to them during the noon-day heat, so that most of the buildings have something of the aspect and stench of an ill-kept farm-yard."—*Porter.* There are remains of palaces, temples, churches, theaters, tombs, etc. The theater is one of the most striking ruins in all Syria, and must have been capable of accommodating more than six thousand spectators.

2. A town in the hill-country of Judah, named with Kirjath-Jearim, Josh. xv, 60. It is unknown.

Rab'bath-Ammon. See RABBAH.

Rab'bath-Moab. See AR.

Rab'bith, *multitude,* a town in Issachar, probably on the boundary, Josh. xix, 20. It is unknown.

Ra'chal, *traffic,* a town in Judah, mentioned only in 1 Sam. xxx, 29, as one of those to which David sent portions of the spoil captured in his raid against the Amalekites. No traces of the name have been found.

Ra'chel's Tomb (Map 6) is about a mile distant from Bethlehem, Gen. xxxv, 16-20. "The building is modern, but the authenticity of the sepulcher cannot be questioned. It is one of the few shrines which Moslems, Jews, and Christians agree in honoring, and concerning which their traditions are identical."—Porter's *Hand-book.*

Ra'gau, a place and its mountains, Judith i, 3, 15; probably identical with Rages.

Ra'ges, a noted city and province in north-eastern Media, deriving its name, according to Strabo, from *chasms* made by earthquakes. The city was not far from the site of the modern *Teheran.* It is connected with the later history of the Jews, as one of the places in which they were located during the captivity, and is mentioned only in the Apocrypha, Tob. i, 14; v, 5; vi, 9, 12; Judith i, 5, 15. Rages is mentioned by very many profane writers. The ruins bear the name of *Rhey,* and consist of walls of prodigious thickness, which seem to have been flanked by strong towers, and are connected with a lofty citadel at their north-eastern angle. Colossal sculptures are also found on the rocks. *Teheran* has been to a great extent built from the ruins of Rages.

Ra'hab, *sea-monster, pride, insolence, violence,* a term used as a symbolical name for Egypt, Psa. lxxiv, 13, 14; lxxxvii, 4; lxxxix, 10; Isa. li, 9, 10; compare 15; and sometimes for its king, Ezek. xxix, 3; xxxii, 2; compare Psa. lxviii, 31. Under this metaphorical designation allusion is probably made to the crocodiles and other aquatic creatures of the Nile. The passage in Isa. xxx, 7, probably referring to this name, is thus translated by Gesenius: "Egypt helpeth in vain; therefore I call her: violence, that is, the violent, (*Rahab* in the original,) they sit still;" that is, they are cowards, and their help will not avail.

Rak'kath, *shore,* one of the fortified towns of Naphtali, grouped between Hammath and Chinnereth, Josh. xix, 35. The Rabbins state that it stood where Tiberias was afterward built. According to Josephus ancient tombs had to be removed to make room for Tiberias. Mr. Porter (in *Kitto*) says: "Rakkath may have stood close on the shore (of the Sea of Galilee) where there were no tombs; while Tiberias, being much larger, extended some distance up the adjoining rocky hill-sides, in which the tombs may still be seen."

Rak'kon, *thinness,* a city of Dan, apparently not far from Joppa, Josh. xix, 46. Unknown.

Ra'ma, the Greek form of Ramah, used in Matt. ii, 18, in reference to Jer. xxxi, 15. The latter passage alludes to the massacre of Benjamites or Ephraimites, at the Ramah in Benjamin or in Mount Ephraim, (compare verses 9, 18.) The mourning over that slaughter may be considered as typical of the massacre of the innocents at Bethlehem, near to which was the tomb of Rachel; and the spirit of the departed Rachel is represented by the evangelist as rising from her tomb and mourning her murdered children. Some of the infants of Benjamin were also slain, for Herod's wrath included both Bethlehem and "all the coasts thereof." So loud was the "lamentation, and weeping, and great mourning," that it resounded throughout the whole land of Benjamin, and hence "in Rama." See RAMAH (1.)

Ra'mah, (Map 5,) *a high place, a height.* Many of the ancient towns of Palestine were built on the top of a hill. Thus several places are called Gibeah, which means *a hill.* Not less than five prominent towns also bear the name of Ramah, and the term enters into composition with the name of many other places situated on an eminence.

1. A city in Benjamin, grouped between Gibeon and Beeroth, Josh. xviii, 25. In the list of 1 Esdr. v, it is called Cirama. In the sad story of the Levite recorded in Judges xix, its position is clearly marked as near to Gibeah; compare verse 13 with Map 6; see also 1 Sam. xxii, 6; Hos. v, 8; Isa. x, 28–32. It occupied a very strong position, commanding the great road from the north to Jerusalem, and was fortified by Baasha, king of Israel. Alarmed at the erection of a fortress so close to his capital, the king of Judah stopped the work by bribing the Syrians to invade northern Palestine, and then carried off the building materials, 1 Kings xv, 17–22; 2 Chron. xvi, 1–6. When Nebuchadnezzar invaded Judea he made his headquarters at Riblah, (Jer. xxxix, 5,) and sent thence his generals to capture Jerusalem. While the conquerors devastated the temple and the city the chief inhabitants who had escaped the sword were placed under guard at Ramah, the prophet Jeremiah being one of the captives, Jer. xxxix, 8–12; xl, 1. Here was fulfilled the prophecy uttered many years before: "A voice was heard in Ramah, lamentation and bitter weeping," Jer. xxxi, 15. [See RAMA; compare Matt. ii, 17, 18.] The lamentation was made not only over those just slain in Jerusalem, but doubtless, also, over the slaughter at Ramah of such captives as from age or sickness were not worth transporting across the desert to Babylon. After the captivity Ramah was again occupied, Ezra ii, 26; Neh. vii, 30. The Ramah of Neh. xi, 33, occupying a different position in the list, is supposed by Mr. Grove to refer to a distinct place lying further west, nearer the plain. But this is conjecture.

Ramah has been identified with the village of *Er-Ram,* a small and miserable place about five miles north of Jerusalem. Broken columns and other ancient remains lie around the fields, while in the foundations and walls of the houses are many large hewn stones.

2. A city on the border of Asher, apparently near the sea-coast, and not far from Tyre, Josh. xix, 29. Dr. Robinson identifies this Ramah with a modern village called *Rameh,* about seventeen miles south-east of Tyre, containing some ancient remains. Kiepert's map thus locates it. Van de Velde's map locates it at the site of another *Rameh,* on a little tell about two miles south-east of modern Tyre. This latter identification seems to agree best with the Scripture requirements.

3. One of the nineteen fortified places of Naphtali, grouped between Adamah and Hazor, Josh. xix, 36. This city is probably identical with the large modern village of *Rameh,* lying about six miles west by south of *Safed,* on the road leading to *Akka.* The village stands on the lower slope of a mountain whose summit commands one of the most extensive views in all Palestine.

4. 1 Sam. i, 19; etc. See RAMATHAIM-ZOPHIM.

5. 2 Kings viii, 29; 2 Chron. xxii, 6. See RAMOTH-GILEAD.

Ra'math-Le'hi, *the hill or height of Lehi,* that is, as in the margin of our version, *the lifting up of the jaw-bone,* or *casting away of the jaw-bone,* Judg. xv, 17. See LEHI.

Ra'math-Miz'peh, *the high place of the watch-tower,* a town in Gad, mentioned only in Josh. xiii, 26, apparently as a landmark on the northern border. The place where Jacob and Laban vowed to each other was marked by a heap of stones, and received the names of Galeed, Jegar-Sahadutha, and Mizpah, and it was somewhere in this region, Gen. xxxi, 25, 48, 49. Probably all these names are identical with Ramoth-Gilead, but certainty cannot be reached until further explorations east of the Jordan are made. The term Maspha in 1 Macc. v, 35, possibly refers to this place.

Ra'math-Ne'geb, or **Ramath of the South,** *height of the south,* a place apparently in the extreme southern border of Simeon, Josh. xix, 8; and doubtless only another name for BAALATH-BEER, which see. The "south Ramoth" of 1 Sam. xxx, 27, is doubtless the same place.

Ramatha'im-Zo'phim, (Map 20,) *the double height of Zophim,* 1 Sam. i, 1. The same as Ramah, (4,) the shortened form, in which the name occurs always, except as above. Ramathaim seems to be the dual of Ramah, and Zophim is added by way of distinction. Zophim is explained by some as "of the prophets," or "of the watchers;" referring in part to the school of the prophets at Naioth in Ramah. It is also thought to have reference to *the land of Zuph,* 1 Sam. ix, 5; and Ramah, being the chief town of that district, was thus "Ramah of the Zuphites." This seems a natural explanation, but it is not established. See ZUPH.

"The position of Ramathaim-Zophim is one of the puzzles of biblical geography." Stanley says, "It is, without exception, the most complicated and disputed problem of sacred topography." All that we know with certainty concerning the place is that it was the residence of Elkanah, and the birthplace, residence, and burial-place of the prophet Samuel, 1 Sam. i, 1, 19; ii, 11; vii, 17; viii, 4; xv, 34; xvi, 13; xix, 18; xxv, 1; xxviii, 3. In 1 Sam. i, 1, 19, it appears that Ramah was "of Mount Ephraim," but the extent of this region is nowhere defined. Possibly, also, it was Elkanah that was "of Mount Ephraim," and he may have migrated thence. Ramah has been located at *Soba,* about six miles west of Jerusalem; at *Rameh,* (Ramah,) north of Hebron; at *er Ram,* on the road from Jerusalem to Bethel; at *Ramleh,* (near Lydda,) which is erroneously considered identical with Arimathæa; at *Jebel Fureidis,* the Frank Mountain, three miles south-east of Bethlehem; at *Ramah,* a hill a short distance above Bethlehem; at *Ramè,* a village three and a half miles west of *Sanur;* at *Ram-Allah,* a small village one mile west of Beroth, (Map 6;) and at *Neby Samwil,* the traditional site of Samuel's tomb, about five miles west of north from Jerusalem—nine sites in all. Each has its learned advocates, but there are no conclusive arguments in behalf of any. Several of them are quite improbable. In 1 Sam. ix, x, we have an account of Saul's visit to Samuel, the anointing of Saul as king, and his return "home to Gibeah." How to reconcile these three Scripture incidents with any of the above sites is the difficulty, and the contradictory assumptions of various commentators only serve to make the difficulty greater. The identity of Ramah with *Soba,* one of the most plausible sites, is thus disposed of by Mr. Porter: "A man hastening home from *Soba* to *Tuleil el-Fûl,* the ancient Gibeah, would not, if in his senses, go round by

Rachel's sepulcher at Bethlehem, yet Saul must have done so if *Soba* be Ramah."—*Hand-book*, p. 269. Mr. Grove inclines to locate Ramah on the peak of *Neby Samwil*, but he claims that Saul's anointing was not necessarily at Ramathaim-Zophim. See Smith's *Dictionary*. This lofty peak, " the culminating point of the mountain region round the Holy City," is crowned by a neglected mosque, with a little hamlet of about twelve houses on the eastern side. The height of the peak and the Mohammedan tradition are in its favor, but its identity with Ramah can be established neither by the Scripture narrative nor otherwise. It is not improbable that it may be identical with Mizpeh, where Saul was made king, 1 Sam. ii, 17–21. See MIZPEH, (6.)

Rame'ses, or **Ram'eses**, (Maps 2, 8,) *son of the sun;* in Exod. i, 11, Raamses; in Judith i, 9, Ramesse. This name was borne by several of the kings of Egypt, by one of whom probably the city of Rameses was founded. Rameses was situated in Lower Egypt, in the land of Goshen, and was built, or at least fortified, by the labor of the Israelites, Gen. xlvii, 11; Exod. i, 11. In Gen. xlvii, 11, the first occurrence of the name, the term is applied to a province, " the land of Ramesse," by which is doubtless meant a part of Goshen, or, more probably, the whole of it, comp. verse 6. It was from this province that the Israelites commenced their march out of Egypt, though they were probably massed about the chief town, Exod. xii, 37; Num. xxxiii, 3, 5. The name of Pithom, employed in the same connection with Rameses, indicates the region near Heliopolis. Lepsius thinks Rameses is to be sought in the ruins of *Aboo-Kesheyd*, north-east of Heliopolis, where there is a group of three figures cut out of a granite block representing the gods Tum and Ra, and between them Rameses II., who was probably there worshiped, and who is thought to be the Pharaoh of Moses. See Stanley's *Jewish Church*, first series, p. 100. Other sites have been proposed, but none is wholly satisfactory.

Rames'se, Judith i, 9. See RAMESES.
Ra'moth, 1 Sam. xxx, 27. See RAMATH-NEGEB.
Ra'moth, 1 Chron. vi, 73. See REMETH.
Ra'moth-Gil'ead, and **Ra'moth in Gil'ead**, (Maps 4, 5, 20,) *heights of Gilead*, called also Ramah, 2 Kings viii, 29; 2 Chron. xxii, 6. One of the chief cities of Gad, east of the Jordan, allotted to the Levites, and made a city of refuge, Deut. iv, 43; Josh. xx, 8; probably it was identical with Ramath-Mizpeh, Josh. xiii, 26. Ramoth was the scene of many sieges and battles in the struggles between the Israelites and the Syrians. It was the seat of one of Solomon's commissariat officers, 1 Kings iv, 13. Being afterward taken by the Syrians, the kings of Israel and Judah united to drive out this common enemy, and it was in this unsuccessful attempt to recover the city that King Ahab was mortally wounded, 1 Kings xxii, 3, 34; 2 Chron. xviii. King Joram was wounded in a battle here, 2 Kings viii, 28, 29; ix, 14, 45; 2 Chron. xxii, 5, 6, and Ramoth was taken from the Syrians. While Joram went to Jezreel to be healed, leaving Jehu in command of his army, Jehu was anointed king at Ramoth by order of Elisha, and drove from Ramoth to Jezreel, being commissioned to execute vengeance on the wicked house of Ahab, 2 Kings ix. The city appears no more in Jewish history after this event. Among the various opinions concerning the site of Ramoth, the most probable is that which locates it at *Es-Salt*, a little village of about three thousand inhabitants. There are but few ancient

remains in the town itself, but in the cliffs and ravines beneath it are great numbers of tombs and grottoes. On the summit of the hill is a rectangular castle, with towers at the corners. About two miles north-west of *Es-Salt* is the highest peak of the mountain range still bearing the name *Jebel Jil'ad*, "Mount Gilead." Mr. Grove says: "If Ramoth-Gilead and Ramath-Mizpeh are identical, a more northern position than *Es-Salt* would seem inevitable, since Ramath-Mizpeh was in the northern portion of the tribe of Gad, Josh. xiii, 26."

Ra'phon, a city of Gilead where Judas Maccabeus obtained a victory over Timotheus, 1 Macc. v, 37. Possibly it is identical with the Rephana mentioned by Pliny as one of the cities of the Decapolis. It appears (verse 4) to have been near to Carnaim, (probably Ashtaroth-Carnaim,) and also near a torrent.

Ras'ses, CHILDREN OF, a people whose country Holofernes ravaged, Judith ii, 23. The Vulgate reads *Tharsis*, by which some infer that Tarsus is meant. The old Latin has *Thiras et Rasis;* the Syriac, *Thiras* and *Ra'msis*. These people are named next to Lud, (Lydia,) and apparently south thereof. Some construe Rasses as Rosos, and, connecting this term with Meshech and Thiras or Tiras in Gen. x, 2, suppose Rosos to signify Russia, (Map 12 ROSH.)

Re'ai'ah, whom *Jehovah cares for*, a family of Nethinim who returned from Babylon with Zerubbabel, Ezra ii, 47; Neh. vii, 30. In 1 Esdr. v, 31, the name is Airus.

Re'chabites, *riders, horsemen*, the family of Kenites, whom Jonadab, the son of Rechab, subjected to a new rule of life; or, rather, bound to the continued observance of ancient usages which were essential to their separate existence, but which the progress of their intercourse with towns seemed likely soon to extinguish, 1 Chron. ii, 55; 2 Kings x, 15, 16, 23. For three hundred years this tribe fully obeyed the injunction to drink no wine, to build no houses, but to dwell in tents. At the Chaldean invasion they were forced to quit the open country and live in Jerusalem, Jer. xxxv. Doubtless they afterward withdrew to the desert. As a reward for faithful obedience to their vows a promise was made them that their family should never be extinct, Jer. xxxv, 19. Travelers report the present existence of an Arabian tribe who claim descent from Rechab, and profess a modified Judaism; but this report needs fuller confirmation.

Re'chah, *the side, utmost part*. In 1 Chron. iv, 12, are mentioned the "men of Rechah." The Targum of Rabbi Joseph calls them "the men of the great Sanhedrim." Rechah would seem to be a place, but nothing is known of it.

Red Sea. See SEA.

Re'hob, *street, broad place*.

1. A city on the northern border of Palestine, first mentioned in connection with the mission of the spies as the extreme northern point of their journey, Num. xiii, 21. It was called also Beth-Rehob, 2 Sam. x, 6, 8. Dr. Robinson would identify Rehob with the village and castle of *Hûnîn*, in the mountains north-west of the plain of *Huleh*, the upper district of the Jordan valley. This lacks confirmation. About twenty-five miles north-east of Damascus is a place called *Ruhaibeh*, which some propose as the site.

2. A town allotted to Asher, Josh. xix, 28, apparently near to Zidon, but no traces of it have yet been found.

3. Another city of Asher, on the southern border of the tribe, Josh. xix, 30. It was probably this Rehob which was allotted to the Levites, Josh. xxi, 31; 1 Chron. vi, 75; but from which the old Canaanites were not driven, Judg. i, 31. Its site is also unknown.

Reho'both, *roomy places, streets.*

1. "The city Rehoboth," or *Rehoboth-Ir*, one of the four cities founded by Asshur, or by Nimrod in Asshur, Gen. x, 11, 12. The translation of the passage is difficult. As Nineveh and Calah stood on the Tigris, it seems natural to place the other two cities, Resen and Rehoboth, in the same vicinity. No ruins have been found on the plain of the Tigris that seem to mark the site of this city, nor any traces of its name. Kalisch and others seek to identify it with *Rahabeh-Malik*, a place said to contain extensive ruins, lying on the eastern bank of the Euphrates, about four miles south-west of the town of *Mayadin*. (See No. 2 below.) Sir H. Rawlinson suggests *Selemiyah*, near *Kaluh*, with extensive ruins. Possibly Rehoboth may have been a part of that "great city," Nineveh. See RESEN: NINEVEH.

2. "Rehoboth by the river," the city of a certain Saul or Shaul, one of the early kings of the Edomites, Gen. xxxvi, 37; 1 Chron. i, 48. "The river" is doubtless the Euphrates; (compare Gen. xxxi, 21; xv, 18; Deut. i, 7; Exod. xxiii, 31.) This city probably lay on the west bank of the Euphrates, between Circesium and Anah, at the site now called *er-Rahabeh*. *Rahabeh-Malik*, on the east bank, is also proposed as the site. (See No. 1 above.) Certainty cannot be attained without further explorations.

3. (Map 5,) Rehoboth, the third of the series of wells dug by Isaac, Gen. xxvi, 22. The most probable site is at the *Wady Ruhaibeh*, containing the ruins of a large town of the same name. Dr. Stewart and Mr. Rowlands both claim to have here found a well, which Dr. Robinson could not find. The place is about twenty-three miles south-west of Beersheba. Dr. Robinson thinks the spot too far south, and Mr. Grove seems to agree with him; while Mr. Porter says, "It seems in the highest degree probable that this is the place where the patriarch had his station." Palmer inclines to this view.

Re'kem, *variegated*, perhaps a *flower-garden*, a town of Benjamin, Josh. xviii, 27. Mr. Grove asks, "May there not be a trace of the name in *Ain Karîm*, the well-known spring west of Jerusalem?"

Re'meth, *a height*, a city of Issachar, grouped with En-Gannim, Josh. xix, 21. It is thought by some identical with the Ramoth of 1 Chron. vi, 73. No place has yet been discovered which can be plausibly identified with either. Mr. Porter inclines to identify Remeth with *Wezâr*, a little village on one of the rocky summits of Mount Gilboa, about five miles north of En-Gannim.

Rem'mon, Josh. xix, 7. See RIMMON, (1.)

Rem'mon-Meth'oar, Josh. xix, 13. See RIMMON, (2.)

Reph'aim and Reph'aims, probably *giants, healers, chiefs*. An ancient tribe noted for their gigantic stature, dwelling, in the time of Abraham, beyond the Jordan, Gen. xiv, 5, 15, 20. One of the last remnants of this race was Og, King of Bashan, although in after ages there lived men of huge stature who were doubtless of the same stock. See REPHAIM, VALLEY OF.

Reph'aim, THE VALLEY OF, (Map 6.) In Josh. xv, 8, and xviii, 16, "the valley of the giants." For the probable signification see REPHAIM. This valley seems to have derived its name from the ancient nation of the Rephaim, a race of gigantic stature, who, dwelling in Palestine in the earliest ages, left their traces in the names, history, and traditions of various sections of the country both east and west of the Jordan. They had settlements in Bashan at a very remote period, and that country was called "the land of the Rephaim" at and even after the conquest, Gen. xiv, 5; Deut. iii, 11-13; Josh. xiii, 12 The Ammonites' country was also called "the land of the Rephaim," ii, 11, 20. The same name was given also to a section of western Palestine adjoining the mountains of Ephraim, Josh. xvii, 15. The valley, which much longer bore the name of this tribe, lay between Jerusalem and Bethlehem. Possibly these "giants" settled here after being driven from their seats east of the Jordan, and before they found their more secure home among the wooded districts of the north. David twice defeated the Philistines in this valley, 2 Sam. v, 17-25; xxiii, 13; 1 Chron. xi, 15, 16; xiv, 9-16. The place was noted for fertility, Isa. xvii, 5.

According to the *Memoir of the Rephaim* by Miss Corbaux, their chief metropolis was Salem, afterward Jerusalem; and this lady would identify them with the shepherd race of kings who held dominion at one time in Egypt. From Josh. xv, 8, and xviii, 16, it would seem that this valley lay on the south of the hill which inclosed the Valley of Hinnom on the west. Mr. Porter, who has surveyed the region in question with great care, says: "On the west side of the Valley of Hinnom rises a bare rocky ridge, beyond which commences an upland plain, considerably lower than the ridge, but almost on a level with the city. It extends southward toward Bethlehem more than a mile. Declining gradually on the south-west, it contracts at length into a narrow and deep valley called *Wady el-Werd*. The plain is flat and fertile, but is shut in on all sides by rocky hill-tops and ridges. This appears to be the Valley of Rephaim; and its position certainly agrees well with all the notices in the Bible and in Josephus." See PERAZIM, MOUNT.

Reph'idim, (Map 2,) *stays, refreshments, rests,* a noted encampment of the Israelites, near to Horeb, and the place where the people complained most bitterly to Moses for bringing them out of Egypt, Exod. xvii, 1, 8; xix, 2; Num. xxxiii, 14, 15. Here occurred the miracle which gave the wondrous supply of water; and here too the triumph, by a miracle, of Israel over the Amalekites. Here, also, Moses learned from Jethro how to marshal the whole host of Israel.

Geographers find much difficulty in locating Rephidim. Dean Stanley says: "We know not the spot with certainty. Yet of all localities hitherto imagined, that which was believed to be so in the fifth century at least answers the requirements well — the beautiful palm-grove now and for many ages past called the Valley of Paran or *Feirân*." E. H. Palmer, Lepsius, Ritter, and Stewart hold this opinion. *Feirân* is near the base of Mount *Serbâl*. Stanley thinks that, wherever Rephidim may be, it was evidently a place of sufficient importance to induce the Amalekites to defend it to the uttermost. Perhaps Amalek contended for the water with which Israel was supplied. Dr. Robinson places Rephidim at a narrow gorge in the *Wady esh-Sheikh,* not far from Horeb; and thinks Horeb was the name not of a single mountain but of the whole group. Mr. Porter, assuming *Jebel-Mûsa* to be Sinai, (or Horeb,) says: "Perhaps the solitary sanctuary of *Sheikh Saleh,* one of the most sacred spots in the whole peninsula, and which gives its name to the great valley, may mark the position of Rephidim. The valley is here of considerable width, and it opens out still more toward Sinai, affording space for the conflict of armies." The smitten rock was at a considerable distance from the camp; and the miracle was performed, not in the sight of all the people, but before chosen elders who went to the place with Moses.

Claiming *Feiran* as the site of Rephidim, Palmer says: "It is in fact the most fertile part of the Peninsula, and one which the Amalekites would be naturally anxious to defend against an invading force; in this respect it answers to the position of Rephidim." Palmer discovered a rock, hitherto unnoticed by travelers, called *Hesy el Khattâtin*, which may have been the rock smitten by Moses. In the valley also is a hill called *Jebel Táhúneh*, (the Mountain of the Windmill,) about seven hundred feet high, and affording a commanding view. Here possibly Moses stood when he viewed the battle of Israel with Amalek. It is situated on the northern side of the valley. At short intervals along the ascent are several chapels, and on the summit is a small church with some ruined out-buildings. See *Desert of the Exodus*, pp. 158–163, 276.

Re'sen, (Map 1,) *a bridle*, an ancient town of Assyria lying between Nineveh and Calah, and called "a great city," Gen. x, 12. Larissa, mentioned by Xenophon as a desolate city on the Tigris, several miles north of the Lycus, has been proposed as the site of Resen; but this identification cannot be established. "As, however," says Mr. G. Rawlinson, "the *Nimrud* ruins [see NINEVEH] seem really to represent Calah, while those opposite Mosul are the remains of Nineveh, we must look for *Resen* in the tract lying between these two sites. Assyrian remains of some considerable extent are found in this situation, near the modern village of *Selamiyeh*, and it is perhaps the most probable conjecture that these represent the Resen of Genesis." Mr. Fergusson believes that Calah is to be identified with *Kalah Sherghat*, and Resen with *Nimrud*. Certainty of identification seems impossible. See CALAH.

Reu'ben, (Map 5,) *behold a son*, one of the tribes of the Israelites, named from the eldest son of Jacob by Leah, Gen. xxix, 32; xxxv, 23; xlvi, 8. Although Reuben was Jacob's first-born, yet the tribe was the least distinguished of the twelve in nearly every respect. This was the result of the unnatural crime of the head of the tribe, which left its stain on the whole race, Gen. xlix, 4; 1 Chron. v, 1. The census at Sinai shows that at the exodus the number of Reubenites was 46,500, Num. i, 20, 21. Their encampment was to the south of the tabernacle. On the march they were to head the second division of the host, Simeon and Gad being joined with them, Num. ii, 10–16; x, 18. On the borders of Canaan, after the plague which punished the idolatry of Baal Peor, the number was 43,730, Num. xvi; xxvi, 5–11. Near the close of the wandering, after the kingdoms of Og and of Sihon had been conquered, the tribes of Reuben and Gad requested that they might settle east of the Jordan, Num. xxxii, 5. Their cattle had accompanied them in the flight from Egypt, Exod. xii, 38; and there are frequent allusions to these on the journey, Exod. xxxiv, 3; Num. xi, 22; Deut. viii, 13, etc. The other tribes having relinquished a taste for the possession of cattle, and Reuben, Gad, and half-Manasseh being now the owners of the cattle, (Num. xxxii, 1,) Moses gave them the rich, well-watered territory east of the Jordan as an ample pasture land, Num. xxxii, 33. But Moses located them there only in consideration of their undertaking to aid in the conquest of the western country—Canaan proper.

The country allotted to the Reubenites extended on the south to the river Arnon, which divided it from the Moabites, Josh. xiii, 8, 16. On the east

VIEW FROM JEBEL TAHUNEH.

it touched the desert of Arabia. On the west were the Dead Sea and the Jordan. The northern border was probably marked by a line running eastward from the Jordan through *Wady Hesbân*, Josh. xiii, 17-21; Num. xxxii, 37, 38. The Moabites had originally conquered and occupied this country; but they were driven out a short time before the exodus by Sihon, King of the Amorites, who was in his turn expelled by the Israelites, Deut. ii; Num. xxi, 22-31. Generally speaking, the towns of Reuben are noted in Num. xxxii, 37, 38; Josh. xiii, 17; four of them being assigned to the Merarite Levites, Josh. xxi, 36, 37; 1 Chron. vi, 78, 79; and one, Bezer, was a refuge city, Deut. iv, 43; Josh. xx, 8. Moses invoked a prophetic blessing upon Reuben, expressing a hope of life and population for the tribe, Deut. xxxiii, 6.

The Reubenites aided their brethren west of the Jordan in the conquest of Canaan, Josh. iv, 12, 13. Returning home after the conquest, and fearing that the deep valley of the Jordan, which formed an almost impassable barrier between eastern and western Palestine, might prove to be a barrier between the brotherhood of the ten tribes and themselves, the Reubenites and their eastern brethren raised up at the ford of the river a vast altar-shaped mound, to serve in all generations as a witness of common origin and of common rights, Josh. xxii, 10-34. Afterward, for not aiding the western tribes against Sisera, the Reubenites were reproved, Judg. v, 15, 16. In the days of Saul, in conjunction with their neighbors, this tribe made some successful forays on the Hagarites, and extended their pastures even to the Euphrates, 1 Chron v, 1-10, 18-22. "An hundred and twenty thousand men of war" from Reuben, Gad, and Manasseh marched with their brethren to Hebron, to put David upon the throne, 1 Chron. xii, 37, 38. David placed a separate ruler over the Reubenites, while Solomon included them with Gad in one of his commissariat departments, 1 Chron. xxviii, 16; 1 Kings iv, 19. On the division of the kingdom they attached themselves to the northern state. Their territory was invaded by the Syrians under Hazael, about B. C. 884, 2 Kings x, 32, 33; and about a century later the whole people were taken captive by Tiglath-Pileser, and carried off to Halah, Habor, and Hara, in Assyria, 1 Chron. v, 6, 26; 2 Kings xv, 29. Then the Moabites returned to their old country, and occupied their old cities. Thus Jeremiah in pronouncing curses upon Moab embraces many of the cities of Reuben. This whole region is now desolate, there being no settled inhabitants in all its borders; while its great cities, though mostly bearing their ancient names, are heaps of ruins.

Reu'benites. See REUBEN.

Re'zeph, (Map 4,) a *stone*, (heated to roast meat or bake bread upon.) A city whose name occurs among those subdued by the Assyrians, 2 Kings xix, 12; Isa. xxxvii, 12. There were nine cities by this name. The most probable supposition locates the ancient Rezeph at *Rasapha*, a day's march west of the Euphrates on the road from Racca to Emesa, (*Hûms*.)

Rhe'gium, (Map 8,) a *breach, broken off*, a city on the south-western coast of Italy, mentioned in Paul's journey to Rome, Acts xxvii, 13. It now has ten thousand inhabitants, and bears the name of *Reggio*.

Rhodes, (Map 8,) a *rose*, an island in the Mediterranean, near the coast of Asia Minor. It is celebrated from the remotest antiquity as the seat of commerce, navigation, literature, and the arts. The city of Rhodes was built in the fifth century before Christ. Over the entrance to the harbor was the celebrated Colossus, a brass statue of Apollo one hundred and five feet high, erected B. C. 290, and overthrown by an earthquake B. C. 224. For a long period the fleets of the Rhodians ruled the seas. In the times of the Maccabees we find Jewish residents in Rhodes, 1 Macc. v, 23. At length, during the reign of Vespasian, the island became a Roman province. St. Paul touched at Rhodes about A. D. 58, on his return voyage from his third missionary journey, Acts xxi, 1. During the Middle Ages Rhodes was famous as the home and fortress of the Knights of St. John. The most prominent remains of the city and harbor are memorials of those knights. The present population of the island is about twenty thousand.

Rib'lah, (Maps 3, 4,) *fertility*, a very ancient city in the northern part of Canaan, in the territory of Hamath, Num. xxxiv, 10, 11; 2 Kings xxiii, 33; xxv, 21; Jer. lii, 9. In Ezek. vi, 14, Diblath. At Riblah the Babylonian monarchs were accustomed to wait while directing their military operations in Palestine and Phenicia. It was here that the Egyptian king, Pharaoh-Necho, put the youthful Jehoahaz in chains, and made Eliakim king, 2 Kings xxiii, 29-35. Here Nebuchadnezzar encamped while his general invaded Judah and captured Jerusalem. To this city Zedekiah was brought captive, and, after being compelled to witness the murder of his sons, his eyes were put out, and he was bound in fetters of brass, 2 Kings xxv, 6, 7; Jer. xxxix, 5-7.

Mr. Grove claims that the Riblah, the border city of Canaan, mentioned in Num. xxxiv, 11, is not the same with the Riblah in the land of Hamath, which is mentioned much later in Bible history. He thinks the former may have been near the Sea of Chinnereth, in the neighborhood of *Banias*. To this Mr. Porter objects: "There is nothing whatever in Num. xxxiv, 11, to indicate that Riblah was near the Sea of Chinnereth." The reader is referred to Smith's *Dictionary* and Kitto's *Cyclopædia* for the discussion by these eminent scholars. To us the weight of argument is with Mr. Porter, who holds there was but one Riblah.

Traces of Riblah are found in the "land of Hamath," in the little village of *Riblah*, lying on the right bank of the Orontes, about twelve miles east by north of its great fountain, which still bears the name *el-Ain*. The only remains of antiquity are the ruins of a square tower, called by the people *el-Kiniseh*, "the church."

Rim'mon, (Map 5,) *a pomegranate*.

1. A city in the extreme south of Palestine, originally allotted to Judah, and afterward to Simeon, Josh. xv, 21, 32; xix, 7, (where the name is Remmon;) 1 Chron. iv, 32; Neh. xi, 29. See also Zech. xiv, 10. It is highly probable that this place is identical with *Er-Rummanim*, ("mother of pomegranates,") a ruined village about thirteen miles south of Eleutheropolis. About a mile south of it are two tells, both of which are covered with ruins.

2. (Hebrew, *Rimmônô*.) A city of Zebulun, assigned to the Merarite Levites, 1 Chron. vi, 77. In our translation of Josh. xix, 13, it is called Remmon-Methoar; but "methoar" is no part of the name: the words of the clause should be rendered, "it (the border) passed on to Rimmon, and stretched to Neah." It is probably identical with the little village of *Rummâneh*, situated about six miles north of Nazareth, on the edge of the upland plain of *Buttauf*.

3. "The Rock Rimmon," (Map 6.) A rock or peak north-east of Geba

THE COLOSSUS AT RHODES.

and Michmash, near the desert, to which the remnant of the Benjamites retreated after the destruction of their tribe, Judg. xx, 45, 47; xxi, 13.

This place is doubtless identical with the modern village of *Rummon*, which stands upon a conspicuous white limestone tell about ten miles north of Jerusalem, and nearly four east of Bethel. Along the sides of the tell are found some large caverns.

Rim'mon-Pa'rez, (Map 2,) *pomegranate of the breach*, a station of the Israelites in the wilderness. Num. xxxiii, 19, 20. Unknown.

Ri'phath, (Map 12,) *a crusher* (?), a northern people descended from Gomer, Gen. x, 3. In 1 Chron. i, 6, margin, it is Diphath, by a transcriber's error. It seems impossible to locate this people with certainty. The weight of opinion appears to compare the name with the *Rhipæan* mountains, in the remotest northern regions. Some good authorities, however, identify this nation with the *Rhiphathæans*, the ancient name of the Paphlagonians. See *Kitto*, art. *Nations, Dispersion of.*

Ris'sah, (Map 2,) *a ruin*, a station in the wilderness, Num. xxxiii, 21, 22. Possibly identical with *Rasa*.

Rith'mah, (Map 2,) *broom*, a station of the Israelites, Num. xxxiii, 18, 19. Unknown.

Riv'er of Egypt, (Maps 1, 2.) This compound term occurs eight times in the Old Testament. In Gen. xv, 18, the word translated "river" is *nahar*, which always signifies a perennial stream. In all the other passages *nakhal* is employed. *Nakhal* is translated "river" in Num. xxxiv, 5; Josh. xv, 4, 47; 1 Kings viii, 65; 2 Kings xxiv, 7; and "stream" in Isa. xxvii, 12. In Gen. xv, 18, reference is undoubtedly made to the Nile as the boundary of the territory promised to Abraham, although this extent of territory was never occupied by the seed of Abraham. As to the meaning of *Nakhal Mitzraim* (River of Egypt) in the other passages, the best authorities differ. *Nakhal* primarily signifies a "torrent-bed," a "brook," or a "valley," and sometimes both a brook and the valley in which it flows. In 1 Kings xvii, 3, it is used in both senses. Its modern equivalent is the Arabic word *wady*, signifying a valley, glen, or ravine of any kind, whether the bed of a perennial stream or of a winter torrent, or permanently dry; and *wady* is sometimes (though not so commonly as *nakhal*) applied to the river or stream which flows in the valley. By some *nakhal*, in the above passages, is considered to refer generally, though not always, to the Nile; others think it invariably signifies the Nile, because this signification would be in harmony with the theory that the Egyptian kingdom never extended eastward of the eastern branch of the Nile. See Smith's *Dictionary*, vol. iii, pp. 1046-1048. But *Nokhal Mitzraim* must be identified with the *Wady el-Arish*, a valley and small winter stream which falls into the Mediterranean near Rhinocolura. Thus this "torrent," "wady," or "river" of Egypt, was the boundary between Egypt and the land promised to Moses, and gained its notoriety from being the dividing line between two great countries.

Ro'gel. 1 Kings i, 9, margin. See EN-ROGEL.

Roge'lim, *fullers'* place, a town in Gilead, the residence of Barzillai, 2 Sam. xvii, 27; xix, 31. Unknown.

Rome, (Maps 1, 8, 19,) the CITY and the EMPIRE. The name is by some derived from 'Ρώμη, the Greek word for "strength." Cicero says the name was taken from that of its founder, Romulus.

The renowned city of Rome stands on the river Tiber, about fifteen miles from its mouth, in the plain which is now called the Campagna. It was founded, according to tradition, in 753 B. C., by Romulus, to whom mythology ascribes a divine parentage. By degrees the city was extended from the Palatine Hill, on which it was founded, so as to include within its limits six other hills. Rome was then called *Urbs Septicollis*, "City of the Seven Hills." In B. C. 390 the city was entirely destroyed by the Gauls; but it was immediately rebuilt, yet with no attention to regularity. In the course of time many noble structures adorned the city. Augustus Cæsar boasted that he had found the city of brick and had left it of marble. In Nero's reign occurred the great fire (A. D. 64) which destroyed nearly two thirds of Rome. Nero rebuilt the city with great splendor. The population has

ANCIENT ROME—THE FORUM, (RESTORED.)

been computed to have been, in the time of Augustus, at least one million three hundred thousand; and in the reigns of Vespasian and Trajan, about two millions.

The name of Rome does not occur in the Old Testament; but the prophet Daniel mentions the Empire under the name of "the fourth kingdom," Dan. ii, 40; vii, 7, 17, 19; xi, 30–40. Compare Matt. xxiv, 15; Dan. ix, 27; xii, 11; and Deut. xxviii, 49–57. In the Apocrypha mention is made of one of Rome's hostages, "a wicked root, Antiochus, surnamed Epiphanes," 1 Macc. i. 10. Various references to the empire occur in the books of the Maccabees. Syria became a Roman province B. C. 65, and soon afterward Jerusalem was captured by the Romans. "In the second century of the Christian era the Empire of Rome comprehended the fairest part of the earth, and the most civilized portion of mankind. The frontiers of that extensive monarchy were guarded by ancient renown and disciplined valor."

—*Gibbon*. The population of the empire in Christ's time has been estimated at eighty-five millions; and in the reign of Claudius, (A. D. 41-54,) one hundred and twenty millions. Concerning the connection of Jewish history with the Empire, see JERUSALEM.

In the New Testament frequent reference is made to the city of Rome. In Jerusalem on the day of Pentecost there were strangers from Rome, Acts ii, 10. Claudius banished Jews from Rome, Acts xviii, 2. Paul's purpose to visit Rome, Acts xix, 21; xxiii, 11; Rom. i, 15. Paul a prisoner there for two years, Acts xxviii, 14-21. Paul was there aided by Onesiphorus, 2 Tim. i, 16, 17. Converts to the Gospel in Rome, Rom. xvi, 5-17; Phil. i, 12-18; iv, 22; 2 Tim. iv, 21. John calls Rome "that great city which reigneth over the kings of the earth," Rev. xvii, 18.

Our chief interest in Rome lies in the fact that the Saviour of the world lived under its government, and at the period of its greatest prosperity; and also in the fact that here the great apostle Paul lived for two years a prisoner and a preacher of Christ's Gospel. Here Paul wrote several of his epistles to the Churches; and here, at length, in his second imprisonment, he was beheaded—dying a glorious martyr for Jesus. It is also believed that St. Luke here, under the eye of St. Paul, wrote the Acts of the Apostles. By the Roman Catholics it is claimed that St. Peter was associated with St. Paul, and that they were fellow-prisoners for nine months in the Mamertine prison at Rome. But in the New Testament there is not the slightest evidence that Peter was ever in Rome at any time. The only Scripture passage upon which Romanists pretend to rely to show that Peter was in the city is that found in 1 Peter v, 13: "The Church that is at Babylon elected together with you saluteth you." They here interpret Babylon to mean Rome, for which interpretation there is not the shadow of proof. It signifies the Babylon in Asia, where, at the very time that Peter wrote, Josephus shows there was a very large colony of Jews. "Within three centuries after Christ the great seat of Rabbinical learning was fixed at Babylon, and then and there the famous Babylonian Talmud was produced."

At the time St. Paul was carried to Rome Nero was Emperor, and the state of society was fearful to contemplate, Emperor and people being alike sunk in the lowest social degradation. One of the fathers of the Church has thus described it: "The infamy of the circus, the indecency of the theater, the cruelty of the amphitheater, the atrocity of the arena, and the folly of the games." From a volume of lectures delivered in Rome by Rev. C. M. Butler, D. D., and entitled *St. Paul in Rome*, we make the following instructive extracts: "The contemplation of Paul, a slight, worn, and weary man in chains, stepping from the ship Castor and Pollux on the crowded quay of Puteoli, testifies in the most striking way that not by power nor might, but by the Spirit of the Lord, does God confound the mighty. We walk amid the ruins of that mighty empire; but the kingdom which Paul planted is spreading over the world, and will at last become the everlasting kingdom of righteousness and peace which shall cover all the earth." Of Paul's nearer approach to the city Dr. Butler says: "The beautiful blue Alban range of hills, with its then conspicuous Temple of Jupiter upon Monte Cavo, on the spot now disfigured by the hideous monastery of the Passionists, rose before him as the road wound around its southern slope, which was covered with villas, to the point now called Albano. From that position, not too high or distant for the view to be intelligible, he gazed upon a scene of beauty rarely surpassed, and upon the signs and evidences of power concentrated at its imperial seat, never before or since in the history of nations equaled. The vast Campagna, even now singularly and mysteriously lovely in its desolation, was then bright and fresh in all the charms which cultivation, luxury, and art could add to those of nature. It was a scene of solid, palatial villas, of slighter 'houses of pleasure,' as they were called, of temples and converging roads, and stately, far-stretching aqueducts, in the midst of meadows and vineyards and gardens. It must have been then an era in any man's life when he first saw Rome in her glory, as it is now when he first sees her in her desolation.

"The first distinct point at which the city would plainly appear, and at which a traveler would naturally pause, was that at which the lofty monument of Pompey, erected by his widow, stood, as its stripped and desolate shaft now stands. At his left he would see the villa of the great Triumvir, whose ruins can still be traced, transformed into an imperial summer residence. Before him the road would be seen to lie straight as an arrow—as the same road, recently opened, can still be seen—to its entrance into the city at the Porta Capena. But how changed its aspect from then to now! Now a street of scattered, broken tombs; then the most thronged and splendid avenue to a city of probably two millions of inhabitants, through fifteen miles of intervening villas and gardens, which were themselves almost a continuous city, in the midst of groves and vineyards. . . . The tombs were structures of the utmost elegance and beauty. . . . Upon the slopes of these tombs, which were fashioned after the Etruscan manner, trees and parterres of flowers were planted. . . . Between the tombs, as they passed, the travelers must have been constantly regaled with the view of the villas and gardens that were placed behind them. . . . The uplifted Palatine Hill, with its far-stretching line of palaces, its white gleaming Temple of Apollo, and its innumerable porticoes and colonnades; the theater and portico of Pompey, the portico of Octavia, the mausoleum of Augustus, with its gardens; and, high eminent over all the city, the arx of the steep Capitol Hill, and the resplendent temple of Jupiter Capitolinus—what a scene of unequaled magnificence it must have been! The one dome of the Pantheon could scarcely have been overlooked, and the eyes of Paul, no doubt, rested upon that shining heathen bronze, which has since been converted into the sacred baldachino of St. Peter's and the orthodox cannon of St. Angelo."

"And now within the city, and leaving the crowded Aventine Hill on the left, and passing between the Cælian and the southern portion of the Palatine Hill, he emerges on the ridge Velia, where the Arch of Titus was subsequently built, and the famous Forum, the very beating heart of Rome, with all its architectural magnificence, is before him. On the left, the Palatine Hill, with its connected imperial palaces and temples around its entire circuit, and covering with their dependent gardens and areas all its surface. In the Forum itself the immense Basilica Julia, commenced by Cæsar and completed by Augustus, and the opposite, almost equal Basilica Æmilia, and between them, and above and below them, temples, porticoes, altars. and rostra; and above, dominating over all, on the abrupt high hill of the Capitol, the resplendent temple of Jupiter Capitolinus, all in its unparalleled magnificence, burst upon the view of Paul the prisoner." Now, when the devout Christian visits Rome, "his first thought is not of Romulus, Cæsar, or Augustus, of Gregory or of Leo, but of Paul."

BIBLE GEOGRAPHY. 405

The most striking of the remains of the ancient city is the Coliseum, grand in its size, and still sublime even it. ruins. Within its vast circuit hundreds of thousands congregated to witness the fearful death of the early Christians as they were torn asunder by ravenous beasts. Among the triumphal arches is that of Titus, whose inscriptions and figures are a memorial of the destruction of Jerusalem.

ARCH OF TITUS.

In Revelation the sacred writer calls this city by the name of Babylon, because in their hatred of Rome the Jews compared her tyranny to the fearful captivity in Babylon, Rev. xiv, 8; xvi, 19; xvii, 5; xviii, 2. The expression "seven mountains, on which the woman sitteth," in Rev. xvii, 9, undoubtedly refers to the seven-hilled city of Rome. The woman, whose character vividly personifies the profligacy of Rome, is described in Rev. xvii.

JEWISH TROPHIES—FROM THE ARCH OF TITUS.

For centuries this great city has been the capital of what Protestants call the "Papal Beast," the Pope of Rome. Calling himself the "Vicar of Christ," and the "Head of the Church on Earth," uttering his anathemas, and fulminating Papal bulls against all unbelievers in the unholy Romish dogmas, and held on his throne for years by foreign bayonets—at length, July 18, 1870, Pope Pius IX., by the vote of his Œcumenical Council in Rome assembled, was declared to be "Infallible." The decree closes with these words: "If then any one—which may God forbid!—have the temerity to contradict our definition, let him be anathema." Let the student compare with this fact *Conybeare and Howson's* version of 2 Thess. ii, 4: "Who opposes himself, and exalts himself against all that is called God, and against all worship; even to seat himself in the temple of God, and take on himself openly the signs of Godhead."

War breaking out between France and Prussia at the same time with the adoption of this decree, the French troops were immediately withdrawn from Rome. As a result, the King of Italy, Victor Emanuel, at once aimed at the unity of the Italian States. After a very brief and almost bloodless campaign the troops of Victor Emanuel entered the gates of the city of Rome, September 20, 1870, in the name of the "King and Italian Unity." The victorious army was received with the wildest delight. Assembled thousands shouted, "Long live Rome, the capital of Italy." In a few days the king called for the voice of the entire nation. The returns showed that the Papal city itself, as well as the provinces, had almost unanimously voted against the Pope. Thus the "States of the Church" are no longer a separate kingdom, and the Pope himself is reduced to a merely spiritual overseer or bishop.

Rosh, (Map 12,) *head, chief.* The Authorized Version, in Ezek. xxxviii, 2, 3; xxxix, 1, translates the Hebrew term "Rosh" as "chief" or "head." In verse 2, "Magog, the chief prince of Meshech and Tubal," should undoubtedly read "Magog, the prince of Rosh, Meshech, and Tubal," thus making Rosh the first of the three great Scythian tribes. Probably the name occurs also in Judith ii, 23, as RASSES, which see. Gesenius and other eminent scholars are inclined to identify Rosh with the Russians. The Bible does not mention the name of any other modern nation. The first certain notice of the Russians under this name occurs A. D. 839 in a Latin Chronicle.

Ru'mah, *lofty,* the native place of Pedaiah, the father of King Jehoiakim's mother, 2 Kings xxiii, 36. Keil and others think it may be the same with ARUMAH, which see. Possibly it is identical with Dumah, near Hebron.

Sabe'ans. See SEBA and SHEBA.

Sab'ta and **Sab'tah,** *striking,* that is, terror to foes; the third in order of the sons of Cush, and founder of one of the nations of antiquity, Gen. x, 7; 1 Chron. i, 9. It is very difficult to fix the locality of this nation. Some locate it in Ethiopia, on the river Astaboras, (now *Takazze,*) which flows through the province of Meroe. Others trace the ancient name in Sabbatha, a noted city in south-eastern Arabia, containing not less than sixty temples. The western shores of the Persian Gulf are suggested, where stood a town called Saphtha. Other theories are advanced. The most probable opinion settles the tribe in Africa, while some families in their wanderings left their traces along the shores of Arabia

Sab'techa, and **Sab'techah,** *striking,* that is, terror to foes; the fifth son of Cush, and progenitor of a tribe, Gen. x, 7; 1 Chron. i, 9. Gesenius suggests that the territory must be sought in Ethiopia. On Egyptian monuments the word SBTK, or Sabatoca, appears as the proper name of the Ethiopians. Bochart proposes the northern shore of the Persian Gulf, but both etymology and history seem opposed to this theory. The Targum of Jonathan renders Zingetani, *Zanguebar.*

Sa'la, Luke iii, 35, the Greek form of **Sa'lah,** *shoot. extension.* The father of Eber, Gen. x, 24, (margin, Shelah;) xi, 12–15. Shelah also in 1 Chron. i, 18, 24. The tribe sprung from this patriarch settled in Mesopotamia.

Sal'amis, (Map 8,) *shaken, beaten,* one of the chief cities of Cyprus, situated on a plain at the eastern end of the island. It was the first place visited by Paul and Barnabas, on the first missionary journey, after leaving the mainland at Seleucia, Acts xiii, 45. Probably many Jews resided in Cyprus, attracted thither by the copper-mines. See 1 Macc. xv, 23. Salamis was ruined by an earthquake in the time of Constantine the Great, and when rebuilt it was called Constantia. Its remains are yet to be seen, not far from the modern *Famagousta.*

Sal'cah, and **Sal'chah,** (Map 4,) *a pilgrimage,* a city on the extreme eastern limit of Bashan, and of the tribe of Gad, Deut. iii, 10; Josh. xii, 5; xiii, 11; 1 Chron. v, 11. Salcah is identified with the modern *Sulkhad,* which occupies a strong and commanding position on a conical hill at the southern extremity of the range of *Jebel Hauran.* Ruins exist, among which are many houses still perfect, with stone roofs and stone doors, but without inhabitants. An inscription found on a gate bears the date 246 A. D.; another on a tombstone A. D. 196. Mr. Porter says that "the view from the summit of the Castle of Salcah is one of the most remarkable for desolation in all Palestine." Near the city begins the great Syrian desert which extends to the Persian Gulf. See ARGOB.

Sa'lem, *peace, peaceful.*

1. A poetical abbreviation of Jerusalem, Psa. lxxvi, 2. It is said that the Arab poets use the same abbreviation. In Gen. xiv, 18, and Heb. vii, 1, 2, reference is made to Melchizedek as "King of Salem." All Jewish commentators affirm that this Salem thus joined with the name of Melchizedek is identical with the Salem of the Psalmist. Christians generally hold the same opinion with the Jews. St. Jerome, however, claims that the Salem of Gen. xiv, 8, was that "Shalem, a city of Shechem," upward of seventy miles to the north of Jerusalem, in the neighborhood of Scythopolis, (or Bethshan,) Gen. xxxiii, 18. Mr. Grove (in Smith's *Dictionary*) says: "That a Salem existed where St. Jerome thus places it there need be no doubt. Indeed, the name has been recovered at the identical distance below *Beisân* by Mr. Van de Velde, at a spot otherwise suitable for Ænon. But that this Salem, Salim, or Salumias was the Salem of Melchizedek is as uncertain as that Jerusalem was so." The use of the term in Heb. vii, 2, seems to indicate that possibly Salem may be merely a title of the king, and not a place at all. If the Salem of Genesis and Hebrews is not Jerusalem, we cannot express our ignorance more tersely than Mr. Grove does in speaking of this word: "Possibly a place, but very doubtful, and if so, not known."

2. A place seized and fortified by the Jews on the approach of Holofernes, Judith iv, 4. It is uncertain what place is intended, perhaps a *Salim* near Jezreel.

Sa'lim, *peace.* In John iii, 23, it is stated that "John also was baptizing in Ænon, near to Salim." The site of each of these places is uncertain. See ÆNON. Dr. Barclay identifies Salim with Wady *Selim,* a wild ravine running down from Anathoth into Wady Farah, and *Ænon* with a large fountain in that ravine. Mr. Grove inclines to this opinion. Mr. Grove thinks Salim may be "perhaps *Sheikh Salim,* near the Jordan," about six or eight miles south of Scythopolis, (*Beisân.*)

Sal'mon, (Hebrew, Tsalmon,) *shady,* the name of a hill, Psa. lxviii, 15. It is possibly, though not probably, the same as ZALMON, which see.

Salmo'ne, (Map 8,) the eastern point of the island of Crete, mentioned in the account of Paul's voyage to Rome, Acts xxvii, 7. This promontory still bears the ancient name.

Salt, CITY OF, (Map 5,) one of the six cities in the wilderness of Judah, Josh. xv, 62. Its name was probably taken from salt-works or mines. It was probably near Engedi, with which it is grouped. At the south-western extremity of the Dead Sea stands a remarkable range of hills of pure salt, near which, perhaps, this city was situated. At the northern end of the range, at the mouth of *Wady Zuweireh,* are ancient ruins, and also at *Um Baghek,* five miles farther north. One or other of these places may mark the site of "the City of Salt."

Salt, VALLEY OF, a name employed five times in Scripture, and referring to two events occurring at the place. Its position is not indicated by the Bible narrative. A more accurate rendering would substitute "ravine" for "valley." In 2 Sam. viii, 13, and 1 Chron. xviii, 12, is an account of the slaughter of eighteen thousand Edomites by the army of David in "the Valley of Salt." See Psa. lx, title. In 2 Kings xiv, 7, and 2 Chron. xxv, 11, Amaziah is said to have slain ten thousand Edomites in this valley, and then, with ten thousand prisoners, to have proceeded to the stronghold of the nation at *Has-Sela,* "the cliff," that is, Petra, and, after taking it, to have massacred them by hurling them down the precipice which gave its ancient name to the city. Using the more appropriate term "glen," or " ravine," it is possible that the place may be the *Wady Zuweireh,* a well-known pass at the northern end of the salt range *Khashm Usdûm,* though the scope of the narrative would rather seem to locate it nearer Edom.

Sama'ria, (Map 5,) (Hebrew, Shomeron,) *watch-height.*

1. A city situated near the middle of Palestine. It was built by Omri, King of Israel, on a mountain or hill of the same name, about B. C. 925. It was the metropolis of the kingdom of Israel, or of the ten tribes. The site of the city is one of rare attractiveness, combining strength, fertility, and beauty. The hill was purchased from the owner, Shemer, from whom the city took its name, 1 Kings xvi, 23, 24. For two centuries Samaria continued to be the capital of Israel till the carrying away of the ten tribes by Shalmaneser, about B. C. 720, 2 Kings xviii, 3, 5. During this period it was the seat of idolatry. "On that beautiful eminence, looking far over the plain of Sharon and the Mediterranean Sea to the west, and over its own fertile vale to the east, the kings of Israel reigned in a luxury which, for the very reason of its being like that of more eastern sovereigns, was sure not to be permanent in a race destined for higher purposes."—*Stanley.* Samaria was the seat of a temple of Baal, built by Ahab and destroyed by Jehu, 1 Kings xvi, 32, 33; 2 Kings x, 18-28. In the reigns of Ahab and Joram the city was unsuccessfully besieged by the Syrians, 1 Kings xx, 1-21; 2 Kings vi, 24-33; vii; but it was ultimately taken by the Assyrians, after a siege of three years, in the reign of Hoshea, 2 Kings xvii, 5, 6; xviii, 9, 10. The inhabitants were carried away into captivity and colonists put in their place, 2 Kings xvii, 24; Ezra iv, 9, 10. For some time after the Babylonish exile Samaria continued to be a place of importance. It was then taken by Alexander the Great, who placed in it a body of Syro-Macedonians. Subsequently John Hyrcanus took the city, after a year's siege, and razed it to the ground. Yet it must soon have revived, as in the time of Alexander Jannæus it was reckoned one of the cities possessed by the Jews. Pompey restored it to the province of Syria, and it was afterward rebuilt by Gabin-

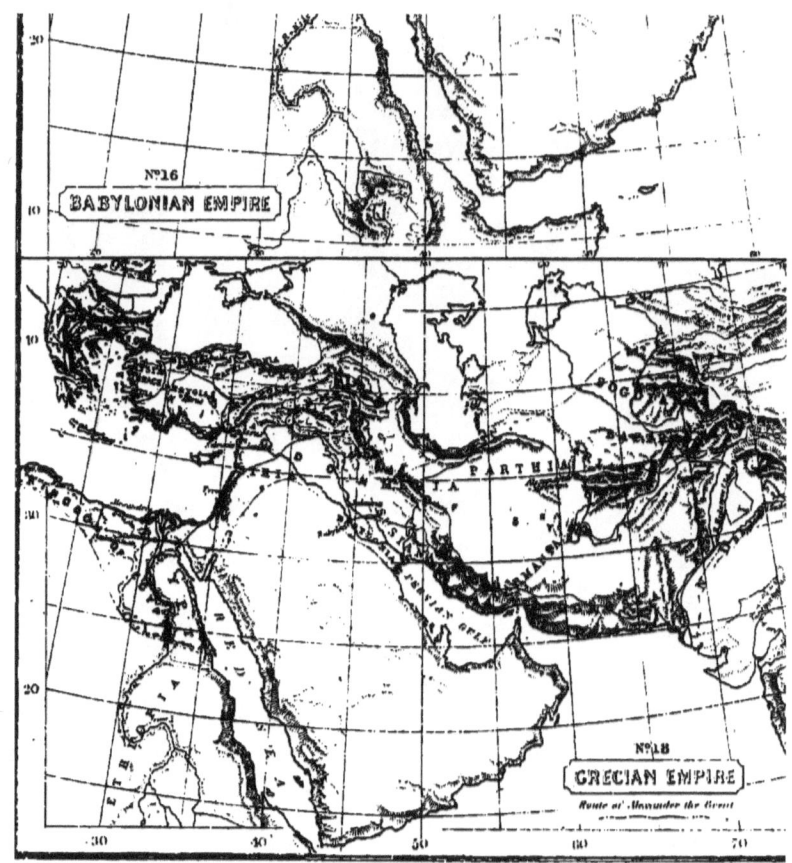

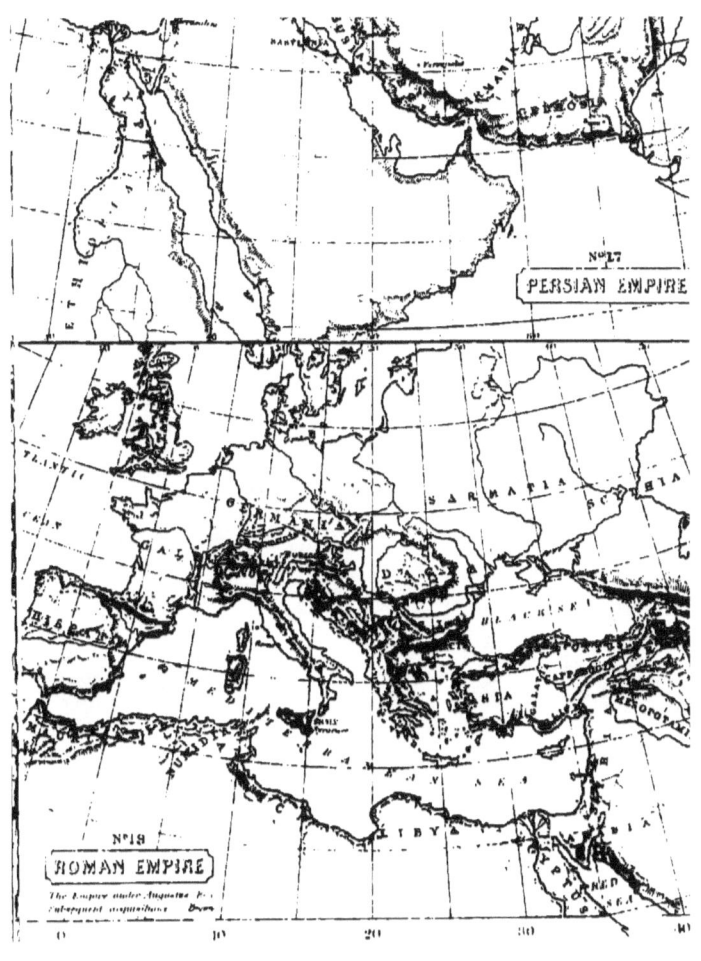

ins. Augustus bestowed Samaria on Herod, who eventually rebuilt the city with great magnificence, and gave it the name of Sebaste, (the Greek translation of the Latin name Augustus.) Here Herod settled a colony of six thousand persons, composed partly of veteran soldiers, and partly of people from the environs. He enlarged the circumference of the city, surrounding it with a strong wall. Such was Samaria in the time of the New Testament, where Philip preached the gospel, and where a Church was gathered by the apostle, Acts vii, 5, 9. But, overshadowed by its neighbor, *Nablûs*, Samaria soon began to decay, and the place that once was so resplendent in beauty, "a crown of pride," (Isa. xxviii, 1,) is now only a mass of ruins. Compare Micah i. 6; Hosea xiii, 16. These ruins are adjacent to the modern village of *Sebastîyeh*. Sebaste is scarcely mentioned by Eusebius as extant, but it is often named by Jerome, and other writers of the same and a later age. Along with *Nablûs*, the city fell into the power of the Moslems during the siege of Jerusalem, and we hear but little more of it till the time of the Crusades. All the notices of the fourth century and later lead to the inference that its destruction had already taken place. The Crusaders established a Latin bishopric at Sebaste. Saladin marched through it A. D. 1184. Notices of the place occur in the records of travelers of the fourteenth, sixteenth, and seventeenth centuries. In the eighteenth century the place appears to have been left unexplored, but lately it has often been visited and described.

"The remains of the ancient city consist mainly of colonnades, which certainly date back to the time of the Herods, and perhaps many of the columns are much older. . . . The grand colonnade runs along the south side of the hill, down a broad terrace, which descends rapidly toward the present village. The number of columns, whole or broken, along this line, is nearly *one hundred*, and many others lie scattered about on lower terraces. They are of various sizes and quite irregularly arranged, but when perfect it must have been a splendid colonnade. The entire hill is covered with rubbish, indicating the existence and repeated destruction of a large city. The modern village is on the south-eastern slope, adjacent to the ruined Church of St. John. . . . The church . . . is an interesting specimen of medieval architecture."—*The Land and the Book*, vol. ii, p. 198.

2. The Samaria of 1 Macc. v, 66, can hardly be the celebrated city above noted. An error has been supposed for Marissa, that is, Mareshah.

Sama'ria, KINGDOM AND PROVINCE OF, (Map 5.) The extent of this kingdom varied very greatly in different periods of its history. The name was borrowed from the capital city. Samaria at first included that portion of the Holy Land which embraced all the tribes over which Jeroboam made himself king, whether east or west of the River Jordan, 1 Kings xiii, 32; Hosea viii, 5, 6; Amos iii, 9; Ezek. xvi, 53. Then the term Samaritan must have indicated every one subject to the king of the northern capital. The kingdom became more and more limited in extent by the loss of section after section from Jeroboam's old kingdom. The territory "beyond Jordan" was invaded first by Pul, and thirty years later by Tiglath-Pileser, King of Assyria, and the Israelites were taken captive. The country thus taken from under the jurisdiction of Samaria was no more called by its name, 1 Chron. v, 26; compare 2 Kings xv, 19, 29. It received the distinctive appellation Peræa, "beyond." Tiglath-Pileser also invaded northern Palestine, captured the province of Galilee, and removed its old inhabitants to

Assyria, 2 Kings xv, 29. This section was then cut off from the kingdom of Israel, and no longer bore the name of Samaria. This name was thus confined, after the conquests of Tiglath-Pileser, (B. C. 738,) to the central portion of Palestine lying between Judah and Galilee. On the capture of the city of Samaria, and the final overthrow of the kingdom of Israel by Shalmaneser, (B. C. 721,) the Jews were removed, and strangers were brought from Assyria "and placed in the cities of Samaria," 2 Kings xvii, 24; compare Ezra iv, 10. These colonists took the name of their new country, and thenceforth were called Samaritans. Samaria now became a province instead of a kingdom. Its extent cannot be exactly defined. The political geography of Palestine was undergoing changes every year in consequence of incessant wars and conquests, and it was not until the period of Roman dominion that the boundaries of provinces began to be accurately defined.

The province is thus described by Josephus: "The district of Samaria lies between Judea and Galilee. Commencing at a village called Ginæa, [the modern *Jenîn*,] situated in the Great Plain, [Esdraelon,] it terminates at the territory of the Acrabatanes. In its natural characteristics it differs in no respect from Judea, hills and plains being interspersed through both; the soil, moreover, being arable and extremely fertile, richly wooded, and amply supplied with fruits, both wild and cultivated."—*Bell. Jud.* iii, 3, 4. The geographical position of the province is incidentally mentioned in Luke xvii, 11, and in John iv, 4; showing that our Lord "passed through the midst of Samaria" on his way from northern Palestine to Jerusalem; and that from this latter city to Galilee "he must needs go through Samaria." Paul and Barnabas "passed through Phenice and Samaria," on a special mission from Antioch to Jerusalem, Acts xv, 3. The name of Samaria as a province appears to have passed away after the time of Roman rule in Syria. It is now wholly unknown to the natives of the country. See SAMARIA (1,) the city.

Samar'itans. In the Old Testament the word Samaritan occurs but once, in 2 Kings xvii, 29. Here it has a wider significance than in its later use in the New Testament. The meaning of the term might vary with the varying extent and history of the kingdom. (See SAMARIA, KINGDOM AND PROVINCE OF.) The origin of these people is obscure. On this point Dr. Hessey (in Smith's *Dictionary*) says: "Shalmaneser, as we have seen, (2 Kings xvii, 5, 6, 26,) carried Israel, that is, the remnant of the ten tribes which still acknowledged Hoshea's authority, into Assyria. This remnant consisted . . . of Samaria, (the city,) and a few adjacent cities and villages. Now, 1. Did he carry away all their inhabitants, or no? 2. Whether they were wholly or only partially desolated, who replaced the deported population? On the answer to these inquiries will depend our determination of the question, Were the Samaritans a mixed race, composed partly of Jews, partly of new settlers, or were they purely of foreign extraction?" Discussing these questions, the writer alluded to concludes that "the cities of Samaria were not partially, but wholly, evacuated of their inhabitants in B. C. 721, and that they remained in this desolate state until, in the words of 2 Kings xvii, 24, 'the king of Assyria brought men from Babylon, and from Cuthah, and from Ava, (Ivah, 2 Kings xviii, 34,) and from Hamath, and from Sepharvaim, and placed them in the cities of Samaria instead of the children of Israel; and they possessed Samaria, and dwelt in the cities thereof.' Thus the new Samaritans . . . were Assyrians by birth or subjugation, were utterly strangers in the cities of Samaria, and were exclusively the inhabitants of those cities." This writer's line of argument, (for which we have not space,) supported as it is by eminent names, and plausible as it is in some respects, cannot, it seems to us, be substantiated from Scripture Dr. Davidson (in *Kitto*) says: "From 2 Kings xvii, 24, it cannot be inferred that the Israelites were removed to the last man, because we learn from 2 Chron. xxxiv, 9, that a remnant of Israel existed in the cities of Manasseh, Ephraim, and Simeon, of whom the Levites collected money for the repair of the temple in Josiah's reign. The same king sent to search the houses in the cities of Manasseh, and Ephraim, and Simeon, even as far as Naphtali, and to destroy the high places and idolatrous altars in the land, (2 Chron. xxxiv, 6, 7;) showing that there was still a remnant of Israelites in the land, after the times of Esarhaddon, that had not been carried away."

Thus the new race became owners of the soil, the Israelites who remained being no longer the chief inhabitants. The removal of all the *priests* does not indicate the removal of all the *inhabitants*. It was the posterity of this new population, intermingled with the Israelites who remained, that afterward, in New Testament times, bore the name of Samaritans. Although, doubtless, the heathen element predominated in this intermixture of Jewish blood, yet the Samaritans never ceased to claim descent from Jacob, John iv, 12. These Eastern tribes, utterly ignorant of the true God, and earnestly worshiping their own false deities, found the Israelites only too ready to fall at once into all their idolatrous practices. For their abominations the Lord sent lions among them and sorely punished them. On their application, one of the captive priests was brought back to teach the people "the manner of the God of the land." Jehovah was then worshiped by this people, but only as one among their many gods, the idols of each respective tribe being equally honored by them, 2 Kings xvii, 25-41. Thus continued this mixture of Hebrews and heathen—their religion a wretched commingling of truth and error, in which "the false and foul far overbore the pure and true."

After the Jews' return from Babylon the Samaritans desired to take part with Zerubbabel in rebuilding the temple, probably relying on the Hebrew element among them. Being refused, they were filled with envy and rage. They represented to the Persian kings the danger of allowing Jerusalem to rise again to honor and influence, and thus for several years the work at Jerusalem was forbidden, Ezra iv. Later still they manifested the same hostility, Neh. iv, vi.

The envy and malice of the Samaritans culminated in the erection of a rival temple on Mount Gerizim. About 409 B. C. a certain Manasseh, of priestly lineage, on being expelled from Jerusalem by Nehemiah for an unlawful marriage, obtained permission from the Persian king of his day, Darius Nothus, to build this temple. It is not certain that the temple was erected during the days of Manasseh. Possibly it was not built till the time of Alexander the Great. The celebrated Samaritan Pentateuch, for which the very highest antiquity is claimed, may possibly have been carried to the people by Manasseh; but it seems more probable that they may have had copies of the same before. The animosity of the two races now became more bitter than ever. The Samaritans annoyed the Jews in every possible mode. They refused hospitalities to pilgrims, as in the case of our Lord; and many, through fear, were compelled to take the longer route to and from Jerusalem, by the east of Jordan. As various Jewish apostates from time to time resorted to them, the Samaritans possessed additional claims to Hebrew descent, and, holding superstitiously to their copy of the Pentateuch, they professed to observe the law more strictly than the Jews themselves. The latter were not less blameworthy in their conduct. The products of Samaria, and all articles of diet among them, were pronounced by the Jews as unclean as swine's flesh. The Samaritans were never to be received as proselytes to the Jews' religion, and they were declared incapable of partaking of the resurrection to eternal life.

The condition of the two rival races above noted will throw much light on many Scripture passages; as, for instance, our Lord's first charge to his apostles not to enter into a city of the Samaritans, Matt. x, 5. Thus James and John showed their Jewish dislike to the Samaritans on account of the inhospitality of the latter, Luke ix, 52-56. The surprise of the Samaritan woman that a Jew should ask her for a drink of water, and the wonderful fact that these Samaritans should listen kindly to the words of Jesus, are narrated in John iv, 1-42. How forcible in the light of this history is the parable of the Good Samaritan! Luke x, 25-37. Then, again, of the ten lepers that were cleansed the only one that gave thanks and glorified God was a Samaritan, Luke xvii, 11-19. By command of Christ, after his resurrection the Gospel was preached in Samaria, Acts i, 8; and when Philip preached Christ in the city of Samaria "there was great joy in that city," Acts viii, 5-22.

The Samaritans were very troublesome both to their Jewish neighbors and to their Roman masters in the first century A. D. Pilate chastised them with a severity which led to his own downfall; and a slaughter of ten thousand and six hundred of them took place under Vespasian. Still they continued to be numerous, and were considered the determined enemies of Christianity. After a while they sank into an obscurity which, though they are just noticed by travelers of the twelfth and fourteenth centuries, was scarcely broken until the sixteenth century. At present the Samaritans number only about two hundred persons. They have now a settlement at *Nablûs*, where they still observe the Law, and still, on a sacred spot on Mount Gerizim, celebrate the Passover with the most tenacious minuteness of ceremonial observance. See SHECHEM.

Sa'mos, (Map 8,) an island in the Ægean Sea, near the coast of Lydia, about five miles from the promontory of Trogyllium, over against Miletus, 1 Macc. xv, 23. It was celebrated as the seat of Juno-worship, for its valuable pottery, and as the birth-place of Pythagoras. St. Paul touched at the island on his voyage from Greece to Syria, Acts xx, 15. Whether he landed or not is uncertain. At the time of Paul's visit Samos was a free city in the province of Asia. Some years ago it contained sixty thousand people, inhabiting eighteen large villages and about twenty small ones. At the present time the wine of Samos ranks high among Levantine wines, and is largely exported, as are also grapes and raisins.

Samothra'cia, (Map 8,) an island in the north-east part of the Ægean Sea, above the Hellespont, with a lofty mountain and a city of the same name. Anciently it was called Dardana, Leucania, and also Samos; and, to distinguish it from the other Samos, the name of Thrace was added from its vicinity to that country. It was formerly celebrated for the mysteries of Ceres and Proserpine. St. Paul touched at this island in his first voyage to

Europe, Acts xvi, 11. It is now called *Samotraki* or *Samandraki*. It is but thinly peopled, and contains only a single village.

Samp'sames, 1 Macc. xv, 23. Probably a place: possibly now *Samsun*, on the Black Sea.

Sansan'nah, *palm branch* (?), a town in the south of Judah, Josh. xv, 31. In Josh. xix, 5, and 1 Chron. iv, 31, for it and Madmannah, with which it is here classed, we have Hazar-Susah, ("horse village,") and Beth-Marcoboth, ("house of chariots.") Mr. Wilton thinks it identical with Hazar-Susah, and locates it in the modern *Wady es-Suny* or *Sunieh*.

Saph'ir, *fair*, one of the villages addressed by the prophet Micah, Micah. i, 11. It is described by Eusebius and Jerome as "in the mountain district between Eleutheropolis and Ascalon." Possibly it is identical with *es-Sawâfir*, between Ascalon and *Beit-Jibrin*. In this vicinity Robinson found three villages of that name, two with affixes.

Sar'amel, 1 Macc. xiv, 28. A place of whose location nothing is known. Possibly it was not a place, but simply a title of Simeon the high priest.

Sar'dis, (Map 8,) the capital of the ancient kingdom of Lydia, situated at the foot of Mount Tmolus, in a fine plain watered by the river Pactolus. In the time of Omphale its name was Hyde'. From its wealth and importance Sardis was often an object of envy to warlike kings. Under Crœsus, its last king, it was one of the most splendid and opulent cities of the East. After its conquest by Cyrus the Persians always kept a garrison in the citadel on account of its natural strength, which induced Alexander the Great, when it was surrendered to him in the sequel of the battle of the Granicus, similarly to occupy it. In the dynasties which arose after the death of Alexander Sardis more than once changed hands. It was sacked by the army of Antiochus the Great in the year 214 B. C. Afterward it passed under the kings of Pergamus. During the reign of Tiberius Sardis was destroyed by an earthquake, but was rebuilt by the Emperor's assistance.

Here was one of the "seven churches of Asia," to which John addressed his apocalyptic message: "Thou hast a few names, *even in Sardis*, which have not defiled their garments," Rev. iii, 4. The ancient inhabitants of this city bore an ill repute among the ancients for their voluptuous habits of life. This worldliness contaminated the Church, doubtless, and hence the cutting words of the revelator: "I know thy works, that thou hast a name that thou livest, and art dead," Rev. iii, 1.

The ravages of the Saracens and Turks, together with successive earthquakes, have made this proud city a heap of ruins. The modern name is *Sert-Kalessi*. A few miserable cottages exist amid the remains of former grandeur. The ruins are chiefly those of the theater, stadium, and of some churches. Two remarkable pillars, which are supposed to have belonged to the massive Temple of Cybele, still bear witness to the wealth and architectural skill of the people that raised it.

Sar'dites, THE. The descendants of Sered the son of Zebulun, Num. xxvi, 26.

Sarep'ta, Luke iv, 26. See ZAREPHATH.

Sa'rid, *a survivor*, a place in Zebulun, west of Chisloth-Tabor, Josh. xix, 10, 12. Unknown.

Sa'ron, Acts ix, 35. See SHARON.

Scyth'ian, (Map 12,) a word employed in Col. iii, 11, as a generalized term for rude, ignorant, degraded. Compare 2 Macc. iv, 47. The Scythians were probably descendants of Magog. They roamed over the regions of Asia north of the Black and Caspian seas, and were, in fact, the ancient representatives of the modern roving Tartars. According to Herodotus the Scythians invaded Egypt, passing through Palestine, under Psammetichus, the contemporary of Josiah. From this fact it is generally believed that Beth-Shean derived its classical name of Scythopolis.

Scythop'olis, (Map 20,) *city of the Scythians,* Judith iii, 10. See BETH-SHEAN.

Sea. Among the Hebrews the term "sea" was used for large bodies of water, and "pool" for smaller. Thus sea (Hebrew, *yâm*) is applied to what we regard as the ocean, Gen. i, 2, 10; also to various parts of the ocean, to large inland lakes, even to smaller lakes, Job xiv, 11; and to great rivers, as the Nile, Isa. xix, 5; Amos viii, 8, (A. V. "flood;") Nah. iii, 8; Ezra xxxii, 2, and the Euphrates, Jer. li, 36.

1. THE SEA OF CHINNERETH, Num. xxxiv, 11; THE SEA OF TIBERIAS, John xxi, 1. See GALILEE, SEA OF.
2. THE MEDITERRANEAN. See MEDITERRANEAN SEA.
3. THE RED SEA, (Maps 1, 2, 8.) This body of water was often called simply "the sea," where there was no danger of confounding it with the Mediterranean, Exod. xiv, 2, 9, 16, 21, 28; xv, 1, 4, 8, 10, 19; Josh. xxiv, 6, 7; and in many other passages. In Isa. xi, 15 it is, "the Egyptian Sea." Its special name in Hebrew is "the sea of Sûph," Exod. x, 19; xiii, 18; xv, 4, 22; xxiii, 31; Num. xiv, 25; xxi, 4; etc. In the New Testament it bears its usual Greek name, the Erythræan Sea, that is the Red Sea, Acts vii, 36; Heb. xi, 29. Compare 1 Macc. iv, 9. The Hebrew name "Sûph" is supposed to mean "weedy;" hence "the weedy sea." Sea-weed is at this day thrown up abundantly on its shores. It has been thought also to include a fluvial rush, such as the papyrus. Many conjectures are made concerning the application of the term "red" to this sea. Some derive it from Edom, which signifies "red," the Edomitish territory being washed by the northeastern arm of the sea. Some take the term from the red color of the mountains on the western shores, or from the red coral, or the red appearance of the water occasioned by certain zoophytes. Others again hold that as the Himyaric tribes of Southern Arabia bear a name implying red, the sea derived its name from these red men. Dean Stanley says: "The appellation 'Red Sea,' as applied distinctly to the two gulfs of Suez and 'Akaba, is comparatively modern. It seems to have been applied to them only as continuations of the Indian Ocean, to which the name of the Erythræan or Red Sea was given at a time when the two gulfs were known to the Hebrews only by the name of the 'Sea of Weeds,' and to the Greeks by the name of the Bays of Arabia and Elath. This in itself makes it probable that the term 'Red' was derived from the corals of the Indian Ocean, and makes it impossible that it should have been from Edom, the mountains of Edom, as is well known, hardly reaching to the shores of the Gulf of Akaba, certainly not to the shores of the ocean. 'As we emerged from the mouth of a small defile,' writes the late Captain Newbold, in describing his visit to the mountains of Nakûs near Tôr, 'the waters of this sacred gulf burst upon our view; the surface marked with annular, crescent-shaped and irregular blotches of a purplish red, extending as far as the eye could reach. They were curiously contrasted with the beautiful aqua-marina of the water lying over the white coral reefs. This red color I ascertained to be caused by the subjacent

red sandstone and reddish coral reefs; a similar phenomenon is observed in the Straits of Babel-Mandeb, and also near Suez, particularly when the rays of the sun fall on the water at a small angle.'—*Journal of Roy. Asiat. Society*, No. xiii, p. 78. This accurate description is decisive as to the origin of the name, though Captain Newbold draws no such inference. The Hebrew word 'sûph,' though used commonly for 'flags' or 'rushes,' could by an easy change be applied to any aqueous vegetation."—*Sinai and Palestine*, p. 6, note.

The Red Sea lies between Egypt and Arabia. The two gulfs into which its northern end divides hold between them the Sinaitic Peninsula. Its length is about fourteen hundred miles, its average breadth one hundred and fifty miles, with an area of about one hundred and eighty thousand square miles. The western arm, now called the Gulf of Suez, across which the Israelites made their escape, is about one hundred and ninety miles long, with an average width of about twenty-one miles. The eastern arm, the Gulf of Akaba, is about one hundred and twelve miles long, with an average width of fifteen miles. The sea is very deep, being more than six thousand feet at its deepest soundings. Groups of islands, coral-reefs, sandbanks, and the prevailing winds, render navigation difficult. The coral so abundantly found is generally white, though some of it is red, and occasionally it is beautifully variegated. Chains of mountains on both sides rise at some distance from the shore to the height sometimes of six or seven thousand feet.

The passage of the Israelites over the western arm of the sea is recorded in Exodus xiv, xv. This miraculous event is frequently referred to in the Scriptures: Num. xxxiii, 8; Deut. xi, 4; Josh. ii, 10; Judg. xi, 16; 2 Sam. xxii, 16; Neh. ix, 9-11; Psa. lxvi, 6; Isa. x, 26; Acts vii, 36; 1 Cor. x, 1, 2; Heb. xi, 29, etc. After spying the land the Israelites return "into the wilderness by the way of the Red Sea," Num. xiv, 25. They "journeyed from Mount Hor by the way of the Red Sea to compass the land of Edom," Num. xxi, 4. From the way of the Red Sea came locusts, Exod. x, 12-19; and also quails, Num. xi, 31. King Solomon "made a navy of ships . . . on the shore of the Red Sea," 1 Kings ix, 26; x, 22; 2 Chron. viii, 17, 18. The ports of Elath and Ezion-Geber were toward the extremity of what is now called the Gulf of Akaba.

To the Christian reader the chief interest in the Red Sea centers in the stupendous miracle by which the children of Israel passed over it, while "the floods stood upright as an heap, and the depths were congealed in the heart of the sea," Exod. xv, 8. The route of the Hebrews' "wandering" is not yet accurately determined, nor is the precise place fixed where the Israelites crossed the sea. "The passage of the Red Sea, as Niebuhr has well remarked, is fixed wherever the traveler puts the question to his Arab guides. The 'Wells of Moses,' the 'Baths of Pharaoh,' the 'Baths of Moses,' all down the Gulf of Suez, and the 'Island of Pharaoh,' in the Gulf of Akaba, equally derive their names from traditions of the passage at each of these particular spots." "There is unquestionably a general atmosphere of Mosaic tradition every-where. From Petra to Cairo, from the northern platform of the peninsula to its southern extremity, the name and the story of Moses is still predominant. There are two groups of 'Wells of Moses,' one on each side of the Gulf of Suez; there are the 'Baths of Pharaoh,' and the 'Baths of Moses' farther down the coast; there is the 'Seat of Moses' near Bisâtîn, and in the Wady Feirân; there is the 'Mountain of Moses' in the cluster of Sinai; the 'Cleft of Moses' in Mount St. Catharine; the 'Valley' and the 'Cleft of Moses' at Petra. . . . There is the romantic story told to Burckhardt, that the soughing of wind down the Pass of *Nuweybi'a*, on that gulf, is the wailing of Moses as he leaves his loved mountains."—Stanley's *Sinai and Palestine*, pp. 29, 30, 32.

On nearly all maps of the "wanderings" the route is marked as just across the head of the Gulf of Suez. The present limit of this gulf could not have been the same in the time of Moses. Since the Christian era the head of the gulf has retired for a distance of at least fifty miles from its ancient head. Hence it may be possible that the passage of the sea was where there is at present a sandy waste. The prediction of Isaiah has been fulfilled: "And the Lord shall utterly destroy the tongue of the Egyptian Sea," Isa. xi, 15; "the waters shall fail from the sea," xix, 5. An ancient canal conveyed the waters of the Nile to the Red Sea, flowing through the *Wady et-Tumeylat*, and irrigating with its system of water-channels a large extent of country; and it also conveyed the commerce of the Red Sea to the Nile, thus avoiding the risks of the desert journey. The drying up of the head of the gulf appears to have been one of the chief causes of the neglect and ruin of this canal. The land north of the ancient head of the gulf is a plain of heavy sand, merging into marsh-land near the Mediterranean coast, and extending to Palestine. The old bed of the sea is indicated by the *Birket-et-Timsâh*, or "Lake of the Crocodile," and the more southern Bitter Lakes, the northernmost part of the former probably corresponding to the head of the gulf at the time of the Exodus. Possibly the Israelites marched through what is now the *Wady et-Tumeylat*, or, it may be, along the *Wady et-Teeh*. which leads to the Red Sea from opposite Memphis.

The constant and zealous explorations of Christian travelers may, and doubtless will, fix with certainty the yet disputed route of the Israelites, To those who assail the miracle itself we offer the comprehensive words of Bonar: "*Deny* the miracle, and the circuitous route remains to be accounted for. *Dilute* the miracle, and reduce it to its minimum by the gratuitous hypothesis of an extraordinary ebb-tide, still the westward march is a mystery. Admit the miracle, and the narrative is as consistent and intelligible as the event is marvelous and Divine." See WILDERNESS.

4. THE SALT SEA, (Maps 2, 4, 5.) This noted inland sea bears also the following names: Sea of the Plain, Deut. iv, 49; 2 Kings xiv, 25. The Salt Sea, Deut. iii, 17; Josh. iii, 16; xii, 3. The Sea, Ezek. xlvii, 8. The East Sea, Joel ii, 20; Ezek. xlvii, 18; Zech. xiv, 8. The Sodomitish Sea, 2 Esdr. v, 7. In the Talmud it is the Sea of Sodom; in Josephus, the Asphaltic Lake. By the Arabs it is called the Dead Sea from its character, and the Sea of Lot (*Bahr Lût*) from its history. The name "Dead Sea" appears to have been first used in Greek by Pausanias and Galen; and in Latin by Justin, or rather by the older historian, Trogus Pompeius, (about 10 B. C.,) whose work he epitomized. Eusebius also employed it. This is now its recognized and established name, arising from the general belief in the many very exaggerated stories of its gloomy aspect and deadly character.

This sea is forty geographical, or forty-six English miles long. Its greatest width is nine geographical, or ten and one third English miles. Its area embraces about two hundred and fifty geographical miles. These dimensions vary according to the time of the year. Its greatest depth is about thirteen hundred feet. The Dead Sea is the final receptacle of the river

THE DEAD SEA. VIEW FROM 'AIN JIDY, (ES-GEDI,) LOOKING SOUTH.

BIBLE GEOGRAPHY. 423

JEBEL USDUM.

Jordan. On its eastern side it receives the *Zŭrka Ma'in*, the *Mojib*, (the Arnon of the Bible,) and the *Beni-Hemâd*. On the south the *Kurâhy* or *El-Ahsy*; and on the west, that of *Ain Jidy*. Along the western side are also a number of springs—some fresh, some warm, some salt and fetid—which appear to run continually, and all find their way, more or less absorbed by the sand and shingle of the beach, into its waters. This large body of water has no visible outlet; and it is believed there can be no invisible one; indeed, the evaporation is amply sufficient to carry off the supply without an outlet.

In shape the Dead Sea is an irregular oval. The shores are much indented in parts. A tongue of land, about five miles wide where it leaves the straight coast, projects into the sea about seven miles, and then curves toward the north; and at its end, near the west shore, it is nine miles long. South of this peninsula the Dead Sea is a lagoon, with a variable depth of from ten to fourteen feet. The surface of the sea is "thirteen hundred feet below the level of the Mediterranean Sea, and thus is the most depressed sheet of water in the world; as the Lake Sirikol, where the Oxus rises, ... is the most elevated."—*Stanley.* The exact depression, according to Lieut. Lynch, (1848,) is 1,316.7; but the report of the Royal Engineers who lately surveyed the country makes it 1,289 feet.

Besides the Scripture references above given, there are other allusions, some of which connect the Dead Sea with events among the most striking in Bible history. Lot chose the borders of this sea as his home, Gen. xiii, 12. Here occurred the famous battle of four kings against five, in which Lot was taken prisoner, Gen. xiv, 1-12. Here were destroyed Sodom and Gomorrah, with the other "cities of the plain," when God rained "brimstone and fire from the Lord out of heaven," Gen. xix, 24. Then followed the strange fate of Lot's wife, xix, 26. The coast of the Dead Sea was a border of the land, Num. xxxiv, 2-12, and the east boundary of Judah, Josh. xv, 1-5. Here also was the scene of the prophet's vision recorded in Ezek. xlvii. Of this Mr. Stanley (*S. and P.*, p. 288) remarks: "The imagery of this vision is often used in illustration of the spread of philanthropic or missionary beneficence; but its full force, as the prophet first delivered it, can only be appreciated by those who have seen the desolate basin of the Salt Sea, and marked the features of its strange vicinity."

The excessive saltness of the water is remarkable. The principal causes of this saltness are found in the remarkable salt-hills called *Jebel Usdum*, situated at the south-west corner of the sea. The saline particles of the water of the ocean are four per cent. while the Dead Sea contains twenty-six and a quarter per cent. Mr. Stanley, referring to Peterman's *Atlas*, and Ansted's *Elementary Geology*, cites two lakes whose waters are still more salt. "Lake Elton (which is situated on the steppes east of the Volga, and supplies a great part of the salt of Russia) contains twenty-nine per cent."—*S. and P.*, page 286, note. The other is Lake Urumia, whose per cent. of salt is not stated. "But Moritz Wagner, in his travels in Persia, (ii, 136, Leipsic, 1852,) . . . says that the salt and iodine of the water of this lake far surpass those of the Dead Sea," p. 286, note.

The specific gravity of this sea is, according to Herepath, 1,172. Mr. Porter says that he floated in it "easily in an upright position, with head and shoulders above the water." Says Lieut. Lynch, "Eggs which would have sunk in the ocean floated here with only two thirds immersed." It has been thought that no life could subsist about the sea; that no bird could fly across its waters; that the waters were dull and motionless, and their steam deadly. These notions are now nearly all exploded. The heights surrounding are often wild, but the general view of the lake is beautiful. Sometimes the waters are as blue as in other lakes. "Living creatures, though of a low type, have been found in them; and animals, birds, and especially reptiles, throng the neighboring thickets, while ducks and

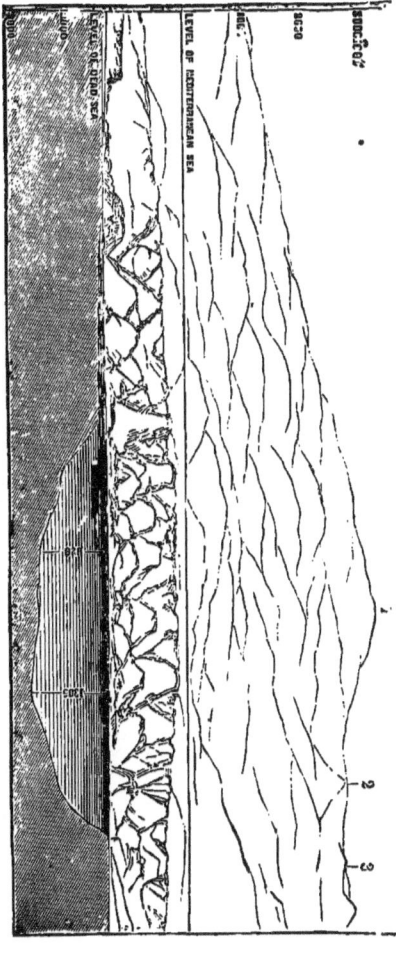

LONGITUDINAL SECTION OF THE DEAD SEA FROM NORTH TO SOUTH.

1. FRANK MOUNTAIN. 2. BETHLEHEM. 3. JERUSALEM.

other aquatic birds have been observed swimming and diving in the water. Most of these are said to be of a stone color, so as easily to escape notice. Lighted up by the rising or setting sun, the tints of the mountains are often gorgeous."—*Ayre.* Concerning the question of animal life being supported in the sea, Mr. Porter thinks that the "fact has not yet been established on conclusive evidence," Kitto, vol. iii, p. 800. Mr. Stanley says: "The birds that pass over it without injury have long ago destroyed the belief that no living creature could survive the baneful atmosphere which hung upon its waters."—*S. and P.*, p. 284. Concerning the general aspect of the sea, Mr. Grove (in Smith's *Dictionary*) remarks: "With all the brilliancy of its illumination, its frequent beauty of coloring, the fantastic grandeur of its inclosing mountains, and the tranquil charm afforded by the reflection of that unequaled sky on the no less unequaled mirror of the surface—with all these there is something in the prevalent sterility, and the dry, burnt look of the shores, the overpowering heat, the occasional smell of sulphur, the dreary salt marsh at the southern end, and the fringe of dead drift-wood round the margin, which must go far to excuse the title which so many ages have attached to the lake, and which we may be sure it will never lose."

The generally received opinion has been that the "cities of the plain" lie engulfed beneath the waters of the Dead Sea. Recent investigations have led some eminent scholars to reject this view. They hold that, if submerged at all, these cities must be under the northern part, and that the southern part of the lake, instead of being anciently dry land, was really much deeper than at present. On the origin of the Dead Sea, with regard specially to supposed volcanic agencies, the view of Mr. Tristam, in his *Land of Israel*, will be interesting to the student. "I think there can be no question," he says, "but that the old notions of volcanic agencies about the Dead Sea were erroneous, and that many writers, like De Saulcy, have been misled by endeavoring to square their preconceived interpretation of Scripture with the facts they saw around them. . . . Such traces are not to be found. . . . The whole region has been slowly and gradually formed through a succession of ages, and . . . its peculiar phenomena are similar to those of other salt lakes in Africa, or referable to its unique and depressed position. But, setting aside all preconceived notions, and taking the simple record of Gen. xix as we find it, let us see whether the existing condition of the country throws any light upon the biblical narrative. Certainly we do observe by the lake sulphur and bitumen in abundance. Sulphur springs stud the shores; sulphur is strewn, whether in layers or in fragments, over the desolate plains; and bitumen is ejected in great floating masses from the bottom of the sea, oozes through the fissures of the rocks, is deposited with gravel on the beach, or, as in the *Wady Mahawat*, appears with sulphur to have been precipitated during some convulsion. We know that at the times of earthquakes in the north the bitumen seems even in our own day to be detached from the bottom of the lake, and that floating islets of that substance have been evolved coincident with the convulsions so frequent in north-eastern Palestine. Every thing leads to the conclusion that the agency of fire was at work, though not the overflowing of an ordinary volcano. The materials were at hand, at whichever end of the lake we place the doomed cities, and may probably have been accumulated then to a much greater extent than at present. The kindling of such a mass of combustible material, either by lightning from heaven or by other electrical agency, combined with an earthquake ejecting the bitumen or sulphur from the lake, would soon spread devastation over the plain, so that the smoke of the country would go up as the smoke of a furnace. There is no authority whatever in the biblical record for the popular notion that the site of the cities has been submerged, and Mr. Grove (in his able and exhaustive article in the *Biblical Dictionary*, 'Sodom') has justly stated 'that there is no warrant for imagining that the catastrophe was a geological one, and in any other case all traces of action must at this distance of time have vanished.' The simple and natural explanation seems—when stripped of all the wild traditions and strange horrors with which the mysterious sea has been invested—to be this, that, during some earthquake, or without its direct agency, showers of sulphur, and probably bitumen, ejected from the lake or thrown up from its shores, and ignited perhaps by the lightning which would accompany such phenomena, fell upon the cities and destroyed them. The history of the catastrophe has not only remained in the inspired record, but is inscribed in the memory of the surrounding tribes by many a local tradition and significant name." From Dr. Porter's able article in Kitto's *Cyclopedia* we present a brief extract expressing his view on the question of submergence. "It was manifestly," he says, "the opinion of Moses that the Vale of Siddim was submerged. . . . It is said 'the Vale of Siddim was full of bitumen pits.' . . . There is no part of the valley north of the sea to which this would apply; nor, indeed, is there any plain or vale along its shores 'full of bitumen pits at the present day.' These facts render it impossible that the Vale of Siddim could have been in the Plain of Jericho; and they seem to confirm the previous statement that Siddim was submerged." Quoting, then, from Dr. Robinson's latest work, (published since his death,) in which Robinson says, "It seems to be a necessary conclusion that the Dead Sea extended no farther south than the peninsula, and that the cities destroyed lay on the south of the lake as it then existed," Dr. Porter adds: "Notwithstanding the arguments and almost contemptuous insinuations of some recent writers, not a single fact has been adduced calculated to overthrow this view; but, on the contrary, each new discovery seems as if a new evidence in its favor. It must be admitted, however, that these are still subjects for observation and scientific research rather than for speculation and dogmatic affirmation. It is greatly to be desired that some accomplished practical geologist should undertake a thorough examination of the valley of the Jordan and Dead Sea. He would reap a rich harvest, and he would confer a rich boon as well upon science as upon biblical literature." See SIDDIM; SODOM; GOMORRAH.

5. Sea of Jazer, Jer. xlviii, 32. See JAAZER.

Se′ba, (Map 12,) *man*, a son of Cush, (Gen. x, 7; 1 Chron. i, 9,) whose descendants appear to have formed a nation in the distant south, Psa. lxxii, 10. In Isa. xliii, 3, they are mentioned as of equal importance with Egypt and Ethiopia. In Isa. xlv, 14, they are termed Sabeans. The term Sabeans in Ezek. xxiii, 42, is "drunkard" in the margin. According to Josephus, Cambyses gave to Seba, the royal city of Ethiopia, the name of Meroe, after his sister. Meroe was an extensive region inclosed by the rivers Astapus (*Bahr el-Azrak*) and Astaboras, (*Tacazze*,) extending to the narrow tract where the latter river joins the Nile. This country appears to answer all the conditions required for the identification of Seba. Meroe, the capital city, was about ninety miles south of the junction of the Nile and the

Astaboras. About twenty miles north-east of the Nubian town *Shendy* are extensive ruins which mark the site of Meroe. See SHEBA.

Sec'acah, *inclosure,* a town in the wilderness of Judah, probably near to the Dead Sea, Josh. xv, 61. Unknown.

Se'chu, *watch-tower,* a place apparently lying on the route between Saul's residence, Gibeah, and that of Samuel, Ramathaim-Zophim. It was noted for its "great well," 1 Sam. xix, 22. Possibly *Bîr Neballa,* (the Well of Neballa,) near *Neby Samwil,* may mark the place.

Se'ir, (Maps 2, 3,) *hairy, bristly,* the mountain district on the east of the Arabah, anciently inhabited by the Horites, Gen. xiv, 6; Deut. ii, 12. The name may come either from Seir, the Horite chief, Gen. xxxvi, 20, or from the rough aspect of the whole region. Afterward Seir was the possession of Esau and his posterity, Gen. xxxii, 3; xxxiii, 14, 16; xxxvi, 8, 9; Deut. ii, 4, 22; 2 Chron. xx, 10. Hence Seir is sometimes put for Edom, or the Edomites, Ezek. xxv, 8, but the old name of Seir was not lost. This district extended from the Dead Sea to the Elanitic Gulf. See EDOM. The northern part of Seir is now called *Jebal,* and the southern *Esh-Sherah.*

2. Another Mount Seir is named as one of the landmarks on the north boundary of Judah, Josh. xv, 10. It lay westward of Kirjath-Jearim, and between it and Beth-Shemesh. The site is unknown.

Se'irath, *a she-goat, shaggy,* the place where Ehud fled after his murder of Eglon, Judg. iii, 26, 27. Perhaps it was the same as Seir, (2,) but nothing is known of it.

Se'la and Se'lah, (Maps 2, 4,) *rock,* a city in Edom, probably the capital taken by Amaziah, King of Judah, and by him named Joktheel, (*subdued of God,*) 2 Kings xiv, 7; 2 Chron. xxv, 11, 12. It was afterward possessed by Moab, Isa. xvi, 1. In Judg. i, 36, 2 Chron. xxv, 12, and Obad. iii, Sela is designated by the term "rock."

Sela is without doubt identical with the city of Petra, whose wonderful ruins are in the *Wady Mousa,* about two days' journey to the north of the Gulf of Akabah, and somewhat farther to the south of the Dead Sea. Petra was celebrated as the chief city of the Nabathæans in the fourth century B. C., and as a central station for the commerce of the East. Afterward it became the residence of the Arabian princes who bore the name of Aretas, and was subjected to the Roman power by Trajan. From Adrian it received the name of Adriana.

The ruins lie in a narrow valley surrounded by lofty and, for the most part, perfectly precipitous mountains. A great many small recesses or side valleys open into the principal one, thus enlarging, as well as varying almost infinitely, the outline. These with one or two exceptions have no outlet, but come to a speedy and abrupt termination among the overhanging precipitous cliffs. The whole circumference of Petra, including these irregularities, may be four miles or more. In one of the ravine-like valleys is a most wonderful structure, *el-Khuzneh,* probably formerly used as a temple, one of the wonders of the East. Its façade consists of "two rows of six columns over one another, with two statues between, with capitals and sculptured pediments, the upper one of which is divided by a little round temple crowned with an urn." Behind this temple are seen other beautiful and varied façades, leading to apartments in the cliffs. In a wider part of the valley, on its left side, is the magnificent Greek theater, entirely hewn out of the solid rock, one hundred and twenty feet in diameter at the base, with more than

PETRA—LOOKING TOWARD THE THEATER.

thirty rows of seats, in the native rock, red and purple alternately, and holding upward of three thousand spectators—surrounded by tombs, and overgrown in the sides with the wild fig-tree and the tamarisk. "Astounding and almost numberless excavations are every-where wrought in the front of the mountain, in its ravines and recesses, and even in the precipitous rocks around it, in many cases one rising over the other, and sometimes several hundred feet above the level of the valley, with steps cut in the solid rocks; some widely conspicuous, others hidden in the most inaccessible cliffs. These excavations shine in all the magic of variegated, though not uniformly light, colors, equaling in softness those of flowers or of the plumage of birds, and exhibiting a gorgeous crimson, streaked with purple, and often intermixed, ribbon-like, with yellow and blue; they are of the most various dimensions, and serve the most manifold purposes ... The cloister (*deir*) at the north-western extremity of the cliffs ... also hewn out of the rock, with a most splendid façade, and a vast urn on the summit, is accessible through a long and tortuous ravine, by a path five or six feet broad, and steps cut in the stone with immense exertion; is surrounded by ruins, covered with inscriptions in the Sinaitic character, crosses, and figures of the wild goat or ibex, indicating its sacred character; but rather modern in effect." See *Kitto; Ayre;* Kalisch's *Commentary on Old Testament, Genesis*, pp. 479, 480; also, specially, Stanley's *Sinai and Palestine*, pp. 88–92.

Se'la-Ham'mahle'koth, *cliff of escapes* or *of divisions*, a rock in the wilderness of Maon, the scene of one of those remarkable escapes which are so frequent in the history of Saul's pursuit of David, 1 Sam. xxiii, 28. Unknown.

Seleu'cia, (classical, *Seleuci'a,*) (Maps 1, 8,) a town on the Mediterranean, about five miles north of the mouth of the Orontes, and sixteen west of Antioch, of which it was the port, 1 Macc. xi, 8. It also bore the name of Seleucia Picria, from the neighboring Mount Pierus, and also Seleucia ad Mare, in order to distinguish it from several other cities of the same name, all of them denominated from Seleucus Nicator. From this port Paul and

Barnabas embarked for Cyprus, Acts xiii, 4. Some ruins of Seleucia are found by the modern village *Kepse*.

Sena'ah, *thorny,* a place whose inhabitants returned in large numbers from captivity with Zerubbabel, Ezra ii, 35; Neh. vii,38. In Neh. iii, 3, the word occurs with the article—"has-Senaah." Unknown.

Se'neh, *thorn-rock,* a rock in the pass of Michmash, 1 Sam. xiv, 4. The name may also signify "a tooth," and thus might have been applied on account of its pointed top. Several such pointed rocks or crags exist in this wild pass.

Se'nir, *coat of mail,* or *cataract,* the Amorite name for Mount Hermon, 1 Chron. v, 23; Ezek. xxvii, 5. Called also Shenir, Deut. iii, 9; Sol. Song iv, 9. See HERMON.

Se'phar, (Maps 1, 8,) *a numbering, census,* a city or a "mountain of the east" which formed the eastern boundary of the Joktanites, Gen. x, 30. Its site is probably marked by *Zafar* or *el-Beleed,* in the province of *Hadramawt,* on the Indian Ocean. The extent of the ruins here attest the prosperity of the ancient city.

Seph'arad, *separation, boundary* (?). A region to which the exiles from Jerusalem were taken, Obad. xx. Among other conjectures some consider this locality as Spain; others as Sparta; and still others (with most probability) as Sardis in Lydia.

Seph'arva'im, *the two Sipparas,* (one being on each bank of the river,) a city of the Assyrian empire whence colonists were brought into the territory of Israel, afterward called Samaria, 2 Kings xvii, 24; xviii, 34; xix, 13; Isa. xxxvi, 19; xxxvii, 13. Some locate it in Syria; but it is without doubt identical with the celebrated town of Sippara on the east bank of the Euphrates above Babylon, which was near the site of the modern *Mosaib.*

Se'pharvites, 2 Kings xvii, 31. The inhabitants of Sepharvaim.

Sephe'la, 1 Macc. xii, 38. The Greek form of the ancient word *has-Shĕfēlāh,* which in our version is invariably treated as an appellative, and is rendered "vale," "valley," "plain," "low plains," "low country," Deut. i, 7; Josh. ix, 1; x, 40; xi, 2, 16; xii, 8; xv, 33; Judg. i, 9; 1 Kings x, 27; 1 Chron. xxvii, 28; 2 Chron. i, 15; ix, 27; xxvi, 10; xxviii, 18; Jer. xvii, 26; xxxii, 44; xxxiii, 13; Obad. xix; Zech. vii, 7. The Sephela was the low fertile district of Judah, lying between the central hill-country and the Mediterranean. The term Shephelah probably did not originally denote a plain, or, if it did, it was sometimes employed to signify not only the plain, but the hills by which it might be inclosed. Thus of the cities of the Shephelah enumerated in Josh. xv, 33-47, some are in the hilly region at the northern end of the plain, and some in the southern part of the hill-region. See PHILISTIA.

Shaalab'bin, *city of foxes* or *jackals,* a city of Dan, Josh. xix, 42; called also Shaalbim, Judg. i, 35; 1 Kings iv, 9. It lay on the hills not far from Ajalon. The inhabitants found great difficulty in dispossessing the Amorites; but, being at length subdued, the city was included in one of King Solomon's commissariat districts. Its people were possibly called Shaalbonites, 2 Sam. xxiii, 32; 1 Chron. xi, 33.

Shaara'im, *two gates; barley* (?).

1. A city of Judah lying in the Shephelah, near Azekah, 1 Sam xvii, 52; called Sharaim in Josh. xv, 36. Mr. Grove says: "Not known, but probably west of *Shuweikeh* in *Wady es-Sumt.*"

2. In Simeon, 1 Chron. iv, 31. See SHARUHEN and SHILHIM.

Shahaz'imah, *heights*, a border-place in Issachar, apparently between Tabor and the Jordan, Josh. xix, 22.

Sha'lem, (Map 3,) *safe, peaceful*, Gen. xxxiii, 18. Some suppose this term to denote a city, and thus would identify it with the modern *Salim*, east of *Nablûs*, (Shechem.) The best critics, however, prefer to translate the word Shalem, "in peace;" so that the passage would read "Jacob came in peace to the city of Shechem."

Sha'lim, LAND OF, *jackals' region*, 1 Sam. ix, 4. It may be the same as "the land of Shual," 1 Sam. xiii, 17; but neither is known. Conjecture places this tract a few miles north of Michmash.

Shal'isha, LAND OF, *a triad, triangular* (region,) a district bordering on Mount Ephraim, (1 Sam. ix, 4,) in which possibly the city of Baal-Shalisha was situated, 2 Kings iv, 42. Eusebius places this city fifteen Roman miles north of Diospolis, (Lydda.)

Shal'lecheth, *a casting down*, one of the gates of the "House of Jehovah" leading to the "causeway of the ascent," 1 Chron. xxvi, 16. The causeway being still in existence, it is thought highly probable that this gate is identical with the *Bab Silsileh* or *Sinsleh*, which enters the west wall of the *Haram* area about six hundred feet from the south-west corner.

Sha'mir, *a sharp point, a thorn*. 1. A town in the mountains of Judah, Josh. xv, 48. Unknown.

2. A place in Mount Ephraim where Tola lived and was buried, Judg. x, 1, 2. Unknown.

Sha'pher, Mount, (Map 2,) *mount of pleasantness*, a station of the Israelites in the Arabian desert, Num. xxx, 23, 24. Unknown.

Shar'aim. Josh. xv, 36. See SHAARAIM.

Shar'on, (Map 5,) *even, the plain*. In Acts ix, 35, Saron. The maritime lowland tract north of Jaffa (Joppa) extending to Cæsarea, (whence it is frequently in Scripture coupled with Carmel,) and reaching from the central hills to the Mediterranean. It is the northern continuation of the Shephelah. See SEPHELA. It was fertile and well adapted to pasturage, 1 Chron. xxvii, 29; xxxiii, 9; xxxv, 2; Isa. lxv, 10; and celebrated for its roses, Sol. Song. ii, 1. Dr. Thomson, regarding the rose as a species of mallow, says, "I have seen thousands of Solomon's roses on Sharon." The prophet Isaiah, (xxxiii, 9,) in order to show the severity of God's vengeance, exclaims, "Sharon is like a wilderness." All travelers speak of "the luxuriance of its grass and the beauty of its flowers."

In 1 Chron. v, 16, a Sharon is coupled with "Gilead in Bashan," east of the Jordan. Its location is difficult to ascertain. Mr. Stanley (in *S. and P.*, App., § 7) thinks that Sharon may here be a synonym for "the Mishor" of Gilead and Bashan.

Sharu'hen, *pleasant dwelling-place*, a city in Simeon, Josh. xix, 6. See SHAARAIM (2) and SHILHIM.

Sha'veh, *a plain*. A valley, called also "the King's Dale," Gen. xiv, 17; compare 2 Sam. xviii, 18. See KING'S DALE.

Sha'veh Kiriatha'im, *plain of Kiriathaim*, a plain or valley near the city of Kirjathaim in Moab, Gen. xiv, 5. Subsequently it belonged to Reuben, Num. xxxii, 37; Josh. xiii, 19.

She'ba, (Map 12,) *man* (?), or *red* (?).

1. A Cushite people, Gen. x, 7; 1 Chron. i, 9. See SEBA.

2. An Arabian people, descendants of Keturah, Gen. xxv, 3; 1 Chron. i, 32. The same name also occurs in Isa. lx, 6; Jer. vi, 20; Ezek. xxvii, 22, 23; xxviii, 13; but it is uncertain which people is referred to in each case. See the following article.

She'ba, (Map 12,) *man* (?), or *red* (?), a Shemite people, descendants of Joktan, mentioned genealogically in Gen. x, 28; 1 Chron. i, 22. They doubtless inhabited the south of Arabia. The visit of the Queen of Sheba to King Solomon is recorded in 1 Kings x, 1-13; 2 Chron. ix, 1-12; where it is said that "she came to Jerusalem with a very great train, with camels that bare spices, and very much gold, and precious stones." Reference to the same Sheba is made in Psa. lxxii, 15; and probably in Job vi, 19. The other passages which seem to refer to this Joktanite Sheba occur in Isa. lx, 6; Jer. vi, 20; Ezek. xxvii, 22, 23; xxxviii, 13; Matt. xii, 42; Luke xi, 31. The kingdom of Sheba embraced the greater part of the *Yemen*, or Arabia Felix. Its chief cities, and probably successive capitals, were Seba, San'â, (Uzal,) and *Zafâr*, (SEPHAR, which see.) Sheba was long regarded as the most southern country of the habitable earth; it was very wealthy and luxurious, its commerce most extended, and its capital, Seba, (or *Marib,*) a splendid city. Difficulties occur in distinguishing the several tribes which bear the name of Sheba; but for an extended discussion of these the reader must consult larger works.

She'ba, *seven,* or *an oath,* a city in the territory of Simeon, Josh. xix, 2. It occurs between Beersheba and Moladah. In Josh. xv, 26, a Shema is mentioned next to Moladah, which is probably identical with this Sheba. Gesenius suggests that the words in Josh. xix, 2, may be rendered "Beersheba, the town, with Sheba, the well;" but, as Mr. Grove says, "this seems forced, and is, besides, inconsistent with the fact that the list is a list of 'cities.'" Lieut. Conder identifies it with *Tell el Seb'a.*

She'bah, (Map 5,) *seven,* or *an oath,* (feminine,) the name of the well dug by Isaac's servants, and which gave its name to Beersheba, Gen. xxvi, 33. See BEERSHEBA.

She'bam, *coolness,* or *fragrance,* a town on the east of Jordan, Num. xxxii, 3. Not known. Perhaps the same as SHIBMAH and SIBMAH, which see.

Sheb'arim, *breaches, ruins,* a place or spot near Ai, to which the men of Ai chased the Israelites, Josh. vii, 5. Unknown.

She'chem, (Map 5,) *the shoulder-blade; ridge* of heights, a town of the Canaanites; called also Sichem, Gen. xii, 6; Sychar, John iv, 5; and Sychem, Acts vii, 16. From Vespasian it received the name of Neapolis, which it still retains in the Arabic form of *Nablûs.*

Shechem lay in the narrow valley between Mount Ebal and Mount Gerizim, in Samaria, within the tribe of Ephraim, being distant from Jerusalem thirty-four miles north, and from Samaria seven miles south. See Josh. xx, 7; xxi, 20; 1 Kings xii, 25; Judg. ix, 7.

Shechem was a very ancient place. It appears from Gen. xii, 6, at the time of Abraham's visit to the place, that the region, if not the city, was already in possession of the aboriginal race: "The Canaanite was then in the land." At the time of Jacob's arrival here, after his sojourn in Mesopotamia, Shechem was a Hivite city, of which Hamor, the father of Shechem, was the head man, Gen. xxxiii, 18, 19. At this time Jacob bought from this chieftain "the parcel of the field" which he afterward bequeathed as a special patrimony to his son Joseph, Gen. xliii, 22; Josh. xxiv, 32; John iv, 5. The capture of Shechem and the massacre of all the male inhabitants by Simeon and Levi are recorded in Gen. xxxiv. Jacob condemned this bloody act, and reprobated it with his dying breath, Gen. xlix, 5-7. "The oak which was by Shechem," under which Abraham had worshiped, survived to Jacob's time; and there Jacob buried the images which some of his family had brought with them from Padan-Aram. When Joseph came from Hebron to the neighborhood of Shechem and Dothan to look after the welfare of his brethren, he was seized and sold to the Ishmaelites, Gen. xxvii, 12-28. It is an interesting coincidence that Joseph was also buried in Shechem, Josh. xxiv, 32. After the conquest of the land by the Hebrews Shechem fell to the lot of Ephraim, Josh. xx, 7; but it was assigned to the Levites, and became a city of refuge, Josh. xxi, 20, 21; 1 Chron. vi, 67; vii, 28. During the life-time of Joshua it became a center of union to the tribes, Josh. xxiv, 1, 25; probably because it was the nearest considerable town to the residence of that chief in Timnath-Serah. After the death of Gideon, Abimelech, his bastard son, induced the Shechemites to revolt from the Hebrew commonwealth and elect him as king, Judg. ix. In revenge for his expulsion, after a reign of three years, Abimelech destroyed the city, and, as an emblem of the fate to which he would consign it, sowed the ground with salt, Judg. ix, 34-45. It was soon restored, for we find that Rehoboam went thither to be inaugurated king; it was there that, in consequence of his folly, the revolution broke out; and Shechem, fortified by Jeroboam, was at first the seat of the new monarchy, 1 Kings xii, 1-19, 25; 2 Chron. x.

VIEW IN NABLOUS.

Ishmael slew men "from S h e c h e m," Jer. xli, 5. After the return from captivity the city became the center of Samaritan worship. See SAMARITANS; GERIZIM. Jesus visited this place, and remained two days, preaching the word, while many believed on him, John iv, 5, 39-42. In Acts vii, 16, Stephen reminds his hearers that certain of the patriarchs were buried at Sychem. It is an interesting fact, in this connection, that Justin Martyr was born at Shechem. The modern town, which is called *Nablous*, or *Nablûs*, contains about eight thousand inhabitants, but not more than from fifteen to twenty Samaritan families. The streets are narrow; the houses high, and, in general, well built, all of stone,

NABLOUS, (ANCIENT SHECHEM.)

with domes upon the roofs, as at Jerusalem. The bazars are good, and well supplied. There are no ruins which can be called ancient in this vicinity, but there are remains of a church of fine Byzantine architecture, and a handsome arched gateway, both apparently of the time of the first Crusades. Through the whole extent of the main street a stream of clear water rushes down—a rare circumstance in the East. The celebrated MS. of the Samaritan Pentateuch is found in *Nablûs,* guarded with very great care.

All travelers unite in admiration of the scenery about *Nablûs.* Dean Stanley (*S. and P.*, p. 230) says: "A valley, green with grass, gray with olives; gardens sloping down on each side, fresh springs rushing down in all directions; at the end a white town embosomed in all this verdure, lodged between the two high mountains, which extend on each side of the valley—that on the south, Gerizim; that on the north, Ebal—this is the aspect of *Nablûs,* the most beautiful, perhaps the only very beautiful spot in central Palestine."

Nearly two miles to the east lies a small village, *Balâta,* where Joseph's tomb is believed to be; (Josh. xxiv, 32; compare Gen. xlviii, 22;) and, at a little distance south-east, Jacob's well. This well is about seventy-five feet deep. It was one hundred and five feet deep at Maundrell's visit in 1697. It is fast filling up with the stones cast in by travelers and others. The well is perfectly round, nine feet in diameter, excavated in the solid rock, with the sides hewn smooth and regular. Sometimes it contains a few feet of water; but at other times it is quite dry. The tomb "is a little square area inclosed by a white wall, and having a common Moslem tomb placed diagonally across the floor.... There is nothing about it to interest one, or to give evidence of antiquity; yet it is most probably genuine."—Porter's *Hand-book,* p. 327. But from a note on page 237 of Stanley's *Sinai and Palestine* it appears that a later Joseph is also commemorated in this sanctuary.

She'chemites, a family of Gilead, of the tribe of Manasseh, descended from Shechem, Num. xxvi, 31.

Sheep Gate, THE, (Map 9,) one of the ancient gates of Jerusalem, Neh. iii, 1, 32; xii, 39. Its position is very uncertain. It probably stood between the tower of MEAH (which see) and the Prison Gate to the north-east.

Sheep Market, THE, at Jerusalem, John v, 2. "Market" is supplied by the translators, and should probably be "gate," as in the foregoing.

She'lanites, the descendants of Shelah, the youngest son of Judah by the daughter of Shuah, the Canaanite, Num. xxvi, 20.

She'leph, *drawn out, selected,* a Joktanite tribe, Gen. x, 26; 1 Chron. i, 20. They probably inhabited the district of *Sulaf* or *Sulafiyeh,* in South Arabia.

She'ma, *rumor,* a city in the extreme south of Judah, Josh. xv, 26, (compare Josh. xix, 2;) 1 Chron. ii, 43, 44. See SHEBA.

Shen, *tooth,* the place—probably a tooth-shaped rock or peak—between which and Mizpeh Samuel erected the stone called Ebenezer, to commemorate the conquest of the Philistines, and the restoration of the cities to the Israelites, 1 Sam. vii, 12.

She'nir, *coat of mail,* or *cataract,* Deut. iii, 9; Sol. Song iv, 8. See SENIR.

She'pham, *a bare region, spot bare of trees,* a place on the eastern boundary of the Promised Land, the first landmark from Hatser-Enan, at which the northern boundary terminated, and lying between it and Riblah, Num. xxxiv,

10, 11. Mr. Grove (in *Smith*) says: "Mr. Porter would fix Haiser-Enan at *Kuryetein*, seventy miles east-north-east of Damascus. . . . The writer ventures to disagree with this and similar attempts to enlarge the bounds of the Holy Land to an extent for which, in his opinion, there is no warrant in Scripture."

Shephe'lah, The. See SEPHELA.

She'shach, a symbolical name of Babylon, Jer. xxv, 26; li, 41. Its etymology and proper signification are doubtful. Von Bohlen thinks the word synonymous with the Persian "Shih-shah," ("house of the prince.") Some critics think it is written on the cabalistic plan of putting the last letter of the alphabet for the first, the last but one for the second, etc. Thus Sheshach would become Babel or Babylon. According to Sir H. Rawlinson the name of the moon-god, which was identical, or nearly so, with that of the city of Abraham, Ur, (or Hur,) "might have been read in one of the ancient dialects of Babylon as *Shishaki*," hence " a possible explanation of the Sheshach of Scripture."

Shib'mah, *fragrance,* a town east of Jordan, in Reuben, Num. xxxii, 38. See SIBMAH; SHEBAM.

Shi'cron, *drunkenness,* a landmark of the north boundary of Judah, lying between Ekron and Jabneel, Josh. xv, 11. Unknown.

Shi'hon, *a ruin,* a city in Issachar, Josh. xix, 19. Unknown.

Shi'hor OF EGYPT, 1 Chron. xiii, 5. See SIHOR.

Shi'hor-Lib'nath, Josh. xix, 26. One of the landmarks on the boundary of Asher. This is generally considered to be a river. As Libnath means "white," some interpret Shihor-Libnath as "glass river," which they naturally identify with the Belus of Pliny, the present *Nahr Naman*, (on whose banks glass was first made,) which enters the Mediterranean a short distance below *Akka*. Mr. Grove and others think it was not a river at all, and that, if a river, the *Naman* is too far north. Mr. Porter says: "Perhaps the sacred writer may have given this name to some little town upon the banks of one of the streamlets which fall into the Mediterranean between Carmel and Dor. The sand there is white and glistening."

Shil'him, *armed men.* A city in the southern part of Judah, Josh. xv, 32. See SHARUHEN; SHUARAIM. Wilton would connect the word with the idea of waters *sent* or *flowing forth*, and he thinks that some ruins now styled *Khirbet es-Serâm*, close to *el-Birein*, may probably mark the site.

Shilo'ah, THE WATERS OF, Isa. viii, 6. See SILOAH; SILOAM.

Shi'loh, (Map 5,) *place of rest,* peace, a city in Ephraim, lying among the hills to the north of Bethel, and eastward of the great northern road. Here the tabernacle was set up, Josh. xviii, 1; Judg. xxi, 19. To this fact Shiloh owed all its importance, and thus it was the ecclesiastical center where solemn assemblies were held and theocratic acts performed, Josh. xviii, 8–10; xix, 51; xxi, 2; xxii, 12; not, however, to the exclusion of other places, Josh. xxiv, 1, 25, 26. Here remained the tabernacle and the ark from the days of Joshua, during the ministry of all the judges, down to the end of Eli's life, Judg. xx, 18, 26, 27; 1 Sam. i, 3, 9, 24; ii, 14; iii, 21; iv, 3, 4, 12; 1 Kings ii, 27. After the ark was taken from Shiloh by the Philistines it was never returned, and the city is seldom noticed. The tabernacle itself was removed from Shiloh, and Jerusalem became ultimately the Lord's chosen city, 2 Chron. i, 3, 4. The ark was sometimes with the army, 1 Sam. xiv, 18; but its resting place was awhile with Abinadab at Kirjath-Jearim,

1 Sam. vii, 1, 2. Ahijah the prophet resided at Shiloh; but for the idolatry of Israel this once-favored city was forsaken and brought to ruin, Psa. lxxxviii, 60; Jer. vii, 12, 14; xxvi, 6, 9; xli, 5. This last reference shows that it survived the exile.

The place of Shiloh was completely forgotten from the time of Jerome till the year 1838. Its present name is *Seilun.* "Its ruins are scattered over a slight eminence which rises in one of those softer and wider plains . . . noticed as characteristic of this part of Palestine—a little removed from the great central route of the country—its antiquity marked by the ruins of the ancient well, probably the very one by which the 'daughters of Shiloh' danced in the yearly festival, (Judg. xxi, 19, 21, 23,) when the remnant of the neighboring tribe of Benjamin descended from their hills to carry them off, and also by the approach from the East through a valley of rock-hewn sepulchers, some of which, in all probability, must have been the last resting-place of the unfortunate house of Eli. Its selection as the sanctuary may partly have arisen from its comparative seclusion, still more from its central situation."—*Stanley.*

Shi'lonite. 1. A native or inhabitant of Shiloh, 1 Kings xi, 29; xii, 15; xv, 29; 2 Chron. ix, 29; x, 15. 2. The word is used to designate the descendants of Shelah, (1 Chron. ix, 5,) otherwise called Shelanites.

Shim'eathites, a family dwelling at Jabez, who seem to be reckoned among the Kenites, 1 Chron. ii, 55.

Shim'ron, *watch-post,* one of the ancient cities of Canaan, whose king joined with Jabin, King of Hazor, in the attempt to resist the conquests of Joshua, Josh. xi, 1; xix, 15. It is possibly identical with *Simûniyeh,* between Bethlehem and Nazareth. The Shimron-Meron of Josh. xii, 20, is probably the same with Shimron.

Shim'ron-Me'ron. Josh. xii, 20. See SHIMRON.

Shi'nar, (Maps 1, 8,) *casting out* (?), *country of two rivers* (?), the district of country between the Euphrates and Tigris, in which were the cities of Babel, (Babylon,) Erech, (Orchoë,) Calneh, (probably Niffer,) and Accad, Gen. x, 10. It was a plain country where "they had brick for stone, and slime [mud (?), bitumen (?)] used they for mortar," Gen. xi, 2, 3. See also Gen. xiv, 1, 9; Isa. xi, 11; Dan. i, 2; Zech. v, 11. In later times this tract was known as Chaldea or Babylonia.

Shit'tim, *acacias.*

1. A tract of acacias in the Jordan Valley opposite Jericho, the place where the Israelites encamped for the last time before they crossed the river, Num. xxv, 1; compare Mic. vi, 5; Deut. xxxii, 49. From this place Joshua sent spies to spy the land as far as Jericho, Josh. ii, 1. See ABEL-SHITTIM.

2. The "Valley of Shittim" mentioned in Joel iii, 18, was probably west of the Jordan, possibly near to Jerusalem. The reference may simply mean that some dry valley (such as acacias thrive in) shall become well watered.

Sho'a, *opulent,* apparently a district of Assyria, Ezek. xxiii, 23. Some critics explain the word as an appellative used to signify the wealth of the Babylonians. See KOA; PEKOD.

Sho'cho, 2 Chron. xxviii, 18; **Sho'choh,** 1 Sam. xvii, 1; **Sho'co,** 2 Chron. xi, 7. See SOCOH.

Sho'phan, a town in Gad, Num. xxxii, 35. Probably this word is simply an affix to the preceding word. See ATROTH.

Shu'al, a *fox* or *jackal; hollow land* (?). Of the Philistine spoilers who went forth from the garrison at Michmash it is said, "One company turned unto the way of Ophrah, unto the land of Shual," 1 Sam. xiii, 17. If Ophrah lay, as has been suggested, about six miles north-east of Bethel, Shual was probably in the same region. But nothing is known concerning it. See SHALIM.

Shu'hite, from Shuah, a *pit*. A descendant of Shuah, a son of Abraham by Keturah, Job ii, 11; viii, 1; xviii, 1; xxv, 1; xlii, 9. The Shuhites are probably (but not certainly) identical with the Tsukhi, a powerful people located in the Assyrian inscriptions above Hit and on both sides of the Euphrates.

Shu'nem, *two resting-places*, a town in Issachar, where the Philistines encamped before Saul's last battle, Josh. xix, 18; 1 Sam. xxviii, 4. Abishag, David's last wife, belonged to Shunem, 1 Kings i, 3; and "the Shunammite woman" with whom Elisha lodged, 2 Kings iv, 8-37; viii, 1-6. It is identified with *Solam*, three miles north of Jezreel, on the south-west flank of *Jebel Duhy*, (Little Hermon,) in the midst of rich grain fields. No ruins are found.

Shur, (Maps 1, 2,) a *fort* or *wall*, a place apparently east of the Red Sea and not far from it, Gen. xvi, 7; xxi, 1; xxv, 18; 1 Sam. xv, 7; xxvii, 8. The desert extending from the borders of Palestine to Shur is called in Exod. xv, 22, the "wilderness of Shur," but in Num. xxxiii, 8, the "wilderness of Etham." The latter is a *part* of the former. Shur (the station) is probably identical with *'Ayún Músa*, (Moses' Wells,) two hours from Suez. From Ayun Musa an unbroken desert plain extends a three days' journey to *'Ain Hawwarah*, (see MARAH.) The mountains *Er Rahah* and *Et-Tih*, forming a "long wall-like escarpment," doubtless gave to Shur its name—*a wall*.

Shu'shan, (Maps 1, 8, 14,) *a lily*, called by the Greeks Susa; a very celebrated city in the province of Elam or Elymais, a portion of the ancient Susiana, or Cissia. It lay on the banks of the river Choaspes. Susa was one of the most important cities of the East; its foundation is thought to date from a time anterior to Chedorlaomer, as the remains found on the site have often a character of very high antiquity. It seems to have been taken by Asshur-Bani-Pal, who filled the Assyrian throne about 650 B. C. Next we find Susa possessed by the Babylonians, to whom Elam had probably passed at the division of the Assyrian Empire made by Cyaxares and Nabopolassar. In Belshazzar's last year (B. C. 538) Daniel, while still a Babylonian subject, was there on the king's business, and "at Shushan in the palace" had his famous vision of the ram and he-goat, Dan. viii, 1, 2, 27. After the conquest of Babylon by Cyrus, Susa was transferred to the Persian dominion, and it was not long before the city became the capital of the whole empire. It was then the chief residence of the kings during part of the year. It seems probable that this transfer of the capital was effected by Darius Hystaspis, who is found to have been the originator of the great palace there—the building so graphically described in Esther i, 5, 6. It was at Shushan, during the reign of Ahasuerus, that most of the events recorded in the book of Esther occurred. This king is now generally believed to have been identical with Xerxes. Susa retained its pre-eminence until the Macedonian conquest. Here Alexander the Great, after the battle of Arbela, found vast wealth—above twelve millions sterling, and all the regalia of the great king. Alexander's preference for Babylon caused the decline of Susa, and it was never again made the capital city. Antigonus conquered it B. C. 315, and obtained about three million and a half sterling. In B. C. 221 Susa was attacked by Molo in his rebellion against Antiochus the Great;

he took the town, but failed to capture the citadel. In the Arabian conquest of Persia the city was bravely defended by Hormuzan. Being captured by the Mohammedans, 640 A. D., it soon fell into ruins, and its site was for a long period uncertain.

The best geographers now unite in identifying Shushan with the modern *Sus* or *Shush*, a mass of ruins or mounds lying between the *Shapur* and the river of *Dizful*. According to Mr. Loftus, (*Chaldæa and Susiana:*) "The principal existing remains consist of four spacious artificial platforms, distinctly separate from each other. Of these the western mound is the smallest in superficial extent, but considerably the most lofty and important. . . . Its highest point is one hundred and nineteen feet above the level of the *Shaour*, (Shapur.) It is apparently constructed of earth, gravel, and sun-dried brick, sections being exposed in numerous ravines produced by the rains of winter. The measurement round the summit is about two thousand eight hundred and fifty feet. In the center is a deep circular depression, probably a large court, surrounded by elevated piles of buildings, the fall of which has given the present transfiguration to the surface. Here and there are . . . traces of brick walls, which show that the recent elevation of the mound has been attained by much subsequent superposition." This writer supposes this mound to mark the site of the famous citadel of Susa, so often mentioned by ancient writers. At the foot of the mounds is the so-called tomb of Daniel.

Farther to the east are other ruins, probably of the mass of the city, sinking gradually to the level of the plain. Excavations have been made in a large square mound to the north which disclose the remains of an immense structure believed to be the magnificent palace erected by Darius Hystaspis and his successors. No traces are found of the walls of Shushan. Wild beasts and game abound, and the whole place is but a gloomy wilderness.

Sib'mah, *coolness* or *fragrance*, a town on the east of the Jordan assigned to the Reubenites, by whom it was built or fortified, Josh. xiii, 19. It is called also Shebam and Shibmah, Num. xxxii, 3, 38. During the main part of Jewish history, Sibmah, like most of the trans-Jordanic places, disappears. But we hear of it again in the prophets' lament over Moab, Isa. xvi, 8, 9; Jer. xlviii, 32. It was then a Moabite town, famous for the abundance and excellence of its grapes.

Jerome states that Sibmah was very near to Heshbon, and one of the very strong cities of that region. Its site is unknown, but De Saulcy found several nameless ruins in the vicinity of Heshbon.

Sib'raim, *twofold hope*, one of the landmarks on the northern boundary of the Holy Land, Ezek. xlvii, 16. Unknown.

Si'chem, Gen. xiv, 6. See SHECHEM.

Si'cyon, a city lying on the north coast of the Peloponnesus, to the west of Corinth, and capital of the small State, Sicyonia, 1 Macc. xv, 23.

Sid'dim, THE VALE OF, (Map 3.) Siddim is variously interpreted: "the valley of the fields," "a valley filled with rocks and pits," "a plain cut up by stony channels, difficult of transit." The location of the vale is even more a subject of doubt than the meaning of the name. It "was full of slime pits," (Hebrew, "wells, wells of bitumen,") Gen. xiv, 10. It was the battle-field in which the King of Sodom and his allies were vanquished, Gen. xiv, 3, 8, 10. Probably (although it is not stated) Sodom and Gomorrah lay in this vale. The almost universally received opinion has hitherto been that the vale of

Siddim was identical with the present southern end of the Dead Sea, below the peninsula, and that the vale was submerged when "the Lord rained upon Sodom and upon Gomorrah brimstone and fire from the Lord out of heaven," Gen. xix, 24. Recent geological investigations along the shores of the sea have led some eminent scholars to discredit this theory. They think it highly probable that both the vale and the "cities of the plain" lay to the north-west or north of the Dead Sea. Scholars of equal note, however, still maintain that the vale lay south of the sea, that it was submerged, and that scientific research goes far to establish *this* view. See GOMORRAH; SODOM; ZOAR; and especially SEA, SALT.

Si'de, a place mentioned in 1 Macc. xv, 23, among the list of places to which the Roman Senate sent letters in favor of the Jews. It lay on the coast of Pamphylia, and was a city of importance, the ruins of which attest its former wealth. Its present name is *Esky Adalia.*

Si'don, Gen. x, 15, 19; Acts xxvii, 3, etc. See ZIDON.

Sido'nians, Josh. xiii, 4, 6; Judg. iii, 3; 1 Kings v, 6. See ZIDON.

Si'hor, (Maps 1, 2, 12;) accurately Shi'hor, once The Shihor, *black, turbid* river. [See NILE.] Sihor is one of the terms employed in Scripture to designate the great river of Egypt, the Nile, Isa. xxiii, 3; Jer. ii, 18; though it sometimes denotes the smaller "river of Egypt," the modern *Wady el-Arish,* which is the south-western boundary of Canaan, Josh. xiii, 3; 1 Chron. xiii, 5. The Nile is often referred to in the Bible by other terms, as follows: "Yeor," an Egyptian word translated "river" and "flood," which almost always, when in the singular number, denotes the Nile; for example, in Gen. xii, 1; Exod. i, 22; ii, 3; vii, 1, 15, 18; Isa. xxiii, 3; Amos viii, 8. In Dan. xii, 5, 6, 7, this word designates some other river, possibly the Tigris or the Ulai. In the plural, as "brooks of defense," "rivers," "streams," it is always used for the canals of the Nile; Exod. vii, 19; viii, 5; 1 Kings xix, 24; Job xxviii, 10; Psa. lxxviii, 44; Isa. vii, 18; xxxiii, 21; xxxvii, 25; Ezek. xxix, 3, 4, etc. Mr. Poole (in Smith's *Dictionary,* art. *Sihor*) questions the common interpretation of "Yeor," and suggests it to be the extension of the Red Sea. The "River of Egypt" in Gen. xv, 18, is doubtless the Nile. This term also signifies the *Wady el-Arish.* See RIVER OF EGYPT. The "Rivers of Ethiopia" in Isa. xviii, 1, must be the tributaries of the Nile in the upper part of its course. The Egyptians called this river Hapi-Mu, "the genius of the waters." The main stream is the White Nile, *(Bahr-el-Abyad.)* At *Khartoom* it is joined by the Blue Nile, *(Bahr-el-Azrak,)* which rises in the mountains of Abyssinia, and brings down a large quantity of alluvial soil. The *Atbara, (black river,)* which also rises in Abyssinia, joins the Nile at the north point of the island of Meroë. The river flows down over rapids or cataracts, and, entering Egypt, is divided a short distance below Cairo into several branches, which water what is known as the Delta and empty into the Mediterranean. The ancients mention seven of these branches: hence for ages the river was known as the "seven-mouthed Nile."

The allusions to the Nile are very frequent in Scripture. It was by this "river's brink" that Moses was laid in the "ark of bulrushes," Exod. ii, 3. The waters of the river were generally drank by the Egyptians, and considered peculiarly delicious; on this account the plague of turning the water into blood must have been especially grievous, Exod. vii, 20, 21. The destruction of the fish of the Nile (Psa. civ, 29) was also a severe visitation, as is indicated by the Israelites in their murmuring in the wilderness,

THE NILE. THE SPEOS OF IBSAMBOUL—THE CLEARED FRONTS SEEN FROM THE RIGHT BANK.

Num. xi, 5. The prophet denounced judgments against Pharaoh, "the great dragon that lieth in the midst of his rivers," Ezek. xxix, 3. Reference is here made to the crocodile. Various allusions are made also to the inundations of the Nile, Jer. xlvi, 7, 8; Amos viii, 8; ix, 5. The Nile is referred to when the prophet warns Nineveh by the ruins of Thebes, (No-Amon,) Nah. iii, 8.

No mention is made of the Nile in the New Testament; but possibly our Lord in his childhood dwelt by its banks. Tradition says that when Jesus was brought into Egypt his mother came to Heliopolis. See ON.

The great annual phenomenon of the Nile is the inundation, the failure of which produces a famine; for Egypt is virtually without rain, Zech. xiv, 17, 18. The modern Arabic name is *Bahr-en-Neel*, "the river Nile." The Egyptians call it *Bahr*, or "the river;" and the inundation they call *En-Neel*, or "the Nile."

From the time of Herodotus, the first great African traveler, in the fifth century before Christ, the source of the Nile has been sought from time to time with boundless zeal and toil. Among others, "Nero, early in his reign, sent a remarkable exploring party under two centurions, with military force.... Assisted by an Ethiopian sovereign, (Candace, no doubt,) they went through the district now known as Upper Nubia, to a distance of 890 Roman miles from Meroë.... After this Pliny, Strabo, and other Roman authors took notice of this portion of Africa, but without giving us any thing important or new."—*H. M. Stanley.* The more distinguished modern explorers have been Burton, Speke, Grant, Livingstone, and Stanley. On the 30th of July, 1858, Captain Speke discovered the Victoria Nyanza, claiming it as the fountain of the Nile. Four years later, at the close of his second expedition, he thus wri es: "I saw that old Father Nile without any doubt rises in the Victoria Nyanza, and as I had foretold that lake is the great source of the holy river." In 1871–74 M. Stanley made a thorough exploration of Equatorial Africa, fully corroborating Capt. Speke's hypothesis. Stanley says: "Is the Victoria Nyanza one lake, or does it consist of five lakes, as reported by Livingstone, Burton, and others? This problem has been satisfactorily solved, and Speke has now the full glory of having discovered the largest inland sea on the continent of Africa, also its principal affluent, as well as the outlet." Speke's hypothetic sketch made this lake 29,000 square miles in extent. Stanley's survey has reduced it to 21,500 square miles, with a mean level above the sea of 4,168 feet. "How steamers afloat on the lake might cause Ururi to shake hands with Usongora, and Uganda with Usukuma, make the wild Wavuma friends with the Wazinza, and unite the Wakerewé with the Wagana!"

Sil'la, *twig, basket,* the scene of the murder of King Joash, 2 Kings xii, 20. It seems to have been in the valley below Mount Zion.

Silo'ah, THE POOL OF, that is, of Shelach, (*dart*,) Neh. iii, 15. See SILOAM.

Silo'am, (Maps 7, 10,) or Shilo'ah, *sent, a sending,* (as of water.)

1. A pool of water near Jerusalem. In Isa. viii, 6, it is spoken of as running "waters;" in Neh. iii, 15, (Siloah,) and John ix, 7–11, as a "pool." These passages (the only ones in which the word is used as referring to water) give us no clue to the situation of the pool. Josephus, however, who frequently mentions it as a fountain, tells us that it was at the termination or mouth of the Tyropœon.

Siloam is still called by the Arabs *Silwân*. It is a mere suburban tank or reservoir. Its length, according to Robinson, is fifty-three feet, its width eighteen feet, with a depth of nineteen feet. The western end is partly broken away. "The masonry is modern; but along the side are six shafts of limestone, of more ancient date, projecting slightly from the wall, and probably originally intended to sustain a roof."—*Porter.* This reservoir is supplied by an aqueduct with water from a higher source. Subterranean channels have been discovered leading from the city to the fountain of the Virgin, (Map 10,) and thence to the Pool of Siloam. Drs. Robinson and Barclay explored the passage between these two fountains, "sometimes walking erect, sometimes kneeling, and sometimes crawling." According to Robinson this rocky conduit, which twists considerably, is seventeen hundred and fifty feet long. Dr. Barclay, who traced one of the other passages (leading into this one) up near the *Mugrabin* gate, where it became so choked with rubbish that it could be traversed no further, says of it: "I there found it turn to the west, in the direction of the south end of the cleft or saddle of Zion; and if this channel was not constructed for the purpose of conveying to Siloam the surplus waters of Hezekiah's aqueduct, [2 Chron. xxxii, 3, 4,] I am unable to suggest any purpose to which it could have been applied."—*City of the Great King.*

The waters of the "pool" sometimes manifest a kind of ebb and flow, varying with the season and the supply. See OPHEL; JERUSALEM.

2. Mention is made in Luke xiii, 4, of a tower "in Siloam." Historians give us no account of the tower or its fall. It cannot be determined whether it was some fortification near the pool, or whether "in Siloam" refers to the district in the vicinity of the pool. A village now exists east of the Kidron which takes its name from the pool—*Kefr-Silwân*: this may be the place of the tower. The village is not mentioned in ancient times. It is a filthy place, with square hovels huddled together "like the lairs of wild beasts," and "inhabited by a tribe as mean and repulsive as their dwellings." That part of the Mount of Olives on which *Silwân* stands may probably mark the site of the idol-shrines built by Solomon to Chemosh, Ashtoreth, and Milcom. This was the "Mount of Corruption," 2 Kings xxiii, 13, the hill that was before (east of) Jerusalem, 1 Kings xi, 7. But the tradition which makes this identification is of recent date.

Sim'eon, (Map 5,) *a hearkening,* one of the tribes of Israel, descended from Simeon, the second son of Jacob, by Leah, Gen. xxix, 33. At the time of the exodus the tribe numbered 59,300 able-bodied men, Num. i, 23; but before entering Palestine it was reduced to 22,200, Num. xxvi, 14. This immense decrease reduced Simeon from the third rank to the lowest of all in point of numbers. The decrease was doubtless caused by the visitation of the Divine displeasure, probably for crimes committed in the wilderness. See, for example, Num. xxv, 6–8, 14. On the journey this tribe marched and encamped under the standard of Reuben, south of the tabernacle, Num. ii, 12; x, 18, 19.

The assignment of Simeon in the Promised Land was "within the inheritance of the children of Judah," seventeen cities in the south of Palestine spread round the venerable well of Beersheba, Josh. xix, 1–9; 1 Chron. iv, 28–33. With Judah's help the Simeonites gained possession of these places, Judg. i, 3, 17; and here they were found, doubtless, by Joab in the reign of David, 1 Chron. iv, 31. At David's installation at Hebron, 7,100 Simeonite warriors were present, 1 Chron. xii, 23–37. The tribe was not able to hold all its towns. Hormah and Beersheba, noted as belonging to it, were afterward possessed by Judah, 1 Sam. xxx, 30; 1 Kings xix, 3. Ziklag be-

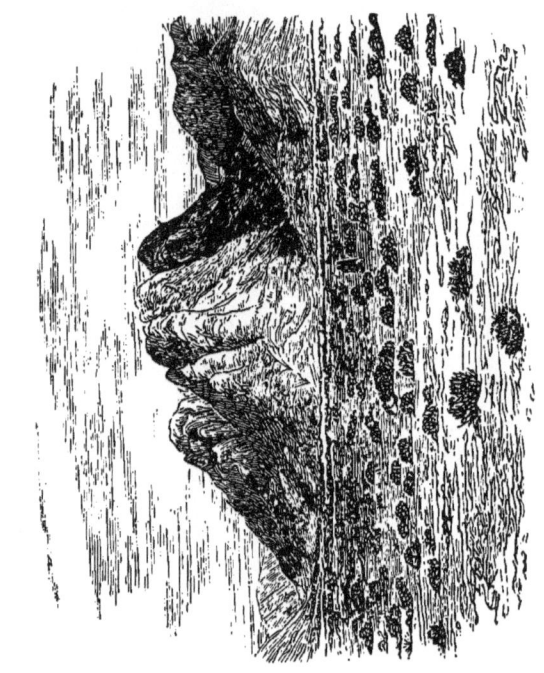

THE RAS SUFSAFEH FROM THE PLAIN OF ER RAHAH.

came first a Philistine, then a Judean, city, 1 Sam. xxvii, 6; and subsequently the Simeonites seem to have been well nigh absorbed in Judah, 2 Chron. xv, 9. The warlike spirit of their progenitor seemed to revive in the tribe, when, rousing themselves, they went forth in two expeditions in search of more eligible territory, 1 Chron. iv, 34–43. In the second expedition, which was against the Amalekites, they were successful, and took possession of the quarters of the remnant of Amalek in the distant fastnesses of Mount Seir. Simeon is mentioned in the catalogues of the restoration after the captivity, Ezek. xlviii, 24, 25; Rev. vii, 7. (Compare Judith vi, 15; ix, 2.)

Sim'eonites. Num. xxv, 14; xxvi, 14; 1 Chron. xxvii, 16. See SIMEON.

Sin, (Map 2,) *mire, clay,* a city of Egypt, called by the Greeks Pelusium. It is mentioned in Ezek. xxx, 15, 16, as "Sin, the stronghold of Egypt." Pelusium was anciently a place of great importance. It lay among the swamps and morasses on the most easterly estuary of the Nile, and stood about two or three miles from the sea. The site is now approachable only by boats during a high Nile, or by land when the summer sun has dried the mud left by the inundation. Some ruins, consisting of mounds and a few fallen columns, at *et-Tineh* or *el-Furma,* are generally supposed to mark the site, but the identification cannot be wholly established.

Sin, WILDERNESS OF, (Map 2,) between the "Red Sea" and Rephidim or Dophkah, Exod. xvi, 1; xvii, 1; Num. xxxiii, 11, 12. Here the manna was first gathered. It is probably the narrow strip of desert which fringes the coast south of *Wady Taiyebeh.* (See Palmer's *Desert of the Exodus,* pp. 274, 275.)

Si'na, MOUNT, Judith vii, 14; Acts vii, 30, 38. The Greek form of Sinai

Si'nai, (Map 2,) *bush of the Lord,* the mountain from which the law was given. This name seems to have been nearly supplanted by Horeb after the forty years' wandering; compare Exod. xx, with Deut. v; Exod. xix, 16–19, with Deut. iv, 10–13. The mention of Horeb in later books, as in 1 Kings viii, 9, and xix, 8, seems to show that it had then become the designation of the mountain and region generally. Yet later, as in Neh. ix, 13, reference is still made to Sinai. Horeb may have been the name of the mountain group, while Sinai denoted a single peak. The Sinaitic mountains lie nearly in the center of the peninsula which is embraced between the two arms of the Red Sea, Exod. xvi, 1; Deut. i, 2.

The Israelites encamped before Sinai, and "Moses went up unto God," Exod. xix, 1, 2, 3, 20. Here God spake all the words of the law amid "the thunderings, and the lightnings, and the noise of the trumpet, and the mountain smoking," Exod. xx, 1–18. Moses ascended the mount again, taking unto him "Aaron, Nadab, and Abihu, and seventy of the elders of Israel," Exod. xxiv, 1, 2, 9–11. Moses and Joshua also went up, Exod. xxiv, 12, 13, 15, 18; xxxii, 15, 17. Again Moses went alone "early in the morning" to the mount, Exod. xxxiv, 2, 4, and was vouchsafed that wonderful revelation in the covenant of the Almighty, as recorded in Exod. xxxiv, 5–27. Moses remained "there with the Lord forty days and forty nights," and when he came down "his face shone, and they were afraid to come nigh him," Exod. xxxiv, 29–31. The people were forbidden to approach the mount, or even to "touch the border of it," Exod. xix, 12, 13, 21–24; xxxiv, 3; Heb. xii, 20. The clouds, darkness, lightnings, and thunders on Sinai are frequently alluded to, Exod. xix, 9, 16–19; xx, 18, xxiv, 15–17; Deut. xxxiii, 2; Judg. v, 5; Psa. lxviii, 8, 17; Heb. xii, 18–21; (Horeb) Deut. iv, 10–13, 33, 36; v, 4. The giving of the law on Sinai is referred to in various parts of the Scriptures, Exod. xx, 31, 18; Lev. vii, 38; xxv, 1; xxvi, 46; xxvii, 34; Num. iii, 1; xxviii, 6; Neh. ix, 13; Acts vii, 30, 38; (Horeb) Deut. iv, 15; v, 2–6; xxix, 1; 1 Kings viii, 9; Mal. iv, 4.

Horeb was called the mountain of God, and there, in a burning bush, Moses saw the angel of the Lord when God called to him and declared that he should deliver Israel from Egypt, Exod. iii, 1–10. It was from a smitten rock in Horeb that water miraculously flowed, Exod. xvii, 6. On Horeb also the Israelites worshiped the golden calf, Exod. xxxiii, 6; Deut. ix, 8. Elijah fled to Horeb when threatened by Jezebel, 1 Kings xix, 8.

As to which is the particular peak of this mountain region whereon the Lord "descended in fire," while the people "stood at the nether part of the mount," much difference of opinion exists. There are three claimants for the name of Sinai. 1. *Mount Serbâl*, 6,720 feet high. Of this Mr. Porter (in *Kitto*) says: "The nature of the country around *Serbâl* is sufficient of itself to show that it could not possibly have been Sinai. . . . *Wady Alyât*, which leads up to *Serbâl*, is narrow, rugged, and rocky, affording no place for a large camp, . . . and, as there is no other valley or plain at the base of the mountain, it follows that *Serbâl* cannot be Sinai." 2. *Jebel Mûsa* (Mount of Moses) is the Sinai of recent ecclesiastical tradition. Its height is about 7,363 feet. It presents some strong claims, according to a few modern travelers. It lies in the very center of the mountain group, "but it is neither so lofty nor so commanding as some of the peaks around it." Moreover, as in the case of *Serbâl*, above, there is no spot sufficiently extensive for the people to encamp upon. Of the spot claimed for the camping place, *Wady es Sebayeh*, Mr. Stanley (*Sinai and Palestine*, p. 76) says: "It is rough, uneven, narrow . . . the mountain never descends upon the plain." 3. *Ras es-Sufsâfeh*, 6,830 feet, the highest point of a range of magnificent cliffs, on the north-western point of the ridge of which *Jebel Mûsa* is the south-eastern. This peak overlooks the plain of *er-Râhah*, measuring more than two miles in length, and ranging from one third to two thirds of a mile in breadth. Travelers give graphic accounts of the view from the peak in question. Dean Stanley says: "The effect on us, as on every one who has seen and described it, was instantaneous. It was like the seat on the top of *Serbâl*, but with the difference that here was the deep, wide, yellow plain sweeping down to the very base of the cliffs, exactly answering to the plain on which the people 'removed and stood afar off.'" Dr. Durbin (*Observations in the East*) says: "When we . . . cast our eyes over the plain we were more than repaid for all our toil. One glance was enough. We were satisfied that here and here only could the wondrous displays of Sinai have been visible to the assembled hosts of Israel; that here the Lord spoke with Moses; that here was the mount that trembled and smoked in the presence of its manifested Creator!"

The explorations by Prof. Palmer (1868–1869) are the most valuable of any that have been made. Of the rival mountains, Jebel Músa and Serbal, a special survey was made on a scale of six inches to the mile. Palmer claims *Rás Sufsáfeh* to be "Mount Sinai itself, the very mountain, in all probability, upon which 'the glory of the Lord rested in the sight of all the people.' A stately, awful-looking, isolated mass it is, rearing its giant brow above the plain. . . . At the base of the bluff is a long semicircular mound,

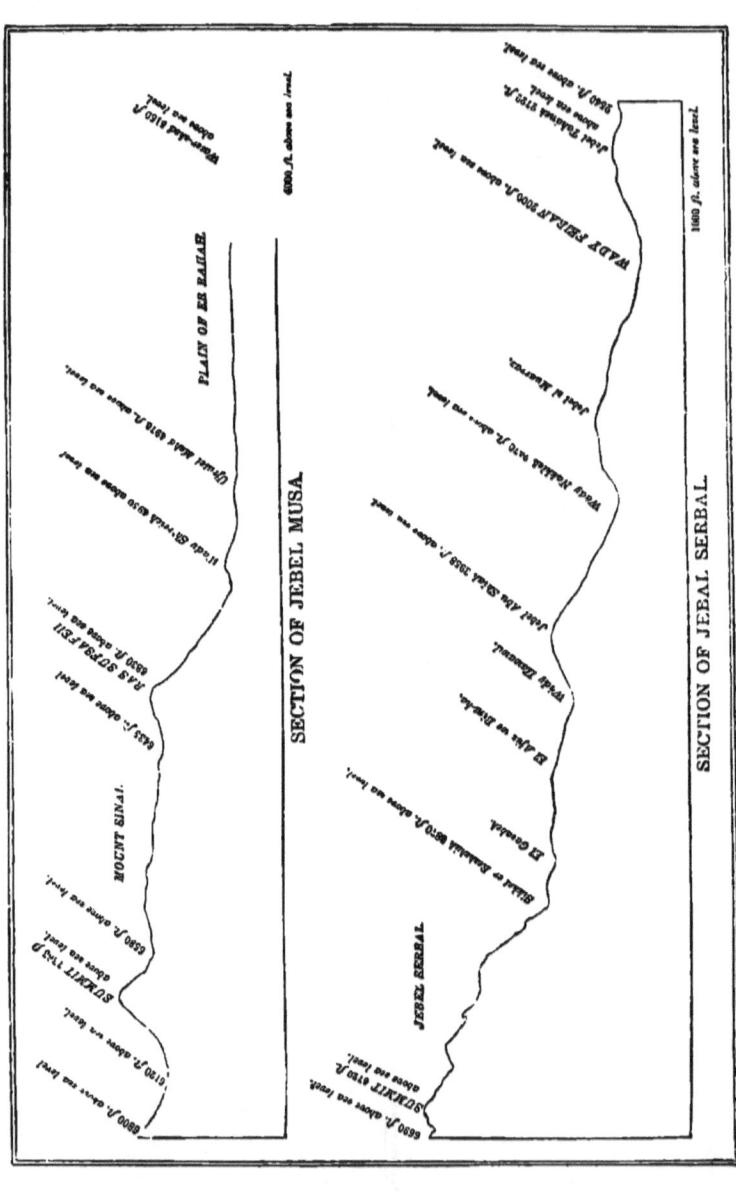

SECTIONS OF JEBEL MUSA AND JEBEL SERBAL.

forming a sort of amphitheater, from which a select congregation of elders might obtain a nearer view of the mountain. The full proportions of the Rás Sufsáfeh are best seen from the approach by the great plain of Er Ráhah."—*Desert of the Exodus.* Palmer holds that Jebel Musa was probably the scene of the *delivery* of the law to Moses, while from Sufsáfeh the law was *proclaimed* to the people. He says: "This indeed seems almost implied in the words of the Bible. . . . [See Exod. xix. 20.] First, there is the awful descent of the Lord in thunder and fire upon the mountain in the sight of the assembled host; then Moses is called up to the secluded summit to receive the words of the law from God's own mouth, and again he is sent down to proclaim them to the people." A calculation made by Captain Palmer, from measurements taken on the spot, proves that the plain of Er Rahah, in "the space extending from the base of the mountain to the water-shed or crest of the plain, is large enough to have accommodated . . . two million souls, with an allowance of a square yard for each individual."

In the wild ravine under the northern brow of Sinai exists the famous Convent of Mount Sinai. Tradition ascribes its erection to the piety of the Emperor Justinian, A. D. 527. The walls exhibit the motley patchwork of various ages from that period till the time of Napoleon. The space inclosed is cut up into a number of little courts and passages, bewildering in their irregularity. Mr. Porter (*Hand-book,* p. 27) says of the convent: "A day may be well spent in wandering amid the labyrinth of buildings, viewing the curiosities of the old church and its chapels, visiting the tomb and relics of the patron saint, contemplating the grim horrors of the charnel-house, and lounging beneath the delicious shade of garden bowers; such a day's comparative rest, too, prepares one for the fatiguing excursions to the Mountain of the Law, and the various spots of interest round it." It was in the library of this convent that Tischendorf discovered the now very celebrated *Codex Sinaiticus,* the only complete uncial MS. of the New Testament we possess, and one of the oldest and most valuable. Other manuscripts are within the convent, but very few travelers have been permitted to inspect the literary treasures in the care of the old monks. Professor Palmer thus writes from the convent, December 31, 1869, (see *Palestine Exploration Fund, Statement,* March, 1870:) "We have succeeded in gaining admittance to the Archbishop's apartments, in which the most valuable part of the MS. treasures are kept, and have inspected some of the most important ones. The wellknown Codex Aureus is a beautifully written copy of the four Gospels, containing illuminated portraits of the evangelists and other sacred personages. It is attributed to the Emperor Theodosius, the colophon giving the date and transcriber's name in the abbreviated uncial characters. . . . There are other very interesting works in the collection, among them an ancient copy of the Psalms in Georgian, written on papyrus, and a curious copy of the Psalms, written in a small female hand in six small pages without a date."

Si'nim. Isa. xlix, 12. The Chinese are probably intended. A dynasty called *Tshin* reigned in China 249 to 206 B. C.

Sin'ite, a Canaanite people, Gen. x, 17; 1 Chron. i, 15; probably located near Mount Lebanon. As late as the fifteenth century a village called *Syn* still existed near the river Arca; this may have been the seat of the Sinites.

Si'on, *lofty.*

1. A name (perhaps the ancient name) of Mount Hermon, Deut. iv, 48.

2. The Greek form of Zion, Matt. **xxi**, 5; John xii, 15, etc.; and frequently in the Apocryphal books. See ZION.

Siph'moth, *bare places,* a town in the south of Judah to which presents were sent by David, 1 Sam. xxx, 28. Unknown.

Si'rah, *retreat,* the name of a well—the spot from which Abner was recalled by Joab to his death at Hebron, 2 Sam. iii, 26. It lay apparently north of Hebron. About one mile out of Hebron there is a spring and reservoir called *Ain Sara,* which may be a relic of the well.

Sir'ion, *breastplate,* the Sidonian name for Mount Hermon, given, perhaps, from a fancied resemblance to a breastplate, Deut. iii, 9; Psa. xxix, 6.

Sit'nah, *accusation, hatred,* the second of Isaac's wells. The herdmen of Gerar strove for it, and therefore Isaac removed, Gen. xxvi, 21. Identified with *Shutneh,* between Rehoboth and Beersheba.

Smyr'na, (Map 8,) *myrrh,* a celebrated city of Ionia, situated about forty miles north of Ephesus, at the mouth of the small river Meles. Having been destroyed by the Lydians, it lay waste for four hundred years, until Alexander, or Antigonus after the great conqueror's death, rebuilt it, at a short distance from the ancient site. During the reign of the first Roman emperors Smyrna was one of the finest cities of Asia. At this period it became the seat of one of "the seven churches of Asia," Rev. i, 11; ii, 8–11. Some of St. John's expressions in these passages seem to refer to rites practiced by pagan inhabitants of the city. Smyrna was destroyed by an earthquake in A. D. 177, and, although rebuilt with more than its former splendor, it has since greatly suffered from earthquakes and conflagrations.

The Turks now call the city *Ismir.* The population is computed at from 120,000 to 130,000. Anciently Smyrna was called "the lovely—the crown of Ionia—the ornament of Asia." Possibly the modern town, whose houses of wood are giving way in all directions to mansions of stone, may yet represent the ancient city.

So'cho, *branches, hedge,* 1 Chron. iv, 18. Probably Socoh of Judah

So'choh, *branches, hedge,* 1 Kings iv, 10. See SOCOH.

So'coh, (Map 13,) *branches, hedge.*

1. A city in the low country (Shephelah) of Judah, Josh. xv, 35; also with the forms of Shoco, 2 Chron. xi, 7; Shocho, 2 Chron. xxviii, 18; and Shochoh, 1 Sam. xvii, 1. This was the place where the Philistines were gathered for the campaign in which Goliath was slain. In 1 Kings iv, 10, it is mentioned (Sochoh) as included in one of Solomon's commissariat districts. It was fortified by Rehoboam, but seized by the Philistines in the reign of Ahaz, 2 Chron. xi, 7; xxviii, 18. It has been identified with the ruins of *Esh-Shuweikeh,* in the *Wady Sumt,* about $3\frac{1}{2}$ miles south-west of Jerusalem.

2. A town also in Judah, but in the mountains, Josh. xv, 48. It is identified with *Esh-Shuweikeh,* ten miles south-west of Hebron.

Sod'om, (Map 3,) (Hebrew, S'dom.) The most probable signification is *burning, conflagration,* or *vineyard,* but the etymology still remains very obscure. The Bible does not definitely locate Sodom. It was in the "plain of Jordan," Gen. xiii, 10, and was first mentioned in describing the borders of the Canaanites, Gen. x, 19. Lot first pitched his tent close by Sodom, in the plain that was "well watered . . . as the garden of the Lord," Gen. xiii, 10–13. At a later period he dwelt in the city. Sodom was plundered by Chedorlaomer and his associates, but the captives and booty were recovered by Abraham, Gen. xiv. The great sinfulness of this city, together with its singular and fearful overthrow, are recorded in Gen. xviii, 16-38; xix, 1-29. Sodom is frequently afterward referred to by Moses, by the prophets, and the New Testament writers, and held up as a warning of the terrible vengeance of God upon sinners, Deut. xxix, 23; xxxii, 32; Isa. i, 9, 10; ii, 9; xiii, 19; Jer. xxiii, 14; xlix, 18; l, 40; Lam. iv, 6; Ezek. xvi, 49, 50; Hosea xi, 8; Amos iv, 11; Zeph. ii, 9; Matt. x, 15; xi, 23, 24; 2 Peter ii, 6-8; Jude 7; Rev. xi, 8.

The testimony of ancient writers concerning the site of Sodom is conflicting. By some it is regarded as having been engulfed by the waters of the Dead Sea; by others it is located on the shore. They agree, however, in locating it at the southern end of the Dead Sea. This has always been the generally received opinion. Recently a number of able critics have maintained that Sodom and the rest of the cities of the plain of Jordan stood on the *north* of the Dead Sea, and that neither the cities nor the district were submerged by the lake, but that the cities were overthrown and the land spoiled, and that the land may still be seen in its desolate condition. Mr. Grove, who strongly favors the northern site for Sodom, remarking that no satisfactory conclusion concerning the location can be reached, adds: "How the geological argument may affect either side of the proposition cannot be decided in the present condition of our knowledge." Dr. J. L. Porter, one of the ablest advocates for the location of Sodom toward the south end of the sea, remarks: "The most careful survey of the shores of the Dead Sea has failed to bring to light a single vestige of Sodom. It is in the highest degree probable that the city stood somewhere near the range of *Khashm Usdum*, [Sodom,] and gave to it the name which it has handed down to our own day. But whether the site was on the shore and has been completely obliterated by the action of the fiery shower and the lapse of well-nigh four thousand years, or whether the waters of the Dead Sea, as they covered the vale of Siddim, covered also the scathed ruins of Sodom, it is now, and probably ever will be, impossible satisfactorily to determine." See SEA, SALT, SIDDIM; ZOAR.

Sod'oma, Rom. ix, 29, the Greek form of Sodom.

Sod'omite. In 2 Esdras vii, 36, this word denotes an inhabitant of Sodom. But in the Bible it refers to those (males) who practiced as a religious rite the abominable and unnatural vice from which the inhabitants of Sodom and Gomorrah have derived their lasting infamy. See Deut. xxiii, 17; 1 Kings xiv, 24; xv, 12; xxii, 46; 2 Kings xxiii, 7; Job xxvi, 14, (margin.) The female form occurs in Gen. xxxviii, 21, 22; Deut. xxxiii, 17; Hosea iv, 14.

Sod'omitish Sea. 2 Esdr. v, 7. The Dead Sea.

Sol'omon's Pools, (Map 6,) three in number, lie in a narrow valley a few miles south-west of Bethlehem on the road to Hebron. The Arabs call them *el-Burak*, "the pools." In the valley, which falls away eastward, is a large castellated Saracenic building called *Kasr-el-Burak*. This castle stands near the north-west corner of the upper pool. The pools, or tanks, are each on a different level, some distance apart, as indicated in the accompanying cut. The native rock forms the bed. The walls are built of large hewn stones. As seen from without they appear as massive structures built up above the ground, the upper, or western end of each being slightly higher than the eastern. The bottom and sides have been carefully coated with cement. In various places flights of steps lead down into the pools. A large fount-

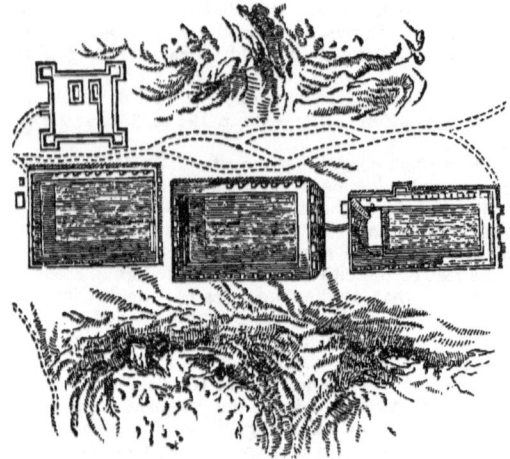

ain not far from the north-west corner of the upper pool is the main source of supply. The waters gathered from the surrounding country into this fountain are thence conducted by an underground passage to the pools. From the pools a conduit carries off the water, until it finally enters the south-west corner of the temple area at Jerusalem. Although these gigantic structures are not mentioned in Scripture, yet we may safely trace them to Solomon's time. Compare Eccles. ii, 4–6. The fountain noted above is, according to tradition, referred to in Sol. Song, iv, 12, as the "spring shut up, the fountain sealed." The following are the measurements of the pools as taken by Dr. Robinson in 1838:

1. *Eastern or lower pool.* Length, 582 feet. Breadth, east end, 207 feet, west end, 148 feet. Depth at east end, 50 feet, of which 6 feet water. Dr. Thomson says: "When full it would float the largest man-of-war that ever plowed the ocean."

2. *Middle pool.* Distance above lower pool, 248 feet. Length, 423 feet. Breadth, east end, 250 feet, west end, 160 feet. Depth at east end 39 feet, of which 14 feet water.

3. *Upper pool.* Distance above middle pool, 160 feet. Length, 380 feet. Breadth, east end, 236 feet, west end, 229 feet. Depth at east end, 25 feet, of which 15 feet water.

Sol'omon's Porch, or **Cloister,** John x, 23; Acts iii, 11; v, 12. The range of pillars on the east side of the outer court of the temple.

So'rek, (Map 5,) *choice vine,* a valley where lived a woman whom Samson loved—Delilah, Judg. xvi, 4. It was doubtless to the north of Eleutheropolis, not far from Zorah, the native place of Samson.

South Ra'moth, 1 Sam. xxx, 27. See RAMATH-NEGEB.

Spain, (Map 12,) the well-known country of Europe. Anciently the name was applied to the whole peninsula which now comprises Spain and Portugal. It is alluded to in 1 Macc. viii, 3, in describing the conquest of the Romans. With the position and mineral wealth of Spain the Hebrews were acquainted from the time of Solomon. This province belonged to Rome in the time of Paul, and many Jews appear to have settled there. The great apostle announced his intention of visiting Spain, Rom. xv, 24, 28; but it is uncertain whether he ever accomplished his design. Many oriental customs still exist in this country. See TARSHISH.

Spar'ta, (Map 8,) 1 Macc. xiv, 16. A celebrated city of Greece, between whose inhabitants and the Jews a relationship was believed to subsist. Between the two nations a correspondence ensued.

Suc'coth, (Maps 2, 5,) *booths.*

1. A place, probably on the east of the Jordan, in the tribe of Gad, where Jacob, after his interview with Esau, constructed a habitation for himself and made booths for his cattle, Gen. xxxiii, 17; Josh. xiii, 27. The inhabitants of Succoth churlishly refused assistance to Gideon when pursuing the Midianites, for which on his triumphant return they were severely punished, Judg. viii, 5–8, 14–16. The place is mentioned in 1 Kings vii, 46, and 2 Chron. iv, 17, as marking the spot at which the brass founderies were placed for casting the metal-work of the temple. It is also alluded to in Psa. lx, 6; cviii, 7.

The ruins of a place called *Sukkot* were discovered by Burckhardt, which from his narrative appear to have been east of the Jordan; but, being about six miles south of Bethshan, they seem too far north for the account in Genesis. Dr. Robinson and Van de Velde discovered another ruin called *Sâkût,* on the west bank of the Jordan, about ten to fifteen miles south of *Beisan.* Mr. Porter says: "Its position on the west bank prevents its being identified with the Succoth of the Bible, but it is just possible that the name may have been transferred from the ancient town on the east side to a more modern village on the west."

2. The first camping-place of the Israelites on their departure from Egypt, Exod. xii, 37; xiii, 20; Num. xxxiii, 5, 6. Its exact position has not been satisfactorily determined.

Sud, Bar. i, 4. A river near to Babylon on whose banks lived Jewish captives. Possibly the Euphrates.

Suk'kiims, *dwellers in tents,* one of the three great nations which composed the army of Shishak, King of Egypt, when he came up against Rehoboam in Jerusalem, 2 Chron. xii, 3. It seems probable that these were a nomad people, and more probably an Arab tribe than Ethiopians.

Sur, a place on the sea-coast of Palestine, Judith ii, 28. Unknown.

Su'sa, Rest of Esther xi, 3; xvi, 18. See SHUSHAN.

Su'sanchites. Ezra iv, 9. The people of Susa or Shushan.

Sy'char, *falsehood*(?), *drunken*(?). The common opinion is that Sychar is but another name for the better known Sychem or Shechem. Dr. Robinson says: "In consequence of the hatred which existed between the Jews and the Samaritans, and in allusion to their idolatry, the towns of Sichem received, among the Jewish common people, the by-name Sychar," John iv, 5. But Dr. Thomson supposes that Sychar is identical with the little village of *Aschar,* on the south-eastern declivity of Mount Ebal.

Sy'chem, Acts vii, 16, the Greek form of Shechem.

Sy'chemite, Judith v, 16. The people of Sychem.

Sye'ne, (Map 1,) *opening* or *key,* (of Egypt,) a city of Egypt, in the southern extremity, on the eastern bank of the Nile. Its ancient Egyptian name was SUN, that is, "opening" (into Egypt.) The prophet speaks of the desolation of Egypt "from Migdol to Syene," Ezek. xxix, 10, margin; xxx, 6, margin.

The modern town of *Aswan,* or *Assouan,* lying a little to the north-east of the old city, represents Syene. A few remains of the ancient city are still found. There are also Arab and Roman ruins.

Syr'acuse, (Map 8,) a celebrated city on the south-east coast of Sicily.

The extensive trade of Syracuse, carried on while an independent State under its own kings, rendered it very wealthy and populous. About B. C. 200 it was taken by the Romans, after a siege rendered famous by the mechanical contrivances whereby Archimedes protracted the defense. On his way to Rome as a prisoner St. Paul spent three days here, Acts xxviii, 12. The city still exists under the name of *Syracusa.* It is a place of some importance, and a few ruins of the ancient city yet remain.

Syr'ia, (Maps 1, 5, 12,) the region of country known to the Hebrews as Aram. The name Syria is probably derived from *Tsur,* or Tyre, the first of the Syrian towns known to the Greeks. Hence Syria would signify the "region of Tyre."

The extent of Syria is not easily determined. Aram extended from the Mediterranean to the Tigris, and from Canaan to Mount Taurus. The Greek geographers gave a much wider signification to Syria, extending it on the one side to Egypt and on the other to the Euxine; but it is doubtful if they were ever agreed as to its exact boundaries. In New Testament times Syria seems to have nearly corresponded with the more ancient Aram. Its boundaries may be given as follows: Palestine on the south, the Mediterranean on the west, Cilicia and Mount Amanus on the north, the Euphrates and Desert of Palmyra on the east. Thus its length was nearly three hundred miles from north to south, with an average breadth of about one hundred and thirty miles. Syria is generally mountainous. Lebanon is the most interesting of its mountain ranges. [See LEBANON.] The most important part of Syria, and on the whole its most striking feature, is the great valley which reaches from the plain of *Umk,* near Antioch, to the narrow gorge in which the river Litany enters in about lat. 33° 30'. Its more southern part was known to the ancients as Cœle-Syria, "the Hollow Syria." See CŒLE-SYRIA. This valley, and especially its southern part, is the most fertile tract of Syria. The region on the coast is hot, and is said to be unwholesome. In the great Syrian desert stretching to the east are some fertile oases, in the most noted of which is Palmyra.

Syria was colonized by the Canaanites and the Arameans. The former settled on the coast and on the heights of Lebanon, and had one inland station at Hamath. The latter occupied Damascus and spread over the remaining portions of the country, Gen. x. When we first hear of Syria in Scripture it seems to have been broken up among a number of petty kingdoms. Joshua doubtless made war often with the Syrian chiefs or kings, Josh. xi, 2–18; but afterward the Syrians were probably undisturbed till the time of David. In 2 Sam. viii, we have the account of David's victory over the "king of Zobah" and "the Syrians of Damascus." A few years later David reduced Syria to general submission, 2 Sam. x, 6–19. The country continued subject to Solomon, who "reigned over all the kingdoms from the river (Euphrates) unto the land of the Philistines and unto the border of Egypt," 1 Kings iv, 21. Afterward, probably in the later days of Solomon, an independent kingdom was formed at Damascus, 1 Kings xi, 23–25. Damascus was now the leading State, and a succession of its kings became formidable to Israel, sometimes being in alliance with the southern State of Judah. See 1 Kings xv, 18–20; xx; xxii, 1–38; 2 Kings vi, 8–33; vii; ix, 14, 15, x, 32, 33; xiii, 3, 14–25. In the reign of Jeroboam II. Israel had some success against the Syrians, 2 Kings xiv, 27, 28. Finally the king of Syria leagued with the king of Israel to overthrow Judah, but Ahaz invoked the aid of the king of Assyria, and the struggle resulted in attaching Syria to the great Assyrian empire. Thence Syria passed successively under the dominion of the Babylonians and the Persians, and, at last, in B. C. 333, it submitted to the conquering legions of Alexander the Great. After his death it fell with other territories to one of his generals, Seleucus Nicator, who founded Antioch 300 B. C., and made it the capital of a great kingdom. The wealth and magnificence of Antioch were extraordinary—it being in fact the most splendid of all the cities of the East. A long line of kings, with more or less success, maintained the dominion of Syria. Of these Antiochus Epiphanes was the most cruel oppressor of the Jews. The latter, however, by the valor of the Asmonean princes, established their independence. At length the wealth of Syria being dissipated—in costly wars, in bribes to Rome, in the wastefulness of luxurious kings—it became a Roman province, B. C. 64. Still, however, under the Romans, there were free cities, and petty sovereignties assigned from time to time to subject princes, such as Chalcis, Abilene, Damascus, and others. Palmyra maintained its independence so late as between A. D. 114 and A. D. 116. Sometimes Judea was attached to Syria, its procurator being subordinate to the president or governor of Syria. St. Paul's visits to the Churches in Syria are several times mentioned, Acts xv, 41; xviii, 18; xxi, 3; Gal. i, 21. In connection with the above history we see the fulfillment of prophecy; Isa. vii, 8-16; viii, 4-7; xvii, 1-3; Jer. xlix, 23-27; Amos i, 3-5; Zech. ix, 1. Syria remained under Roman and Byzantine rule till A. D. 634, when it was overrun by the Mohammedans under Khaled. For many years this country was the theater of fierce contests, and at length, in A. D. 1517, it was captured by the Turks under Sultan Selim I., and it has since remained a portion of the Ottoman empire.

Syr'ia-Ma'achah. 1 Chron. xix, 6. See ARAM; MAACHAH.

Syr'ian, Syr'ians, *people of a high region.* The inhabitants of Syria, Gen. xxv, 20; Deut. xxvi, 5; 2 Sam. viii, 5, 6, 13; 1 Kings xx, 20; 2 Kings v, 2, 20; Ezra iv, 7; Isa. ix, 12; Amos ix, 7; Matt. iv, 24; Luke iv, 27, etc.

Sy'ro-Phœnic'ian. This term is employed to distinguish the Phœnicians of Syria from those of Africa, (the Carthagenians.) The woman described in Mark vii, 26, as Syro-Phœnician, is called in Matt. xv, 22, a Canaanitish woman, because Phœnicia was still occupied by the descendants of Canaan, of whom Sidon was the eldest son.

Ta'anach, (Map 5,) *sandy soil;* in Josh. xxi, 25, Tanach, a royal city of the Canaanites, whose king Joshua destroyed, Josh. xii, 21. It was in the territory of Issachar, but assigned to Manasseh, and then allotted to the Levites, Josh. xvii, 11-21; xxi, 25; Judg. i, 27. Barak's victory was gained near Taanach, Judg. 5, 19. In later times, with Megiddo and other places, this city formed a part of one of Solomon's commissariat districts, 1 Kings iv, 12. The Aner of 1 Chron. vi, 70, may possibly be the same with Taanach. *Ta'annuk,* a small modern village on the south-west border of the plain of Esdraelon, four miles south of Megiddo, marks the site of ancient Taanach.

Ta'anath-Shi'loh, *approach to Shiloh,* a place named in Josh. xvi, 6, as one of the landmarks on the border-line of Ephraim. It is not known, but is considered as possibly identical with Shiloh.

Tab'bath, *celebrated,* a place mentioned in describing the flight of the

Midianite host after Gideon's night attack, Judg. vii, 22. Possibly it is identical with *Tubukhat-Fahil*, a remarkable mound or bank, about six hundred feet high, opposite *Beisan*, (Beth-Shean.)

Tab'erah, (Map 2,) *a burning,* a place in the wilderness of Paran, where a judgment by the "fire of the Lord" was inflicted on the Israelites, Num. xi, 3; Deut. ix, 22. Unknown.

Ta'bor, (Map 5,) *mound, mountain height.*

1. A mountain of Palestine. Among Greek and Roman writers the name appears as Itabyrion and Atabyrion. Tabor lies on the confines of Zebulun and Naphtali, rising abruptly from the north-eastern arm of the Plain of Esdraelon, Josh. xix, 22. It stands entirely insulated, except on the west, where a narrow ridge connects it with the hills of Nazareth. Seen from a distance it presents a most beautiful appearance, being very symmetrical in its proportions, and rounded off like a hemisphere or the segment of a circle, yet varying somewhat as viewed from different directions. The southern face of the mountain is almost naked limestone rock, but the northern slope is covered with forests of oak, terebinth, and syringa to the very summit.

It was on Tabor that Barak, at the command of Deborah, assembled his forces. On the arrival of the opportune moment he descended thence with "ten thousand men after him" into the plain, and conquered Sisera on the banks of the Kishon, Judg. iv, 6–15. In the wars of Gideon Tabor is again mentioned, Judg. viii, 18, 19. It is also alluded to in Psa. lxxxix, 12; Jer. xlvi, 18; Hosea v, 1.

Although the name of Tabor does not occur in the New Testament, yet from the fourth century it has been traditionally believed to be the scene of our Lord's transfiguration. "If one might choose a place which he would deem peculiarly fitting for so sublime a transaction, there is none certainly which would so entirely satisfy our feelings in this respect as the lofty, majestic, beautiful Tabor." But this theory seems highly improbable from the fact that just a little before this glorious event Jesus was far away from Tabor, near Cæsarea Philippi, Matt. xvi, 13. Moreover the summit of Tabor was at the time occupied by a fortified town. It may also be remarked that this part of Galilee abounds with "high mountains apart," so that there is no difficulty in providing other suitable sites for the transfiguration. Possibly it may have occurred on one of the spurs or recesses of Hermon.

The modern name of Tabor is *Jebel et-Tûr.* On the summit, which rises about one thousand nine hundred feet, " are the foundations of a thick wall built of large stones, some of which are beveled, showing that the entire wall was perhaps originally of that character."—*Robinson.* There are also remains of "towers, vaults, cisterns, and houses, some of which indicate the sites of the convents and churches erected by the Crusaders."—*Thomson.* Several of these vaults have been converted into a Greek chapel, with a residence for the priest. The Latin Christians have also an altar here, at which an annual mass is celebrated by their priests from Nazareth.

2. A Levitical city in the tribe of Zebulun, (1 Chron. vi, 77,) and probably identical with CHISLOTH-TABOR, which see.

3. An oak or grove of oaks in the territory of Benjamin, 1 Sam. x, 3. Unknown.

Tad'mor, (Maps 1, 4, 8,) *city of palms,* a city in the wilderness, built by Solomon, 1 Kings ix, 18; 2 Chron. viii, 4. The form Tamar also occurs, and it

MOUNT TABOR.

seems more ancient than that of Tadmor. According to an Arabic tradition this city existed at an earlier age, and Solomon rebuilt and fortified it as a barrier fortress.

Tadmor lay between the Euphrates and Hamath, to the south-east of that city, in a fertile tract or oasis of the desert. Thus, being at a convenient distance from both the Mediterranean Sea and the Persian Gulf, it was sure to secure the advantages of caravan traffic. Without doubt, Tadmor is identical with the renowned Palmyra of the Greeks and Romans. Palmyra, after various fortunes, at length, under Odenathus and his martial queen Zenobia, expanded into a mighty sovereignty, rivaling and defying for a time the Roman power. Finally, however, Zenobia was defeated and taken captive by the Emperor Aurelian, (A. D. 273,) who left a Roman garrison in the city. The garrison was massacred in a revolt. For this Aurelian executed not only those who were taken in arms, but common peasants, old men, and even women and children. Although there are proofs that Palmyra continued to be inhabited until the downfall of the Roman Empire, yet from this blow it never recovered. The grandeur and magnificence of Palmyra are abundantly attested by the vast ruins which remain. These are found about one hundred and forty miles east-north-east from Damascus. The old name was never superseded among the natives, who to this day give the spot the name of *Thadmor*.

Tahap'anes. Jer. ii, 16. See TAHPANHES.

Ta'hath, (Map 2,) *place, station,* one of the halting places of Israel in the wilderness, Num. xxxiii, 26, 27. Probably identical with *Elt'hi.*

Tah'panhes, (Map 2.) The etymology of the word is obscure. It has been conjectured to mean, *The head or beginning of the age or world.* It is also called Tahapanhes, and Tehaphnehes, and Taphnes; and it is possibly the Hanes of Isa. xxx, 4. The name clearly resembles that of the Egyptian Queen TAHPENES referred to in 1 Kings xi, 18–20.

This was a city of Lower Egypt, near the eastern border, Jer. ii, 16; xliii, 7, 8, 9; xliv, 1; xlvi, 14; Ezek. xxx, 18. To this place Johanan and his party repaired, taking Jeremiah with them, after the murder of Gedaliah. It is considered as possibly identical with the Daphne of the Greeks, a strong boundary city on the Pelusiac arm of the Nile. The site of Daphne is supposed to be marked by a mound called *Tel Defenneh,* which lies nearly in a direct line between the modern *Zan* and Pelusium.

Tah'tim-Hod'shi, THE LAND OF, *nether or low land newly inhabited* (?) a place visited by Joab while taking the census of the land of Israel, 2 Sam. xxiv, 6. "The name has puzzled all the interpreters." Some make it a proper name; some translate it as above; others translate the first part, and make Hodshi a proper name. Mr. Porter (in *Kitto*) says it was "manifestly a section of the upper valley of the Jordan, probably that now called *Ard el-Hûleh,* lying deep down at the western base of Hermon."

Ta'mar, *palm-tree,* a place on the south-eastern frontier of Judah, Ezek. xlvii, 19; xlviii, 28. It is identified by Dr. Robinson with the ruins at *Kûrnûb,* a place about a day's journey south of *el-Milh,* (Malatha or Moladah.) Wilton identifies it with Hazar-Gaddah; but both these sites are as yet only conjectural.

Ta'nach, Josh. xxi, 25. See TAANACH.

Ta'nis, Ezek. xxx, 14, margin; Judith i, 10. See ZOAN.

Taph'nes, Judith i, 9. See TAHPANHES.

Ta'phon, a city in Judea, fortified by Bacchides, 1 Macc. ix, 50. It was probably identical with Beth-Tappuah, near Hebron.

Tap'puah, *apple* or *citron region.*

1. A city in the Shephelah or plain country of Judah, Josh. xv, 34; situated about twelve miles west of Jerusalem. Unknown.

2. A city on the border of Ephraim and Manasseh, Josh. xvi, 8; xvii, 8; probably the same as En-Tappuah, Josh. xvii, 7. Attached to the city was a district called the land of Tappuah; the city belonged to Ephraim, and the land to Manasseh, Josh. xvii, 8. Both are unknown. Which of the two places above mentioned is referred to in Josh. xii, 17, is uncertain.

Ta'rah, (Map 2,) *station,* a halting place in the wilderness, between Tahath and Mithcah, Num. xxxiii, 27, 28. Unknown.

Tar'alah, *a reeling,* a city in Benjamin, Josh. xviii, 27. Unknown.

Tar'pelites, The, an Assyrian people sent by Asnapper to colonize Samaria, Ezra iv, 9. They are by some supposed to be the Tapyri, east of Elymais; by others the Tarpetes, a race near the Mæotic marsh.

Tar'shish, (Map 12,) *hard,* that is rocky, *ground* (?). In 1 Kings x, 22; xxii, 48, Tharshish. Concerning the exact position of this city or country opinions have been much divided, but it is highly probable that it was located in the south of Spain. In the table of genealogies given in Genesis we find it placed among the sons of Javan: "Elishah and Tarshish, Kittim and Dodanim. By these were the isles of the Gentiles divided in their lands," Gen. x, 4, 5. In Psa. lxxii, 10, we read, "The kings of Tarshish and of the isles shall bring presents;" and in 2 Chron. ix, 21, "The king's (Solomon's) ships went to Tarshish with the servants of Hiram; every three years once came the ships of Tarshish bringing gold and silver, ivory, and apes, and peacocks." In Isa. lxvi, 19, Tarshish is mentioned among *distant* places, "the isles afar off." Evidently this place must have been on the sea-coast, for we frequently read of the "ships" and the "navy" of Tarshish. See 1 Kings x, 22; Psa. xlviii, 7 · Isa. ii, 16; xxxiii, 1-14; lx, 9; Ezek. xxvii, 25.

ANCIENT TRADING VESSELS.

The passage in Ezek. xxvii, 12-25, describes this region as abounding in wealth. "Tarshish was thy (Tyre's) merchant, by reason of the multitude of all riches; with silver, iron, tin, and lead, they traded in thy fairs... The ships of Tarshish did sing of thee in thy market; and thou wast replenished, and made very glorious in the midst of the seas." From Jer. x, 9, we learn that Tarshish produced "silver spread into plates," and from the connection the silver was doubtless elaborately wrought, thus implying a high state of the art. We learn more of its opulence from

TARSUS.

Ezek xxxviii, 13. When the prophet Jonah refused to go to Nineveh he doubtless would flee in an opposite direction: thus he "rose up to flee unto Tarshish . . . and went down to Joppa; and he found a ship going to Tarshish," Jonah i, 3; iv, 2.

The following extract, from an article in Kitto's *Cyclopædia* by Dr. J. R. Beard, will be read with interest: "It appears, then, clear . . . that Tarshish was an old, celebrated, opulent, cultivated commercial city, which carried on trade in the Mediterranean and with the seaports of Syria, especially Tyre and Joppa, and that it most probably lay on the extreme west of that sea. Was there, then, in ancient times any city in these parts which corresponded with these clearly ascertained facts? There was. Such was Tartessus in Spain, said to have been a Phœnician colony . . . a fact which of itself would account for its intimate connection with Palestine and the biblical narrative. As to the exact spot where Tartessis (so written originally) lay authorities are not agreed, as the city had ceased to exist when geography began to receive attention; but it was not far from the Straits of Gibraltar, and near the mouth of the Guadalquiver, consequently at no great distance from the famous Granada of later days. The reader, however, must enlarge his notion beyond that of a mere city, which, how great soever, would scarcely correspond with the ideas of magnitude, affluence, and power that the Scriptures suggest. The name, which is of Phœnician origin, seems to denote the district of south-western Spain, comprising the several colonies which Tyre planted in that country, and so being equivalent to what we might designate Phœnician Spain. We are not, however, convinced that the opposite coast of Africa was not included, so that the word would denote to an inhabitant of Palestine the extreme western parts of the world." Other arguments might be adduced in support of the site indicated; but space is afforded simply for reference to the fact that this theory gains force by the testimony of ancient writers to the great wealth of Spain. Says Pliny: "Nearly all Spain abounds in the metals—lead, iron, copper, silver, gold." Heeren says: "Spain was once the richest land in the world for silver; gold was found there in great abundance, and the baser metals as well." From 1 Kings xxii, 48, it appears that Jehoshaphat had "ships of Tarshish" constructed at Ezion-Geber, on the eastern arm of the Red Sea, to go to Ophir and in 2 Chron. xx, 36, it is said they were to go to Tarshish. The supposition (of Keil) that these ships were intended to be transported across the land to the Mediterranean, and thus to sail to Spain, seems improbable. It is still more improbable that they were designed to circumnavigate Africa. Some think there must have been *two* places called Tarshish, one in Spain, the other in the Indian Ocean. The most probable theory, however, is that first suggested by Vitringa, and now adopted by the best critics, namely, that the term "ships of Tarshish" had come (at the time the Chronicles were compiled) to signify "large Phœnician ships, of a particular size and description, destined for long voyages, just as in English 'East Indiaman' was a general name given to vessels some of which were not intended to go to India at all."

Tar'sus, (Map 8.) The signification may possibly have some connection with Tarshish. This was a celebrated city, the capital of Cilicia, in Asia Minor. Cæsar changed its name to Juliopolis. It lay on the banks of the river Cydnus, which flowed through it and divided it into two parts. Tarsus was a distinguished seat of Greek philosophy and literature, and from the number of its schools and learned men was ranked by the side of Athens and Alexandria. Many Jews appear to have settled here; and the most distinguished citizen of Tarsus was Saul, afterward the Apostle Paul, Acts ix, 11, 30; xi, 25; xxi, 39; xxii, 3. Augustus made Tarsus free; but this freedom did not convey any right as a Roman colony of Roman citizenship to the natives, so that Paul was a citizen of Rome by virtue of some other franchise. Tarsus, indeed, eventually became a Roman colony. The modern town is called *Tarsous*, and is a poor and filthy place, inhabited by Turks, the population being estimated at from 20,000 to 30,000. Only a few ruins of the ancient city remain.

Tav'erns, THE THREE, (Map 8,) a place on the Appian road, about thirty-three miles from Rome. The name is probably derived from three large inns, or eating-houses, for the refreshment of travelers passing to and from Rome. Some of the "brethren" came thither to meet Paul, and by their coming the apostle took fresh courage, Acts xxviii, 13--15. The place still remains under the name *Tre Tuverne*, near the modern *Cisterna*.

Tehaph'nehes, Ezek. xxx, 18. See TAHPANHES.

Teko'a and Teko'ah, (Map 6,) possibly *a pitching of tents*, or *trumpet-clang*. In 1 Macc. ix, 33, Thecoe. A city about six miles south of Bethlehem, on the borders of the desert to which it gave its name, 2 Chron. xx, 20; Jer. vi, 1. It was colonized by Asher, of the tribe of Judah, 1 Chron. ii, 24; iv, 5; and fortified by Rehoboam, 2 Chron. xi, 6. The "wise woman" who interceded for Absalom resided here, 2 Sam. xiv, 2, 4, 9; and here also lived the prophet Amos as a herdman when he was visited by the prophetic word, Amos i, 1. The site still bears the name of *Teku'a*. It is an elevated hill, not steep, but broad at the top, and covered with ruins to the extent of four or five acres. These consist chiefly of the foundations of houses built of squared stones, some of which are beveled. There are also cisterns and broken columns.

Teko'ites, the inhabitants of Tekoah, 2 Sam. xxiii, 26, etc.

Tel-a'bib, *corn-hill,* a city of Chaldea or Babylonia, on the river Chebar; the residence of Ezekiel, with other Jewish captives, Ezek. iii, 15. Unknown.

Tel'aim, *young lambs,* the place at which Saul collected and numbered his forces before his attack on Amalek, 1 Sam. xv, 4. Possibly it may be identical with TELEM, (which see.)

Telas'sar, *the hill of Asshur;* also Thelasar, a city inhabited by the "children of Eden," and conquered by the Assyrians, 2 Kings xix, 12; Isa. xxxvii, 12. It lay, probably, in the hill country, above the upper Mesopotamian plain. Ewald identifies it with *Teleda*, a heap of ruins south-west from Racca; but this lacks confirmation.

Te'lem, *oppression,* a city in the extreme south of Judah, occurring between Ziph and Bealoth, Josh. xv, 24. It is possibly identical with Telaim. Mr. Wilton supposes that a trace of Telem is found in the Arab tribe *Dhulâm*, which gives its name to a district lying south-east of Beersheba: a supposition not altogether improbable.

Tel-Hare'sha, and Tel-Har'sa, *forest hill,* a place in Babylonia, probably in the low country, near the sea. In 1 Esdr. v, 36, Thelersas. From this town some Jews who could not prove their pedigree returned to Judea with Zerubbabel, Ezra ii, 59; Neh. vii, 61. Unknown.

Tel-Me'lah, *salt-hill;* in 1 Esdr. v, 36, Thermeleth; a place in Babylonia, from which also returned persons of doubtful pedigree, Ezra ii, 59

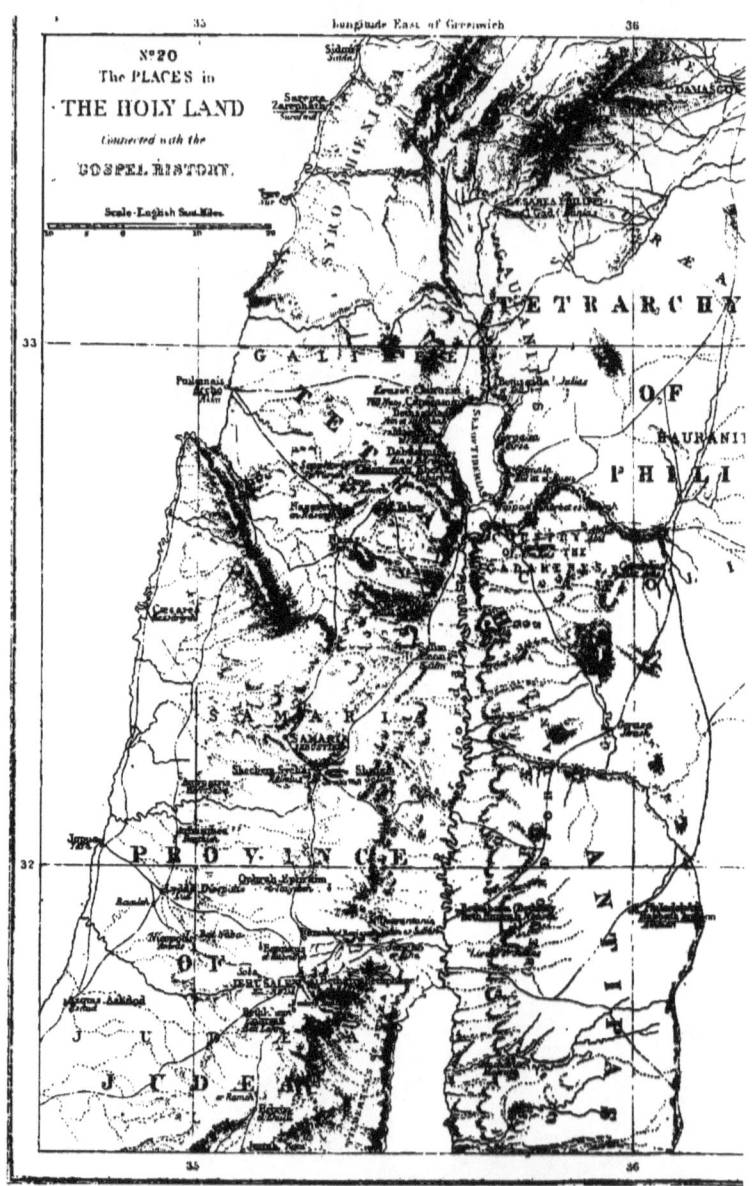

HUNT & EATON, NEW YORK.

Neh. vii, 61. It was probably near the Persian Gulf; but it is not identified.

Te'ma, (Map 12.) *south, desert,* an Ishmaelite tribe descended from Tema, Gen. xxv, 15; 1 Chron. i, 30. They peopled a district of Arabia. Tema is coupled with Sheba, Job vi, 16; and with Dedan, Isa. xxi, 14; Jer. xxv, 23; and it appears to have furnished caravans for commerce between Damascus and Mecca. Possibly the ancient Tema corresponds with *Teyma,* a small town on the *Haj* route, outside the borders of Syria.

Te'man, *south, desert,* the name of a people and country taking their appellation from the oldest son of Eliphaz, the son of Esau. Gen. xxxvi, 11. In Bar. iii, 22, 23, Theman. These people were called Temani, or Temanites, and were noted for their wisdom and valor. They formed the stronghold of Idumean power: hence they are specially mentioned in the predictions against Edom, Jer. xlix, 7; Ezek. xxv, 13; Amos i, 12; Obad. 9; Hab. iii, 3. The exact bounds or locality of Teman cannot be determined by the Scripture allusions; but it is probable that this region was a southern portion of the land of Edom, or, in a wider sense, that of the sons of the East, the Bene-Kedem. A town called Teman is mentioned by Jerome and Eusebius as lying a few miles from Petra, and having a Roman garrison. Some think this may mark the region of the Temanites. Wilton would place Teman at the northern extremity of Edom, among the mountains of the '*Azâzimeh.*

Te'mani and **Te'manite,** Gen. xxxvi, 24; Job ii, 11, etc. See TEMAN.

Tham'natha, 1 Macc. ix, 50, probably the ancient Timnah and the modern *Tibneh,* half way between Jerusalem and the Mediterranean.

Thar'shish, 1 Kings x, 22; xxii, 48. A more accurate form of Tarshish.

Thebes. See NO-AMON.

The'bez, *brightness,* a town not far from Shechem, where Abimelech was killed, Judg. ix, 50; 2 Sam. xi, 21. It is now *Tubâs,* eleven miles northeast of *Nablous,* surrounded by olive groves, and said to be a thriving place.

Theco'e. 1 Macc. ix, 33. See TEKOA.

Thela'sar. 2 Kings xix, 12. See TELASSAR.

Theler'sas. 1 Esdr. v, 36. See TEL-HARESHA.

The'man. Bar. iii, 22, 23. See TEMAN.

The'ras. 1 Esdr. viii, 41, 61. Corruption of AHAVA, which see.

Ther'meleth. 1 Esdr. v, 36. See TEL-MELAH.

Thessaloni'ca, (Map 8,) a city of Macedonia, anciently called Therma. On the ancient site a new city was built by Cassander, who called it after his wife, Thessalonica, the daughter of Philip. Under the Romans it was one of the four divisions of Macedonia, and the usual station of a Roman prætor and quæstor. Here the Jews had a synagogue; and it was to the Church gathered here that Paul wrote his earliest epistles. The Church was organized by Paul and Silas, most of the persons who believed being Gentiles and Jewish proselytes, Acts xvii, 1–4; 1 Thess. i, 9. The apostle after a short stay was driven from the city by the violence of the Jews, who followed him even to Berea, and stirred up a persecution against him there, Acts xvii, 5–10, 13. No doubt he visited Thessalonica at least once again, Acts xx, 1–3. The place is also referred to in Phil. iv, 6; 2 Tim. iv, 10. In Acts xvii, 6, 8, the rulers of the city are called (in the original) *politarchai;* and this same word remains to this day on an ancient arch which spans the street of the modern city. Thessalonica continued an important city; it was regarded as the capital not only of Macedonia, but of all Greece, till the building of Constantinople. During several centuries after Christ it was known as the "Orthodox City." Its modern name is *Saloniki*. The population numbers about 70,000, including many Jews. The present town stands on the acclivity of a steep hill, rising at the north-eastern extremity of the bay to which the city gives its name. It presents an imposing appearance from the sea, with which the interior by no means corresponds. The principal antiquities are the propylæa of the hippodrome, the rotunda, and the triumphal arches of Augustus and Constantine.

Thim'nathah, (Map 5.) Josh. xix, 43. See TIMNAH, (1.)

This'be, a city of Naphtali, Tob. i, 2. Some suppose this city has the honor of being the birthplace of Elijah the Tishbite. (See 1 Kings xvii, 1.) This, to say the least, is very doubtful. The site is not identified.

Thra'cia, (Map 8,) 2 Macc. xii, 35. Thrace, the country between the Ægean, the Propontis, and Euxine, and the rivers Strymon and Danube, now *Bulgaria* and *Roumelia*, 2 Macc. xii, 35.

Three Taverns. See TAVERNS, THE THREE.

Thy'ati'ra, (Map 8,) a city known in earlier times by the names Pelopia, Semiramis, and Euhippa. It is situated on the northern border of Lydia, about twenty-seven miles from Sardis. From Acts xvi, 14, it appears to have been noted for the art of dyeing. Inscriptions still exist of the guild of dyers at Thyatira. This city was the seat of one of the seven Apocalyptic Churches, Rev. i, 11; ii, 18. The seductive teachings of Jezebel mentioned in Rev. ii, 20–23, are said to refer to the worship of a Chaldean Sibyl, symbolically called Jezebel. Compare 1 Kings xvi, 31; xxi, 23, 25; 2 Kings ix, 7. The modern name of the city is *Ak Hissar*, ("white castle.") The place has a reputation for the manufacture of scarlet cloth, large quantities of which are sent weekly to Smyrna. The town consists of about two thousand houses, besides two or three hundred small huts. The population is about fifteen thousand. There are nine mosques and one Greek church. Ruins of the ancient city still remain; fragments of sculptures are found built into modern walls.

Tibe'rias, (Map 5,) a town of Galilee situated on the western bank of the Lake of Genesareth, John vi, 1, 23; xxi, 1. It was built by Herod Antipas, and named by him in honor of the Emperor Tiberius. Some suppose it was built on the site of a more ancient city, but this theory is not established. See *The Land and the Book*. Tiberias was the principal city of the province from the time of Herod Antipas to the commencement of the reign of Herod Agrippa II. It was adorned with buildings, a royal palace and a stadium. The inhabitants were a motley race, deriving their maintenance chiefly from the navigation of the adjoining lake and its fisheries. After the destruction of Jerusalem, Tiberias was noted during several centuries for its famous rabbinical academy. It was here that the *Mishna* was compiled. Here also originated the celebrated work called the *Masorah*, (traditions,) a collection of notes, mainly critical, on the Hebrew text of the Old Testament. Many of these Masoretic notes are introduced in the margin of our version. Some of them are worthy of much respect. See, as a specimen, margin, Psa. c, 3. Not far from Tiberias, in the immediate neighborhood of the town of Emmaus, were warm mineral springs, whose celebrated baths are sometimes spoken of as belonging to Tiberias itself. These springs contained sulphur, salt, and iron, and were employed for medicinal purposes.

It is a remarkable fact that the Gospels give us no information that the

Saviour, who spent so much of his public life in Galilee, ever visited Tiberias. The present city, *Tubarieh*, stands about four miles from the southern end of the lake at the northeast corner of a small plain. The walls inclose an irregular parallelogram, and are strengthened by round towers, ten on the west, five on the north, and eight on the south. There were also towers along the shore. It is described as a filthy place, fearfully hot in summer, and, according to Dr. Thomson, contains about two thousand inhabitants.

TIBERIAS.

The site of the present town does not fill the area of the ancient city, of which some insignificant vestiges still exist. By an earthquake on New Year's Day, 1837, *Tubarieh* was nearly destroyed, and six hundred persons perished in the ruins.

Tibe'rias, THE SEA OF, John xxi, 1. See GALILEE, SEA OF.

Tib'hath, *butchery,* 1 Chron. xviii, 18. See BETAH.

Ti'gris, (Map 1,) *velocity,* or *an arrow,* Tobit vi, 1; Judith i, 6; Ecclesiasticus xxiv, 25. The river Hiddekel of Scripture. See HIDDEKEL. The prophet Daniel had to cross this river in his journey to and from Susa, (Shushan.) Daniel had some of his greatest visions by the side of the Hiddekel. See Daniel x-xii.

Tim'nah, (Map 5,) *portion assigned.*

1. A town on the northern border of Judah, Josh. xv, 10. In the time of King Ahaz it was occupied by the Philistines, 2 Chron. xxviii, 18. This is probably the same place which is called Thimnathah, Thamnatha, and Timnath, and which belonged apparently to Dan. It is now believed to be represented by the modern *Tibneh,* a deserted village about two miles to the west of *Ain Shems,* (Bethshemesh.)

2. A town in the mountains of Judah, south of Hebron, Josh. xv, 57.

Tim'nath, and **Tim'nathah,** (Map 5,) *portion assigned.*

1. The place to which Judah was going up when he was met by his daughter-in-law Tamar, Gen. xxxviii, 12-14. It is very probably identical with TIMNAH, 1.

2. The residence of Samson's wife, Josh. xiv, 1, 2, 5. By some it is considered identical with the preceding.

Tim'nath-He'res. Judg. ii, 9. See TIMNATH-SERAH.

Tim'nath-Se'rah, *portion of abundance;* in Judg. ii, 9, Timnath-Heres, *portion of the sun.* A city in the mountains of Ephraim which was assigned to Joshua, and became the place of his residence and burial, Josh. xix, 50; xxiv, 30. The tomb of Joshua was still pointed out in the time of Eusebius, who was inclined to identify this city with Timnah, (1); and this identification at present seems probable.

Tim'nite, THE, Judg. xv, 6. An inhabitant of Timnah, (1).

Tiph'sah, (Map 4,) *passage, ford.*

1. A large and opulent city on the western bank of the Euphrates, the frontier of Solomon's dominions, 1 Kings iv, 24. Doubtless this city is identical with the Thapsacus of the Greeks and Romans, situated at the point where it was usual to cross the Euphrates. From the time of Seleucus Nicator it was called Amphipolis. The Euphrates expedition has shown that the only ford in that part of the course of the Euphrates here indicated is at *Suriyeh,* one hundred and sixty-five miles above *Deïr,* which doubtless marks the site of Thapsacus. Here, on either side of the river, a paved causeway is visible, and a long line of mounds may be traced, disposed in the form of an irregular parallelogram, something like those of Nineveh.

2. In 2 Kings xv, 16, it is said that Menahem, king of Israel, "smote Tiphsah and all that were therein, and all the coasts thereof." This place is usually identified with the above, but it seems rather to have been in the land of Israel, and near to Tirzah.

Ti'ras, *desire* (?), a people descended from Tiras, one of the sons of Japheth, Gen. x, 2; 1 Chron. i, 5. They are usually supposed to have peopled the regions of Thrace. Kalisch identifies Tiras with the great Asiatic mountain-chain of Taurus, which includes many Asiatic tribes. Several other localities are assigned. See Smith's *Dictionary,* art. *Tiras;* and Kitto, art. *Nations, Dispersion of.*

Tir'zah, *delight, pleasantness,* an ancient royal city of the Canaanites, captured by Joshua, Josh. xii, 24. Jeroboam seems to have chosen it as his principal residence, 1 Kings xiv, 17. His successors resided at Tirzah till the royal palace was burned by Zimri; then, the city being probably despoiled, Omri chose another capital, and built Samaria, 1 Kings xv, 21, 33; xvi, 6, 8, 9, 15, 17, 23, 24. A brief notice of Tirzah occurs again in the time of Menahem, 2 Kings xv, 14, 16. The site of the city seems to have been noted for its beauty, Sol. Song vi, 4. Dr. Robinson and others would identify Tirzah with *Tellûzah,* a thriving town north of *Nablous.* This place lies in a sightly and commanding position surrounded by immense groves of olive trees. Scarcely any remains of antiquity are found.

Tish'bite, THE. 1 Kings xvii, 1. See THISBE.

Ti'tans, Judith xvi, 7. According to classical legend, the children of Uranus (heaven) and Gaia, or Terra, (earth,) vanquished by the gods of Olympus.

Tob, *good,* a "land" or district beyond the Jordan into which Jephthah withdrew when expelled from Gilead, Judg. xi, 3, 5. It is called also Ish-Tob, 2 Sam. x, 6, 8; Tobie, 1 Macc. v, 13; Tubieni, 2 Macc. xii, 17. See ISH-TOB.

To'bie, THE PLACES OF. See TOB.

To'chen, *a measure,* a place in Simeon, 1 Chron. iv, 32. Unknown.

Togar'mah, (Map 12,) *breaking bones* (?), *Armenian tribe* (?). The descendants of a son of Gomer of the family of Japheth, Gen. x, 3; 1 Chron. i, 6. They are represented as an agricultural tribe, breeding horses and mules, in which they traded with Tyre, Ezek. xxvii, 14; also as a well-armed and military nation, Ezek. xxxviii, 6. Some identify this people with the Taurians; but Togarmah is more probably the ancient name of ARMENIA, which see.

To'lad, *birth, generation.* 1 Chron. iv, 29. See EL-TOLAD.

To'phel, *lime,* a place east of the Arabah, Deut. i, 1. It is probably identical with *Wady et-Tufileh,* in a well-watered, fertile valley south-east of the Dead Sea.

To'phet, and more accurately **To'pheth** (once, 2 King xxiii, 10.) Various interpretations are given, namely: *drum; garden; place of burning or burying; abomination; place to be spit upon; pleasant; tabret grove.* Tophet lay somewhere east or south-east of Jerusalem. It was in "the Valley of the Son of Hinnom," which is "by the entry of the east gate," Jer. vii, 31; xix, 2. It was *in* Hinnom, and was perhaps a music, or tabret grove. At first, possibly, it formed a part of the royal garden, a spot of special beauty. Afterward, being defiled by idols and polluted by the sacrifices of Baal and the fires of Moloch, it thus became exceedingly abominable, Isa. xxx, 33; Jer. vii, 31, 32; xix, 6, 11–14. See HINNOM.

Trachoni'tis, (Maps 5, 20,) *a rugged region,* a name occurring only once in the Bible, Luke iii, 1. It was probably the Greek equivalent for Argob. This country was placed by Augustus under the authority of Herod the Great, that it might be cleared of the banditti with which it was overrun. Afterward it was a part of the tetrarchy of his son Philip. The modern *Lejah,* south of Damascus, is doubtless identical with Trachonitis. See ARGOB.

Trip'olis, (Map 8,) the Greek name of an important Syrian city on the coast north of Sidon, at one time the point of federal union for Aradus, Sidon, and Tyre, 2 Macc. xiv, 1. It was destroyed by Sultan El-Mansour, A. D. 1289. The modern representative of Tripolis is *Tarablous,* a city of about fifteen thousand souls; but the ancient site is probably occupied by the small fishing place *El Myna.*

Tro'as, (Maps 1, 8,) a city of Lesser Mysia, in Asia Minor, built by King Antigonus and by him called Antigonia Troas. Afterward the name was changed, in honor of Alexander the Great, to Alexandria Troas. It lay south of the site of ancient Troy, opposite the south-east end of Tenedos. Paul was twice at Troas, Acts xvi, 8, 11; xx, 5, 6; 2 Tim. iv, 13. Here he had the heavenly vision which induced him to carry the Gospel message into Europe; and here also occurred the fall and restoration of Eutychus, Acts xx, 9, 10. Troas is represented by the modern *Eski-Stamboul.* Its ruins, which are considerable, are now concealed in the heart of a thick wood of oaks.

Trogyl'lium, (Map 8,) a town and cape on the western coast of Asia Minor, opposite Samos, at the foot of Mount Mycale. Here St. Paul spent a night, Acts xx, 15. An anchorage here is still called *St. Paul's Port.*

Tu'bal, (Map 12,) *a flowing forth,* a Japhetic people, Gen. x, 2; Isa. lxvi, 19; Ezek. xxvii, 13; xxxii, 26; xxxviii, 2, 3; xxxix, 1. They were probably the ancestors of the Tibareni, on the south of the Euxine Sea.

Tubie'ni, Jews of Tob. 2 Macc. xii, 17. See TOB

Tyre, and **Ty'rus,** (Maps 1, 5, 8,) *rock.* Hebrew, Tsor. A celebrated city of Phœnicia on the eastern coast of the Mediterranean Sea. In Isa. xxiii, 12, it is called the daughter of Zidon. Tyre was situated on an island;

but there was also a city on the shore, and it is questioned which is the more ancient. The town on the shore was called Palæ-Tyrus, (Old Tyre,) not from its being founded before the other—for, indeed, Island-Tyrus was probably the older—but from its having achieved a high renown long before its less favorably situated island sister. According to Pliny the circumference of both cities was reckoned at about nineteen Roman miles. Tyre was a very ancient and splendid city, Isa. xxiii, 7, 8; Zech. ix, 3, 4. In the division of Canaan the border of Asher is described as reaching to the "strong city Tyre," Josh. xix, 29. We do not hear of Tyre again till the reign of David, at which time we find it under King Hiram. From Tyre were obtained both timber and skilled workmen for the splendid edifices built at Jerusalem, 2 Sam. vi, 11; 1 Chron. xiv, 1; and up to this city David's census extended, 2 Sam. xxiv, 7. Hiram was in the most friendly alliance, also, with King Solomon; and the perfection of the Tyrian arts and artisans was of great value to the Hebrew monarch in carrying out his magnificent projects at the Jewish capital, 1 Kings v; vii, 13, 14; 2 Chron. ii. The timber from Lebanon was taken in floats to Joppa, on the Mediterranean, a distance of less than seventy-four geographical miles; while the distance from Joppa to Jerusalem was about thirty-two miles. Thus these two friendly sovereigns were not widely separated, and it is possible that they may have frequently met. After Solomon's buildings were completed he presented to King Hiram twenty cities in Galilee, but they did not please the Tyrian king. Hence they were restored to Solomon, who fortified them and colonized them with Israelites, 1 Kings ix, 10-14; 2 Chron. viii, 2. The friendship of the two kings, however, was not interrupted; and their respective fleets were together in the habit of making trading voyages, 1 Kings ix, 25-28; x, 11-22; 2 Chron. viii, 17, 18; ix, 21. Possibly it was from this close intercourse with the Phœnicians that Solomon was led to go after the Zidonian goddess, and to have Zidonian women in his harem, 1 Kings xi, 1, 5.

Later we learn of the marriage of Ahab, the king of Israel, with Jezebel, daughter of the king of Tyre, or "king of the Zidonians;" a title undoubtedly referring to Ithobalus, king of Tyre and Sidon, 1 Kings xvi, 31. The consequences of this marriage proved most fatal. Idol-worship was thus established in Israel; and it was also introduced into Judah by the marriage of Jehoram with Athaliah, Jezebel's daughter, 2 Kings viii, 18, 26, 27. But whatever friendship existed between the Tyrians and the two Israelitish kingdoms would be ended by the revolution in Samaria which placed Jehu on the throne, and the deserved execution of Athaliah in Jerusalem. The notice of Tyre as hostile to Judah, in Psa. lxxxiii, 7, has been supposed to be of an earlier date than the period just alluded to. This is generally referred to the great war of Moab and others against Jehoshaphat, 2 Chron. xx, 1. In later times unquestionably there was bitter enmity between the Tyrians and the Hebrews. See Joel iii, 4-8; Amos i, 9, 10; and Isaiah's "burden of Tyre," Isa. xxxiii. Some critics suppose that Isaiah's prophecy referred to the siege of Tyre by Shalmaneser, (not long after 721 B. C.) Others, with less probability, we think, refer it to a later siege by Nebuchadnezzar. After the siege by Shalmaneser Tyre remained a powerful State, with its own kings, Jer. xxv, 22; xxvii, 3; Ezra xxvi, 4, 6, 8, 10, 12; xxvii, 11; xxviii, 5; Zech. ix, 3. The prophecies concerning Tyre are some of them singularly full, giving us details such as have scarcely come down to us respecting any city of antiquity. See especially Ezek. xxvii. Nebu-

RUINS OF TYRE.

chadnezzar, whose siege Ezekiel predicted, beleaguered Tyre for thirteen years; and the city, which had just rejoiced over the fall of Jerusalem, was now herself to drink the bitter cup of suffering; but it is still a disputed point whether Nebuchadnezzar actually took it. However this may be, it is probable that, on some terms or other, Tyre submitted to the Chaldees, a vassal prince being allowed to hold the government. Afterward it passed under the Persian rule; and again, by the decree of Cyrus, it supplied the materials of the temple at Jerusalem, Ezra iii, 7, when other trade with the Jews sprang up, Neh. xiii, 16. Alexander the Great found Tyre in his path to glory, and laid siege to the city. This memorable siege was resisted by the Tyrians for seven months. The harbors of Tyre (there are said to have been two) were blockaded, and a mighty mound was constructed which joined the island to the continent. The city was taken, and multitudes of its inhabitants were put to death or sold for slaves. Ever since Tyre has stood upon a spit of land running out into the sea, with no appearance, so far as ordinary observation goes, of having ever been surrounded by the waters. Yet Tyre again revived and was flourishing, first under the Syrian monarchy, and then under the Romans, who professed to respect its freedom; though Augustus is said to have taken away some of its liberties. A few other notices in the Old Testament besides the above may be found: Psa. xlv, 12; Ezek. xxix, 18; Hos. ix, 13; and several in the Apocrypha: 1 Esdr. v, 56; 2 Esdr. i, 11; Judith ii, 28; 1 Macc. v, 15; 2 Macc. iv, 18, 33, 44, 49. In the time of Christ Tyre was still a populous place. The prophetic curse was yet resting upon the city, but our Lord declared that if the mighty works which were done in Chorazin and Bethsaida had been done in Tyre and Sidon they would have repented, Matt. xi, 21, 22. Christ once visited "the coasts of Tyre," and there performed an act of mercy; but it is not probable that he ever entered the city, Matt. xv, 21–29. See also Mark iii, 8; vii, 24–31; Luke vi, 17. Yet the Gospel was received there, Acts xxi, 3–6; and in later times Tyre was an episcopal see.

In 1291 A. D. the Saracens gave the final blow to Tyre, from which it sank into its present miserable state of ruin. The modern name is *Sûr*. The site of Tyre, "the Queen of the Sea," is now unoccupied, except by fishermen as "a place to spread nets upon." Says Mr. Porter, (*Hand-book*, p. 370:) "The modern town contains about three thousand to four thousand inhabitants, about one half being Metâwileh, and the other Christians. Most of the houses are mere hovels; the streets are narrow, crooked, and filthy; and the walls and houses of a superior class are so shattered by earthquakes that they look as if about to fall to pieces. One is reminded at every footstep, and by every glance, of the prophecies uttered against this city." "A mournful and solitary silence now prevails along the shore which once resounded with the world's debate."—*Gibbon.* Among the ruins are huge stones, and granite columns, with other remains of splendid edifices. Many fine stones have been removed to other cities. About a mile and a half distant from Tyre is the so-called tomb of Hiram, an immense sarcophagus of limestone, supposed to contain the remains of that king.

U'lai, (Map 1,) *strong water* (?). A river of Susiana, on whose banks Daniel had one of his visions, Dan. viii, 2, 16. It is doubtless the *Eulæus* of the Greeks and Romans. Mr. Loftus (*Chaldea and Susiana*) believes it to be a river or artificial channel which connected the *Kerkhah* (Choaspes) and the *Kárún*, (Pasatigris.) The ancient channel may yet be traced, though now there is but a small run of water in it. And as the Eulæus is said to have surrounded the citadel of the Susians, the Kerkhah and this old channel were the two streams intended. This may explain the words of Daniel, "between the two banks of Ulai," that is, between the two streams. But the identity of the Eulæus with any existing stream is a point of dispute among geographers.

Um'mah, *community,* a city of Asher, Josh. xix, 30. Possibly the site is marked by *'Alma,* where many ruins exist, on the top of the Ladder of Tyre, near the cape *Ras en Nakhura.*

U'phaz, (Map 12,) Jer. x, 9; Dan. x, 5. See OPHIR.

Ur of the Chaldees, (Map 1,) *fire,* or *light,* a place where resided the family of Terah, Abraham's father, and from which they departed and came unto Haran, Gen. xi, 28, 31; xv, 7; Neh. ix, 7; Acts vii, 2. Much difference of opinion exists concerning the location of Ur. Josephus calls it "a city of the Chaldeans." He says that Chaldea was in Mesopotamia, and quotes authority to show that it was "above Babylon." Four localities are presented as the site of Ur: 1. The modern *Urfa,* or *Oorfa,* the classic *Edessa.* This city is about twenty-five miles north of Haran, and contains about sixty thousand inhabitants. Ancient Jewish tradition, together with some local sanctuaries dedicated to Abraham, its nearness to Haran, the fact that it is *east* of the Euphrates, (compare Josh. xxiv, 3,)—these are the chief claims of *Oorfa.* Several prominent American missionaries and travelers are among those who favor this site. Chaldea was a country of very variable bounds at different epochs, and some have thought that it may have reached as far north as the spot in question. As to the traditions at *Oorfa,* Dean Stanley says these "are at least as strong as those elsewhere."—*Jewish Church,* i, p. 528. 2. A fortress or city on the Tigris, supposed to have been called Ur in the fourth century after Christ. This is the modern *El Hathr,* and it seems to represent the ancient *Adur* (not Ur) mentioned by Ammianus Marcellinus, (xxv, 8.) 3. *Warka,* or *Irak,* on the present eastern bank of the Euphrates; but this is doubtless identical with the ancient ERECH, which see. 4. *Mugeyer,* or *Umgeyer,* ("the mother of bitumen,") on the *west* of the confluence of the Euphrates with the Tigris. The grounds on which Sir H. Rawlinson identifies this site with Ur are, (1,) From the name of *Urukh,* or *Hur,* found on cylinders in the neighborhood; (2.) From the remains of a "Temple of the Moon," whence, perhaps, the name of *Camarina* given to Ur by Eupolemus; (3.) From the existence of a district called *Ibra,* whence he derives the name of Hebrew. Here are found extensive ruins, comprised in a large circuit of low mounds, half a mile in diameter. The chief ruin is that of the temple, which was built of large bricks cemented with bitumen. It measures one hundred and ninety-eight feet in length and one hundred and thirty-three in width. The cylinders, containing inscriptions, which were found among the ruins, are now in the British Museum. On one of the bricks was this inscription: "Orchamus, King of Ur, is he who has built the temple of the Moon-god." Many of the ruins are tombs. Whether *Mugeyer* occupies the site of Ur or not is still an open question; but the inscriptions on the cylinders found here have proved to be invaluable in sustaining the authenticity and truth of Scripture concerning the Babylonian realm.

Uz, THE LAND OF, perhaps *fertile land,* the country of Job, Job i, 1. The location of this land has been a subject of much dispute. Uz is first mentioned in Gen. x, 23, and it was evidently settled by a son of Aram; compare 1 Chron. i, 17. The sacred writer declares that Job was "the greatest of all the men of the East," Job i, 3. Here "men of the East" is in Hebrew *Bene-Kedem;* and the Bene-Kedem were the people who dwelt in Arabia, and especially in the country to the east and south-east of Palestine; compare Job i, 15–17. In Jer. xxv, 20, Uz is grouped with Egypt, Philistia, Edom, and Moab; and in Lam. iv, 21, either Uz seems to have been a part of Edom, or some of the Edomites in the prophet's days inhabited Uz. Job's friend Eliphaz lived in Teman, and Teman was probably in the southern part of Edom. (See TEMAN.) Uz is by some located in Idumea. Others place it in northern Mesopotamia, near *Oorfa,* (Ur?) where the name of Job is familiar. All through the *Jebel Hauran,* adjoining the Trachonitis, intelligent natives hold the old tradition that theirs is the country of the patriarch Job. They point out "Job's pasture-ground," "the summer palace of Job," "the home of Job," and "the tomb of Job." Mr. Porter has located Uz as definitely, perhaps, as it can now be done. He says: "On the whole, therefore, it would appear from the statements and allusions of the sacred writers, combined with the remarks of Eusebius and Jerome and the result of modern research, that the land of Uz was in Arabia, bordering on Edom westward, on Trachonitis northward, and extending perhaps indefinitely across the pasture-lands of Arabia toward the Euphrates."

U'zal, perhaps *a wanderer,* a son of Joktan, (Gen. x, 27; 1 Chron. i, 21,) whose descendants seem to have settled in Yemen. The capital of this district of Arabia long had the name of Uzal. It is now *Sanaa.* The correct reading of Ezek. xxvii, 19, following the Septuagint, would seem to be "Dan and Javan, *of Uzal,* conveyed to your markets," etc., (see VEDAN.) At *Sanaa* there are still about fifteen thousand Jews. The commanding position of *Sanaa,* "its strong fortifications, the number of its mosques and minarets, and the size of its houses, render it one of the most imposing cities in Arabia."

Uz'zen-She'rah, *ear of Sherah,* a city founded by Sherah, the daughter or descendant of Ephraim, 1 Chron. vii, 24. Probably it was near Beth-Horon, and its site may be marked by *Beit Sira,* a place to the south-east of the Upper Beth-Horon.

Ve'dan. In Ezek. xxvii, 19, "Dan also" is considered by some critics an incorrect translation. "Dan" seems here entirely out of place. It would be better not to translate the Hebrew copulative *ve,* but, joining it to Dan, read↓Vedan. Thus Vedan would be considered an Arabian city trading in "bright iron, cassia, and calamus." Gesenius and others incline to identify this city with the modern *Aden,* in the province of *Yemen.*

Vineyards, PLAIN OF THE, Judg. xi, 33. Possibly marked by *Beit el-Kerm,* east of the Jordan, and north of *Kerak,* where some ruins are found.

Wilderness of the Wandering, (Map 2.) From the time the Israelites left Egypt, until they crossed the Jordan into Canaan, was a period of forty years, Deut. i, 3: viii, 2; Josh. v, 6. Had they proceeded in a direct course from Egypt to Canaan the journey might have been accomplished in about ten or twelve days. The reason for this long and fearful wandering is given in Num. xiii, xiv. In Num. xxxiii may be found a list of many stations on the way to Canaan. Other notices occur in different chapters of the Penta-

touch. The Bible does not give us a full history of the wandering, nor are all the places through which this people passed mentioned. Especially have we no record of that "great and terrible wilderness" through which the Israelites wandered thirty-eight years after leaving Kadesh. For ages this whole region has borne the name of *Bedu et-Tih*, " the wilderness of wandering." Professor E. H. Palmer has made (1869-1870) a very thorough exploration of *Et-Tih*, with results of the greatest value. (See Palmer's *Desert of the Exodus*.) Although many stations still remain unknown, yet some have been so clearly identified in various portions of the route that the general line of march has been somewhat satisfactorily determined. The student is referred to the notice of the places named in the passages above alluded to, especially GOSHEN; RAMESES; SEA, RED; SINAI; KADESH; PARAN; EDOM; MOAB; NEBO.

Zaana'im, *removals*, a "plain," but more accurately an oak, where Heber the Kenite pitched his tent, Judg. iv, 11. See ZAANANNIM.
Za'anan, *place of flocks*, Micah i, 11. See ZENAN.
Zaanan'nim, *removals*, Josh xix, 33. An oak on the border of Naphtali, not far from Kedesh, identical with ZAANA'IM, which see. There are to this day large oak-trees in the green pastures around Kedesh.
Zabade'ans, 1 Macc. xii, 31, an Arab tribe whose name probably survives in *Zebdany* and *Kefr Zebad*, two villages on Anti-Lebanon. See ABANA.
Zab'ulon, Matt. iv, 13, 15; Rev. vii, 8. The Greek form of Zebulun.
Za'ir, *small*, a place in Idumea where Joram defeated the Edomites, 2 Kings viii, 21. Unknown.
Zal'mon, (Hebrew, Tsalmon,) *shady*, a hill near Shechem, Judg. ix, 48. Whether the Salmon of Psa. lxviii, 14, is identical with Zalmon is disputed. The Psalmist's words, "as snow in Salmon," are by some critics rendered, "there was snow in the darkness;" that is, "there is brightness where there was darkness," or, "light in calamity." Possibly, but not probably, Salmon may be the same as Zalmon.
Zalmo'nah, (Map 2,) one of the camping places in the wilderness, Num. xxxiii, 41, 42. Unknown.
Zamzum'mims, (Map 3,) *noisy people*, a race of giants dwelling anciently in the territory east of Jordan between the Arnon and the Jabbok. They were extirpated by the Ammonites before the time of Moses, Deut. ii, 20, 21. See ZUZIMS.
Zano'ah, *marsh, bog*.
1. A town in Judah in the lowland district, Josh. xv, 34; Neh. iii, 13; xi, 30. The site is doubtless marked by *Zana'a* in the *Wady Ismail*, on the slope of a low hill east of *Ain Shems*, (Beth-Shemesh.)
2. A town in the highlands of Judah, Josh. xv, 56. Possibly the site is at Khirbet Sa'nût. See Qr. St. Pal. Ex. Fd., Jan., 1875.
Za'phon, *the north*, a city of Gad east of the Jordan, Josh. xiii, 27. Lost. By the term "northward," in Judg. xii, 1, Zaphon may perhaps be intended.
Za'reah, *hornet's town*, Neh. xi, 29. See ZORAH.
Za'red, *exuberant growth*, Num. xxi, 12. See ZERED.
Zar'ephath, (Maps 5, 20,) *smelting-house* (?); in Luke iv, 26, Sarepta. A Phenician town between Tyre and Sidon. It is the place whither Elijah was sent to dwell, and where he performed two miracles, 1 Kings xvii, 8-24. The name occurs in Obad. xx. Possibly the Canaanitish woman, whose

BIBLE GEOGRAPHY. 485

daughter Jesus healed, came from the neighborhood of this city, Matt. xv, 21-28. Sarepta was made a Latin bishopric by the Crusaders. The ancient Zarephath is represented by the modern village of *Surafend*. Dean Stanley thus speaks of it: " It is a village seated aloft on the top and side of one of the hills, the long line of which skirts the plain of Phœnicia, conspicuous from far by the white domes of its many tombs of Mussulman saints. . . .

ZAREPHATH, (SURAFEND.)

It may be worth while to record, as characteristic, the curious confusion of the story [of Elijah] which lingers in the Mussulman traditions of the neighborhood. Close on the sea-shore stands one of these sepulchral chapels dedicated to 'El-Khudr,' or 'Mar Elias.' There is no tomb inside, only hangings before a recess. This variation from the usual type of Mussulman sepulchers was, as we were told by the peasants on the spot, 'Because El-Khudr is not yet dead; he flies round and round the world, and those chapels are built wherever he has appeared. Every Thursday night and Friday morning there is a light so strong within the chapel that no one can go in.'"—*Sinai and Palestine*, p. 271.

Zar'etan, perhaps *cooling*, Josh iii, 16. See ZEREDA.

Za'reth-Sha'har, *splendor of the dawn*, a city in Reuben on a hill in a valley, Josh. xiii, 19. *Zara*, in *Wady Zurka Main*, three miles south of the mouth of the Callirrhoe, is doubtless the ancient site.

Zar'tanah, *cooling*, 1 Kings iv, 12, apparently near Beth-Shean. See ZEREDA.

Zar'than, *cooling*, 1 Kings vii, 46, apparently near Succoth, in the Jordan Valley. Perhaps identical with *Tell Sarem*, 3m. s. of *Beisan* (Beth-Shean).

Zeba'im, *the gazelles*. In Ezra ii, 57; Neh. vii, 59, we read of a person named "Pochereth of Zebaim." Some suppose this name to be identical with Zeboim. Others translate Zebaim as the plural of the Hebrew word signifying *antelope* or *gazelle*, and read " Pochereth of the antelopes." This seems plausible. Possibly this man was a mighty hunter.

Zabo'im and **Zebo'im,** perhaps *roes*, one of the "five cities of the plain," generally grouped with Sodom and Gomorrah, Gen. x, 19; xiv, 2, 8; Deut. xxix, 23; Hos. xi, 8. Unknown. See SIDDIM; SEA, SALT.

Zebo'im, THE VALLEY OF, *valley of hyenas*, a gorge or ravine east of Mishmas, 1 Sam. xiii, 18. The name is, in Hebrew, totally distinct from that of Zeboim, the city. The valley must be looked for among the wild gorges that run from the eastern slopes of Benjamin into the Jordan plain.

Zeb'ulun, (Map 5,) *a habitation*, the tribe of Israel descended from the sixth and last son of Leah, and the tenth born of Jacob, Gen. xxx, 20; xxxv, 23. Jacob's prophetic blessing upon Zebulun declared that he should dwell "at the haven of the sea," and "his border should be unto Zidon," Gen. xlix, 13. At the census of the wilderness Zebulun numbered 57,400, Num. i, 30, 31. In the encampment their position was to the east of the tabernacle, Num. ii, 5, 6; and on the march they followed third under the standard of Judah, Num. x, 14–16. At the second census their number was 60,500, Num. xxvi, 26. Previous to the settlement in Palestine Zebulun was one of the six tribes stationed on Ebal to pronounce the curses, Deut. xxvii, 13.

The territory assigned to Zebulun was one of the richest and most beautiful sections west of the Jordan. The borders are described in Josh. xix, 10–16; but from the fact that many of the ancient cities have disappeared, the exact limits of the tribe cannot now be determined. It is doubtful whether it touched the Sea of Galilee on the east, Matt. iv, 13. On the west it reached to the Kishon and Mount Carmel, and if not to the Mediterranean, yet, at least, to the territory of Phenicia, called "Zidon" above, from the chief city. It embraced a part of the fertile plain of Esdraelon. The beautiful wooded hills and ridges extending from Tabor by Nazareth to the plain of Akka were also in Zebulun. The four northern tribes, Zebulun, Issachar, Asher, and Naphtali, were very much isolated from the other tribes. Their peculiar position threw them into closer intercourse with their Gentile neighbors—especially with the commercial Phenicians. Thus they became somewhat different in manners and customs from their brethren of the southern tribes. Their speech also became peculiar. Thus it was said to Peter, "Thy speech bewrayeth thee," Matt. xxvi, 73. Much of the purity of their religion was also lost, 2 Chron. xxx, 10–18. Although this tribe was slow, as were many of their brethren, to drive out their enemies, yet Zebulun became distinguished among the northern tribes for warlike spirit and devotion. The noble ode of Deborah and Barak in Judg. v, recounts the splendid triumph in which Zebulun bore so prominent a part. Scientific skill seems also to have been acquired by this tribe, and there came "out of Zebulun they that handle the pen of the writer," Judg. v, 14. In David's army there were "of Zebulun . . . expert in war, with all instruments of war, fifty thousand which could keep rank, not of double heart," 1 Chron. xii, 33. Of their liberality in supplying the wants of the army honorable mention is made, verse 40.

The northern tribes were first carried away captive into Assyria by Tiglath-Pileser, 2 Kings xv, 29; and from this point the history of distinct tribes ceases. On the return from captivity the term Jews was applied to all the tribes in common. The territory of Zebulun was greatly honored in later times by the frequent presence of Jesus. Here he performed miracles, and here were uttered many of his parables and discourses. The beautiful prophecy of Isaiah (ix, 1, 2) was fulfilled, and "the people which sat in darkness saw great light," Matt. iv, 13-16.

Ze'dad, (Map 4,) *mountain-side*, a city on the northern boundary of Palestine, Num. xxxiv, 8; Ezek xlvii, 15. It is probably identical with *Sudud*, on the road from Baalbec to *Hums*, (Emesa.)

Ze'lah, *a rib, the side*, a city of Benjamin, Josh. xviii, 28. Here was the family tomb of Kish, the father of Saul, 2 Sam. xxi, 14; and Zelah was probably the native place of Saul, the first king of Israel. Its site is unknown.

Zel'zah, *shade from the sun*, a place on the boundary of Benjamin, not far from Rachel's tomb, 1 Sam. x, 2. About half a mile westward from this sepulcher is the village of *Beit Jala*; this may probably be identical with Zelzah.

Zemara'im, perhaps *double mount*.
1. An ancient town in Benjamin, Josh. xviii, 22. Possibly the site is marked by *Es-Sumra*, four miles north of Jericho.
2. Mount Zemaraim, in the highlands of Ephraim, 2 Chron. xiii, 4. Unknown.

Zem'arite, THE. A tribe of Hamites, Gen. x, 18; 1 Chron. i, 16. These people may have lived at the ancient Simyra. The site of this city is possibly marked by the ruins called *Sumrah*, north of *Tripolis*. The Zemarites possibly emigrated southward and gave their name to Zemaraim.

Ze'nan, *place of flocks*, a place in the lowlands of Judah, apparently near the western coast, Josh. xv, 37. It is perhaps the same as the Zaanan of Micah i, 11. A few miles south-east of Ascalon is a modern village called *Jenin*, and this possibly may represent Zenan.

Ze'phath, *watch-tower*, Judg. i, 7. See HORMAH.

Zeph'athah, VALLEY OF, *vale of the watch-tower*, near Mareshah, 2 Chron. xiv, 10. A deep valley is found near the site of Mareshah, running down to *Beit Jibrin*, (Eleutheropolis,) and thence into the plain of Philistia. See MARESHAH.

Zer, *flint*, a city of Naphtali, probably near the Lake of Genesareth, Josh. xix, 35.

Ze'red, *exuberant growth*, or *willow-brook*, a valley separating Moab and Edom, Deut. ii, 13, 14; in Num. xxi, 12, Zared. Perhaps it is identical with the *Wady el-Ahsy*.

Zer'eda, *cooling*, a town in Ephraim, in the plain of Jordan, 1 Kings xi, 26; 2 Chron. iv, 17. Possibly it is the same as Zaretan, Josh. iii, 16; Zererath, Judg. vii, 22; Zartanah, 1 Kings iv, 12; Zeredathah, 2 Chron. iv, 17, and Zarthan, 1 Kings vii, 46. While these places are probably identical, yet there are difficulties in the way. Some place Zarthan east of Jordan. Others claim that Zereda was on a hill, while the other places seem to have been in the plain. The site of Zereda is unknown.

Zered'athah, 2 Chron. iv, 17. See ZEREDA.

Zer'erath, Judg. vii, 22. See ZEREDA.

Zid'dim, *the sides*, a place in Naphtali, Josh. xix, 35. The site is possibly marked by the village of *Kefr-Hattin*, a few miles west of the Sea of Galilee.

Zi'don, (Maps 5, 20,) *a fishery*. Hebrew, Tsidon. In Josh. xi, 8, Great Zidon, (margin, Zidon-Rabbah.) Sidon (the Greek form) in Gen. x, 15, 19; in the Apocrypha generally, and in the New Testament. Zidon was an ancient and opulent Phenician city. It was situated on the Mediterranean coast, on the northern slope of a small promontory which juts out from a

SIDON.

low plain (less than two miles broad) between the Lebanon and the sea. It was nearly twenty miles north of Tyre, and about forty miles south of Berytus, (*Beirût.*) Zidon, though usually associated in Scripture with Tyre, was of earlier origin; and probably the latter city was originally a colony of the former. In Isa. xxiii, 12, Tyre is styled the "daughter of Zidon." At the conquest of Canaan the Israelites found "Great Zidon" the metropolis of a district which seems to have embraced the States of Zidon, Tyre, and Aradus. The inhabitants of this district are called Zidonians, or Sidonians, and are distinguished from the residents of the city, Deut. iii, 9; Judg. iii, 3; x, 12, etc.

At the division of Canaan among the tribes Asher's inheritance is said to have reached "unto great Zidon," Josh. xix, 28. (See ZEBULUN; compare Gen. xlix, 13.) But Asher did not possess Zidon, Judg. i, 31; iii, 3, and the Zidonians oppressed Israel, at least for a time, Judg. x, 12. These people were noted for their luxurious habits—their "careless manner," Judg. xviii, 7; and celebrated for their manufactures and works of art, and for their commerce, 1 Kings v, 6; 1 Chron. xxii, 4; Ezra iii, 7. Profane authors also testify to their wealth and skill. Thus Homer speaks of the Zidonian silver bowl bestowed by Achilles as a prize; and he tells also of another similar bowl of silver, gold-edged, a gift from the king of the Zidonians, which Menelaus gave Telemachus. Hecuba also offered to Minerva a beautiful robe wrought by Zidonian women. Pliny and others speak of the merchants of Zidon, of their linen, glass, etc. Zidon long remained a place of power and wide sovereignty; but it was at length eclipsed by its own colony, Tyre, to which city her noblest and most skillful children seem to have fled. Thus, for a time, Zidon almost disappeared from history.

In the time of David and Solomon we find that, although Zidon still retained her kings, nevertheless the kings of Tyre gradually assumed the title of "king of Zidon," and embraced both cities under their jurisdiction. Tyre manned her fleets with Zidonian sailors, and Hiram furnished Zidonian workmen for Solomon's temple, 1 Chron. xxii, 4; 1 Kings v, 6; compare Ezek. xxvii, 8. But when Shalmaneser marched against Phenicia, Zidon probably regained its former rank; for then we read again of "Kings of Zidon," Jer. xxv, 22; xxvii, 3. Doubtless, however, these kings were not independent, but, by submitting to its conquerors, Zidon was enriched at the expense of Tyre. In the expedition of Xerxes against Greece the Sidonians furnished the best ships in the whole fleet. When Xerxes reviewed his fleet he sat in a Sidonian galley, under a golden canopy; and at his council, next to Xerxes sat the king of Sidon, above the king of Tyre. Sidon revolted against Artaxerxes Ochus, and was then nearly destroyed, (B. C. 351.) Compare the predictions in Jer. xxvii, 6, 11; xlvii, 4; Ezek. xxviii, 21–23; xxxii, 30; Joel iii, 4–8. The city was rebuilt, and became a provincial town, but of little importance, and, happy to rid itself of the Persian yoke at any cost, gladly opened its gates to Alexander the Great. Under Alexander's Syrian successors the place rose in population and importance, sometimes under Syrian, and again under Egyptian kings. At length Sidon fell under Roman dominion; but still it retained much of commercial importance. At this period we find it referred to in the New Testament. Jesus preached "in the coasts of Tyre and Sidon," and wrought there a miracle, Matt. xv, 21–28; Mark vii, 24–31; though we have no evidence that he ever entered the cities themselves. From Sidon many people went out to hear Christ, Mark iii, 8; Luke vi, 17; and the Saviour declared "it shall be more tolerable for Tyre and Sidon at the judgment" than for Chorazin and Bethsaida, where so many mighty works had been wrought, Luke x, 13, 14. The Sidonians having displeased Herod, they flattered him, Acts xii, 20. When St. Paul "touched at Sidon" he found there Christian friends, Acts xxvii, 3.

Sidon was afterward known as *Saida*, and *Sageta* or *Sogitta*. The invading army of the Crusaders did not dare to attack the city at first in 1099; and eight years later, when vast preparations were made, they were bought off by the inhabitants for a high price. In 1111, however, the place was captured after a defense of six weeks. For seventy-six years it was held by the Christians, when it was seized and its fortifications destroyed by Sultan Saladin. After various fortunes, it became in the fifteenth century a port of Damascus, and a link between Europe and Asia. In the many wars that afterward occurred between the Druses and the Turks this city suffered greatly; yet down to the close of the eighteenth century it was the central point for export and import. At length (in 1790) the rebellious Jezzâr Pasha gave a fatal blow to *Saida* by expelling from the city not only the French consulate, but also the French merchants.

Saida is now a poor and miserable place, without trade or manufactures worthy of the name; yet it presents a beautiful appearance, surrounded as it is by fragrant gardens and orchards. The population is estimated at about nine thousand, of whom seven thousand are Moslems, and five hundred Jews. The streets are narrow, crooked, and dirty; but the houses are large, and some of them even elegant. The architectural ruins about Saida are not extensive; but this is the only spot in Phenicia where Phenician monuments with Phenician inscriptions have as yet been found. In one of the many sepulchral caves which abound in the vicinity a very remarkable sarcophagus was discovered, January, 1855. It is of black syenite, the lid of which represents the form of a mummy, with the uncovered face of a man. On the top of the lid is a Phenician inscription of twenty-two lines, each line containing about forty-five letters, all in perfect preservation. Another inscription in six very long lines is at the upper end of the sarcophagus beneath the head. After adjuring posterity not to disturb the remains of the great king which lie within, the inscription proceeds: "I am Ashmanezer, King of the Sidonians; son of Tabinth, King of the Sidonians; grandson of

BIBLE GEOGRAPHY.

SARCOPHAGUS FOUND AT SAIDA.

Ashmanezer, King of the Sidonians; and my mother, Immiashtoreth, priestess of Astarte, our sovereign Queen." Other interesting points follow. No date is found, but its age is variously estimated from the eleventh to the fourth century B. C. This exceedingly valuable monument is now in the Museum of the Louvre, Paris.

Speaking of the Phenician tombs at Saida, Captain Warren (*Palestine Exploration Fund, Quar. Statement*, Dec., 1869) says: "I was disappointed to find that the nature of the rock in which they are cut prevents their being finished off in any manner, and the sides in many cases have been coated with plaster, so that they now have a very dilapidated appearance. I could neither see nor hear of any *red paint* marks on the plaster, similar to those we have found on the walls of the *Haram Esh-Sherif.* The sarcophagi are generally cut out of the solid mountain limestone, (the tombs being sandstone,) and have devices on them which I have seen in Palestine." Concerning some small pieces of pottery also found at Saida he says: "They are precisely similar to what we find at Jerusalem in the middle of our sections, below the early Christian pottery, and above the pottery found at the southeast angle of the Haram." On the pedestal of an exhumed column seen by Captain Wilson he found an inscription in Greek dedicated to the Emperor Hadrian. Masons' marks were also discovered on some of the stones.

Zik'lag, (Map 2,) perhaps *outpouring of a fountain*, a city in the south of Judah, Josh. xv, 31, but afterward given to Simeon, xix, 5. It was at times, however, subject to the Philistines of Gath, whose king, Achish, bestowed it upon David for a residence; after which it was re-incorporated with Judah, 1 Sam. xxvii, 6; xxx, 1, 14, 26; 2 Sam. i, 1; 1 Chron. iv, 30; Neh. xi, 28. Its site is supposed by some to be marked by '*Aslûj* or *Kaslûj*.

Zin, (Map 2,) *a low palm-tree*. The wilderness of Zin was a part of the Arabian desert on the south of Palestine, Num. xiii, 21, 22; xxxiv, 3. It joined the territory of Judah, Josh. xv, 1, 3, and lay west of Idumea, Num. xx, 1; xxvii, 14; xxxiii, 36. In the last named passages it is said that

Kadesh was in Zin, while in Num. xiii, 26, Kadesh was in Paran. This apparent contradiction is readily explained from the fact that Zin was the northern part of the great wilderness of Paran.

Zi'on, (Maps 7, 9,) *dry, sunny mount,* (in the New Testament, Sion.) The citadel of Jerusalem, or the "upper city." This height was held by the Jebusites until the reign of David, who took it by storm. "Then David dwelt in the fort and called it the city of David. And David built round about from Millo and inward," 2 Sam. v, 9; 1 Chron. xi, 7. Zion was the highest point within the city limits, having an elevation of two thousand five hundred and thirty-nine feet above the level of the Mediterranean, (see Map 11.) On Zion David's house was built; and the household for his families was there; and the houses for the ark of God, 1 Chron. xiv, 1; xv, 1, 29; 1 Kings viii, 1; 2 Chron. v, 2; Psa. ix, 11; xiv, 7. During the latter part of King David's life Moriah was chosen as the abode of God's name, 1 Chron. xvii; 2 Chron. iii, 1. Thus we find the term Zion sometimes employed so as to include the whole city, thus meaning Jerusalem, Psa. cxlix, 2; lxxxviii, 2; Isa. xxxiii, 14; Joel ii, 2, etc. After the captivity the name of Sion was given to the eminence on which the Temple was built. In Heb. xii, 22, and Rev. xiv, 1, Mount Sion is employed symbolically to express the glorious habitation of the redeemed. Zion is almost universally understood to be the south-western hill of Jerusalem. Some, however, have attempted to identify it with the Temple Hill, and others with Akra, on the northern side of the Holy City. But these attempts are so far complete failures.

"On the summit of Zion is a level tract extending in length, from the Citadel to the Tomb of David, about 600 yards; and in breadth, from the city wall to the eastern side of the Armenian convent, about 250 yards. A much larger space, however, was available for building purposes, and was at one time occupied. Now not more than one half of this space is inclosed by the modern wall, while fully one third of that inclosed is taken up with the barrack-yards, the convent-gardens, and the waste ground at the city gate.

MOSQUE OF DAVID ON ZION.

All without the wall, with the exception of the cemeteries and the cluster of houses round the Tomb of David, is now cultivated in terraces, and thinly sprinkled with olive-trees." "At the *Yáfa*

Gate the traveler will also notice the massive walls and deep fosse of the citadel, (see cut on page 174.) One of its towers claims attention from the antique masonry of the lower part, consisting of very large stones beveled like those of the temple walls. Recent researches have shown that this tower, as well as that at the north-west angle of the citadel, is founded on a scarped rock, which rises about forty feet above the bottom of the fosse. This appears to be that 'rocky crest' on which Josephus informs us the three great towers on the northern brow of Zion were founded. The researches of the Count de Vogüé have contributed greatly to increase our knowledge of this section of the Tyropœon Valley. He found that its depth near the citadel is thirty-three feet below the present surface, and farther eastward the bottom of the valley is twenty-six feet beneath the level of the Street of David, and nearly eighty feet lower than the top of Zion. At one spot a fragment of the ancient northern wall was laid bare. It was built close against the precipitous side of the hill, and though no less than thirty-nine feet in height, only rose to the top of the cliff behind it. Here, then, are data sufficient by which to determine the northern limits of Zion."—Porter's *Hand-book,* p. 87. The tower above-mentioned is generally called the "Tower of David," and is considered identical with *Hippicus,* one of the three massive towers built by Herod the Great.

The Mosque of David is supposed to cover the tombs of David, Solomon, and the other kings of Judah. Various other localities, however, are assigned (with very faint probability) as the burial place of the kings. In 1839 Sir Moses Montefiore and his party were admitted to the mosque. Through a trellised doorway they saw the "tomb," but they were not permitted to enter. A few years ago an American lady, daughter of the eminent missionary, Dr. Barclay, was enabled by the kindness of a Mohammedan lady to enter and sketch the tomb. Miss Barclay describes the room as small, but gorgeously furnished. "The tomb is apparently an immense sarcophagus of rough stone, and is covered by green satin tapestry, richly embroidered with gold. A satin canopy of red, blue, green, and yellow stripes hang over the tomb, and another piece of black velvet tapestry, embroidered in silver, covers a door in one end of the room, which they said leads to a cave underneath. Two small silver candlesticks stand before this door, and a little lamp hangs in a window near it, which is kept constantly burning."—*City of the Great King,* p. 212. See JERUSALEM.

Zi'or, *smallness,* a city in the highlands of Judah, perhaps near Hebron, Josh. xv, 54. Possibly the site is marked by *Sa'ir,* between Hebron and *Tekua.*

Ziph, *a flowing.*
1. A city in the south of Judah, Josh. xv, 24. Unknown.
2. A city in the highlands of Judah, Josh. xv, 55. When pursued by Saul, David frequented the wilderness of Ziph, 1 Sam. xxiii, 14, 15, 24; xxvi, 2. This place was fortified by Rehoboam. 2 Chron. xi, 8. Conder, with much plausibility, identifies Ziph with *Khirbet Khoreisa,* near *Tell Ziph.* Here are some very ancient bell-mouthed cisterns; also some more modern ruins. See American Palestine Exploration Statement, January, 1875.

Zi'phron or **Ziph'ron,** *sweet odor,* a city in the north of Palestine, Num. xxxiv, 9. It lay south-east of Hamath, toward Palmyra. There is a modern village called *Zifrân,* about fourteen hours north-east of Damascus. Here are found extensive ruins which may represent the ancient Ziphron.

Ziz, *a flower*, 2 Chron. xx, 16, a pass, possibly the large ruin near modern Yutta, called *Khirbet Aziz*.

Zo'an, (Map 8,) perhaps *low region*, or *place of departure*, a very ancient city of Lower Egypt, Num. xiii, 22, called by the Greeks Tanis. This city seems to have been one of the chief capitals, or royal abodes of the Pharaohs, Isa. xix, 11, 13 ; xxx, 4. The Psalmist speaks of the "field of Zoan" as the scene of God's marvelous works in the time of Israel's deliverance, Psa. lxxviii, 12, 43. Tradition says it was the residence of the court in the time of Moses. The overthrow predicted by Ezekiel (xxx, 14) overtook the city; "fire has been set in Zoan," and the "field" is desolate. The modern name of the site is *San*. Very extensive ruins remain. There are mounds of unusual height, which are filled with fragments of pottery. Remains of a vast temple and its inclosure bear the name of Rameses the Great. Of the ruins of Zoan Mr. Macgregor (*Rob Roy on the Jordan, Nile*, etc., 1870) says: "They are wide-spread, varied, and gigantic. Here you see about a dozen obelisks, all fallen, all broken ; twenty or thirty great statues, all monoliths of porphyry and granite, red and gray ; a huge sarcophagus (as it seemed to me) was of softer stone, and enormous pillars, lintel and wall stones are piled in heaps one over the other, most of them still buried in the earth. The polished statues are of various sizes, and of beautiful workmanship. Some sit with half the body over the ground, others have only a leg in the air. One leans its great bulk sideways, covered up to the ear ; another lies with its chair and legs appearing, but the head is buried deep out of sight in the mud. The buildings seem to have formed a temple with three outlying edifices. Some of the obelisks must have fallen long before the dust and refuse of ages had filled the courtly halls, then tenantless. Others fell on this new stratum, and these now lie, say ten feet higher than the floor, while a few of the taller columns lasted perhaps for another thousand years, and then they toppled over on the lonely plain with a crash unheard by a regardless world. . . . Many as are the celebrated ruins I have seen, I do not recollect any that impressed me so deeply with the sense of fallen and deserted magnificence." Although the name of Rameses the Great most frequently occurs amid the ruins, yet other names are found, among them that of Osirtasen III., whose time ascends nearly to that of Joseph.

Zo'ar, (Map 5,) *smallness*, one of the "cities of the plain," Gen. xiii, 10, originally called Bela, Gen. xiv, 2, 8. By the intercession of Lot this "little city" was spared from the destruction which overtook Sodom and the other cities, Gen. xix, 20-30. Zoar was the limit of Moses's view from Pisgah in one direction, Deut. xxxiv, 3. The prophets Isaiah (xv, 5) and Jeremiah (xlviii, 34) reckon Zoar among the cities of Moab.

Much controversy exists concerning the position of the cities of the plain. See SIDDIM; SODOM : SEA. SALT. Zoar is generally located at the southeastern angle of the Dead Sea. Josephus places it east of the Dead Sea. Jerome's notices of the place indicate a site near this sea in the southern border of Moab. Eusebius describes the Salt Sea as between Jericho and Zoar. Ptolemy locates Zoar in Arabia Petræa. Abulfeda, the Arab historian, says that Zoar (or Zoghar) lay near the Dead Sea and the Ghor.

Late travelers find ruins about the site, as indicated in our map. Recently, however, some eminent scholars locate Zoar near the north end of the Dead Sea, eastward. Dr. Tristram claims (1873) to have discovered the site of Zoar in the extensive ruins at *Zi'ara*, a little west of Nebo. On the etymology of the names Tristram observes: "There is an identity, more exact than often occurs in ancient and modern nomenclature, between the Hebrew ... Zo'ar and the Arabic Zi'ara."—*The Land of Moab*, pp. 340-345.

Zo'ba, and **Zo'bah,** *station,* a portion of Syria. It was one of the powerful kingdoms of Aram, hence its full name Aram-Zobah. See ARAM. It embraced that section of Northern Syria which lies between Hamath and the Euphrates, and it was so closely connected with Hamath that that great city was sometimes called Hamath-Zobah. Compare 1 Chron. xviii, 3-9; xix, 6; 2 Chron. viii, 3. The king of Zobah was defeated by Saul, 1 Sam. xiv, 47. The people of Zobah were very hostile to King David, and especially troublesome to Solomon, 1 Kings xi, 23-25. David defeated their king, taking from him his chariots and horses, shields of gold, and much brass, 2 Sam. viii, 3, 5, 12; compare x, 6, 8; 1 Chron. xviii, 3-9; xix, 6. Solomon also "prevailed against" Hamath-Zobah, 2 Chron. viii, 3. One of David's warriors is said to be the son of Nathan of Zobah, 2 Sam. xxiii, 36. Zobah is mentioned in the title of Psalm lx. "The rich plains of Hamath and Zobah are now swept by the Bedawin; yet some remnants of industry and civilization linger round the walls of *Aleppo, Hamâh,* and *Hums."—Porter.*

Zo'heleth, *serpent,* a stone "by En-Rogel," by which Adonijah "slew sheep and oxen and fat cattle," 1 Kings i, 9. On the western face of the rocky plateau, which slightly overhangs the valley of the village of Siloam, steps are rudely cut, by which one can climb directly from the valley to the midst of the village. Along this troublesome and even dangerous way habitually pass the women of Siloam who come to fill their vessels at the so-called "Virgin's Fount." This passage and the ledge of rock in which it is cut are called by the fellahin "*Ez Zehwele.*" This is doubtless the stone of Zoheleth. If this identity be established, En-Rogel must be put at the *Virgin's Fountain,* and not at *Bîr Eyub.* See EN-ROGEL.

Zo'phim, *watchers.* The "field of Zophim" was the place on the "top of Pisgah" to which Balak brought Balaam, that this false prophet might see the camp of Israel. Num. xxiii, 14.

Prof. Paine locates Zophim between *Jebel Nebâ'* and *'Ayûn Mûsâ.* "For the purpose of observation the place is peculiarly adapted. Evidently it was the point from which Moab in its alarm and distress looked down upon the vast array of the children of Israel, abiding over against them."—*Identification of Pisgah,* (January, 1875.)

Zo'rah and **Zo'reah,** *hornets' town;* in Neh. xi, 29, Zareah; a town in the low country of Judah, afterward assigned to Dan, Josh. xv, 33; xix, 41. This was the birthplace of Samson, and also his burial place, Judg. xiii, 2, 25; xvi, 31. The Danites sent a marauding expedition from Zorah to seek an inheritance, Judg. xviii. It was fortified by Rehoboam, 2 Chron. xi, 10; and inhabited after the return from captivity, Neh. xi, 29. The place still exists under the name of *Sur'ah.* It is now a miserable hamlet, lying on a sharp, conical hill two miles north of Beth-Shemesh.

Zo'rathites, 1 Chron. iv, 2. Perhaps inhabitants of Zorah.

Zo'reah, Josh. xv, 33. See ZORAH.

Zo'rites, 1 Chron. ii, 54. Probably inhabitants of Zorah.

Zuph, *flag, sedge,* Deut. i, 1, margin. See SEA, RED.

Zuph, *honey-comb,* a district visited by Saul, 1 Sam. ix, 5. The "land of Zuph" was doubtless south of Benjamin; but its precise location is not yet determined. Possibly the name may be preserved in *Soba*, about seven miles west of Jerusalem. See RAMATHAIM-ZOPHIM.

Zu'zims, (Map 3,) perhaps *throwing out*, (as sprouts,) possibly so named from the *fertility* of the country; but the etymology is very obscure. The Zuzims were an ancient people living on the east of the Jordan, Gen. xiv, 5. Their territory is supposed to have been the same as that afterward occupied by the Ammonites, and thus the tribe itself appears to have been identical with the Zamzummims, Deut. ii, 20, 21. Doubtless they were allied by blood to the Rephaim, and those other races of giants who were the original possessors of the Land of Canaan.

THE END.

www.ingramcontent.com/pod-product-compliance
Lightning Source LLC
Chambersburg PA
CBHW021417300426
44114CB00010B/532